Corporate Governance

Jurisdictional Comparisons **First Edition 2013**

General Editor:
Akira Kawamura, Anderson Mori & Tomotsune
Immediate Past President of International Bar Association

with a Foreword by
Martin Lipton, a founding partner of Wachtell, Lipton, Rosen & Katz

THOMSON REUTERS

General Editor
Akira Kawamura,
Anderson Mori & Tomotsune

Commercial Director
Katie Burrington

Managing Editor
Emily Kyriacou

Commissioning Editor
Michele O'Sullivan

Chief Sub-editor
Paul Nash

Publishing Assistant
Magdalena Wika

Design and Production
Dawn McGovern

Published in 2013 by Sweet & Maxwell,
100 Avenue Road, London NW3 3PF
part of Thomson Reuters (Professional) UK Limited
(Registered in England & Wales, Company No 1679046.
Registered Office and address for service:
Aldgate House, 33 Aldgate High Street, London EC3N 1DL)

A CIP catalogue record for this book is available from the British Library.

ISBN: 978-0-414028-98-2

Contents

Preface

Akira Kawamura **Anderson Mori & Tomotsune**

Global corporate governance

Good corporate governance is a necessary precondition for corporate culture to flourish. It ensures that companies comply with the law and the ethical rules of societies, and therefore be good corporate citizens.

Good corporate governance is also a key factor for companies to raise funds from the most suitable capital markets in the world or to trade their financial commodities in the marketplace. Unless they can prove themselves to be highly and legitimately managed under the commonly accepted corporate governance rules, businesses may no longer be admitted to the major markets.

It is also a key consideration for the regulators of the recipient countries to introduce the rules according to the global standards into their own jurisdictions because these are critical criteria looked at by foreign investors when deciding where to invest. They owe substantive responsibilities to commit themselves with their own corporate governance rules prevailing in their own home jurisdiction. Therefore, the globally recognised rules can be considered to be an important business infrastructure of the recipient countries.

Another trend is that not only companies but also investors are increasingly becoming more global. Hence, the corporate governance rules must also be of a global standard. They influence each other and become very much the same in most of the world's leading markets, although, needless to say, the US law has been, among those, the most influential and has in many ways dominated the global rule making. We may say that global corporate governance is emerging and is well accepted in many jurisdictions around the world.

Thus, I think, we could infer that good corporate governance is essential for the sustainable growth of the world economy.

Global financial crisis

Corporate governance became a critical agenda item for regulators and lawmakers worldwide in the years of the global financial crisis (GFC), which took place following the collapse of Bear Stearns Co. Inc. and Lehman Brothers Holding Inc. in 2008. It triggered, as is well known, the collapse of the many financial institutions, banks and investment banks in major jurisdictions in the USA, Europe and then in other parts of the globe. The serious aftermath of the GFC is still being felt in many jurisdictions, such as Spain, Greece and Italy.

While there were many different reasons why rescue packages were or were not applied to the failed financial institutions, there was a common and important criterion, which was the ethical fairness of the corporate governance adopted by the board of that failed entity. It was observed that the peoples and their governments were not persuaded to help the collapsed entities unless they were able to prove that they had been properly managed under a healthy corporate governance structure. If not, they were no longer admitted to play a role as corporate citizens.

Enron and the Sarbanes-Oxley Act

As early as 2002, the so-called 'Sarbanes-Oxley Act' (SOX Law or Act) was introduced in the USA to react to a number of large corporate scandals revealed in that year. The largest one was the accounting fraud orchestrated by the board of Enron Corporation. It was said that it would have triggered a second Great Depression following the 1929 crisis, if a comprehensive reform was not introduced by ways of the Act, into the management of corporate boards as well as into the accounting and audit systems and into the professional services rendered by accountants and lawyers.

The Round Table Discussion on the rule making to enforce the Act was held at the historical building of the United States Security Exchange Commission in Washington D.C. just before the Christmas holidays in 2002. I was invited to the Round Table as a panellist by the SEC. We discussed the scope of the cross-border reach that may be given to the Act and its subordinate rules. It was noted that the Act was intended to be a global rule and not just a national rule. As is seen in the following chapters of this book, the major principles of the Act are now introduced and enforced in most of the major jurisdictions including Japan, Germany and so on.

Common issues

There are many commonalities in the corporate governance rules of the jurisdictions covered in this book. The committees system of the board coupled with the independent directors, especially the independent audit committee, have been introduced in many jurisdictions after the introduction of the SOX Law and its subordinate rules. The power and functional support to the independent committees may have to be introduced in many more jurisdictions.

Executive compensation is another hot issue. It is a problem of so-called 'say on pay'. A large number of litigations have been instituted in many jurisdictions, especially in the USA. It is hoped that a sound standard for executive compensation will be established through those court cases.

Effective enforcement of the compliance programme developed under the SOX Law regime must be strengthened in many jurisdictions. In this regard, boards may have more practical powers to oversee the management of the companies.

Thus, the topic of corporate governance is now an acute concern for the companies and their boards around the world. It is especially important for the companies that are active in multi-jurisdictional markets and hence, for their in-house counsels and outside legal counsels. They should keenly watch developments in corporate governance rules as an important part of the changing business environment.

General Editor's thanks

I am very much honoured to undertake the general editorship of this new book on present-day global corporate governance. This should be a unique and excellent source of legal information on this topic. The authors, who have kindly agreed to contribute their valuable time to making this book, are literally the best and most prominent lawyers on the topic in each of the jurisdictions and are very well known as such throughout the world.

This publication should be the best and most practical first-hand reference material for the lawyers and the in-house counsels who may have opportunities to counsel the clients on their business in the foreign jurisdictions. I thank the authors for their valuable contributions to this book.

The most important point I wish to note about this publication is the Foreword given by Marty Lipton of Wachtell, Lipton, Rosen & Katz. He is the legendary M&A lawyer of our time and a prominent advisor to the boards of major US and global entities. He kindly agreed to contribute to this book in his inspiring way. I thank him very much.

Akira Kawamura, Anderson Mori & Tomotsune
Immediate Past President of International Bar Association

Foreword

Martin Lipton **Wachtell, Lipton, Rosen & Katz**

The core purpose of corporate governance is to build long-term sustainable growth in corporate and shareholder value for the benefit of all stakeholders. The vitality of the global economy depends upon our fostering a long-term orientation and resisting the pressure to measure success on the basis of myopic benchmarks. Corporate governance practices can, and should, vary across jurisdictions, and the treatment of the following key issues by boards, management, stakeholders and regulators has global relevance in determining a corporate governance profile that facilitates the creation of sustainable value and is fine-tuned to specific country and company circumstances.

- Establishing an appropriate 'tone at the top' to actively cultivate a corporate culture that gives high priority to ethical standards, principles of fair dealing, professionalism, integrity, full compliance with legal requirements and ethically sound strategic goals.
- Partnering with management and advisors to review the company's business and strategy and identifying and developing talent as part of robust succession planning.
- Organising the business, and maintaining the collegiality, of the board and its committees so that each of the increasingly time-consuming matters that the board and board committees are expected to oversee receives the appropriate attention of the directors.
- Understanding, and effectively evaluating, the ever-evolving legal rules, stock exchange requirements and aspirational 'best practices' that have come to have almost as much influence on board and company behaviour.
- Developing an understanding of shareholder and stakeholder perspectives on the company and fostering long-term relationships with shareholders and other stakeholders, as well as coping with escalating requests for meetings to discuss governance and business proposals, including employee lay-offs, stock buy-backs, special dividends, spin-offs and other corporate transactions.
- Objective evaluation of activist agendas, notwithstanding the threat of proxy contests, with-hold-the-vote campaigns and other pressure tactics, to determine what will in fact further the best interests of the company and all of its constituents.
- Developing an understanding of how the company and the board will function optimally in the event of a crisis and proactively planning for a crisis.
- Ensuring appropriate procedures for review of transactions involving related persons or that could otherwise involve a conflict.

- Retaining and recruiting directors who meet the requirements for experience, expertise, diversity, independence, leadership ability and character, and providing compensation for directors that fairly reflects the significantly increased time and energy that they must now spend in serving as board and board committee members.
- Coping with the proliferation of new regulations and changes in the general perception of business that have followed the financial crisis.
- Addressing conflicts of proxy advisory firms and the shortcomings of one-size-fits-all governance checklists and resisting unsound demands of corporate governance activists that are not linked to true value creation.
- Achieving the delicate balance of enabling the company to recruit, retain and incentivise the most talented executives while avoiding media and populist criticism for inappropriate compensation.
- Dealing with populist demands, such as criticism of risk management, and the demands of the public with respect to health, safety, environmental and other socio-political issues in a manner that will pre-empt increased regulation and avoid escalation of unsound demands, while at the same time furthering the best interests of the company.

Considerable attention has been devoted to searching for lessons learned from the global financial crisis and ways to improve board functioning. Perhaps one of the most valuable 'lessons learned' is that boards and regulators need to focus on what works, without the undue distraction of reform for reform's sake and standardised mandates that pay lip service to 'best practices' but add little if any real value. Some of the other 'lessons learned' include a renewed focus on risk management, a better understanding of the challenges faced by highly complex, global businesses, and a rethinking of the experience and skill sets needed for an effective board.

In order to promote effective governance, the institutional, regulatory and governance environment must facilitate an adequate supply of quality directors who: (i) have sufficient knowledge of, and experience with, the company's businesses, even if this requires a re-examination of whether the trend towards boards with only one non-independent director makes sense and results in boards with a greater percentage of directors who are not 'independent'; (ii) are in sufficient number to staff the requisite standing and special board committees that handle much of the board's work; (iii) are able to devote sufficient time to board and committee meetings, and the preparation for them; (iv) receive regular tutorials by internal and external experts as part of expanded director education; and (v) are encouraged to maintain a true collegial relationship among and between the company's senior executives and the members of the board.

Martin Lipton, Wachtell, Lipton, Rosen & Katz
Founding Partner

Australia

Hiroyuki Kano & Andrew Hay **Clayton Utz**

1. GENERAL PRINCIPLES

1.1 What are the general principles of corporate governance in your jurisdiction? What are the main objectives of corporate governance principles in your jurisdiction? State also whether your legal system is based on common law or civil law.

There is no agreed statutory definition of the phrase 'corporate governance' in Australia. The concept of corporate governance is a very broad one, and the phrase can be used in both a narrow and broad context. In a narrow sense, the phrase can refer to the ways in which investors to a company ensure a return on their investment. In a broad sense, the phrase covers matters concerning interests of stakeholders, such as the relationship between a company, its management, its members and other stakeholders, such as creditors and auditors.

The Australian Securities Exchange (ASX) Corporate Governance Principles and Recommendations (Principles and Recommendations) developed by the ASX Corporate Governance Council define corporate governance as '*the framework of rules, relationships, systems and processes within and by which authority is exercised and controlled in corporations*', and that it encompasses the mechanisms by which companies, and those in control, are held to account.

The laws in Australia in this area cover rights and obligations that each stakeholder has and owes to others, and it might be right to state that the development of laws in this area is an ongoing and evolving process with lawmakers and regulators seeking to strike a balance of conflicting interests held by different stakeholders.

Australia (consisting of both Federal and State or Territory levels) is a common law jurisdiction.

1.2 Have there been any recent developments in the law, codes and rules of corporate governance?

While there have not been any fundamental changes to the laws concerning corporate governance since 2004, there have been numerous amendments to relevant legislations, legislative instruments, guidance, rules and recommendations in specific areas from time to time.

Notable recent changes to corporate governance laws include amendments to provisions concerning the remuneration of key management personnel of listed companies, the 'two-strikes rule' in relation to the remuneration report contained in a listed company's annual report (ie, the ability to spill the board where 25 per cent or more of shareholders disapprove of the board's determination of the remuneration for the key management personnel), changes to the rules for payment of dividends and the publication by the ASX of updated Principles and Recommendations in 2010, representing guidelines for best practice.

1.3 Outline recent court cases and incidents involving corporate governance issues. Were there any significant corporate scandals or large unlawful corporate cases?

There have been numerous Australian court cases and administrative decisions concerning various corporate governance issues, such as member's rights, responsibilities of board of directors and managements, validity of constitution and powers of courts conferred by relevant legislations.
In recent years, there have been a few notable court cases concerning breaches of directors' duties in Australia.

In *Australian Securities and Investments Commission v Ingleby* [2012] VSCA 49, the chief financial officer of AWB Ltd was held to have contravened his statutory duty of care and diligence by authorising payments for bribes to the then Iraqi government in breach of a United Nations resolution that dealt with trade between United Nations members and Iraq.

In *Australian Securities and Investments Commission v Healey* (2011) 196 FCR 291; 83 ACSR 484; [2011] FCA 717, the court held that the chief executive officer, who was also a director, and six non-executive directors had contravened their statutory duty of care and diligence and other statutory obligations by approving the consolidated financial statements of certain companies and other entities within Centro group which failed to disclose significant matters at board meetings. The chief financial officer also admitted contravening his statutory duty of care and diligence in this case.

In several related court cases, certain officers and directors (executive and non-executive) of James Hardie Industries Ltd were held to have breached their statutory duties of care in connection with the company's announcement to the Australian Securities Exchange, which was substantially inaccurate.

1.4 Which law enforcement agency is in charge of enforcing corporate governance? May a criminal sanction be levied upon infringement of the corporate governance rules?

The Australian Securities and Investments Commission (ASIC) is the Federal government body responsible for ensuring compliance with laws concerning corporate governance, including the ASX listing rules. ASIC's powers include powers to investigate alleged contravention of the law, power to issue infringement notices to alleged offenders, and power to seek civil and criminal penalties from the Australian courts. Enforcement of the laws, including those concerning corporate governance, is the role of the Australian courts.

The Corporations Act 2001 (Cth) (Corporations Act) makes certain contraventions of the Corporations Act an offence and a criminal sanction is imposed on a person who is held to have committed such an offence, usually where a breach of a provision involves strict liability or the breach is intentional or reckless. In addition, the Corporations Act provides for civil penalty provisions for contravention of certain provisions of the Corporations Act.

2. SOURCES OF LAW

2.1 Which laws, codes or statutes govern company structures and organisations? Are there statutes like the Companies Act or other forms of law? Is there much relevant case law?

The Corporations Act is the principal legislation governing company structures and body corporates in Australia. The Corporations Act is supplemented by legislative instruments such as the Corporations Regulations 2001 (Cth). In addition, the Corporations Act confers on ASIC the power to issue class orders or provide case-by-case relief which provides ASIC with the power to amend certain provisions of the Corporations Act or to exempt the application of certain provisions of the Corporations Act in accordance with such class orders or relief.

ASIC also issues regulatory guides which set out ASIC's interpretation of relevant corporate legislation (mostly the Corporations Act) and how ASIC will exercise its powers under such legislation.

Companies or entities listed on the official list of a securities exchange in Australia are also subject to the listing rules of the relevant exchange, such as the ASX Listing Rules, which set out provisions concerning governance and structures of the listed companies or entities. In addition, notably, companies listed on the ASX are expected to adopt the Principles and Recommendations.

Court cases are also a source of law in Australia, although statutes and legislation take precedence over case laws. Court cases often provide for the interpretation of statutory provisions, and fill any gaps not covered by statute.

2.2 Which laws, codes or statutes regulate capital markets in your jurisdiction?

In the context of regulating capital markets in Australia, the Corporations Act sets out rules in relation to matters such as fundraising by a company (whether or not it is listed on a securities market) and other entities, continuous disclosure by a listed company, licensing of financial markets and clearing and settlement facilities, and supervision of financial markets. The Corporations Act is supplemented by relevant legislative instruments, ASIC's class orders and individual relief and regulatory guides.

Companies listed on a securities exchange in Australia (such as ASX) are also subject to listing rules of the relevant securities market. Operations of such securities markets, such as the obligations of trading participants, are governed by a separate set of operation and market rules relating to each.

2.3 Are there any public interest laws which apply to or influence corporate governance?

While Australia (at both Federal and State and Territory levels) has various pieces of legislation and government policies dealing with specific areas which are arguably considered to be for the 'public interest', such as environmental protection, anti-discrimination, consumer protection, civil liberties, native title and so on, there is no legislation which is designed to apply to or influence governance of companies in Australia for the 'public interest' in a general sense.

2.4 Have there been any recent developments in any of the above laws? What are the recent changes to the above laws or rules and the reasons for such changes?

In Australia, legislation and other regulations and rules, including those concerning corporate governance or capital markets, are continuously reviewed and amended. For instance, in 2012 alone, the Commonwealth Parliament passed at least eight pieces of legislation amending the Corporations Act. In addition, ASIC amends, repeals and issues class orders and regulatory guides on a regular basis.

An example of recent notable changes is the introduction of an amendment to the Corporations Act known as the 'two-strikes rule'. Under the rule, if at least 25 per cent of the members of a listed company who cast their votes reject the company's remuneration report at two consecutive annual general meetings, then the members must decide whether to convene another general meeting to determine whether the board members are to be replaced. The introduction of such a rule was intended to address community and investor concerns regarding excessive remuneration of company senior executives and senior management.

3. SHAREHOLDERS AND THE SHAREHOLDERS' MEETING

3.1 How are shareholders' interests represented in the company? How are the shareholders assured exercise of their rights? What is the highest governing body within the company structure if it is not the shareholders' meeting?

In the context of corporate governance, interests of the members of a company are primarily represented by participating in and voting at general meetings or passing a members' resolution without a meeting (provided that shares held by the members confer on them the right to vote).

The Corporations Act sets out various matters which require member approval, such as buying back the company's own shares, a capital reduction, amending the constitution or voluntarily winding up a solvent company. Listing rules of securities exchanges in Australia provide additional matters which require member approval for listed companies, such as the issue of securities in certain circumstances, the disposal of the company's main undertaking and proposed transactions with persons in a position of influence.

Apart from matters which require member approval under the Corporations Act and relevant listing rules, a company does not have to confer on its members any powers to make corporate decisions. An unlisted company and its members may choose to enter into a 'Shareholders Agreement' to regulate how the company is to be owned, controlled and possibly financed. It is common in such agreements to list certain matters which require member approval, and certain other matters which are specifically delegated to the board.

Members are arguably the 'highest governing body' within the company structure in a sense that they have the ultimate say in most important decisions concerning the company. However, for many listed companies, shareholdings are so widely dispersed that no member or group of members has any real control over the company. It is, therefore, also arguable that in such cases day-to-day control of the company lies with the directors.

3.2 How is the shareholders' meeting conducted? Who may chair the meeting? May attendance (not voting) at the meeting be restricted only to the shareholders? Are the shareholders allowed to be accompanied by legal or other counsel?

The Corporations Act permits a company (whether it be a proprietary company, eg closely held, or a public company) which has only one member to pass a resolution by the member recording it and signing the record. Since one member cannot hold a 'meeting' by him/her/itself, no meeting can take place.

The Corporations Act also permits a proprietary company (but not a public company) with more than one member to pass a written resolution without holding a meeting if all the members entitled to vote on the resolution sign a document containing a statement that they are in favour of the resolution set out in the document.

There are limited mandatory provisions in the Corporations Act concerning the manner of conducting a meeting of members, such as the requirements to hold a meeting for a proper purpose and at a reasonable time and place. The Corporations Act also allows a company to hold a meeting at two or more venues using any technology that gives the members as whole a reasonable opportunity to participate. The manner of conducting a meeting of members is usually set out in a company's constitution (if the company has one). If a company does not have a constitution, or if the constitution does not set out manner in which a meeting of members is to be conducted, certain provisions in the Corporations Act known as 'replaceable rules' apply to the company. The replaceable rules, however, have limited provisions concerning the manner of conducting a meeting of members, such as the required quorum of two members and the right of the directors to elect a person to chair the meeting.

Matters concerning eligibility and a way to select a chairperson are, again, usually set out in a company's constitution. Typically, a general meeting of members of a listed company is chaired by the chairperson of the company's board, although this may not always be the case.

There are no legal restrictions as to who may be present at a meeting of members, although a constitution (if the company has one) will usually give members who have a right to vote at the meeting an entitlement to be present at the meeting. A constitution may also give the chair the ability to restrict access to the meeting.

3.3 How are minority shareholders' rights protected?

The Corporations Act confers on a member or former member of a company (whether the member be a majority or minority member) the right to apply to the court for a remedy where conduct carried on against the member by the company, or those who control the company, is either contrary to the interests of the members as a whole, or oppressive to, unfairly prejudicial to, or unfairly discriminatory against the member. If the court is satisfied that such conduct has taken place, it can make various kinds of order it considers appropriate, such as an order restraining or requiring a person to do a specified act, and an order to wind up a company.

Other rights the Corporations Act confers on minority members of a company include:

- the right of members with at least 5 per cent of the votes to direct a small proprietary company to prepare a financial report and directors' report and send them to all members of the company;
- the right of members with at least 5 per cent of the votes (or at least 100 members who are entitled to vote) to give a company a notice of a resolution that they propose to move at a general meeting; and
- the right of a member (regardless of the proportion of the member's share in the company) to have access to a copy of minutes of members' meetings and written resolutions without a meeting.

In addition, the Corporations Act provides for a number of matters which require a special resolution of members, which to be passed requires at least 75 per cent of votes cast by members entitled to vote on the resolution. Matters requiring a special resolution includes a change of the company's constitution and the voluntary winding up of the company. Such rights effectively gives a minority member with more than a 25 per cent interest in a company to block the passing of the special resolution.

3.4 Is shareholder activism encouraged or discouraged? If not encouraged, how is it regulated?

While it is difficult to state objectively whether the Australian government actively encourages or discourages the shareholder activism, the current legal framework and policies do provide opportunities for investors to be heard and have a say in relation to affairs of companies to which they invest as members. In Australia, there are organisations which encourage and assist shareholder activism, such as the Australian Shareholders' Association and a number of proxy advisory service providers. Further, ownership of shares by institutional investors such as superannuation funds and life insurance companies have grown in recent years – a factor which contributes to shareholder activism in Australia.

There is no law in Australia which is specifically designed to regulate or control the level of shareholder activism.

3.5 How are professional shareholders (those minority shareholders who seek some extra benefit from companies by unduly and habitually influencing management by using their shareholding) treated by the law? Are they excluded from attending the shareholders' meeting? Are they criminally or otherwise publicly sanctioned?

So far as listed companies in Australia are concerned, applicable laws, market rules, guidelines and policies seek to ensure that a board discloses information that has an effect on the company's affairs and value to the market. Given this position in Australia and resultant corporate practice, the practice by a minority member to obtain a benefit in return for the member's silence at a company's general meeting is virtually unheard of in Australia.

While there is no law to specifically deal with such minority members, such conduct by members may amount to extortion under the criminal law and, depending on the circumstances, the provision of a benefit by the directors may also result in criminal liability including for breach of statutory and common law duties of directors.

3.6 Are shareholders' benefits given to some of the shareholders by the company without resolution by the shareholders' meeting prohibited or regulated by the law or other rules?

Generally, a payment by a company to its members is ultimately determined by the board of directors as opposed to the members, unless the company's constitution or the law requires that a particular kind of payment requires member approval. Only limited types of payments by a company to its members require a member approval under the Corporations Act.

The Corporations Act contains provisions concerning related party transactions which require a public company (but not proprietary company) to obtain member approval before the giving of a financial benefit (which is not on arm's length terms or subject to another exception) to a 'related party'. 'Related parties' include members which control the company and members who are directors, their close relatives, or entities controlled by them. The giving of financial benefit to a non-related party member of a public company, or to a member of a proprietary company, does not require member approval.

4. DIRECTORS AND BOARD OF DIRECTORS

4.1 What are the functions and responsibilities of the directors and the board of directors? Do you have a one- or two-tier board system? What are the outside directors called?

Companies in England and Wales have a single-tier board structure. There Companies are so diverse in many respects, such as the size and nature of the business, the number and composition of investors, and the complexity (or otherwise) of internal structure, that the functions and responsibilities of directors differ significantly from one company to another. Generally, however, the inherent powers of a board of directors of a company are extremely broad, and subject to limitations imposed by law and the company's constitution (if any), the board can determine virtually every aspect or affair of the company. The Corporations Act provides by way of 'replaceable rule' that the business of a company is to be managed by or under the direction of the directors, and that they may exercise all powers of the company except those that the Corporations Act or the company's constitution (if any) require to be exercised in general meeting.

It should be noted, however, that it is common in Australia for a company, especially a larger company, to have a structure where administration of the company's affairs is undertaken by a management team (typically headed by a chief executive officer) which is accountable to the board of directors while the board supervises the management and determines the general direction of the company. In Australia, larger companies, especially listed companies, tend to have very few overlaps between board members and the management team.

Australian companies have a one-tier board system.

A member of a board of directors of a company who is not an employee of the company is generally known as a 'non-executive director', although this is not a defined term under the Corporations Act. There is also a term called an 'independent director', although, again there is no definition of the term in the Corporations Act. There is no set of compulsory rules or tests which determines whether a director is independent or not, although in the case of companies listed on ASX, the Principles and Recommendations provide guidance as to what constitutes an independent director and examples of relationships affecting independent status. The Principles and Recommendations provide that an independent director is a non-executive director who is not a member of management and is free of relationships that could materially interfere with the independent exercise of their judgement (or could reasonably be perceived to do so). Whether a director is independent is usually determined taking into account of factual circumstances, such as absence of any ownership, material contractual, managerial or advisory relationship between the director or his/her family members and the company.

4.2 What are the rules that may give rise to civil and criminal liability of the director(s)? How are those liabilities sought?

There are numerous legal grounds on which a person can bring an action against a director of accompany on a civil basis, such as for breach of contract, conduct giving rise to tortious liability, breach of trust or fiduciary duty and breach of various common law and statutory duties imposed on a director of a company. As for criminal liabilities, any conduct which is an offence under common law or statutes committed by a director can give rise to the director's criminal liability.

Generally, both civil and criminal proceedings concerning a director's liability are heard before the Australian courts.

In the context of a liability arising out of breach of duties imposed on directors of a company, both common law and the Corporations Act set out circumstances under which directors may be liable. For example, a director is subject to common law fiduciary duties such as a duty of care, skill and diligence, a duty to act honestly, a duty to exercise powers for a proper purpose and a duty to avoid conflicts of interest with the company. In parallel with common law, the Corporations Act also sets out director's duties. Such duties include a duty of care and diligence, a duty of good faith and to exercise powers for a proper purpose, a duty to avoid misuse of position and company information and a duty to prevent a company from trading while insolvent. In addition to civil liabilities, the Corporations Act makes a contravention of certain provisions an offence. For example, it is an offence under the Corporations Act if a director intentionally or recklessly misuses his or her position or information obtained as a director, and such a conduct involves dishonesty.

The Corporations Act provides for extensive provisions concerning civil and criminal procedures in connection with the Corporations Act, such as who is entitled to make what sort of claims and under what circumstances, what procedures must be followed before and during an action, and what kind of orders or actions the courts can and cannot take.

4.3 Does the board of directors have a committee system, eg, nomination committee, compensation committee, audit committee? If not required, is it common practice for companies? How does it function?

Although there is a concept of board committees in Australia, there is no requirement under the Corporations Act that the board of directors of a company establish any committees. Whether a board of a company establishes a committee is, to a large extent, discretionary.

However, under the ASX Listing Rules a listed company which is included in the S&P All Ordinaries Index must have an audit committee. A listed company included in the S&P/ASX 300 Index must have a remuneration committee comprised solely of non-executive directors.

The ASX Principles and Recommendations also provide recommendations that the board of a company listed on ASX establish three board committees: a nomination committee, audit committee and remuneration committee. While, in general, a company's adoption of the Principles and Recommendations is not mandatory (although a listed company included in the S&P/ASX 300 Index must comply with the Principles and Recommendations in relation to the composition, operation and responsibility of the audit committee), companies listed or to be listed in ASX are required under the ASX Listing Rules to show ASX the extent to which they have followed the Principles and Recommendations, and where they have not adopted all the recommendations, they must identify the recommendations that have not been adopted and give reasons for not adopting them. This effectively encourages ASX-listed companies to adopt the Principles and Recommendations and gives a company the flexibility to adopt alternative corporate governance practices as it considers appropriate to its particular circumstances, if it explains the reasons for doing so.

While recommended matters concerning each of these committees, such as purposes, compositions, roles and responsibilities vary, one notable common feature of the committees is that they consider matters concerning the company or its board that require a degree of independence and make recommendations to the full board of directors.

The Principles and Recommendations recommend that each committee have a charter that clearly sets out its role and responsibilities, composition, structure and membership requirements, and the procedures for inviting non-committee members to attend meetings. The Principles and Recommendations also provide that each committee should be allowed to have access to adequate internal and external resources necessary to achieve its purposes.

4.4 Is it a legal requirement to have an independent director or a third-party director? If so, how are they appointed? Is it required for listed companies?

There is no requirement under the Corporations Act that a company have a non-executive director or an independent director.

However, the ASX Principles and Recommendations recommend that a majority of the directors on the board of companies listed on ASX should consist of independent directors, that the chairperson of the board be an independent director, and that the nomination, audit and remuneration committees consist of a majority of independent directors and be chaired by an independent chairperson (in the case of the audit committee, who is not also the chairperson of the board).

An independent director is appointed in the same way as other directors are appointed. How to appoint a director is usually set out in a company's constitution, if it has one. In the absence of a constitution or provisions regarding appointment, the Corporations Act contains 'replaceable rules' for the appointment of directors and mandatory rules regarding the appointment of public company directors and the appointment of directors in single director/shareholder proprietary companies.

4.5 How is the compensation for directors or officers determined? Can it be contested by the shareholders or the regulatory authorities? What are the common rules or practices for the compensation of officers?

Unless a company's constitution provides otherwise, the remuneration of the directors is determined by a resolution of members. It is possible for either the constitution or the members' resolution to delegate to the board the amount and form of remuneration.

In the case of a public company, remuneration to a director who is also an officer or an employee of the company cannot be paid without member approval unless the remuneration is reasonable in the circumstances.

For a company listed on ASX, the ASX Listing Rules provide that an executive director's salary or director's fee must not include a commission on, or percentage of, operating revenue and if a non-executive director is paid, such payment must be a fixed sum.

Members of companies may obtain information about the remuneration paid to directors. A company must disclose the remuneration paid to each director of the company or a subsidiary (if any) by the company if the company is directed to disclose the information by members with at least 5 per cent of the votes or at least 100 members who are entitled to vote.

The position of remuneration of an officer is different because the terms 'director' and 'officer' are defined differently under the Corporations Act. The definition of an 'officer' includes not only a director but also a person who holds positions such as a company secretary, an external administrator (such as a liquidator, administrator and receiver), and, more relevantly in this context, a person who can make decisions affecting the whole or substantial part of the company's affairs or the company's financial standing. This latter category of officer falls roughly into the definition of persons usually classified as 'key management personnel'.

The terms of remuneration of an officer differ from one position to another. For example, the terms of remuneration of a company secretary are usually determined by the board unless the company's constitution provides otherwise, and the Corporations Act provides for a statutory procedure to determine a remuneration of a liquidator or an administrator.

With regard to key management personnel, the Corporations Act provides a process for determination of the remuneration of key management personnel of listed companies. Under the Corporations Act, if a listed company engages a remuneration consultant (as is commonly the case), the remuneration consultant must be free of any undue influence by members of key management personnel and its appointment must be approved by the board of directors or the remuneration committee. The remuneration consultant must make remuneration recommendations for key management personnel to either or both of the non-executive directors (unless the board consists only of executive directors) and/or the remuneration committee. The Corporations Act also prohibits hedging of key management personnel's remuneration against their exposure to incentive remuneration (such as the use of derivatives to hedge against a drop in the company's share price).

Under the Corporations Act, adoption of a listed company's directors' report concerning the remuneration of key management personnel must be put to a vote before the company's annual general meeting. Although the vote on the resolution is advisory only and does not bind the company, if at least 25 per cent of the votes cast on the adoption of the remuneration report are against the resolution at two consecutive annual general meetings, then the members can vote as to whether another members' meeting will be held, and the votes at such a meeting will determine whether the directors of the company (other than the managing director) should be replaced. This rule is called the 'two-strikes rule'.

4.6 How will the board handle a corporate crisis like an internal criminal case, violence, social media exposure or dawn raid by the authorities?

There is no single set of rules which prescribe how a board of directors needs to handle an extraordinary event although, as a basic rule, the directors owe a duty to the company to minimise any adverse effect on the company as the result of occurrence of an extraordinary event. The means used by the board to handle such an event depend on the circumstances. If, for instance, there is a crisis management procedure in place dealing with the occurrence of an event which has happened, the board is expected to follow the procedure. If the board of a listed company becomes aware of any information that a reasonable person would expect to have a material effect on the price or value of the listed securities, then the board needs to immediately disclose the information to the relevant securities market.

5. BOARD OF AUDITORS, AUDIT COMMITTEE, ACCOUNTING AUDITORS

5.1 How is the internal accounting and legal audit structured and conducted? Is an outside accounting audit required and, if so, how is it structured? Are there requirements to change the auditor each five years?

Australia does not have the concept of a purely internal audit of a company. The Corporations Act prohibits a party interested in a company from auditing the financial statements of the company. The Corporations Act sets out very detailed and stringent independence requirements with which a company's auditor must comply.

The Corporations Act requires that a company which must prepare an annual financial report to have the financial report audited by an independent auditor and obtain an auditor's report. All public companies and proprietary companies which are classified as a 'large proprietary company' must prepare an annual financial report and lodge with ASIC an audited report, among other documents. A proprietary company classified as a 'small proprietary company' is not required to prepare an annual financial report unless directed by at least 5 per cent of its members or by ASIC, or unless the company is controlled by a foreign company. While a small proprietary company is not required to prepare a financial report and thus have it audited, the company's board must pass a resolution once a year declaring whether or not the company is in their opinion solvent.

In addition to having a financial report audited, the Principles and Recommendations recommend that companies listed on ASX should establish an audit committee which consists only of non-executive directors (ie, directors who are not also employees of the company) and a majority of independent directors of the company, and which is chaired by a committee member who is not also the chairperson of the board. Having an audit committee is compulsory for companies which are included in S&P All Ordinaries Index or S&P/ASX 300 Index at the beginning of the relevant financial year.

Generally, the Corporations Act prohibits an individual who plays a significant role in the audit of a listed company for five successive years from playing a significant role in the audit of the company for a later financial year. This provision does not apply to an individual who plays a significant role in the audit of an unlisted company.

5.2 Do you have supervisory auditors? What is the function of the supervisory auditors' board?

As referred to in paragraph 4.3 above, there is a concept of an audit committee in Australia. An audit committee is one of board committees which companies listed on ASX are recommended to have by the Principles and Recommendations. Having an audit committee is mandatory for companies on the S&P All Ordinaries Index. Being a board committee, an audit committee is an organ of the company, although its function requires a degree of independence from the management of the company.

The role of the audit committee is to ensure the integrity of the company's financial reporting and oversee the independence of external auditors. An audit committee's role also includes reporting to the board as to matters such as its opinion on adequacy of the external auditors' report and assessment of the performance and independence of the external auditors, and of the management processes supporting external reporting. It also makes recommendations to the board as to matters such as appointment or removal of the company's external auditor.

6. MARKET DISCLOSURE/TRANSPARENCY TO THE SHAREHOLDERS AND THE PUBLIC

6.1 What are the disclosure requirements for companies in your jurisdiction under company law, capital markets law or any other rules?

As mentioned in paragraph 5.1 above, all public companies and large proprietary companies as well as some small proprietary companies are required under the Corporations Act to lodge their audited financial statements (and other prescribed documents) with ASIC. The financial statements and other documents lodged with ASIC are recorded and kept on ASIC's computer-based database, and copies of the documents are accessible by the general public. These companies are also required to make the documents available to their members and to notify the members of the documents' availability each year. The board of directors of a public company must also lay before the company's annual general meeting the documents for the last financial year that ended before the meeting.

Listed companies are also required to prepare half-year financial statements and other prescribed documents, have the financial statements audited and lodge the documents with ASIC. Copies of the documents lodged with ASIC are accessible by the general public.

Listed companies are also subject to disclosure requirements under the listing rules of securities markets. In the case of companies listed on ASX, they are subject to, among other things, continuous disclosure obligations and periodical disclosure obligations. Very broadly, continuous disclosure obligations refer to a listed company's obligation to notify the market via ASX of any information which a reasonable person would expect to have a material effect on the price or value of their securities immediately after becoming aware of such information. Periodical disclosure obligations refer to a listed company's obligation to inform of their financial standing periodically, and include obligations to lodge with ASX the financial statements that are lodged with ASIC. In addition, companies listed on ASX are required to notify ASX of the occurrence of certain events, such as proposed transactions affecting share capital, takeover offers and changes in a material part of their business.

The Corporations Act also sets out disclosure rules in relation to fundraising conducted by companies and other entities, for example the requirement to prepare and issue a prospectus or product disclosure statement for certain offers of securities or financial products in Australia.

6.2 What is the liability or responsibility of the board in relation to the company's disclosure requirements?

Under the Corporations Act, if directors of a company fail to take all reasonable steps to comply with the obligation to lodge financial statements and other prescribed documents with ASIC, and the failure has a material adverse effect on the company or on the company's ability to pay debt, or is otherwise serious, the directors are subject to a civil penalty not exceeding A$200,000. A breach of this obligation involving dishonesty constitutes an offence, and the directors are subject to a fine not exceeding A$340,000 or five years' imprisonment, or both, as well as disqualification from managing a corporation.

If a listed company fails to comply with continuous disclosure obligations required under the relevant listing rules of a securities market and the failure has a material adverse effect on the company or on the company's ability to pay debt, or is otherwise serious, a person involved in the failure (which may include directors of the company) become subject to a civil penalty not exceeding A$200,000. The failure also constitutes an offence punishable by a fine not exceeding A$34,000 or five years' imprisonment, or both, as well as disqualification from managing a corporation.

If a director of a company knowingly makes or authorises the making of a false or materially misleading statement to ASIC, the market or a stakeholder of the company such as a director, member and auditor, the director is guilty of an offence. The offender is subject to a fine not exceeding A$34,000 or five years' imprisonment, or both. Further, it is also an offence for a director to fail to have taken reasonable steps to ensure that such a statement is not false or materially misleading. The offender is subject to a fine not exceeding A$17,000 or two years' imprisonment, or both.

In the fundraising context, there are multiple areas of potential civil and criminal liability under the Corporations Act for directors of a company, including deemed liability for directors in relation to misleading and deceptive statements and omissions in a prospectus.

7. M&A AND CORPORATE GOVERNANCE

7.1 Upon an M&A offer, how are the transparency and fairness rules of the company provided under the company and stock market laws

and rules?

The Corporations Act provides that the purposes of Australian takeover laws are to ensure that the acquisition of control over a target company takes place in an efficient, competitive and informed market, and that members and directors of the target company know the identity of proposed bidders, have a reasonable time to consider the proposal and are given enough information to enable them to assess the merits of the proposal.

The Corporations Act seeks to achieve the above objectives by prescribing detailed procedures for and conditions of a takeover bid of a listed company or an unlisted public company with more than 50 members. There are also a number of ASIC regulatory guides to supplement the provisions of the Corporations Act and to help stakeholders understand their rights and obligations. In addition, the Takeovers Panel, which is a peer-review body that regulates takeovers of companies and is the primary forum for resolving disputes about a takeover bid, also seeks to achieve the purposes by declaring certain circumstances in relation to a takeover unacceptable.

Very broadly, an off-market takeover bid under the Corporations Act requires a bidder to send copies of a 'bidder's statement' to the target company, ASIC and the market in which the target company is listed (if the target is listed), before the bidder sends the bidder's statement to the members of the target company to offer to purchase the securities held by them. The Corporations Act then requires the target company to prepare a 'target's statement' and send the target's statement to the bidders in response to the takeover bid, and also send copies of the target's statement to its members, ASIC and the market in which it is listed. The bidder's statement and the target's statement must contain information prescribed by the Corporations Act so that the members of the target company can make an informed decision as to whether to accept the bid offer. The Corporations Act also provides for the timing of steps to be taken to ensure that the members of the target have sufficient time to consider their options, while avoiding the process becoming unnecessarily protracted. The Corporations Act also contains provisions concerning formulation and consideration for the target's security the subject of the bid, and other procedural rules to achieve the objectives of the Corporations Act.

There is no prescribed procedure for a takeover of a proprietary company or a public company with 50 or less members.

The Corporations Act also contains general prohibitions on misleading and deceptive conduct, and making false or misleading statements, in relation to securities.

8. PROXY FIGHTING

8.1 Is proxy fighting customarily conducted for control of the company management or what other items? How is it regulated under the company law or market regulations?

In Australia, the term 'proxy fight' or 'proxy fighting' is rarely used, and members of a company lobbying at the company's general meeting in their own interests is recognised as a form of shareholder activism. Such shareholder activism, however, is not very common in Australia. There are no rules specifically regulating members of a company lobbying other members to vote at a general meeting in a particular way.

9. OFFICERS' REMUNERATION RULES

9.1 How is remuneration of officers determined? By whom? Is there a role for the shareholders' meeting? Is there any mechanism for an independent body to review and evaluate them?

Rules pertaining to remunerations of officers are discussed in paragraph 4.5 above.

9.2 Is the mechanism of officers' remuneration publicly debated?

There has been significant community concern in Australia about remuneration practices of senior executives of listed companies, both in terms of their excessiveness and the level of remuneration not being directly linked to a company's performance.

One result of such community concern is the amendment of the Corporations Act in 2011 which introduced the 'two-strikes rule', concerning remuneration consultants and the prohibition of hedging of key management personnel's remuneration, as described in paragraph 4.5 above.

10. DIRECTORS' LIABILITIES, LIABILITY INSURANCE, INDEMNIFICATION

10.1 What are the directors' responsibilities and liabilities under the law? Can those liabilities be covered by insurance? Can it be indemnified by the company or other related parties?

A director primarily owes responsibilities to the company. However, this does not mean that the director is free from any civil or criminal liabilities arising out of his or her performance of duties or position as a director of the company brought by parties other than the company itself. Some of the duties and obligation of directors under Australian law have been discussed earlier.

A company may indemnify a director in respect of certain liabilities incurred by the director while acting in such a capacity. While it is not compulsory, companies often enter into Deeds of Indemnity, Insurance and Access with directors which provide for such an indemnity, and may also require the company to arrange insurance for the benefit of the director and provide rules for access by the director to corporate records.

Directors' and officers' liability insurance is available in Australia. However, the Corporations Act prohibits a company from paying a premium for a contract insuring a present or former director of the company against a liability arising out of conduct involving a wilful breach of duty in relation to the company or misuse of the position as a director of the company or misuse of information obtained as a director of the company.

The Corporations Act prohibits a company from exempting a person from a liability to the company incurred as a director of the company. A company is also prohibited from indemnifying a person against liabilities owed to the company or a related body corporate as a director, liability arising out of contravention of certain director's duties under the Corporations Act, or a liability that did not arise out of conduct in good faith as a director.

11. SHAREHOLDERS' DERIVATIVE SUITS

11.1 Is a shareholder's derivative suit provided for by law in your jurisdiction? How is it enforced by the shareholders?

The Corporations Act provides for the right of a member (among others) of a company to bring proceedings on behalf of the company, or intervene in any proceedings to which the company is a party for the purpose of taking responsibility on behalf of the company for those proceedings. However, such an action by the member requires leave (ie, permission) of the court. The applicant for leave must satisfy the court of things such as:

- the unlikeliness of the company to bring the proceedings itself or take proper responsibility;
- that the grant of leave is in the best interest of the company; and
- that there are serious questions to be tried.

Unless proven otherwise, the court does not grant leave to the member if the company's decision not to bring or defend the proceeding was made by an informed, good faith decision of all of the directors that such inaction is in the best interest of the company.

Even if members of the company ratify the inaction of the company concerning the proceedings, such ratification does not prevent a member from bringing a derivative suit and does not automatically disqualify the member from being granted leave.

Once leave for a member's derivative action is granted, the court may make any orders and give any directions that it considers appropriate in relation to such proceedings.

11.2 Have there been any recent relevant court cases on the subject?

A number of recent court cases have dealt with a member's right to bring a derivative action.

For example, in *Vinciguerra v MG Corrosion Consultants Pty Ltd* (2010) 79 ACSR 293; [2010] FCA 763, the company unsuccessfully sought to challenge the member's submission to the court for leave for the derivative action.

In *Re Wan Ze Property Development (Aust) Pty Ltd* (2012) 90 ACSR 593 [2012] NSWSC 722, the court confirmed that it can determine whether the applicant honestly believes that a good cause of action exists and has a reasonable prospect of success.

12. SOCIAL INTEREST IN CORPORATE BEHAVIOUR

12.1 How is a company in your country expected to deal with the following issues? Corporate social responsibility; gender, racial and social diversification; environmental issues; ecology and corruption?

The Corporations Act does not have any direct reference in relation to Australian companies' behaviour concerning social responsibilities, although this issue has been considered by the Corporations and Markets Advisory

Committee (CAMAC) in 2006. CAMAC does not support any revision of the Corporations Act in relation to corporate social responsibilities because it considered that the established formulations of directors' duties allows sufficient flexibility to take relevant interests and broader community considerations into account. In CAMAC's view, the most effective response to concerns that arise from time to time about the environmental and social impact of business behaviour is through specific legislation directed to the problem area.

In Australia, at both the Federal, State and Territory level, there are various pieces of legislation and government policies concerning social and other issues of community concern in such areas as environment and biodiversity conservation, climate change, anti-discrimination on various grounds (such as discrimination based on gender, race, religion, sexual orientation, marital status, and so on), anti-competitive practices, anti-bribery and corruption. The directors of Australian companies are expected to comply with such legislation and policies.

For companies listed on ASX, the Principles and Recommendations provide that listed companies should establish a diversity policy (which may include, but is not limited to, gender, age, ethnicity and cultural background diversity) and the policy should include requirements for the board of the listed entity to establish and assess measurable objectives for achieving gender diversity.

Brazil

Marta Viegas **Tozzini Freire**

1. GENERAL PRINCIPLES

1.1 What are the general principles of corporate governance in your jurisdiction? What are the main objectives of corporate governance principles in your jurisdiction? State also whether your legal system is based on common law or civil law.

Brazil is a civil law country, which means that the legal system is based on legislation rather than court decisions. Brazilian courts have little room for innovating in their decisions, although they do provide different interpretations of the legislation on a case-by-case basis. With a few exceptions, decisions from higher courts are not binding upon lower courts, but are important guidelines and often used as an interpretation tool.

The corporate governance principles in Brazil are based on the pillars accountability, fairness, transparency and corporate responsibility. Concepts such as 'interest of the company', 'shareholder interest', 'stakeholder interest', 'good faith', 'business judgment rule', 'duty of loyalty', 'fiduciary principles', 'duty of skill', 'negligence', 'care', 'honesty', 'fairness', 'transparency' are provided for in the Brazilian Civil Code (Law 10.406/02), the Brazilian Corporations Law (Law 6.404/76) and regulations enacted by the Brazilian Securities and Exchange Commission (*Comissão de Valores Mobiliários* – CVM), in addition to the voluntary Code of Best Corporate Governance Practices, issued by the Brazilian Institute of Corporate Governance (*Instituto Brasileiro de Governança Corporativa* – IBGC), a highly reputable not-for-profit organisation aimed at improving corporate governance practices in Brazil.

Among the most important principles of corporate governance in Brazilian legislation is the one providing that all shareholders have to exercise their voting rights at shareholders meetings in the best interest of the company. When there are conflicts of interest, certain cases require the shareholder to refrain from voting; others do not prevent voting, but may subject shareholders to damages claims.

The same principle applies to directors and officers, who must exercise their voting rights on the best interest of the company, regardless of the interests of those who elected them. Directors and officers have fiduciary duties such as duty of loyalty and duty of care, and may be held liable for damages to the company and the other shareholders in case of failure to observe such duties.

Controlling shareholders have duties towards the company, the other shareholders and all of the company's stakeholders. They may be liable for abusive conducts, such as conducts that deviate from the company's purpose, threaten the company's continuity, cause losses to the company in favour of related parties, corrupting or trying to corrupt managers or authorities, among others.

The main objectives of the current corporate governance principles are to create checks and balances to minimise incentives for controlling shareholders to seek private benefits of control in detriment of minority shareholders.

Although the Brazilian capital markets have significantly developed in the last years and there are today companies with fully dispersed capital, the reality in Brazil is still one of concentrated ownership, in which most of the companies have clearly identified controlling shareholders.

This reality provides for a different spectrum in the so-called agency problem. In Brazil, the agency problem is verified more between controlling and minority shareholders, rather than management and shareholders as seen in other countries.

The legislation, therefore, assumes the existence of controlling shareholders and contains protections for the relationship between them and minorities.

The development of the Brazilian capital markets and the rise of companies with dispersed capital provide a challenge to this system, as new situations arise that may not be easily addressed in existing legislation. Among these situations are issues with minority abuses, agency problems between management and shareholders, efficiency of the board of directors and hostile takeovers.

1.2 Have there been any recent developments in the law, codes and rules of corporate governance?

Yes. Corporate governance in Brazil has undergone a significant improvement in the last 15 years. This is a result of many factors, among which important economic and regulatory reforms implemented since the 1990s, which resulted in macro-economic stability, ended a long period of hyperinflation, provided for minority shareholder protections and were key for attracting and giving comfort to investors.

Before 2000, Brazil was seen as having fragile corporate governance practices. Many Brazilian corporations were controlled by shareholders with a majority of voting shares, but smaller total economic interest due to the issuance of preferred non-voting shares – which used to be allowed up to two-thirds of the total corporate capital. This scenario existed with a relatively weak minority shareholder protection framework, which allowed for abuses and expropriations of minority interests by controlling shareholders.

In 2001, the Brazilian Corporations Law (Law 6.404/76) was amended to reduce the proportion of preferred non-voting shares relatively to the common voting shares, so currently they are allowed up to half of the total corporate capital. Another important change was the creation of the so-called tag-along rule, under which a purchaser taking control of a listed company must also make a tender offer for the remaining voting shares at a price equal to at least 80 per cent of the price paid for the controlling shares.

Private sector initiatives have also helped modify the then prevailing market and investment culture. The Brazilian Institute of Corporate Governance (IBGC) published in 1999 the Code of Best Corporate Governance Practices, which was revised in 2001, 2004 and again in 2009. The Code raised the bar and established a number of good corporate governance practices above and beyond legal requirements. The compliance with the Code is voluntary, but the Code has had a significant impact on what was considered good corporate governance among Brazilian companies.

In addition, perhaps the most important recent development was the creation in 2001 by the São Paulo Stock Exchange (BM&FBOVESPA) of different listing segments based on corporate governance criteria ('Novo Mercado', 'Level 1' and 'Level 2'). The idea underlying these special markets is that investors would be more inclined to invest in companies that have adopted specific governance standards, including greater protection to minority shareholders and more transparency in corporate affairs.

The creation of such different listing segments contributed to a rise of initial public offerings, significantly increasing trading volume and liquidity. The great majority of new listings are currently made in one of these three premium listing segments.

Also, in 2008, BMF&BOVESPA created another special listing segment, 'BOVESPA Mais', with rules to attract listing requests of medium-market companies. In general lines, the disclosure rules are more flexible than other levels and the shares can be offered gradually to free float, being mandatory 25 per cent of the shares until the 7th year after the IPO. 'BOVESPA Mais' is yet to take off, with only a handful of companies listed in this level. Nevertheless, there is a significant effort from the market to create incentives for middle-market companies to thrive and list their securities in the stock exchange.

In 2007, the Brazilian Corporations Law was amended to provide for accounting obligations in harmony with International Financing Reporting Standards (IFRS).

Finally, the Brazilian Securities and Exchange Commission (CVM) issued important regulations in 2009. CVM Instruction 480/09 created new disclosure requirements with the so-called reference form, or *formulário de referência*. The new disclosure requirements include additional financial information, risk factors, market risks, information on related party transactions and information on the policy for directors' and officers' compensation, including variable compensation and disclosure of minimum and maximum amounts. CVM Instruction 481/09 regulates proxy voting and information that companies need to provide before shareholders' meetings.

It is also worth mentioning that the Brazilian Anti-corruption Law was enacted quite recently, in August 2013, and will come into force in February 2014 (Law 12.846/2013). This law introduces administrative penalties and civil liability on legal entities that engage in fraud or corruption of public officials, particularly involving public tenders and government contracts.

1.3 Outline recent court cases and incidents involving corporate governance issues. Were there any significant corporate scandals or large unlawful corporate cases?

One of the most important recent scandals involving corporate governance was that of Sadia. Sadia was a very successful meat-processing company in Brazil, but in 2008, in just a few months, it became financially insolvent and was eventually merged into its main competitor in the market.

Sadia is such an emblematic case because it was apparently a great company in which to invest. It had a large and growing market share, was steadily showing profits, listed in BM&FBOVESPA Level 1 and had American Depositary Receipts (ADRs) traded in the New York Stock Exchange. It had a board with a majority of independent directors and four committees to assist the board, including a financial and an audit committee.

Sadia had a practice of purchasing derivative instruments to protect revenues in foreign currency, due to large exports operations. The problem arose when Sadia began to use some exotic derivative instruments as a financial source of income, rather than protection against currency variations. Sadia bet in the continuing appreciation of the Brazilian currency against the dollar – when the financial crisis of 2008 blew over, the dollar appreciated and such exotic derivative instruments left Sadia with financial losses of approximately R$3.8 billion.

Corporate governance was the heart of the problems that contributed to Sadia's failure. The conclusion was that Sadia had an empty corporate governance structure that did not function adequately in practice. The case discussions orbited around issues such as fiduciary duties, segregation of functions, compensation based on financial short-term results, lack of adequate functioning of the board of directors and its financial and audit committees, lack of adequate internal controls and compliance, and inadequate disclosure.

The CVM punished the chief financial officer (CFO) with a three-year suspension from exercising office in listed companies and nine board members with penalties of R$400,000 and R$200,000. Sadia settled a class action of ADR holders in the USA for $27 million. The shareholders of Sadia proposed a derivative suit against the CFO, but the decision was favourable to the CFO on the grounds that the shareholders' meeting in that particular fiscal year had approved the management accounts with no remarks.

A similar situation occurred with Brazilian cellulose-producing company Aracruz. The dealing with exotic derivative instruments resulted in losses of approximately R$4.3 billion. Aracruz was at that time under a sale negotiation with one of its competitors, Votorantim Papel e Celulose (VCP). The corporate scandal stressed the negotiations, but eventually Aracruz was merged into VCP to create a new company, currently called Fibria.

The CVM initiated administrative proceedings against 17 individuals, all directors and officers of Aracruz. Differently from Sadia, 16 from the 17 individuals settled the cases before a final decision. The settlements were higher than the penalties applied to the directors and officers of Sadia, ranging from R$800,000 to R$1.2 million. In addition, Fibria settled a $37.5 million class action with a pension fund in Miami, which had significant losses with Aracruz securities. The shareholders of Aracruz filed a derivative suit against the CFO, which was eventually settled for R$1.5 million.

Another case worth mentioning was that of Banco Cruzeiro do Sul, blown in 2012. This case involves allegations of fraud and crimes against the Brazilian financial system.

Banco Cruzeiro do Sul was a bank listed in BM&FBOVESPA Level 1 since 2007. After the IPO, the controlling shareholders, in conjunction with management, allegedly initiated a series of illicit transactions involving false loans. The investigations revealed approximately 320,000 false loan transactions, which justified the accounting of R$1.25 billion in non-existing assets. In yet another fraud, Banco Cruzeiro do Sul assigned loan receivables to investment funds having the bank itself as quota-holder. The accusation alleges that the investment funds would purchase the loans in unfavourable conditions, generating artificial profits to the bank. The controlling shareholders and management were also able to artificially inflate the demand for the bank's securities in the BM&FBOVESPA, by financing a number of people to negotiate bank's securities and future contracts.

The Central Bank of Brazil initiated an investigation in Banco Cruzeiro do Sul in 2009, involving the federal police and the public prosecutors shortly thereafter. The CVM also investigated and disclosed the fraud involving investment funds. Eventually, in 2012, the Central Bank decided to declare the intervention of Banco Cruzeiro do Sul, discharging management and taking over the operations. In the same year, the Central Bank mandated the bank's liquidation.

There are currently criminal prosecutions against the controlling shareholders and other 15 members of the bank's management for a number of crimes, including racketeering, crimes against the financial system and capital markets, money laundering and evasion of foreign exchange.

It is estimated that the amount that may have been deviated by the controlling shareholders and the management since the IPO until the bank's intervention by the Central Bank of Brazil reached approximately R$575 million.

1.4 Which law enforcement agency is in charge of enforcing corporate governance? May a criminal sanction be levied upon infringement of the corporate governance rules?

The CVM is the agency in charge of supervising listed companies and is generally considered the 'market sheriff' – although it only regulates and supervises listed companies. The BM&FBOVESPA also supervises compliance with the many requirements for listing and having securities traded in the stock exchange.

With respect to private companies, the courts are the legitimate arena for corporate governance disputes.

Criminal sanctions may be levied, but they require the occurrence of a crime and a criminal prosecution imputing such crime to the individual or to the company. The company and its directors and officers may be held criminally liable in case wilful misconduct or negligent actions constitute a crime.

2. SOURCES OF LAW

2.1 Which laws, codes or statutes govern company structures and organisations? Are there statutes like the Companies Act or other forms of law? Is there much relevant case law?

The Brazilian Civil Code (Law 10.406/02) is the most general legislation governing company structures and organisations. It provides for many corporate types, among which the two most utilised are the *Sociedade Limitada* and the *Sociedade Anônima*, roughly comparable in other jurisdictions to limited liability companies and corporations. Other corporate types are rarely used because they do not provide for limited liability of the shareholders. The Civil Code also governs not-for-profit organisations.

The Brazilian Corporations Law (Law 6.404/76) applies both to listed and privately held corporations. Limited liability companies are governed by the Civil Code, but may choose to be supplementarily governed by the Corporations Law in instances where the Civil Code is silent.

The CVM issues a number of regulations applicable to listed corporations, such as those governing the issuance and trading of securities, tender offers, disclosure requirements, press releases, related party transactions and proxy voting.

The BM&FBOVESPA sets the rules for trading in the stock exchange and in the different listing segments (Traditional, Level 1, Level 2 and Novo Mercado).

Finally, the IBGC has issued the Code of Best Corporate Governance Practices, which is voluntary, but establishes a benchmark for good corporate governance practices among private and listed companies.

2.2 Which laws, codes or statutes regulate capital markets in your jurisdiction?

The main legislation governing capital markets in Brazil is the Capital Markets Law (Law 6.385/76). This law, together with other rules and regulations, establish the requirements for disclosure of information applying to issuers of securities listed on stock exchanges, the criminal penalties for insider trading and price manipulation, the protection of minority shareholders, licensing procedures, supervision of brokerage firms, and governance of the Brazilian stock exchanges.

The Brazilian capital markets are regulated and monitored by the National Monetary Council (*Conselho Monetário Nacional* – CMN), which has general authority over the stock exchanges and securities markets. The CMN regulates and supervises the activities of the CVM, foreign investment and foreign exchange transactions and has, among other powers, licensing authority over brokerage firms.

2.3 Are there any public interest laws which apply to or influence corporate governance?

The most relevant public interest laws influencing corporate governance are the Consumer Protection Code (Law 8.078/90) and the Environmental Law (Law 9.605/98).

They both establish specific rules allowing the disregard of legal entity, to attribute personal liability of controlling shareholders, directors and officers for damages to consumers and to the environment.

Although both laws require elements of fraud or gross negligence before the corporate veil may be pierced, the public nature of consumer and environmental protection causes courts to seek compensation from other sources when the company does not have sufficient funds, which oftentimes leads to the attribution of personal liability.

2.4 Have there been any recent developments in any of the above laws? What are the recent changes to the above laws or rules and the reasons for such changes?

There have not been recent developments in the above mentioned laws – the Consumer Protection Code and the Environmental Law. Rather than changes in the laws, what is still under development is the general understanding of the courts when attributing personal liability to controlling shareholders, directors and officers based on such laws, given the controversial nature of this matter.

3. SHAREHOLDERS AND THE SHAREHOLDERS' MEETING

3.1 How are shareholders' interests represented in the company? How are the shareholders assured exercise of their rights? What is the highest governing body within the company structure if it is not the shareholders' meeting?

The shareholders' interests are represented in the company through the exercise of voting rights. The shareholders' meeting is the highest governing body within the company.

In limited liability companies, each share entitles its holder to one vote at the shareholders' meetings.

Corporations may have voting and non-voting rights, at the ratio of 50:50, unless they are traded in the Novo Mercado segment, which only allows voting shares.

Non-voting shares must have advantages over voting shares, which normally consist in priority in the receipt of dividends or capital reimbursement; listed companies with non-voting shares must grant additional advantages consisting on either dividends 10 per cent higher than those of voting shares, dividends of at least 25 per cent of net income or tag along right on sale of control equivalent to at least 80 per cent of the per-share price paid to the control block.

Non-voting shares may acquire voting rights if during a period covered in the bylaws, not to exceed three consecutive years, the company fails to pay dividends to which the shares are entitled – the voting rights will continue until dividends are paid. Non-voting shares will also have voting rights in certain special cases, such as creation of additional classes of non-voting shares or changes in the rights of the existing class of non-voting shares.

3.2 How is the shareholders' meeting conducted? Who may chair the meeting? May attendance (not voting) at the meeting be restricted only to the shareholders? Are the shareholders allowed to be accompanied by legal or other counsel?

Brazilian privately held companies (corporations and limited liability companies) must call shareholders' meetings at least eight days in advance. Listed corporations must observe a minimum 15 days' period. The IBGC recommends that the shareholders' meetings are called at least 30 days in advance. When all shareholders are present at the meeting, the call requirements are waived.

Shareholders' meetings are usually conducted in the head offices of the company. Recently, the Corporations Law was amended to allow shareholders' meetings to be conducted electronically, with online voting, but this has not yet been widely implemented.

The meeting must be chaired by a person chosen by the attending shareholders.

Attendance at the meeting is restricted to shareholders and management of the company, except in cases where the presence of an outsider (the independent auditor or a consulting firm, for example) is justified. Shareholders must evidence their status of shareholders and vote in person (presently or online) or be represented by an attorney-in-fact, who may be a shareholder, a director, an officer or a lawyer; in listed companies, the shareholders may also be represented by a financial institution. Shareholders are not forbidden to be accompanied by legal or other counsel.

3.3 How are minority shareholders' rights protected?

The Brazilian Corporations Law provides for a number of rights to minority shareholders. Some of these rights are also provided by the Brazilian Civil Code and applicable to shareholders of limited liability companies.

The following essential rights are applicable to all voting shareholders, regardless of their equity stake in the company:

- to participate in any profit distribution;
- to participate, equally and pro-rata, in any remaining residual assets in the event of the liquidation of the company;
- to participate in shareholders' meetings and discuss the matters of the agenda;
- pre-emptive rights in the event of an issuance of new shares, convertible debentures and subscription warrants (*bônus de subscrição*), except in certain specific circumstances;
- to withdraw from the company in certain cases, such as reduction in the percentage of the minimum mandatory dividend, change in the

corporate purpose and acquisition of a controlling stake of another company if the acquisition price is outside certain limits;
- to call a shareholders' meeting, if the directors fail to do so within 60 days from the date they were required;
- for listed companies, to be included in a tender offer when there is a sale of control of the company, for a per-share price equivalent to at least 80 per cent of the price paid for the control block (this percentage is increased to 100 per cent in the Novo Mercado of BMF&BOVESPA);
- to monitor the management of the company; and
- to propose derivative suit against directors and officers, in case such suit is not proposed within three months from approval by the shareholders' meeting.

In addition to the above essential rights, minority shareholders have additional rights exercisable in accordance with their equity stake:

- General Meetings
  - Shareholders representing 5 per cent or more of the capital stock may call a shareholders' meeting if directors or officers fail to do so within eight days after receipt of a justified request or a request to install a fiscal council.
  - Shareholders representing 0.5 per cent or more of the capital stock may require a list with contact information of other shareholders for purposes of proxy solicitation.

- Board of Directors
  - Shareholders representing at least 10 per cent of the voting capital may require the adoption of cumulative voting for election of the board of directors; in listed companies, these percentages are reduced in accordance with the capital stock.
  - In a separate election, shareholders representing at least 15 per cent of the voting capital or 10 per cent of the total capital may each elect one director; in case the holders of voting and non-voting shares do not reach the required percentages, they may combine their participations and may exercise the right with 10 per cent of the total capital.

- Fiscal Council
  - Shareholders representing 10 per cent of the voting capital or 5 per cent of the non-voting capital may request the installation of a fiscal council; in listed companies, these percentages are reduced in accordance with the capital stock.
  - In a separate election, holders of non-voting shares and holders of 10 per cent of the voting capital will have each the right to elect one fiscal council member.
  - Members of the fiscal council must provide information about matters of their responsibility whenever required by shareholders representing at least 5 per cent of the capital.

- Others
  - Shareholders representing at least 5 per cent of the capital stock may require in a shareholders' meeting that directors and officers disclose information about shares acquired and sold in the last fiscal year, including stock option plans, benefits received from affiliated companies, conditions of the employment agreement and material facts related to the company.
  - If the shareholders' general meeting decide not to propose a derivative suit against a director or officer, shareholders representing at least 5 per cent of the capital may do so directly.

The different listing segments of BM&FBOVESPA provides for additional rights to minority shareholders.

Companies listed in Novo Mercado are required to have only voting shares, a minimum of 25 per cent free-float, a board of directors with a maximum term in office of two years, tag-along rights to minority shareholders with a price 100 per cent equivalent to the price paid for the controlling shareholder stake, separation between the roles of chair of the board of directors and CEO, valuation based on economic value in tender offers for delisting or freeze-outs, disclosure on trades made by controlling shareholders and senior management, and arbitration as dispute-resolution method. Level 2 maintains most of the requirements of Novo Mercado, but allows companies to have preferred non-voting shares. Level 1 companies need to have a minimum 25 per cent free-float and disclosure beyond legal requirements, including annual agenda for corporate events.

3.4 Is shareholder activism encouraged or discouraged? If not encouraged, how is it regulated?

Shareholder activism in Brazil has increased over the years, in line with the development of capital markets and corporate governance practices.

As mentioned above, the reality in Brazil is still that of a clearly identified controlling shareholder, but currently there is an increased number of companies with fully dispersed capital, especially in the Novo Mercado segment of BM&FBOVESPA. This scenario promotes greater shareholder activism.

In 2009, the CVM issued CVM Instruction 481/09, which is the first regulation about proxy solicitation ever enacted in Brazil. In addition to governing proxy solicitation, this new rule entitles shareholders owning at least 0.5 per cent of the totality of the company's shares to include nominees for the board of directors in the company's proxy material.

According to the CVM, the goal of this new rule is to create a simple framework able to lower the cost of voting and to facilitate the shareholder participation on the company's business oversight.

The Association of Capital Markets Investors (*Associação de Investidores no Mercado de Capitais* – AMEC) is a not-for-profit entity that congregates many institutional investors and plays an important role in advocating for greater shareholders' activism in Brazilian listed corporations.

3.5 How are professional shareholders (those minority shareholders who seek some extra benefit from companies by unduly and habitually influencing management by using their shareholding) treated by the law? Are they excluded from attending the shareholders' meeting? Are they criminally or otherwise publicly sanctioned?

The Brazilian Civil Code establishes that a holder of a right commits an illegality if it exercises such rights in a manner that exceeds the limits imposed by its social and economic purposes, good faith and ethics.

In addition, the Corporations Law contains the principle that all shareholders, including minority shareholders, must exercise their voting rights in the best interest of the company.

The situation where minority shareholders seek extra benefits from companies by unduly and habitually influencing management by using their shareholding would fall into these legal principles. Such shareholders may, therefore, be subject to damages claims from the company or other shareholders.

3.6 Are shareholders' benefits given to some of the shareholders by the company without resolution by the shareholders' meeting prohibited or regulated by the law or other rules?

Limited liability companies cannot have different types or classes of shares, so all shareholders shall be treated equally. Corporations may have different types and classes of shares, but shares of the same type and class shall confer the same rights to their holders. Therefore, the company cannot grant benefits to some of the shareholders, without an actual shareholders' meeting that decides on a change of the bylaws and the features of the entire class of shares.

4. DIRECTORS AND BOARD OF DIRECTORS

4.1 What are the functions and responsibilities of the directors and the board of directors? Do you have a one- or two-tier board system? What are the outside directors called?

The Civil Code, applicable to limited liability companies, does not establish a formal management structure for such companies, simply stating that they are to be managed by one or more Brazilian resident individuals. Limited liability companies therefore usually have a simplified structure, with no board of directors and managers elected by and reporting to the shareholders' meeting.

The Corporations Law establishes that corporations are to be managed by a board of directors and executive officers. The board of directors is only mandatory for listed companies, companies with authorised capital (a pre-agreed limit for capital increases) and companies with control shared by the government (*sociedades de economia mista*). In the absence of a board of directors, the executive officers are elected by and report to the shareholders' meeting.

The attributions of the board of directors include determining the general strategy for the company's business, electing and dismissing executive officers, establishing their duties, examining books and records, requesting information on contracts and so on.

The executive officers are responsible for the day-to-day management of the company and the company's representation before third parties.

Brazilian companies may also have the so-called fiscal council, a separate body, not part of the board of directors, to investigate the company's financial reporting and provide a separate opinion on the financial statements. The fiscal council may be permanent or temporary and installed at the request of minority shareholders, based on minimum percentage participations.

Directors and officers have fiduciary duties to the company. These duties encompass basically a duty of care in avoiding harm to the company and a duty of loyally placing the company's interests ahead of their own. Acting in the best interest of the company and avoiding any potential conflict of interests are also notions that must follow all directors' and officers' decisions. In summary, the fiduciary duties are the following:

- Duty of Care and Misuse of Power: directors and officers shall employ the care and diligence which a diligent and honest man customarily employs in the administration of his own affairs; they must use their powers to achieve the corporate purposes and to support the company's best interests.
- Duty of Loyalty: directors and officers shall serve the company with loyalty, treat its affairs with confidence and shall not: (i) use commercial opportunities coming to his knowledge by virtue of his position, for his own benefit or that of a third party; (ii) fail to exercise or protect companies rights or, in seeking to obtain advantages for himself or for a third party, fail to make use of a commercial opportunity which he knows to be of interest to the company; or (iii) acquire for resale at a profit property or rights which he knows the company needs or which the company intends to acquire.
- Conflict of Interest: directors and officers shall not take part in any corporate transaction in which they have an interest which conflicts with an interest of the company, nor in the decisions made by the other officers on the matter. They shall disclose their disqualification to the other officers and shall cause the nature and extent of their interest to be recorded in the minutes of the meeting.
- Duty to Inform: this is specific for listed corporations – upon taking office, directors and officers of listed corporations shall declare the number of shares, subscription bonuses, options to purchase shares and convertible debentures issued by the corporation, by a controlled corporation or by a corporation belonging to the same group, which they own. They must also sign a statement attesting compliance with the terms and conditions imposed by the Corporation Law. This duty also requires directors and officers to comply with public announcement requirements.

These duties must also be observed by members of the fiscal council and members of any other corporate body created by the company.

4.2 What are the rules that may give rise to civil and criminal liability of the director(s)? How are those liabilities sought?

The general rule is that directors and officers may not be held personally liable for debts of the company. However, they respond whenever damages arise from actions taken with gross negligence or wilful misconduct or in violation of fiduciary duties, law or bylaws. There must be evidence that they have somehow contributed, whether intentionally or upon malpractice, imprudence or negligence, for the occurrence of the damage.

Certain Brazilian laws and court precedents establish further grounds for attributing personal liability of directors and officers in certain circumstances, directly or through the application of the disregard of legal entity doctrine. This is usually seen in labour, tax, environmental and consumer protection cases.

The attribution of personal liability should only take place in case of evidenced fraud, malpractice, imprudence or negligence. However, up to the present moment, precedents vary in establishing the guidelines for directors and officers being held personally responsible pursuant to the disregard doctrine. Specifically in labour courts, precedents have been unanimous in applying the disregard doctrine in a very broad way.

Criminal liability depends on whether a crime has occurred and whether such crime may be specifically imputed to the director or officer. There are a number of crimes that may be imputed to directors and officers of a company, among others issuing false trade bills (Penal Code – Decree-Law 2.848/40), bankruptcy crimes (Law 11.101/05), white-collar crimes (Law 7.492/86), crimes against consumers (Law 8.078/90), crimes against the environment (Law 9.605/98) and insider trading (Law 6.385/76).

4.3 Does the board of directors have a committee system, eg, nomination committee, compensation committee, audit committee? If not required, is it common practice for companies? How does it function?

The creation of committees to assist the board of directors is not a general legal requirement, although it is considered a good corporate governance practice, contributing to enhance board performance.

In certain regulated sectors – such as financial institutions and insurance companies – there are rules requiring the creation of an audit committee.

CVM Instruction 509 also contains an incentive for the creation of an audit committee in listed companies: those companies with an audit committee may contract an independent auditor for up to 10 consecutive years, while the general rule is that independent auditors must be replaced every five years.

The IBGC Code provides that having committees is good practice, but the number of committees should depend on the size of the company. An excessive number may create inappropriate interference in management. They must be accessory bodies and not imply in a delegation of responsibilities, which remain with the board as a whole.

The number of Brazilian companies with committees is still considerably low. It is worth mentioning that many companies have created a fiscal council, which is an interesting substitute for an audit committee, although their nature is different.

4.4 Is it a legal requirement to have an independent director or a third-party director? If so, how are they appointed? Is it required for listed companies?

There is no requirement in the Corporations Law for companies to have independent directors. The law establishes only that no more than one-third of the board members may also serve as officers.

The regulation of the Novo Mercado of BM&FBOVESPA contains a requirement that corporations traded in this segment must have at least 20 per cent of the board seats reserved to independent directors.

The existence of independent directors is considered a good corporate governance practice by the IBGC. According to the IBGC Code, the number of independent directors should depend on the level of maturity of the company, its life cycle and its particular features. The IBGC nevertheless recommends that a majority of the board members be independent and lists 12 qualifications that would make an individual independent.

4.5 How is the compensation for directors or officers determined? Can it be contested by the shareholders or the regulatory authorities? What are the common rules or practices for the compensation of officers?

The aggregate annual compensation of directors and officers is determined by the shareholders' meeting taking into account their duties and liabilities, the time dedicated to the function, professional reputation and the value of their services in the market.

Once this determination is made, the board of directors is responsible for distributing the aggregate annual amount among the directors and executive officers.

Listed corporations must disclose the compensation of directors and officers to the market. CVM Instruction 480/09 provides for disclosure through the reference form (*formulario de referência*), which must be updated annually. The compensation must be disclosed in aggregate, in two blocks, one for board of directors and another for executive officers. The compensation is not disclosed on an individual basis, but the minimum and maximum compensation in each block is disclosed.

The compensation disclosure was one of the most discussed aspects when CVM Instruction 480/09 was under public scrutiny – the initial draft provided for disclosure on an individual basis, but this was eventually changed after much discussion and pressure.

The IBGC advocates for the formality and transparency of the procedures to determine board compensation and recommends that incentive payment structures be different than those applied to executive officers, saying that short-term result-based compensation should be avoided. Further, the IBGC shows a preference for disclosure on an individual rather than aggregate basis or, at least, minimum, average and maximum amounts. Disclosure should comprise all types of compensation and targets and metrics of variable compensation should be measurable, disclosed and explained.

4.6 How will the board handle a corporate crisis like an internal criminal case, violence, social media exposure or dawn raid by the authorities?

The members of the board of directors have fiduciary duties and must handle corporate crisis strictly following such duties. Depending on the crisis, the board must make sure that the market is duly informed through the publication of the so-called 'material fact' notice. A material fact must be published whenever there is a fact that may substantially influence the value of the company's securities, the decision of investors in trading such securities or the decision of investors in exercising any rights inherent to the ownership of such securities. The company may refrain from publishing a material fact only when the issue is confidential and its disclosure would significantly jeopardise the company's interest.

5. BOARD OF AUDITORS, AUDIT COMMITTEE, ACCOUNTING AUDITORS

5.1 How is the internal accounting and legal audit structured and conducted? Is an outside accounting audit required and, if so, how is it structured? Are there requirements to change the auditor each five years?

Brazilian companies are required to follow International Financial Reporting Standards (IFRS). The Corporations Law contains a number of accounting-related rules, which are supplemented by regulations issued by the Federal Accounting Council (*Conselho Federal de Contabilidade* – CFC). The Committee for Accounting Opinions (*Comitê de Pronunciamentos Contábeis* – CPC) also provides valuable information on the interpretation of accounting rules – such committee was born as an initiative of a few market agents, among which the CFC and BM&FBOVESPA.

Listed corporations and companies considered as 'large companies' (those with assets totalling R$240 million or annual gross revenues in excess of R$300 million) are required to have independent audits.

According to CVM Instructions 509 and 308, listed corporations must rotate their independent auditors every five years, unless they have an audit committee, in which case they may keep the same independent auditor for 10 years.

Rotation of independent auditors is also provided for in the regulations of certain regulated sectors – such as financial institutions and insurance companies.

5.2 Do you have supervisory auditors? What is the function of the supervisory auditors' board?

Brazilian companies may have a fiscal council, which is a corporate body separated from the board of directors, elected by and reporting to the shareholders. The main attribution of the fiscal council is to investigate the company's financial reporting and provide a separate opinion on the financial statements.

6. MARKET DISCLOSURE/TRANSPARENCY TO THE SHAREHOLDERS AND THE PUBLIC

6.1 What are the disclosure requirements for companies in your jurisdiction under company law, capital markets law or any other rules?

Limited liability companies have to disclose financial statements to the shareholders, for approval at the annual shareholders' meeting. There is currently a market discussion on whether large limited liability companies (those with assets totalling R$240 million or annual gross revenues in excess of R$300 million) must also publish financial statements in the official gazette and a local newspaper, but this is still not a settled issue.

Corporations must have their financial statements, including an annual balance sheet, accumulated profit-and-loss statement, income statement, cash flow statement (except for a privately held corporation with a net worth of less than R$2,000,000) and value-added statement (in the case of a listed corporation), published in the official gazette and a local newspaper. A privately held corporation with less than 20 shareholders and a net worth of less than R$1,000,000 is exempted from such publication, but its financial statements must nonetheless be filed with the competent Board of Trade.

Listed corporations have a number of additional disclosure requirements. They are required to provide the CVM, the BM&FBOVESPA and the public in general with periodic and specific information in respect of the company, its activities and financials. Periodic information includes, for instance, financial statements, the annual reference form (*formulário de referência*), management accounts, minutes of annual shareholders' meetings, quarterly information reports, among others. Specific information includes, for instance, minutes of any special shareholders' meeting, shareholders' agreements and information on bankruptcy.

In addition, listed corporations are required to disclose any 'material facts', save for situations where the disclosure would jeopardise corporate interests. For purposes of Brazilian law, a 'material fact' refers to any decision taken at a shareholders' meeting or by management bodies, or any other business fact that could substantially influence the value of the company's securities, the decision of investors in trading such securities or the decision of investors in exercising any rights inherent to the ownership of such securities.

Among the facts that trigger such duty to inform the market we have changes in company stock control, merger or spin-off, delisting of shares, execution or termination of a shareholders' agreement, significant changes in the company asset composition, creation of a stock option plan, serious disagreements among directors and officers, investments for the opening of new facilities, changes to the rights or benefits of securities, signing or cancellation of a significant contract, or failure to obtain such contract, when expectations were known to the public, acquisition of company shares for holding in treasury or cancellation, or the sale of shares.

In addition, the CVM also requires that any person that reaches at least 5 per cent of total of any class of shares, a listed corporation discloses such fact to the market.

6.2 What is the liability or responsibility of the board in relation to the company's disclosure requirements?

Failure to comply with disclosure requirements constitutes a breach of fiduciary duties of directors and officers, subjecting them to damages claims from stakeholders. Directors and officers of listed companies may also face penalties from the CVM.

7. M&A AND CORPORATE GOVERNANCE

7.1 Upon an M&A offer, how are the transparency and fairness rules of the company provided under the company and stock market laws and rules?

M&As involving privately held companies enjoy much flexibility in the law, so purchaser and seller may freely discuss price, terms and conditions (subject, naturally, to provisions of bylaws and shareholders' agreements, if any).

M&As involving listed companies may be negotiated between sellers and purchasers in private transactions or through public tender offers (friendly or hostile); they may also involve a corporate restructuring, such as merger (*fusão or incorporação*) or merger of shares (*incorporação de ações*). They must comply with the Corporations Law, the Capital Markets Law and CVM Instruction 361/02.

The acquisition of control of a listed company requires the purchaser to make a tender offer for the remaining common shares at a price equal to at least 80 per cent of the price paid for the controlling shares (or 100 per cent, for companies traded at Novo Mercado).

Tender offers must observe equitable treatment to all shareholders holding the type and class of shares subject to the offer and must provide adequate information to allow for an informed decision.

There is flexibility on the proposed price if the tender offer is voluntary, implemented by independent parties and in cash. If the tender offer is mandatory, or made by parties related to the company or its controlling shareholder or involves payments with share swap, the offer must be registered with the CVM and supported by independent valuation reports.

Specifically in the cases where the transaction involves related parties, the CVM has issued an opinion (*Parecer de Orientação* No. 35), establishing guidelines to be followed by directors and officers when reviewing the transaction terms and conditions, including obtaining fairness opinions and creating independent committees.

It is also worth mentioning that in 2012, BM&FBOVESPA, IBGC, AMEC and the Brazilian Association of Entities of the Financial and Capital Markets (*Associação Brasileira das Entidades dos Mercados Financeiro e de Capitais –*

ANBIMA) entered into an agreement to create the Brazilian M&A Committee (*Comitê de Aquisições e Fusões* – CAF), a voluntary organisation, inspired in the UK Takeover Panel.

The purpose of the CAF is to ensure equitable treatment to shareholders of listed companies during public tender offers and corporate restructuring. Adhesion to the CAF is voluntary, but its decisions will certainly establish a benchmark for fairness in public M&A transactions.

8. PROXY FIGHTING

8.1 Is proxy fighting customarily conducted for control of the company management or what other items? How is it regulated under the company law or market regulations?

Proxy fighting is a new phenomenon in Brazil. It is expected to become more common given the increased number of companies with dispersed capital, but it is still rare. The first rule concerning proxy solicitation in Brazil was issued in 2009 – CVM Instruction 481/09. In addition to governing proxy solicitation, this new rule entitles shareholders owning at least 0.5 per cent of the totality of the company's shares to include nominees for the board of directors in the company's proxy material.

9. OFFICERS' REMUNERATION RULES

9.1 How is remuneration of officers determined? By whom? Is there a role for the shareholders' meeting? Is there any mechanism for an independent body to review and evaluate them?

See paragraph 4.5.

9.2 Is the mechanism of officers' remuneration publicly debated?

The issue of directors' and officers' remuneration has been much in the spotlight of public debate, especially because of the recent CVM Instruction requiring disclosure of compensation for listed companies, even if not on an individual basis. The IBGC has also played an important role in the public debate, given its recommendations in the Code of Best Corporate Governance Practices and annual researches published with the results of the compensation disclosure to the CVM.

10. DIRECTORS' LIABILITIES, LIABILITY INSURANCE, INDEMNIFICATION

10.1 What are the directors' responsibilities and liabilities under the law? Can those liabilities be covered by insurance? Can it be indemnified by the company or other related parties?

For directors' responsibilities and liabilities, see paragraph 4.1.

Brazilian laws are silent on the issue of whether or not a company is permitted to indemnify its directors and officers in case they face damages resulting from actions taken on behalf of the company, but hold harmless letters providing for such indemnification from controlling shareholders are quite common, especially in cases where directors and officers are called to respond to liabilities of the company towards third parties due to joint liability or disregard of legal entity doctrine.

There are many insurance companies offering directors' and officers' (D&O) coverage in Brazil. D&O insurance is considered to be an effective source of protection to directors and officers, but some exclusions apply, such as for cases involving fraud, wilful misconduct and penalties applied by governmental authorities.

11. SHAREHOLDERS' DERIVATIVE SUITS

11.1 Is a shareholder's derivative suit provided for by law in your jurisdiction? How is it enforced by the shareholders?

Shareholders' derivative suits are provided for by the Corporations Law. As a general principle, suits by the company against a director or officer must be approved by the shareholders' meeting. If approved by the shareholders' meeting and not filed by the company within three months, any shareholder may directly propose the suit. If not approved by the shareholders' meeting, the suit may be proposed by shareholders representing at least 5 per cent of the capital stock.

The favourable results of a derivative suit filed by a shareholder will revert to the company, but the company must indemnify the shareholder, up to the amount of such results, of all costs and expenses incurred by such shareholder in connection with the suit.

The Corporations Law also provides for derivative suits that can be filed by minority shareholders against the controlling shareholder for damages caused to the company in case of abusive exercise of control power.

11.2 Have there been any recent relevant court cases on the subject?

Derivative suits in Brazil are not very common. Among recent relevant court cases are those involving Sadia and Aracruz, discussed in paragraph 1.3.

12. SOCIAL INTEREST IN CORPORATE BEHAVIOUR

12.1 How is a company in your country expected to deal with the following issues? Corporate social responsibility; gender, racial and social diversification; environmental issues; ecology and corruption?

Pursuant to the Corporations Law, the controlling shareholder must lead the company to fulfil its social function and has duties with regard to stakeholders, including the community within which the company carries out its purpose. Directors and officers must also use their powers to achieve the corporate purposes and to fulfil the company's social function, observing the needs of stakeholders in general. Directors and officers may authorise gratuitous actions by the company to the benefit of its employees and the community.

Stakeholder interests include the employees working within the company, which, pursuant to the Consolidation of Labor Laws in Brazil (CLT), must be treated equitably, regardless of gender, race, disabilities or background.

Corruption is a crime established in the Penal Code (Decree-Law 2.848/40). The Environmental Law (Law 9.605/98) provides for ecology and protection to the environment, establishing a number of environment-related crimes.

Corruption is a crime established in the Penal Code (Decree-Law 2.848/40). The recent Brazilian Anti-corruption Law (Law 12.846/2013) establishes administrative penalties and civil liability on legal entities that engage in fraud or corruption of public officials, particularly involving public tenders and government contracts. The law also prohibits companies from frustrating or defrauding the public tender process in any way, gaining an undue advantage or benefit from fraudulent modifications or manipulations of government contracts, or hindering the government's investigation or auditing activities.

Administrative penalties comprise fines of up to 20 per cent of the entity's gross revenues in the year prior to that in which the administrative proceeding is initiated, or up to R$60 million in circumstances in which it is not possible to calculate gross revenues. Other administrative sanction includes publication of the condemnatory decision on media of wide circulation.

Judicial sanctions include loss of assets, rights and valuables, suspension or partial interdiction of company's activities and prohibition to receive incentives, grants, donations or financing from public entities and financial institutions owned or controlled by the government, for a period of one to five years. The law also provides for mechanisms to avoid that new legal entities incorporated by the shareholders of previously punished entities contract with the Public Administration.

The government may enter into leniency agreements with companies that collaborate effectively with the investigations, reducing or exempting certain sanctions. Also, the law encourages the implementation of compliance programmes, as their existence may be taken into account when applying administrative sanctions.

There are many initiatives concerning corporate social responsibility. One of the most interesting is BM&FBOVESPA's sustainability index (*Índice de Sustentabilidade Empresarial* – ISE) for comparing listed companies' performance based on corporate sustainability, economic efficiency, social justice and corporate governance.

The Ethos Institute (*Instituto Ethos de Empresas e Responsabilidade Social*) is a not-for-profit entity that plays an important role in encouraging companies to be ethically responsible and advocating for an investment environment compatible with contemporary society's need for sustainable development.

Canada

Jay M. Hoffman & James M. Klotz*
MILLER THOMSON LLP

*The authors gratefully acknowledge the assistance provided by their associate Mara Banack in the preparation of this chapter.

1. GENERAL PRINCIPLES

1.1 What are the general principles of corporate governance in your jurisdiction? What are the main objectives of corporate governance principles in your jurisdiction? State also whether your legal system is based on common law or civil law.

The board of directors of a Canadian corporation manage or oversee the management of a corporation, appoint the corporation's officers and delegate tasks to the corporation's officers, where appropriate.

A director of a corporation has two fundamental duties imposed by Canadian corporate statutes. The first is a fiduciary duty to act in good faith with a view to the best interests of the corporation. This duty requires a director to act in the interest of the corporation and not in his or her own interest or the interest of any one particular stakeholder group. The fiduciary duty also contemplates a duty to treat individual stakeholders fairly and equitably.

A director's second fundamental duty is to exercise the care, diligence and skill that a reasonably prudent person would exercise in comparable circumstances. This duty imposes an objective standard on directors and requires a director to make fully informed judgements on behalf of the corporation. Directors should only rely on the expertise of management or other advisors where reasonable.

Directors who discharge these statutory duties properly may benefit from the 'business judgment rule'. Canadian courts have stated that they will not intervene when a director has made a decision that is independent of any conflict of interest, made in good faith and that is within the range of reasonable possibilities given the information available to the director at the relevant time. Further, courts have confirmed that directors will not be held to a standard of perfection but rather a standard of reasonableness. However, if a court determines that a director did not act in accordance with his or her statutory duties to the corporation, the onus shifts to the director to prove that a decision was not only reasonable but also the best possible alternative. Therefore, directors should carefully consider the possible application of the business judgment rule and should ensure that processes are implemented to document a director's actions in reaching a decision and discharging his or her duties.

Canada's legal system is based on common law with civil law in the province of Quebec. Canadian corporations are formed as limited liability companies or unlimited liability companies.

1.2 Have there been any recent developments in the law, codes and rules of corporate governance?

Election of directors

Canada's corporate governance regime is constantly evolving. For public companies listed on the Toronto Stock Exchange, a new requirement was implemented in December 2012 which requires all directors to be elected individually instead of by slate and for the corporation to disclose the voting results for each director individually. Corporations are also required to disclose if the corporation has a majority voting policy for its directors. A majority voting policy stipulates that if a nominee director does not receive a majority of votes in favour of his or her election, then the nominee will resign as director, regardless of the fact that he or she was validly elected under the applicable corporate statute. Recently, the Ontario Securities Commission, the largest securities regulator in Canada, issued a statement supporting the Toronto Stock Exchange's plan to introduce regulations to address majority voting. Lastly, the amendments impose a requirement that elections be held on an annual basis. This requirement prohibits 'staggered' boards which are still permissible under Canadian corporate statutes.

Notice and access

Recently, Canadian securities regulators amended National Instrument 54-101 *Communication with Beneficial Owners of Securities of a Reporting Issuer* to modernise the method for delivery of proxy materials. Canadian public corporations are now permitted to post proxy materials on the corporation's website (as opposed to sending it by regular mail). These 'notice and access' amendments became available to public corporations holding shareholders' meetings after 1 March 2013.

Advance notice by-laws

Another recent development in Canadian corporate governance is the implementation of advance notice by-laws for nominee directors proposed by shareholders. An advance notice by-law is a tool used by corporations to prevent surprises at the annual meeting of shareholders. An advance notice by-law will impose a deadline by which a shareholder must submit a director's nomination to the corporation's management prior to the annual shareholders' meeting of the corporation. A number of stakeholder groups have supported advance notice by-laws. For example, Institutional Shareholder Services supports advance notice by-laws when the nomination period for shareholder nominees is no less than 30 days and no more than 65 days prior to the meeting date. While advance notice by-laws are common in the USA, they are a new development in Canada.

Emerging market issuers

Recently, Canadian corporations with operations in emerging markets have faced increased scrutiny by Canadian regulators. In late 2012, the Ontario Securities Commission published OSC Staff Notice 51-720 *Issuer Guide for Companies Operating in Emerging Markets*. Shortly thereafter, the Toronto Stock Exchange and TSX Venture Exchange published their own consultation papers on the subject. These publications reinforce the existing continuous disclosure obligations for Canadian companies operating in emerging markets and highlight potential risks associated with operating in an emerging market including: corporate governance practices, financial reporting and auditing issues, corporate structures and issues relating to risk management and internal controls.

The OSC Staff Notice recommends that appropriate modifications be made to a corporation's governance when it operates in an emerging market. For example, when the language and culture of the market in which a company conducts its operations is significantly different than Canada, it is recommended that the corporation have a director with knowledge of the culture and business environment. Similarly, corporations operating in an emerging market using complex or unusual structures (for example, structures involving many subsidiaries or special purpose entities) should ensure that internal controls are appropriate. Further, the impact of operating in an emerging market should be appropriately disclosed in a corporation's continuous disclosure documents.

Say on pay

A recent trend in Canadian corporate governance is the introduction of non-binding shareholder votes on executive compensation. These 'say on pay' votes are receiving a lot of attention in Canadian media as well as the business community. For further discussion of this issue, refer to paragraph 9.1.

Empty voting

Empty voting is the term used to describe a number of circumstances that, whether intentionally or not, decouple the economic interest in a share from the voting rights attached to it. Empty voting can occur in various ways, including when an investor sells shares between the record date and the meeting date so that he or she no longer has an economic interest in the outcome of the shareholder vote but retains the ability to affect the outcome of the meeting. The type of empty voting that triggers the most policy concerns arises when an investor employs hedging techniques that insulate against the economic risk of holding shares or that result in the investor having a large voting interest with a relatively small economic interest. Empty voting, especially empty voting that is intentionally employed to affect the outcome of a proxy battle, causes concern because of the misalignment created between voting rights and the investor's economic interest. A Canadian court recently considered the issue of empty voting and while it expressed concern about the misalignment of economic interests of the hedge fund that had engaged in empty voting and other shareholders, it concluded that the practice does not violate any law and there was no legal basis for judicial intervention.

Canadian securities regulators have attempted to address the issue by proposing requirements for security holders to aggregate holdings and disclose any use of derivatives or security lending arrangements that could lead to empty voting. However, these amendments are not currently in effect and it remains to be seen if the proposed amendments will effectively address the issue.

1.3 Outline recent court cases and incidents involving corporate governance issues. Were there any significant corporate scandals or large unlawful corporate cases?

Currently, the auditors of Livent Inc. (Livent), formerly a live theatre production company, are the subject of a C$450 million lawsuit filed on behalf of Livent's creditors and shareholders. In 2009, the co-founders of Livent were found guilty of fraud and forgery for artificially inflating Livent's profits and understating its costs to improve the company's financial position for every quarter between 1993 and 1998. Investors lost approximately C$500 million as a result of the scheme. Both co-founders were sentenced to four- and five-year jail sentences respectively. The current allegation is that the auditors ignored signs of fraud and were negligent in their review of Livent's financial statements. The case is being closely watched in Canada because it has the potential to be a precedent-setting decision regarding the potential liability for an auditor's failure to detect fraudulent accounting.

Another scandal that has received much attention involves Canadian engineering firm, SNC-Lavalin Group Inc. (SNC-Lavalin). It is alleged that SNC-Lavalin made improper payments to secure construction contracts in a number of countries including Libya, Tunisia, Mexico, Switzerland, Algeria, Cambodia and Bangladesh. SNC-Lavalin's former CEO and a number of other former executives of the company have also been arrested and charged with fraud in connection with other construction projects. It is also alleged that SNC-Lavalin was involved in corrupt political donations domestically. The company has already settled a complaint from the World Bank that bars one subsidiary of the company from bidding on any projects funded by the World Bank for at least 10 years. The company also faces potentially crippling bans from participating in public works contracts in the province of Quebec. While the full extent of SNC-Lavalin's alleged impropriety is still unknown, it highlights the need for increased enforcement of Canada's anti-bribery laws.

The Supreme Court of Canada's landmark decision in *BCE Inc. v 1976 Debentureholders* continues to be an important case in Canadian corporate governance. The *BCE* decision states that the duty of a board of directors is owed to the corporation and not any particular constituency. While a board is not required to consider the interests of any particular stakeholder groups, boards may and, as a practical matter, should assess the reasonable expectations of various stakeholders including shareholders, employees, suppliers and creditors. The decision also provides that while a corporation is entitled to act in a manner that will maximise profit and shareholder value, a corporation is not entitled to treat any particular stakeholder unfairly. The decision is considered to be positive for Canadian boards of directors because it recognises the inherent difficulty of balancing the interests of various stakeholder groups while acknowledging the important role played by shareholders in approving proposed transactions. The decision affirms that Canadian courts will not intervene where directors have weighed the various competing interests and exercised sound business judgement.

1.4 Which law enforcement agency is in charge of enforcing corporate governance? May a criminal sanction be levied upon infringement of the corporate governance rules?

The enforcement of corporate governance falls within a number of different areas. Criminal laws are enforced by local, provincial and federal police agencies. Securities laws are enforced by provincial securities regulators. Other governmental authorities may also impose sanctions or fines for infringement of environmental, labour, and competition laws. Liability for directors and officers may arise under corporate statute. Corporate law regulators are empowered under corporate statutes to enforce breaches of corporate law. For example, Canadian corporate law statutes provide that any person who makes or assists in making a report, return, notice or other document required by the statute that contains an untrue statement or omits a material fact is guilty of an offence and liable for a fine or imprisonment. However, the statute also provides a due diligence defence that states that there is no liability for a misstatement or omission when the person exercised reasonable diligence. As a result, it is very rare for liability to arise under these statutes in Canada. It is much more common for private parties to enforce corporate law statutes among themselves by seeking judicial intervention to settle disputes; for example, see discussion of the oppression remedy in paragraph 3.1.

2. SOURCES OF LAW

2.1 Which laws, codes or statutes govern company structures and organisations? Are there statutes like the Companies Act or other forms of law? Is there much relevant case law?

Corporations in Canada are governed by either federal or provincial corporate statutes, provincial securities laws, applicable stock exchange rules and common law. These sources of law are supplemented by recommendations and best practices from various industry groups, institutional shareholder groups and professional associations.

Corporate statutes provide the general framework in which a corporation operates. Most Canadian corporations are formed by articles of incorporation which serve as the primary rules governing the corporation. The articles of incorporation set out the legal name of the corporation, the location of its registered office, any restrictions on the business of the corporation, the number of directors, and rights and restrictions attaching to the corporation's shares. Most corporations will also enact by-laws that specify many of the 'mechanics' associated with governing the corporation including the appointment of corporate officers, the authority of corporate officers and the procedure for meetings of directors.

Canadian common law provides further guidance on many corporate governance issues. For example, the common law has interpreted the duty and scope of directors' duties and affirmed the use of the 'business judgment rule' by directors. The 'business judgment rule' provides that a Canadian court will not interfere with a reasonable business decision made by a corporation's directors as long as the directors exercised reasonable care and diligence and acted honestly and in good faith when making the decision. Similarly, Canadian courts have clarified that directors of a corporation owe their duty to the corporation and not any stakeholder group in particular.

Canadian public companies are also subject to regulation by provincial securities laws and regulations and stock exchange rules. For further discussion of regulation in the public company context, see paragraph 2.2 below.

2.2 Which laws, codes or statutes regulate capital markets in your jurisdiction?

Canadian capital markets are regulated by provincial securities regulators. Each province and territory of Canada has its own securities legislation. There are national rules that have been adopted to harmonise and streamline the regulatory system. The provincial system has faced significant criticism. However, there is no national securities regulator in Canada. In December 2011, the Supreme Court of Canada ruled that the federal government's proposal to create a national securities regulator was unconstitutional. As a result, while there are still some efforts to create a national securities regulator, in the near term, it is likely that the status quo will continue.

With respect to corporate governance, all public companies in Canada are subject to National Policy 58-201 *Corporate Governance Guidelines* (NP 58-201), which addresses issues relating to the composition, mandate and conduct of a corporation's board of directors, nomination of board members and compensation of officers. While NP 58-201 is called a 'guideline', corporations are required to comply or explain any non-compliance in the corporation's annual disclosure documents. Failure to disclose is considered a breach of securities law. National Instrument 58-101 *Disclosure of Corporate Governance Practices* specifies the ongoing disclosure requirements for public companies with respect to corporate governance.

In addition to provincial regulators, the Canadian securities industry is regulated by two self-regulatory organisations: the Investment Industry Regulatory Organisation of Canada and the Mutual Fund Dealers Association of Canada. These two bodies regulate the standards of practice and conduct of its members in order to protect investors and the public interest.

Canada also has five exchanges – the Toronto Stock Exchange (TSX), the Montreal Exchange, the TSX Venture Exchange (TSXV), the ICE Futures Canada and the Canadian National Stock Exchange. The TSX is the only stock exchange for senior issuers. The exchanges impose additional requirements on listed issuers. For example, the TSX requires corporations to seek shareholder approval for certain transactions. The TSXV also has its own policy manual for issuers.

2.3 Are there any public interest laws which apply to or influence corporate governance?

Corporations in Canada are required to comply with a variety of laws that indirectly influence corporate governance. For example, the Canadian Charter of Rights and Freedoms, human rights legislation, environmental laws and anti-corruption laws are all applicable to corporations.

2.4 Have there been any recent developments in any of the above laws? What are the recent changes to the above laws or rules and the reasons for such changes?

Public interest legislation in Canada is well established and has not undergone any recent significant changes that would affect the governance of corporations in a material way.

3. SHAREHOLDERS AND THE SHAREHOLDERS' MEETING

3.1 How are shareholders' interests represented in the company? How are the shareholders assured exercise of their rights? What is the highest governing body within the company structure if it is not the shareholders' meeting?

Shareholders elect the directors who manage or supervise the management of the business and affairs of the corporation. Typically, the management of a public company will nominate director candidates for election by the shareholders with recommendations from the board of directors or a nominating committee. Under Canadian corporate statutes, certain fundamental changes require shareholder approval, including: changes to the corporation's constating documents, amalgamations, sale of all or substantially all of the corporation's assets and the continuance of the corporation into another jurisdiction. For public corporations, the rules of the stock exchange may require shareholder approval in additional circumstances. The TSX Company Manual states that securityholder approval may be required for transactions that materially affect the control of the corporation. For example, securityholder approval is required by the TSX in an acquisition transaction where the acquirer issues more than 25 per cent of the number of its own issued and outstanding shares as consideration for an acquisition.

A shareholder may submit a proposal to raise a matter at a shareholders' meeting. In some circumstances, a corporation is required to include a proposal submitted with materials circulated by management. Under Canadian corporate statutes, shareholders who hold at least 1 per cent of the total number of voting shares or whose shares have a fair market value of $2,000 and have held the shares for at least six months are entitled to have a proposal presented to other shareholders at a corporation's annual meeting. The main advantage of this approach is that it is very cost efficient. Management is obliged to give notice of these proposals in its proxy solicitation materials and to include a brief statement in support of the proposal if it is supplied by the shareholder. Management does not have to include materials that are not submitted in a timely manner or do not constitute business that relates to other shareholders.

A shareholder holding 5 per cent of the issued voting shares of a corporation is entitled to requisition a shareholders' meeting as long as the shareholder provides notice of the meeting to all directors and the registered office of the corporation indicating the business to be transacted at the meeting.

In Canada, there are many different avenues for a shareholder to pursue to protect his or her rights. A shareholder can undertake a derivative action, which involves the shareholder applying to a court to compel the corporation to take action against a director. Alternatively, a shareholder may rely on the oppression remedy. It is available to a complainant (as defined in corporate legislation) who can establish that the corporation or its affiliates have acted in a way that is oppressive or unfairly prejudicial to or unfairly disregards the interests of the complainant. The oppression remedy gives a court broad discretion to enforce fairness and rectify the complaint. A third option available to a shareholder is to apply to a court to compel a director, officer or employee of a corporation to comply with corporate statutes, the corporation's constating documents or a shareholders' agreement.

3.2 How is the shareholders' meeting conducted? Who may chair the meeting? May attendance (not voting) at the meeting be restricted only to the shareholders? Are the shareholders allowed to be accompanied by legal or other counsel?

In Canada, regular shareholders' meetings must be held on an annual basis. Corporate statutes require a meeting of shareholders to be held not later than 15 months after the last preceding annual meeting of shareholders. Generally, shareholders' meetings are called by the directors of the corporation, but may be requisitioned by shareholders who meet minimum ownership thresholds. Canadian corporate statutes prescribe the amount of notice required to be provided to shareholders of an upcoming meeting. For public companies, these notice requirements may be more stringent because of applicable securities regulation.

The chairperson of an annual meeting of shareholders is commonly determined by the corporation's by-laws which may specify which officer of the corporation will act as the chairperson. Some corporate legislation specifies that if the corporation's by-laws do not specify who will chair the meeting, the president, or in his or her absence, a vice-president who is a director shall preside as chair. If there is no person who meets the criteria provided by applicable corporate legislation, the shareholders present are entitled to choose a person to act as chair. The chairperson of the meeting of shareholders is under a general duty to assist the meeting in achieving its objectives by preserving order, ensure that the proceedings are being conducted in an orderly manner and to determine any incidental matters that arise during the course of the meeting. The chairperson is required to act in good faith and to be impartial throughout the meeting.

The agenda of an annual meeting of shareholders must include the election of the board of directors, the appointment of auditors and a review of the corporation's financial statements. After these matters have been completed, directors or management may put forward issues for shareholder consideration or shareholders may raise other issues of concern to them.

Generally, in order to attend a shareholders meeting one must have the right to vote at the meeting. In addition to shareholders, proxyholders, directors and auditors of the corporation are entitled to attend a meeting. Others may attend by invitation of the chairperson or with consent of the shareholders. Alternatively, the corporation's by-laws may specifically entitle a 'stranger' to attend. Shareholders are not regularly permitted to attend with legal counsel; however, this requirement is easily circumvented by appointing legal counsel as a proxyholder.

In addition to annual meetings, a corporation may hold special meetings of shareholders. These meetings are usually called to address a specific issue that requires shareholder approval. For example, a special meeting of shareholders may be held to approve a fundamental change to the corporation or to approve a change of control transaction. Practically, special meetings are frequently held in conjunction with the annual meeting of shareholders. In order to call a special meeting of shareholders, notice must be provided that states the location and time of the meeting and provides shareholders with information about the specific topic that they will be asked to consider and vote on at the special meeting of shareholders.

3.3 How are minority shareholders' rights protected?

Minority shareholders are protected by the requirement for either a simple majority or two-thirds of shareholders voting at a shareholders' meeting to approve certain transactions which would constitute a fundamental change to the corporation under corporate and securities statutes and the rules of the TSX.

Additionally, in Ontario and Quebec, Multilateral Instrument 61-101 *Protection of Minority Security Holders in Special Transactions* will apply to protect the interests of minority shareholders by requiring minority approval and independent valuations in the context of certain business combinations and related party transactions and takeover bids made by insiders or issuers.

3.4 Is shareholder activism encouraged or discouraged? If not encouraged, how is it regulated?

In Canada, shareholder activism is on the rise and the increased participation of shareholders in the governance of the corporation is generally viewed as a positive. This trend can be attributed to a number of 'activist friendly' attributes of the regulatory regime for Canadian corporations. For example, there are generally no staggered boards of directors in Canada and an entire board of directors can be removed by a simple majority vote of shareholders. Similarly, shareholders with a 5 per cent ownership interest are entitled to requisition a shareholders' meeting. There are also fewer defences available to fend off potential takeover bids in Canada compared with the US system.

A recent development in securities law that will impact the strategy shareholder activists undertake involves changes to the early-warning regime. Currently, a shareholder is not required to disclose its ownership position in a public company until they acquire a 10 per cent ownership interest. The proposed amendments would bring this threshold down to 5 per cent which is in line with the equivalent US requirements. The proposed amendments are intended to provide greater transparency about significant holdings of a corporation's securities. These changes are not currently in effect but they have been generally viewed as positive by securities law practitioners.

Canadian securities regulators have also recently published new proposals regarding the regulation of shareholder rights plans or 'poison pills' under proposed National Instrument 62-105 *Security Holder Rights Plans*. These changes, if implemented, will change the tactics employed by parties involved in takeover bids and as a result, will likely impact shareholder activism. For further discussion of the proposed legislation, see paragraph 7.1.

3.5 How are professional shareholders (those minority shareholders who seek some extra benefit from companies by unduly and habitually influencing management by using their shareholding) treated by the law? Are they excluded from attending the shareholders' meeting? Are they criminally or otherwise publicly sanctioned?

In Canada, there is no legislation regulating professional shareholders. However, as shareholder activism continues to rise, this issue may garner more attention. As regulators consider the issue, it will be essential to balance the legitimate right of shareholders to actively participate in the governance of a corporation and the desire to prevent professional shareholders from employing abusive tactics that hinder the proper management of the corporation.

Empty voting continues to be an issue for corporations in Canada. As discussed above in paragraph 1.2, empty voting typically occurs when a shareholder's economic interest is not aligned with his or her voting rights. While a Canadian court determined that it could not intervene to prevent empty voting, recently, Canadian securities regulators have attempted to address the issue by proposing requirements for security holders to aggregate holdings and disclose any use of derivatives or security lending arrangements that could lead to empty voting. However, these amendments are not currently in effect and it remains to be seen if the proposed amendments will effectively address the issue.

3.6 Are shareholders' benefits given to some of the shareholders

by the company without resolution by the shareholders' meeting prohibited or regulated by the law or other rules?

The rights of shareholders are dictated by the type of shares held. The starting point in Canadian corporate law is that all holders of a class of shares shall be treated equally. The terms, conditions, rights, privileges and restrictions that attach to a corporation's shares are set out in the share terms which form part of the constating documents of a corporation. Directors or officers of the corporation only have authority to vary the terms conditions, rights, privileges and restrictions outlined in the corporation's constating documents in limited circumstances. For example, the by-laws of a corporation can be amended by the board of directors and become effective pending shareholder approval. However, most other changes to a corporation's constating documents would be considered fundamental changes, and as a result, require shareholder approval under Canadian corporate law.

4. DIRECTORS AND BOARD OF DIRECTORS

4.1 What are the functions and responsibilities of the directors and the board of directors? Do you have a one- or two-tier board system? What are the outside directors called?

A corporation's board of directors is tasked with providing stewardship and oversight to the corporation's management team. Board members are not expected to devote their full time or attention to the daily business of the corporation. Daily responsibilities are typically delegated to the corporation's management but must still be supervised by the board of directors. Appointing and evaluating the performance of the corporation's management is considered an important function of the board of directors. Unlike in the USA, the role of chair of the board of directors and chief executive officer of the corporation are usually separated and held by different individuals in Canada.

While delegation of daily responsibilities to management is common, there are certain functions that a board is not permitted to delegate under the governing corporate statute. These functions include: issuing securities, purchasing or redeeming shares, declaring dividends, approving financial statements and certain disclosure documents, making changes to the corporation's by-laws and filling vacancies on the board of directors. Ultimately, the board must always retain ultimate control over the corporation and be able to intervene in any material issue facing the corporation.

Canada has a one-tier board system. Under corporate law applicable in most Canadian provinces, in order to act as a director in Canada, a director must be a natural person, over the age of 18, of sound mind and not bankrupt. Some Canadian corporate legislation imposes a requirement that the board of directors include at least 25 per cent resident Canadians. Several Canadian jurisdictions do not impose a residency requirement. Therefore, this requirement frequently becomes an important consideration when determining where to incorporate in Canada.

Outside directors are known as 'outside directors', 'independent directors' or 'non-executive directors.' Generally, Canadian corporate statutes require public corporations to have at least two directors who are 'outside', meaning that they are not employees, partners, family members of executive officers, or in receipt of remuneration from the company in excess of specified amounts from the corporation or its affiliates. NP 58-201 recommends that a majority of directors be independent. However, it has become common in Canada for boards to have two-thirds independent directors. For further discussion of independent directors, see paragraph 4.4 below.

NP 58-201 provides additional guidelines that impact the functions and responsibilities of a board of directors of a public company. For example, NP 58-201 provides that a board should adopt a written mandate that acknowledges the directors' responsibilities, implements internal controls and adopts processes for receiving feedback from stakeholders. While audit committees are required by securities law, NP 58-201 also recommends that directors form other committees including a nominating committee, compensation committee and corporate governance committee.

In addition, a board of directors may determine that it is appropriate for an independent special committee to be formed in specific circumstances. Special committees are commonly formed to consider potential change of control transactions, corporate crises, and insolvency proceedings. A special committee is required by law in limited circumstances, for example, an insider bid. In that context, a bidder will be required to obtain a formal valuation which will be supervised by the special committee. In a related party transaction, it is considered a best practice to form a special committee of independent directors.

4.2 What are the rules that may give rise to civil and criminal liability of the director(s)? How are those liabilities sought?

Directors must be aware of potential exposure to personal liability in the civil and criminal context. As discussed above, directors owe the corporation a duty of care and loyalty and can be held personally liable for breaches of these duties if it can be proven that the directors acted unreasonably, dishonestly or adversely to the best interests of the corporation. A breach of these duties is usually enforced in the civil context by a derivative action brought by the corporation's shareholders. For further discussion of derivative actions, see paragraph 11.1 below. Directors may also face civil liability if they are found to have acted negligently in the performance of their duties.

In the criminal context, directors can be found guilty of theft or fraud under Canada's Criminal Code. For an example, see discussion of Livent Inc.'s founders above in paragraph 1.3.

Statutorily, directors may be held liable for unpaid employee wages and benefits and, in some jurisdictions, accrued vacation pay and other benefits. Directors may also be liable for funds that are not remitted to the appropriate governmental authority for income taxes, pensions, unemployment insurance, registered retired savings plans and withholding taxes. Other potential sources of personal liability for directors arise from non-compliance with health and safety requirements, environmental laws, competition laws, and anti-spam legislation.

Directors of public companies must also be aware of potential liability (including fines or imprisonment) that arises from breaches of securities law. Directors may face liability in connection with continuous disclosure documents, takeover bid circulars and prospectuses if these documents contain fraudulent information or material misrepresentations. Directors may face additional penalties related to insider trading or other offences under securities law.

For a director, the best defence against the risk of personal liability is ensuring that the corporation has appropriate corporate governance policies and procedures in place and he or she is aware of a director's obligations and is diligent in ensuring that they are discharged and maintained.

4.3 Does the board of directors have a committee system, eg, nomination committee, compensation committee, audit committee? If not required, is it common practice for companies? How does it function?

Public companies are required to have an audit committee. The audit committee must consist of a minimum of three financially literate independent directors. Other committees that are common for Canadian public companies include: governance committees, compensation committees, health and safety committees, pension committees and nominating committees. While there is no requirement at law to have these committees, it is generally recommended by the Canadian Securities Administrators and considered a best practice in corporate governance. If a public company forms a nominating or compensation committee, NP 58-201 recommends that all members of the committee be independent. For corporate governance committees, NP 58-201 recommends that it be formed by a majority of independent directors and all other members be 'non-management' directors.

The board of directors of private companies are not required to have any committees; however, committees are a practical method of dividing responsibilities and expertise among directors and, as a result, are commonly formed.

4.4 Is it a legal requirement to have an independent director or a third-party director? If so, how are they appointed? Is it required for listed companies?

Generally, corporate statutes impose a requirement on public companies to have at least two 'independent' directors. 'Independent' means that the director is not an employee of the corporation and the director has no 'material' relationship with the corporation. The Canadian Securities Administrators recommend that a board of directors should be composed of a majority of independent directors. Under the federal corporate statute, a corporation that offers securities to the public must have at least three directors and at least two of those directors must be independent.

4.5 How is the compensation for directors or officers determined? Can it be contested by the shareholders or the regulatory authorities? What are the common rules or practices for the compensation of officers?

The compensation of directors is determined by the board of directors. There is no requirement to obtain shareholder approval for the remuneration of directors. However, for public companies, the remuneration of directors will be subject to disclosure requirements. Generally, directors' compensation in Canada is relatively modest.

The compensation of officers is also determined by the board. The CEO of the corporation will frequently provide a recommendation for remuneration of other officers. Many Canadian corporations have adopted non-binding shareholder 'say on pay' votes which allow shareholders to participate in the process of determining officers' compensation. See paragraph 9.1 below for a full description of officers' remuneration.

4.6 How will the board handle a corporate crisis like an internal criminal case, violence, social media exposure or dawn raid by the authorities?

When a corporate crisis arises, the most common response of a prudent board of directors is to form a special committee of independent directors to handle the crisis. The mandate of the special committee should be clear and tailored to address the specific crisis in order to ensure that the special committee has the requisite authority to address the issue. The formation of a special committee generally is viewed favourably by courts and tribunals as it supports the presumption that the corporation's directors are discharging their obligations by ensuring that the corporation's interests are being protected. Depending on the nature of the crisis, it may be prudent to grant the special committee authority to obtain its own legal counsel and financial advisors or other experts. For directors serving on the special committee, it may also be prudent to obtain an additional indemnity from the corporation and additional directors' insurance because frequently the decisions of a special committee are scrutinised by the public and reviewed by courts or regulatory bodies.

5. BOARD OF AUDITORS, AUDIT COMMITTEE, ACCOUNTING AUDITORS

5.1 How is the internal accounting and legal audit structured and conducted? Is an outside accounting audit required and, if so, how is it structured? Are there requirements to change the auditor each five years?

For public companies, the corporation is required to appoint an auditor. The shareholders of a private corporation are entitled to dispense with the audit requirement. In order to be appointed as auditor, the auditor must be registered with the applicable regulatory bodies. Auditors are appointed by the shareholders for annual terms which expire at the next annual meeting of shareholders.

It is a statutory requirement for a public corporation to appoint an audit committee. The audit committee is comprised of at least three independent directors of the corporation who possess special duties to review the corporation's financial statements and act as a liaison between the board of directors and the corporation's auditors.

There is no requirement in Canada to change auditors after a specific period of time. This issue was recently considered as part of an industry consultation regarding audit standards. The Enhancing Audit Quality (EAQ) steering group recommended that it is more appropriate to require audit committees to review their audit firm every five years and leave it to the discretion of the committee to either keep or replace their current auditors. The EAQ steering group also recommended public disclosure of the results of the audit committee's review.

5.2 Do you have supervisory auditors? What is the function of the supervisory auditors' board?

Not applicable.

6. MARKET DISCLOSURE/TRANSPARENCY TO THE SHAREHOLDERS AND THE PUBLIC

6.1 What are the disclosure requirements for companies in your jurisdiction under company law, capital markets law or any other rules?

Private corporations in Canada have limited disclosure obligations consisting of delivery of annual financial statements and a notice of an annual shareholders' meeting.

Public companies in Canada have ongoing disclosure requirements for shareholders and the public under Canadian securities law. Public companies are required to file: financial statements (annually and quarterly) with management's discussion and analysis, an annual information form outlining the corporation's business and information circulars for shareholders' meetings.

In addition to the regular disclosure requirements outlined above, public companies in Canada are required to disclose any material changes in the business of the corporation that would reasonably be expected to have a significant effect on the market price of any of the corporation's securities by filing a material change report and press release. For public companies listed on the TSX, there is an additional requirement to promptly disclose by press release any fact that would be reasonably expected to have a significant effect on the market price or value of any of the corporation's securities.

In addition to the corporation's disclosure obligations, directors and some officers are required to file insider reports outlining their holdings of the corporation's securities including any compensation based holdings or indirect holdings of the corporation's securities or related financial instrument.

6.2 What is the liability or responsibility of the board in relation to the company's disclosure requirements?

If a public company does not comply with its ongoing and timely disclosure obligations outlined in paragraph 6.1 above, the corporation may be subject to enforcement proceedings by the applicable securities regulator. In addition, directors and officers may be held liable for damages to investors if the corporation makes misleading or untimely disclosure. Class-action proceedings in Canada against public companies, directors and officers are becoming much more common.

7. M&A AND CORPORATE GOVERNANCE

7.1 Upon an M&A offer, how are the transparency and fairness rules of the company provided under the company and stock market laws and rules?

In Canada, there are several ways to acquire a target company including plans of arrangement, amalgamations and takeover bids. We will focus here on takeover bids. Canadian takeover bid rules are engaged when the securities subject to a potential bid together with the current holdings of an acquirer (together with any joint actors), constitute 20 per cent or more of the outstanding voting or equity securities of a particular class. If the takeover bid rules apply, the acquirer must offer to all shareholders of the target corporation to acquire shares on the same terms, unless an exception is available to, and relied on, by the acquirer. The policy rationale for Canada's takeover bid rules is to ensure that the interests of the target company's shareholders are protected while ensuring that any takeover bid is conducted in an open and transparent manner. Takeover bid legislation is intended to enhance a shareholder's ability to make a fully informed decision based on the merits of a potential offer and ensure the equal treatment of all shareholders. Canadian takeover bid rules have been criticised for favouring bidders and, in some cases, conflicting with the fiduciary duties of the board of directors by limiting the defensive measures it may employ in an unsolicited bid.

Under Canadian securities law, a takeover bid can be commenced by either publishing an advertisement or, more commonly, by mailing an offer to purchase to the target's shareholders. In the offer to purchase, the acquirer is required to disclose relevant background information about the negotiations of the offer, future plans for the target and any other material information for shareholders. All shareholders of a particular class of shares must be offered identical consideration. The directors of the target will then deliver a director's circular either recommending that shareholders accept the offer or request that shareholders take no action while the bid is considered by the board of the target corporation. The director's circular must be mailed within 15 days of the acquirer's commencement of the bid and it must disclose any information that would reasonably be expected to affect the shareholder's decision to accept or reject the offer. A bid must remain open for acceptance for a minimum of 35 days.

National Policy 62-202 *Defensive Tactics* outlines the securities regulators views on defensive tactics taken by a potential target's board of directors. A shareholder rights plan (or 'poison pill') is a defensive tactic that is triggered when a person acquires more than a specified percentage of outstanding shares (typically 20 per cent). When triggered, the shareholder rights plan allows existing shareholders to acquire additional shares of the target at a deep discount to their market price, which effectively prevents a bidder from acquiring a control position in a target corporation unless the target board agrees to waive the shareholder rights plan or the Canadian securities regulator terminates it. Historically, the position of Canadian securities regulators has been that a shareholder rights plan should be used as a tool to allow a target's board of directors time to seek out alternatives to a hostile bid, including a white knight or other alternative. However, these plans are generally terminated by securities regulators within 45–70 days of the commencement of a bid based on the rationale that shareholders should be given the opportunity to decide if they wish to tender to a hostile bid. The defensive tactics available under Canadian securities law are relatively limited compared with US laws.

Recently, the Canadian securities regulators published for comment a new regulatory framework involving the treatment of shareholder rights plans in Canada. As discussed above, 'poison pills' are currently permitted for up to 70 days to provide the directors of a target time to respond to a hostile bid. Under the new proposed framework, a shareholder rights plan becomes effective when it is adopted by the board of directors of the target, but it must be approved by a majority of shareholders within 90 days of its implementation. If shareholder approval is not obtained, the shareholder rights plan will automatically be removed after 90 days. Under this proposal, the shareholder rights plan must be approved annually by shareholders and can be terminated at any time by a majority vote of shareholders (excluding the shares of a bidder and any joint actors in a formal takeover bid). The proposed amendments would align Canada's regime more closely with the rules in the USA. The comment period for the proposed amendments was still open at the time of publication of this chapter.

The Quebec securities regulator, the *Autorité des Marchés Financiers* in Quebec (AMF), published its own consultation paper proposing an alternative policy that would reduce securities regulators' intervention in defensive tactics by increasing reliance on a target's board of directors. The AMF proposal would limit securities regulatory intervention to situations where there is an abuse of shareholders' rights or the efficiency of capital markets. The reasonableness of a target board's recommendation would be reviewed by considering: the use of special committees of independent directors to review bids, the engagement of financial and legal advisors by the special committee and the disclosure to shareholders regarding the bid process and recommendation of directors. The AMF proposal would also require an irrevocable minimum tender condition of 50 per cent of the target's shares held by independent shareholders. If the 50 per cent threshold is satisfied, the bidder would then be required to extend its offer for an additional 10 days to give other shareholders the opportunity to deposit his or her shares.

At the present time, it is unclear which proposal, if any, will be adopted by Canadian regulators.

8. PROXY FIGHTING

8.1 Is proxy fighting customarily conducted for control of the company management or what other items? How is it regulated under the company law or market regulations?

Shareholder activism is on the rise in Canada. In the last five years, proxy contests have become increasingly more common and dissidents have been successful in more than half of the proxy contests. Proxy contests in Canada have affected issuers of all sizes in a wide variety of industries.

The methods of proxy solicitation have also been receiving increased attention in recent years. For example, in a recent case in British Columbia, *International Energy and Mineral Resources Invest (Hong Kong) Company Limited v Mosquito Consolidated Gold Mines Limited*, the British Columbia Supreme Court found that the management's use of a telephone-based proxy system for a contested directors election was oppressive and unfairly prejudicial to the dissident shareholders because it was not a reliable method for identifying the shareholder giving instructions and ensuring that the shareholder's vote was private and fully informed.

The increased use of proxy advisory firms by mainly institutional investors has also raised corporate governance concerns related to potential conflicts of interest, lack of transparency and incomplete disclosure. Canadian securities regulators issued a consultation paper for comment in August 2012 and proposed a number of possible regulatory frameworks to address these issues. Recently, a number of industry groups have made recommendations for the regulation of proxy advisory firms. These recommendations include implementing proficiency standards for analysts making recommendations and a similar regulatory regime for proxy advisory firms to the current regulations in place for investment bankers regarding disclosure of potential conflicts of interest.

As discussed above in paragraph 1.2, the process for delivery of proxy materials in Canada was recently amended to allow for proxy materials to be posted on a company's website. These 'notice and access' amendments should improve the proxy solicitation process and may ultimately improve shareholder engagement.

9. OFFICERS' REMUNERATION RULES

9.1 How is remuneration of officers determined? By whom? Is there a role for the shareholders' meeting? Is there any mechanism for an independent body to review and evaluate them?

The board of directors is responsible for determining the remuneration of the corporation's officers. However, in the last five years, many large Canadian corporations have adopted a policy whereby shareholders are entitled to a non-binding 'say on pay' vote. Shareholder participation in executive compensation decisions continues to be controversial in Canada.

Those in favour of 'say on pay' voting argue that it is a means of increasing dialogue and engagement with shareholders. Many consider it to be a best practice that should be voluntarily adopted as part of a corporation's governance regime. Those opposed to 'say on pay' voting argue that it is inappropriate for shareholders to usurp the responsibilities of the board of directors. Further, for those corporations who have already adopted 'say on pay' voting in Canada, shareholders have supported the board of director's recommendation in almost all cases and so many argue that these votes are largely rubber stamps and are not effective.

Recently, Barrick Gold Corp.'s shareholders voted against its executive compensation plan at the corporation's annual meeting by an overwhelming majority. However, while the vote clearly expresses its shareholders' dissatisfaction, it is not binding on the board of directors.

9.2 Is the mechanism of officers' remuneration publicly debated?

The mechanism for determining the remuneration of a corporation's officers is publicly debated and frequently discussed in the Canadian press. Canadian public corporations are required to disclose its executives' compensation as a part of its continuous disclosure obligations. Specifically, public corporations must disclose all compensation paid to its executive officers from any source. The corporation is also required to disclose the objectives and rationale of its compensation strategy and the methodology used for determining compensation.

10. DIRECTORS' LIABILITIES, LIABILITY INSURANCE, INDEMNIFICATION

10.1 What are the directors' responsibilities and liabilities under the law? Can those liabilities be covered by insurance? Can it be indemnified by the company or other related parties?

As discussed above in paragraph 4.2, directors are at risk for personal liability from a number of sources. Therefore, it is common for corporations to obtain insurance against personal liability which may be incurred by current or former directors. Frequently, the corporation will pay the premium on these insurance policies.

Under corporate statutes, a corporation may indemnify its current and past directors for most liabilities for which they may be responsible by virtue of acting as a director of the corporation. The indemnification is usually qualified by the condition that the director acted in good faith with a view to the best interest of the corporation. A corporation cannot indemnify a director for a breach of his or her fiduciary duty or criminal or administrative penalties unless the director reasonably believed that the conduct was lawful.

Corporations indemnify directors for litigation costs related to actions in which the director acted in good faith in accordance with his or her duties. Under some corporate statutes, there is a requirement that the court find that the director was not at fault in order to be eligible for indemnification by the corporation.

11. SHAREHOLDERS' DERIVATIVE SUITS

11.1 Is a shareholder's derivative suit provided for by law in your jurisdiction? How is it enforced by the shareholders?

Canadian corporate law statutes allow certain stakeholders to bring a derivative action on behalf of the corporation or its affiliates to enforce the corporation's rights when the corporation does not take action on its own behalf. Shareholders, directors of the corporation, former shareholders (in specific circumstances) or any other person whom a court determines is a 'proper person' is entitled to bring a derivative action. These actions are viewed as a mechanism for protecting the corporation and ensuring corporate accountability.

In order to commence a derivative action, a complainant must seek leave of a court and provide notice of the action to the corporation's directors not less than 14 days prior to commencing the action. If the court is satisfied that the complainant is acting in good faith and that the action appears to be in the best interest of the corporation, leave will be granted.

While derivative actions are available, in Canada it is more common to bring an action under the oppression remedy as opposed to a derivative action. The oppression remedy is framed broadly and, unlike derivative actions, there is no requirement to obtain leave of the court before commencing an oppression remedy. Further, the oppression remedy is a broad equitable remedy that affords the court the power not only to enforce legal rights but also to determine a fair outcome for the parties involved.

Interestingly, there have been situations where Canadian courts have found it appropriate to bring both a derivative action and an oppression remedy when the corporation and a particular shareholder have been directly harmed.

11.2 Have there been any recent relevant court cases on the subject?

In recent examples of derivative actions, Canadian courts have reaffirmed the principles outlined above and have allowed actions to proceed as long as the complainant has standing to bring the action and is acting in the best interest of the corporation.

12. SOCIAL INTEREST IN CORPORATE BEHAVIOUR

12.1 How is a company in your country expected to deal with the following issues? Corporate social responsibility; gender, racial and social diversification; environmental issues; ecology and corruption?

A public corporation in Canada must annually report to its shareholders on social and environmental policies that have been implemented that are fundamental to operations. A large number of both public and private Canadian corporations have adopted codes of ethics, conduct and best practices for their employees to achieve greater diversity and equality within corporations.

Canadian anti-corruption laws have recently been receiving increased attention by corporations and the Canadian media. Anti-corruption legislation in Canada falls under the Criminal Code or the Corruption of Foreign Public Officials Act (CFPOA). Many Canadian companies implemented compliance programs after CFPOA was introduced in 1999. Recently, there has been a surge in Canadian investigations by the Royal Canadian Mounted Police which created an International Anti-Corruption Unit. As a result, there has been a renewed focus for Canadian corporations to have robust anti-corruption compliance programmes.

China

Xu Ping & Wei Kao **King & Wood Mallesons**

1. GENERAL PRINCIPLES

1.1 What are the general principles of corporate governance in your jurisdiction? What are the main objectives of corporate governance principles in your jurisdiction? State also whether your legal system is based on common law or civil law.

It is increasingly difficult to characterise China's evolving legal system as belonging to either the civil law family or common law family, simply because the contemporary Chinese legal system has been tremendously influenced by Western laws. China remains a civil jurisdiction, at least insofar as sources of law are concerned.

Corporate governance in China has emerged and developed as China has shifted from a planned economy to a market economy. The establishment and growth of China's capital market and the evolution of Chinese enterprises from government affiliates to modern companies have made it necessary to establish a new corporate governance framework.

Until 1978, most Chinese enterprises were state-owned. A major characteristic of the state-owned enterprise management mechanism was its administration-driven, unified and collective governance.

The Company Law, which was promulgated in December 1993, provided legal support to the establishment of a modern enterprise system and laid the groundwork for China's corporate governance framework.

In 2001, China joined the World Trade Organisation and undertook to adopt the OECD Principles of Corporate Governance.

The China Securities Regulatory Commission (CSRC) and the National Economic and Trade Commission jointly issued the Code of Corporate Governance of Listed Companies in early 2002, which was based on the OECD Corporate Governance Principles.

In 2006, the Company Law was revised with its main objectives including 'regulating the organization and operation of companies; protecting the legitimate rights and interests of companies, shareholders and creditors; maintaining the socialist economic order; and promoting the development of the socialist market economy'.

This revised Company Law improved companies' governance structures and mechanisms to protect lawful shareholders' rights and public interests. It highlighted the legal obligations and responsibilities of those in actual control of the company, the directors, senior management and supervisors. It incorporated general principles of good faith, duty of care, diligence and loyalty, the fiduciary principles, honesty, fairness and transparency. While ensuring the lawful rights and interests of the shareholders, the company and the creditors are also well protected.

1.2 Have there been any recent developments in the law, codes and rules of corporate governance?

In recent years, there has been a proliferation of corporate governance literature and discussions among and studies being carried out by the legal pundits and scholars to improve corporate governance in China, especially in the area of corporate social responsibility (CSR), and these recommendations are slowly being reflected in the legislation. The latest developments in the law, codes and rules with respect to corporate governance are the revised Company Law and the revised Securities Law in 2006.

1.3 Outline recent court cases and incidents involving corporate governance issues. Were there any significant corporate scandals or large unlawful corporate cases?

Most of the significant corporate scandal cases are related to financial crimes.

In May 2013, Ping An Securities, the sponsor of Wanfu Biotechnology (Hunan) Agricultural Development Co. Ltd's IPO in 2011, was fined 76.65 million RMB. The fine was the largest handed out to an IPO sponsor since 2004. It was found that Wanfu Biotechnology had started falsifying its books as early as 2008 in preparation for its listing. From 2008 to 2011, the agricultural company from Hunan province inflated its revenues by a total of 740 million RMB and net profits by 160 million RMB. In 2011, its real net profits were only 1.1 million RMB, while it claimed they were 60.3 million RMB. It is the first time that the CSRC has set up an independent investigation on a sponsor institution, and it is the first case that any sponsor has also been banned for three months from submitting any new IPO application.

The following case relates to penalties imposed on the director of a listed company. In 2009, the CSRC won the case against a director of a listed company for the breach of his duty of care and diligence. Ding Liye, a board director with the meat-processor Shenzhen Shenxin Taifeng Group, sued the regulator at Beijing No. 1 Intermediate People's Court after he was fined 30,000 RMB in August 2007 for not properly compiling the company's earnings reports in 2003 and 2004. Mr Ding refused to pay the fine, claiming he was not responsible for the false reports because he did not personally sign, inspect or enquire about the financial statements (he has nominated the chairman as his proxy to sign the financial statements). The Court ruled that Mr Ding had breached his duty of care and diligence and the CSRC's fine was reasonable. According to the CSRC statement, Shenxin Taifeng overstated its inventory by 20 million RMB in the interim earnings report in 2003 and did not properly release information on its guarantees for other companies' bank loans worth 25.2 million RMB in the full-year report for 2004.

The following is one of the most significant corporate scandals in China. In September 2001, the CSRC investigated Ying Guang Xia, a blue-chip company, after the media voiced suspicions about its profit increase from 178 million RMB in 1999 to 567 million RMB in 2002. In May 2002, the

CSRC reported that from 1998 to 2001, the company had 'fabricated sales receipts and disclosed false information about various production facilities that actually never existed', leading investors to believe they were investing in blue-chip stock.

It was this case – known as China's Enron – which highlighted the importance of corporate governance and depicted the failed state in China at that time. From then and throughout the next decade, the concept of corporate governance moved from being a 'virtual unknown' to 'centre stage' in China's economic reform. Various government agencies have since issued numerous laws and normative documents to standardise the corporate governance practices of Chinese enterprises, including, most significantly, the promulgation of the Code of Corporate Governance for Listed Companies in 2002 and the revision of the Company Law and Securities Law in 2006.

1.4 Which law enforcement agency is in charge of enforcing corporate governance? May a criminal sanction be levied upon infringement of the corporate governance rules?

The institutional framework of China's corporate governance is composed of three parts: the China Securities Regulatory Committee (CSRC), the agency in charge of securities and futures markets; corporate governance-related government agencies, such as the Ministry of Finance (MOF), the Ministry of Commerce (MOFCOM), the State-owned Assets Supervision and Administration Commission (SASAC) and the General Administration of Industry and Commerce (SAIC); and the stock exchanges.

- CSRC – is a public agency directly under the State Council. Pursuant to relevant laws and regulations, and with the mandate of the State Council, it performs a unified regulatory function over China's securities and futures markets to supervise the public listed companies to make sure that market order is maintained and capital market operations comply with the law.
- MOF – is a department of the State Council. It is responsible for drafting and supervising the implementation of accounting rules and regulations, the accounting system governing administrative institutions and industries, and guiding and supervising the work of accountants and accounting firms.
- MOFCOM – is the body in charge of China's domestic and foreign trade, international economic cooperation and foreign investment, including joint venture companies and wholly foreign-owned enterprises.
- SASAC – is the body supervising and administering state-owned shares, assets and investments, including managing state-owned enterprises as well as performing the shareholders' responsibilities according to the Company Law and other laws and administrative regulations pursuant to the State Council.
- SAIC – is the body in charge of market supervision and regulation to maintain market order and it protects the rights and interests of businesses and consumers.

Criminal sanctions may be levied upon infringement of the corporate governance rules (see paragraph 4.2)

2. SOURCES OF LAW

2.1 Which laws, codes or statutes govern company structures and organisations? Are there statutes like the Companies Act or other forms of law? Is there much relevant case law?

China's legal framework for corporate governance comprises four levels: basic laws, administrative regulations, regulatory provisions, and self-disciplinary rules.

The first level comprises some fundamental laws, formulated either by the National People's Congress or its Standing Committee. They include the Company Law (2006), the Securities Law (2006), the Equity Joint Venture Law (2001), the Contractual Joint Ventures Law (2000), the Foreign-funded Enterprises Law (2000), the Criminal Law Amendment Act (sixth amendment) (2006) and the Accounting Law (2000).

The second level includes State Council administrative regulations, notably: Opinions on Promoting the Reform, Opening and Steady Growth of Capital Markets (2004) and Circular of the State Council on its Approval of the CSRC's Opinion on Improving the Quality of Listed Companies (2005).

The third level involves departmental provisions formulated by the ministries, commissions, auditing administration and other agencies with administrative jurisdiction directly under the State Council. These include: the Code of Corporate Governance of Listed Companies (2002) (Code), Regulations on Information Disclosure of Listed Companies (2007), Guidelines on Articles of Association of Listed Companies (2006) (AoA Guidelines), Rules on Shareholders' Meetings of Listed Companies (2006), Guiding Opinions on the Establishment of the System of Independent Directors in Listed Companies (2001), Provisions on Strengthening the Protection of the Rights and Interests of Public Shareholders (2004), Measures on the Takeover of Listed Companies (2006) (Takeover Measures), Regulations on the Registration and Settlement of Securities (2006), Rules for the Implementation of the Law of the People's Republic of China on Foreign-funded Enterprises (2001) and Administrative Measures for the Establishment of Partnership Enterprises within China by Foreign Enterprises or Individuals (2009).

The fourth level of self-disciplinary rules refers to the Listing Rules (2006) made by the stock exchanges.

2.2 Which laws, codes or statutes regulate capital markets in your jurisdiction?

See paragraph 2.1.

2.3 Are there any public interest laws which apply to or influence corporate governance?

A wide range of standards are in place in the area of CSR, including standards for environmental protection, product quality, women's equality protection, minimum wage and workplace safety, to give rights to the social communities and stakeholders to assert against the companies. Penalties for violation of CSR obligations are defined, including forced closure, revocation of business licences, compensation for economic loss and execution of criminal liability.

2.4 Have there been any recent developments in any of the above laws? What are the recent changes to the above laws or rules and the reasons for such changes?

13 November 2005 witnessed one of the biggest environmental disasters in China's modern history. An explosion occurred at a PetroChina chemical plant in the north-western province of Jilin, pouring 100 tons of Benzene into the Songhua River and creating a toxic slick stretching more than 80 kilometres into the Amur River in Russia. This disaster inaugurated a new era in Chinese environmental activism: seeking legal recourse for environmental harm and encouraging businesses to disclose environmental information. The State Administration on Environmental Protection (SEPA) issued the Guiding Opinion on Strengthening the Regulatory Work on Listed Companies in Respect of Environmental Protection in 2008, which provides that listed companies shall immediately disclose to investors who have no prior knowledge of major events with potential substantial impacts on the transaction price of securities and derivatives, and relevance to environmental protection.

3. SHAREHOLDERS AND THE SHAREHOLDERS' MEETING

3.1 How are shareholders' interests represented in the company? How are the shareholders assured exercise of their rights? What is the highest governing body within the company structure if it is not the shareholders' meeting?

Pursuant to the Company Law, in China, the shareholders' meeting is the highest governing body within the company structure and shareholders' interests are mostly represented in the shareholders' meeting. However, it is interesting to note that the board of directors is the highest authority in a sino-foreign joint venture company, of which there are no shareholders' meetings. The appointment of members of the board of directors is generally done in proportion to each party's equity contribution to the joint venture.

For a company, the shareholders' rights include the right to request the distribution of a dividend, the right to request the distribution of residual assets, the right to transfer shares and the right to request share purchases. Shareholders' rights are assured through voting (maybe through cumulative voting) in the shareholders' meeting, bringing shareholders' derivative suits, making a proposal in the shareholders' meeting, making an enquiry to the directors, revoking the decisions of the shareholders' meeting, revoking the decisions of the board of directors, and inspecting the books and records of the company.

3.2 How is the shareholders' meeting conducted? Who may chair the meeting? May attendance (not voting) at the meeting be restricted only to the shareholders? Are the shareholders allowed to be accompanied

by legal or other counsel?

There are two types of companies under the Company Law – the limited liability companies and joint stock companies which include the listed companies.

For limited liability companies, pursuant to Article 39 of the Company Law, the first shareholders' meeting shall be convened and presided over by the shareholder who made the largest capital contributions.

Pursuant to Article 40, the shareholders' meetings shall be classified into regular meetings and interim meetings. The regular meetings shall be timely held according to the articles of association. Where an interim meeting is proposed by the shareholders representing one-tenth of the voting rights or more or by directors representing one-third of the voting rights or more, or by the board of supervisors, or by the supervisors of the company with no board of supervisors, an interim meeting shall be held.

Article 103 provides that in order to hold a general meeting of shareholders, notice concerning the time, venue and matters to be considered at the meeting shall be given to each shareholder 20 days in advance. In the event of an interim meeting of shareholders, the notice may be given 15 days in advance.

Article 41 stipulates that shareholders' meetings shall be convened by the board of directors and presided over by the chair of the board of directors. If the chair is unable or fails to perform his duties, the meetings shall be presided over by the deputy chair. If the deputy chair is unable or fails to perform his duties, the meetings shall be presided over by a director jointly recommended by half or more of the directors.

For joint stock companies, specifically the listed companies, the AoA Guidelines further improves the procedures for convening general shareholders' meetings in that listed companies may, according to their actual circumstances, decide whether to include in their articles of association a procedure for a public summons. Article 55 of the AoA Guidelines provides that the notice shall include the date, location and length of the general shareholders' meeting as well as matters and proposals submitted to the meeting for deliberation.

The Listing Rules of Shenzhen and Shanghai Stock Exchanges also require listed companies to make available on designated websites other information necessary for shareholders to make reasonable judgement on matters to be discussed.

With respect to who may attend the shareholders' meeting, unless the articles of the association, bylaws or rules of procedures stipulate otherwise, the Company Law does not prohibit other persons (non-shareholders) from attending the shareholders' meeting. However, for non-listed companies, due to confidentiality reasons, before attending the shareholders' meeting, such non-shareholders should inform other shareholders of their intention and the reasons to participate in the meeting. Hence, if there is a particular need for shareholders to be accompanied by legal or other counsel, such shareholders should inform the other shareholders beforehand.

3.3 How are minority shareholders' rights protected?

The Company Law strengthens minority shareholders' rights by:

- Exercising voting rights at general shareholders' meetings.
- Allowing companies to use cumulative voting, if desired, thereby empowering minority shareholders to appoint directors and/or supervisors. Listed companies that are more than 30 per cent owned by controlling shareholders are required to adopt a cumulative voting system to reflect the opinions of minority shareholders.
- Granting shareholders the right to bring a derivative suit or direct suit against directors, supervisors, and senior management.
- Increasing minority shareholder protection by granting shareholders the right to check and copy the company's account books and meeting minutes, allowing share buybacks under certain circumstances (such as the merger or division of the company), and granting shareholders the right to petition for liquidation of a company.
- Granting shareholders the right to petition the court to revoke any illegal resolutions passed by the company's board or shareholders' meeting.
- Granting the shareholders inspection and enquiry rights concerning the way the company operates.
- Granting shareholders individually or jointly holding 3 per cent of the shares of the company, 10 days prior to the general meeting of shareholders, to submit a written proposal to the board of directors to be discussed in the general meeting.
- The resolution with regard to an amendment to the articles of association, an increase or reduction of registered capital, a merger, division or dissolution of the company or change in the form of the company as well as any purchase or sale of major assets within one year or provision of a security in an amount in excess of 30 per cent of the total assets for a listed company, should be adopted by an absolute majority of voting rights accounting for at least two-thirds of the voting rights represented.

3.4 Is shareholder activism encouraged or discouraged? If not encouraged, how is it regulated?

Shareholder activism is neither directly encouraged nor discouraged under the People's Republic of China (PRC) laws and regulations. But, over the past few years, we have seen emerging shareholder activism from the minority shareholders pushing for an improved and sustainable business strategy and responsible investment from the company. However, due to the ownership structure of companies, the laws indirectly deter certain shareholders from building up their ownership in a company, thus making shareholders' activism less common.

In China, the major shareholders are likely to be institutions and the state rather than individuals, and a lot of the publicly traded companies are state-controlled. Among the shareholders, most institutions have been passive. Many factors may have led to the passivity of Chinese institutions.

One possible explanation for institutional passivity is the highly concentrated ownership structure of Chinese listed companies. The prevailing model is that two-thirds of all outstanding shares are non-tradable and concentrated in the hands of one or two majority shareholders. Of these tradable shares, securities investment funds hold an average of about 15 per cent. In a lot of the listed companies, the funds hold a larger proportion of tradable shares. The institutional shareholding, therefore, represents only a relatively small stake in the listed companies. Hence, voting against, for example, a proposal that advances the interests of the majority shareholders to the detriment of other investors will not prevent the proposal from being adopted. Thus, institutional investors often times lack the incentives to be active.

3.5 How are professional shareholders (those minority shareholders who seek some extra benefit from companies by unduly and habitually influencing management by using their shareholding) treated by the law? Are they excluded from attending the shareholders' meeting? Are they criminally or otherwise publicly sanctioned?

The relevant PRC laws and regulations make no distinction and do not treat professional shareholders any differently than the normal shareholders. Hence, they enjoy the same rights, including the right to participate and vote in the shareholders' meeting as other shareholders and generally are not subject to criminal or public sanctions, except in certain extreme cases.

3.6 Are shareholders' benefits given to some of the shareholders by the company without resolution by the shareholders' meeting prohibited or regulated by the law or other rules?

Article 35 of the Company Law specifically stipulates that the dividends shall be distributed in proportion to each shareholder's respective paid-in capital contributions. Hence, unless the articles of association stipulated otherwise, the dividends must be distributed to each shareholder pro rata.

Under the Company Law, unless otherwise provided in the articles of association, the shareholders' meeting has the power to approve the profit distribution plans of the company by receiving affirmative votes of the shareholders that represent more than one half of the voting rights. Alternatively, if all the shareholders agree in writing, a resolution on such matters may be made directly instead of convening a shareholders' meeting and all the shareholders shall affix their signatures and seals to such resolution.

4. DIRECTORS AND BOARD OF DIRECTORS

4.1 What are the functions and responsibilities of the directors and the board of directors? Do you have a one- or two-tier board system? What are the outside directors called?

The Company Law adopted a two-tier control system comprised of the board of directors and the board of supervisors. It introduces a framework of management duties resembling common law fiduciary duties, under which corporate directors, supervisors and senior-management personnel owe the company a duty of care, diligence and loyalty.

As provided under the PRC Company Law, the directors of a company will exercise their rights mainly in the form of exercising their voting rights in the board of directors' meetings, and the board of directors shall have the following enumerated powers and authorities:

- to report work to the shareholders;
- to implement the resolutions/decisions of the shareholders;
- to decide on the business and investment programmes of the company;
- to formulate plans for annual financial budget and final accounts of the company;
- to formulate plans for profit distribution and loss making-up of the company;
- to formulate plans for the increase or reduction of the registered capital and issuance of company bond of the company;
- to formulate plans for the merger, split, dissolution and liquidation of the company or changing the form of the company;
- to decide on the establishment of the company's internal management organisations;
- to decide on appointment and dismissal of the company's general manager and his/her remuneration, and, upon recommendation of the general manager, to decide on appointment and dismissal of the company's deputy manager(s) and person(s) in charge of the financial affairs and the matters concerning their remuneration;
- to formulate the basic management system of the company; and
- other powers and authorities provided in the articles of association of the company.

The outside director is called the independent director, which is required for listed companies – see paragraph 4.4.

The board of supervisors, on the other hand, is responsible for supervising the company's affairs as well as the exercise of powers by directors and senior managers. However, compared with the board of supervisors in other jurisdictions, the authority and function of the board of supervisors in China remains weak.

In addition, there is a concept of 'legal representative' that is unique to Chinese companies. Companies in China must have a 'legal representative' – an individual with broad powers and potentially unlimited liability. The legal representative has the same duties as the director, as discussed above; he is also authorised to perform all acts regarding the general administration of a company according to the company's aims and objectives. This may include:

- acting (legally) to conserve the company's assets;
- executing powers of attorney on the company's behalf;
- authorising legal representation of and litigation by the company;
- executing any legal transactions that are within the nature and scope of that company's business; and
- entrusting with the company chop, which is necessary for approving decisions relating to the operations and management of a company in China and provides the legal capacity to make and execute agreements,

provide guarantees, transfer assets, and legally bind the company.

4.2 What are the rules that may give rise to civil and criminal liability of the director(s)? How are those liabilities sought?

Civil Liabilities

In China, civil liabilities of directors or supervisors are similar to tort liability under the common law jurisdictions. Normally, there are four elements that must be met: (i) the existence of a duty; (ii) a breach of that duty; (iii) damage suffered by the company, its shareholders or third parties; and (iv) causation between the breach and the damage.

If a director or a supervisor violates the provisions of PRC law or the company's articles of association and the company or the shareholder suffers loss as a result, such director or supervisor is liable for damages caused to the company or the shareholder, respectively. In addition, if a director or general manager carries out a certain prohibited action, any income derived from such action will be given back to the company.

In China, certain serious wrongful acts in the management of a company may result in criminal liability. The directors or supervisors may be held criminally liable for their own acts as well as the crimes committed by the company if they are the 'persons who are directly responsible' or the 'persons who are in charge'.

Below is a non-exhaustive list of crimes provided for in the PRC Criminal Law which might result in criminal liability for a company as well as its director or supervisor:

- smuggling;
- disrupting the order of company and enterprise administration;
- undermining the order of financial management;
- financial fraud;
- impairing the collection and administration of taxes;
- manufacturing and selling fake and shoddy goods;
- infringing upon intellectual property rights;
- disrupting market order, such as providing false information in advertisement which causes severe consequences;
- encroaching on property; or
- bribery.

If a company commits a crime and is prosecuted, the company will need to pay a monetary fine depending on the severity of such crime. Those 'persons who are directly responsible' or 'in charge' may also be subject to criminal liability, including imprisonment.

In practice, however, it is likely that the 'persons who are directly responsible' are those who directly committed the violation. 'Persons who are directly responsible' might be understood to be the decision-makers who participated in decisions which led to the violation of law. If interpreted broadly, this term may also include those who oversaw the division of the company but failed to take preventive or remedial steps and ensure full compliance with the legal requirements.

4.3 Does the board of directors have a committee system, eg, nomination committee, compensation committee, audit committee? If not required, is it common practice for companies? How does it function?

The Code stipulates that, according to the resolution of the general shareholders' meeting, a listed company's board may set up special committees on strategy, audit, nomination, remuneration and appraisal, etc. All of the special committee members are directors. Thereinafter, independent directors shall account for more than half of the committee members and act as conveners in the committees. In audit committees, at least one independent director should have an accounting background.

The main duties of the audit committee are (i) to recommend the engagement or replacement of the company's external auditing institutions; (ii) to review the internal audit system and its execution; (iii) to oversee the interaction between the company's internal and external auditing institutions; (iv) to inspect the company's financial information and its disclosure; and (v) to monitor the company's internal control system.

4.4 Is it a legal requirement to have an independent director or a third-party director? If so, how are they appointed? Is it required for listed companies?

For Chinese listed companies, Article 123 of the Company Law expressly mandates the independent director institute for listed companies. In addition, the Guidelines for Introducing Independent Directors to the Boards of Directors for Listed Companies formally established the institution of the independent director in China and provide the relevant details.

The above Guidelines stipulate that independent directors shall account for more than one-third of the board in a listed company and at least one of the independent directors should be a professional accountant.

Board of directors, supervisory board and shareholders who independently or jointly hold more than 1 per cent of the shares issued by the listed company may nominate independent directors, who will be voted at the shareholders' meeting.

The term of office is the same as other directors, but cannot consecutively exceed six years. The board of directors, board of supervisors and shareholders who independently or jointly hold more than 1 per cent of shares can nominate an independent director. Meanwhile, Article 5.5 of the above Guidelines provide that dismissal before expiry of the term shall not occur without proper reason.

4.5 How is the compensation for directors or officers determined? Can it be contested by the shareholders or the regulatory authorities? What are the common rules or practices for the compensation of officers?

According to the Company Law, at the general shareholders' meeting, shareholders are entitled to decide directors' remuneration. For listed companies, the Code stipulates that the board of directors may establish a remuneration and appraisal committee. The committee shall be composed solely of directors and chaired by an independent director, and independent directors shall constitute the majority of the committee. The main duties of the remuneration and appraisal committee are to study the appraisal standard for directors and management personnel, to conduct an appraisal and make recommendations, and to study and review the remuneration policies and schemes for directors and senior managers.

Although currently there are no regulatory authorities to contest the remunerations of the directors, supervisors and senior officers, the total pre-tax remuneration (including basic pay, bonuses, allowances, subsidies, welfare benefits, insurance premiums, accumulation funds, annuities and other forms of payment by the company) received by the directors, supervisors and senior officers of a listed company within the reporting period shall be disclosed to the public eye. Apart from remuneration information, all listed companies shall also disclose information on the decision-making process concerning the remuneration of directors, supervisors and senior managers, the basis on which remuneration is established, and the actual payment of the remuneration.

With respect to equity incentive packages, in accordance with the Administration Measures on Equity Incentives of Listed Companies, a listed company's equity incentive plan shall be approved by a vote of more than two-thirds of the shareholders attending the shareholders' meeting.

The common practices for the compensation of officers in China beside salary are: (i) stock options; (ii) bonuses; (iii) promotions; and (iv) administrative expenses, such as on-duty consumption.

4.6 How will the board handle a corporate crisis like an internal criminal case, violence, social media exposure or dawn raid by the authorities?

There are no regulatory guidelines on how the board will handle a corporate crisis such as internal criminal violence and social media exposure. However, for listed companies, they usually have internal guidelines on how to handle these different corporate crises, which may include establishing an independent committee to investigate and prohibit the employees from contacting the media. With respect to dawn raid, since the Anti-Monopoly Law only came out in 2008 and the procedures for dawn raid in 2009, the concept of dawn raid by authorities in China is relatively new and in its infancy. Hence, currently a lot of companies are relatively inept and do not have proper internal guidelines to handle such a situation. However, we are beginning to see more companies making an effort to adopt sound internal guidelines to handle this situation.

5. BOARD OF AUDITORS, AUDIT COMMITTEE, ACCOUNTING AUDITORS

5.1 How is the internal accounting and legal audit structured and conducted? Is an outside accounting audit required and, if so, how is it structured? Are there requirements to change the auditor each five years?

In China, internal accounting is not common in practice. For companies that have internal accounting, they structure the internal audit units in the following two ways: (i) the internal audit unit is established parallel to the other departments in the company and is administered by the board of directors; and (ii) the internal audit unit is placed inside the finance unit of the company, as internal auditing is one of the key functions of the finance department.

Pursuant to the Company Law, a company shall, after the end of each fiscal year, formulate a financial report and shall have it audited by an outside accounting firm. Such annual audits should be conducted by an independent, competent and qualified auditor.

With respect to an auditor rotation scheme, China does not currently require companies to change their external auditor every fixed period like in the USA, but it does have a similar scheme in place. Article 15 of the Professional Ethical Code of Chinese Certified Public Accountants Guiding Opinion requires the accounting firm to 'regularly' rotate the responsible auditor of the company to maintain its independence, though the term 'regularly' is not clearly defined.

5.2 Do you have supervisory auditors? What is the function of the supervisory auditors' board?

The board of directors of a listed company may establish an audit committee. The main duties of an audit committee are to recommend the engagement or replacement of external auditors, to review the internal audit system, to oversee the interaction between the internal and external auditors, to inspect the company's financial information and its disclosure, and with the support of external auditors to monitor the company's internal control system. The audit committee shall be chaired by an independent director and composed of a majority of independent directors. It also requires that at least one independent director on the audit committee should be an accounting professional.

6. MARKET DISCLOSURE/TRANSPARENCY TO THE SHAREHOLDERS AND THE PUBLIC

6.1 What are the disclosure requirements for companies in your jurisdiction under company law, capital markets law or any other rules?

Article 146 of Company Law provides that a listed company shall make public its financial conditions, operating conditions and major legal actions in accordance with the relevant laws and administrative regulations, and shall make public its financial and accounting reports half-yearly in each fiscal year.

For listed companies, the Securities Law stipulates that the information disclosed by issuers and listed companies in accordance with the law must be authentic, accurate and complete, and may not contain false records, misleading statements or major omissions. The Securities Law provides three types of disclosure obligations: annual reports, half-yearly reports and ad hoc reports.

Administrative Measures on Information Disclosure by Listed Companies require that where the occurrence of a significant event is likely to have a marked impact on the trading prices of a company's securities and derivatives, and the investors have yet to be informed, the listed company shall make a disclosure to declare the cause, the current status and the likely effect of the event on a timely basis. These events may be divided into transactions and non-transactions, and transactions may be divided into general transactions and related-party transactions.

6.2 What is the liability or responsibility of the board in relation to the company's disclosure requirements?

The Securities Law provides that the directors and senior executives of a listed company shall sign a written opinion for confirmation on the regular reports of the company. The supervisory board of a listed company shall examine and approve the company's regular reports formulated by the board of directors and produce a written opinion.

In addition, under the Securities Law, the directors, supervisors and senior executives of a listed company must ensure the truthfulness, accuracy and completeness of the information disclosed by the company. If the share prospectus, measures for offer of corporate bonds, financial and accounting statements, listing report document, annual report, interim report, ad hoc report or other information disclosure materials announced by an issuer or listed company contain any false records, misleading statements or major omissions, and cause losses to investors in the course of securities trading, the directors, supervisors, senior executives and other personnel directly involved shall be jointly and severally liable for such losses.

7. M&A AND CORPORATE GOVERNANCE

7.1 Upon an M&A offer, how are the transparency and fairness rules of the company provided under the company and stock market laws and rules?

There are certain disclosure requirements if the offer is to purchase stocks from the listed companies. Article 86 of the Securities Law provides that where an investor possesses independently or jointly with other person(s) through agreement or other arrangements 5 per cent of the stocks issued by a listed company through trading on the stock exchange, they shall, within three days, submit a written report to the securities regulatory body of the State Council and the stock exchange, notify the listed company, and make a public announcement. They are prohibited from buying or selling company's stocks in the period prescribed above. Article 88 of the Securities Law further provides that when an investor, through trading on the stock exchange, possesses individually or jointly with other person(s) through agreement or other arrangement 30 per cent of the stocks issued by a listed company and plans to make more purchases, he or she shall make a tender offer for all or part of the company's shares to all shareholders as is required by law. The offer to purchase part of the shares shall include an agreement that when the amount of shares the shareholders commit to sell exceeds the offered amount to be purchased, the purchaser will make the purchase proportionately.

The Takeover Measures contain more detailed procedures and information disclosure requirements for tender offer. The Listing Rules of the stock exchanges have similar provisions on information disclosure concerning the purchase and significant asset restructuring of listed companies.

With respect to the fairness principles in the context of listed companies, Article 8 of the Takeover Measures provides that the directors, supervisors and senior managers of an acquired company shall fulfil the loyalty and diligence obligations and treat all acquirers fairly. The decisions and measures of the acquired company's directors shall be conducive to maintaining the interests of the company and shareholders. The directors must not abuse their authority by setting unnecessary barriers to the acquisition, use the company's resources to provide financial aid in any form to the acquirers, or damage the lawful rights and interests of the company and its shareholders.

8. PROXY FIGHTING

8.1 Is proxy fighting customarily conducted for control of the company management or what other items? How is it regulated under the company law or market regulations?

Proxy fighting for the control of the company management is not common in China.

Under both the Company Law and Securities Law, the shareholders can either be present at the shareholders' meetings in person or they may appoint a proxy to vote on their behalf, and both means of voting have the same legal effect. The proxy shall exercise the voting right within the scope of the authority granted by the shareholders.

9. OFFICERS' REMUNERATION RULES

9.1 How is remuneration of officers determined? By whom? Is there a role for the shareholders' meeting? Is there any mechanism for an independent body to review and evaluate them?

Management compensation in Chinese companies is determined by the board of directors. For listed companies, the Code stipulates that the board of directors of a listed company may establish a remuneration and appraisal committee in accordance with the resolutions of the shareholders' meetings. It shall be composed solely of directors and chaired by an independent director, and independent directors shall constitute the majority of the committee. The main duties of the remuneration and appraisal committee are to study the appraisal standard for directors and management personnel, to conduct an appraisal and make recommendations, and to study and review the remuneration policies and schemes for directors and senior managers.

The shareholders' meeting may determine and approve the equity incentive plan by a confirming vote of more than two-thirds of the shareholders attending the shareholders' meeting. However, there are no mechanisms for an independent body to review and evaluate the remuneration of the officers.

9.2 Is the mechanism of officers' remuneration publicly debated?

Like many countries during the economic downturn, the mechanism of the officers' remuneration for a listed company is often questioned and debated by the Chinese public, including the legal pundits. In fact, a public outcry occurred in 2008 when it was disclosed that the annual salary of Ma Mingzhe, chairman and CEO of Ping An Insurance Group, an insurance and financial services company, was 66 million RMB. However, there has been little government or regulatory intervention to regulate the officers' remuneration in listed companies.

10. DIRECTORS' LIABILITIES, LIABILITY INSURANCE, INDEMNIFICATION

10.1 What are the directors' responsibilities and liabilities under the law? Can those liabilities be covered by insurance? Can it be indemnified by the company or other related parties?

For the full description of the directors' responsibilities and liabilities, see paragraph 4. With respect to insurance, it is optional for companies to purchase insurance to cover directors' liability in the event of breach of duties. In fact, there are a number of Chinese insurance companies that provide such insurance coverage.

The company may indemnify directors, supervisors and officers if so stated in the articles of association of the company.

11. SHAREHOLDERS' DERIVATIVE SUITS

11.1 Is a shareholder's derivative suit provided for by law in your jurisdiction? How is it enforced by the shareholders?

The Company Law provides that the shareholders that individually or jointly hold 1 per cent of the total shares may request in writing for the board of supervisors or the supervisors of a limited liability company to file suit before a people's court against the company.

The Company Law also provides that if a director or senior officer breaches any of its duties, the shareholders that have individually or collectively held more than one per cent of the shares of the company for more than 180 consecutive days may petition in writing the board of supervisors to initiate legal proceedings against such director or senior officer in the people's court; if the supervisor breaches his duties, the aforementioned shareholders may petition in writing to the board of directors or the executive director to initiate legal proceedings against such supervisor in the people's court.

If the board of supervisors or the board of directors or the executive director refuses to initiate any legal proceedings upon receipt of the written petition as referred to in the preceding paragraph, or fails to initiate any legal proceedings within 30 days of receipt of such petition, or the situation is so emergent that the company will suffer irreparable losses if legal proceedings are not initiated immediately, the aforementioned shareholders shall have the right to directly initiate legal proceedings in the people's court in their own name for the benefit of the company.

11.2 Have there been any recent relevant court cases on the subject?

Since 1 January 2006, after the promulgation of the revised Company Law, the Chinese courts at all levels have accepted derivative pleadings and rendered judgments on them.

In 2009, plaintiffs attempted to sue derivatively on behalf of Sanlian

Shangshe Company, Ltd. against the former controlling shareholder of that listed company, Sanlian Group. The lawsuit also concerned the dispute over the infringement of the exclusive right to use the trademark filed by the company's small and medium shareholders against the company's major shareholder Shandong Sanlian Group – the damages claimed by plaintiffs were estimated to be 50 million RMB.

This case was accepted by the Shandong High People's Court on 11 December 2009 (after a large minority shareholder and one independent director were able to convince 1.56 per cent of the listed company's shareholders to join the action) but, eventually, the plaintiffs were not successful.

12. SOCIAL INTEREST IN CORPORATE BEHAVIOUR

12.1 How is a company in your country expected to deal with the following issues? Corporate social responsibility; gender, racial and social diversification; environmental issues; ecology and corruption?

CSR and environment issues

CSR has drawn increasing attention from different sectors across the country.

The Code calls specific attention to the importance of CSR. There are also certain specially designed provisions that provide taxation, credit and other policy incentives for CSR enforcement. For instance, the purchasing costs of facilities for the purposes of environmental protection, water or energy conservation, and workplace safety are subject to certain tax allowances.

Moreover, according to the Measures for the Administration of Initial Public Offerings of Shares and the Listing Thereof and Administrative Measures for the Issuance of Securities by Listed Companies, companies that have violated laws and administrative regulations on environmental protection within the recent 36 months and were subject to administrative penalties with serious circumstances shall not be allowed to apply for initial public offerings.

Corruption

Under the Law against Unfair Competition published in 1993, companies are required to observe the principle of voluntariness, equality, justice, honesty and integrity and the agreed commercial morals. In 1996, the Interim Provision on Banning Commercial Bribery was published by the State Administration for Industry and Commerce. In 2005, China joined the United Nations Convention against Corruption and has enhanced international cooperation against corruption. The Criminal Law also defines severe criminal punishments of bribery.

Discrimination in the workplace

There is no specific anti-discrimination law in the PRC. However, certain general anti-discrimination provisions are included in various laws and regulations.

The Labour Law, the Employment Promotion Law, the Labour Contract Law, the Provisions on Employment Services and Employment Management, and the Law on the Protection of Women's Rights and Interests are the major laws cited as the legal basis for fighting against discrimination in the workplace. They deal with different aspects of employment from recruitment to promotion and termination.

Although the above laws illustrate the PRC government's efforts to promote equal rights to all citizens, those regulations remain too general. They do not provide any steps to implement these principles or specify penalties for violations, thereby hindering the enforcement process.

Article 13 of the PRC Labour Law prescribes that employees or applicants for employment must not be discriminated against on the basis of nationality, race, gender or religious belief.

The PRC Employment Promotion Law prescribes that the employer shall offer equal employment opportunities, terms and conditions to each employee. This law expressly restricts any employment discrimination against women and ethnic minorities.

Finally, on 28 June 2012, the Shenzhen Municipal People's Congress Standing Committee passed the Regulation to Promote Gender Equality in the Shenzhen Special Economic Zone (Gender Equality Regulation), which came into effect on 1 January 2013. The media and scholars considered it as the first piece of legislation that exclusively addresses the issue of gender equality in every aspect of daily life. Furthermore, legislative measures such as the Gender Equality Regulation, as well as the draft regulation in Beijing, are enacted or expected to be enacted to tackle gender discrimination and ensure equal opportunities for women in the workplace.

France

Jacques Buhart & Nicolas Lafont **McDermott Will & Emery**

1. GENERAL PRINCIPLES

1.1 What are the general principles of corporate governance in your jurisdiction? What are the main objectives of corporate governance principles in your jurisdiction? State also whether your legal system is based on common law or civil law.

The French legal system is based on civil law.

The following are some of the key general corporate governance principles prevailing under French law:

- corporate interest: directors and officers must act in the best interest of the company;
- duty of loyalty: directors must be diligent in carrying out their duties; and
- equal treatment of shareholders: special procedures apply to any benefits offered to some, but not all, of the shareholders.

In addition, transparency is a key principle for companies whose shares are listed on a French stock market. These companies must comply with strict financial communication rules and must make other information, including on corporate governance, available to the public (see paragraph 6 below).

1.2 Have there been any recent developments in the law, codes and rules of corporate governance?

On 26 July 2012, the French government issued a Decree that capped the salaries of corporate officers in state-owned companies at EUR 450,000 a year.

New regulations on officers' remuneration, including a 'say on pay' mechanism are also expected to be implemented.

The French government recently announced that there would be no law imposing the 'say on pay' principle. Instead, the 'say on pay' principle should be introduced through the two major corporate governance codes voluntarily applied by companies whose shares are listed on a French stock market. It is expected that the codes will recommend the following:

- introduction of a 'say on pay' mechanism allowing the shareholders to approve officers' remuneration, it being said that (i) the shareholders will only be able to vote on the overall compensation policy and not on the amount itself, and (ii) such consultation of the shareholders will only be advisory and not binding;
- setting-up of an independent supervisory body to deal with disputed cases.

1.3 Outline recent court cases and incidents involving corporate governance issues. Were there any significant corporate scandals or large unlawful corporate cases?

Following public controversy on the EUR 16 million compensation package allocated to the chairman and CEO of French communication group Publicis in 2012, Publicis put in place a 'say on pay' mechanism pursuant to which the remuneration policy applicable to its main officers would be subject to the advisory vote of the shareholders.

1.4 Which law enforcement agency is in charge of enforcing corporate governance? May a criminal sanction be levied upon infringement of the corporate governance rules?

The French financial markets authority (the *Autorité des Marchés Financiers*, AMF) is in charge of enforcing the rules of corporate governance applicable to companies whose shares are listed on NYSE Euronext Paris and Alternext.

Each year, the AMF publishes a report on corporate governance highlighting the good and bad practices of public companies. In 2012, for the first time, the AMF named those companies that do not fully comply with corporate governance rules.

The AMF comprises a sanctions commission (*Commission des Sanctions*) that can impose penalties upon infringement of the corporate governance rules laid down in the AMF General Regulations (*Règlement Général de l'AMF*). However, the AMF cannot levy criminal sanctions (eg, an insider-trading claim would be reviewed by the criminal courts).

2. SOURCES OF LAW

2.1 Which laws, codes or statutes govern company structures and organisations? Are there statutes like the Companies Act or other forms of law? Is there much relevant case law?

Company structures and organisations are mainly governed by the French Commercial Code, the French Civil Code and the companies' articles of association. French courts play a role in so far as they interpret and complete those rules when necessary.

The above legal sources set out the rules applicable to all forms of companies existing under French law. However, in the rest of this questionnaire, we will focus on the rules applicable to joint stock companies (*sociétés anonymes*), which is by far the most common corporate form for public companies.

2.2 Which laws, codes or statutes regulate capital markets in your jurisdiction?

Regulation of capital markets is mainly found in the French Monetary and Financial Code and in the AMF General Regulations.

In recent years, the regulation of corporate governance and capital markets has increasingly been developing by reference to soft law. Professional organisations have developed non-binding corporate governance codes, which are today widely applied by French public companies:

- the corporate governance code for public companies dated December 2008 (last review in April 2010) usually referred to as the Afep-Medef code provides a set of recommendations relating to board of directors, the role of independent directors, specialised committees, and the remuneration of directors and managers; and

- the Middlenext corporate governance code for small and medium sized companies dated December 2009 (usually referred to as the Middlenext code) applies to companies with a market capitalisation of less than EUR 1 billion; the structure and scope of the document are similar to that of the Afep-Medef code.

Any company (public or private) can chose to voluntarily comply with the provisions of a governance code. Those companies whose shares are listed on NYSE Euronext Paris must specify in the management report submitted by the board of directors to the shareholders, the terms of the corporate governance code that they have not complied with, if any, and explain the reason for such deviation (so-called 'comply or explain' principle). Should such companies decide not to comply with a governance code, they must explain the rationale for not doing so and also describe what rules are applied by in relation to corporate governance. Almost all French companies whose shares are listed on the SBF120 Index (the 120 largest companies on NYSE Euronext Paris in terms of market capitalisation) have adopted the Afep-Medef code of corporate governance.

2.3 Are there any public interest laws which apply to or influence corporate governance?

Companies whose shares are listed on NYSE Euronext Paris (as well as large private companies exceeding certain thresholds in terms and employees and revenue) must ensure that they reach a balance between men and women in their board of directors.

Under the law of 27 January 2013, public companies will need to have at least 20 per cent of directors of each gender on the day of the ordinary shareholders' meeting held in 2014 and at least 40 per cent of directors of each gender on the day of the ordinary shareholders' meeting held in 2017. In addition, by 2017, if the board of directors consists of no more than eight members, the difference between the number of directors of each gender should be no higher than two.

Similarly, as of 1 January 2017, private companies with revenues or a balance sheet more than EUR 50 million and employing at least 500 persons for three consecutive years (that is from 2017 to 2020), will need to have at least 40 per cent of directors of each gender on the board. The provision relating to the difference between the number of directors of each gender is also applicable to these companies.

2.4 Have there been any recent developments in any of the above laws? What are the recent changes to the above laws or rules and the reasons for such changes?

See paragraph 1.2 above.

3. SHAREHOLDERS AND THE SHAREHOLDERS' MEETING

3.1 How are shareholders' interests represented in the company? How are the shareholders assured exercise of their rights? What is the

highest governing body within the company structure if it is not the shareholders' meeting?
The shareholders' meeting is the 'sovereign body' of the company. It has the authority to resolve on some of the most important decisions affecting the company, including appointing and dismissing members of the board of directors or supervisory board and amending the company's articles of association.

There are two kinds of shareholders' meetings under French law:

- The ordinary shareholders' meeting: it must meet at least once a year in order to approve the annual financial statements and is also competent to appoint or dismiss the members of the board of directors or supervisory board; the adoption of decisions requires a majority of 50 per cent of the shares present or represented at the meeting.
- The extraordinary shareholders' meeting: it is competent to adopt decisions triggering an amendment to the company's articles of association (eg, capital increase, change in the corporate governance structure, change of registered office...); the adoption of decisions requires a majority of two-thirds of the shares present or represented at the meeting.

The main right of a shareholder is the right to attend and vote at the shareholders' meeting, such right being secured as follows:

- each shareholder must be convened to the shareholders' meeting;
- each shareholder is entitled to receive or consult certain documents and information prior to the meeting;
- each shareholder is entitled to (i) attend the meeting in person or by videoconference, (ii) vote by mail (or by email if the company's articles of association allow) or (iii) be represented by its spouse or by another shareholder, unless the company's shares are listed on NYSE Euronext Paris or on Alternext, in which case the shareholder can be represented by any person of its choice; and
- a shareholders' meeting cannot be validly held unless the following quorum is met: (i) for an ordinary shareholders' meeting, one-fifth of the voting rights (and no quorum if the meeting is convened on second notice); and (ii) for an ordinary shareholders' meeting, one-quarter of the voting rights (and one-fifth if the meeting is convened on second notice).

3.2 How is the shareholders' meeting conducted? Who may chair the meeting? May attendance (not voting) at the meeting be restricted only to the shareholders? Are the shareholders allowed to be accompanied by legal or other counsel?
The shareholders' meeting is conducted by a chairman, who is usually the chairman of the board of directors or management board.

A bureau also ensures that the meeting is conducted in accordance with applicable rules, ie (i) that the quorum is met, (ii) that the agenda is complied with, and (iii) that the shareholders can freely exercise their voting rights. It also settles any conflicts arising during the meeting. The bureau is composed of the chairman and the two shareholders holding the highest number of voting rights (or if they refuse, the shareholders coming immediately after). The bureau appoints a secretary.

In companies where a works council is in place (*comité d'entreprise*), two representatives of the works council are entitled to attend the shareholders' meeting. They do not have the right to vote or to speak at the meeting (unless they are invited to speak by the chairman).

Apart from these works council representatives, the chairman can restrict attendance to the shareholders only (or their proxy holders). Members of the press, for example, may be prevented from attending a shareholders' meeting. In practice, many public companies allow their presence as they consider that the meeting shall be public. If a shareholder complains about the presence of the press, the question would have to be submitted to the vote of the shareholders.

Similarly, a shareholder may be allowed, but is not entitled, to be accompanied by a bailiff or a lawyer.

3.3 How are minority shareholders' rights protected?

French law offers limited protection to minority shareholders. It is not uncommon for the main shareholders, including in companies whose shares are listed, to enter into a shareholders' agreement offering protection that goes beyond that provided by law.

Among the legal provisions offering protection to minority shareholders, the following can be highlighted:

- Minority shareholders can convene a shareholders' meeting and put resolutions on the agenda under certain conditions. Article L. 225-103, II-2 of the French Commercial Code entitles one or several shareholders holding 5 per cent or more of the company's share capital to petition the competent commercial court in summary proceedings in order to convene a shareholders' meeting. Provided the request is made in the company's interest, as opposed to the sole interest of the petitioning shareholders, the court will have to appoint an agent who will in turn convene the shareholders' meeting. In addition, shareholders representing 5 per cent or more of the company's share capital are entitled to propose resolutions to be included in the shareholders' meeting agenda (note that in company's whose share capital exceeds EUR 750,000, the threshold to propose resolutions is lower than 5 per cent and calculated in accordance with a complex formula).
  When the company's shares are listed on NYSE Euronext Paris, a shareholders' association composed of shareholders representing 5 per cent or more of the share capital can exercise similar rights.
- Any shareholder, whatever its equity participation, can ask questions to the board of directors or the managing board, which must be answered during the shareholders' meeting.
- The adoption of decisions at the extraordinary shareholders' meeting requires a majority of two-thirds of the shares present or represented at such meeting. This means that minority shareholders holding more than one-third of the shares present or represented can veto any decision

submitted to the vote of the extraordinary shareholders' meeting. In practice, the blocking minority can be achieved by shareholders holding less than one-third of the voting rights if a significant number of shareholders are neither present nor represented at the meeting.

- Finally, another noteworthy feature is the 'abuse of majority' concept, which can trigger the annulment of a decision adopted by the shareholders' meeting. In short, any shareholder can ask a court to annul a decision which was adopted by the majority shareholder(s) solely in its (their) own interest and is contrary to the company's interest. The 'abuse of majority' is not easy to prove but was established by French courts for instance in the case of majority shareholders who refused to distribute any dividends for 20 years and did not invest the corresponding funds, or in the case of a decision of majority shareholders to fund the losses of the company's subsidiary which was managed by one of them.

3.4 Is shareholder activism encouraged or discouraged? If not encouraged, how is it regulated?

Shareholder activism in France has significantly increased in the recent past, mainly through the rise of proxy advisors and investor associations.

Although shareholder activism is not heavily regulated, a few key legislative changes have enabled its development:

- In 2001, the threshold allowing minority shareholders to propose resolutions at the shareholders' meeting has been lowered to 5 per cent of a company's share capital (and even less than 5 per cent in company's whose share capital exceeds EUR 750,000); this allows institutional investors to be more active at the shareholders' meetings.
- Since 2003, investment management companies are required to put in place an investment policy applicable to the shares held by their funds and to report on the implementation of such policy to their investors; today, these policies and their implementation are heavily influenced by proxy advisors.
- While shareholders used to be required to freeze the trading of their shares within the five-day period preceding the shareholders' meeting, a 'record date' system was implemented in 2005 pursuant to which shareholders who record their shares three days before the shareholders' meeting are admitted to vote; this significantly increased the rate of participation of shareholders, in particular foreign institutional investors, in the shareholders' meetings.
- Since 2010, French law recognises the right for shareholders to be represented by any third party at the shareholders' meeting of companies whose securities are listed on NYSE Euronext Paris or on Alternext; this facilitates proxy fighting (before 2010, a proxy holder had to acquire at least one share in the company).

The rise of proxy advisors' influence over shareholders' meetings has raised some concerns. The AMF issued a recommendation on 18 June 2011 asking proxy advisors to be more transparent with respect to their policies and to use their best efforts to prevent conflicts of interest.

3.5 How are professional shareholders (those minority shareholders who seek some extra benefit from companies by unduly and habitually influencing management by using their shareholding) treated by the law? Are they excluded from attending the shareholders' meeting? Are they criminally or otherwise publicly sanctioned?

There are no specific rules applicable to 'professional shareholders' and, as a general rule, shareholders cannot be prevented from attending a shareholders' meeting. However, minority shareholders shall not abuse their right to vote at a shareholders' meeting. The 'abuse of minority' is a situation where minority shareholders prevent the adoption of a decision that is essential for the company in order to satisfy their own interest. Examples of abuse include the refusal by a minority shareholder to allow a capital increase of an undercapitalised company, creating a risk that the company will be wound up or the refusal to allow the company's profits to be allocated to the reserve when the company urgently needed cash. When the 'abuse of minority' is found, the minority shareholder(s) can be ordered to pay damages to the company. The court could also appoint an agent who will represent the minority shareholder(s) at the next shareholders' meeting and will vote in its (their) name in the interest of the company.

3.6 Are shareholders' benefits given to some of the shareholders by the company without resolution by the shareholders' meeting prohibited or regulated by the law or other rules?

The company must ensure equal treatment of all shareholders. Any benefits given to some of the shareholders must be approved by a resolution of the shareholders' meeting on the basis of a report by a special auditor (eg, issuance of preferred shares).

4. DIRECTORS AND BOARD OF DIRECTORS

4.1 What are the functions and responsibilities of the directors and the board of directors? Do you have a one- or two-tier board system? What are the outside directors called?

French joint stock companies may either adopt a unitary or a dual system. A one-tier structure consists in a single board of directors (*conseil d'administration*), headed by a chairman. A general manager (*directeur general*) appointed by the board of directors, who may also be the chairman of the board, runs the company along with his management team.

A two-tier structure consists in a management board (*directoire*), which manages the company, and a supervisory board (*conseil de surveillance*), which oversees the actions of the management board. The management board members and its chairman are appointed by the supervisory board, whose members are appointed by the shareholders.

Most public companies (80 per cent) are managed under a one-tier board system.

The board of directors is a collegial body composed of at least three directors, with a maximum of 18.

The mission of the board of directors is as follows:

- it contributes to the development of the general strategy by determining the overall orientations of the company; and
- it supervises the implementation of the company's strategic orientations by the management through control or verification of the management's actions as it deems appropriate.

In addition, although the company's day-to-day management is handled by the general manager, the board of directors can make business decisions (provided such decisions are implemented by the general manager, eg a lawsuit decided by the board of directors can only be brought by the general manager or a person to whom the general manager has delegated his authority). It must also draw the annual accounts and a management report to be submitted to the shareholders' meeting.

By contrast, a supervisory board operates as a permanent supervisory body and is not involved in the management of the company, which is solely carried out by the management board. Accordingly, the supervisory board does not prepare the annual accounts. Nonetheless, it can make observations on the management report and annual accounts prepared by the management board.

The powers of the board of directors and the management and supervisory board are subject to the sovereign power granted to the shareholders (see paragraph 3.1 above).

Outside directors are commonly referred to as independent directors (see paragraph 4.4 below for further details).

4.2 What are the rules that may give rise to civil and criminal liability of the director(s)? How are those liabilities sought?

Civil liability

Directors can be held liable towards the company and/or the shareholders on the following grounds:

- breach of applicable laws and regulations;
- breach of the company's article of association; and
- mismanagement, ie an action or a failure to act that is contrary to the interest of the company.

Directors may only be liable towards third parties if they commit a wrongdoing that is separate from their corporate duties.

According to the French highest court (*Cour de cassation*), each director is presumed liable towards the company and/or the shareholders in case of improper decisions, whether intentional or resulting from negligence and, in order to escape liability, a director should prove that he disagreed with the improper decision. Directors can also be considered liable for not overseeing properly the management of the company.

Such liability may either be individual or collective, depending on the nature of the misconduct. If the judge considers that the liability is collective, that is when several directors are responsible for the misconduct, the court will determine to which extent each of these directors is liable.

As far as supervisory board members are concerned, they have no liability towards the company or third parties other than for personal negligence, tortious acts in the performance of their duties or mismanagement. They have no liability for managerial acts and their consequences.

Directors' civil liability may be engaged either:

- by a shareholder who suffered harm that is separate and different from the harm suffered by the company; or
- through a claim introduced by the company itself through its legal representatives; or
- through a claim introduced by one or several shareholders on behalf of the company.

Criminal liability

In addition to general rules of criminal law, directors' criminal liability may be triggered for misuse of corporate assets or power, payment of fictitious dividends and introduction of false corporate accounts.

Misuse of corporate assets is the most common criminal offence found against directors. It consists in deliberately using the company's assets against the company's interest and for one's personal benefit. Is it punishable by a five-year prison sentence and a fine amounting to EUR 375,000.

Other cases of liability

Directors may incur civil and criminal liability for breach of securities law, including disclosure of false or misleading information, insider trading, failure to declare the crossing of shareholding thresholds, etc.

Finally, directors may be held liable in the following cases:

- in the context of bankruptcy proceedings, corporate officers may be held liable for corporate losses in case of mismanagement and may be subject to measures preventing them from holding management positions; and
- breach of health and safety regulations, environmental regulations and/ or antitrust regulation.

As a result of the increasing number of lawsuits brought against corporate officers, an increasing number of companies subscribe to an insurance policy known as RCMS (civil liability of corporate officers). Cases of fraud, intentional improper actions and fines resulting from criminal practices are not covered by directors' insurance.

4.3 Does the board of directors have a committee system, eg, nomination committee, compensation committee, audit committee? If not required, is it common practice for companies? How does it function?

There is a legal requirement for companies whose shares are listed on NYSE Euronext Paris to appoint an audit committee to oversee the preparation of financial information, the effectiveness of internal control procedures and risk management, and the certification of the accounts by the statutory auditor. The audit committee also makes recommendations on the appointment of the statutory auditors.

French law provides that the audit committee must be composed of non-executive directors and that at least one member of the audit committee must be an independent director. However, the Afep-Medef corporate governance code, which is applied by almost all companies whose shares are listed on the CAC40 index, recommends that two-thirds of the members of the audit committee be independent directors.

French law does not require that other committees be put in place. But, as the workload of boards of directors has expanded considerably in recent years, it has become common practice for the board of directors to delegate certain powers to specialised committees. The following committees are increasingly common among companies whose shares are listed on the CAC40 index: remuneration committee, nominations committee, strategic committee, ethics committee, governance committee, risk committee, etc.

4.4 Is it a legal requirement to have an independent director or a third-party director? If so, how are they appointed? Is it required for listed companies?

There is no legal obligation to appoint independent or third-party directors.

However, the corporate governance codes recommend such appointment in order to guarantee the independence of the board of directors. In particular, companies applying the Afep-Medef code shall ensure that (i) half of the directors are independent in companies where there is a scattered shareholding and no controlling shareholder, and (ii) at least a third of the directors are independent in controlled companies. The code defines an independent director as a person who has no relationship of any kind with the company, its management or the corporate group to which it belongs.

4.5 How is the compensation for directors or officers determined? Can it be contested by the shareholders or the regulatory authorities? What are the common rules or practices for the compensation of officers?

This section will only address the compensation of directors. See paragraph 9 for officers' compensation.

Under French law, directors can only be granted the following remuneration:

- an annual fixed attendance fee called *'jetons de presence'*, which is a lump-sum amount for the entire board determined by the general meeting, such amount being then allocated by the board between its members; and
- remuneration for specific missions carried out by some of the directors.

Any other form of remuneration of directors would be deemed null and void. In two-tier structures, the fees payable to supervisory board members are allocated in a similar manner to the directors' fees.

The Afep-Medef code recommends that remuneration granted to directors be tied to their contribution to the board, including attendance to board meetings and membership in specialised committees.

The publication of the remuneration policy applicable to directors is now a well-established practice.

4.6 How will the board handle a corporate crisis like an internal criminal case, violence, social media exposure or dawn raid by the authorities?

In any situation involving a corporate crisis, the board of directors, or any specialised committee such as an audit or risk committee, as the case may be, will be urgently convened in order to discuss the solutions that shall be implemented, and define a communication strategy.

5. BOARD OF AUDITORS, AUDIT COMMITTEE, ACCOUNTING AUDITORS

5.1 How is the internal accounting and legal audit structured and conducted? Is an outside accounting audit required and, if so, how is it structured? Are there requirements to change the auditor each five years?

Companies publishing consolidated accounts and public companies must appoint two statutory auditors. Other limited liability companies must have at least one statutory auditor.

The statutory auditor(s) is in charge of:

- certifying the company's accounts;
- ensuring that the shareholders have been treated equally;
- ensuring compliance of the company's accounts with applicable accounting standards; and
- ensuring the accuracy of the accounting information provided to the shareholders.

They are appointed by the shareholders' meeting for six financial years.

As mentioned above, public companies must also set up an audit committee, which will review the financial information prepared by the statutory auditors.

5.2 Do you have supervisory auditors? What is the function of the supervisory auditors' board?

Not applicable.

6. MARKET DISCLOSURE/TRANSPARENCY TO THE SHAREHOLDERS AND THE PUBLIC

6.1 What are the disclosure requirements for companies in your jurisdiction under company law, capital markets law or any other rules?

Any French company must make public, through the commercial registry, its annual financial statements and its up-to-date articles of association.

In addition, companies whose shares are listed on NYSE Euronext Paris or on Alternext are required to inform the public (i) periodically, about their business activity and results (periodic reporting obligations) and (ii) at all times, whenever circumstances which may affect the market price of their stock arise (permanent disclosure obligations).

Permanent disclosure obligations imply that any information which could be considered as inside information should be disclosed by the issuer through a press release or a prospectus to the general public as soon as possible. Inside information is defined by article 621-1 of the AMF General Regulation as *'information of a precise nature that has not been made public, relating directly or indirectly to one or more issuers of financial instruments, or to one of more financial instruments, and which, if it were made public, would be likely to have a significant effect on the price of the relevant financial instruments or on the price of related financial instruments'*.

Periodic reporting obligations applicable in NYSE Euronext Paris involve the following (disclosure obligations on Alternext are much less significant):

- Filing with the AMF of a registration document (*document de reference*), which includes the annual financial report (audited financial statements, management report), a report on internal control procedures, information on the remuneration of directors and officers and information on the fees of the statutory auditors.
- Disclosure to the AMF and the public of an annual financial report (included in the registration document mentioned above), a half-year financial report and a quarterly financial report.
- Disclosure to the AMF and to the public of information on the total number of voting rights and shares, the description of any share buyback programmes, news releases setting out the arrangements for supplying the prospectus, news releases indicating how the information relating to upcoming shareholders' meetings is made available or may be consulted.
- Informing the AMF and, if applicable, the managers of EEA-regulated markets on which their shares are listed of any proposed amendments to their articles of association.
- Submitting to the AMF a written list of all persons and third parties who have regular or occasional access to inside information.

6.2 What is the liability or responsibility of the board in relation to the company's disclosure requirements?

The board of directors must ensure compliance with the disclosure obligations described above.

7. M&A AND CORPORATE GOVERNANCE

7.1 Upon an M&A offer, how are the transparency and fairness rules of the company provided under the company and stock market laws and rules?

Preliminary negotiations of an M&A transaction involving a French issuer whose shares are listed on NYSE Euronext Paris or Alternext may have to be disclosed as 'inside information' when such negotiations become sufficiently defined so as to have a reasonable chance of success.

The AMF has ruled that entering into a non-disclosure agreement (NDA) does not constitute information sufficiently precise to be inside information.

However, the execution by the French issuer of a non-binding LOI/MOU setting forth the main terms and conditions of the contemplated transaction, which are sufficient to assess the potential effect of the contemplated transaction on the issuer's stock price, constitutes inside information and must be disclosed by the issuer.

8. PROXY FIGHTING

8.1 Is proxy fighting customarily conducted for control of the company management or what other items? How is it regulated under the company law or market regulations?

Proxy fighting is not very common within French companies. One of the only high profile cases in which proxy fighting was – successfully – conducted is the Eurotunnel case, in which a group of minority shareholders gathered proxies to finally obtain the removal of management in 2004.

The Eurotunnel proxy fight occurred at a time when French law allowed shareholders to give proxy to other shareholders, but not to third parties. As explained above in paragraph 3.4, the rule changed in 2010 and it is today possible for shareholders to give a proxy to any third-party proxy holder. Yet, this change should not significantly increase the number of proxy fights in France, as there remains two hurdles making proxy fights difficult to carry out:

- The proxy holder cannot easily identify the minority shareholders: as a general rule, shares traded on NYSE Euronext Paris or Alternext must be registered with an authorised book keeper and the company does not have any obligation to identify the holders of such shares (as opposed to the shares that are not traded, in which case the identity of their holders must be communicated to other shareholders at least 16 days before the meeting).
- The shareholders giving proxies run the risk of being considered as 'acting in concert': if the purpose of the proxy fight is to take control of the company, the shareholders could be deemed as jointly liable in case of breach of any applicable legal provisions.

Proxy fighting is further regulated as follows:

- Proxy holders must inform the shareholders giving the proxy of any fact or circumstances likely to create a conflict of interest, eg, that the proxy holder is an employee or a director in the company.
- Proxy holders who solicit proxies must publish on their website their voting policy.
- Proxies can be given for any specific shareholders' meeting and cannot have an indefinite term.

9. OFFICERS' REMUNERATION RULES

9.1 How is remuneration of officers determined? By whom? Is there a role for the shareholders' meeting? Is there any mechanism for an independent body to review and evaluate them?

In one-tier structure companies, the fixed and variable part of the officers' remuneration is set by the board of directors whereas in two-tier structure companies, the fixed and variable part of the management board members' remuneration is set by the supervisory board.

Some components of the remuneration such as stock-options and gratuitous shares must be authorised by the shareholders.

Finally, additional benefits granted by public companies to a departing officer, such as a golden parachute, are subject to the procedure applicable to related-party agreements, ie transactions entered into between the company and one of its officers. In this case, the board of directors approves such benefits, which are thereafter ratified by the shareholders. If the shareholders disagree with the board decision, these benefits would remain valid and enforceable but the board of directors may be held liable for any negative consequences suffered by the company.

In private companies, this procedure is not applicable, provided that the benefits granted to the departing officer meet the following conditions:

- the benefit is granted to the officer in exchange for specific services rendered to the company while the officer was still exercising his or her functions within the company;
- the benefit is proportional to the services the officer provided; and
- the benefit does not constitute an excessive burden for the company.

The corporate governance codes also recommend complying with certain criteria when determining the remuneration of officers. For instance, the Afep-Medef code suggests that golden parachutes should not exceed an amount equal to two years of remuneration and should be awarded only in case of forced departure or change of control of the company.

The Afep-Medef code also recommends that listed companies set up a remuneration committee mainly composed of independent directors.

Currently, the law does not provide for any independent body that would be in charge of reviewing and evaluating the remuneration granted to corporate officers. However, as mentioned above in paragraph 1.2, the Afep-Medef code is expected to be amended shortly in order to recommend (i) the creation of an independent body that would be in charge of dealing with disputes and (ii) the implementation of a 'say on pay' mechanism.

9.2 Is the mechanism of officers' remuneration publicly debated?

As mentioned in paragraph 9.1 above, certain components of the remuneration must be approved or ratified by the shareholders.

In addition, it is expected that public companies will soon be urged to implement the 'say on pay' principle. Accordingly, as described in paragraph 1.2 above, the mechanism of officers' remuneration will be subject to a shareholders' vote.

10. DIRECTORS' LIABILITIES, LIABILITY INSURANCE, INDEMNIFICATION

10.1 What are the directors' responsibilities and liabilities under the law? Can those liabilities be covered by insurance? Can it be indemnified by the company or other related parties?

See paragraphs 4.1 and 4.2 above.

11. SHAREHOLDERS' DERIVATIVE SUITS

11.1 Is a shareholder's derivative suit provided for by law in your jurisdiction? How is it enforced by the shareholders?

French law recognises the possibility for one or several shareholders to sue directors or officers on behalf of the company (*action sociale ut singuli*).

Shareholders' derivative suits can be brought in the case of mismanagement by a director or an officer that caused harm to the company itself. It is valid provided the company has not already brought suit against the relevant director or officer.

Shareholders holding at least 5 per cent of the company's share capital can bring a derivative suit jointly by electing one or several representatives. In addition, in a company whose shares are listed on NYSE Euronext Paris, a shareholders' association can also bring a derivative lawsuit.

Any damages for the harm caused by the officer or director would be awarded to the company, and not to the shareholders.

11.2 Have there been any recent relevant court cases on the subject?

In February 2013, Lagardère sued the management of Canal + to obtain EUR 1.6 billion in damages on behalf of Canal +. Lagardère is a minority shareholder of Canal +, with 20 per cent of the share capital, the remaining 80 per cent being held by Vivendi. Lagardère claimed that a cash-pooling agreement entered into between Canal + and a wholly owned subsidiary of Vivendi is invalid, as a result of which Vivendi should return EUR 1.6 billion of treasury to Canal +.

12. SOCIAL INTEREST IN CORPORATE BEHAVIOUR

12.1 How is a company in your country expected to deal with the following issues? Corporate social responsibility; gender, racial and social diversification; environmental issues; ecology and corruption?

The rules on corporate social interest are rather limited. In practice, many French public companies voluntarily undertake some efforts to act as good citizens in relation to these issues.

On gender, companies whose shares are listed on NYSE Euronext Paris (as well as large private companies exceeding certain thresholds in terms and employees and revenue) must ensure that they reach a balance between men and women in their board of directors (see paragraph 2.3 above).

In companies whose shares are listed on NYSE Euronext Paris (as well as large private companies exceeding certain thresholds in terms and employees and revenue), the management report submitted by the board of directors to the shareholders must provide specific information set out in the Commercial Code relative to the social and environmental consequences of the company's operations, as well as the company's commitments in terms of sustainable development, the fight against discriminations and the promotion of minorities. Public companies must also provide an independent third-party report opining on the company's assessment.

Finally, any company with more than 20 employees must have at least 6 per cent of people with disabilities in its workforce. Companies that do not reach that threshold can make a financial contribution to a dedicated non-profit organisation associated with the public authorities.

Germany

Prof. Dr Jörg Rodewald & Dr Jörgen Tielmann
Luther Rechtsanwaltsgesellschaft mbH

1. GENERAL PRINCIPLES

1.1 What are the general principles of corporate governance in your jurisdiction? What are the main objectives of corporate governance principles in your jurisdiction? State also whether your legal system is based on common law or civil law.

The legal system in Germany is based on civil law. Corporate governance rules are incorporated in the German Stock Corporation Act (*Aktiengesetz*), the Limited Liability Companies Act (*Gesetz über Gesellschaften mit beschränkter Haftung*) the Commercial Code (*Handelsgesetzbuch*) and in some financial market regulations.

The general principles of corporate governance in Germany have been summarised in the Corporate Governance Codex, a regulation issued by the Corporate Governance Commission. The Corporate Governance Commission was established in 2001 by the Federal Minister of Justice in Germany in order to develop the principles of corporate governance in Germany. The Corporate Governance Commission in 2002 published and later on from time to time amended the Corporate Governance Codex which summarises the general principles of corporate governance as provided for in German law and those principles the Corporate Governance Commission deems to be common and appropriate for listed companies in Germany. Consequently, only listed companies are the addressees of the Corporate Governance Codex. Nevertheless, even the principles laid down not being already mandatory as part of the legal system in Germany turn out to have a benchmark effect also for German companies not being listed on a stock market. In order to understand better the German specifics of the corporate governance principles it is helpful to know that the organisation of stock corporations in Germany is based on a two-tier system, ie an executive board forming the company's management and a supervisory board being responsible for the control of the management and having an advisory function towards the management.

The general principles are:

- protection and execution of shareholders' rights, in particular voting rights, enabling shareholders' participation in the general assembly;
- care for shareholder interest and stakeholder interest;
- good cooperation between executive board and supervisory board;
- information to and transparency towards supervisory board and shareholder meeting (specific attention is paid to the executives' remuneration matters);

- management of the company by the executive board (and the supervisory board with regard to its responsibilities) according and in line with the principles of loyalty (to the company), duty of skill and good faith;
- business judgment rule;
- diversity;
- conflict of interest;
- professionalism and independence; and
- importance of financial accounting and annual audit.

1.2 Have there been any recent developments in the law, codes and rules of corporate governance?

The recent legislation developments in the field of corporate governance are related to the matter of remuneration of executives. In June 2013, the Lower House of German Parliament adopted a binding say of the shareholder assembly of a stock corporation by approval of the remuneration system negotiated between the supervisory board and the executive directors, and by resolving a maximum amount (cap) for such remuneration. The sole responsibility of the supervisory board for the executives' remuneration will be limited by such approval of the shareholder assembly (see section 120 paragraph (4) German Stock Corporation Act) if this latest Stock Corporation Act reform adopted passes the Upper House of German Parliament and is enacted before the upcoming elections to the German Federal Parliament.

While a few years ago the remuneration system was focused on maximising the shareholder value, the success-based components of the remuneration for executives and supervisory board members was most important. In a turn to a more stakeholder value-related approach, the sustainable development of corporations recently became more important. Thus, the German Corporate Governance Codex does no longer recommend a success-based remuneration for supervisory board members.

In Germany, also a discussion on fixed quotas for women as members of executive and supervisory boards has taken place. While some stakeholders prefer a mandatory obligation for corporations to have at least a quota of 30 per cent women as members of the aforesaid boards, others are satisfied with a voluntary commitment of German corporations. Legislation on this matter does not yet exist.

1.3 Outline recent court cases and incidents involving corporate governance issues. Were there any significant corporate scandals or large unlawful corporate cases?

In the last decade there was a long line of corruption or bribery scandals involving major corporations and global players, such as Siemens, Deutsche Bahn, Thyssen Krupp, MAN and others. These cases gave reason to start an intensive discussion on corporate compliance in Germany and to establish compliance structures in German corporations. As a further consequence executives and supervisory board members have been subject to legal proceedings by which they were sentenced to have violated criminal law (breach of trust – *Siemens* (2009), *Mannesmann/Vodafone* (2006)). Following such verdicts significant compensation payments for damages to the companies are usual.

1.4 Which law enforcement agency is in charge of enforcing corporate governance? May a criminal sanction be levied upon infringement of the corporate governance rules?

In Germany, a law enforcement agency enforcing corporate governance standards does not exist. The Corporate Governance Commission only issues the relevant standards (Corporate Governance Codex) and has no powers to enforce the standards. According to section 161 of the German Stock Corporation Act, listed companies have to confirm to the public that the corporation is in compliance with the Corporate Governance Codex and to the extent of non-compliance the corporation has to explain the reasons for such non-compliance ('comply or explain' approach). In case of a wrong compliance statement a specific sanction does not exist and the corporation is not subject to any liability. A false compliance statement does not trigger a personal liability of the executives per se. However, if the non-compliance with the Corporate Governance Codex comes along with a violation of civil or criminal law rules the personal liability is caused by such violation. In the case of criminal offences the executives are subject to public prosecution.

2. SOURCES OF LAW

2.1 Which laws, codes or statutes govern company structures and organisations? Are there statutes like the Companies Act or other forms of law? Is there much relevant case law?

Unlike the law in the UK (Companies Act) there is no homogeneous law on companies in Germany. While smaller companies using the legal form of a limited liability company are governed by the German Limited Liability Companies Act, in particular listed companies which have to use the legal form of stock corporation (or *Societas Europaea* (SE)) are governed by the German Stock Corporation Act. The German Stock Corporation Act contains the relevant rules on structure and organisation of a stock corporation, in particular the two-tier system consisting of an executive board of directors and a supervisory board, which is specific for this type of German legal form. With regard to the SE, a group of rules is relevant: EU decree on SE (No. 2157/2001 as of 8 October 2001), German legislation on implementation of the SE in Germany and the Stock Corporation Act.

With regard to companies' structure and organisation, the relevance of jurisprudence and case law in Germany is limited. There is a certain influence with regard to competences of boards, rules of interaction of executive boards and supervisory boards – in particular, information rights and obligations and procedures in case of potential damage claims against members of the executive or the supervisory board. Also the applicability of the business judgment rule (see No. 10 hereof) was initially based on a verdict of the German Federal Civil Court. However, the German case law does not have the same impact on organisation and structure of a company than it has under common law.

2.2 Which laws, codes or statutes regulate capital markets in your jurisdiction?

The German Securities Trading Act (WpHG) provides for rules for all market participants, including insider trading, insider information disclosure, shareholders' disclosure and publication and disclosure obligations of listed companies. The German Takeover Act (WpÜG) contains the regulations applicable in a case of a bidder acquiring control, ie 30 per cent in a listed company, in particular with regard to voluntary and mandatory takeover offers.

2.3 Are there any public interest laws which apply to or influence corporate governance?

There are no specific public interest laws which apply to or influence corporate governance. As mentioned earlier (see above paragraph 1.1) the German way of implementation of corporate governance structures to a significant extent relies on the influence of the Corporate Governance Commission. This commission although established by the Federal Minister of Justice has no function as legislator but aims to influence the German corporate governance culture via statements by a group of experts (the members of the Corporate Governance Commission). Consequently, Germany places emphasis on progressing with corporate governance matters not via legislator activities.

2.4 Have there been any recent developments in any of the above laws? What are the recent changes to the above laws or rules and the reasons for such changes?

Not applicable.

3. SHAREHOLDERS AND THE SHAREHOLDERS' MEETING

3.1 How are shareholders' interests represented in the company? How are the shareholders assured exercise of their rights? What is the highest governing body within the company structure if it is not the shareholders' meeting?

The shareholders' meeting is the highest governing body of the company. It is in charge of resolving on the distribution of profits, discharging the management, approving of any structural measures as well as electing the auditor and the supervisory board. The supervisory board being composed of shareholders' representatives and, if applicable, employees' representatives is in charge of monitoring the management board thereby taking into account the shareholders' interests as long as they are in accordance with the German law and the articles of association. In addition, shareholders have intensive information rights and can make motions in the annual shareholders' meeting.

3.2 How is the shareholders' meeting conducted? Who may chair the meeting? May attendance (not voting) at the meeting be restricted only to the shareholders? Are the shareholders allowed to be accompanied by legal or other counsel?

In general, the shareholders' meeting will have to be convoked 30 to 37 days prior to its date by a published invitation in the German federal gazette or private letter to each shareholder. Such invitation must include the agenda of the shareholders' meeting and proposals for the resolutions. In the case of listed companies, a notary will be required to take the minutes.

Generally, only shareholders are allowed to attend the shareholders' meeting. By giving proxies, a shareholder can also be accompanied by legal or other counsels. Guests may be admitted at the discretion of the chairman. The meeting is generally chaired by the chairman of the supervisory board unless the shareholders' meeting resolves otherwise.

3.3 How are minority shareholders' rights protected?

Depending on certain quotas, there are minority rights, such as (i) to amend the agenda, (ii) to demand a special audit, or (iii) to have an individual voting on the discharge for each board member or to have the voting on candidates to the supervisory board in a certain order. In addition, any shareholder with just one share may ask questions in relation to all topics to the management, may challenge resolutions before court not to be compliant with German law or the company's articles of association and may make alternative proposal for resolution on the topics suggested by the management. If such rights are infringed and such infringement is relevant for the way a resolution is drawn, such resolution can be challenged before court on this basis.

3.4 Is shareholder activism encouraged or discouraged? If not encouraged, how is it regulated?

Shareholder activism is rather encouraged due to the fact that shareholders are able (i) to ask questions with regard to any topic relating to the company or its business during the shareholders' meeting, (ii) challenge resolutions or (iii) to put a specific topic on the agenda, if they reach the necessary quota.

3.5 How are professional shareholders (those minority shareholders who seek some extra benefit from companies by unduly and habitually influencing management by using their shareholding) treated by the law? Are they excluded from attending the shareholders' meeting? Are they criminally or otherwise publicly sanctioned?

In the past years, there have been a series of legislative reforms to the Stock Corporation Act to limit such unduly shareholder actions by introducing preliminary proceedings to overrule such actions if it is evidently unjustified or if the plaintiffs do not hold certain minimum quotas or by enabling the chairman to restrict the time each shareholder may speak during meetings. Still, the equal-treatment principles must be observed. Any settlement in shareholders' action must be published in the federal gazette (*Bundesanzeiger*) and will be void if not published. Professional shareholders may only be excluded from attending a particular shareholders' meeting if their unruly behaviour endangers the further progress of the meeting. This caste of shareholders is known to the public and the respective listed stock companies, *inter alia* by press reports. In individual cases, there has been criminal prosecution on the basis of blackmailing.

3.6 Are shareholders' benefits given to some of the shareholders by the company without resolution by the shareholders' meeting prohibited or regulated by the law or other rules?

Benefits can only be granted to shareholders on the basis of shareholders' resolutions to distribute profits shown in the balance sheet. Such resolutions must treat all shareholders equally. Any other benefit granted which is not at arm's length will be regarded as a repayment of equity and can be claimed to be repaid.

4. DIRECTORS AND BOARD OF DIRECTORS

4.1 What are the functions and responsibilities of the directors and the board of directors? Do you have a one- or two-tier board system? What are the outside directors called?

A German stock corporation generally has a two-tier board system, which provides for a managing board and a supervisory board. In addition, the so-called European stock corporation (SE) can be organised as a one- or two-tier board system.

The members of the managing board of a German stock corporation independently run the company's business and are hereby controlled by the members of the supervisory board. The supervisory board is, in particular, in charge of appointing and dismissing management board members, of approving the annual reports and certain operational measures, and of advising the board.

4.2 What are the rules that may give rise to civil and criminal liability of the director(s)? How are those liabilities sought?

The members of the managing and supervisory boards are obliged to run the company's business in accordance with the diligence of a prudent businessman pursuant to sections 93 and 116 of the German Stock Corporation Act. A breach of this obligation can cause indemnification or compensation claims of the company, if the respective board member acted culpably. The members of the boards are not obliged to a damage or indemnification payment, if the actions of the members were based on a lawful resolution of the shareholders' meeting. Such liability is enforced either by the respective other board or on the basis of a shareholders' resolution.

In addition, the managing board is obliged to file for insolvency, if the company is bankrupt or heavily indebted. In the case of omission to file for insolvency, the respective member of the managing board can be accused of delayed filing of insolvency or bankruptcy and will be personally liable for any payment made at this stage.

4.3 Does the board of directors have a committee system, eg nomination committee, compensation committee, audit committee? If not required, is it common practice for companies? How does it function?

A committee system is known for the supervisory board, eg a nomination committee, compensation committee or an audit committee. Besides, the managing board can be organised by establishing various departments as long as the direction of the company is not transferred to one special committee, ie the final decisions have to remain with and be made by the entire managing board.

4.4 Is it a legal requirement to have an independent director or a third-party director? If so, how are they appointed? Is it required for listed companies?

There is no legal requirement to have an independent director or a third-party director in the managing board. However, at least one of the members of the supervisory board has to be independent and to possess expert knowledge in accounting and audit, if the company is capital market-orientated. In addition, no former management board member may change into the supervisory board within two years after his appointment as a management board member has terminated, unless 25 per cent of all shareholders support such election.

4.5 How is the compensation for directors or officers determined? Can it be contested by the shareholders or the regulatory authorities? What are the common rules or practices for the compensation of officers?

The compensation for members of the managing board is negotiated and agreed upon on behalf of the company by the supervisory board. The compensation cannot be contested by the shareholders or the regulatory authorities, but members of the supervisory board might be liable, if the compensation exceeds an appropriate amount.

In the case of a premature termination, the overall compensation shall according to a recommendation of the German Corporate Governance Codex not exceed two annual salaries of the respective member of the managing board, including all additional benefits granted to the managing board member.

4.6 How will the board handle a corporate crisis like an internal criminal case, violence, social media exposure or dawn raid by the authorities?

If such a corporate crisis is related to the wrongful actions of an individual member of the board, his appointment will be revoked with cause. Otherwise, law does not provide for specific patterns of behaviour.

5. BOARD OF AUDITORS, AUDIT COMMITTEE, ACCOUNTING AUDITORS

5.1 How is the internal accounting and legal audit structured and conducted? Is an outside accounting audit required and, if so, how is it structured? Are there requirements to change the auditor each five years?

In compliance with section 238 of the German Commercial Code, companies have to maintain an appropriate accounting system. The accounting department and the risk-management system of a stock corporation in Germany have to be organised in a way which enables the management to have clear view on the financial situation of the company at any time (sections 90 and 91 German Stock Corporation Act). In addition, for listed companies section 100, paragraph 5 of the German Stock Corporation Act requires at least one financial expert as member of the supervisory board. There is no binding obligation for stock corporations to establish an audit committee as part of the supervisory board. However, the Corporate Governance Codex (section 5.3.2) recommends such a committee. If a listed company has an audit committee, at least one member of such a committee has to be a financial expert in the meaning of section 100, paragraph 5 of the Germen Stock Corporation Act (see section 107, paragraph 3 German Stock Corporation Act).

Due to section 316 of the German Commercial Code, the annual (external) audit regarding the financial statement of a German company is mandatory. Smaller companies are excluded. The annual audit is focused on the compliance of the financial statement with national and (to the extent applicable) international accounting rules and standards. Only persons or companies qualified as certified accountants or auditing firms may act as a statutory auditor.

Based on a recommendation by the supervisory board, the statutory auditor is elected by general assembly on an annual basis. After such election, the assignment for the statutory auditor has to be issued by the supervisory board.

There is no requirement to change the statutory auditor after a certain period of time under German law. However, public and state-owned companies increasingly tend to follow a rule of change providing for a new statutory auditor after five years. Major private companies such as Siemens seem to follow this example and changed a couple of years ago from KPMG (which maintained this assignment for more than 15 years) to Ernst & Young. Any efforts at EU level to bring forward an EU directive and a decree on mandatory rotation of the statutory auditor for companies of public interest (combined with the mechanism of a joint audit) have not been successful so far.

5.2 Do you have supervisory auditors? What is the function of the supervisory auditors' board?

Supervisory auditors are not required or foreseen under German law. However, the mechanism of a joint audit (instead of a supervisory auditor) may become subject of an EU directive and an EU decree (see above under paragraph 5.1). Apart from that, financial statements of German companies are subject to review by the Financial Reporting Enforcement Panel (FREP) according to section 342(b) of the German Commercial Code. The FREP is a private institution established by the Federal Minister of Justice to investigate violation of accounting standards. The FREP takes a sample of financial statements for review on an annual basis. Due to the means available to the FREP, its review activities are limited.

6. MARKET DISCLOSURE/TRANSPARENCY TO THE SHAREHOLDERS AND THE PUBLIC

6.1 What are the disclosure requirements for companies in your jurisdiction under company law, capital markets law or any other rules?

Each German corporation has to publish its annual report along with a profit-and-loss account with the German federal gazette. Depending on the company's size and/or legal form, the annual report with an operation review, the supervisory board's report and/or notes and appendices will have to be added.

If the company is listed, there are additional disclosure requirements stipulated by the capital markets law. Listed companies also have to publish quarterly financial reports within certain dates. Moreover, the respective listed company has to publish immediately by way of ad hoc disclosure any insider information it becomes aware of unless there are valid reasons to suspend such publication in the company's best interest and confidentiality regarding such insider information can be secured.

6.2 What is the liability or responsibility of the board in relation to the company's disclosure requirements?

If the managing board does culpably not comply with its responsibility to fulfil any disclosure requirements, it will be liable to the company. Moreover, in the case of listed companies, any investor may hold the managing board directly liable for damages it suffers because he or she has relied in its investment decision on an incorrect or belated ad hoc disclosure of the company.

7. M&A AND CORPORATE GOVERNANCE

7.1 Upon an M&A offer, how are the transparency and fairness rules of the company provided under the company and stock market laws and rules?

The German takeover regulation (section 3 of the German Takeover Act) provides for the following principles:

- equal treatment of all shareholders of the target company (ie the same offer has to be made to all shareholders of the target);
- transparency (further defined in the takeover regulation – such as obligations of the tenderer to immediately announce the offer and to provide all relevant information to the shareholders);
- obligation of the management of the target company to observe and to act in the best interest of the target;
- rapid execution of the offering procedure (short timeline for the parties involved to conduct their activities, provision addressed to the bidder regarding the covering of the financing matters); and
- contortion of the market shall strictly be avoided (this refers to the shares of the bidder, the target and other parties affected by the takeover bid – special rules exist with regard to insider business and market manipulation).

8. PROXY FIGHTING

8.1 Is proxy fighting customarily conducted for control of the company management of what other items? How is it regulated under the company law of market regulations?

The German Stock Corporation Act does not provide for a system enabling shareholders to a proxy fight or a similar proceeding, but primarily to a portfolio voting system. If the company offers that an employee will serve as a voting representative for shareholders, such nominee may only exercise the voting rights if and to extent he has detailed instructions thereby preventing a proxy fight since the representatives have no discretion in exercising their proxies.

9. OFFICERS' REMUNERATION RULES

9.1 How is remuneration of officers determined? By whom? Is there a role for the shareholders' meeting? Is there any mechanism for an independent body to review and evaluate them?

The remuneration of officers is determined by the respective managing board member and the supervisory board in a service agreement between the managing board member and the company represented by the supervisory board. The shareholders' meeting only has a non-binding say on the remuneration system. The remuneration has to be (i) appropriate in view of the duties, responsibilities as well as benefits and the company's business situation, and (ii) shall not exceed the common remuneration. In addition, the remuneration needs to be adequate in relation to the company's financial situation and in a vertical and horizontal comparison. In cases of crisis, the supervisory board is authorised to decrease the remuneration. The supervisory board may consult a remuneration expert as to the adequateness of the remuneration. Variable remunerations are required to be connected to predominately sustainable aims. The shareholders' meeting is informed about the managing board members' remuneration on an individualised basis in the annual report and during the annual shareholders' meeting.

9.2 Is the mechanism of officers' remuneration publicly debated?

There is a current ongoing debate on granting the shareholders' meeting the right to resolve on the remuneration as introduced in Switzerland. The Lower House of German Parliament has adopted in June 2013 a concept of having an annual binding resolution on the remuneration system also outlining maximum amounts of possible wages, rather than just a voluntary non-binding say on such a system, as provided for by law before. Such latest Stock Corporation Act reform will only be enacted if it passes the Upper House of German Parliament before the upcoming elections to the Lower House of German Parliament.

10. DIRECTORS' LIABILITIES, LIABILITY INSURANCE, INDEMNIFICATION

10.1 What are the directors' responsibilities and liabilities under the law? Can those liabilities be covered by insurance? Can it be indemnified by the company or other related parties?

In general, any executive director (as well as any supervisory board member) has to officiate with the care of a diligent businessman. This general rule is provided for in section 93 of the German Stock Corporation Act (for German stock corporations – similar rules for limited liability companies are provided for in section 43 of the German Limited Liability Companies Act). This general rule is supplemented by several special directors' duties provided for in the Law on Stock Corporations and Limited Liability Companies (such duties related to the preservation of the company's nominal capital or the obligation to file for insolvency in due time if the case may be, establishment of a risk-management system, reporting obligations *vis-à-vis* the supervisory board and the general assembly). With regard to the general rule, multiple case law exists by which certain standards of ruling an office as executive director or member of a supervisory board have been established (such as conducting the business within the limits given by the business purpose of the company, preserving the company's assets, complying with the applicable laws, etc.). Further rules for executive directors can be found in the German takeover regulation (see above under No. 7 hereof) and in various rules on specific matters (such rules on trade in securities/bonds/shares, rules for banks and insurance companies and service providers in the financial market). Also a business judgment rule exists which excludes those directors' decision and activities from the liability regime which are business decision and activities (given the business decision was based on an appropriate level of information, in the company's best interest and not motivated by private interest).

In the case of violation of duties and obligations, the director as well as any member of the supervisory board is liable to the company. Such liability leads to the obligation to compensate all damages the company suffered due to the misconduct. Beyond this a personal liability *vis-à-vis* third parties who suffered a damage is possible if the director or member of the supervisory board directly harmed the third party while not properly officiating.

A directors' or supervisory board members' liability may be covered by a directors' and officers' (D&O) insurance policy. The respective insurance coverage grants protection with regard to any liability of the director or the supervisory board member for damages based on negligent misconduct. The insurance protection does not cover any damages caused by intentional misconduct. Any insurance coverage has a limit. The limits vary from EUR 10 million for smaller companies up to EUR 100 million for large listed companies. Beyond these limits insurance coverage becomes rare due to the extremely expensive insurance fees. According to section 93, paragraph 2 of the German Stock Corporation Act an excess of at least 10 per cent of the compensation payment (limited to an amount equalling 150 per cent of his or her annual remuneration) has to stay with the executive director of a German stock corporation. For companies being a limited liability company the aforesaid rule is not applicable.

The company may waive towards the director or member of the supervisory for a claim but not earlier than three years after the claim of the company for damages came into existence. Furthermore, such waiver requires the approval of the general assembly of the stock corporation (section 93, paragraph 4 German Stock Corporation Act). Such a shareholder resolution regarding a waiver can be blocked by a minority of shareholders representing at least 10 per cent of the nominal capital of the corporation. Also, a director is protected from a liability towards the corporation if his or her decision is based on a shareholder resolution adopted by the general assembly of the corporation (such exemption from liability only being valid if the decision made by the director did not violate mandatory law). Alternatively, or in addition, a related party may hold the director or the supervisory board member harmless. Such indemnification by a related party is a rare occurrence. However, any waiver by the company or indemnification by the company or related parties does not block any third parties' claims against the director or supervisory board member.

11. SHAREHOLDERS' DERIVATIVE SUITS

11.1 Is a shareholder's derivative suit provided for by law in your jurisdiction?

A specific shareholders' derivative suit is provided for (i) certain claims with regard to the foundation and post-foundation of the corporation against the founders of the corporation and certain other persons legally defined, (ii) indemnification/damage claims with regard to the management of the corporation against the members of the managing and supervisory board, and (iii) indemnification claims against persons who intentionally suborn the members of the managing or supervisory board, a *prokurist* or an authorised agent to damage the corporation by using his/her influence in the corporation. Shareholders with a minimum quota will be able to file an action against the respective person in their own name with regard to the previously mentioned claims of the company.

How is it enforced by the shareholders?

This shareholders' derivative suit has to be brought to the responsible district court by the shareholders. The district court will accept this filing, if the shareholders are able to prove (i) their holding of shares previous to the filing, (ii) their unsuccessful request towards the corporation to file an action by its own in accordance, and (iii) facts exist, which justify the suspicion that the corporation was damaged by disingenuousness or gross violation of law or the articles of association, and (iv) the enforcement of the claims are not blocked by prevailing reasons of the company's best interest. Once the filing has been accepted, the company has to take over proceedings as a party against the plaintiff. At any time, the company is also entitled to file an own action in accordance with section 147 of the German Stock Corporation Act or to take over the shareholders' action in accordance with section 148 of the German Stock Corporation Act.

11.2 Have there been any recent relevant court cases on the subject?

Since the shareholders' derivative suit was only introduced in 2009, only one major court decision was released by the Higher Regional Court of Munich in 2010 (file reference: 7 W 2040/10) with regard to recall of a special representative (*besonderer Vertreter*).

12. SOCIAL INTEREST IN CORPORATE BEHAVIOUR

12.1 How is a company in your country expected to deal with the following issues? Corporate social responsibility; gender, racial and social diversification; environmental issues; ecology and corruption?

Corporate social responsibility (CSR) has so far not been a field of legislator activities in Germany. Nevertheless, the general expectation is that companies act responsible and with care towards their employees, their customers and with regard to natural resources. Initiatives to comply with the (undefined) rules of CSR have been initiated *inter alia* by the German federal government (CSR in Deutschland – initiated by the Federal Minister of Labour and Social Matters). Climate change, pollution and conservation of nature are permanent topics in Germany. In light of the ongoing social discussion on these matters, it is difficult for companies in Germany not to profess to the principles of CSR.

Gender, racial and social diversification is also not the subject of legal provisions. However, a fundamental principle in German law and, in particular, constitutional law is the non-discrimination of human beings. Nobody shall be discriminated against because of his gender, race or nationality. In this regard a special law on non-discrimination is in place in Germany. Indeed, supporting non-discrimination does not automatically lead to diversification. In particular, there is no positive obligation in place to have a certain mix of people employed or to comply with a minimum quota for women, non-German employees or alike.

Environmental and ecological matters are also important for German companies. Germany has detailed legislation on environmental matters (such as protection of water, waste-water management and emission protection). Moreover, the occurrence of polluted areas (not only) in Germany's eastern region and the experience of cleaning such areas (and of the cleaning costs) triggered a rising sensitiveness to environmental and ecological matters.

Corruption and the avoidance of corruption is a very important topic for German companies. Due to a lot of corruption scandals in Germany and a steady rise in prosecutors' activities, almost all major companies down to mid-size organisations have implemented compliance management systems in general and anti-corruption management systems, in particular. Germany appears to be have one of the most competitive anti-corruption advisory markets in the world (although it does not rank the highest on the Transparency International Corruption Index).

Hong Kong

George A. Ribeiro, Dominic W. L. Hui & Ricky W. K. Sun
Ribeiro Hui

1. GENERAL PRINCIPLES

1.1 What are the general principles of corporate governance in your jurisdiction? What are the main objectives of corporate governance principles in your jurisdiction? State also whether your legal system is based on common law or civil law.

Hong Kong Special Administrative Region of the People's Republic of China (PRC) (Hong Kong), being a past British Dependent Territory prior to 1 July 1997, inherited its corporate governance model and principles from Britain. With its ever-growing importance in international business as well as the gateway to China prior to and after the 1997 Handover, international norms on corporate governance have also played a key role in shaping its corporate governance regime.

In addition to the traditional keys of fiduciary duties on the management, transparency, fairness, accountability and protection of the rights of minority shareholders and creditors, corporate governance is also viewed as a necessity for a healthy corporate image that practises controls against managers' opportunistic behaviour and which in turn leads to better management that maximises shareholders' value.

1.2 Have there been any recent developments in the law, codes and rules of corporate governance?

Corporate governance principles and rules are contained in legislation, common law and regulatory codes. The principal legislation and codes are:

- the Companies Ordinance, Chapter 32 of the Laws of Hong Kong;
- the Securities and Futures Ordinance, Chapter 571 of the Laws of Hong Kong; and
- the Listing Rules of the Stock Exchange of Hong Kong Limited (Listing Rules), including the Corporate Governance Code made under it and the Listing Agreement (the Listing Rules govern the main board listings and there are also the Growth Enterprise Market Listing Rules).

Since its implementation in 1984, the Companies Ordinance has not undergone any major change until it was re-written last year. The New Companies Ordinance received legislative blessing in July 2012 and is expected to commence in 2014. The major amendments to enhance corporate governance include:

- the requirement of having at least one individual director to serve as member on the board whereas currently, directors can be corporations established in jurisdictions where information on directors and

shareholders of corporations incorporated there are not open to public inspection;
- the imposition of the duty on directors to exercise reasonable care, skill and diligence to the standard that would be exercised by a reasonable diligent person having the knowledge of a person carrying out the function of a director and the standard of the care, skill and diligence that the director has, in the conduct of the company's affairs;
- the threshold for members to demand a poll will be reduced from 10 per cent to 5 per cent of the total voting rights attached to issued shares; and
- widening the range of persons required to provide information and explanations reasonably required to the company's auditors, such as officers of the company's subsidiary.

1.3 Outline recent court cases and incidents involving corporate governance issues. Were there any significant corporate scandals or large unlawful corporate cases?

There have been a number of recent cases involving listed and private companies and notable individuals, where management officers abused their positions in securing excessive remuneration structures, related-party transactions without disclosure and/or falsifying records or books in that connection or to inflate the value of the company for ulterior purposes. Some of such cases where criminal conduct is involved will be proceeding to trial or on appeal, and the resulting court decisions are hoped to provide deterrence against such conduct and guidance for improvement of ethical standards to be observed and corporate governance.

1.4 Which law enforcement agency is in charge of enforcing corporate governance? May a criminal sanction be levied upon infringement of the corporate governance rules?

The Registrar of Companies is empowered to enforce compliance of the provisions of the Companies Ordinance and has authority to prosecute where the offence may attract criminal sanction. Most offences are however dealt with administratively, such as imposition of a late filing fee, eg in respect of late filing of an annual return, although for serious and repeated delays, a higher penalty and daily default fine can be imposed. Criminal offences under the Companies Ordinance that may be penalised by both a fine and imprisonment are generally directed to protection of investors or creditors and proper accounting. Examples are:
- authorising the issue of a prospectus for subscription of shares with an untrue statement;
- provision of financial assistance by the company to purchase its own shares that do not come within any of the permitted exceptions;
- reduction of share capital in breach of the Companies Ordinance (such as concealing name of a creditor entitled to object to the proposed reduction);
- a director failing to ensure proper books of accounts are kept;

- a director failing to take reasonable steps to ensure the accounts are tabled at the annual general meeting;
- an officer knowingly or wilfully omitting an entry in the register of charges of the company; and
- an officer recklessly or knowingly making a false statement to auditors.

As for insider dealing of shares in a listed company, the regulatory authority is the Securities and Futures Commission. A convicted insider dealer can be subject to heavy fines and imprisonment of up to 10 years.

Contravention of the Listing Rules or the Listing Agreement may result in issue of private reprimands or public statements denouncing the particular contravention, suspension of trading and de-listing the listed company.

2. SOURCES OF LAW

2.1 Which laws, codes or statutes govern company structures and organisations? Are there statutes like the Companies Act or other forms of law? Is there much relevant case law?

For statutory laws and codes, see paragraph 1.2 above.

As for the sources of law in Hong Kong, Hong Kong is a common law jurisdiction and hence there is common law which is also modelled from British rules and concepts. Prior to the Handover in 1997, decisions of the House of Lords in England were binding in Hong Kong, but since then, while English precedents need not be followed, they are highly persuasive.

Case law is relevant in the interpretation of legislation and on numerous issues, such as the nature and extent of fiduciary duties of directors and senior-management officers, how they have been discharged, what may amount to reckless or wilful conduct, what constitutes oppression against the minority and just and equitable grounds for dissolution of the company, remedies available and criteria to be satisfied for injunctive, tracing, disclosure and accounting orders.

Of particular importance is the common law right of minority shareholders to sue management officers and shareholders in the name of the company for their wrongdoings to the company by way of derivative action. The major difficulty in the past is that the asset and/or operating company is usually the subsidiary, and the minority is the shareholder of the parent. Hence, the minority shareholder may not have the *locus standi* to complain and issue a derivative action. Further, fraud on the minority has to be shown and that may be difficult to prove.

In 2009, the Court of Final Appeal in *Waddington Limited v Chan Chun Hoo Thomas and others* (2009 HKC 381) ruled that such proceedings were possible. *Waddington*'s case is one of the first reasoned decisions on multiple derivative suits made in Asia. It began years before it reached the Hong Kong Court of Appeal, and during the course of the proceedings, statutory derivative actions were made available in 2005 through the introduction of Part IVAA of the Companies Ordinance. However, multiple derivative actions were then not possible by way of statutory law. Amendments were made in 2010 that enabled this by affording a member of a related company (which includes a holding company, a subsidiary of the holding company and a subsidiary of the holding company of the subject company) with the right to sue in the name of the company.

Statutory derivation actions are generally considered wider than common law derivation actions because a shareholder of a company can sue for general misfeasance. However, there are still certain limitations. In Hong Kong, it is typical to find the holding company to be an offshore company for various reasons, eg tax. In *East Asia Satellite Television (Holdings) Ltd v New Cotai, LLC and others* [2011 HKC 115], the Hong Kong Court of Appeal ruled that the right of a member of a parent company to bring proceedings for wrongdoings to its subsidiary has to be governed by the law of the place of incorporation of the subsidiary. Accordingly, even if the relevant foreign law permits this, expert evidence has to be adduced and with the time involved in additional procedures and evidence, injunctive remedies sought against the act complained may be met with difficulties with the court leaning towards maintaining the status quo.

Another limitation is that the member has to be a member on the register of members of the company in question or the relevant related company. The right is therefore not conferred on the beneficial owner of shares which for any reason is not registered as a member of the company, eg the registered owner passed away and the beneficiary under his will or intestacy has yet to obtain grant of probate or letters of administration or the board has not approved registration. If the board of the company refuses to register the beneficial owner as a member, proceedings have to be first issued for rectification of the share register. That again may have to depend on the law of a foreign jurisdiction, if the shares are in a company incorporated outside Hong Kong.

2.2 Which laws, codes or statutes regulate capital markets in your jurisdiction?

The principal legislation and codes are:

- the Securities and Futures Ordinance, Chapter 571 of the Laws of Hong Kong;
- the Codes on Takeovers, Mergers and Share Repurchases issued by the Securities and Futures Commission (Takeover Code); and
- the Listing Rules of the Stock Exchange of Hong Kong Limited and the Listing Agreement (the Listing Rules govern the main board listings and there are also the Growth Enterprise Market Listing Rules).

2.3 Are there any public interest laws which apply to or influence corporate governance?

The above-mentioned laws are the principal ones. There are, of course, also the Crimes Ordinance, Chapter 200 of the Laws of Hong Kong, which prohibits forgery and falsifying documents for unlawful purposes, and the Prevention of Bribery Ordinance, Chapter 201 of the Laws of Hong Kong, which prevents abuse of one's position to secure an advantage.

2.4 Have there been any recent developments in any of the above

laws? What are the recent changes to the above laws or rules and the reasons for such changes?
See paragraphs 1.2 and 2.1 above.

3. SHAREHOLDERS AND THE SHAREHOLDERS' MEETING

3.1 How are shareholders' interests represented in the company? How are the shareholders assured exercise of their rights? What is the highest governing body within the company structure if it is not the shareholders' meeting?

Management of the company is vested in the board of directors, and they are appointed by the members of the company through members' resolutions but in the case of vacancies, the articles of association (articles) of the company may provide for appointment by the members of the board. As to which matters must be determined by members in general meeting and the proportion of votes required, reference should be made to the articles, the relevant shareholders' agreement (if any) and the Companies Ordinance. In the case of private companies, the shareholders' agreement can override the articles, except where certain minimum standards are required under the Companies Ordinance, eg matters that are required to be passed by special resolution and a special resolution requires at least 75 per cent vote of the members having the right to vote at general meetings present at the meeting.

There are two types of resolutions, namely ordinary resolutions and special resolutions. Ordinary resolutions only require a simple majority of the members present to be effective, whereas special resolutions require at least 75 per cent of the members voting at the meeting under the Companies Ordinance. Matters that do not require a special resolution to be effective can be passed by an ordinary resolution. The shareholders of the company may, through the articles, require for a higher proportion of votes for any particular matter or even unanimous consent.

There are various matters that require a special resolution under the Companies Ordinance. Examples are: (i) amendment of the articles; (ii) voluntary winding up; (iii) reduction of capital; (iv) provision of financial assistance to purchase the company's shares under the permitted exceptions to the financial assistance prohibition; and (v) payment out of capital for share repurchase. The notice calling the meeting where a special resolution is proposed should be given at least 21 days before the meeting unless a 95 per cent waiver of the requirement is given. Further, a company must hold an annual general meeting (AGM) each year (although under the New Companies Ordinance, members can consent to dispense with an AGM), except for the first AGM which may be held within 18 months of incorporation.

At the AGM, the directors should table the accounts of the company for the ensuing year, unless there is a reasonable excuse not to do so. Depending on the articles, directors and auditors are generally elected or re-appointed at the AGM by ordinary resolution and directors may be deemed to retire by rotation. A director has a statutory right of access to all books and records of the company. Thus, if a minority shareholder has the right or sufficient votes to have its director on the board, protection of its rights may be enhanced notwithstanding such director or itself may be outvoted on matters in board or general meetings respectively. Such statutory right has been construed liberally by the court, and cases indicate that such right will be allowed even if it may be inconsistent with provisions in the articles and the director needs not have to demonstrate good faith or basis for the inspection despite objections by the other board members.

All ordinary resolutions and special resolutions can be passed through written resolutions without the need of the members to physically meet and cast their votes at the meeting. However, for written resolutions, the company and every officer have to ensure they are entered into the books of the company, failing which a fine (including a default daily fine) can be imposed.

Certain resolutions require special notice. If directors or members propose resolutions to be passed (and in fact members holding in the aggregate not less than 1/20 of the total paid-up capital having voting rights can requisition a general meeting seeking resolutions to be passed) for the appointment or removal of the auditors or the removal of a director, notice of such resolutions must be given to the company at least 28 days in advance prior to the meeting at which the motion is moved.

3.2 How is the shareholders' meeting conducted? Who may chair the meeting? May attendance (not voting) at the meeting be restricted only to the shareholders? Are the shareholders allowed to be accompanied by legal or other counsel?

Whether shareholders' meetings can be conducted through electronic means such as telephone or videoconferencing in addition to physical meeting depends on the articles or the shareholders' agreement (if any). As noted above, resolutions sought to be passed at a members' meeting can be made through written resolutions.

The individual to chair a members' meeting is again subject to the articles or the shareholders' agreement (if any). Otherwise, he is elected by ordinary resolution at the meeting. The chairman of the meeting does not have a casting vote unless the articles provide so.

Although a members' meeting should be restricted to members, in practice most companies allow a member to bring his lawyer or counsel to accompany him if there is a reason and advance notice has been given. This is to minimise exposure to an allegation of minority oppression. However, the lawyer or counsel should generally be an observer. If he wishes to speak or raise issues, the member should appoint him as a proxy and deposit the proxy form within the time prescribed under the articles.

3.3 How are minority shareholders' rights protected?

As mentioned above, certain matters of the company have to be determined by members in general meeting, a special resolution may be required, a minority shareholder may requisition a members' meeting, an annual general meeting must be held and derivative actions may be brought. A minority shareholder also has the right to bring minority shareholders' proceedings under section 168A of the Companies Ordinance on oppression against the minority, and if successful, the court may grant various orders such as an injunctive order restraining the continuation of the act complained of, rectification and/or a buying-out order. Where the quasi partnership principle under common law can be established, proceedings for winding up can further be brought on the just and equitable ground. Issue of such proceedings can be a powerful remedy by way of procedure, as the winding order, if granted, dates back to the presentation of the petition and may invalidate transactions occurring after that date. Hence, third parties generally will not enter into contracts or conduct transactions with a company that is the subject of a winding-up petition in Hong Kong. Bank accounts of the company are also frozen. In order for the company to conduct business in the usual course, it has to apply for a validation order.

There are also certain rules on requiring the shares of the minority to be bought or purchased in the case of takeover under the Companies Ordinance. In the case of a listed company's takeovers, mergers and privatisations, the general offer is principally governed by the Takeover Code and the Listing Rules. Further details are contained in paragraph 7 below.

3.4 Is shareholder activism encouraged or discouraged? If not encouraged, how is it regulated?

There is no particular policy to encourage or discourage shareholder activism. There is, however, a growing tendency for public shareholders to attend members' meetings of listed companies to express concerns. For private companies, it basically depends on the relevant shareholders, and where there are anticipated challenges by a minority shareholder, calling shareholders' meetings and putting forward resolutions on the relevant subject may help in fending off an allegation of minority oppression if there are also shareholders other than the management shareholders that support the proposed resolution.

3.5 How are professional shareholders (those minority shareholders who seek some extra benefit from companies by unduly and habitually influencing management by using their shareholding) treated by the law? Are they excluded from attending the shareholders' meeting? Are they criminally or otherwise publicly sanctioned?

Professional shareholders are not treated differently from other shareholders under the law for influence on the management or related-party transactions, but if professional advice is given, there is the usual duty of care. With respect to special benefit that is not enjoyed by other shareholders, in practice the subject would be regulated by the shareholders' agreement and/or the articles. Whether or not an interested shareholder or its appointed board member is allowed to vote or abstain from voting on a resolution relating to the interested transaction is governed by such instruments.

The question of whether the appointed director of interested party in voting upon a transaction that benefits his shareholder needs to have the company's interest as the overriding one depends on the facts and purpose of the venture.

In the case of listed companies, however, where the professional shareholder is also a substantial shareholder or has its director appointed to the board, disclosures and shareholders' approval of the transaction may be required.

3.6 Are shareholders' benefits given to some of the shareholders by the company without resolution by the shareholders' meeting prohibited or regulated by the law or other rules?

Shareholders' benefits are attached to the shares they hold, eg there should be pro rata offer and allotment of new shares unless the members in a general meeting have resolved otherwise. However, there can be class rights with special benefits attaching to certain classes of shares, eg special voting rights, right to distribution of assets to other shareholders on dissolution of the company, right of first refusal to new shares, right of appointment of directors etc. These rights can be contained in the articles or partly in the articles and the shareholders' agreement. While certain procedural formalities may have to be complied with under the Companies Ordinance, eg a shareholders' resolution in the case of allotment of shares non-pro rata, the shareholders will have to pass the resolution contractually pursuant to the relevant shareholders' agreement.

4. DIRECTORS AND BOARD OF DIRECTORS

4.1 What are the functions and responsibilities of the directors and the board of directors? Do you have a one- or two-tier board system? What are the outside directors called?

The directors are entrusted with the general management of the company and in doing so, each owes fiduciary duties to the company, such as honesty and not to allow his interest to conflict with that of the company. The New Companies Ordinance will further clarify and fortify this through introduction of the dual objective and subjective standard of diligence and knowledge mentioned in paragraph 1.2 above.

There is neither a one-tier nor two-tier system but companies can, if they so wish, have committees that take care of the management and business of the company with report to and seeking approval from the board of the company on designated major matters. There can also be executive and non-executive directors but non-executive directors owe fiduciary duties to the company. External directors are generally either called non-executive directors, or independent non-executive directors if they are appointed because of their particular expertise and are not related to any shareholder.

For listed companies, the Listing Rules require the establishment of an audit committee and a remuneration committee, which will be discussed below.

4.2 What are the rules that may give rise to civil and criminal liability of the director(s)? How are those liabilities sought?

Civil proceedings can be brought for breach of fiduciary duties but cases in practice concern conflict of interest or diversion of business opportunities of the company. The company will be the plaintiff, and if the directors are controlled by the majority who refuse to take action, the minority shareholders can bring an action on behalf of the company through a derivative action. The usual remedies are an injunction order, damages and account of profits. Where the funds have been dissipated, a claim based on constructive trust can be made with seeking a tracing order and making other third parties liable as constructive trustees as well, eg a company controlled by the director used as the receptacle of the benefits of the transaction.

Criminal proceedings are generally forgery, falsification of books and records, misleading information in prospectuses, embezzlement of funds, and in case of listed companies, there have been insider-dealing cases. These are undertaken by the relevant regulatory authorities, and the offender may be penalised with fines and imprisonment orders, the severity of which depends on the criminal act and funds involved. The fines and amounts under related confiscation orders belong to the government but depending on the circumstances, and if civil proceedings have also been issued, the government may consider releasing a portion of the recovered funds to the victim corporation.

4.3 Does the board of directors have a committee system, eg, nomination committee, compensation committee, audit committee? If not required, is it common practice for companies? How does it function?

Private companies are not required by law to have a committee system. However, they are free to have committees that are appointed to take care of the management and business of the company with report to and seeking approval from the board of the company on designated major matters. A committee system is not common but there are substantial companies and joint-venture companies that practise this.

For listed companies, they are obliged to have an audit committee under the Listing Rules comprising only of non-executive directors. There should be a minimum of three of whom at least one has to be an independent non-executive director with the appropriate qualifications in accounting/ financial-related management. Terms of reference must be issued to the committee, and such terms set out matters such as the duties, authority and frequency and procedures of meetings. The authority includes the power to investigate any activities the committee determines appropriate, seek information from any officer or employee, obtain independent legal or other professional advice and monitor the external auditor's independence and objectivity with recommendations for change if required. Audit committee members should be familiar with the Guide to Effective Committees issued by the Hong Kong Institute of Certified Public Accountants.

4.4 Is it a legal requirement to have an independent director or a third-party director? If so, how are they appointed? Is it required for listed companies?

There is no legal requirement for a private company to have any third-party or independent director.

For listed companies, they are obliged to have at least three independent non-executive directors and independent non-executive directors must be at least one-third of the board. Due to the requirements of an audit committee, there must at least be one independent non-executive director with the appropriate qualifications in accounting/financial-related management. Independent non-executive directors of listed companies are expected to be familiar with the Guide for Independent Non-executive Directors issued by the Hong Kong Institute of Directors and Corporate Governance Code under the Listing Rules.

4.5 How is the compensation for directors or officers determined? Can it be contested by the shareholders or the regulatory authorities? What are the common rules or practices for the compensation of officers?

There is no particular rule or benchmark for determining the rate of compensation of directors. Much depends on the relative bargaining position of the parties, the size of the business and the qualifications and experience of the relevant director. However, as a director owes fiduciary duties to the company, excessive remuneration that is not commensurate to his expertise, level of work and industry norm may amount to a breach.

For listed companies on the main board, a remuneration committee has to be established to determine the policy of remuneration for the directors and senior management of the company. This committee has to be chaired by an independent non-executive director and members must comprise a majority of independent non-executive directors. Share-option schemes are common and the initial scheme is approved by members in a general meeting. Having mentioned this, there are instances where the recommendations and approvals have been manipulated to secure excessive packages in favour of executive directors.

4.6 How will the board handle a corporate crisis like an internal criminal case, violence, social media exposure or dawn raid by the authorities?

Crisis-management policies of companies differ significantly in Hong Kong. Many private companies and even local subsidiaries of global companies do not have such policies.

5. BOARD OF AUDITORS, AUDIT COMMITTEE, ACCOUNTING AUDITORS

5.1 How is the internal accounting and legal audit structured and conducted? Is an outside accounting audit required and, if so, how is it structured? Are there requirements to change the auditor each five

years?

Every company in Hong Kong is required to have external auditors and have audited financial statements annually after it has commenced business. Under the New Companies Ordinance, the following are disqualified for appointment as auditor of a company:

(a) a person who is an officer or employee of the company; and
(b) a person who is a partner or employee of a person mentioned in paragraph (a).

There is no requirement to change auditors every five years.

See paragraph 4.3 on audit committees of listed companies.

5.2 Do you have supervisory auditors? What is the function of the supervisory auditors' board?

There is no requirement for having supervisory auditors. PRC companies that list in Hong Kong, however, have supervisory committees.

6. MARKET DISCLOSURE/TRANSPARENCY TO THE SHAREHOLDERS AND THE PUBLIC

6.1 What are the disclosure requirements for companies in your jurisdiction under company law, capital markets law or any other rules?

6.2 What is the liability or responsibility of the board in relation to the company's disclosure requirements?

For a listed company on the main board, one of the most important aspects of its continuing obligations is its general duty of disclosure. Disclosure may be required to be made to the Stock Exchange and/or shareholders.

Generally, a listed company must inform the Stock Exchange as soon as possible of information relating to the company or its group which is necessary to enable the public to be appraised of the position of the company, to avoid establishment of a false market for its securities or which might reasonably be expected to materially affect market activity in the company's securities. There should be prompt and even disclosure of price-sensitive information and prior to public announcement, the directors have to ensure that the information is kept confidential. In the case of offers for the listed company's shares, the following circumstances may trigger a mandatory announcement of offers:

- if there is reasonable ground to believe that rumours of such an offer cause movement of share price of the offeree company; or
- if negotiations and/or discussions involve more than a restricted number of individuals.

A draft announcement has to be sent to the Stock Exchange for clearance and thereafter publication after the same has been confirmed by the board which takes responsibility for its contents.

Other required notifications to the Stock Exchange prior to public announcement include proposals for the change of directorship, class of listed securities, constitutional documents or nature of business of company and publication of periodical results and insolvency-related matters that may affect the group.

The listed company is further subject to various general financial disclosures. Its accounts and annual report have to be published and which must contain various detailed financial disclosures, such as particulars of directors' remunerations, particulars of directors' interest in the company's securities, contracts of significance and directors' interest in them. Certain acquisitions, disposals and connected transactions are subject to size tests that determine whether disclosure through announcement is sufficient or circulars followed by general meeting to secure approval by the company in general meeting is required. A very substantial acquisition or major transaction should be accompanied by recommendation supported by accountants' and valuation reports.

In addition to the above which are required under the Listing Rules, there is a new disclosure regime under Part V of the Securities and Futures Ordinance whereby disclosures of interest in the listed company's securities have to be made by persons who control or are in a position to control the company or who may benefit from transactions involving assets of the company. The objective is to require corporate insiders to give notice of their interest in the securities including on short positions, and the provisions of the Ordinance catch substantial shareholders, directors and the chief executive officer.

The above are only illustrations of the disclosure requirements applicable to listed companies and are not exhaustive.

Private companies are subject to few disclosures to its shareholders. In practice, the issue only arises in cases where there are minority shareholders who have complaints against the management. Unless pursuant to shareholders' agreements, shareholders have limited rights to detailed information of the company if they do not have a board member who represents them. The board or management shareholders are not obliged to provide detailed information on management matters and decisions, and thus, while annual accounts should be tabled at the annual general meeting and shareholders are provided with a copy, the management does not have to answer all questions on the audited accounts raised by a minority shareholder. Repeated requests made reasonably but ignored may, however, help to build a case of oppression.

7. M&A AND CORPORATE GOVERNANCE

7.1 Upon an M&A offer, how are the transparency and fairness rules of the company provided under the company and stock market laws and rules?

Whether a general offer of securities in a listed company has to be made is governed by the Takeover Code. The following circumstances may trigger a mandatory offer:

- the offeror purchases 30 per cent or more of the voting shares of the listed company; or
- the offeror holds between 30 per cent to 50 per cent of the voting rights and increases the holding by more than 2 per cent in any 12-month

period.

As mentioned in paragraph 6, certain circumstances may further trigger a mandatory announcement of offers.

Care should also be taken to determine if the shareholding held by parties may be considered as parties in concert. Advance determinations may be obtained from the Stock Exchange.

For private companies, under the Companies Ordinance, rights are given to a company that acquires at least 90 per cent of the outstanding shares of a private company to purchase the shares of the remaining shareholders upon the same terms. The offer must be made within the prescribed time and followed by a court application if the same is not accepted. On the other hand, the remaining shareholders are also provided with the corresponding right to be bought out on the same terms of the outgoing shareholders through making the request within the prescribed time.

There is an alternative of a scheme of arrangement for a complete takeover. However, the procedures can be complicated and a scheme of arrangement is not commonly adopted.

8. PROXY FIGHTING

8.1 Is proxy fighting customarily conducted for control of the company management or what other items? How is it regulated under the company law or market regulations?

There are no specific laws on proxy fighting. In practice, it only happens on odd occasions and depends on the shareholding structure of the particular company in question.

9. OFFICERS' REMUNERATION RULES

9.1 How is remuneration of officers determined? By whom? Is there a role for the shareholders' meeting? Is there any mechanism for an independent body to review and evaluate them?

9.2 Is the mechanism of officers' remuneration publicly debated?

See paragraph 4.5 above.

10. DIRECTORS' LIABILITIES, LIABILITY INSURANCE, INDEMNIFICATION

10.1 What are the directors' responsibilities and liabilities under the law? Can those liabilities be covered by insurance? Can it be indemnified by the company or other related parties?

See the relevant paragraphs above on directors' responsibilities and liabilities.

With respect to indemnification, under section 165(1) of the Companies Ordinance, any provision under the articles or a contract with the company or otherwise providing for indemnification of the directors of the company or its related company for any liability owed to that company or related company on account of negligence, default, breach of duty or breach of trust is void. However, it appears that indemnity can be provided by a third party and section 165(3) allows insurance against the liability to be purchased and maintained by the company for the director. Directors' and officers' liability insurance is offered by a number of reputable insurers in Hong Kong. Care should be taken in the reviewing and negotiation of the removal of exclusions.

11. SHAREHOLDERS' DERIVATIVE SUITS

11.1 Is a shareholder's derivative suit provided for by law in your jurisdiction? How is it enforced by the shareholders?

11.2 Have there been any recent relevant court cases on the subject?

See paragraph 2.4 above.

12. SOCIAL INTEREST IN CORPORATE BEHAVIOUR

12.1 How is a company in your country expected to deal with the following issues? Corporate social responsibility; gender, racial and social diversification; environmental issues; ecology and corruption?

There are specific laws on equal opportunities against discrimination of gender, race and disability, as well as environmental laws in Hong Kong. Also, as mentioned above, there is the Prevention of Bribery Ordinance prohibiting corruption.

Hungary

Richard Lock & Pál Rahóty **Lakatos, Köves & Partners**

1. GENERAL PRINCIPLES

1.1 What are the general principles of corporate governance in your jurisdiction? What are the main objectives of corporate governance principles in your jurisdiction? State also whether your legal system is based on common law or civil law.

Hungary is a civil law jurisdiction. See paragraph 2 for the sources of law.

The general principles of corporate governance in Hungary are as follows:

- *Due care and diligence.* Directors shall conduct the management of the company with due care and diligence as generally expected from persons in such positions.
- *Interests of the company.* Directors shall give priority to the interests of the company. This term refers to the interests of the company as a separate legal entity, ie interests that may be different from the interests of its shareholders or the interests of its management. There may be situations when the shareholders also need to support the interests of the company: shareholders who support a resolution, in respect of which they knew, or should have known given reasonable care, that such resolution was clearly contrary to the significant interests of the company, shall bear unlimited and joint and several liability toward the company for resulting damage to the company, unless otherwise prescribed by law.
- *Interests of the creditors.* In the event of an imminent threat of the insolvency of the company, directors shall conduct the management of the company giving priority to the interests of the company's creditors (not those of the company or the shareholders). There will be a change to this principle introduced in 2014 by the New Civil Code (as referred to in paragraph 2.1 below) (see paragraph 10 below for further details).
- *Purpose of the company.* This principle is very similar to the 'interests of the company' principle: the shareholders may determine specific activities or purposes for the company in the articles of association. More generally, the purpose of the company is to aim to continue the sound operation of the company (eg a member of a limited liability company may be excluded from the membership of the company by the court, based on a claim launched by the company, if the continued membership of the person in question would gravely endanger the achievement of the company's purpose).

According to the Companies Act (as defined in paragraph 2.1 below), the purpose of the general principles of corporate governance in Hungary is to lay down an appropriate legal framework to support the consolidation and further strengthening of the market economy in Hungary, to enhance the productivity of the national economy and the success of enterprises, and to promote fair competition among companies without creating any dominant position, and to operate in harmony with the equitable interests of creditors and with public interests.

1.2 Have there been any recent developments in the law, codes and rules of corporate governance?

Yes. The Hungarian parliament adopted Act V of 2013 (the New Civil Code), which will enter into force on 15 March 2014 and will replace the existing corporate law provisions. The Hungarian parliament needs to adopt further legislation so that the New Civil Code can enter into force and provisions that are dealing with transitional issues. As of the end of July 2013, the parliament has not adopted this implementing legislation yet.

The Hungarian parliament also enacted a new Criminal Code and a new Labour Code in 2012, and both have already become effective and impact corporate governance issues.

1.3 Outline recent court cases and incidents involving corporate governance issues. Were there any significant corporate scandals or large unlawful corporate cases?

There are no recent significant court cases and incidents involving corporate governance issues in Hungary. See paragraph 2.1 below.

1.4 Which law enforcement agency is in charge of enforcing corporate governance? May a criminal sanction be levied upon infringement of the corporate governance rules?

The enforcement of corporate governance is in the hands of courts.

Companies are registered with the 'courts of registration' in Hungary. The courts of registration are authorities established in every county court dealing with the initial registration of the companies and with the registration changes in the corporate data of the companies, and supervising whether the companies are operated in accordance with the relevant laws. The courts of registration may run legal supervisory procedures and pass sanctions.

Corporate litigations are dealt with by the ordinary courts, in particular by the county courts at the first instance. This involves the following types of corporate disputes:

- all legal disputes arising out of or in connection with the corporate relationship between the company and its shareholders (quotaholders), including former quotaholders excluded from, or shareholders (quotaholders) otherwise withdrawing from, the company;
- legal disputes among the shareholders (quotaholders) in connection with the articles of association, or the operation of the company;
- the judicial review of resolutions passed by the bodies of a company; and
- the legal disputes concerning *de facto* (non-recognised) company groups.

Infringement of the corporate governance rules in certain cases may be considered as a crime (eg fraudulent bankruptcy, breaching of accounting regulations, misuse of equity, etc.) and may involve criminal sanctions. The criminal procedures are conducted before normal courts with the participation of the public prosecutor. In addition, public prosecutors have a very limited role in supervising the legal operation of the company (eg public prosecutors start an action against the company if the registered data of company or any underlying document thereof does not comply with legal regulations).

2. SOURCES OF LAW

2.1 Which laws, codes or statutes govern company structures and organisations? Are there statutes like the Companies Act or other forms of law? Is there much relevant case law?

Company structures are governed by Act IV of 2006 on business associations (the Companies Act) (which together with Act IV of 1959 on the Civil Code (Civil Code) will be replaced by the New Civil Code, as referred to in paragraph 1.2).

There is not much relevant case law in the recent past. Every seven to nine years, a new companies act is adopted to reflect the economic, legal, etc. changes that have occurred in the meantime and also to integrate the jurisprudence of the courts.

2.2 Which laws, codes or statutes regulate capital markets in your jurisdiction?

Capital markets in Hungary are regulated by Act CXX of 2001 (the Hungarian Capital Markets Act).

2.3 Are there any public interest laws which apply to or influence corporate governance?

Yes, such public interest provisions can be found in various acts and regulations. The most important ones are, as follows: (i) publication requirements in Act V of 2006 on public company information, company registration and solvent liquidation proceedings; (ii) liability-related provisions in Act XLIX of 1991 on bankruptcy proceedings and insolvent liquidation proceedings; and (iii) specific provisions applicable to publicly owned companies in Act CXXII of 2009 on the more efficient operation of publicly owned companies.

The Budapest Stock Exchange published Recommendations for Sound Company Governance for public companies limited by shares listed in the Budapest Stock Exchange. If the shares of a public company limited by shares are admitted for trading on the Budapest Stock Exchange, the management board of a company shall present to the shareholders' meeting the company governance and management report together with the annual report. The company governance and management report shall contain the management board's report on the company's policy adopted with a view to sound governance and management in the previous financial year, and shall explain any deviation from the Recommendations of the Budapest Stock Exchange for Sound Company Governance. The report shall be posted on the official website of the company. The report should be approved by a separate resolution of the shareholders' meeting.

2.4 Have there been any recent developments in any of the above laws? What are the recent changes to the above laws or rules and the reasons for such changes?

The New Civil Code will replace the existing Civil Code and the Companies Act, and brings a new approach to the corporate legislation. The existing approach is that the parties may only deviate from the provisions of the Companies Act if the Companies Act explicitly allows that. The new approach is that the parties may generally deviate from the provisions of the New Civil Code, except when it is explicitly prohibited.

In addition to this change in approach, the New Civil Code will introduce some other changes to the current provisions of the Companies Act.

The reason behind the new approach is that the corporate law provisions will be included in the New Civil Code, and civil law generally leaves significant freedom for the parties to elaborate the provisions covering their contractual etc. relationship.

This chapter presents the effective provisions as of end of July 2013. However, we indicate where such provisions will be changed significantly by the entering into force of the New Civil Code.

3. SHAREHOLDERS AND THE SHAREHOLDERS' MEETING

3.1 How are shareholders' interests represented in the company? How are the shareholders assured exercise of their rights? What is the highest governing body within the company structure if it is not the shareholders' meeting?

The shareholders' interests and rights differ to some extent in case of the different company forms. The most convenient and usual types of corporate forms in Hungary are the company limited by shares (*'Részvénytársaság'* or *'Rt.'*) and the limited liability company (*'Korlátolt felelősségű társaság'* or *'Kft.'*). This chapter focuses on the provisions applicable to company limited by shares, with an indication if the applicable provisions are different for limited liability companies.

Companies limited by shares

The company limited by shares is the most likely choice of corporate vehicle in cases of substantial investments. It is broadly similar to the English plc, the German AG, the French SA or the Russian AO. Whether the company is public (open) or private (closed) must be reflected in its name (ie *'Nyilvánosan Működő Részvénytársaság'* or *'Nyrt.'* (public) or *'Zártkörűen Működő Részvénytársaság'* or *'Zrt.'* (private).

The company limited by shares has a share capital divided into shares of a predetermined amount and nominal value. The company can issue various types of shares (ordinary shares, preference shares, employees' shares, interest-bearing shares, shares granting pre-emption rights and redeemable shares) granting different rights. Hungarian company law does not stipulate a statutory pre-emption right *vis-à-vis* the shareholders. A shareholder may exercise its shareholders' rights only if it is registered in the 'book of shareholders' kept by the board of directors of the company. Ownership of shares is evidenced by share certificates. Such certificates are in a registered form and need to be produced in a printed or an electronic form (and the book of shareholders can also be maintained in electronic form). It is possible to have a company limited by shares formed with only one shareholder, called a 'one member' company. The liability of the shareholders is limited to the higher of the nominal or issued value of their shares. A court, however, may declare the liability of a shareholder holding more than 75 per cent of the votes in the company to be unlimited in certain situations, for example, where a dominant shareholder makes the company pursue a business policy which is detrimental to the company or the dominant shareholder is jeopardising the company's ability to meet its liabilities.

A company limited by shares is controlled through its general meeting of shareholders (or, instead, the resolutions of a sole shareholder). The general meeting of shareholders is the governing body of a company limited by shares. Certain rights may be exercised only by the shareholders in general meeting, such as amendments to the articles of association, increases and reductions of share capital (except where the board of directors has authority to do so), mergers, dissolutions or transformations, etc.

Limited liability companies

The limited liability company is broadly similar to the German GmbH, the French SARL, or the Russian OOO. This type of company is generally used for investments in which the number of investors is relatively small. The limited liability company has capital consisting of 'quotas'. There are no certificates issued to certify ownership of the quotaholders. (For ease of reference, if the provisions are the same for shareholders and quotaholders, we use the term shareholder.) It is possible to define and create quotas providing different rights. Any other quotaholder, the company and any third person designated by the quotaholders' meeting shall, in that order, have pre-emption rights over the quotas to be transferred by means of a contract of sale, provided that this is not precluded or restricted by the company's articles of association.

The quotaholders' liability is limited to providing a primary investment and any other contributions referred to in the company's articles of association. Similarly to the company limited by shares, it is possible to have a limited liability company formed with only one quotaholder, and abuse of limited liability may result in lifting the corporate veil and make a quotaholder liable for the debts of the company.

A limited liability company is controlled by the meeting of the quotaholders (or resolutions of the sole quotaholder). The powers of the quotaholders' meeting are similar to those of the shareholders' meeting in a company limited by shares, ie that is the ultimate governing body.

Representation of the shareholders' interests
Representation of the shareholders' interests in Hungarian companies are twofold: (i) all shareholders of the company have the right to participate in the activities of the highest governing body; and (ii) for the purpose of the supervision of the company's management the shareholders shall have the possibility (or in certain cases specified in paragraph 4.1 below, the obligation) to establish a supervisory board.

The basic rights of shareholders are: (i) attending the shareholders' meeting; (ii) voting at the shareholders' meeting; (iii) requesting information; (iv) making remarks and proposals at the shareholders' meeting; and (v) receiving dividends.

Shareholders may exercise their shareholders' rights through representatives. The auditor may not function as such representative. Unless otherwise provided for in the articles of association, directors, executive employees of the company and supervisory board members may not serve as representatives. A person acting as a proxy holder may hold a proxy from more than one shareholder; however, one shareholder may appoint only one proxy holder. The proxy holder shall cast votes in accordance with any instructions issued by the appointing shareholder. Unless otherwise prescribed in the articles of association, authorisations for representation may be valid for one shareholders' meeting or a fixed period of time not exceeding 12 months.

The articles of association may restrict or exclude voting rights attached to a specific class of shares, and in public companies limited by shares the maximum level of voting rights which may be exercised by a single shareholder and/or by any group of shareholders can be stipulated in the articles of association

The shareholders' meetings are usually chaired by a director elected to this function by the shareholders' meeting.

3.2 How is the shareholders' meeting conducted? Who may chair the meeting? May attendance (not voting) at the meeting be restricted only to the shareholders? Are the shareholders allowed to be accompanied by legal or other counsel?

The shareholders' meeting is generally convened by the management of the company (see paragraph 3.3 below). The shareholders' meeting is convened and held at least once a year and in addition if it is deemed necessary with a view to the interest of the company or is so prescribed by law.

The invitation of shareholders to the shareholders' meeting shall contain the agenda of the meeting. Unless otherwise provided for in the articles of association, the invitation shall be sent at least 15 days in advance. In case of public companies limited by shares the shareholders' meeting is convened by way of a public notice published in accordance with the articles of association – published on the company's official website as a minimum requirement, or by other means – at least 30 days in advance.

The shareholders' meeting may discuss any issues that were not included in the agenda sent with the invitation (public notice) only if all shareholders are present at the meeting and if they unanimously agree to discuss such issues on the agenda.

The articles of association may allow a shareholders' meeting to be held in a way that allows the shareholders to participate by way of electronic means of communication, designed to handle dialogues between shareholders and providing adequate facilities for debates without any restriction whatsoever. The articles of association may specify certain specific issues which may not be debated in this manner.

Meetings of the shareholders' meeting may be attended by the shareholders of the company, and – without voting rights – any person invited according to the applicable legal provisions (eg the auditor in certain cases) or the articles of association. Shareholders may be accompanied by legal or other counsel.

Meetings are generally chaired by a director elected by the shareholders' meeting.

The articles of association of limited liability companies and those of private companies limited by shares may define the matters which may be resolved without having to hold a meeting, where the decision of the shareholders is fixed in writing or by any other means containing authentic proof about the statements made in the decision-making process. The draft of a proposed decision shall be conveyed to the shareholders in writing, allowing at least eight days for making a decision unless a shorter period is prescribed in the articles of association. Shareholders shall cast their votes in writing or in some other verifiable manner.

3.3 How are minority shareholders' rights protected?

Shareholders having at least 5 per cent of the voting rights may request the convening of the shareholders' meeting, indicating the reason and the purpose thereof. The articles of association may also grant this right to shareholders controlling a lesser percentage of the votes. If the management fails to comply with such request within 30 days, upon the request of the shareholders making the proposal, the court of registry shall convene the meeting of the company's shareholders' meeting within 30 days after the submission of a request to this effect, or shall empower the requesting shareholders to convene the meeting. The ruling of the court of registry in favour of the request may not be appealed.

Shareholders of a private company limited by shares and quotaholders of a limited liability company having 5 per cent of voting rights and shareholders of a public company limited by shares having 1 per cent of the voting rights may add additional items to the agenda of the general meeting, and may request the appointment of an independent expert to examine the annual report of the company, any particular management action of the previous two years, and also whether a particular payment to a shareholder (quotaholder) has been performed in line with the accounting and corporate regulations, including the specific requirement that the equity cannot decrease below the share capital as a result of the payment.

For details of shareholders' derivative suits, see paragraph 11 below.

3.4 Is shareholder activism encouraged or discouraged? If not encouraged, how is it regulated?

Hungarian law is neutral in this respect.

3.5 How are professional shareholders (those minority shareholders who seek some extra benefit from companies by unduly and habitually influencing management by using their shareholding) treated by the law? Are they excluded from attending the shareholders' meeting? Are they criminally or otherwise publicly sanctioned?

No special treatment is determined.

If shareholders are unduly and habitually influencing the management, such shareholders are not excluded from attending the shareholders' meeting. However, if the management follows the instructions or direct orders of a shareholder, any other shareholder of the company may request the judicial review of resolutions adopted by the management on the grounds that such resolution violates the provisions of the Hungarian legal regulations, or the articles of association. Such shareholders may also be considered as shadow directors (see paragraph 10.1 below). Criminal sanctions may be imposed in case of eg bribery.

No claims may be lodged for the exclusion of shareholders. A quotaholder may not be expelled from a limited liability company, if the company has only two quotaholders. A quotaholder holding three-quarters or more of the votes cannot be expelled from a limited liability company.

The quotaholders' meeting of a limited liability company may pass a resolution to file an action for the expulsion of a quotaholder, for which a majority of three-quarters of the votes shall be required (the member affected may not vote on the issue of lodging the claim). The member shall excluded from the company by the court based on a claim launched by the company only, if the continued membership of the person in question would gravely endanger the achievement of the company's purpose (see paragraph 1.1 for more details on this principle).

3.6 Are shareholders' benefits given to some of the shareholders by the company without resolution by the shareholders' meeting prohibited or regulated by the law or other rules?

Giving benefits to shareholders is prohibited in the absence of a resolution of the shareholders' meeting, eg dividends can be paid if the shareholders' meeting passed a resolution in this respect (and if the conditions to pay dividends are satisfied).

Unless otherwise provided by the articles of association, any resolution of the shareholders' meeting of a private company limited by shares that discriminates against the rights attached to a certain series of shares may only be passed if, according to the procedure set out in the articles of association, the shareholders of the share series in question grant their explicit consent.

A resolution of the quotaholders' meeting of a limited liability company adopted by unanimous decision shall be required to increase the obligations of quotaholders contained in the articles of association, to establish new obligations, or to restrict special rights of certain quotaholders.

4. DIRECTORS AND BOARD OF DIRECTORS

4.1 What are the functions and responsibilities of the directors and the board of directors? Do you have a one- or two-tier board system? What are the outside directors called?

Public or private companies limited by shares

A company limited by shares is managed by a board of directors that is elected by the general meeting, and the board of directors consists of at least three but not more than 11 members. As an alternative, one may replace the board of directors with one sole general director. There is no restriction on foreigners serving as directors, and directors need not be shareholders of the company. The board of directors represents the company *vis-à-vis* third parties and manages the operations of the company. Each director is entitled to represent (solely or jointly, depending on the provisions of the articles of association) the company *vis-à-vis* third parties. The power of the directors to represent the company *vis-à-vis* third parties may be further limited by the articles of association. However, such limitations do not currently affect the rights of third parties against the company. This rule will be changed by the New Civil Code: the limitation of the representation rights of the director is valid *vis-à-vis* third parties, provided that the third party knew or should have known about the limitation (eg from the published articles of association).

The board of directors (i) is responsible for presenting the annual report of the company to the shareholders' meeting; (ii) is obliged to prepare a report on the management, the financial situation and the business policy of the company at the intervals set out in the articles of association, or at least once every year for the shareholders' meeting, and at least once every three months for the supervisory board (if any); and (iii) ascertain that the books of the company are kept according to the rules.

In private companies limited by shares, the powers of the board of directors could be conferred under the deed of foundation upon a single executive officer (chief executive officer).

The shareholders are allowed to (or, in certain cases defined below in this paragraph, are obliged to) establish a supervisory board.

Establishment of a supervisory board is mandatory (i) for public companies limited by shares, except if controlled by the *one-tier system* (see below in this paragraph); (ii) for private companies limited by shares if requested by the shareholders controlling at least 5 per cent of the total number of votes; and (iii) if the annual average of the number of full-time employees employed by the company exceeds 200. The supervisory board consists of at least three members, but not more than 15 members, elected by the shareholders at their annual general meeting. One-third of the members of the supervisory board must be elected from among the employees. The principal role of the supervisory board is to supervise the operation of the management of the company for the benefit of the shareholders. The articles of association of the company may grant the supervisory board power to (i) elect and remove directors and to determine their remuneration, and (ii) approve certain transactions.

The articles of association of public companies limited by shares may contain provisions to confer management and supervisory functions upon the board of directors (this is called the 'one-tier system' operation). Such companies have no supervisory board, and the members of the board of directors are treated as executive officers. This type of corporate governance system is not common in Hungary.

Limited liability companies

The management of a limited liability company is carried out by one or more managers who are responsible for the day-to-day running of the company, similarly to the board of directors of a company limited by shares. Unlike the board of directors, the managers of a limited liability company do not operate as a body (the New Civil Code will bring a change to that position). Managers are individually or jointly authorised to act on behalf of the company, and represent the company *vis-à-vis* third parties.

Similarly to the position of companies limited by shares, if the number of employees is more than 200 (and also in other circumstances), a supervisory board must be established, and, depending on turnover, an auditor may also be needed.

It is not possible in Hungary to appoint a legal entity as a managing director or as a member of the board of directors. The New Civil Code disperses with this express prohibition.

4.2 What are the rules that may give rise to civil and criminal liability of the director(s)? How are those liabilities sought?

See paragraph 10.

4.3 Does the board of directors have a committee system, eg, nomination committee, compensation committee, audit committee? If not required, is it common practice for companies? How does it function?

The board of directors in companies limited by shares is not required to have a committee system, except for the establishment of an audit committee which is mandatory for public companies limited by shares (for details see paragraph 5.1 below).

It is not common practice to have a committee system in Hungary except for the largest companies.

The shareholders' meeting (or the company's management body if authorised) may contract the services of organisations other than the company organs specified above (eg committees, advisory boards) in connection with the preparation of decisions. The activities of these contracted organisations have no relevance concerning the powers and competencies of the corporate bodies described above.

The New Civil Code will explicitly allow the establishment of committees, or other corporate organs (if this possibility is stipulated in the articles of association). However, the establishment of such committees and corporate organs does not have an effect on the scope of authority and the liability of the shareholders' meeting, the directors and the supervisory board.

4.4 Is it a legal requirement to have an independent director or a third-party director? If so, how are they appointed? Is it required for listed companies?

There is no such legal requirement that the companies must have an independent director or a third-party director. The only exception is when a public company limited by shares is operated in a one-tier system (ie the duties of the board of directors and of the supervisory board are carried out by one single corporate body). In this case, the majority of the directors must be independent. A director is considered to be independent if he/she has no other legal relationship with the company other than his/her board membership.

4.5 How is the compensation for directors or officers determined? Can it be contested by the shareholders or the regulatory authorities? What are the common rules or practices for the compensation of officers?

The remuneration of the directors, supervisory board members, and independent auditor is generally determined by the shareholders' meeting. The articles of association of limited liability companies or private companies limited by shares may contain provisions enabling the supervisory board to determine the remuneration of the management.

Shareholders and the regulatory authorities may challenge the decisions regarding the remuneration in accordance with the general rules (ie may file an action against the company alleging that the decision is either unlawful or adopted contrary to the provisions of the articles of association).

4.6 How will the board handle a corporate crisis like an internal criminal case, violence, social media exposure or dawn raid by the authorities?

No specific rules are provided. The management needs to comply with the relevant laws and regulations especially with the reporting obligations. To the extent legally possible it needs to prioritise the interest of the company.

5. BOARD OF AUDITORS, AUDIT COMMITTEE, ACCOUNTING AUDITORS

5.1 How is the internal accounting and legal audit structured and conducted? Is an outside accounting audit required and, if so, how is it structured? Are there requirements to change the auditor each five

years?

In general, it is not mandatory to appoint an internal legal and accounting auditor, except when sector-specific laws provide otherwise (eg in case of financial institutions).

It is also not mandatory to appoint an external (outside) accounting auditor. However, it is mandatory to appoint an outside auditor if: (i) the company's annual net revenue (calculated for the period of one year) exceeds HUF 200 million (approx. EUR 666,675) on the average of the two financial years preceding the financial year under review, and the average number of employees of the company of the two financial years preceding the financial year under review exceeds 50 persons; or (ii) if the articles of association provides so.

The external auditor is responsible for carrying out the audits of financial documents, including – first and foremost – to determine whether the annual report of the company is in conformity with legal requirements, and whether it provides a true and fair view of the company's assets and liabilities, financial position and profit or loss.

External auditors may be appointed for the maximum period of five years. An auditor may be appointed for successive terms.

Public companies limited by shares are required to have an audit committee consisting of three members elected by the shareholders' meeting from the board of directors or from the independent members of the supervisory board, where applicable. At least one member of the audit committee must be a professional accountant and/or auditor. The scope of activities of the audit committee consists, *inter alia*, in monitoring: (i) the audit of the annual report prepared according to the act on accounting; (ii) the services of the auditor other than auditing the annual report; and (iii) the effectiveness of the internal monitoring and risk management. The articles of association may confer additional duties upon the audit committee.

5.2 Do you have supervisory auditors? What is the function of the supervisory auditors' board?

Hungarian law does not recognise the term 'supervisory auditor'. The company's financials are audited by outside accounting auditor (see paragraph 5.1 above) and are also reviewed by, the supervisory board of the company (see paragraph 4.1 above) and the audit board (see paragraph 5.1 above).

6. MARKET DISCLOSURE/TRANSPARENCY TO THE SHAREHOLDERS AND THE PUBLIC

6.1 What are the disclosure requirements for companies in your jurisdiction under company law, capital markets law or any other rules?

Notification is required both to the issuer and the Hungarian regulator within two calendar days, if voting rights directly or indirectly reach, exceed or decrease below the following thresholds: 5 per cent, 10 per cent, 15 per cent, 20 per cent, 25 per cent, 30 per cent, 35 per cent, 40 per cent, 45 per cent, 50 per cent, 75 per cent, 80 per cent, 85 per cent, 90 per cent, 91 per cent, 92 per cent, 93 per cent, 94 per cent, 95 per cent, 96 per cent, 97 per cent, 98 per cent, and 99 per cent.

For the calculation of voting rights held either directly or indirectly by a shareholder, the following voting rights must be taken into account:

- Voting rights which can be exercised by the shareholder himself or by a company being controlled by the shareholder on the basis of:
  - an agreement between the shareholder and a third party acting in concert;
  - a temporary transfer of the voting rights;
  - shares which are deposited to the shareholder as security; and
  - an agreement on rights of use, under which the shareholder is entitled to exercise the voting rights attached to the shares which are owned by the company.
- Voting rights exercised by the shareholder acting as a custodian.
- Voting rights exercised by a third party on behalf of the shareholder.
- Voting rights exercised by the shareholder acting as a proxy without having specific instructions.
- Voting rights attached to shares belonging to a stock or portfolio managed by a fund management company, an investment service provider or a credit institution. If the entities holding these shares are controlled by the shareholder they need to be calculated together, as long as they exercise the voting rights on the basis of direct or indirect instructions received from the shareholder or a company controlled by the shareholder.

Credit institutions and investment service providers are exempted from notification requirements in respect of shares recorded in the trading book, if: (i) they ensure that voting rights cannot be exercised by anyone; (ii) they do not participate in decisions appointing or removing members of the managing, supervisory, decision-making bodies of the issuer; and (iii) voting rights attached to the shares recorded in the trading book do not exceed 5 per cent.

Shareholders are exempted from notification requirements if the notification is performed on their behalf as well as by their parent undertaking.

When shareholdings reach certain specified levels, disclosure must be made to the court of registration and published in the *Companies Gazette* within 30 days.

6.2 What is the liability or responsibility of the board in relation to the company's disclosure requirements?

The general rules are applicable (see paragraph 10).

7. M&A AND CORPORATE GOVERNANCE

7.1 Upon an M&A offer, how are the transparency and fairness rules of the company provided under the company and stock market laws

and rules?

General transparency rules

The bidder and the brokerage company must send the public offer to the Hungarian Financial Supervisory Authority (HFSA) for approval and a copy must be sent to the target's directors. A legislative proposal has been submitted by the government recently aiming at the merger of HFSA into the Hungarian National Bank in a way that the Hungarian National Bank will take over the responsibilities of the HFSA (eg authorisation of financial and investment services, monitoring the market, etc.) with effect from 1 October 2013.

The publishing of the offer must be initiated at the same time. The HFSA has 10 business days to check that the offer complies with the Capital Markets Act and, if necessary, to prohibit the transaction, or to give the bidder another three business days' notice for the correction or the supplementation of the offer. If a bidder does not hear anything from the HFSA within the 10 and three business-day periods, approval is deemed to be given by the HFSA. The offer must be published promptly after obtaining HFSA approval and the offer shall also indicate the starting and closing date of the acceptance period.

Every announcement must be published either in a Hungarian national daily newspaper, on the homepages of both issuer and distributor (where available), or on the homepage of the Budapest Stock Exchange or the HFSA.

In addition, a bidder must also prepare its business plans regarding the future operations of the target and an information memorandum, giving shareholders details of the bidder's business. All such information must be made available to the target shareholders at the place set out in the offer documents.

Duties of the management

The management of the target must comply with the following principles during a takeover:

- free competition between bidders;
- equal treatment between shareholders;
- all disclosures being true and fair; and
- due attention being paid to the corporate interests/benefit of the target.

The target board is required to issue either a statement or a document giving its opinion on the offer.

The articles of association of the target company may provide that the board cannot take frustrating actions which may interfere with the offer (eg increasing the share capital of the target or acquiring its own shares) from the receipt of the offer or, if earlier, from becoming aware of the intended offer, until the end of the acceptance period. Even if the articles of association restrict the target board in doing so the resolutions adopted by the general meeting may still allow the board to take frustrating actions. The implementation of such a decision does not necessarily fall within the exclusive competence of the shareholders' meeting, enabling the quick reaction of the target company to the offer.

The target board is also entitled to proceed with a view to encouraging the submission of competing proposals, or to making a decision in relation to the execution of resolutions passed by the members' meeting, provided that they fall within the common business activities of the target company.

Even after the takeover bid is launched or after receiving information concerning the bid, the target board may undertake actions in the cases and in the manner specified in a resolution adopted by its shareholders' meeting, convened in due observation of the relevant provisions of the Companies Act.

The members of the board of directors of the bidder are subject to the normal duties owed by the directors to the company. There are no specific additional responsibilities imposed in preparing for an acquisition.

8. PROXY FIGHTING

8.1 Is proxy fighting customarily conducted for control of the company management or what other items? How is it regulated under the company law or market regulations?

Proxy fighting is not regulated, and not customarily conducted in Hungary.

9. OFFICERS' REMUNERATION RULES

9.1 How is remuneration of officers determined? By whom? Is there a role for the shareholders' meeting? Is there any mechanism for an independent body to review and evaluate them?

See paragraph 4.5.

9.2 Is the mechanism of officers' remuneration publicly debated?

Not applicable.

10. DIRECTORS' LIABILITIES, LIABILITY INSURANCE, INDEMNIFICATION

10.1 What are the directors' responsibilities and liabilities under the law? Can those liabilities be covered by insurance? Can it be indemnified by the company or other related parties?

General civil law liability

According to the general corporate law rules, the director shall conduct the management of the company with due care and diligence as generally expected from persons in such positions, and give priority to the interests of the company.

The director is liable to the company in accordance with the general rules of civil law for damages caused by any infringement of the law or any breach of the articles of association, the resolutions of members' meeting, or their management obligations. As a general rule the company shall be liable for damages caused to third persons by its director when acting as a representative of the company. The New Civil Code will establish the joint and several liability of the company and the director in such cases.

The company (or in certain limited cases detailed in section 11, the shareholders itself) can sue its director for damages, which are attributable to the conduct or omission of the director. The Hungarian civil law liability is based on fault, thus there may be an exemption for the director if he/she can prove that acted in a way that was generally expectable in such situation. The New Civil Code will change this to some extent and the director may be exempted if he/she proves that the damage was due to an unforeseeable event that was outside the scope his/her control and it was not expectable to foresee the occurrence of the damage.

If the directors represent a company jointly or if a body manages the company, the liability of these directors is joint and several for the damage caused. If the damage results from a decision of the management body, any member of such body who has not taken part in the decision-making process or voted against it shall be exempt from liability.

The liabilities of the directors can be covered by insurance.

Specific corporate law liability towards the company

Beyond the general requirements, there are other grounds of liability for a director. Unless expressly permitted by the supreme body, the Companies Act prohibits the directors from the following:

- acquisition of shares by the director or a stake in another company that pursues similar activities to the company, except in public companies limited by shares;
- being a director in another company that pursues similar activities to the company;
- conclusion of transactions by the director or its close relatives in their own name or for their own benefit, that fall within the scope of the company's activities; and
- the director or its close relative being at the same time the member of the company's supervisory board.

A claim for damages by the company as a result of a breach of these obligations may be made within one year after the damage was incurred.

Liability in case of insolvency or bankruptcy

If the director is of the view that the company is threatened with insolvency, he needs to prioritise the interests of the creditors. According to the New Civil Code, the director does not need to prioritise the interests of the creditors, but needs to also take into account the creditors' interests. The determination of the time when the threat of insolvency has occurred is difficult. In the course of the insolvency process creditors may bring an action for the establishment of the director's liability and the amount of the indemnification. The judgment of such litigation can be enforced after the completion of the insolvency procedure, if the company's assets are not sufficient to satisfy the creditors' claims. Creditors may have claims against not only the directors but also those, who had actual influence on the management of the company (so-called 'shadow directors'). Such shadow directors can be, for example, the directors of the parent company or an influential shareholder of the company, who have actively influenced the acts of the directors.

11. SHAREHOLDERS' DERIVATIVE SUITS

11.1 Is a shareholder's derivative suit provided for by law in your jurisdiction? How is it enforced by the shareholders?

If the supreme body of a company has refused the request to enforce a claim against the shareholders, executive officers, supervisory board members or against the auditor of the company, or, if the supreme body of the company failed to adopt a decision regarding a proposal that has been properly presented, a group of shareholders controlling at least 5 per cent of the votes may enforce the claim themselves on behalf of the company by filing a lawsuit within a period of 30 days after the meeting of the company's supreme body.

11.2 Have there been any recent relevant court cases on the subject?

Not applicable.

12. SOCIAL INTEREST IN CORPORATE BEHAVIOUR

12.1 How is a company in your country expected to deal with the following issues? Corporate social responsibility; gender, racial and social diversification; environmental issues; ecology and corruption?

A company, either international or Hungarian, operating in Hungary is obliged to comply with the relevant national as well as international (primarily EU) regulations and guidelines in these respects. Anti-discrimination, anti-corruption, and to some extent, environmental issues, are catered for in terms of legislation and, therefore, by default, are expected to be observed by corporations.

India

Rajiv K. Luthra, Sundeep Dudeja & Vaibhav Kakkar
Luthra and Luthra Law Offices

1. GENERAL PRINCIPLES

1.1 What are the general principles of corporate governance in your jurisdiction? What are the main objectives of corporate governance principles in your jurisdiction? State also whether your legal system is based on common law or civil law.

The legal and regulatory framework of corporate governance in India is based on various principles like primacy of interest of the company and its shareholders, fiduciary duties, duty of skill, fairness and transparency. In India, accountability, transparency and equality of treatment for all stakeholders are recognised as the key principles of corporate governance. Generally, the shareholders of a company, the board of directors (BoD) and the management are identified as the three constituents of corporate governance.

Thus, in pursuance of the general principles of corporate governance in India, the BoD owes a fiduciary duty to the company and is expected to act in good faith and exercise reasonable skill and care to promote the best interests of the shareholders and other stakeholders. Further, companies are mandated to disclose accurate information on matters like performance and financial position within time by way of various filings with the regulatory authorities of India. It is pertinent to mention that broadly the applicable corporate governance norms are most stringent in cases of listed companies, are comparatively relaxed for public unlisted companies and are most relaxed for private companies.

As per the publicly available government sources, the corporate governance norms in India broadly seek to achieve the following objectives:

- a properly structured board capable of taking independent and objective decisions is in place at the helm of affairs;
- the board is balanced as regards the representation of adequate number of non-executive and independent directors who will take care of their interests and well-being of all the stakeholders in listed companies;
- the board adopts transparent procedures and practices and arrives at decisions on the strength of adequate information;
- the board has an effective machinery to subserve the concerns of stakeholders;
- the board keeps the shareholders informed of relevant developments impacting the company;
- the board effectively and regularly monitors the functioning of the management team; and

- the board remains in effective control of the affairs of the company at all times.

The Indian legal regime is based largely on common law principles and comprises of various codified statutes. Indian courts often refer to the common law jurisprudence as a guide in construing provisions of Indian statutes and in areas where the Indian law appears to be silent.

1.2 Have there been any recent developments in the law, codes and rules of corporate governance?

In India, except for listed companies, there are, as such, no specific corporate governance norms. Thus, the legal and regulatory framework of corporate governance in India is governed by a host of legislation, including the Companies Act, 1956 (Companies Act), Securities and Exchange Board of India Act, 1992 (SEBI Act) and rules and regulations framed there under, the Securities Contract (Regulations) Act, 1956 (SCRA) and the rules and regulations framed there under including the Listing Agreement, and as amended from time to time.

It is pertinent to mention that the Central Government of India is proposing to repeal the Companies Act and to enact a new legislation to meet the changed national and international economic environment. For this purpose a bill, namely, the Companies Bill, 2012 (Bill) passed by the *Lok Sabha* (lower house of the Indian parliament) on 18 December 2012 is pending before the *Rajya Sabha* (upper house of the Indian parliament), and once ratified will be the law of the land for operation of companies and other related matters. The Bill seeks to strengthen the corporate governance regime in India by introducing certain crucial governance norms like mandatory provisions on corporate social responsibility, a lucid definition of 'independent director' and on the strengthened role of independent directors to ensure effective functioning of the BoD and to protect the best interest of all stakeholders.

The Securities and Exchange Board of India (SEBI) has recently issued a 'Consultative paper on review of corporate governance norms in India, 2012'. This consultative paper proposes wide-ranging overhaul of corporate governance norms for listed companies, through measures like checks against unjustifiable remunerations, greater powers to minority shareholders and hefty penalties for non-compliance of corporate governance norms.

Further, in 2010, the SEBI had amended the Equity Listing Agreement, vide circular no. CIR/CFD/DIL/1/2010 dated 5 April 2010 requiring listed companies to ensure that the limited review/audit reports submitted to the stock exchanges be given only by an auditor who has subjected himself to the peer-review process of the Institute of Chartered Accountants of India (ICAI) and holds a valid certificate issued by the Peer Review Board of the ICAI.

Also, the SEBI, vide circular no. CIR/CFD/DIL/10/2010 dated 16 December 2010 has mandated all listed companies to maintain a functional website that contains certain basic information about them, duly updated for all statutory filings, including agreements entered into with media companies.

Further, in 2009, the Ministry of Corporate Affairs (MCA) of India had issued the 'Corporate Governance Voluntary Guidelines' in 2009 in order to encourage companies to adopt better corporate governance practices and the 'Corporate Social Responsibility Voluntary Guidelines'. This was the first step towards mainstreaming the concept of business responsibilities. Although recommendatory in nature, these guidelines are significant for the development of corporate governance norms in India.

1.3 Outline recent court cases and incidents involving corporate governance issues. Were there any significant corporate scandals or large unlawful corporate cases?

The Satyam Computer Services Limited (now Tech Mahindra) fraud, in 2009,was one of the biggest corporate frauds in the recent times in India. The managing director and other high-level officials were involved in inflating the cash flows and falsifying accounts for several years. This scandal witnessed breach of several corporate governance norms like protection of shareholders' and stakeholders' interests, director's liability and his fiduciary duty towards the company, duty of care, good faith and transparency. Serious corporate governance issues related to working of BoD and auditors, their transparency and accountability were also raised.

Sahara's dispute with the SEBI triggered in 2009 was the fallout of another corporate fraud. On reviewing the initial public offering (IPO) prospectus filed by the group's Sahara Prime City Ltd, the SEBI discovered that two affiliated companies the Sahara group had been selling convertible debentures to about 30 million investors in the guise of a 'Private Placement' without complying with the requirements applicable to the public offerings of securities. The Supreme Court observed that if the offer is made to 50 persons or more, then it will have to be treated as public issue and not a private placement and directed the company to refund monies to investors.

In 2009, Subhiksha's nationwide multibrand network of retail stores collapsed owing to financial mismanagement and severe cash crunch. The company has been probed for fraud and misrepresenting the actual financial condition of the company following a series of litigations, mostly filed by lenders and investors. The Madras High Court had, in 2012, ordered the winding up of the company after a winding-up petition was filed by Kotak Mahindra Bank, lender to Subhiksha.

1.4 Which law enforcement agency is in charge of enforcing corporate governance? May a criminal sanction be levied upon infringement of the corporate governance rules?

As set out above, the regulatory framework relating to corporate governance is governed by a host of legislation and accordingly there are multiple authorities who are in charge of enforcing the corporate governance norms. Under the Companies Act, the Registrar of Companies (RoC) and the Serious Fraud Investigation Office (SFIO), a multidisciplinary organisation under the Ministry of Corporate Affairs (for detecting and prosecuting white-collar crimes/frauds) are the authorities responsible for enforcing corporate governance norms in India. In case of listed companies, in addition to the above, the SEBI and the stock exchanges on which the company is listed, are the first level of regulatory compliance mechanism for enforcing the corporate governance norms.

The Companies Act imposes both civil and criminal liabilities on directors and officers in default depending upon the specific violation. Apart from the basic provisions of the Companies Act, every listed company needs to comply with the provisions of the SEBI Act and SCRA, including the Listing Agreement. Non-compliance with the same, may at times lead to delisting or monetary penalties.

2. SOURCES OF LAW

2.1 Which laws, codes or statutes govern company structures and organisations? Are there statutes like the Companies Act or other forms of law? Is there much relevant case law?

The Companies Act, including the circulars and notifications issues thereunder, is the principal legislation governing all companies in India. The listed companies in India are, along with the Companies Act and the circulars and notifications issued thereunder, regulated by the SEBI under the provisions of the SEBI Act and the rules and regulations framed thereunder. Clause 49 of the Listing Agreement issued under the SCRA, which is entered into between the company and the relevant stock exchange on which it is proposed to be listed, also prescribes the composition of the BoD of listed companies.

In addition, there are other sector specific laws and regulations that govern company structures and organisations. For instance, the Insurance Regulatory and Development Authority of India, RBI and the Department of Telecommunications, under the Ministry of Communications and Information Technology, under the respective statutes and applicable regulations, govern structures of insurance companies, companies engaged in the financial sector and the telecommunications sector respectively.

2.2 Which laws, codes or statutes regulate capital markets in your jurisdiction?

The securities market in India is governed by the Companies Act, the SCRA, the SEBI Act and the Depositaries Act, 1996 (the Depositaries Act), and the rules and regulations framed under each of them such as the Securities and Exchange Board of India (Substantial Acquisition of Shares and Takeovers) Regulations, 2011 (Takeover Code), Securities and Exchange Board of India (Issue of Capital and Disclosure Requirements) Regulations, 2009 (ICDR) and Securities and Exchange Board of India (Prohibition of Insider Trading) Regulations, 1992.

2.3 Are there any public interest laws which apply to or influence corporate governance?

Under the current legal framework pertaining to corporate governance in India, as such there are no specific public interest laws. However, most

Indian laws and regulations, including the Companies Act especially in the context of corporate governance have been enacted to promote the interest of the shareholders and other stakeholders, including the employees. For example, the laws and regulations, regulating the capital market, namely the Takeover Code, ICDR and the Insider Trading Regulations are meant to protect investors and other market players. Further, under the Companies Act, the judicial and quasi-judicial authorities, while assessing the legality of corporate actions, must ensure the safeguarding of public interest as a consequence of such corporate actions.

2.4 Have there been any recent developments in any of the above laws? What are the recent changes to the above laws or rules and the reasons for such changes?

It may be relevant to note that corporate governance norms in India are at a fluid stage, and hence there are constant reviews and changes being brought about in these rules/regulations. Accordingly, various amendments to the SEBI regulations including the Listing Agreement, the ICDR and the Takeover Code and other laws and regulations mentioned above are made from time to time, to cater for the needs of the changing business environment, in pursuance of the protection of interest of the investors. With respect to the corporate governance norms under the Companies Act, the recent changes include changes in the law relating to provision of managerial remuneration, limitation of liability of non-executive directors, the 'Green Initiative in the Corporate Governance' relating to clarification regarding sending copies of Balance Sheets and Auditors Report through electronic mode and the Director's Relative (Office or Place of Profit) Rules, 2011.

3. SHAREHOLDERS AND THE SHAREHOLDERS' MEETING

3.1 How are shareholders' interests represented in the company? How are the shareholders assured exercise of their rights? What is the highest governing body within the company structure if it is not the shareholders' meeting?

The corporate structure of every company as set out in the Companies Act comprises the BoD and the shareholders of the company. The powers relating to the affairs of a company are divided between the BoD and the shareholders of the company.

The general powers of shareholders ensuring representation of their interests in the company are elaborated below.

Shareholders meetings and voting rights

As per the Companies Act, certain corporate actions can be taken only pursuant to passing of a resolution by the shareholders. Thus, the shareholders exercise their powers through resolutions passed in meetings. Every member has a right to attend any general meeting of the company and to speak and vote on any resolution before the meeting notwithstanding any provision in the memorandum and articles of association. Resolutions need to be voted by a simple majority or a special majority, depending on the nature of the business proposed to be transacted. Also, certain businesses transacted by a listed company are mandated to be voted on by postal or electronic mode. Resolutions once passed become binding upon the company and all its members. Shareholders also have the power to requisition for convening an extraordinary general meeting (EGM) to consider matters which, due to their urgency cannot be kept pending till the next annual general meeting(AGM). This meeting may be convened at the requisition of the prescribed number of shareholders.

Further, balance sheet and profit-and-loss accounts of a company are laid before the members at every AGM of the company. Thus, shareholders' meetings provide a forum for them to express the shareholders' will in regard to the management of the affairs of the company. It is pertinent to mention that failure to call meetings in accordance with the Companies Act is an offence punishable by fine and, in certain cases, the shareholders have the power to apply to the central government, which may call or direct the calling of the meeting.

Appointment of directors and auditors by shareholders

The shareholders are given the powers to appoint directors and auditors in a general meeting, who may safeguard them from possible manipulations. Shareholders also have the power to remove the directors and auditors so appointed before the expiry of their period of office.

Shareholders' right of inspection

Shareholders have the right to access the register and index of members and debenture holders, copies of annual returns with annexed certificates and documents, minute books of general meetings and the register of directors during business hours at the registered office of the company.

3.2 How is the shareholders' meeting conducted? Who may chair the meeting? May attendance (not voting) at the meeting be restricted only to the shareholders? Are the shareholders allowed to be accompanied by legal or other counsel?

One of the basic requirements under the Companies Act relating to shareholders' meetings is that the shareholders of a company can exercise their powers only when they act as a body at a validly convened and held meeting. Accordingly, the Companies Act requires meetings to be convened by persons having such authority by giving proper and adequate notice, containing the agenda and the explanatory statement, to all those entitled to attend the meetings. Further, the Companies Act prescribes certain rules of quorum which must be complied with for a meeting to be validly constituted. Every meeting needs a person to act as chairman to control and superintend the conduct of the meetings. The chairman is elected by members present in person at the meeting from within themselves. The Companies Act classifies shareholders' meetings as AGM, and EGM. Each of them is briefly discussed below.

AGMs

The Companies Act provides that every company must a hold a general meeting of the shareholders every year as its AGM. The AGM provides a forum for shareholders to exercise control over the affairs of the company, review the working of the company and take necessary measures for protecting their interests. Routine matters of the business of the company like adoption of annual accounts of the company, reports of the BoD, declaration of dividend, appointment of directors and auditors and fixing their remuneration, are discussed and approved by way of appropriate resolutions passed by the shareholders.

EGMs

EGMs are convened to consider matters which, due to their urgency cannot be kept pending till the next AGM. This meeting may be convened at the requisition of the prescribed number of shareholders as well.

As per the Companies Act, every member of a company is entitled to appoint another person or persons (whether a member or not) as his proxy to attend and vote on his behalf; however, the shareholders do not have any legal right to be accompanied by legal or other counsel. However, by way of practice, the chairman of the meeting may on specific request of any of the shareholders permit the same.

3.3 How are minority shareholders' rights protected?

While the shareholders' democracy is supreme, the Companies Act and the decided judicial decisions suggest that the majority shall not be allowed to act in an unfair, fraudulent or oppressive manner against the interests of minority shareholders. The Companies Act extends protection to minority shareholders by granting them various rights as discussed below.

Oppression and mismanagement

A member who complains that the affairs of the company are being conducted in a manner oppressive to some of the members, including himself, that the affairs of the company are being conducted in a manner prejudicial to public interest or to the interests of the company may apply to the CLB by way of a petition and obtain adequate relief. Further, in cases of mismanagement by the company, ie where the members complain. The CLB normally entertains such complaints only from a group of shareholders who are at least 100 in number or constitute 10 per cent of the shareholders by number or by value. The CLB is empowered to make any such order as it thinks fit. Thus, the power of the CLB to grant relief is fairly wide. These measures, *inter alia*, include purchase of shares or interests of any members of company by other members, termination, setting aside or modification of agreements, setting aside of transactions relating to transfer, delivery of goods etc. or any other matter for which the CLB feels that provisions should be made.

Further, public companies and private companies which are subsidiaries of public companies are provided with an option to adopt the principle of proportional representation for the appointment of not less than two-thirds of the total number of directors. Further, on a reference or on an application by the requisite number of members of the company, the CLB, to prevent oppression to any shareholders, may direct the company to amend its articles of association to provide for appointment of directors according to the principle of proportional representation and make fresh appointments in pursuance of the articles of association so amended.

Small shareholders' director
For special representation of the interests of small shareholders, the Companies Act prescribes that a public company having a paid-up capital of Rs. 50 million or more and having 1,000 or more small shareholders (holding shares of nominal value of Rs. 20,000 or less) may have a director elected by such small shareholders. This is, however, not a mandatory requirement under the Companies Act.

Variation of class rights
The rights attached to the shares of any class can be varied only with the written consent of the holders of not less than three-fourths of the issued shares of that class or with the sanction of a special resolution passed at a separate meeting of the holders of the issued shares of that class. As a protection measure of all members, the Companies Act empowers the holders of not less than 10 per cent of the shares of that class who had not assented to the variation to apply to the high court for cancellation of the variation.

Information disclosure and audit
Company law provides for regular accounting information to be supplied to the shareholders along with a report by the auditors. It also requires that when shareholder approval is sought for special business, the company must provide all material facts relating to these resolutions including the interest of directors and their relatives in the matter.

Special majority
Another safeguard in the Companies Act is the requirement that certain major decisions, for instance amending the articles of association, amending the objects clause/registered office clause of the memorandum of association and reduction of share capital, have to be approved by a special majority, ie the votes actually cast in favour of the resolution are three times or more than the votes against the resolution.

3.4 Is shareholder activism encouraged or discouraged? If not encouraged, how is it regulated?

Shareholder activism, a hitherto non-existent phenomenon in India, has become pervasive in recent years and is primarily led by the institutional investors. The regulatory reforms in India such as voting by postal ballot introduced for certain types of resolutions and the option to companies to hold shareholders' meetings through videoconference and other electronic means, have focused on promoting shareholder participation in corporate decision-making. All these measures are towards increasing the participation of shareholders in shareholders' meetings, thereby increasing their ability to influence corporate decisions. Further, lately, shareholder activism can also be seen specifically in cases of IPO, wherein the retail investor writes to the SEBI in relation to its grievances on the basis of which the SEBI takes appropriate actions against the relevant company. The activist investors are now effectively aided by proxy advisory firms which analyse corporate proposals and make recommendations to their clients on the manner in which they should exercise their votes at shareholders' meetings. The firms also publicly announce their recommendations on specific proposals, for the benefit of the retail shareholders. While proxy advisors play a significant part in influencing corporate decision-making, their role in the Indian context is still very limited.

3.5 How are professional shareholders (those minority shareholders who seek some extra benefit from companies by unduly and habitually influencing management by using their shareholding) treated by the law? Are they excluded from attending the shareholders' meeting? Are they criminally or otherwise publicly sanctioned?

While in practice, India has begun to witness the rise of professional shareholders, who take a keen interest in the affairs, the number of such instances is miniscule. Under law, there is no prescription for any differential treatment for such shareholders who seek some extra benefit from companies by unduly and habitually influencing management by using their shareholding. They are treated similarly as any other minority shareholders.

3.6 Are shareholders' benefits given to some of the shareholders by the company without resolution by the shareholders' meeting prohibited or regulated by the law or other rules?

The promoters of a company may, by way of private contractual arrangement confer certain rights to some shareholders without passing resolutions in the shareholders' meetings; however, such rights in respect of the company cannot be specifically enforced against the company unless the articles of association of the company are amended accordingly, which requires the special resolution to be passed by the shareholders of the company.

4. DIRECTORS AND BOARD OF DIRECTORS

4.1 What are the functions and responsibilities of the directors and the board of directors? Do you have a one- or two-tier board system? What are the outside directors called?

Section 2(13) of the Companies Act, defines a director to include '*...any person occupying the position of a director by whatever name called*'. Broadly, the functions and responsibilities of directors arise under the relevant provisions of the Companies Act and as per the relevant judicial decisions following the common law principles. There exist a host of other legislations relating to the specific sector/business of the company, which prescribe duties of a director.

Common law

Indian courts often refer to common law jurisprudence as a guide in construing provisions of Indian statutes (including the Companies Act) and in areas where the Indian law appears to be silent, particularly because the Companies Act is largely inspired from the UK Companies Act 1948. Accordingly, directors are required to adhere to principles of common law while performing their statutory duties. Consequently, in the performance of their statutory duties, directors are required, inter alia, to act in good faith, exercise reasonable skill and care, and to act within the powers of the company.

Further, directors are expected to act in fiduciary capacity, in the best interests of the company and to safeguard the interests of the stakeholders. They are duty-bound to refrain from placing themselves in a position where their personal interests may conflict with their duties to the company. Directors are liable to the company for all personal profits or gains made by them if they have been found to have taken advantage of their position as directors.

Duties under the Companies Act

The company as a separate legal entity is subject to statutory controls and the directors are responsible for ensuring compliance with such statutory controls. For the purposes of imposing certain liabilities under the Companies Act, reference is often made to the term 'officers in default', who have been defined as follows:

(i) managing director(s);
(ii) whole-time director(s);
(iii) manager;
(iv) secretary;
(v) any person in accordance with whose directions or instructions, the BoD of the company is accustomed to act;
(vi) any person charged by the board with the responsibility of complying with a particular provision, provided that such person has consented to act; and
(vii) where any company does not have any of the officers specified in (i) to (iii) above, any director or directors who may be specified by the board of directors in this behalf or where no director is so specified, all the directors.

Any violation under the Act would make the directors and officers in default liable to monetary penalties and/or imprisonment.

Some significant statutory duties of directors include ensuring appropriate filings with the RoC in relation to change in directorship of the company, appointment of first auditor of the company, return of allotments, annual return, and charge created on the properties of the company. Further, directors are obligated to make a disclosure of their personal interests in any contracts/arrangements, which the company is proposing to enter into. Further, no such interested director can participate or vote in the board's proceedings. Directors must not fail to attend three consecutive meetings or all meetings for three months, whichever is longer, without the permission of the board. Failure in this regard would lead to automatic vacation of his office of directorship. Directors have a duty to convene board meetings in every quarter and call the AGM for every year. Further, they must ensure that the annual accounts, balance sheet and profit-and-loss account of the company are presented to the shareholders at every AGM in the prescribed manner. Directors also have an obligation to distribute dividend with 30 days from the date of declaration of dividend, except in certain specified cases.

It is pertinent to mention that the Master Circular on Prosecution of Directors issued by the MCA has recognised the need for extra protection to non-executive directors including nominee directors of financial institutions and banks having participation in equity of a company, in whose cases extra care is required while examining liability as officers in default.

Duties under other legislations

Duties of directors are prescribed under host of other legislations such as the Foreign Exchange Management Act, 1999 (FEMA), the Negotiable Instruments Act, 1881 (NI Act), and the various labour and environment laws. Broadly, under this legislation in case of contravention of any of the provisions of such legislation by a company, the person who at the time of the contravention was in charge of and was responsible to the company for the conduct of the business of the company is be deemed to be guilty of the provisions and is liable to be proceeded against. If the offence committed was in the knowledge of the director and he himself had consented or connived of it, then the director is deemed to be guilty and liable.

Tier-based structure

India does not have a tier-based BoD structure. It is, however, pertinent to mention that the BoD is mandated to delegate certain matters to specialised committees, for instance the audit committee, as discussed in greater detail in subsequent responses. In India, as a general principle, there is no concept of outside directors as such for private or unlisted public companies. In case of listed public companies, directors having no pecuniary relationship with the company or the promoters are called 'independent directors'. Also, nominee directors appointed in certain circumstances and directors appointed by the government in order to prevent oppression and mismanagement are also deemed to be independent directors.

4.2 What are the rules that may give rise to civil and criminal liability of the director(s)? How are those liabilities sought?

Directors can be held liable for every act, commission or omission which is not in accordance with the provisions of the relevant statutes.

Personal liability

It is a general rule of company law that the liability of a company is different from that of the director and accordingly there exists no personal liability of the director for the acts of the company. However, under certain specific circumstances, a director can be held liable on behalf of the company. Instances where directors are held personally liable include the case where taxes are due from a private company in respect of any income of any previous year that cannot be recovered from such private company under the Income Tax Act, 1961. A director can, however, escape liability if such non-recovery of tax cannot be attributed to any gross neglect, misfeasance or breach of duty on his part. Further, directors can be held personally liable in case of recovery of sales taxes due from liquidated company in case of winding up (under the Central Sales Tax Act and certain state Sales Tax laws).

A director is not personally liable for any debt of the company unless fraud on the part of such director can be established. Also, a director is personally liable along with the company to repay the share application or excess share application money, as the case may be, if the same is not repaid within the stipulated time limit.

Civil liability of directors

Civil liability can be imposed on a director, to pay compensation to every person who subscribes for any shares or debentures on the faith of the prospectus for any loss or damage he may have sustained by reason of any untrue statement in the prospectus of a public company, if he or she is a director at the time of the issue of the prospectus, unless it was issued without his consent or knowledge or that the consent was withdrawn after giving reasonable public notice of the same.

Criminal liability

Certain provision of the Companies Act imposes criminal liability on directors for wilful acts of omission or commission, not in accordance with the provisions of the Companies Act, such as, on any person who was responsible for a mis-statement in the prospectus of a public company thereunder, failure to all reasonable steps to keep books of account in the manner prescribed therein, failure to distribute the dividend with 30 days from the date of declaration of dividend, except in certain cases specified thereunder and failure to take all reasonable steps to prepare a balance sheet and profit-and-loss account showing a true and a fair view of the state of affairs of the company. The director can be made liable and punished with imprisonment for dishonour of a cheque issued on behalf of a company under the NI Act. Similarly, under the provisions of the various labour welfare legislation, environmental protection legislation and anti-corruption legislation, directors and officers-in-charge of companies may be made subject to the penal provisions provided thereunder.

4.3 Does the board of directors have a committee system, eg, nomination committee, compensation committee, audit committee? If not required, is it common practice for companies? How does it function?

The BoD may form committees and delegate certain powers to the committee set up for the purpose. These committees are usually formed as a means of improving board effectiveness and efficiency. Further, certain restrictions are placed on the extent of delegation of some powers of the BoD. For example, certain powers such as the power to make calls on shares, power to issue debentures cannot be delegated and must be exercised by the board.

As per the provisions of the Companies Act, all public companies having paid up capital of 50 million of more are required to constitute audit committee.

Further, for listed companies, clause 49 of the Listing Agreement provides for the constitution of mandatory and non-mandatory committees, discussed below:

Mandatory committees

Audit committee

The primary role of the audit committee is to have an overview on the reporting process of the company's financial and accounting matters, and the disclosure of its financial statements in a correct, sufficient and credible format. The recommendations of the audit committee on any matter relating to the financial management including the audit report are binding on the BoD.

Shareholders' grievance committee

A board committee under the chairmanship of a non-executive director must be formed to specifically look into the redressal of shareholder and investor complaints such as transfer of shares, non-receipt of balance sheet and non-receipt of declared dividends.

Further, under the Companies Act, in case the listed and subsidiaries of listed companies have no profits or inadequate profits then the approval of the remuneration committee is required for payment of managerial remuneration.

Non-mandatory committees

Clause 49 also provides for the constitution of non-mandatory committees, such as the nomination committee, remuneration committee, corporate compliance committee and the corporate governance committee.

4.4 Is it a legal requirement to have an independent director or a third-party director? If so, how are they appointed? Is it required for listed companies?

With respect to private and public unlisted companies, there is no concept of independent directors as such. With respect to listed companies, clause 49 of the SEBI's Listing Agreement mandates the appointment of independent directors (who are to be determined in accordance to the negative criteria provided) on the BoD of a listed company. Clause 49 mandates that, where the chairman of the board is a non-executive director, at least one-third of the board should comprise independent directors and, in case the chairman of the board is an executive director or where the non-executive chairman is a promoter of the company or is related to any promoter or person occupying management positions at board level or one level below the board, at least one half of the board should comprise independent directors. Independent directors are appointed by the shareholders/BoD, as per the constitutional documents of the company and the recommendations of the nomination committee.

4.5 How is the compensation for directors or officers determined? Can it be contested by the shareholders or the regulatory authorities? What are the common rules or practices for the compensation of officers?

The remuneration payable to the directors of a company, including any managing or whole-time director, is governed, by the articles of the company, or by a resolution or, if the articles so require by a special resolution passed by the company in general meeting and is determined by the BoD and is appointed by the shareholders. A director who is in whole-time employment of the company or a managing director may be paid remuneration which cannot exceed 5 per cent of the net profits of the company, except with the approval of the central government in case of one director and 10 per cent for all executive directors.

Private limited companies are not subject to any limits on managerial remuneration which require central government approval. In a recent relaxation, no such restriction is placed on an unlisted public company. However, listed companies or their subsidiaries with no/inadequate profits who wish to pay managerial remuneration, beyond a specified limit to a director who is not a professional director, are required to approach the central government for approval.

The total managerial remuneration payable by a public company or a private company which is a subsidiary of a public company to its directors and its manager in any financial year cannot exceed 11 per cent of the net profits of the company calculated in the prescribed manner. Further, non-executive directors can be paid remuneration either by way of a monthly, quarterly or annual payment with the approval of the central government or by way of commission if the company by special resolution authorises such payment. Remuneration payable to such directors cannot exceed 1 per cent, of the net profits of the company, if the company has a managing or whole-time director or a manager, in any other case, 3 per cent of the net profits of the company. For the purposes of calculation of remuneration payable to directors, any remuneration paid to directors for professional services rendered by them to the company, is excluded, provided that director possesses the requisite professional qualification.

4.6 How will the board handle a corporate crisis like an internal criminal case, violence, social media exposure or dawn raid by the authorities?

The BoD responds to a corporate crisis on a case-by-case basis. For listed public companies, the BoD is obligated to keep the shareholders and the stock exchanges informed of any such corporate crisis. Further, in specific instances, the BoD typically appoints specialists such as professional data analysts, auditors and legal advisors in order to examine the issue and suggest risk-mitigation strategies.

5. BOARD OF AUDITORS, AUDIT COMMITTEE, ACCOUNTING AUDITORS

5.1 How is the internal accounting and legal audit structured and conducted? Is an outside accounting audit required and, if so, how is it structured? Are there requirements to change the auditor each five years?

With respect to audit requirements under the Companies Act, the management of the company is required to prepare books of accounts, which are then audited by the auditors appointed by the shareholders of the company.

Internal audit

As per clause 49 of the Listing Agreement, the audit committee is required to review various aspects of the internal audit function of the company such as its adequacy and internal audit reports. The audit committee needs extensive support from the internal audit function to provide the primary assurance about controls and compliances before giving the required reports/certificates or to appropriately review the necessary aspects and make informed decisions. In addition, as per the Companies (Auditor's Report) Order, 2003, notified by the central government (in case of listed companies and/or other companies having paid-up capital and reserves exceeding Rs. 5 million, or having an average annual turnover exceeding Rs. 50 million for a period of three consecutive financial years), the auditor must report whether the company has an internal audit system commensurate with its size and nature of its business. Although the clause does not by itself mandate internal audit in the subjected companies, a company would incur a negative remark from the auditor if it does not have an internal audit system. Further, the internal auditor is required to attend and participate at the meetings of audit committees.

The Companies Act provides for compulsory appointment of an auditor by the shareholders of every company, at each AGM, except the first auditors who may be appointed by the BoD. It is pertinent to mention that while the existing Companies Act does not have any requirement for a change in auditors every five years, the proposed Bill advocates rotation of auditors of listed companies, after five years with the flexibility to extend it to 10 (in case of an audit firm), after which there is a mandatory cooling off for five years. Further, there are more stringent norms applicable to the appointment of auditors in government companies.

5.2 Do you have supervisory auditors? What is the function of the supervisory auditors' board?

Although there is no concept of supervisory auditors in India and only statutory audit is required to be conducted for every company, it is pertinent to mention that the SEBI, in 2009,had in the wake of the Satyam scandal, ordered a review of financial statements of companies constituting National Stock Exchange Nifty-50 and Bombay Stock Exchange Sensex-30 by peers, chosen from a panel of specialist auditors nominated by the SEBI.

6. MARKET DISCLOSURE/TRANSPARENCY TO THE SHAREHOLDERS AND THE PUBLIC

6.1 What are the disclosure requirements for companies in your jurisdiction under company law, capital markets law or any other rules?

Periodical and event-based disclosure obligations of Indian companies arise from more than one statute. Importantly, the Companies Act prescribes disclosures for all Indian companies while regulations issued by the SEBI and the listing agreement stipulates disclosure rules for companies whose securities are traded on Indian exchanges.

Examples of matters required to be publicly disclosed under the Companies Act include capital structure, managerial remuneration, shareholding pattern, balance sheet and (in case of public companies) statement of income, encumbrances on properties and special resolutions passed by the company. Disclosures required under the SEBI's regulations in relation to listed companies include shareholding levels of significant shareholder groups, price-sensitive information and disclosures of material information in tender offers. The Listing Agreement (illustratively) requires listed companies to publish financial statements and their shareholding pattern on a periodical basis, price sensitive information on an immediate basis and to intimate the exchanges before some matters are considered by the company's board. Ordinarily, such disclosures are publicly available on the stock exchange websites as well as the company websites. Further disclosures, which may be mandated under the Companies Act, are generally disclosed to the RoC and the MCA.

The SEBI's regulations and (to a lesser extent) the Companies Act contain very detailed disclosure obligations in relation to the issuances of securities. The extent and nature of these disclosures depends on the type of issue. Predictably, the most stringent disclosure and oversight regime is reserved for offer documents in relation to the IPOs of securities.

6.2 What is the liability or responsibility of the board in relation to the company's disclosure requirements?

There is no general rule of law that makes directors vicariously liable for the acts of an Indian company. Different statutes have different provisions to deal with the liability of individual officers or directors for acts and omissions of an Indian company. For example, as has been set out in paragraph 4.1, the Companies Act stipulates a seven-tier 'cascading' structure of liability, of which the first six tiers are occupied by different classes of officers. It is only if a company has none of the first six classes of officers that ordinary (non-executive) directors become liable for violations of the Companies Act.

Again, different statutes prescribe different consequences for breaches of their disclosure obligations. Fines imposed under the Companies Act are generally lower than those under the SEBI Act. Illustratively, under the Companies Act, a default in filing annual returns or balance sheets is punishable by a fine of up to Rs. 500 for each day of the continuing default and a default in filing the return of allotment attracts a fine of up to Rs. 5,000. On the other hand, illustratively, the SEBI Act punishes a failure to furnish certain documents and delays in filing them with a penalty of Rs. 10 million or Rs. 100,000 for each day of continuing default, whichever is lower. Further, as has been set out in paragraph 4.2, any mis-statement in the prospectus by the directors may also lead to certain liability being imposed.

7. M&A AND CORPORATE GOVERNANCE

7.1 Upon an M&A offer, how are the transparency and fairness rules of the company provided under the company and stock market laws and rules?

A few examples of transparency and fairness rules of Indian corporate law that apply to M&A are as follows:

Under the Companies Act, when an application is made to a high court to sanction a scheme of merger, a disclosure of all material facts relating to the company, such as the latest financial position of the company, the latest auditor's report, the pendency of any investigation proceedings in relation to the company has to be disclosed. Merger schemes involving listed Indian companies have to be filed with the stock exchanges and with the SEBI, for their comments before they are filed with a high court. Further, in case of mergers involving listed companies, there is a requirement to obtain a fairness opinion from an independent merchant banker on valuation of assets/shares done by the valuer for the transaction.

Open offers for shares of listed Indian companies are governed by the SEBI's Takeover Code. The open offer itself is administered by a SEBI-registered intermediary. The offer documents follow SEBI-prescribed formats, which lay down material facts about the target and the acquirer in the proposed transaction, and guidelines on contents and are scrutinised by the SEBI. Relevant material documents are required to be made publicly available for inspection by shareholders. Further, as per the Takeover Code, the committee of independent directors is required to provide its written reasoned recommendations on the open offer to the shareholders of the target company and such recommendations are to be made publicly available.

8. PROXY FIGHTING

8.1 Is proxy fighting customarily conducted for control of the company management or what other items? How is it regulated under the company law or market regulations?

Normally, proxy fighting is not prevalent in India as the concept of such proxy advisory firms is still at its nascent stage and as such not regulated. However, in the limited context of hostile takeovers, there have been a few instances of proxy fighting.

9. OFFICERS' REMUNERATION RULES

9.1 How is remuneration of officers determined? By whom? Is there a role for the shareholders' meeting? Is there any mechanism for an independent body to review and evaluate them?

The provisions of the Companies Act regulate the remuneration payable to managers and, as has been detailed above in paragraph 4.5, to the directors of a company. The remuneration payable to directors is determined primarily by the BoD and requires the approval of the shareholders. For all categories of officers below directors, remuneration is determined by the BoD or the person delegated by the same.

The Companies Act also lays down a specific procedure to be followed for persons who are related to a director of the company and who are appointed to an office or place of profit in the company, in which case the approval of the shareholders, accorded by a special resolution passed in a general meeting as well as the approval of the central government where applicable is mandatory.

In general, the company and its BoD are free to determine the remuneration to be granted to officers and shareholders do not have a role as such in the determination of remuneration for officers. There is no particular mechanism for an independent body to review and evaluate the same, though generally the remuneration is paid as per market trends and is evaluated internally by the human resources department in the company.

However, the role of the central government, as an independent body, when determining remuneration of executive directors of a listed company and a company which is a subsidiary of a listed company is pertinent to note. Further, the role of the remuneration committee, as discussed above in paragraph 4.3, in the determination of payment of remuneration to executive directors in listed companies and subsidiaries of listed companies, when the company is making no profits or when the profits are inadequate, is relevant.

Furthermore, clause 178 of the Bill provides for the constitution of a nomination and remuneration committee by the BoD of a company, consisting of three or more non-executive directors out of which not less than half shall be independent directors, which will determine a specific policy for determining remuneration for the directors, key managerial personnel and other employees, and which is similar to the definition of a remuneration committee under the extant Companies Act.

9.2 Is the mechanism of officers' remuneration publicly debated?

While there is no such concept of a public debate in this area, it is pertinent to note that approval by the shareholders of a company is standard when determining the remuneration of all categories of officers, including whole-time directors. Further, there is a requirement as per the Companies Act as well as the Listing Agreement to make disclosures regarding the remuneration paid to directors and key employees.

10. DIRECTORS' LIABILITIES, LIABILITY INSURANCE, INDEMNIFICATION

10.1 What are the directors' responsibilities and liabilities under the law? Can those liabilities be covered by insurance? Can it be indemnified by the company or other related parties?

The primary principle behind the directors' responsibilities and liabilities under the law can be traced to the concept that a company is a juristic person, which means that the actions of the company and all the decisions relating to the running of affairs of the company are made by the BoD of the company, and when specifically authorised to do so, by the individual directors of the company. The actual extent of powers of the directors of the company is delineated in the Companies Act itself and the articles of association of the company. See paragraph 4.1 above for more detail.

The Companies Act renders void any provision, whether contained in the articles of a company or in an agreement with a company or in any other instrument, for exempting any officer of the company or any person employed by the company as auditor from, or indemnifying him against, any liability which, by virtue of any rule of law, would otherwise attach to him in respect of any negligence, default, misfeasance, breach of duty or breach of trust of which he may be guilty in relation to the company. However, a company may indemnify any officer or auditor against any liability incurred by him in defending any proceedings, whether civil or criminal, in which judgment is given in his favour or in which he is acquitted or discharged.

Hence, any payment to a director or officer of a company (even the cost of the defence) before there has been a finding in the director's favour will be void. This may pose a challenge to a company wishing to indemnify directors for defence costs if there are allegations of negligence, default, misfeasance, breach of duty or breach of trust, which is often the case when proceedings are brought by the regulators. However, a more liberal interpretation of the aforesaid provision allows a company to pay a premium for procuring directors' and officers' insurance to recompensate the loss such individuals may suffer because of the liability accruing to the company. In such cases, as the company is not agreeing to indemnify the directors per se, but merely agreeing to meet the expenses of procuring an undertaking from the insurer to do so, the provisions of section 201 are unlikely to be attracted.

This view is bolstered by common market practice as well as a clause in the Bill, which acknowledges a premium paid by companies for insurance taken by a company on behalf of its managing director, whole-time director, manager, chief executive officer, chief financial officer or company secretary, for indemnifying any of them against any liability in respect of any negligence, default, misfeasance, breach of duty or breach of trust for which they may be guilty in relation to the company. Further, the SEBI has also expressed a view in the past of making directors' and officers' insurance mandatory for listed companies.

In India, the practice of providing directors' and officers' insurance policies (D&O insurance policy) is quite prevalent and is significant in light of the fact that a director is jointly and severally liable, and losses suffered by the company following an act which is either wrong or negligent or outside the company's authority or beyond the power of the directors or which evidences insufficient skill and care in managing the company's affairs, are to be borne by the directors personally.

Generally, a D&O insurance policy provides coverage for damages and defence costs in the event directors and officers suffer losses as a result of a lawsuit for alleged wrongful acts while acting in their capacity as directors and officers for the organisation. Further, a general D&O insurance policy may be extended depending on the product being offered on the payment of an enhanced premium to cover special excess protection for non-executive directors, entity securities cover, entity employment practice liability cover and outside entity directors. Claims relating to breach of fiduciary duty, neglect, mis-statements in the prospectus, wrongful dismissal of employee and misrepresentation are typically made.

11. SHAREHOLDERS' DERIVATIVE SUITS

11.1 Is a shareholder's derivative suit provided for by law in your jurisdiction? How is it enforced by the shareholders?

There is no specific provision recognising shareholders' derivative suits in the general scheme of corporate law in India. As a consequence, the derivative action mechanism has not been frequently utilised in India. However, there have been instances where shareholders have initiated such actions, primarily relying on common law principles like the established exceptions to the rule of judicial non-interference in a company's management, laid down in *Foss v Harbottle* (1843) 67 E.R. 189. Procedurally, as per Order I, Rule 8 of the Code of Civil Procedure, 1908, derivative actions are considered to be representative actions, and hence shareholders are required to obtain the permission of the court before proceeding with the suit.

11.2 Have there been any recent relevant court cases on the subject?

There are relatively fewer court cases in relation to derivative suits as compared with the other actions that may be taken by shareholders. The Bombay High Court and the Calcutta High Court have both recently passed judgments in relation to derivative suits in 2011 in the cases of *Anil*

Madhavdas Ahuja v Marvel Fragrances Ltd & Ors 2011 (113) BomLR 3142, *Victor Fernandes & Ors v Raghav Bahl of Noida & Ors* MANU/MH/1840/2011 and *Narendra Kumar Berlia & Ors v Om Prakash Berlia & Ors* in 2011(3) CHN147.

The courts have generally held that shareholders cannot ordinarily assume to themselves the right of suing in the name of the company and only the company can sue in its own name for any wrong that may be done to it. However, it has been affirmed that a derivative action is an exception to this rule and that it is founded on the basis that the company, being managed by the miscreant directors or shareholders, will not institute proceedings for protecting or enforcing the rights of the company. Therefore, when a derivative action is filed by a shareholder, the company is required to be joined as a co-defendant and the relief is sought not on behalf of the person bringing the action, but on behalf of the company. Further, the shareholders should be unable to remedy the illegality through any other way.

A derivative action or a suit can also be filed by the minority directors or shareholders, if it is in the interest and welfare of the company and its shareholders and if it is in good faith and is bona fide, in order to check and control unfair action, inefficient management and self-dealing by the majority directors.

It is relevant to note that most cases in India involving derivative suits by shareholders have been adjudged as personal or representative actions which actually seek to personally benefit the petitioners but which have been masqueraded in the form of derivative actions. It is pertinent that the reliefs claimed in such suits should necessarily be in the interest of the company and not for the vindication of the personal rights of the shareholders and have hence not met with much success.

12. SOCIAL INTEREST IN CORPORATE BEHAVIOUR

12.1 How is a company in your country expected to deal with the following issues? Corporate social responsibility; gender, racial and social diversification; environmental issues; ecology and corruption?

In the recent past, India has witnessed a general trend in enhancing domestic laws to promote and to encourage socially responsible companies. The Bill has included a corporate social responsibility (CSR) annual spending requirement, among many other requirements. The CSR spending requirement would apply to companies registered in India with a net worth of Rs. 5 billion or more or a turnover of Rs. 10 billion or more per year or a net profit of Rs. 50 million during any financial year. Such companies will be required to spend at least 2 per cent of the average net profits of the company made during the three immediately preceding financial years, in pursuance of its CSR policy. Such companies are also mandated to form a CSR committee and recommend and monitor a CSR policy or initiative.

Further, in order to provide protection against the sexual harassment of women in the workplace and for the prevention and redressal of complaints of sexual harassment, on 22 April 2013 parliament passed the Sexual

Harassment of Women at Workplace (Prevention, Prohibition and Redressal) Act, 2013 (the Sexual Harassment Act). The Sexual Harassment Act defines sexual harassment in the workplace and creates a mechanism for redressal of complaints. It mandates the employer of a workplace to constitute an 'internal complaints committee'. Employers who fail to comply will be punished with a fine of up to Rs. 50,000. The District Officer is required to constitute a local complaints committee in each district, and if required at the block level. The complaints committees are required to provide for conciliation before initiating an inquiry, if requested by the complainant. Further, there are certain stringent norms relating to corruption, which are also to be followed by the companies.

Further, the Companies Act also requires certain disclosures regarding the conservation of energy absorption of new technology by the company and foreign exchange earnings and outgoings to be made in the report presented by the BoD of a company in the general meeting.

Indonesia

Tony Budidjaja & Juni Dani **Budidjaja & Associates**

1. GENERAL PRINCIPLES

1.1 What are the general principles of corporate governance in your jurisdiction? What are the main objectives of corporate governance principles in your jurisdiction? State also whether your legal system is based on common law or civil law.

Indonesia is a civil law country. The principal source of Indonesian civil law is the Civil Code, which together with the Commercial Code, the Criminal Code and the civil procedural law, is inherited from the Dutch.

The general principles of corporate governance as adopted by the Code of Good Corporate Governance issued by the National Committee on Governance in 2006 include:

- Transparency: A company must provide material and relevant information that are easily accessible and understandable by stakeholders. A company must take the initiative to disclose not only the issues mandated by laws and regulations, but also other information deemed necessary by shareholders, creditors and other stakeholders to form a decision.
- Accountability: A company must be accountable for its performance in a fair and transparent manner. Thus, a company must be managed properly, in such manner that it is aligned with its interest by also considering the interest of shareholders and other stakeholders.
- Responsibility: A company shall abide by laws and regulations and fulfil its responsibility to the communities and environment for the purpose of maintaining long-term sustainability of the business and to be recognised as a good corporate citizen.
- Independency: A company must be managed independently with an appropriate balance of power. No single company's organ shall dominate the other and no intervention from the other party shall be tolerated.
- Fairness: A company must provide the opportunity for stakeholders to give input and opinions in the interest of a company, a fair and equitable treatment to stakeholders in accordance with benefit and contribution given to the company; and shall give equal opportunity in recruitment of employees, in career development and for employees to carry out their duty professionally.

According to the National Committee on Governance, the main objectives of corporate governance principles are as follows:

- achieving sustainable growth of the company through a management system based on the principles of transparency, accountability,

responsibility, independency and fairness;
- empowering the function and independency of each company organ, ie, the board of commissioners, the board of directors and the general meeting of shareholders;
- encouraging shareholders, members of the board of commissioners and members of the board of directors to take decisions and actions based on high moral values and compliance with the law and regulations;
- stimulating the company awareness of social responsibilities, in particular the environmental and societal interests of the communities in which a company operates;
- optimising the value of a company for its shareholders by also taking into consideration the interests of other stakeholders; and
- enhancing the competitiveness of a company, both nationally and internationally, in order to enhance market confidence which may promote investment flow and contribute to the economic growth of the country.

1.2 Have there been any recent developments in the law, codes and rules of corporate governance?

Yes, there have been some developments.

To substitute the role of the Central Bank with regard to banking supervision, the Indonesia's Financial Services Authority (*Otoritas Jasa Keuangan* or OJK) has been established in 2011 with the authority to regulate, supervise, examine and investigate the financial services sector in Indonesia.

On 17 June 2013, the OJK and the International Financial Corporation (a member of World Bank Group) signed an agreement to improve corporate governance standards in Indonesia. To achieve that objective, the Indonesian government has established a Corporate Governance Task Force (CGTF) to implement good corporate governance in financial services companies. The CGTF has the role of preparing the corporate governance road map in Indonesia.

In addition to OJK, the CGTF membership consists of Bank of Indonesia, Ministry of State-Owned Enterprises, the Directorate General of Taxation, the Finance and Development Supervisory Agency (BPK), the Indonesian Institute of Accountants (IAI) and the Indonesia Stock Exchange (IDX).

1.3 Outline recent court cases and incidents involving corporate governance issues. Were there any significant corporate scandals or large unlawful corporate cases?

One of the most controversial financial issues since Indonesia's financial crisis in 1998 was the Bank Century (now 'Bank Mutiara') scandal, known as 'Centurygate'. The Bank Century scandal appears to be the apparent failure of the corporate governance principles in the banking sector.

The bank defaulted on several large loan payments and was declared insolvent and taken over by the government through the Financial Sector Stability Committee on 21 November 2008. The Corruption Eradication

Commission (KPK) confirmed the involvement of several influenced leaders widely suspected of playing a role, after questioning several witnesses, including the then Indonesia's finance minister who was authorizing the IDR 6.7 trillion (approximately $690 million) bailout of Bank Century.

In another case and year (2010), a publicly listed shipping company in Indonesia filed a claim against its former directors and commissioners in connection with the issuance of corporate guarantee. The company claimed that all defendants failed to carry out their fiduciary duty to the company; and also acted beyond their authority in issuing a corporate guarantee in favour of the ship owners to guarantee the due and prompt payment of charter hire by the company's subsidiaries.

The shipping company further claimed that the issuance of the guarantee had been imprudent and lacking in business judgement, as well as having violated the principle of good corporate governance. The court declared that the corporate guarantee does not bind on the company, and all defendants shall be jointly and severally responsible for the issuance of the corporate guarantee.

1.4 Which law enforcement agency is in charge of enforcing corporate governance? May a criminal sanction be levied upon infringement of the corporate governance rules?

As provided by Article 6 Law No. 21 Year 2011 on the Financial Services Authority (OJK), the OJK shall perform regulatory and supervisor duties over financial services activities in the banking sector, the capital market sector, the insurance sector, the pension funds sector, the finance institution sector and other financial services institutions sector.

Yes, criminal sanctions such as fraud and corruption can be levied upon infringement of the corporate governance rules.

2. SOURCES OF LAW

2.1 Which laws, codes or statutes govern company structures and organisations? Are there statutes like the Companies Act or other forms of law? Is there much relevant case law?

Law No. 40 of 2007 on Limited Liability Companies (the Company Law), which replaced the previous Law No. 1 of 1995.

Law No. 19 of 2003 on State-Owned Enterprises, which provides regulations on Indonesian state-owned enterprises.

2.2 Which laws, codes or statutes regulate capital markets in your jurisdiction?

Law No. 8 of 1995 on Capital Market (the Capital Market Law), and its supplementing regulations issued by the Indonesian Capital Market and Financial Institution Supervisory Agency (BAPEPAM LK; now OJK), which applies to publicly listed companies.

2.3 Are there any public interest laws which apply to or influence corporate governance?

Yes. An example of this would be Law No. 14 of 2008 on Transparency of Public Information, which regulates that public institutions are obliged to disclose public information related to activities and performance of the public institutions, including financial reports regularly or at least every six months. Furthermore, Law No. 20 Year 2001 on the Amendment of Law No. 31 Year 1999 on Eradication of Corruption, which provides criminal sanctions for corruption made by public administrators, eg public servants, armies, judges and the police also influence the good corporate governance practices within the government institutions.

Besides, the National Code of Good Corporate Governance, especially the Banking Sector Code (issued in 2004) and the Insurance Sector Code (issued in 2006); also influences corporate governance for the relevant sectors in Indonesia.

2.4 Have there been any recent developments in any of the above laws? What are the recent changes to the above laws or rules and the reasons for such changes?

There has been no change in both the Company Law and Capital Market Law, but the OJK has been drafting an amendment to the Capital Market Law.

3. SHAREHOLDERS AND THE SHAREHOLDERS' MEETING

3.1 How are shareholders' interests represented in the company? How are the shareholders assured exercise of their rights? What is the highest governing body within the company structure if it is not the shareholders' meeting?

The shareholders' interests are represented through the general meeting of shareholders (GMS), which has the highest authority in the Indonesian limited liability companies (*Perseroan Terbatas* or PT). The GMS has the authority to appoint and dismiss the members of the board of commissioners and the board of directors.

3.2 How is the shareholders' meeting conducted? Who may chair the meeting? May attendance (not voting) at the meeting be restricted only to the shareholders? Are the shareholders allowed to be accompanied by legal or other counsel?

In principle, the GMS consists of the following:

- annual GMS, which is required to be held within six months after the end of latest book year; and
- other GMS – commonly called as an extraordinary GMS, which may be convened at any time based on the need to discuss and decide the agenda of the meeting.

A GMS may be convened if the attendance quorum as required by the Company Law or the PT's Articles of Association has been fulfilled.

Place, notice and chairman of GMS: the GMS shall be convened at the company's domicile or at the place where the company runs its main business activities. While for a publicly listed PT, the GMS may be convened at the domicile of stock exchange where the PT's shares are listed in Indonesia.

A notice of GMS must be sent by the board of directors via registered mail and/or through advertisement in newspapers, at least 14 days prior to the date of the GMS, excluding the date of the notice and the date of the GMS. For a publicly listed PT, a notice of GMS must be preceded by an announcement that the notice to a GMS will be issued.

An Indonesian company is free to stipulate the chairman of the GMS in its Articles of Association.

The shareholders may also adopt a binding resolution without convening a GMS, provided that all shareholders have their legal voting rights approved by the resolutions in writing and/or by signing the resolutions concerned. The GMS may also be carried out through teleconferences, videoconferences or other electronic media mechanism, in which all participants can see and hear each other directly, and participate in the GMS, provided that a confirmation letter is made and signed by all participants.

The Company Law must set a restriction on the attendance of the GMS. Shareholders without voting rights are prohibited to attend the GMS. The Company Law does not restrict the shareholders to be accompanied by their counsel. It shall be solely dependent on the shareholders' discretion. The shareholders may, however, be represented in the GMS by their proxies based on a power of attorney. It is important to note that in voting, members of the board of directors, members of the board of commissioners, and employees of the company concerned are prohibited from acting as proxies for shareholders.

3.3 How are minority shareholders' rights protected?

The protection for the PT's shareholders provided by Article 97 paragraph (6) of the Company Law, which states that the holders of 10 per cent of the company's voting shares may bring a derivative action in the name of the company against the directors, if the company suffers loss as a result of their fault or negligence.

In addition, Article 62 of the Company Law provides the right to the company's shareholder to request the company for its shares to be bought at a fair price if the shareholder concerned does not approve the company's actions, which may harm the shareholder or the company, in the form of:

- amendments of the Articles of Association;
- assignment or securing of assets of the company which have a value of more than 50 per cent of the company's net assets; or
- mergers, consolidations, acquisitions or demergers.

3.4 Is shareholder activism encouraged or discouraged? If not encouraged, how is it regulated?

Shareholder activism is encouraged.

3.5 How are professional shareholders (those minority shareholders who seek some extra benefit from companies by unduly and habitually

influencing management by using their shareholding) treated by the law? Are they excluded from attending the shareholders' meeting? Are they criminally or otherwise publicly sanctioned?
There are no specific regulations on this.

3.6 Are shareholders' benefits given to some of the shareholders by the company without resolution by the shareholders' meeting prohibited or regulated by the law or other rules?

Under the Company Law, a company may issue preferred shares which give their holders priority over ordinary shares. For example: shares with voting rights; shares with special rights to nominate members of the board of directors and/or members of the board of commissioners; shares which after a certain period of time will be withdrawn or exchanged for some other classification of shares; shares which give their holder priority over shares with other classifications in receiving dividends in the allocation of dividends cumulatively or non-cumulatively; and shares which give their holders the right to priority over holders of shares with other classifications in receiving allocations of the remainder of the PT's assets in liquidation.

4. DIRECTORS AND BOARD OF DIRECTORS

4.1 What are the functions and responsibilities of the directors and the board of directors? Do you have a one- or two-tier board system? What are the outside directors called?

Indonesia's Company Law applies the 'two-board management system' comprising board of directors that performs the executive role and a board of commissioners that performs the supervisory and advisory roles.

The basic functions of the board of directors are to manage and to represent the company in the interests of and in accordance with the PT's objectives. Whereas, the basic functions of the board of commissioners are to supervise the performance of and policies made by the board of directors in managing the PT, and to provide advice to the board of directors.

The board of commissioners may also have the responsibility of protecting shareholders' interests. In this respect, the board of directors may be required by the PT's Articles of Association to obtain prior approval from the board of commissioners before undertaking certain legal acts (such as obtaining loans, providing guarantees or encumbering company's property).

Outside directors are also known as independent/third-party directors.

4.2 What are the rules that may give rise to civil and criminal liability of the director(s)? How are those liabilities sought?

The Company Law provides a remedy for situations where the directors fail to perform their duties with good faith and a full sense of responsibility with regards the PT's (best) interests.

According to Article 97(3) of the Company Law, the relevant directors shall be personally liable for the consequences of failing to act negligently. Likewise, each member of the board of commissioners shall be personally liable if the company suffers a loss as a result of their fault or negligence in performing their duties.

Moreover, the Indonesian Penal Code provides criminal sanctions for directors and commissioners who committed actions detrimental to the creditors of a company under bankruptcy status.

4.3 Does the board of directors have a committee system, eg, nomination committee, compensation committee, audit committee? If not required, is it common practice for companies? How does it function?

No. In practice, it is quite common in an Indonesian company for specific functions to be assigned to individual directors, such as director of finance, director of operations, director of marketing, director of human resources, etc.

Pursuant to Article 121 of the Company Law, in performing their supervisory duties, the board of commissioners may establish committees, such as an audit committee, remuneration committee, and/or nomination committee, whose members are one or more members of the board of commissioners.

Moreover, a publicly listed company must have an audit committee which consists of one independent commissioner and two other external members.

4.4 Is it a legal requirement to have an independent director or a third-party director? If so, how are they appointed? Is it required for listed companies?

There is no legal requirement to have an independent director for a private PT. The Articles of Association of a company may, however provide for one or more independent commissioners. A publicly listed company must have at least one non-affiliated director and one independent commissioner appointed by the GMS. The independent commissioner must not have the following:

- any affiliation with the PT;
- shareholding in the PT, whether directly or indirectly;
- affiliation with the members of the majority shareholders, members of the board of commissioners and the board of directors; or
- a business relationship or be part of the company's activities in relation to the PT, whether directly or indirectly.

4.5 How is the compensation for directors or officers determined? Can it be contested by the shareholders or the regulatory authorities? What are the common rules or practices for the compensation of officers?

The remuneration and other benefits of the directors and commissioners of the company shall be determined by the GMS.

4.6 How will the board handle a corporate crisis like an internal criminal case, violence, social media exposure or dawn raid by the

authorities?
Generally, the board will handle the corporate crisis internally, for example, by engaging an internal and external auditor or a public relations company. Most Indonesian companies, especially state-owned enterprises, are known to be very sensitive when its problems attract public attention.

5. BOARD OF AUDITORS, AUDIT COMMITTEE, ACCOUNTING AUDITORS

5.1 How is the internal accounting and legal audit structured and conducted? Is an outside accounting audit required and, if so, how is it structured? Are there requirements to change the auditor each five years?

Pursuant to Article 68 of the Company Law, the board of directors is required to deliver the PT's financial statement to be audited by a public accountant if:

- the PT's business is to collect and/or manage the public's funds;
- the company issues acknowledgements of indebtedness to the public;
- the company is a publicly listed company;
- the company is a state-owned enterprise;
- the company has assets and/or a business turnover worth at least IDR 50,000,000,000 (50 billion Indonesian Rupiah); or
- it is obligatory under legislative regulations.

The obligation to deliver financial statements to a public accountant for audit purposes arises from the nature of the relevant company.

Pursuant to Law No. 5 of 2011 on Public Accountant and the Minister of Finance Regulation No. 17 of 2008 on Public Accountant Service, the service of a public accountant firm for auditing the company's financial statement shall be limited to six consecutive years, and the service of a public accountant for auditing the company's financial statements shall be limited to three consecutive years.

5.2 Do you have supervisory auditors? What is the function of the supervisory auditors' board?

As explained above, the board of commissioners carries out the supervisory role. Board of commissioners may establish committees, such as an audit committee, remuneration committee, and/or nomination committee.

6. MARKET DISCLOSURE/TRANSPARENCY TO THE SHAREHOLDERS AND THE PUBLIC

6.1 What are the disclosure requirements for companies in your jurisdiction under company law, capital markets law or any other rules?

The disclosure requirement for a publicly listed company is stipulated in the OJK Regulation No. X.K.1, which states that every public company whose registration statement has become effective must report to the OJK and make public, within two working days of any decision or event, information or material fact that may affect the value of the securities of the company or may affect the investment decision of the investor. According to this Regulation, events, information or material facts that are subject to the disclosure obligation include:

- a merger, acquisition, consolidation or establishment of a joint venture;
- a stock split or distribution of dividends;
- a distribution of a dividend that is unusual in character;
- an acquisition of, or loss of, an important contract;
- a significant new product or innovation;
- a change in control or significant change in management;
- an announcement to repurchase or pay for its debt securities;
- a sale of additional securities to the public or in a private placement;
- the purchase of, or loss from the sale of, a material asset;
- a relatively important labour dispute;
- any important litigation against the company and/or the company's directors or commissioners;
- an offer to purchase securities of another company;
- the replacement of the auditor who audits the company;
- the replacement of the company's trust agent; and
- a change of the company's fiscal year.

6.2 What is the liability or responsibility of the board in relation to the company's disclosure requirements?

As explained above, the board of directors of the company shall be responsible to disclose information or material facts that are subject to disclosure requirements. The OJK can impose any of administrative sanctions to the public company for violation of the disclosure requirement, ie:

- warning letter;
- fines;
- restrictions on business activity;
- suspensions of business activity;
- revocations of business licences;
- cancellations of approvals; and
- cancellations of registrations.

7. M&A AND CORPORATE GOVERNANCE

7.1 Upon an M&A offer, how are the transparency and fairness rules of the company provided under the company and stock market laws and rules?

The transparency and fairness rules upon an M&A offer are reflected in the Company Law and Capital Market Regulations, ie:

- The Company Law, which requires the board of directors of both the acquiring company and the target company, no later than 30 days prior to the date of the notice calling the GMS, to jointly announce in brief the acquisition plan in at least one Indonesian national newspaper and to the employees of each company.
- The OJK Regulation No. IX.G.1 on Merger and Consolidation of

Public Companies, which requires the board of directors and board of commissioners of the public companies involved in the merger or consolidation to submit a statement to the OJK and to the GMS confirming that the merger or consolidation takes into account the interests of the companies, the public, and fair competition, and will guarantee the rights of shareholders and employees.

- The OJK Regulation No. IX.E.1 on Conflict of Interest on Certain Transaction.
- The OJK Regulation No. IX.E.2 on Material Transactions and Core Business Shifting.
- The OJK Regulation No. IX.H.1 on Public Company Takeover.
- The OJK Regulation No. IX.K.1 on Disclosure of Information that Must Be Made Public Immediately.

8. PROXY FIGHTING

8.1 Is proxy fighting customarily conducted for control of the company management or what other items? How is it regulated under the company law or market regulations?

Not regulated.

9. OFFICERS' REMUNERATION RULES

9.1 How is remuneration of officers determined? By whom? Is there a role for the shareholders' meeting? Is there any mechanism for an independent body to review and evaluate them?

Except for the remuneration of the directors and commissioners, which shall be determined by the GMS, there is no specific regulation on the mechanism to determine the officers' remuneration rules.

Under the Regulation of the Minister of State-Owned Enterprises No. Per-07/MBU/2010 (as amended by Regulation No. Per-04-MBU-2013), the remuneration of the directors and commissioners of state-owned enterprises in the form of a limited liability company will be determined by the GMS. The remuneration of the directors and supervisory board of state-owned enterprises in the form of a general company will be determined by the relevant minister.

9.2 Is the mechanism of officers' remuneration publicly debated?

The issue of officers' remuneration within an Indonesian company is usually private and not transparent.

10. DIRECTORS' LIABILITIES, LIABILITY INSURANCE, INDEMNIFICATION

10.1 What are the directors' responsibilities and liabilities under the law? Can those liabilities be covered by insurance? Can it be indemnified by the company or other related parties?

In Indonesia, there has been a widely accepted view that directors are fiduciaries of the PTs they serve. This fiduciary duty is owed to the company and not to the shareholders individually or collectively as shareholders, although it could also be enforced by the company through a shareholders' derivative action.

Article 97 paragraph (2) of the Company Law specifically requires that every director perform his/her duties with good faith and a full sense of responsibility with a view to the PT's (best) interests. Article 114, paragraph (2) of the Company Law provides a similar provision in respect of commissioners.

According to Article 97(3) of the Company Law, the relevant director shall be personally liable for the PT's losses if the relevant director is at fault or is negligent in performing his/her duties. In the event that the board of directors consists of two or more members, the liability shall be joint and several to each member of the board of directors.

It is difficult to procure professional liability insurance in Indonesia.

11. SHAREHOLDERS' DERIVATIVE SUITS

11.1 Is a shareholder's derivative suit provided for by law in your jurisdiction? How is it enforced by the shareholders?

Yes. As explained above, the holders of 10 per cent of the company's voting shares may bring a derivative action on behalf of the company through the district court against the directors, if the company suffers a loss as a result of their fault or negligence.

11.2 Have there been any recent relevant court cases on the subject?

Yes. In early 2013, a minority shareholder filed a derivative action against a publicly listed timber company in Indonesia and its management. The shareholder claimed that the management of the company did not adhere to good corporate governance standards, which has caused the company to incur losses since 2008.

12. SOCIAL INTEREST IN CORPORATE BEHAVIOUR

12.1 How is a company in your country expected to deal with the following issues? Corporate social responsibility; gender, racial and social diversification; environmental issues; ecology and corruption?

Law No. 40 of 2008 on the Elimination of Racial and Ethnic Discrimination provides a framework for the protection of all Indonesians from all forms of racial and ethnic discrimination. Article 19 of Law No. 40 of 2008 provides criminal sanction for corporate action on racial and ethnic discrimination.

Under the Company Law, a company that carries out any business activity in the field and/or related to natural resources must undertake social and environmental responsibilities.

Indonesia's Law No. 32 of 2009 on Environmental Protection and Management requires Indonesian companies to issue an environmental management statement, environmental management efforts – environmental monitoring efforts reports or an environmental impact assessment, depending on their industry and exposure to the environment. In addition to this obligation, the Environmental Law also provides a requirement for companies to carry out an environmental risk analysis or obtain an environmental permit.

Israel

Rachel Levitan & Yael Navon **Levitan, Sharon & Co.**

1. GENERAL PRINCIPLES

1.1 What are the general principles of corporate governance in your jurisdiction? What are the main objectives of corporate governance principles in your jurisdiction? State also whether your legal system is based on common law or civil law.

The Israeli legal system is based on the common law; however, it incorporates aspects of civil law. Most general principles of corporate governance in Israel are set in the Companies Law 1999, which replaced most of the provisions included in the Company Ordinance of 1983 which was based on English Law.

The corporate governance principles set under the law are intended to create mechanisms for the proper management of the company, while protecting the company's creditors and minority shareholders from the expropriation of the controlling shareholders and the company's management.

According to section 11 of the Companies Law:

'The purpose of the company is to act in accordance with business considerations in order to maximize its profits, and it may include among these considerations, inter alia, the interests of its creditors, employees and the interests of the public. In addition the company may donate reasonable sums for an appropriate purpose, even if such donation is not within the framework of business considerations, if such term is included in its Article of Association.'

The Companies Law emphasised the supervisory role of the board of directors over the company's executives. In order to ensure that the board can indeed function as a supervisor, the Companies Law set several rules which were intended to strengthen the independency of the board, specifically in public companies. These rules include the separation between the CEO and the board of directors, the duty to include in the board of directors of public companies independent directors, the duty of each director to execute its voting power in board meetings independently and so on.

In addition, the Companies Law set two main duties for directors and officers towards the company:

- The duty of care, which is the duty of a director or officer of a company to exercise the care and skill which a reasonable director or officer would exercise under the circumstances.
- The duty of trust (a fiduciary duty), which is phrased in the Companies Law as a requirement that the directors and officers *'will act in good faith and for the company's benefit'* and will refrain from any act which

involves their conflict of interests with the company.

In Israel, most public companies are held by controlling shareholders. Therefore, one of the main concerns of the Companies Law is to protect the minority shareholders from inappropriate transactions with interested parties. The main protection provided to the minority shareholders in this respect is the need to receive – prior to such transaction –the approval of a majority of the shareholders who have no interest in the transaction, in addition to the approval of the audit committee.

Another aspect of corporate governance rules is set in the Israeli Securities Law 1968. This Law is based on the principle of full and fair disclosure towards the company's securities holders from the public in the primary and secondary market. The Israeli Securities Law imposes various reporting duties on public companies and set criminal sanctions for the breach thereof.

1.2 Have there been any recent developments in the law, codes and rules of corporate governance?

At the beginning of 2012, the OECD published a report regarding 'Related Party Transactions and Minority Shareholders Rights'. The report referred to corporate governance in five different countries, including Israel. In the report, the OECD stated: 'Israel has taken numerous additional steps to strengthen an already robust framework to prevent the abuse of minority shareholder rights, including for related party transactions in particular.'

Indeed, in the past several years, the Israeli Law went through several amendments, which were intended to improve corporate governance in Israeli entities, and to strengthen the power of the minority shareholders.

On 14 May 2011, several significant amendments to the Companies Law came into force (amendment 16). These amendments were intended to improve the quality of corporate governance in publicly traded companies. The amendments included provisions increasing the power of the disinterested shareholders, placing stricter criteria for approval of transactions with interested parties, strengthening the independence of the board of directors and of the audit committee and granting a stronger role for independent directors.

Amendment 16 provided that a director should use independent judgement and prohibited a director from entering into voting agreements.

In addition, amendment 16 granted the Israel Securities Authority (ISA) new authority to impose monetary sanctions on an individual or corporation for the breach of certain law provisions.

Additional amendments to the Companies Law were meant to apply on companies which issued debentures to the public similar standards, which apply to companies whose shares are publicly traded.

An additional amendment (amendment 20), which came into force on 12 December 2012, set new rules regarding the approval of the employment terms of the company's senior management, and established the duty of the company to appoint a compensation committee.

1.3 Outline recent court cases and incidents involving corporate

governance issues. Were there any significant corporate scandals or large unlawful corporate cases?

Supreme Court judgments, which were handed down recently, examined the effect of amendment 16 over the Court's authority to review the companies' decisions. As mentioned, amendment 16 of the Companies Law increased the voting power of the disinterested shareholders. Prior to the said amendment, approval of transactions with related parties required the approval of one-third of the disinterested shareholder. The amendment increased the majority required to 50 per cent of the disinterested shareholders (a majority of the minority).

In two cases, M&A transactions which were properly approved by the disinterested shareholders were challenged in court. The companies involved in the said cases claimed that since the transactions were approved by the majority of the minority shareholders, there is no justification for a judicial review of the decision. The court rejected the said position and determined that although minority shareholders are entitled to execute their right by voting in the general assembly, they are also entitled, under certain circumstances, to apply for judicial review of the company's decision.

One of the hot issues in respect of corporate governance is officers' remuneration. Several motions to file derivative actions were filed to court based on the allegation that the company's senior-management compensation terms were not properly approved by the company, and thus the managers, who unduly received the said benefits, should return them to the company. In one case (D.A. (Tel Aviv) 32007-08-11) *Efrat v Ben Shaul*, the court has approved the motion to file a derivative action against the company's controlling shareholder who also served as its CEO.

1.4 Which law enforcement agency is in charge of enforcing corporate governance? May a criminal sanction be levied upon infringement of the corporate governance rules?

The main enforcement agency in charge of enforcing corporate governance is the ISA. The ISA was established in the Securities Law 1968 and its main objective is to protect the interests of the investors from the public.

Infringement of corporate governance rules may result in criminal sanctions. For example, in cases of misleading details included in a company's prospectus or financial reports, the company and its directors and officers may be subject to criminal proceedings.

2. SOURCES OF LAW

2.1 Which laws, codes or statutes govern company structures and organisations? Are there statutes like the Companies Act or other forms of law? Is there much relevant case law?

The structures and organisation of a company are set in the third part of the Israeli Companies Law. According to the said Law, the three main organisations of the company are the general assembly, the board of directors and the general manager. There is a lot of case law examining the relationship between the said organs, their duties and liabilities.

2.2 Which laws, codes or statutes regulate capital markets in your jurisdiction?

The law that regulates the capital markets in Israel is the Securities Law enacted in 1968, in addition to the regulations set under the said Law.

2.3 Are there any public interest laws which apply to or influence corporate governance?

The duty to act in good faith, which was set under the Contracts Law 1973, also applies, according to the said Law, to legal actions and duties which do not arise from a contract.

Accordingly, the Israeli courts determined that the duty to act in good faith is a principal duty which applies to all areas of law, including corporate law (see for example: C.A. 2643/97 *Ganz v Britis & Colonial Corp.*; C.A. 779/06 *Kital v Maman*).

2.4 Have there been any recent developments in any of the above laws? What are the recent changes to the above laws or rules and the reasons for such changes?

As mentioned above, in the past few years there have been various changes made to the Companies Law (amendments 16–20 of the Law), which were intended to improve the corporate governance of Israeli companies, by increasing the independence of the board of directors and the audit committee, while reducing the power of the controlling shareholders. The main changes incorporated in the Companies Law include:

- Approving transactions with interested parties–directors, officers and controlling shareholders are obliged to disclose any interest they may have in a transaction presented for the approval of the company. The approval of such transaction requires the approval of the company's audit committee, board of directors and a majority of the shareholders which do not have a personal interest in the transaction (unless the number of shareholder objecting to the transaction is not higher than 2 per cent of the shareholders with voting power in the company).
- Strengthening the position and independency of the board–the amendments prohibited a person who was not appointed as a director to act as such ('shadow director') and imposed on the directors the duty to execute its independent judgement when voting in the board. In addition, the amendments set the terms for the appointment of external directors and set the conditions required to assure their independency. The amendment also prohibits the CEO from serving as the chairman of the board.
- Strengthening the position and independency of the audit committee – according to the amendments, the majority of members of the audit committee will be independent directors. Furthermore, the amendments prohibit the company's chairman of the board or any director employed by the company or by the company's controlling shareholder or who provides services to any of the above from serving as a member of the audit committee. In addition, the amendments increased the authority

of the audit committee in supervising the company's management, and imposed on them the authority to classify a transaction as such which requires special approvals.

- Presenting a proposed corporate governance code to be adopted by the parties– within the framework of the said amendments, the Law was amended to include a corporate governance code to be adopted voluntarily by companies, by their inclusion in the company's articles of association.
- Increasing the supervision over the compensation of the company's senior management –according to amendment 20, the board of directors must appoint a compensation committee; the majority of its members will be external directors. The main goal of the compensation committee is to set a long-term compensation policy, and to examine the compensation terms of the company's executives.
- Strengthening the supervision over debenture companies and over creditors' agreements.

On 17 January 2011, the Law for Improvement of Enforcement Proceedings by the Securities Authorities 2011 came into force. The purpose of the said Law was to improve the enforcement of the Securities Law and Regulations.

Within the framework of the law the ISA was granted the authority to instigate administrative proceedings against companies and individuals for the breach of the Securities Law. The administrative proceedings will be handled by an administrative enforcement committee, which is entitled to impose monetary sanctions and to order limited compensation to injured parties.

In addition, the Law for Improvement of Enforcement Proceedings by the Securities Authorities stated that the CEO of a company must take all reasonable steps to pervert the breaches of the law, or else he will be exposed to personal liability. The existence of an effective enforcement plan in the company can serve as a defence for the CEO.

3. SHAREHOLDERS AND THE SHAREHOLDERS' MEETING

3.1 How are shareholders' interests represented in the company? How are the shareholders assured exercise of their rights? What is the highest governing body within the company structure if it is not the shareholders' meeting?

The shareholders' general assembly is the highest governing body in the company's structure, and represents the interests of the shareholders. The shareholders exercise their rights through their voting power in the general assembly. The general assembly has the power to nominate the board of directors and to exercise the powers of the board if it considers it necessary. It is authorised to nominate the company's accountant and to determine his engagement terms; it is authorised to nominate the external directors, and has the right to change the company's articles of association.

3.2 How is the shareholders' meeting conducted? Who may chair

the meeting? May attendance (not voting) at the meeting be restricted only to the shareholders? Are the shareholders allowed to be accompanied by legal or other counsel?

According to law, a company must hold a shareholders' general assembly every year and not later than 15 months from the last meeting. In addition, the company can hold a special general assembly according to the decision of the board of directors, and in a public company, if demanded by one of the following: (i) two directors; (ii) a quarter of the members of the board of directors; (iii) a shareholder or several shareholders who own 5 per cent of the company's issued shares and 1 per cent of the company's voting shares; or (iv) a shareholder or several shareholders who own 1 per cent of the company's issued shares and 5 per cent of the company's voting shares.

The agenda of the general assembly will be determined by the board of directors. A shareholder or several shareholders owning at least 1 per cent of the voting shares are entitled to request the board to include a certain subject in the agenda.

In a public company, a notice regarding the general assembly shall include the agenda, the proposed decision and the arrangements required for voting through voting papers.

According to the Companies Law, the minimum quorum required for handling the general assembly is at least two shareholders who own at least 25 per cent of the voting shares. At the beginning of every general assembly a chairman of the meeting will be elected. These provisions can be stipulated against in the company's articles of association.

The Companies Law has no limitation regarding a shareholder's right to be accompanied by legal or other counsel.

3.3 How are minority shareholders' rights protected?

The minority shareholders' rights are protected in several ways:

- Increasing their voting power for approving related-party transactions – as mentioned above, approval of transactions of public companies with interested parties requires the approval of the audit committee, board and general assembly. The approval required by the general assembly includes the support of the majority of the voting shareholders who do not have any personal interest in the transaction.
- Increasing their voting power in appointing outside directors – generally, the appointment of an outside director requires the approval of at least 50 per cent of the shareholders who are not controlling shareholders.

In addition, the minority shareholders have been granted several enforcement tools to enforce their rights:

- Shareholder's class action – a class action is a mechanism which enables a private individual to sue in the name of a group of injured individuals unknown to him, provided the same facts and legal questions are common to all members of the group, and the losses are of the same type. Filing a class action requires the approval of the court, which will be granted if the condition set under the Class Action Law 2006 is met.

- Shareholder's derivative action – a derivative claim is a claim filed by a shareholder on behalf of the company. The shareholder in such case does not claim his personal damages but rather executes the company's cause of action on the company's behalf. The main purpose of derivative claims is to serve as a tool for enforcement of legal standards on wrongdoers who have control over the company and therefore are not expected to cause the company to file claims against them. A derivative claim may be filed only with the court's permission, which will be granted if the court is convinced that the claim serves the company's interest and that the plaintiff is acting in good faith.

3.4 Is shareholder activism encouraged or discouraged? If not encouraged, how is it regulated?

The Israeli laws are meant to encourage activism of shareholders, as can be seen, *inter alia*, from the following:

- As mentioned above, the Israeli law increased the voting power of the minority shareholders in several decisions, such as the approval of transactions by interested parties.
- Shareholders were granted the possibility of executing their voting power in writing, without the need to participate in the general assembly.
- According to the law, the ISA is entitled to finance shareholders' class actions and derivative actions.

3.5 How are professional shareholders (those minority shareholders who seek some extra benefit from companies by unduly and habitually influencing management by using their shareholding) treated by the law? Are they excluded from attending the shareholders' meeting? Are they criminally or otherwise publicly sanctioned?

The law does not determine any sanction which applies to 'professional shareholders'; however, such shareholders are required to execute the rights arising from their shares in good faith, and their failure to do so can expose them to civil liability.

3.6 Are shareholders' benefits given to some of the shareholders by the company without resolution by the shareholders' meeting prohibited or regulated by the law or other rules?

Shareholders' benefits must be given equally to all shareholders in accordance with their respective holdings of the company's shares. An unequal allocation of benefits can be considered as a discrimination of the minority shareholders, which allows them to approach the court with a motion to order the removal or prevention of such discrimination.

In general, a company's decision to distribute dividend to its shareholders can be made by the board of directors, unless the company's article of association provides otherwise.

4. DIRECTORS AND BOARD OF DIRECTORS

4.1 What are the functions and responsibilities of the directors and the board of directors? Do you have a one- or two-tier board system? What are the outside directors called?

Israel has a one-tier board system, which includes the executive directors and the non-executive directors. According to the Companies Law, the board of directors will define the company's policy and will supervise over the activities of the company's CEO. Specifically, the board should:

- Determine the strategy of the company as well as the financing of such strategy.
- Review, from time to time, the financial position of the company and decide the range of credit limits which the company is permitted to borrow.
- Determine the organisational structure of the company, including the remuneration policy.
- Be responsible for preparing the financial report and obtaining approval thereof.
- Report to the general assembly about the position of the company – financially and otherwise.
- Hire and fire the CEO.
- Decide (in a public company) on the minimum number of directors who must have special financial and accounting expertise.

The authority of the board of directors cannot be assigned to the CEO of the company.

According to the Companies Law, a public company must appoint at least two outside directors.

An 'outside director', under the Companies Law, is an independent director with accounting or financial expertise. The 'independent directors' in the company include the outside directors, and other independent directors which have not been serving in the company for more than nine years in a row.

The Companies Law includes various provisions which are intended to ensure that the independent directors and the outside directors are not connected to the company, its management and its controlling shareholders, and they do not have any conflict of interest with the company.

4.2 What are the rules that may give rise to civil and criminal liability of the director(s)? How are those liabilities sought?

The legal basis of directors' and officers' liability in Israel derives from both statutory law and court precedents.

Liability towards the company

The directors and officers owe the company as well as its shareholders and any other third party a *duty of care*. The law establishes that the directors and officers duty of care is based on the principles of negligence in the Tort Ordinance. According to clause 253, directors and officers should act with the standard of care which any reasonable director or officer would have used in a similar position and circumstances.

In addition, the director or officer owes the company a *duty of trust* and shall act in good faith for the benefit of the company (clause 254). He or she should refrain from any act which involves a conflict of interest between the performance of his or her duty in the company and his or her other personal interests. Directors and officers should also refrain from any act which involves competition with the company's business, from taking advantage of any business opportunity of the company. It is the duty of director or officer to disclose to the company any information which relates to its affairs which comes to his or her knowledge by virtue of his or her position in the company.

Liability towards third parties

A well-established rule set by the Supreme Court is that a director or officer has no immunity from liability for wrongful tort acts he or she personally committed just because he or she is an organ of the company. Therefore, if directors or officers breached a duty towards a third party, they can be held personally liable for the damage they caused (C.A. 407/89 *Zok Or Ltd v Security Ltd*, PDI 48(5), 661).

In various cases, the Supreme Court discussed scope of liability of directors and officers towards various third parties.

In C.A. 8133/03 *Oded Itzhak v Lotem Distribution Ltd & Others*, PDI 59(3) 66, the Supreme Court examined an officer's liability towards an employee of the company who was injured. Under the circumstances, the Court found that the officer served as the employee's direct manager, and thus had the duty to assure his safety. Since the manager failed to fulfil his duty of care, the Court imposed personal liability on him.

This precedent was followed by many Court rulings which imposed personal liability on directors and officers for employment practice claims.

Director and officer liability for breach of a contract by the company was discussed by the Supreme Court on several occasions. In C.A. 4612/95 *Itamar Matityahu v Shtil Yehudit*, PDI 51(4), 769, managers of a company which was liquidated were sued by a couple which purchased three apartments from the company, and did not receive them. The Supreme Court ruled that since the managers were not a party to the contract signed with the plaintiffs, no contractual liability should be applied. However, the Court continued and examined whether the managers should be held liable in tort. The Court stated that the mere fact that a person serves as a manager of the company does not justify imposing on him or her liability for wrongful act perpetrated by the company. On the other hand, however, a manager does not have immunity from tort liability arising from acts he or she perpetrated in his or her managerial capacity. In order to determine a personal duty of care which applies to the company's manager, the plaintiffs must prove that the manager's actions exceeded the regular and routine activities of a manager. For example, the manager had special expertise in the subject matter of the contract on which the contracting parties relied, or there was a special relationship between the manager and the third parties which led them to trust the manager personally and to believe that the manager takes personal responsibility towards them.

Under the circumstances, the Court ruled that the managers did not act in a manner exceeding their routine actions as managers and thus there was no basis to apply personal liability thereto.

In another case discussed by the Supreme Court, C.A. 10582/02 *Israelben-AbuvDelatot Hamadia* (not published), the Court dealt with a manager's liability for cheques provided by the company which were not honoured by the bank. The Supreme Court ruled that while negotiating with third parties, the company's managers are subject to a duty to act in good faith and in an acceptable manner. Since, under the circumstances, the manager breached the said duty, he is subject to personal liability for the damage caused to the third party.

Directors' and officers' criminal liability

The Israeli law refers to various duties which apply to directors and officers, breach of which may lead to imposing criminal liability on them.

In C.C. (Tel Aviv – District Court) 40213/05, *The State of Israel v Rachel Toledano and Others*, the Court imposed criminal liability on three members of the board of directors who did not ensure that a company, which was managed in a risky manner by its controlling shareholders, filed its financial reports on time.

The District Court criticised the practice of appointing individuals who have no qualifications to serve as directors in public companies, repeating a statement made by the Supreme Court in another case:

'Indeed, being a director is not only a matter of honour or respect. It is not only a reward for services provided in the past to the State or to the society. It is not a respectful way to retire.'

Knowledge, expertise and experience are the basic tools of a director who is required to consider and examine the issues presented to the board. A director should have knowledge regarding the operation of corporations in general, and of the company in which he or she serves, in particular.

Under the circumstances, the Court found that the three directors were not qualified for the job.

The District Court continues by repeating a Supreme Court precedent pursuant to which:

'Each director must incur all the precautions which a reasonable director would have incurred under the circumstances ... a reasonable director must be interested in the Company's affairs and be familiar with them. He must be aware of the company's financial position. A director cannot fulfill his obligations on the board of directors if he has no idea of what is happening in the Company or if his interest is superficial.'

In the said case, the Court found that, when the directors became aware of the company's problem in publishing its financial report on time, they took no steps to understand the problem, to consult with professional experts or to keep updated as to the actions taken to overcome it. The directors should have taken an active role in trying to prevent the company's failure, including taking drastic steps such as taking over the authority for active management of the company. None of these steps were taken. The gatekeepers of the company failed to perform their job, and thus should be held criminally liable.

The Court wished to send a clear message to board members:

'Every director should know that he can serve as such only if he has suitable qualifications. The appointment is not a prize for services he provided in the past, is not a reward for loyalty to someone or for knowing him and is not for the purpose of experiencing a new field. And he should also know that if he signs in this respect and fails to act like a reasonable director, he might be brought to justice for problems he caused or in which he participated.'

Claims against directors and officers upon the insolvency of the company

The Companies Ordinance grants a liquidator appointed to liquidate an entity the authority to investigate the reasons which led to the liquidation, and to file personal claims against its directors and officers.

Section 288 to the Companies Ordinance provides that upon the appointment of a temporary liquidator or the issuance of a liquidation order, the court may order any director or officer to provide information regarding the company's establishment, business or assets and to interrogate such director or officer verbally or in writing. It is common practice for the court to authorise the company's liquidator to execute the interrogation of the directors and officers and to act in this respect as the court's 'long arm'.

Two provisions in the Companies Ordinance refer to potential claims against directors or officers during liquidation:

- *Claims arising from fraudulent acts perpetrated by the directors and officers*

Section 373 to the Companies Ordinance determines that the court finds that a director or officer of the company was knowingly involved in the fraudulent management of the company, it can hold him personally liable for all of the company's obligations.

Under section 373, liability may be imposed on directors or officers. The definition of 'director or officer' for the purpose of this section is broad and includes present and past director or officer and any person who the directors or officers normally acted in accordance with his orders. The sanction set in section 373 is severe. The director or officer may be forced to pay all of the company's debts, including those debts which were not created as a result of their fraudulent acts.

No causal connection is required between the director's or officer's acts and the extent of the debts imposed on them.

In addition, the Companies Ordinance determines that a director or officer who was knowingly involved in the fraudulent management of the company as set above may be subject to criminal liability.

- *Claims arising from the directors' and officers' breach of their duty of care or trust*

According to section 374 of the Company Ordinance, liability can be imposed on a shareholder, director, officer, receiver or liquidator without the need to prove a fraudulent act. The liability may arise from the breach of duty of care or the duty of trust of a director or officer or any of the above officials toward the company. According to court judgments, section 374 is not intended to set a new standard of liability, but is rather intended to provide a procedural framework for claims against directors or officers due to the breach of their duties.

A claim against a director or officer based on section 374 must point out a specific legal duty which was breached by the director or officer and which can be based on the applicability of section 374.

Contrary to section 373, imposing liability according to section 374 requires the existence of causal connection between the director's or officer's wrongful act and the damage for which he is liable.

4.3 Does the board of directors have a committee system, eg, nomination committee, compensation committee, audit committee? If not required, is it common practice for companies? How does it function?

The Companies Law (clause 110) authorises the board of directors to establish committees, unless it was determined otherwise in the company's articles of association. In a public company, the law provides the duty to appoint an audit committee.

In addition, according to a recent amendment to the Companies Law (amendment 20), a public company must appoint a compensation committee.

4.4 Is it a legal requirement to have an independent director or a third-party director? If so, how are they appointed? Is it required for listed companies?

Every public company must appoint at least two outside directors who must be independent and with financial or accountancy expertise. The outside directors are appointed by the 'majority of the minority' of the shareholders' general assembly. In other words, their appointment requires an approval of at least 50 per cent of the votes of the non-controlling shareholders (or that the votes objecting the appointment are not higher than 2 per cent of the non-controlling shareholders).

In addition, the Companies Law allows for the classification of directors which were not appointed in accordance with the above procedure as 'independent directors', if they meet the criteria set by the law for independence.

4.5 How is the compensation for directors or officers determined? Can it be contested by the shareholders or the regulatory authorities? What are the common rules or practices for the compensation of officers?

Since December 2012, all public companies are required to establish a compensation committee, which will be comprised of at least three directors, all independent directors with a majority of outside directors. The committee has the authority to recommend a compensation policy and to approve the compensation of the CEO.

The board of directors has the duty to determine the compensation policy based on the recommendations of the compensation committee. After the board has approved a compensation policy, it is brought to a non-binding vote in the general assembly. If the majority of the minority shareholders object to the presented policy, it is returned to the board of directors, which is required to take into consideration the general assembly's decision.

The final decision as to whether to approve the compensation policy is of the board of directors, if it considers the policy in the company's best interest.

4.6 How will the board handle a corporate crisis like an internal criminal case, violence, social media exposure or dawn raid by the authorities?

The law does not specifically refer to the handling of a corporate crisis. The board of directors is required to act as a reasonable board would have acted under the circumstances, bearing in mind its duties towards the company and third parties. The board of directors has the authority to order the CEO how to act in a certain case, and under certain circumstances, it has the authority to execute the CEO's authorities instead of the CEO.

5. BOARD OF AUDITORS, AUDIT COMMITTEE, ACCOUNTING AUDITORS

5.1 How is the internal accounting and legal audit structured and conducted? Is an outside accounting audit required and, if so, how is it structured? Are there requirements to change the auditor each five years?

The board of directors of a public company must appoint an internal auditor, in accordance with the recommendation of the audit committee. The internal auditor is subject to the authority of the company's CEO or chairman of the board, as determined in the company's articles of association, and in cases there is no such determination – as determined by the board.

The internal auditor shall issue a periodical working plan for the approval of the board of directors or the audit committee. The chairman of the board and the chairman of the audit committee are entitled to order the internal auditor to execute an internal audit of urgent issues which arise.

The internal auditor shall submit a report regarding its findings to the chairman of the board, the CEO and the chairman of the audit committee.

The termination of the internal auditor can be authorised by the board of directors only after it receives the position of the audit committee, and has given the internal auditor the opportunity to present his or her position to the audit committee and the board. The quorum required for such a decision is the majority of the members of the board.

In addition to the internal auditor, a company is required to appoint an outside accounting audit to audit its financial report and provide an opinion regarding thereof.

In a public company, the outside accounting audit shall be appointed by the annual general assembly, or – if required – by a special general assembly scheduled for such purpose. The accounting audit should be totally independent, and should not depend upon the company, whether directly or indirectly. Termination of the outside accounting audit can be decided by the general assembly after hearing the position of the company's audit committee, and after the accounting audit was given a reasonable opportunity to present its position in this respect.

An accounting auditor who resigns from his or her position in the company, due to circumstances which have interest to the company's shareholders, must notify this to the company's board. The company's board of directors shall notify the company's shareholders of the reasons for the resignation of the outside accounting with details it finds as appropriate.

The Israeli law includes no duty to change the auditor every five years.

5.2 Do you have supervisory auditors? What is the function of the supervisory auditors' board?

Not applicable.

6. MARKET DISCLOSURE/TRANSPARENCY TO THE SHAREHOLDERS AND THE PUBLIC

6.1 What are the disclosure requirements for companies in your jurisdiction under company law, capital markets law or any other rules?

The disclosure duties of public companies are set under the Securities Law 1968. According to section 15 of the said Law, a company cannot propose its securities to the public without the publication of a prospectus which was approved by the ISA. Section 16 provides that the prospectus must include all details that might be important to a reasonable investor who is considering purchasing the proposed securities. In addition, the prospectus shall not include any misleading information.

Section 36 of the Securities Law determines the duty of a company whose securities were offered to the public to publish reports and announcements, and authorised the minister of finance to introduce regulations regarding the details which should be included in the said reports, and the time for their submission.

In accordance with the Securities Law, the minister of finance introduced the Securities Regulations (Periodical and Annual Reports) 1970, which refer to the duty to file periodical and annual reports and provide the details which should be included therein. In addition, according to the said Regulations, the report should include every detail which may be important to a reasonable investor who is considering whether to invest in the securities of the company.

6.2 What is the liability or responsibility of the board in relation to the

company's disclosure requirements?
The Securities Law and its Regulations impose personal liability on directors and officers of a company for breach of the company's disclosure duties. For example, in case of misleading particulars in a prospectus or in the company's financial reports, directors are 'jointly and severally liable' together with the issuer (the company) towards any holder of securities for loss or damage caused as a result of the misleading particular.

7. M&A AND CORPORATE GOVERNANCE

7.1 Upon an M&A offer, how are the transparency and fairness rules of the company provided under the company and stock market laws and rules?

According to the Securities Regulations (Periodical and Immediate Reports) 1970, there is a presumption that information regarding M&A is material, and thus must be reported to the public. According to the said Regulations, a report regarding M&A must be published after the approval of the transaction by the board of directors. The report should include various details, including valuations and other financial material which served as a basis for the board's decision to approve the transaction.

According to the Companies Law, a merger decision must be approved by the board of directors of both merged companies and by the shareholders' general assembly. In certain circumstances, the approval required is of the majority of the shareholders which have no personal interest in the merger.

In P.C. 26809-01-11 *Dov Cahana v Machteshim Agan*, the Economical Division of the Tel Aviv District Court ruled that the Court may review a merger agreement reached by the company, even if it was approved in accordance with the procedure set by the law. The Court ruled that despite the 'business judgment rule', pursuant to which the Court will not review business decisions made by the company, in decisions with crucial effect on the minority shareholders, and in which there is a conflict between the controlling shareholders and the minority shareholders, the Court will not avoid from reviewing the company's decisions. The Court stated that while, in general, the trust duties of the directors and officers and fairness duties of the controlling shareholders are duties towards the company, in merger transactions these duties should apply also directly towards the shareholders.

The Companies Law as well as the Securities Regulations (Tender Offer) 2000 refer to the procedures and obligations which apply to tender offers.

In general, when an acquirer publishes a tender offer, the board of directors of the target company should provide an opinion regarding the worthwhileness of the offer, unless it cannot do so. In such case, it must report the reasons for not providing an opinion. A director or officer who takes steps to fail the offer or to harm the chances of its approval, will be liable towards the offerer and the offerees, unless he or she acted in good faith and had a reasonable basis to believe that his or her acts are for the benefit of the company.

A tender offer shall be accepted only if it was approved by the majority of the shareholders who do not have personal interest in the offer.

According to the Companies Law, a full tender offer which enables the purchase of 100 per cent of the company's shares requires the acceptance of at least 95 per cent of the company's shareholders. Six months after the approval of the tender offer, minority shareholders can approach the court with a motion to determine that the value of the shares according to the purchase offer was unfair, and to determine the fair value which has to be paid for the shares.

In MCA 779/06 *Kital v Maman*, the Supreme Court ruled that the fact that 95 per cent of the offerees approved the offer, does not create a presumption that the value offer was fair.

8. PROXY FIGHTING

8.1 Is proxy fighting customarily conducted for control of the company management or what other items? How is it regulated under the company law or market regulations?

Since Israeli companies are characterised with having controlling shareholders, proxy fighting is not customarily conducted in Israel. In order to minimise proxy fighting and to increase the involvement of the minority shareholder, the Companies Law allows shareholders to vote by voting papers, and allows the board of directors or any person at whose demand the board convened a special general meeting to address the shareholders in writing, via the company, in order to convince them of how to vote.

9. OFFICERS' REMUNERATION RULES

9.1 How is remuneration of officers determined? By whom? Is there a role for the shareholders' meeting? Is there any mechanism for an independent body to review and evaluate them?

As mentioned above, according to a recent amendment to the Companies Law, all public companies are required to establish a compensation committee, whose objective is to recommend a compensation policy and to approve the compensation of the CEO.

The board of directors has the duty to determine the compensation policy based on the recommendations of the compensation committee. After the board has approved a compensation policy, it is brought to a non-binding vote in the general assembly. If the majority of the minority shareholders object to the presented policy, it is returned to the board of directors, which is required to take into consideration the general assembly's decision.

The final decision as to whether to approve the compensation policy is of the board of directors, if it considers the policy in the company's best interest.

9.2 Is the mechanism of officers' remuneration publicly debated?

Officers' remuneration is one of the hottest topics among public corporations. This issue was recently amended in view of public criticism regarding officers' employment terms.

10. DIRECTORS' LIABILITIES, LIABILITY INSURANCE,

INDEMNIFICATION

10.1 What are the directors' responsibilities and liabilities under the law? Can those liabilities be covered by insurance? Can it be indemnified by the company or other related parties?

As mentioned, the two main duties of directors and officers towards the company are the duty of trust and the duty of care.

The Companies Law refers to several measures which can be taken to reduce the risk to which the company's directors and officers are exposed: indemnification, exemption from liability and insurance.

In order for a company to exempt its directors, indemnify them or purchase directors' and officers' insurance, the company must include a special provision in its bye-laws allowing the exemption, indemnification or insurance.

Indemnification

The Companies Law allows a company to indemnify a director or officer for financial liability which has been imposed on him due to acts perpetrated in his capacity as a director or officer. In addition, a company may indemnify its directors and officers in respect of reasonable expenses including lawyers' fees which the directors and officers incurred, including defence costs incurred within the framework of a criminal prosecution in which he was acquitted or convicted of an offence which does not require proof of criminal intent.

In addition, a company is permitted to indemnify its directors and officers for legal expenses incurred by them during an investigation or proceedings conducted against the directors and officers by an authorised authority which was concluded without filing a criminal indictment, and without imposing monetary liability (ie fine or penalty) on the directors and officers as an alternative to criminal prosecution.

Insurance

A company is permitted to purchase a directors' and officers' insurance policy which insures the liability of its directors and officers only in respect of acts or defaults which fall within the closed list allowed under the law to be insured:

- Loss or damage which derives from breach of duty of care towards the company or any other third party.
- Loss or damage which derives from breach of duty of trust towards the company, provided that the directors and officers acted in good faith and had reasonable grounds to assume that such an act would not prejudice the interest of the company.
- A monetary obligation which will be imposed on the directors and officers for the benefit of another person.

Invalid stipulations

The Companies Law states that in the following cases any stipulation in the company's articles relating to indemnification or directors and officers insurance will not be valid:

- in case of breach of duty of trust, except if perpetrated in good faith and the directors and officers had reasonable grounds to assume that such act would not prejudice the interest of the company;
- in the event of intentional or reckless breach of duty of care, except if perpetrated with negligence;
- in case of the directors and officers acting with intention to gain personal profit; and
- in case of fine or penalty which is imposed on the directors and officers.

The Companies Law states that the provisions which determine the conditions according to which the company may indemnify or purchase insurance to its directors and officers are cognitive and cannot be stipulated against.

11. SHAREHOLDERS' DERIVATIVE SUITS

11.1 Is a shareholder's derivative suit provided for by law in your jurisdiction? How is it enforced by the shareholders?

The Israeli law allows a shareholder to file a derivative action on behalf of the company.

In general, a party interested in filing a derivative claim must first approach the company and demand that it take steps to exhaust its rights. Only if the company did not act as required, a derivative claim can be filed. However, the potential plaintiff is not required to approach the company if the organ with the authority to decide whether to file a claim has personal interest in the decision, or if there is reasonable risk that an early approach to the company will risk the ability to recover therefrom.

A derivative claim may be filed only with the court's permission, which will be granted if the court is convinced that the claim serves the company's interest and that plaintiff is acting in good faith.

Technically, the derivative claim is filed together with a motion to approve it, and the court will handle the hearing of the claim in two stages: first, it will rule regarding the motion to approve the derivative claim, and only if the derivative claim is approved; second, the court will rule as to its merit.

The Companies Law sets a monitory incentive to plaintiff and his attorney for filing derivative claims. In addition, the Law prohibits a plaintiff from withdrawing a derivative claim which has been filed or to reach a settlement with the defendant, without receiving the court's approval.

Amendment 16 of the Companies Law allows the ISA to financially support the filing of derivative suits. In addition, the said amendment allows the plaintiff to request disclosure of documents from the company prior to the filing of the derivative suit.

11.2 Have there been any recent relevant court cases on the subject?

Recently, several motions to file derivative actions were approved by Israeli courts. For example:

- The court approved a motion to file a derivative action against a company's CEO due to remuneration which he received and which was not properly approved by the company – D.A. (Tel Aviv) *Efrat v Ben Shaul.*

- The court approved a motion to file a derivative action alleging that the company's directors were negligent while approving a transaction for the purchase of real estate in Eastern Europe – D.A. (Central) 11266-07-08 *Shtavinski v Pasifica.*

12. SOCIAL INTEREST IN CORPORATE BEHAVIOUR

12.1 How is a company in your country expected to deal with the following issues? Corporate social responsibility; gender, racial and social diversification; environmental issues; ecology and corruption?

Section 11 of the Companies Law, which deals with the purpose of the company, allows the company to take into consideration the public interests. In addition, it allows companies to donate reasonable sums for an appropriate purpose, even if such donation exceeds the business considerations meant to maximise the company's profits.

In addition, companies, like any other legal entity, must operate in accordance with the laws, including employment laws, environmental laws and so on.

In the past few years there has been a growing interest in the social responsibility of corporations, and there are several Israeli banks and public companies which have started to implement active social responsibility plans.

Italy

Claudio Visco & Ernesto Pucci
Macchi di Cellere Gangemi

1. GENERAL PRINCIPLES

1.1 What are the general principles of corporate governance in your jurisdiction? What are the main objectives of corporate governance principles in your jurisdiction? State also whether your legal system is based on common law or civil law.

Under Italian law, the general principles of corporate governance include 'interest of the company', 'shareholder interest', 'stakeholder interest', 'good faith', 'duty of loyalty', 'fiduciary principles', 'duty of skill', 'negligence', 'care', 'honesty', 'fairness' and 'transparency'. Namely, according to the Italian Civil Code, directors are required to fulfil their duties with the diligence required by the nature of the appointment and their specific competences. They have to act in the interest of the company, the shareholders and stakeholders.

However, Italian law does not sanction directors for committing errors, even in the case of serious errors that more competent and capable directors would possibly not have committed, but only provides for the respect of the duty to manage their company with diligence and to refrain from acting in conflict of interest or without disclosing the existence of an interest in the specific matter, even though not conflicting with those of the company. This principle is similar to the 'business judgment rule' applied in Anglo-Saxon jurisdictions.

Directors' responsibility is only triggered with the breach of their fiduciary duties and responsibilities and not as a result of management errors or wrong business decisions.

As to listed companies, the principle of 'equal treatment' applies. According to this principle, directors of listed companies must guarantee the same terms and conditions to all holders of a class of listed financial instruments.

The main objective of corporate governance is regulating the ownership and control structures of the company, the composition and functioning of the board of directors and the executive committees, monitoring the remuneration and performance of the directors and executives, the operations of the company, the relationships between the various stakeholders (shareholders, board of directors, control bodies, such as internal and external auditors, etc.) involved and the transparency as to disclosure of any interest the directors' may have in the company's affairs. As to listed companies, access by all shareholders to information regarding the company should be guaranteed; listed companies must make available to all holders of financial instruments the tools and information necessary for the exercise of their rights.

Moreover, Consob (ie the Italian securities and financial market regulator) exercises its supervisory powers on listed companies/issuers of listed financial instruments having regard to the investors' protection and to the efficiency and transparency of the market.

The Italian legal system is based on civil law. Nonetheless, as a result of the globalisation of the markets and of the legal services, some concepts which were originally developed in common law jurisdiction systems have been applied to Italian corporate law.

1.2 Have there been any recent developments in the law, codes and rules of corporate governance?

The tendency of rules concerning corporate governance is that of an evolution from the attention that was essentially focused on the interests of the shareholders to an increasing appreciation of all the stakeholders involved, with the subsequent upgrade of the area of responsibility of the company. Signs of this tendency are the importance given to independent directors, disclosure of interests, control bodies' role and rights of minority shareholders. The corporate governance legal framework has greatly improved as a result of the 2003 reform. The reform introduced, *inter alia*, a clearer distinction between joint stock companies (S.p.A.s) and limited liability companies (S.r.l.s), a new regime of the S.p.A.s based on the different level of distribution of shares to the public; three models of corporate governance for S.p.A.s, a well-structured definition of roles and duties of the company's bodies, a new definition of group of companies based on the activity of direction and coordination, and a simple and a clearer discipline of extraordinary transactions such as, for example, mergers or reorganisations of companies.

1.3 Outline recent court cases and incidents involving corporate governance issues. Were there any significant corporate scandals or large unlawful corporate cases?

During the first decade of this century, following Enron, two major scandals (Cirio and Parmalat) affected Italian large corporates and drove a deep reform of the Italian corporate governance rules. These two cases highlighted the lack of effective control systems, ethical codes and proper disclosure rules as to directors' interests in the business of the company. The enactment and full implementation of the Legislative Decree No. 231/2001 which introduced in Italy a sort of administrative/criminal liability of corporate entities requiring the latter to adopt internal organisational models capable of preventing the commission of certain crimes by their employees, contributed significantly to develop a 'culture', especially within large corporates and listed companies.

1.4 Which law enforcement agency is in charge of enforcing corporate governance? May a criminal sanction be levied upon

infringement of the corporate governance rules?
There is no agency in charge to enforce corporate law – only courts can enforce it. However, listed companies fall under the general supervision of Consob and, to a limited extent, *Borsa Italiana*.

Yes, there could be liabilities for the individual directors, officers or directors of the companies in case of violation of certain corporate governance rules such as – for example – false corporate statements, (*'false comunicazioni sociali'*), false statements in prospectus (*'falso in prospetto'*), false statements in the reports or notification by the external audit companies (*'falsità delle relazioni o nelle comunicazioni delle società di revisione'*), blocked control (*'impedito controllo'*), crime against the false capital formation (*'formazione fittizia del capitale'*), unlawful restitution of capital contributions (*'indebita restituzione dei conferimenti'*), market manipulation (*'aggiotaggio'*), and so on.

To this effect, it is important to consider that under the above-mentioned Legislative Decree No. 231/2001, the above infringement may also cause an administrative liability of the company if carried out by officers, representatives or other individuals acting on behalf of, in the interest of, or to the advantage of the company.

In particular, the penalties consist in monetary fines, confiscation and banning measures, which can be imposed also as a precautionary measure.

2. SOURCES OF LAW

2.1 Which laws, codes or statutes govern company structures and organisations? Are there statutes like the Companies Act or other forms of law? Is there much relevant case law?

The primary source of law related to company structures and organisation is the Civil Code; as for listed companies, the legal framework is mainly given by the Legislative Decree No. 58/1998 (TUF), the relevant implementing provisions issued by Consob and self-regulatory codes.

Though the Italian system is a civil law system, case law assumes an extremely important role providing an interpretation of the applicable regulations. In particular, it is worth mentioning the decisions issued by the Supreme Court (ie, Court of Cassation), which has, *inter alia*, the function of providing a consistent interpretation of laws and regulations.

2.2 Which laws, codes or statutes regulate capital markets in your jurisdiction?

The legal framework governing capital markets is a double-level scheme based on the self-regulation of companies within a statutory framework, where the self-regulatory provisions are allowed within the general rules set out by the laws and the regulatory provisions issued by Consob. In particular, the legal framework includes:

- general rules issued within the EU framework (a number of directives and regulations, for example, MiFID Directive, Directive No. 206/73/CE, Regulation No. 1287/2006/CE, etc.);
- Part III of the TUF;

- the relevant implementing provisions issued by Consob, the Ministry of Economy and Finance (MEF) and the Bank of Italy; and
- the provisions issued by the companies managing regulated markets.

Finally, it is worth mentioning the letter circulars, communications, opinions published by the supervisory authorities or by the companies managing regulated markets, even though they are not formally part of the legal framework.

2.3 Are there any public interest laws which apply to or influence corporate governance?

As pointed out, the trend in Italian corporate governance is that of increasing consideration towards the various stakeholders. Given this perspective, even the above-mentioned Legislative Decree No. 231/2001 has witnessed the extension of the list of crimes that may lead to the entity's criminal liability (eg crimes against the personality of individuals such as slavery, dealing with juvenile pornography or other similar crimes; environmental crimes such as the disposal of wastes in breach of the applicable law and regulatory provisions, safety at work; etc.).

The TUF and Consob implementing provisions lay down a regime to protect the balance between genders in the board of directors of listed companies. According to these provisions, the company by-laws set forth that the directors are appointed on the basis of a criterion that ensures a balance between genders. The less-represented gender must be equal to at least one-third of the number of the elected directors. This regime applies for three consecutive mandates. In case of non-compliance, Consob warns the company to comply with it within the maximum term of four months and, subsequently, Consob may apply a fine (from EUR 100,000 up to EUR 1,000,000). In the event of further non-compliance with respect to the new warning, the members elected lose their position. Similar rules apply also to companies controlled by public administrations.

2.4 Have there been any recent developments in any of the above laws? What are the recent changes to the above laws or rules and the reasons for such changes?

The most recent development in corporate law is the discipline concerning 'innovative start-ups', which sets out a number of derogations from the general regulations applicable to corporate governance, recapitalisation (possibility to carry forward the loss of the year or defer recapitalisation); reduced requirements for employment contracts for the start-up period; tax benefits for investments in such companies and incentive schemes and stock options issued by them; support measures on internationalisation, and company risk management; and non-applicability of bankruptcy procedures (only the segregation of the assets applies). There are also exemptions at the incorporation stage concerning the stamp and secretarial duties to be paid to the Company's Register and annual fees to be paid to the Chamber of Commerce.

These derogations apply to non-listed companies incorporated and governed by Italian law (or European companies) under the following limitations: (i) the majority of the corporate capital and voting rights of the ordinary shareholders must be held by individuals; (ii) the status of innovative start-up is limited to four years; (iii) the company's main office must be located in Italy; (iv) the total amount of the annual production shall not exceed EUR 5 million; (v) the companies are prohibited from distributing dividends for the above-mentioned four years; and (v) the company's corporate purpose must be limited to the development and marketing of innovative products or services having a high technological value.

In order to be considered as innovative start-ups, the companies need to fulfil certain prerequisites, such as having incurred research and development expenses equal to or exceeding 30 per cent of the higher value between total expenses and production value; at least a third of the employees and consultants should hold, or should be pursuing a research doctoral degree; the company must be the owner of or have title to at least one industrial patent right relating to an industrial or biotechnological invention, etc.. Innovative start-ups can also finance their activities by raising capital through online portals (so-called 'crowd-funding'). The relevant discipline is set forth by the TUF and by the relevant implementing provisions.

In 2012 a new type of S.r.l. company has been introduced which makes the incorporation easier and cheaper for young entrepreneurs (up to 35 years old). Its specific feature is a very favourable regime about amount of share capital required for the incorporation (ie the minimum amount of capital required is EUR 1).

Furthermore, the legislator increased the competence of the special divisions of the intellectual property courts, creating the so-called 'companies' courts' whose jurisdiction concerns, *inter alia*, S.p.A.s' claims (eg, shareholders and the related rights, actions to claim the invalidity of shareholders' resolutions, shareholders' agreements, derivative suits, etc.).

3. SHAREHOLDERS AND THE SHAREHOLDERS' MEETING

3.1 How are shareholders' interests represented in the company? How are the shareholders assured exercise of their rights? What is the highest governing body within the company structure if it is not the shareholders' meeting?

The interests of the shareholders/quota-holders are represented by shares. Each shareholder is assigned a number of shares in proportion to the corporate capital subscribed and for a value not exceeding that conferred; however the by-laws may provide for a different allocation of shares. The shares cannot be divided.

Every share attributes a right to vote. The by-laws may provide for the creation of shares without the right to vote (saving shares), with the vote limited to particular topics, with a right to vote that is subordinated to the verification of specific conditions or with specific privileges in terms of dividends' distribution or impact of losses (preferred shares) etc., it being understood that the value of such shares in total shall not exceed half of the corporate capital. In any case each class of shares shall grant the owners equal rights. In other cases, as in cooperatives companies and in popular banks, each shareholder exercises one vote in the shareholders' meeting, regardless of the value of the participation held.

Shareholders with voting rights attend ordinary shareholders' meetings to resolve upon the approval of the financial statements, the appointment and removal of the board of directors, of the board of statutory auditors and of the outside auditor, the remuneration of the board of directors and of the board of statutory auditors, resolve upon their responsibility and have further rights (see paragraph 3.3 below). Extraordinary shareholders' meetings resolve upon the amendment of the by-laws, the winding up of the company and the appointment and removal of the liquidator. The law provides for minimum attendance and voting quorum, which differs for extraordinary and ordinary shareholders' meetings and for the first and following calls.

As to saving shares, as mentioned, these do not allow their holders to vote at shareholders' meetings but only at special meetings that concern their class of share (in order to appoint a common representative and to adopt any resolution necessary to protect the rights of savings shareholders; see paragraph 3.2 below). In case of bond's issue by S.p.A.s, special meetings of bondholders are also allowed by law to ensure safeguards of their interests.

With regards to S.r.l. companies (which were intended to be a more flexible tool for family owned or close circle businesses), the participation in the company's capital is represented by quotas; there are no share certificates but the ownership is evidenced by an entry in the Company's Register and in the Stock Ledger, as the case may be. The corporate rights are granted in a measure proportionate to the participation held by each quota-holder. The company's by-laws may provide for the allocation of particular rights to individual quota-holders (eg right to appoint a director or an auditor regardless of the participation held in the company, distribution of dividends non-proportional to the participation held, etc.).

To exercise their corporate rights in stock companies, shareholders shall be registered in the shareholders' book; the by-laws may provide the deposit of the shares at the company's registered office a number of days before the date on which the shareholders' meeting is convened. Shares may also be dematerialised; in such a case, a declaration will be issued by the depository company to enable the participation of the shareholders to the meeting. As to listed companies, the shareholders' meeting is convened by notice published on the company's website and in daily newspapers, the board of directors makes a report on each of the items of the agenda available to the public at the company's registered office, on the company website and by other means. Shareholders shall give evidence of the ownership of shares in order to attend to the meeting. Shareholders of listed companies will have the right to ask questions on any item of the agenda during the period preceding the meeting and the directors will be obliged to respond.

Quota-holders of S.r.l. companies need to be registered with the

Company's Register and on the quota-holders' book if the company's by-laws provide for it.

In general terms, shareholders/quota-holders may delegate third parties (with the exclusion of directors, auditors and employees of the company or of controlled companies of the company or of controlled companies) to vote in their name and on their behalf.

The highest governing body is the board of directors both for S.p.A. and S.r.l. companies (see paragraph 4 below for two-tier and single-tier governance systems). Executive committees may also be established. S.r.l. companies may also be governed by a sole director.

3.2 How is the shareholders' meeting conducted? Who may chair the meeting? May attendance (not voting) at the meeting be restricted only to the shareholders? Are the shareholders allowed to be accompanied by legal or other counsel?

Shareholders' and quota-holders' meetings are conducted by the chairman; however, in his absence the chair can be taken by another person in accordance with the provisions of the by-laws. Attendance of third parties to meetings is not regulated by the law – it is common, however, that the chairman authorises it unless the by-laws provide for limitations. Directors and statutory (internal) auditors have the right to participate to shareholders' meetings even though they cannot cast a vote. However, the favourable opinion of the statutory auditors is necessary with respect to specific resolutions. Special meetings (eg bond-holders' meetings) are reserved to the holders of the financial instrument of the specific class. Holders of preferred shares or saving shares as well as bondholders have the right to appoint a common representative to attend shareholders'/special meetings and take actions on their behalf (eg, challenging resolutions of the shareholders' meeting).

Shareholders may grant lawyers with a proxy to attend shareholders' meetings on their behalf. Lawyers may attend the shareholders' meeting together with the shareholder (the representative of the shareholder if this latter is a legal entity) only where authorised by the chairman and provided that there are no limitations to this effect in the by-laws.

3.3 How are minority shareholders' rights protected?

Some rights are guaranteed by the minority shareholders (with reference to specific percentages of the corporate capital), with differences between S.p.A. and S.r.l. companies.

As to S.p.A. companies, the main rights of minority shareholders are:

(i) Minority shareholders that represent at least 1/40 (or a lower quorum provided by the by-laws) of the share capital in listed companies or companies with open capital (ie companies whose shares are widely distributed to a relevant extent), or at least one-fifth (or a different quorum not exceeding one-third as provided by the by-laws) in other companies may file an action for damage against the members of the board of directors, board of auditors, general manager and external auditor who would have caused a damage by fraud or gross negligence misconduct (see paragraph 11.1 below).

(ii) Shareholders representing at least 1/1000 of the capital in listed companies or companies with open capital (the by-laws may reduce or exclude such a percentage), 5 per cent in other companies, may request the tribunal to acknowledge, where applicable, the invalidity of the shareholders' resolutions.

(iii) Shareholders representing at least 1/20 of the capital listed companies or companies with open capital (1/10 or the lower quorum provided by the by-laws in other companies), may request the directors to convene without delay the shareholders' meeting.

(iv) Shareholders attending the meeting representing one-third of the capital may request a postponement of the shareholders' meeting (not more than five days) should they declare that they were not adequately informed on the items to be resolved upon.

(v) Each shareholder, regardless of the participation held in the company, is entitled to report relevant facts (eg breaches of the law or the by-laws, irregularities or conducts which affect the management of the company) to the board of statutory auditors, which shall record them in the board of statutory auditors and in the report to be attached to the financial statements. Should said relevant facts be reported by shareholders representing at least 1/20 of the capital (or 1/50 for listed companies or companies with open capital), the board of statutory auditors is required to promptly investigate them and submit its conclusions and proposals, if any, to the shareholders' meeting.

(vi) Shareholders representing at least 1/10 of the capital (or 1/20 in listed companies or with open capital) may file a claim with the court in case of founded suspects of serious breach of duties by the members of the board of directors or of the board of statutory auditors.

(vii) Shareholders representing at least one-fifth of the corporate capital (or 1/20 in listed companies or with open capital) may oppose the renunciation or the settlement of the action against the directors.

(viii) Shareholders also have the right to withdraw from the company (to obtain reimbursement of the participation's value) if the shareholders' meeting has approved an amendment of the corporate purpose, the transformation of the company, the cancellation or amendment of the withdrawal clause provided by the by-laws, the amendment of clauses of the by-laws which sets the attending and/or voting rights or relates to limitations to the transfer of shares (eg in terms of pre-emption rights), and so on.

In S.r.l. companies, the main rights of the minority quota-holders are:

(i) the minority quota-holders (representing at least one-third of capital) may request the quota-holders' meeting to resolve on matters, other than those reserved by the law to the quota-holders' meeting;

(ii) the minority quota-holders (representing at least one-third of capital) may request the quota-holders' meeting to resolve on a matter, although according to the by-laws the relevant decision can be adopted by written consultation or written consent among the quota-holders; and

(iii) the minority quota-holders (representing at least 1/10 of capital) may oppose the renunciation to or the settlement of an action for damage against the members of the board of directors or of the board of statutory auditors (the action may be proposed by each of the quota-holders regardless of the quota held in the company).

Moreover, regardless of the quota held in the company, quota-holders:

(iv) have the right to be informed by the directors on the course of corporate business and to have access, also through professionals, to the corporate books and other documents relating to the management of the company (provided that they are not vested with the powers to manage the company);

(v) are entitled to challenge resolutions adopted by the quota-holders' meeting in breach of the law or the by-laws (provided that they were dissenting); and

(vi) are entitled to withdraw from the company in the event of resolutions concerning, *inter alia*, amendments in the company's purposes or type of company, transfer abroad of registered office, amendments of the quota-holders' rights, mergers, demerger, amendments to the provisions concerning withdrawal, if the company is incorporated for an undetermined duration or when the duration is extended, if the transfer of quotas to third parties or *mortis causa* is subject to the approval of the other quota-holders (provided that they were dissenting).

3.4 Is shareholder activism encouraged or discouraged? If not encouraged, how is it regulated?

As mentioned, there are significant differences in the provisions applicable to S.p.A. and to S.r.l. companies where the role of the quota-holders can be relevant even in the management of the company. First of all, unless otherwise provided by the by-laws, the company's management may be entrusted to one or more quota-holders. Furthermore, the by-laws may reserve certain decisions to the quota-holders. On the contrary, as to S.p.A.s, shareholders cannot exceed their role, unless they are also appointed as directors.

3.5 How are professional shareholders (those minority shareholders who seek some extra benefit from companies by unduly and habitually influencing management by using their shareholding) treated by the law? Are they excluded from attending the shareholders' meeting? Are they criminally or otherwise publicly sanctioned?

Professional shareholders are not treated by the law; there may be shareholders pursuing these objectives but this is not common as it is in the common law system.

3.6 Are shareholders' benefits given to some of the shareholders by the company without resolution by the shareholders' meeting prohibited or regulated by the law or other rules?

Only shareholders can adopt the resolution upon the distribution of profits. The directors have no powers to give benefits to the shareholders unless the shareholders' meeting has specifically authorised them.

4. DIRECTORS AND BOARD OF DIRECTORS

4.1 What are the functions and responsibilities of the directors and the board of directors? Do you have a one- or two-tier board system? What are the outside directors called?

In S.p.A. companies, the board of directors (or the sole director where applicable) has any and all powers to manage the company and act as necessary for the achievement of the corporate object. The same rules apply to S.r.l. companies unless the by-laws reserve certain decisions to the quotaholders.

As to S.p.A. companies, Italian law provides for three different types of management structures:

(i) The traditional system, which is the predominant system, is based on a board of directors (or a sole director), the shareholders' meeting and a board of statutory auditors; the management of the company is conferred to the board of directors, and the audit of the company to the board of the auditors or to an external auditor, if appointed. In such a case, the board of statutory auditors continues to perform more limited control functions on compliance with the law and internal organisation.

(ii) A two-tier system is a system based on a management board composed of at least two members and a supervisory board composed of at least three members. The by-laws may require the members of both boards to meet independence, integrity and experience requirements. At least one member of the supervisory board shall be enrolled in the register of legal auditors kept by the MEF and all members shall meet the independence requirements provided for the board of statutory auditors. The supervisory board has monitoring powers and a substantial influence over the choices of the management board; namely, it appoints the members of the management board, establishes their compensation, approves the financial statements, can dismiss and file a legal action against them, can file a complaint with the tribunal and reports to the shareholders at least once a year, establish the strategic plans and strategic transactions of the company to be implemented by the management board (the approval is compulsory for listed companies and where provided by the by-laws). Furthermore, the supervisory board has the power to verify the compliance of the company with the law and by-laws, with fair administration principles, the adequacy of the corporate administrative and accounting system adopted by the company as well as its functioning and can investigate on the activities performed by the management board. They are jointly responsible with the members of the management board if the damage would have not occurred should they have duly accomplished their duties.

(iii) A single-tier system, composed of a board of directors and a supervisory committee ('*comitato per il controllo della gestione*') chosen among the members of the board of directors. The members of the board of directors are in charge of the management of the company. At least one-third of its members shall meet the independence requirements set forth for the members of the board of statutory auditors. The by-laws may require its members to meet further requirements.

The members of the supervisory committee are appointed by the board of directors among the members who (i) meet the integrity and experience requirements provided for by the by-laws, and certain independence requirement provided also for the members of the board of statutory auditors; and (ii) do not have, even de facto, managing powers in the company or in controlled or controlling companies. The number of the members of the supervisory committee is established by the board (a minimum of three members is required for listed companies); however, the by-laws may reserve the appointment to the shareholders' meeting. At least one member of the supervisory committee shall be enrolled in the register of legal auditors kept by the MEF. The supervisory committee shall monitor the adequacy of the corporate administrative and accounting system adopted by the company, as well as its capacity to fairly represent the activities carried out by the company, and shall accomplish the duties entrusted to the same by the board of directors and take care of the relationship with the outside auditor. In listed companies, the supervisory committee or its members can call a meeting of the board of directors and of the executive committee.

As for the limited liability companies, the law provides a large possibility of choices: a board of directors or a system where the management is conferred to one or more directors, jointly or severally among them.

The outside directors (the so-called 'independent directors') must possess the independency requirements set out by law (see below, paragraph 4.4).

4.2 What are the rules that may give rise to civil and criminal liability of the director(s)? How are those liabilities sought?

Pursuant to the Civil Code, directors may be liable towards the company, the company's creditors, the shareholders and third parties for breach of their duties. The Civil Code also provides some example of criminal liability of the directors (among others, see those mentioned under paragraph 1.4 above). Special laws provide further liabilities, both civil and criminal (eg tax and social security laws).

Depending on the structure of the companies, these liabilities might be sought by minority shareholders, by the statutory auditors on the basis of their periodical review of compliance, by the company and, in case of insolvency, by the receivers in bankruptcy, special administrators or extraordinary commissioners. For listed companies and in relation to specific administrative and criminal offences Consob has wide powers of investigation and also the power to sanction directors or employees. In case of administrative liability, the sanction is imposed by Consob; in case of criminal liability, Consob reports the information of crime to the competent public prosecutor.

4.3 Does the board of directors have a committee system, eg, nomination committee, compensation committee, audit committee? If not required, is it common practice for companies? How does it function?

In general terms, committee systems are required by law only for listed companies or companies subject to the supervisory authorities because of the nature of their activity (eg banks, financial intermediaries, insurance companies, etc.). In other circumstances, it is not very common to have such committees in place save for multinational companies; the activities of these committees may, but shall not, be regulated by the by-laws.

4.4 Is it a legal requirement to have an independent director or a third-party director? If so, how are they appointed? Is it required for listed companies?

It is a requirement only for listed companies. The TUF (Article 147-*ter*) provides that at least one of the members of the board of directors (or two if the board has more than seven members) shall meet the conditions of independence provided for the members of the board of statutory auditors. Pursuant to Article 148, paragraph 3 of the TUF, the following persons may not be elected as independent directors (or as members of the board of statutory auditors):

(a) interdicts, disabled persons, bankrupt people and persons who have been sentenced to a penalty entailing the disqualification from office;
(b) spouses, relatives and the like up to the fourth degree of kinship of the directors of the company, spouses, relatives and the like up to the fourth degree of kinship of the directors of the companies it controls, the companies it is controlled by and those subject to common control; and
(c) persons who are linked to the company, the companies it controls, the companies it is controlled by and those subject to common control or to directors of the company or persons under (b) by self-employment or employee relationships or by other relationships of an economic or professional nature that might compromise their independence.

Moreover, the self-regulatory code of listed companies (Article 3, paragraph 3.C.1) sets out further independency requirements.

Article 147-*ter* of the TUF provides that the members of the board of directors of listed companies are elected on the basis of lists of candidates and that the by-laws shall establish the minimum quota of participation requested for the presentation of the lists. Pursuant to the same article and to Article 147-*quinquies* of the TUF, the lists shall indicate who among the directors meet the requirements provided by the law and the by-laws (eg: independency, experience and integrity requirements).

Yes, it is required only for listed companies (see above).

4.5 How is the compensation for directors or officers determined? Can it be contested by the shareholders or the regulatory authorities? What are the common rules or practices for the compensation of officers?

The directors' remuneration is established by the shareholders' meeting at the time of their appointment, as a single amount to be subsequently allocated by the board among its members or individually to each of them. The board of directors may resolve upon the remuneration of directors vested with particular roles in the company (eg chairman, vice-chairman, managing director), having previously obtained the favourable advice of the board of statutory auditors (if any). The by-laws, however, may reserve to the shareholders' meeting to set forth the overall amount of such remuneration.

As to listed companies, these are required to communicate to the public by way of an ad hoc report the amount of the remunerations to be awarded to the members of the board and to the officers entrusted with strategic functions at least 21 days before the date the shareholders' meeting is convened for their approval. This report (which shall cover at least the remuneration for the subsequent financial year) shall outline the company's policy on remunerations including the procedures for the implementation of such policy; indicate each of the items of remuneration; and give evidence of any amounts paid or to be paid to the above individuals for any other title or reason and in any form by the company, by the controlled companies and by the controlling company.

Italian law does not define the concept of 'officer'. In practice, with the term 'officers' we often refer to the 'executives' of the companies (so-called '*dirigenti*', ie, those employees who are entrusted with the responsibility of specific functions or departments).

Their remuneration is agreed by the employer and the employee upon hiring and must be consistent with the minimum amounts provided for in the applicable collective labour agreements. These agreements are negotiated at national level by the labour trade unions and the employers' associations and have binding nature also for companies, which are not members of the trade unions which negotiated the same. They determine, *inter alia*, the minimum salary and the other applicable benefits but, as mentioned, employer and employee can always agree on a different salary, provided that it is not lower than that set forth by the agreements.

Pursuant to Article 123-*ter* of the TUF, the shareholders' meeting of a listed company may refuse to approve the report concerning remuneration. See above.

4.6 How will the board handle a corporate crisis like an internal criminal case, violence, social media exposure or dawn raid by the authorities?

There are no rules established – often these aspects are provided at a soft-law level, by the company's codes of internal conduct, internal policies and procedures. Specific rules apply to banks and financial intermediaries. However, companies, which have adopted Legislative Decree No. 231/2001's organisational model, have detailed procedures to avoid execution of certain crimes by their directors and 'officers' and to manage these situations in the event they have nonetheless occurred, including the imposing of sanctions.

5. BOARD OF AUDITORS, AUDIT COMMITTEE, ACCOUNTING AUDITORS

5.1 How is the internal accounting and legal audit structured and conducted? Is an outside accounting audit required and, if so, how is it structured? Are there requirements to change the auditor each five years?

The structure of the internal audit is decided by the board of directors; however, the board of statutory auditors (where appointed) shall verify the adequacy and effectiveness of the corporate administrative and accounting system adopted by the company. For listed companies or companies subject to supervisory authorities because of their activity (eg banks, financial intermediaries and insurance companies, etc.) the law may require the appointment of an internal audit committee. In general terms, the audit committee cooperates with the board of directors to establish the guidelines for the internal audit, verifies its adequacy and functioning, assesses that the main company risks are identified and properly managed; it also, jointly with the board of directors and the external auditors, evaluates: (i) the adequacy of the accounting principles and their consistency with the financial statements; (ii) the work plans of the person(s) in charge of the internal audit of the company and the internal audit reports; and (iii) the remarks made by the board of statutory auditors and by the outside auditors.

As to legal audit, see below.

The accounting audit of company and of the financial statements (so-called 'legal audit') is mandatory for S.p.A companies and S.r.l. companies (the latter only if certain minimum thresholds have been exceeded). It can be performed internally (by the board of statutory auditors or by the single internal auditor ('*sindaco unico*')) or entrusted to an outside auditor, provided they are enrolled in the register of legal auditors kept by MEF. The outside auditor is appointed by the shareholders' meeting on the basis of the motivated proposal submitted to the same by the board of statutory auditors.

The audit is performed in accordance with the principle of Italian law and with Italian Generally Accepted Accounting Principles (GAAP). Once the review has been performed, the auditor issues a report to assess that the financial statements are drafted in compliance with the law and that they reflect in a true and fair manner the profit and losses, and asset situation of the company. This report is submitted to the shareholders' meeting in due time before the same is held to approve the financial statements.

In general, outside auditors can be re-appointed (the usual duration is three years); in case of listed companies the duration shall not exceed nine years and they cannot be re-appointed before a three-year cooling-off period has expired.

In S.r.l. and S.p.A. companies which have the duty to file the consolidated financial statements (or for S.p.A which are listed companies), the legal audit must be performed by outside auditors.

5.2 Do you have supervisory auditors? What is the function of the

supervisory auditors' board?

Yes, we do have supervisory auditors. In the traditional system the supervisory board is the board of statutory auditors (*'collegio sindacale'*); however, the same is not always compulsory for S.r.l. companies (eg: if the corporate capital is lower than EUR 120,000 and other thresholds are not exceeded and when the company does not have the duty to file consolidated financial statements).

The board of statutory auditors has the duty to supervise the compliance of the company with the law and by-laws, its compliance with fair administration principles, to verify the adequacy of the corporate administrative and accounting system adopted by the company as well as its functioning. The members of the board attend both shareholders' and board of directors' meetings, and can, at any time, proceed to inspections and controls. The board can request updates from the directors, also with reference to subsidiaries. Their members are jointly responsible with the directors for the facts or omissions by the latter, when the damage would not have occurred if they were acting in conformity with their duties. The board shall, *inter alia*, issue a report on the financial statements which is submitted to the shareholders' meeting in due time before the approval of the financial statements. The board can also receive claims by shareholders if the latter deem that the directors may have violated their duties and, where provided by the law, report the violation to the tribunal and/or to the competent supervisory authority.

The same rules provided for external auditors apply to the appointment and re-appointment of the board of statutory auditors.

The supervisory auditors' functions are carried out by the supervisory board in the two-tier governance system and by the supervisory committee in the one-tier governance system (see paragraph 4.1 above).

6. MARKET DISCLOSURE/TRANSPARENCY TO THE SHAREHOLDERS AND THE PUBLIC

6.1 What are the disclosure requirements for companies in your jurisdiction under company law, capital markets law or any other rules?

In general terms, the most important information concerning a company (date of establishment, head office, branches, object of the activity, persons entitled to act on behalf of the company, etc.) and most of the company's acts (deed of incorporation, by-laws, extraordinary resolutions of the shareholders' meetings, etc.), must be filed with the Company's Register which shall make them available to the public upon request (also in electronic form); specific documents are made available to shareholders at the company's offices. Furthermore, certain specific elements which identify the company (registration number, company's office, parties exercising direction and control over the company) must be indicated in the company's letterhead and on the company's website. S.p.A.s may have the duties to publish additional information in the *Official Bulletin* (*Gazzetta Ufficiale*).

Listed companies are subject to a wider regime of disclosure contained in the TUF and in the Consob relevant implementing provisions. Consob publishes on its website much of the information concerning the ownership (shareholders holding, directly or indirectly, more than 2 per cent of the share capital, shareholders' agreements, etc.); share capital, members of the companies' bodies, communication of the parent company on transactions on the shares of the Italian listed subsidiary.

Disclosure requirements for listed companies include a large set of information, which is made available to the public and communicated to Consob. In general, the company shall disclose certain periodic information concerning the company (report of the board of directors, members of the companies' bodies, annual financial report, financial statements, audit report, etc.) and information related to certain transactions carried out by the company (such as, for example, mergers, spin-offs, acquisitions, transactions with related parties, conversion of shares, capital increases, etc.). Furthermore, listed companies disclose to the public the information that may have an impact on the price of their financial instruments and they have the duty to declare if they adhere to self-regulatory codes.

Borsa Italiana's regulations envisage additional duties of communication upon the company and Consob may require additional disclosure of information to a company when it is deemed necessary to inform the public.

Many disclosure duties are applicable also to companies that control listed companies and to the companies whose shares are widely distributed.

6.2 What is the liability or responsibility of the board in relation to the company's disclosure requirements?

Failure to file information with the Company's Register may entail administrative sanctions. Moreover, the main consequence arising from the failure to file mandatory information with the Company's Register is that the circumstances that have not been filed and registered (eg the fact that a given activity does not fall within the corporate purpose of the company) are not enforceable *vis-à-vis* third parties.

Moreover, failure to comply with the disclosure duties may give rise to a criminal liability for instance for false corporate statements, hindrance to the functions of supervisory authorities, etc. Furthermore, as to listed companies, failure to disclose information that may influence the price of financial instruments is punished with administrative sanctions up to EUR 500,000.

7. M&A AND CORPORATE GOVERNANCE

7.1 Upon an M&A offer, how are the transparency and fairness rules of the company provided under the company and stock market laws and rules?

As for the transparency, the relevant resolutions and documents (eg, the merger plan) describing the merger and the steps to implement the same must be filed with the Company's Register.

Special attention is given to the determination of the exchange ratio between the shares of the merging companies by the respective boards of directors. According to case law, such ratio must be fair and should take into consideration also factual elements which are not strictly related to the companies' assets.

In case of mergers, the law envisages a number of mechanisms to protect shareholders, creditors and bondholders of the interested companies and requires the issue by an expert (chosen by the tribunal for S.p.A.s and by Consob for listed companies) of a report to be filed with the Company's Register. Such a report shall state, *inter alia*, the adequacy of the exchange rate applied to the shares/quotas, the criteria adopted.

Proposals to buy, sell, exchange and underwrite financial instruments are regulated by the TUF and by Consob implementing regulations. The ratio of the discipline is to protect investors. The main transparency requirement is the prior publication of a prospectus which contains the information that, depending on the characteristics of the financial products and the issuer, is necessary for investors to make an informed assessment of the issuer's assets and liabilities, profits and losses, financial position and prospects and of the financial products and related rights. The prospectus also contains a securities note which briefly gives key information in the language in which the prospectus was originally drafted. The securities note, together with the prospectus, give proper information on the fundamental features of the financial products.

Public offers to purchase or exchange financial instruments are irrevocable and financial instruments are offered at the same conditions to all the holders of the financial products. The offeror can modify the offer and increase the offer price. Articles 41 and 42 of Consob Regulation No. 11971 set out transparency rules and rules of conduct according to which statements and communications regarding an offer shall indicate the person by whom they are issued and be designed to be clear, complete and knowable by all those to whom they are addressed. During the offer period, the provisions set out a specific regime governing communication to Consob and disclosures by the interested parties.

The information the announcement contains must be clear, correct and it must be consistent with the documentation already disclosed and must not be misleading about the characteristics of the operation or the features of the financial instruments involved. A copy of each announcement must be sent to Consob ahead of its publication.

The interested parties shall adhere to principles of proper conduct and equal treatment of those to whom the offer is addressed which are in identical conditions.

8. PROXY FIGHTING

8.1 Is proxy fighting customarily conducted for control of the company management or what other items? How is it regulated under the company law or market regulations?

Proxy fighting is rare in Italy; however, for listed companies it is disciplined by TUF and the relevant implementing provision issued by Consob.

The request to more than 200 shareholders to obtain the proxy to vote on specific proposals or the request accompanied by recommendations, declarations or other indications that may influence the exercise of vote is defined as 'solicitation'. The promoter shall distribute a prospectus and a proxy form. The prospectus indicates, *inter alia*, proposals for which the solicitation is to be carried out and the relevant reasons, information on the company and the promoter, information on any financing received by the promoter (if any), according to a scheme set out by Consob's regulation. In essence, as a general rule, the information sent out during a solicitation or collection of proxies must enable shareholders to make an informed decision.

Under the Italian law, requests for proxy by shareholders' associations are not regarded as solicitation provided that the shareholders' associations, targeting their own members, (i) are incorporated by means of a notarial private deed, (ii) do not exercise business activities other than those directly instrumental to the purpose of the association, and (iii) are composed of at least 50 natural persons, each of which owning a number of shares not exceeding 0.1 per cent of the share capital represented by shares with voting rights.

9. OFFICERS' REMUNERATION RULES

9.1 How is remuneration of officers determined? By whom? Is there a role for the shareholders' meeting? Is there any mechanism for an independent body to review and evaluate them?

See paragraph 4.5 above.

9.2 Is the mechanism of officers' remuneration publicly debated?

As to listed companies, any plans of remunerations based on the distribution of financial instruments (such as stock options) shall be made available to the shareholders before the shareholders' meeting. The officers' remuneration is publicly debated to the extent that the officers will receive such financial instruments. Furthermore, in the event of public offers, the law provides disclosure obligations on the company *inter alia* with reference to the assignment of financial instruments to the top officers.

10. DIRECTORS' LIABILITIES, LIABILITY INSURANCE, INDEMNIFICATION

10.1 What are the directors' responsibilities and liabilities under the law? Can those liabilities be covered by insurance? Can it be indemnified by the company or other related parties?

Directors are civilly liable towards (i) the company due to failure to fulfil the duties set out by law and by the by-laws of the company; (ii) the company's creditors due to failure to comply with the rules concerning the protection of the company's capital; and (iii) the individual shareholders and third parties who are directly damaged by their behaviour. In addition, directors may be held liable for various criminal or administrative offences related to their role/duties (for example, the offences of false corporate statements, false statements in prospectus, false statements in the reports or notification by the external audit companies, etc.). Civil damages and negligence (other than serious negligence or wilful misconduct) may be covered by insurance, while fines arising from criminal offences or administrative offences cannot be covered by insurance. The company can indemnify only civil sanction and not criminal and administrative offences.

11. SHAREHOLDERS' DERIVATIVE SUITS

11.1 Is a shareholder's derivative suit provided for by law in your jurisdiction? How is it enforced by the shareholders?

Yes, a shareholder's derivative suit is provided for by law against a company's directors, statutory auditors, general manager and external auditor. In particular, derivative actions against the mentioned persons due to the failure to fulfil the obligation set out by law or the by-laws may be brought by:

- the shareholders' meeting or the statutory board of auditors (pursuant to Article 2393 of the Civil Code); and
- minority shareholders (pursuant to Article 2393-*bis* of the Civil Code).

As already explained above, derivative actions of minority shareholders may be exercised by shareholders representing the thresholds indicated under paragraph 3.3(i) above for S.p.A.s. Shareholders appoint one or more representatives for the exercise of the action and the execution of the relevant acts. As mentioned above (see paragraph 3.3(vii)), shareholders representing at least one-fifth of the corporate capital or 1/20 in listed companies or with open capital may waive or settle the claims against the responsible persons.

A single shareholder or a third party is entitled to sue for damages the company's director for non-contractual liability, pursuant to Article 2395 of the Civil Code. Company creditors are also entitled to bring action against the directors under certain circumstances (pursuant to Article 2394 of the Civil Code).

Finally, bankruptcy receivers or extraordinary commissioners may exercise such action on behalf of bankruptcy estates.

11.2 Have there been any recent relevant court cases on the subject?

There is a wide range of case law on the matter – it is worth mentioning, among the others, the Court of Milan's decision which on 27 October 2011 limited the directors' liability in accordance to the so-called 'business judgment rule'. The Court of Milan stated that directors cannot be responsible for wrong business decisions and judges are not allowed to dispute the merits of decisions regarding management. Directors' liability is only triggered with the breach of the fiduciary duties and responsibilities and not as a result of management errors.

12. SOCIAL INTEREST IN CORPORATE BEHAVIOUR

12.1 How is a company in your country expected to deal with the following issues? Corporate social responsibility; gender, racial and

social diversification; environmental issues; ecology and corruption?
In a broad sense, the Legislative Decree No. 231/2001 mentioned above could be regarded as a form of corporate social liability as it introduced the duty to implement an organisational model in order to prevent a wide range of criminal offences, including offences against individuals – such as slavery, dealing with juvenile pornography – or environmental crimes.

Corporate social responsibility is the integration carried out by companies on voluntary basis of social, environmental issues in the commercial transactions and in relationships with the interested parties. An efficient strategy of corporate social responsibility goes beyond the legal duties of the company and is performed on voluntary basis. For example, the company may be known for the actions carried out in social fields, especially, in order to encourage the consumers' goodwill. This can be done by integrating social and environmental requests with the corporate practices, with actions aimed at protecting the environment, building relationships with local institutions, participating to the solution of social problems or through an accurate choice of suppliers.

Japan

Hiroki Kodate **Anderson Mori & Tomotsune**

1. GENERAL PRINCIPLES

1.1 What are the general principles of corporate governance in your jurisdiction? What are the main objectives of corporate governance principles in your jurisdiction? State also whether your legal system is based on common law or civil law.

The general principles of corporate governance in Japan are the interest or value of the company. In this context, as the company is owned by the shareholders, the shareholder interest ought to be respected and given the first priority. In addition, the interests of various other stakeholders of the company, such as employees, creditors and trade counterparties should also be taken into account.

The legal system in Japan is based upon civil law.

1.2 Have there been any recent developments in the law, codes and rules of corporate governance?

Although there is no requirement in the law that at least one independent director be appointed at a listed company, it is expected that new rules of the Tokyo Stock Exchange will require listed companies to make efforts to appoint at least one independent director.

1.3 Outline recent court cases and incidents involving corporate governance issues. Were there any significant corporate scandals or large unlawful corporate cases?

Olympus Corporation, a major optical equipment maker headquartered in Japan, had long covered losses on investments dating back to the 1990s. This accounting scandal was precipitated in October 2011 when a British president of the company, who had been inquiring certain M&A transactions that it subsequently turned out that the company had previously used to manipulate accounting treatments, was removed by the board of directors of the company. Thereafter, the company's stock price plunged while rumour had it that the Tokyo Stock Exchange would disqualify the company from listing its shares on it. Consequently, the listing of its shares on the Tokyo Stock Exchange was maintained to the benefit of the general investors, although the net assets of the company diminished by more than JPY 50 billion as a result of ratification of the company's accounts.

1.4 Which law enforcement agency is in charge of enforcing corporate governance? May a criminal sanction be levied upon

infringement of the corporate governance rules?

The Financial Services Agency of Japan is in charge of enforcing corporate governance as it relates to disclosures required under the Financial Instruments and Exchange Act.

A criminal sanction may be levied upon violation of the corporate governance rules in relation to disclosures required under the Financial Instruments and Exchange Act.

2. SOURCES OF LAW

2.1 Which laws, codes or statutes govern company structures and organisations? Are there statutes like the Companies Act or other forms of law? Is there much relevant case law?

The main sources of law for company structures and organisations are the Companies Act. In addition, the rules of stock exchanges are also relevant in relation to corporate governance of listed companies. Further, principally in the context of disclosures, the Financial Instruments and Exchange Act importantly regulates listed companies. There is not much relevant case law in respect of corporate governance.

2.2 Which laws, codes or statutes regulate capital markets in your jurisdiction?

The Financial Instruments and Exchange Act most importantly regulates capital markets in Japan.

2.3 Are there any public interest laws which apply to or influence corporate governance?

There are no public interest laws which much influence corporate governance in Japan.

2.4 Have there been any recent developments in any of the above laws? What are the recent changes to the above laws or rules and the reasons for such changes?

See paragraph 1.2 above. In addition, it is expected that a bill to amend the Companies Act will sooner rather than later be submitted to the Diet, the Japanese legislative body, which will change some of the rules relating to corporate governance. One of these changes of note is, coupled with the tightening of definition of 'external' director; introduction into the Companies Act of a 'comply or explain' regime with regard to appointment of at least one external director typically at a listed company. Another change of note is the adoption of a third system of corporate governance in addition to the conventional system of statutory auditor and the committee system, details of which are set out in paragraph 4.1 below. This third system resembles the committee system in that there are no statutory auditors required but differs from it as instead of establishing three distinct committees, ie, the audit committee, the nomination committee and the compensation committee, only the audit committee is required to be set up. The changes discussed above partly stem from increasing recognition of importance of independent directors.

3. SHAREHOLDERS AND THE SHAREHOLDERS' MEETING

3.1 How are shareholders' interests represented in the company? How are the shareholders assured exercise of their rights? What is the highest governing body within the company structure if it is not the shareholders' meeting?

The highest governing body within the company is the shareholders' meeting. The shareholders elect the directors by resolutions of the shareholders' meeting. The shareholders of a listed company are generally able to exercise their voting rights either in person or by proxy at the shareholders' meeting or by casting their votes by mail or via the Internet.

3.2 How is the shareholders' meeting conducted? Who may chair the meeting? May attendance (not voting) at the meeting be restricted only to the shareholders? Are the shareholders allowed to be accompanied by legal or other counsel?

The shareholders' meeting is conducted physically. The chairman of the meeting is typically the president or the chairman of the company. Generally speaking, attendance at the meeting is restricted only to the shareholders. Depending upon the company's policies, the shareholders are either allowed or not allowed to be accompanied by legal or other counsel.

3.3 How are minority shareholders' rights protected?

Minority shareholders are granted various rights depending upon how many per cent of the total votes they hold. For example, a shareholder holding 1 per cent or more of the total votes (or 300 votes or more) may, *inter alia*, propose one or more agenda items for any general meeting of shareholders. Further, a shareholder holding 3 per cent or more of the total votes may, among others, ask for convocation of a general meeting of shareholders and inspect financial records. Finally, a shareholder holding 10 per cent or more of the total votes may propose dissolution of the company.

3.4 Is shareholder activism encouraged or discouraged? If not encouraged, how is it regulated?

Shareholder activism is at least not discouraged. For a few years immediately before the financial crisis occurred, many more incidents of shareholder activism had been seen in Japan as compared with the years prior to that period of time, such as shareholders demanding larger dividends. However, since the financial crisis, the level of shareholder activism has continued to be moderate, keeping pace with the level of activity of foreign funds in Japan.

3.5 How are professional shareholders (those minority shareholders who seek some extra benefit from companies by unduly and habitually influencing management by using their shareholding) treated by the law? Are they excluded from attending the shareholders' meeting? Are

they criminally or otherwise publicly sanctioned?
These professional shareholders are not excluded from attending the shareholders' meeting. However, those shareholders who knowingly receive, or request for receipt of, economic benefits from the company or its subsidiaries in connection with exercise of rights of shareholders may be criminally sanctioned.

3.6 Are shareholders' benefits given to some of the shareholders by the company without resolution by the shareholders' meeting prohibited or regulated by the law or other rules?
See paragraph 3.5 above. In addition, regardless of whether resolved by the shareholders' meeting, the equality among the shareholders needs to be achieved unless there is a justifiable reason. Therefore, depending upon the relevant facts, it may be that shareholders' benefits given to some of the shareholders by the company are prohibited.

4. DIRECTORS AND BOARD OF DIRECTORS

4.1 What are the functions and responsibilities of the directors and the board of directors? Do you have a one- or two-tier board system? What are the outside directors called?
The functions and responsibilities of the directors are (i) to decide on execution of business of the company and (ii) to monitor execution of duties of the management. Currently, there are two systems of corporate governance: the statutory auditor system and the committee system. The statutory auditor system is a two-tier board system where the directors execute the management of the company and the board of directors is monitored by the board of statutory auditors, at least a half of the members of which consist of external statutory auditors. On the other hand, the committee system is a one-tier board system where three distinct committees, ie, the audit committee, the nomination committee and the compensation committee, are set up under the board of directors. Each of the committees comprises three or more directors, of which external directors constitute the majority.

4.2 What are the rules that may give rise to civil and criminal liability of the director(s)? How are those liabilities sought?
The directors owe the duty of care and the duty of loyalty to the company. Therefore, the directors are liable to the company for damages arising from a breach of their duty of care or duty of loyalty. The directors are also liable to third parties for damages arising from wilful misconduct or gross negligence of the directors in performing their duties. The directors are criminally liable if, among other things, the directors violate their duty of care or duty of loyalty with the intent of seeking their own benefits thereby causing damages to the company. Civil liabilities of the directors to the company can be sought by way of shareholders' derivative suits. On the other hand, only the public prosecutors can prosecute criminal liabilities of the directors.

4.3 Does the board of directors have a committee system, eg, nomination committee, compensation committee, audit committee? If not required, is it common practice for companies? How does it function?

As regards the committee system, it is required by law to establish the three committees mentioned in paragraph 4.1 above. Under the statutory auditor system, it is not required by law to have such a committee of the board of directors, but in practice, it is often the case that the company establishes a nomination or compensation committee which is commonly designed to play an advisory role as against the board of directors on the nomination or the compensation of directors and typically consists of not only external directors (if any), but also managers of other companies, lawyers or consultants who are necessarily directors of the company.

4.4 Is it a legal requirement to have an independent director or a third-party director? If so, how are they appointed? Is it required for listed companies?

It is not a legal requirement to have an independent director or a third-party director. See also paragraph 1.2 above.

4.5 How is the compensation for directors or officers determined? Can it be contested by the shareholders or the regulatory authorities? What are the common rules or practices for the compensation of officers?

Under the statutory auditor system, the compensation for directors (who concurrently serve as officers in most cases) is commonly determined by a resolution of the shareholders' meeting. On the other hand, under the committee system, the compensation for officers and directors is determined by a resolution of the compensation committee, but not to be contested by the shareholders. Under either system, the compensation for officers or directors cannot be contested by the regulatory authorities. Conventionally, the compensation of officers is not much linked to results of operation of the company. However, it is getting common that performance-linked compensation is put in place for officers, such as stock options.

4.6 How will the board handle a corporate crisis like an internal criminal case, violence, social media exposure or dawn raid by the authorities?

There are no specific laws regulating this issue. For instance, in the case of an internal criminal matter, depending upon the nature thereof, it is, in practice, often the case that the board of directors sets up a third-party committee which is intended to investigate into the matter and report the findings to the board of directors. It is common practice that the directors seek advice from lawyers in the event of any corporate crisis.

5. BOARD OF AUDITORS, AUDIT COMMITTEE, ACCOUNTING AUDITORS

5.1 How is the internal accounting and legal audit structured and conducted? Is an outside accounting audit required and, if so, how is it structured? Are there requirements to change the auditor each five years?

An outside accounting audit is required of a listed company. The management of the listed company is responsible for preparation of financial statements and an outside accounting firm or accountant audits these financial statements. It is generally required to change accountants in charge every seven years.

5.2 Do you have supervisory auditors? What is the function of the supervisory auditors' board?

See paragraph 4.1 above.

6. MARKET DISCLOSURE/TRANSPARENCY TO THE SHAREHOLDERS AND THE PUBLIC

6.1 What are the disclosure requirements for companies in your jurisdiction under company law, capital markets law or any other rules?

Listed companies are subject to continuous disclosure obligations under the Financial Instruments and Exchange Act. More specifically, listed companies are required to file with the authorities annual securities reports and quarterly securities reports, as well as extraordinary reports when and as certain specified significant events occur. In addition, under the rules of stock exchanges, listed companies are obliged to make timely disclosures when and as certain specified significant events occur.

6.2 What is the liability or responsibility of the board in relation to the company's disclosure requirements?

The directors are civilly and criminally liable for false statements in annual securities reports and other statutory documents required pursuant to the continuous disclosure obligations under the Financial Instruments and Exchange Act. In addition, the directors may be liable under the theory of tort or otherwise if the company makes false statements in public announcements made pursuant to the timely disclosure rules under the stock exchange rules.

7. M&A AND CORPORATE GOVERNANCE

7.1 Upon an M&A offer, how are the transparency and fairness rules of the company provided under the company and stock market laws and rules?

In the case of M&A transactions involving conflicts of interest, such as a merger between the parent and a listed subsidiary, heightened disclosure is required pursuant to the Financial Instruments and Exchange Act and/or the stock exchange rules. Further, it is becoming common practice that the board of directors sets up a third-party committee which is designed to play an advisory role as against the board of directors in terms of fairness of the transaction in question, and typically consists of external directors/statutory auditors, lawyers and certified public accountants.

8. PROXY FIGHTING

8.1 Is proxy fighting customarily conducted for control of the company management or what other items? How is it regulated under the company law or market regulations?

Proxy fighting is not customarily conducted for control of the company management or otherwise. See paragraph 3.4 above for the level of shareholder activism. Other than the appointment of directors, the amount of dividends is a common item for which proxy fighting is conducted. Proxy fighting is primarily regulated under the Financial Instruments and Exchange Act from a disclosure perspective.

9. OFFICERS' REMUNERATION RULES

9.1 How is remuneration of officers determined? By whom? Is there a role for the shareholders' meeting? Is there any mechanism for an independent body to review and evaluate them?

See paragraph 4.5 above. Under the statutory auditor system, there is no statutory mechanism for an independent body to review and evaluate remuneration of directors (who concurrently serve as officers in most cases), but some companies voluntarily have a compensation committee (see paragraph 4.3 above).

9.2 Is the mechanism of officers' remuneration publicly debated?

Recently, remuneration of the management of the company has increasingly been publicly debated. However, it should be noted that remuneration of the top management of listed companies in Japan is generally much lower than in, for instance, the USA.

10. DIRECTORS' LIABILITIES, LIABILITY INSURANCE, INDEMNIFICATION

10.1 What are the directors' responsibilities and liabilities under the law? Can those liabilities be covered by insurance? Can it be indemnified by the company or other related parties?

See paragraph 4.2 above. The liabilities of directors can generally be covered by insurance. Indemnification by the company of the liabilities of directors generally is permissible only if certain requirements (eg, a resolution of the shareholders' meeting) are met.

11. SHAREHOLDERS' DERIVATIVE SUITS

11.1 Is a shareholder's derivative suit provided for by law in your jurisdiction? How is it enforced by the shareholders?

A shareholders' derivative suit is provided for under the Companies Act. Plaintiffs' bar has not been much developed and so the number of shareholders' derivative suits is relatively low.

11.2 Have there been any recent relevant court cases on the subject?

The Supreme Court of Japan ruled on 15 July 2010 in a shareholders' derivative suit as to the liability of directors of a company in setting the price of shares of its group company (by which the company purchases such shares), and held that the directors were not liable. Although the purchase price was much higher than the market price, the Supreme Court recognised a broad discretion of directors by applying the 'business judgment rule'.

12. SOCIAL INTEREST IN CORPORATE BEHAVIOUR

12.1 How is a company in your country expected to deal with the following issues? Corporate social responsibility; gender, racial and social diversification; environmental issues; ecology and corruption?

A company, particularly a large, listed company in Japan is increasingly expected to actively deal with these issues. A number of listed companies voluntarily publish corporate social responsibility or other reports to show their commitment to these issues.

Korea

Gene-Oh (Gene) Kim & Heon-Yup Lee **Kim & Chang**

1. GENERAL PRINCIPLES

1.1 What are the general principles of corporate governance in your jurisdiction? What are the main objectives of corporate governance principles in your jurisdiction? State also whether your legal system is based on common law or civil law.

Although the Korean corporate law does not expressly stipulate general principles of corporate governance, generally speaking, many of the principles cited above are recognised in the applicable statutory and case law in Korea (ie, 'interest of the company', 'shareholder interest', 'good faith', 'business judgment rule', 'duty of loyalty', 'fiduciary principles', 'negligence', 'care', and 'fairness', among other things).

One distinguishing feature of the Korean corporate governance regime is that it is generally understood that a company's board of directors (BoD) owes fiduciary duty only to the company (and not to the company's shareholders) and, therefore, directors are supposed to perform their duties for the best interests of the company itself. In this connection, in determining the best interests of the company, the legal commentators generally view that, in principle, the interests of the shareholders should be considered by the directors.

Like other jurisdictions, the Korean corporate governance regime offers various mechanisms to protect the interests of the shareholders in light of possible conflict between the management and shareholders arising from the principal-agent problem. At the same time, in light of the pervasive influence of the *Chaebols* (which are the large business conglomerates in Korea controlled by the members of the founding families), the minority shareholder protection *vis-à-vis* majority shareholders receives substantial attention, as well.

The Korean legal system is based on civil law.

1.2 Have there been any recent developments in the law, codes and rules of corporate governance?

Since the 1997 financial crisis, the Korean government has introduced a number of large-scale changes and reforms in the area of corporate governance, with the goals of improving the transparency and accountability of Korean companies, strengthening the rights of minority shareholders, and instituting systems of oversight in terms of management and financial auditing.

The Korean government's continuing reform initiatives in the corporate governance arena recently took the form of the amendments to the Korean

Commercial Code (the KCC), which took effect in April 2012. The KCC is the statute governing company structures and organisations in Korea. An overview of the principal features of the amendment that relate to corporate governance are described below.

First, the KCC newly introduced the 'executive officer' system that allows companies to choose to appoint an executive officer who will be dedicated to overseeing the executive functions of the company, under the supervision of the BoD. As a result, companies may choose between (i) the traditional system of a BoD plus representative director structure (where the BoD takes the dual role of the executive organ and the supervisory organ) and (ii) the new system of a BoD plus executive officers structure (where the BoD focuses on its supervisory role).

Second, the KCC now prohibits directors of a company from causing certain of their relatives or other third parties from appropriating business opportunities that would be beneficial to the company, unless it is approved by more than two-thirds of the BoD members of the company.

Third, following the amendments, restrictions on self-dealing transactions (which currently apply only to directors) apply to directors and major shareholders, certain relatives of such directors and major shareholders, as well as affiliated companies. Such self-dealing transactions have to be approved by more than two-thirds of the board members and must be fair.

Fourth, the KCC now provides for reduced liability exposure of directors. Prior to these amendments, the KCC did not provide for reduction in director liability, except to allow shareholders to unanimously resolve to exempt a director from liability. The KCC now limits directors' liability to their most recent annual salary multiplied by six (in the case of outside directors, the multiple is three); however, such limitation will not apply to damages resulting from a director's wilful misconduct or gross negligence.

Fifth, the KCC provides for a 'compliance officer' system for all listed companies of a certain size, whereby the companies are required to implement compliance control regulations and to appoint a compliance officer responsible for monitoring compliance with such regulations.

In addition to the foregoing, the Ministry of Justice (the MoJ) is preparing further amendments to the KCC addressing corporate governance, with the goal of introducing them by 2015. The key measures will be to (i) limit the influence of the controlling shareholder over the process of selecting members of the audit committee; (ii) mandate the nomination of executive officers for listed companies of certain size; and (iii) permit multiple derivative suits.

Moreover, other bills are currently pending before the National Assembly to address the corporate governance of financial institutions in response to corporate scandals arising out of embezzlement or fiduciary duty violation by the controlling shareholders of financial institutions. The lawmakers are discussing the following reform measures, among other things: (i) imposing minimum outside director requirement for financial institutions; (ii) requiring the board approval to appoint executive officers performing major functions, such as strategy or finance; (iii) specifying the minimum service term of two years for a compliance officer or a chief risk officer; and (iv) establishing requirement for a periodic review of their major shareholder qualifications.

Finally, to address the issue of the concentration of economic power in the hands of the *Chaebols*, the National Assembly is currently reviewing possible amendments to the Monopoly Regulation and Fair Trade Law (the FTL), which is the primary anti-trust and competition law in Korea. It is contemplated that the proposed amendments will address matters relating to corporate governance of *Chaebol* companies such as (i) reinforcing disclosure requirements, (ii) prohibiting new circular ownership and (iii) encouraging holding company structure for greater transparency.

1.3 Outline recent court cases and incidents involving corporate governance issues. Were there any significant corporate scandals or large unlawful corporate cases?

Recent court cases in Korea involving corporate governance have addressed fiduciary duty violation by company directors as one of the major issues. Under Korean corporate law, a director who breaches his or her fiduciary duties will be liable for damages suffered by the company resulting from the breach. In addition to civil liability, a director can be subject to criminal penalty if he or she commits an intentional breach of his or her fiduciary duty. In this regard, some court cases found fiduciary duty violation in the context of companies with sole shareholders, while others examined whether fiduciary duty violation must be based on actual damages or upon a finding that there existed a reasonable likelihood of damages arising from the alleged wrongdoing.

In particular, the issue of fiduciary duty violation has been at the heart of recent cases concerning leveraged buy-out (LBO) transaction structure, which has been utilised in Korea since the early 2000s. With the Korean Supreme Court ruling in 2006 that an asset-backed type LBO (ie, the target company's assets are provided as collateral for the acquirer's acquisition financing) could result in a breach of fiduciary duty triggering criminal liabilities under Korean criminal law, the debate has continued with respect to the legitimacy and risks of LBO transactions in Korea.

In this regard, the Supreme Court recently held that it was not unlawful for the acquirer to utilise a special purpose company to finance an LBO, and post-closing, to upstream cash from the target to the special purpose company via a capital reduction and dividend-out of the target company in order to repay the acquisition financing.

Please note that the above-mentioned decision is the first Supreme Court decision where a capital reduction or dividend-type LBO was at issue and the directors were found to be not guilty of a breach of their fiduciary duty. However, since the Supreme Court stated that the decision should not be interpreted to have upheld an LBO's legitimacy per se. In this regard, the jurisprudence in this area appears to be evolving and the specific facts and circumstances of the case will likely have a key influence on the outcome of the case.

1.4 Which law enforcement agency is in charge of enforcing corporate governance? May a criminal sanction be levied upon infringement of the corporate governance rules?

The primary law enforcement agencies in charge of enforcing corporate governance are the MoJ and the prosecutor's office. In addition, the Korea Fair Trade Commission plays an active role in regulating the conduct of large companies, including those belonging to the *Chaebols*, in the context of restraining concentration of economic power, one of its duties under the FTL.

Criminal sanctions may be levied upon violation of certain corporate governance rules, including violation of fiduciary duty.

2. SOURCES OF LAW

2.1 Which laws, codes or statutes govern company structures and organisations? Are there statutes like the Companies Act or other forms of law? Is there much relevant case law?

The KCC is the primary statute governing company structures and organisations in Korea.

For the listed companies, the Financial Services and Capital Markets Act (the FSCMA) provides additional regulatory framework that prevails over (or supplements) the KCC. In case of companies in certain regulated industries (eg, financial services, telecommunications and broadcasting), the applicable laws for those industries often establish additional corporate governance rules.

Also, the FTL prescribes certain requirements for the corporate governance of companies belonging to large conglomerates. The FTL has a set of provisions which aim to lessen the concentration of economic power in the hands of the large conglomerates by, among other things, banning cross-shareholding and cross-debt guarantees among affiliates, controlling undue financial assistance between affiliates and providing for a board approval requirement for affiliate transactions.

Although Korea is a civil law jurisdiction, there is a significant body of civil and criminal case precedents concerning corporate governance matters, which functions as an important guide for interpreting and applying the relevant statutory provisions.

2.2 Which laws, codes or statutes regulate capital markets in your jurisdiction?

The FSCMA regulates the capital markets in Korea. The FSCMA regulates the following businesses: (i) the securities and derivatives brokerage business; (ii) the securities and derivatives dealing business; (iii) the collective investment business; (iv) the investment advisory business; (v) the discretionary investment management business; and (vi) the trust business.

Any company that engages in any of the above businesses for Korean residents in Korea will be subject to the FSCMA. The FSCMA also governs activities conducted outside of Korea if the effects of such activities extend to the territory of Korea.

In addition, the FSCMA regulates all financial products with a risk of loss in the invested amount as 'financial investment products' (except deposit and insurance).

2.3 Are there any public interest laws which apply to or influence corporate governance?

The primary public interest laws comprise the FTL, the FSCMA and the Securities-Related Class Action Act.

In addition, as discussed above, the fiduciary duty violation by a director can be punished as criminal conduct in certain cases. Specifically, directors could be indicted for (i) breach of fiduciary duty under the criminal law or (ii) special breach of fiduciary duty under the KCC. Depending on the amount involved, breach of fiduciary duty under (i) above may be subject to more severe punishment under the Act Concerning Aggravated Punishment of Specific Economic Crimes.

2.4 Have there been any recent developments in any of the above laws? What are the recent changes to the above laws or rules and the reasons for such changes?

See paragraph 1.2 above concerning the 2012 amendments to the KCC, the FTL, etc.

3. SHAREHOLDERS AND THE SHAREHOLDERS' MEETING

3.1 How are shareholders' interests represented in the company? How are the shareholders assured exercise of their rights? What is the highest governing body within the company structure if it is not the shareholders' meeting?

The general meeting of shareholders is the highest governing body of a company and determines fundamental corporate matters. Each shareholder is entitled to one vote per share. Generally, the exception applies for preferred shares (which may have no voting right) and for treasury stock (which lack any voting rights). The KCC does not recognise dual class stock with multiple votes for a particular class of stock, and does not permit a particular shareholder to have the casting vote or the power to veto.

The powers of the general meeting of shareholders are circumscribed to those matters specifically provided for in the KCC or the articles of incorporation (AoI) of the company. Depending on the importance of the corporate action in question, a simple majority or super-majority (or even unanimous consent for very exceptional matters) will be required, as prescribed in the KCC and the AoI.

Specifically, certain matters such as election of directors or declaration of dividends must be authorised by an 'ordinary' resolution of the shareholders, which refers to a resolution adopted by a majority of the shares present, representing one-fourth or more of the total number of the shares issued and outstanding. Other fundamental corporate actions such as an amendment of the AoI, merger, dissolution of the company, removal of a director or transfer of an important business asset require a super-majority and must be authorised by a 'special' resolution of the shareholders, which must be adopted by two-thirds or more of the votes of the shareholders present, representing one-third or more of the total number of the shares issued and outstanding.

3.2 How is the shareholders' meeting conducted? Who may chair the meeting? May attendance (not voting) at the meeting be restricted only to the shareholders? Are the shareholders allowed to be accompanied by legal or other counsel?

The general meeting of shareholders may be convened by a resolution of the BoD. In some limited circumstances, a company's minority shareholders, a statutory auditor of such company or a court may also convene a general meeting of shareholders of such company. The shareholders may exercise their votes by proxy or in writing, subject to certain requirements under the KCC.

The question of who presides over the general meeting of shareholders as the chairperson is addressed by the AoI of the company, and it is customary practice for a company's representative director to fulfil such role. It is also possible at a general meeting of shareholders to select the chairperson by shareholder vote.

Since the KCC is generally silent on the manner for proceeding with a general meeting of shareholders, it is possible for matters necessary for holding the shareholders' meeting to be determined pursuant to shareholder vote or by the company's AoI.

It is not customary to find restriction on attendance at a shareholders' meeting, including prohibition on a legal counsel accompanying a shareholder to the shareholders' meeting to provide assistance.

3.3 How are minority shareholders' rights protected?

Minority shareholders in Korea are afforded rights in proportion to their share ownership ratio, with the KCC specifying the relevant ownership thresholds at which the various prescribed rights become exercisable. Examples of the types of rights afforded to minority shareholders include: (i) the right to propose agenda for shareholders' meeting; (ii) the right to demand that the company convene an extraordinary general meeting of shareholders; (iii) the right to bring actions to unwind corporate actions if taken illegally, such as the issuance of new shares or merger; (iv) the right to bring derivative actions; (v) the right to inspect books and records; (vi) the right to apply to court for removal of a director or suspension of a director's authority; and (vii) the right to apply for dissolution of the company.

In some cases, the applicable thresholds are significantly lowered for listed companies. For instance, the right to demand that the company convene an extraordinary general meeting of shareholders requires shareholders holding in the aggregate 3 per cent or more, but in case of listed companies, shareholders with 1.5 per cent of the total number of issued shares continuously held for at least six months can exercise such right.

In addition, under the KCC, certain fundamental actions requires super-majority resolution, and therefore, minority shareholders may have effective veto rights to those actions depending upon their share ownership ratio. In particular, a resolution to discharge or release a director from liability owed to the company may be adopted only by the unanimous consent of all shareholders, and therefore, a shareholder holding at least one share, regardless of the voting right thereof, has an effective veto right to block or prevent such resolution.

3.4 Is shareholder activism encouraged or discouraged? If not encouraged, how is it regulated?

Shareholder activism is generally encouraged in Korea. There are a number of public interest groups that are actively seeking to advance shareholders' rights, monitor the activities of the *Chaebols* and publicly disseminate the results of relevant studies, and provide assistance (including legal assistance) to minority shareholders in bringing derivative suits against companies.

3.5 How are professional shareholders (those minority shareholders who seek some extra benefit from companies by unduly and habitually influencing management by using their shareholding) treated by the law? Are they excluded from attending the shareholders' meeting? Are they criminally or otherwise publicly sanctioned?

At this time, there is no applicable Korean law which expressly addresses 'professional shareholders'. However, under the KCC, the chairperson of a shareholders' meeting is authorised to maintain order at a meeting. Further, such chairperson has the authority to order any person causing undue disturbance at the meeting or intentionally engaging in conduct designed to disrupt the orderly proceeding of the meeting to cease making statements or exit the meeting. It is worth noting that the chairperson is generally expected to exercise his or her powers at the meeting in a deliberate manner, since the validity of relevant shareholder resolution may be challenged if it is later found that the chairperson acted in a manner that unreasonably constrained the exercise of shareholder rights.

In dealing with disruptive conduct by 'professional shareholders' at a shareholders' meeting, one may consider filing a suit for preliminary injunction, civil damages or criminal sanction, depending on the facts of the case.

3.6 Are shareholders' benefits given to some of the shareholders by the company without resolution by the shareholders' meeting prohibited or regulated by the law or other rules?

The concept of equal treatment of shareholders is a fundamental principle in Korean corporate law. Accordingly, any corporate action which violates this principle may be subject to cancellation or nullification for reason of defect in shareholder resolution. Please note that under the KCC, any shareholder having any special interest (eg, personal pecuniary interest) in a shareholder resolution item may not exercise voting right in respect of such item.

4. DIRECTORS AND BOARD OF DIRECTORS

4.1 What are the functions and responsibilities of the directors and the board of directors? Do you have a one- or two-tier board system? What are the outside directors called?

Under the KCC, the BoD of a company occupies the dual role of the executive organ with decision-making authority for important matters and the supervisory organ which exercises oversight over the company's management.

To begin with, under the KCC, all matters concerning management of a company's business including, but not limited to, disposition or transfer of material assets, borrowing a substantial amount, establishment and closing of a branch office, and appointment and discharge of a representative director or executive officers, need to be carried out pursuant to a resolution of the BoD.

Korean legal commentators generally take the position that all of the important matters concerning the management of a company's business are to be decided by a resolution of the BoD unless the KCC or the AoI provide they are to be decided by a resolution of the shareholders. Other matters need not be decided by a BoD resolution but instead may be delegated to another organ or body of the company. In practice, the representative director of the company will be responsible for carrying out the decisions reached by the BoD (or by the representative executive officer if the company adopted the executive officer system).

As mentioned, the BoD has the supervisory authority over the conduct of duties by the directors (including the representative director) of the company. A director may make a demand to the representative director to report to the BoD on the conduct of duties by the other directors or employees, and the directors are required to make a report to the BoD at least once every three months.

Further, a director, as a member of the BoD, participates in the decision-making processes and exercises supervisory oversight over the conduct of the duties by the representative director, among others.

Under the KCC, the directors of a Korean company have various duties and responsibilities towards the company. Such duties and responsibilities include (among others): (i) duty of due care; (ii) duty to be faithful (duty of loyalty); (iii) duty of confidentiality; (iv) duty not to compete with the company; (v) duty against self-dealing; and (vi) duty against appropriation of business opportunities.

The representative director has the general power and authority to represent the company in dealings with third parties, to execute commitments in the name of the company, and to manage the general affairs of the company in the ordinary course of business subject to the general policy and resolutions of the BoD and general meeting of shareholders.

Finally, in case a company adopts the executive officer system pursuant to the 2012 amendment to the KCC, the executive officers are required to carry out the executive role played by the representative director and the management, with the BoD exercising supervisory oversight over the executive officers.

Korean law only recognises a one-tier board, although a BoD may have committees composed of certain directors within it as further discussed in paragraph 4.3 below.

Outside directors in Korea are referred to as *'Sa-Woe-Ee-Sa'* (the term *'Ee-Sa'* means 'director' in Korean), and more direct translation of it is 'outside directors'. The definition of an outside director under Korean law is a director who does not engage in the business of the company on a full-time basis and who does not meet any of the disqualification criteria listed in the relevant statute (such as being the largest shareholder, being declared bankrupt or being an officer of the company).

The duties and responsibilities of directors under the KCC apply equally to both inside and outside directors of the company. In other words, the standard for satisfying such duties and responsibilities are not heightened or lowered for an inside director or an outside director (as the case may be).

4.2 What are the rules that may give rise to civil and criminal liability of the director(s)? How are those liabilities sought?

Article 399 of the KCC sets forth the fundamental principles concerning the civil liability of directors of a Korean company. It provides that if the directors of a company act in contravention of the requirements of law, government regulations or the AoI of the company, or if they neglect to perform their duties, they will be jointly and severally liable for damages incurred by the company as a result such actions or omissions. If such actions were taken pursuant to a BoD resolution, all of the directors who voted for such resolution will be jointly and severally liable. By law, the directors are required to compensate the company for all damages suffered by the company that have a reasonable causal connection to the improper act.

In this regard, if the company does not take proper action to seek damages from the directors, shareholders can initiate a derivative suit as provided in the KCC (see paragraph 11.1 below for further discussion concerning shareholders' derivative suits).

Furthermore, under the KCC, if it appears likely that a director will commit an action that violates the law, government regulations or the AoI of the company, and that the company will suffer irreparable harm as a result, a shareholder(s) holding 1 per cent or more of the total number of issued and outstanding shares of the company (in the case of a listed company, the threshold is lessened) may demand that the director desist from the action in question. Such demand can be made either through or outside of a lawsuit.

In order to protect third parties, the KCC provides that a director will be liable to a third party for any damages incurred by the third party as a result of the director's neglect of his/her duties to the company if such neglect results from wrongful intent or gross negligence. This liability is joint and several for all directors involved in the decision-making process, and in the event of any action taken pursuant to a resolution of the BoD, the directors who voted for such resolution will be jointly and severally liable.

In this regard, directors could be exposed to criminal liability (as well as civil liability) in case of their failure to fulfil their fiduciary duties (eg, breach of trust under the Korean Criminal Code). For directors to be found criminally liable, they would have to be shown to (i) have acted with 'intent' and (ii) either benefited themselves or caused a third party (eg, shareholders) to benefit, resulting in damages or 'threatened damages' to the company. Please note that the above element of 'intent' can be proven by showing that the directors merely had 'awareness' of or 'recognised the possibility' of causing financial harm to the company.

4.3 Does the board of directors have a committee system, eg, nomination committee, compensation committee, audit committee? If not required, is it common practice for companies? How does it function?

The BoD may establish a committee under the BoD, comprising two or more members, and delegate the BoD's authority to such committee. Upon a BoD committee adopting a resolution, the outcome is notified to each director, and any director receiving such notice may request the convening of a BoD meeting to have the BoD resolve on the matter subject to the committee resolution.

In case of a listed company or a financial institution, the KCC and other applicable laws and regulations mandate the establishment of an audit committee and an outside director nomination committee.

For audit committees, at least two-thirds of the members must be outside directors. The boards of listed and non-listed companies have the discretion to establish other types of committees composed of certain directors, but the AoI must provide for the establishment of such non-mandatory committees.

In practice, large companies will generally establish a number of committees under the BoD to seek enhancement of the efficiency of the BoD function (eg, by establishing a management committee or executive committee, made up of executive directors) or to pursue independence of supervision or decision-making with respect to certain specific matters (eg, by establishing inter-affiliate transaction committee or compensation committee).

4.4 Is it a legal requirement to have an independent director or a third-party director? If so, how are they appointed? Is it required for listed companies?

Under the KCC, a listed company must have at least a quarter of its BoD comprised of outside directors. If a listed company's total asset as of the end of the immediately preceding fiscal year exceeds Korean Won 2 trillion, such company must have at least three outside directors, who must account for at least half of the total number of directors.

Moreover, in the case of financial institutions, the appointment of outside director may be required by applicable law. For example, the Bank Act provides for an exception to this rule in that banks are always required to have 50 per cent or more of the directors as outside directors.

4.5 How is the compensation for directors or officers determined? Can it be contested by the shareholders or the regulatory authorities? What are the common rules or practices for the compensation of officers?

Under the KCC, the maximum amount of the remuneration of directors must be determined at the general meeting of shareholders by an ordinary resolution, unless it is provided for under the AoI. The amount of director remuneration need not be determined for each director at the general meeting of shareholders or in the AoI; instead, in practice, the aggregate ceiling will generally be determined at the shareholders' meeting (or in the AoI), with the individual director remuneration being delegated to the BoD. In the case of management personnel who are not directors, the remuneration will be determined in accordance with the internal regulations or criteria established by the BoD or as otherwise determined by the BoD.

The fairness of director and executive compensation is an issue which has received increasing attention in Korea. If the amount of remuneration is deemed excessive in light of the performance of the person concerned, or the company's financial condition, the decision of the BoD approving such payment may be subject to challenge as being contrary to the interests of the company.

Finally, the Korean government is preparing legislation which will mandate public disclosure of executive compensation exceeding certain threshold in the case of large companies (including listed companies) and financial institutions.

4.6 How will the board handle a corporate crisis like an internal criminal case, violence, social media exposure or dawn raid by the authorities?

How the BoD deals with corporate crisis is a matter which is not the subject of any express statutory provision in either KCC or any other Korean law, and, accordingly, one may find a number of different approaches to handling corporate crisis. For example, one company may have a standing department, such as compliance department, and executive officers having responsibility of handling corporate crisis, while others may establish a special committee upon the occurrence of a crisis.

Also, if the corporate crisis involves the incumbent members of the company management, an organ or committee may be established to handle such crisis, with a view to ensuring independence.

5. BOARD OF AUDITORS, AUDIT COMMITTEE, ACCOUNTING AUDITORS

5.1 How is the internal accounting and legal audit structured and conducted? Is an outside accounting audit required and, if so, how is it structured? Are there requirements to change the auditor each five

years?

Korean companies are required to appoint a minimum of one statutory auditor under the KCC, whose term may not exceed three years. The statutory auditor is appointed at a general meeting of shareholders and supervises the management of the company's business and audits the company's accounts. In particular, the statutory auditor must examine the annual financial documents of a company within four weeks from the date of the receipt of such documents by the directors of the company and prepare an audit report two weeks prior to the opening of the ordinary general meeting of shareholders each fiscal year.

At their discretion, privately held companies may establish an audit committee that functions in place of the statutory auditor. Publicly traded companies whose total assets are Korean Won 2 trillion or more are required to organise an audit committee, for which two-thirds or more of the total members must be outside directors.

Under the Joint Stock Company External Audit Law (the JSCEAL), if a joint stock company (which is a most commonly used form of entity type in Korea), among others, is a listed company or its total assets for the preceding fiscal year were at least Korean Won 10 billion, the company must appoint an outside accounting firm as an independent auditor. The appointed independent auditor will be authorised to conduct a financial audit pursuant to the statutory requirements under the JSCEAL.

A certified public accounting firm may not have the same director of such accounting firm serve in the capacity of an external auditor of a company for more than six continuous fiscal years (four fiscal years in the case of listed companies).

Further, the JSCEAL requires that a joint stock company (excluding non-listed company whose total assets for the preceding fiscal year were less than Korean Won 100 billion) adopt an Internal Accounting Management Regulation at its BoD meeting and appoint one of its full-time directors as the internal accounting manager, who must review the implementation and enforcement of the foregoing system and include the results of such review in its annual report.

5.2 Do you have supervisory auditors? What is the function of the supervisory auditors' board?

By law, each company must have one or more statutory auditors, who serves as an independent watchdog over the management of the company. Alternatively, a company may have an audit committee comprised of three or more directors. The KCC empowers the statutory auditor and audit committee to observe and ensure proper management of the company by the BoD and the representative director.

6. MARKET DISCLOSURE/TRANSPARENCY TO THE SHAREHOLDERS AND THE PUBLIC

6.1 What are the disclosure requirements for companies in your jurisdiction under company law, capital markets law or any other

rules?

See below key disclosure requirements that are more frequently triggered with respect to Korean companies.

First, the KCC requires certain disclosures to be made by the companies. Under the KCC, the following documents must be prepared, kept at the corporation's head office (and branch offices, if any) and made available for inspection by the shareholders and the creditors at least one week in advance of the ordinary general meeting of shareholders: (i) business report prepared by the director(s); (ii) financial statements prepared by the director(s); and (iii) internal audit report prepared by the statutory auditor (or the audit committee if applicable).

Second, under the JSCEAL , any corporation with assets equal to greater than Korean Won 10 billion and any listed corporation must have its financial statements audited by its external auditor and make the external auditor's audit report available to the shareholders at its head office and branch offices.

Third, the FSCMA requires various reports to be made by listed companies and their shareholders.

- In terms of periodic reports, a listed company is required under the FSCMA to submit to the Korea Exchange its annual reports within 90 days of the end of each fiscal year and semi-annual and quarterly reports within 45 days of the end of the applicable quarter.
- Furthermore, under the FSCMA, a listed company is required to promptly report to the Financial Services Commission (the FSC) certain events or BoD resolutions that are enumerated in the FSCMA (the general guideline being that such events or resolutions may affect the investors' decision), ie, non-periodical reports (disclosure of important management information). Such reports filed by listed companies under the FSCMA are made available to the public by the FSC and the Korea Exchange via their websites.
- In addition to the reporting obligations noted above, the FSCMA provides for various reporting obligations for listed companies. For example, a listed company is required to file a prior report with the FSC regarding a contemplated merger. In case of a report on merger, the FSC will review whether the merger ratio is calculated in accordance with the criteria set forth in the relevant regulations. The same kind of reporting requirement is triggered in case of business transfer, spin-off or comprehensive stock swap or the acquisition or disposal of treasury shares.
- When the fair disclosure information provider selectively releases certain information to a specific recipient of fair disclosure information, the applicable listed company is required to notify or report such fact and the contents of such information to Korea Exchange, which is then disclosed to the public.
- Once an investor in a listed company (including specially related persons and other parties acting in concert) holds 5 per cent or more of the voting shares or certain other equity securities issued by such

company, the investor must file a report regarding such acquisition with the FSC within five business days. For the purpose of this report, the investor is deemed to hold the shares upon entering into a share purchase agreement. Where the holdings of the investor reaches 10 per cent or more of the issued and outstanding voting shares of the listed Korean company, a separate report should be filed with the Securities and Futures Commission (the SFC) within five business days, and any change in shareholding must be reported to SFC within five business days of such change.

Fourth, the FTL requires that any large-scale affiliate transaction (ie, those with value of Korean Won 5 billion or greater, or as otherwise prescribed by the FTL) to be subject to BoD resolution and subsequent public disclosure.

6.2 What is the liability or responsibility of the board in relation to the company's disclosure requirements?

In general, the sanction for any failure to comply with applicable disclosure requirement is imposed on the company itself. However, if a director is in charge of the preparation of the disclosure information or submission thereof to the government authorities, and fails to fulfil such duty, then such director may face punishment or sanction under applicable law. Further, according to the general provisions under the KCC regarding director's liability, if any violation of disclosure requirement occurs due to a director's act or omission, then such director may be held liable for damages incurred due to such wrongdoing.

7. M&A AND CORPORATE GOVERNANCE

7.1 Upon an M&A offer, how are the transparency and fairness rules of the company provided under the company and stock market laws and rules?

Korean law does not distinguish between hostile and voluntary takeover bids. They are both subject to the same takeover laws and regulations. The board of the target company is allowed, but not required, to express its opinion on the tender offer. In this regard, the FSCMA requires a tender offer statement to be filed in order to launch a takeover bid for a listed company.

In addition, with respect to LBOs, as discussed in paragraph 1.3 above, although the issue is still developing in Korea, recently there have been a couple of meaningful court decisions which may provide more guidance in relation to structuring an LBO in Korea, and considerations and procedures that the BoD needs to give and take to uphold its fiduciary duty.

8. PROXY FIGHTING

8.1 Is proxy fighting customarily conducted for control of the company management or what other items? How is it regulated under the company law or market regulations?

Proxy fights or solicitation in Korea generally occurs for the purpose of procuring the required quorum for a specific agenda item at a shareholders' meeting (at the initiative of the company or the controlling shareholder), or for the smooth conduct of the shareholders' meeting.

Proxy solicitation is also used to propose an agenda to shareholders meeting or to effectively veto an agenda proposed by the company or the controlling shareholder at the shareholders' meeting, as well. Finally, proxy fights have also been utilised as a means of conducting hostile M&A, in a contest for corporate control.

In all instances, proxy fighting must be conducted in accordance with the prescribed requirements under the FSCMA.

9. OFFICERS' REMUNERATION RULES

9.1 How is remuneration of officers determined? By whom? Is there a role for the shareholders' meeting? Is there any mechanism for an independent body to review and evaluate them?

There is no rule on how to set the remuneration of the most senior management, but the general view is that such remuneration should be decided by the BoD. For remunerations of non-director officers, there is no legal requirement for shareholders' approval. However, in order to be treated as expenses for the purpose of Korean tax law, the remunerations for officers should generally be paid in accordance with the standards set by the AoI or the standards that have been approved by the BoD.

The total amount of remuneration of directors and officers must be disclosed in a company's yearly business report. Although some Korean companies establish a compensation committee under the BoD to determine executive compensation, it is not legally required.

9.2 Is the mechanism of officers' remuneration publicly debated?

The issue of executive compensation has become a topic of increasing public scrutiny and debate in Korea, with certain companies and financial institutions becoming subject to allegations that their directors and management are receiving excessive remuneration. In response, there has been some discussion for regulating such executive pay. Particularly, in the case of the *Chaebols*, there have been some cases where the compensation received by the members of the founding families were challenged as being excessive.

Against this background, legislation is currently pending at the National Assembly regarding whether the compensation of individual directors and officers for certain large companies and financial institutions must also be disclosed.

10. DIRECTORS' LIABILITIES, LIABILITY INSURANCE, INDEMNIFICATION

10.1 What are the directors' responsibilities and liabilities under the law? Can those liabilities be covered by insurance? Can it be indemnified by the company or other related parties?

See the discussion in paragraph 4.2 above concerning director duties and liabilities.

Directors' and officers' (D&O) liability insurance is available in Korea, and the subscription of such insurance policies by companies is common practice in Korea. The risk insured by D&O liability insurance in Korea is the liability of directors and statutory auditors of a company for their breach of duty to the company and the company's shareholders subject to specific terms and conditions of the relevant insurance policies.

For the reduced liability or exemption of liability of directors, see paragraph 1.2 above, discussing the relevant parts of the 2012 amendments to the KCC. As to the indemnity by other related parties based on an indemnity agreement with the directors, in principle, such agreement would be enforceable under Korean law, except under special circumstances. However, indemnification of directors by a company is a developing area under Korean law.

Under Korean law, although a company's payment of D&O liability insurance premium is generally viewed as being permissible, it is unclear whether the company is allowed to indemnify its directors for damages incurred by them due to the performances of their duties or whether such indemnification triggers a breach of fiduciary duty of directors, particularly if such indemnification also covers wilful misconduct or gross negligence of such director.

11. SHAREHOLDERS' DERIVATIVE SUITS

11.1 Is a shareholder's derivative suit provided for by law in your jurisdiction? How is it enforced by the shareholders?

Shareholders' derivative suits are provided for under Korean law.

Specifically, if a company does not take proper action to seek damages from the directors, any shareholder(s) holding 1 per cent or more of the total number of issued and outstanding shares (or, in the case of a listed company such, any shareholders(s) holding 0.01 per cent or more of the total number of issued and outstanding shares for a period of at least six months) may demand in writing that the company initiate a suit to hold the directors liable. If the company does not initiate such suit within 30 days from the date of such demand, the shareholder(s) may initiate an action on behalf of the company against the responsible directors (ie, derivative suit).

11.2 Have there been any recent relevant court cases on the subject?

Shareholders' derivative suits have not yet become a mainstream of the Korean litigation activity. However, there have been a few cases where the NGOs have successfully brought shareholders' derivative suits against certain *Chaebols*, seeking damages for losses arising from related party transactions in the past.

12. SOCIAL INTEREST IN CORPORATE BEHAVIOUR

12.1 How is a company in your country expected to deal with the following issues? Corporate social responsibility; gender, racial and social diversification; environmental issues; ecology and corruption?

By way of background, due to growing domestic legal and social pressures, on the one hand, and to increasing sensitivity to reputation and standing in the global marketplace, on the other, many Korean companies have become aware of the issues such as corporate social responsibility, gender, racial and social diversification, environment, corruption, among other issues which did not receive much management attention in the past.

In particular, with the current administration putting a significant emphasis on advancing the interests of the small- and medium-sized enterprises and those economic actors which have occupied positions of inferior economic power in the Korean society, there has been a policy orientation from the government to encourage large businesses to help stimulate the growth and support the viability of such entities aiming at a 'win-win' outcome. Moreover, anti-corruption and other compliance issues referred to above are receiving increasing regulatory and legislative attention, reflecting the changing needs and demands of the Korean society at large.

Given the foregoing, Korean companies are expending greater resources to address the social responsibility and compliance matters due to the changing environment.

Malaysia

Kar Han Lim, Hui Yee Leong & Eng Yeow Lee
Zaid Ibrahim & Co

1. GENERAL PRINCIPLES

1.1 What are the general principles of corporate governance in your jurisdiction? What are the main objectives of corporate governance principles in your jurisdiction? State also whether your legal system is based on common law or civil law.

The corporate governance framework in Malaysia comprises a myriad interlinked legislation and codes (see paragraph 2.1 below). The general principles of corporate governance are statutorily codified into the Malaysian Companies Act 1965 (Companies Act). The legal system in Malaysia is principally based on common law.

Under the Companies Act, every director of a company is under a duty to, at all times, exercise his powers for a proper purpose and in good faith in the best interest of the company. It also describes the manner in which a director is expected to make business judgments. This is further discussed in paragraph 4 below.

The Securities Commission Malaysia (SC) launched the Capital Market Masterplan 2 (CMP2) to expand the role of the capital market in invigorating national economic growth. The SC recognises in the CMP2, that growth is only sustainable if it is underpinned by a proper system of accountabilities and governance. Strengthening corporate governance therefore represents one of the key thrusts to reinforce investor confidence in the Malaysian capital market.

In 2011, the SC released the Corporate Governance Blueprint 2011 (Blueprint) which provides the action plan to raise the standards of corporate governance in Malaysia by strengthening self and market discipline and promoting greater internalisation of the culture of good governance.

1.2 Have there been any recent developments in the law, codes and rules of corporate governance?

The Malaysian Code on Corporate Governance 2012 (MCCG) was issued pursuant to the Blueprint; it sets out the broad principles and specific recommendations on structures and processes which companies should adopt in making good corporate governance an integral part of their business dealings and culture. While the MCCG is specifically targeted at companies listed on the stock exchange, all companies are encouraged to adopt the principles and recommendations of the MCCG and make good corporate governance an integral part of their business dealings and culture.

The exposure draft of the Companies Bill 2013 (Companies Bill) was made available for public consultation and comment in July 2013. The Companies Bill proposes a major and far-reaching reform of the structural framework of companies and is drafted based on policy statements and guiding principles, including:

- simplifying internal decision-making processes;
- strengthening the corporate governance structure: in relation to the affairs of the directorship of a company; through refinement of the auditors' role and responsibilities; and by enhancing and refining rules pertaining to transactions involving directors and substantial shareholders;
- reinforcing the roles, functions and obligations of company secretaries;
- enhancement of shareholders' rights and protection; and
- introducing a comprehensive financial reporting framework which is in line with international accounting standards and practices.

1.3 Outline recent court cases and incidents involving corporate governance issues. Were there any significant corporate scandals or large unlawful corporate cases?

Accounting irregularities

- Accounting irregularities (eg inflated sales and fictitious transactions) were discovered in the accounts of a public-listed cargo carrier. In 2011, two directors sitting on the company's audit committee were sentenced to one year's imprisonment and a fine of RM 300,000 for having authorised the furnishing of a misleading statement to Bursa Malaysia in the company's quarterly report. The judgment of that case emphasised that the audit committee had specific duties, functions and responsibilities, which were relied upon heavily by the investing public. The judge stated that the evidence showed a blatant disregard for the seriousness of the concerns raised by the auditors that certain transactions of the company were unusual and lacked commercial justification.
- In mid-2011, the auditors of a public-listed bakery and confectionery manufacturer company expressed concerns over the validity and recording of certain transactions, for which the auditors were unable to obtain relevant supporting evidence and satisfactory explanations from the management of the company.
  The former managing director and the former executive director of the company were sued by the company for alleged breach of fiduciary duties, breach of duty of fidelity and loyalty, abuse of power, conspiracy to commit fraud, and for facilitating a misappropriation of funds.

Making of a prohibited loan

- In June 2013, a director was convicted of committing offences under section 132(1) (which provides that a director shall at all times exercise his powers for a proper purpose and in good faith in the best interest of the company) and section 133A(1)(a) (which prohibits loans to persons connected to a director) of the Companies Act, when he authorised the making of a RM 500,000 loan to a company, in which he was a majority shareholder, without the approval of the lender-company's board of directors.

1.4 Which law enforcement agency is in charge of enforcing corporate governance? May a criminal sanction be levied upon infringement of the corporate governance rules?

Enforcement of corporate governance is jointly undertaken by a number of regulators including the Companies Commission of Malaysia (CCM), the Malaysian Anti-Corruption Commission, the SC and the Royal Malaysian Police. Financial institutions are further regulated by the Central Bank of Malaysia. Criminal sanctions may be levied depending on the nature of the infringement.

2. SOURCES OF LAW

2.1 Which laws, codes or statutes govern company structures and organisations? Are there statutes like the Companies Act or other forms of law? Is there much relevant case law?

The Companies Act (and its subsidiary instruments) is the primary legislation governing companies in Malaysia. However, there are additional codes and rules which supplement the Companies Act:

- Capital Markets and Services Act 2007 (CMSA);
- MCCG;
- Malaysian Accounting Standards Board's (MASB) Approved Accounting Standards;
- the Code of Ethics for Company Directors (issued by CCM); and
- the Code of Ethics for Company Secretaries (issued by CCM).

Some legislation impose direct responsibility on directors and officers with respect to the company's compliance with certain obligations. For example, under the Employees Provident Fund Act 1991 and the Employees' Social Security Act 1969, the directors of a company are jointly and severally liable for contributions due and payable to the Employees Provident Fund and the Social Security Organisation by such company that remains unpaid.

Additional laws may apply depending on the nature of the company's business (eg financial institutions are subject to the Financial Services Act 2013 and the Islamic Financial Services Act 2013).

Public companies listed on the Main Market of Bursa Malaysia are bound to observe, among others, Bursa Malaysia's Listing Requirements (Listing Requirements). Chapter 15 of the Listing Requirements sets out corporate governance requirements that must be complied with by a listed issuer and its directors. In order to assist directors of listed companies with corporate governance best practices, Bursa Malaysia has published the *Corporate Governance Guide: Towards Boardroom Excellence*.

Civil and criminal cases have been brought before the courts in connection with corporate governance issues.

2.2 Which laws, codes or statutes regulate capital markets in your jurisdiction?

The primary legislation regulating capital markets in Malaysia is the CMSA and its subsidiary legislation. The SC also issues guidelines and circulars from time to time to effect the operation of the CMSA. The Listing Requirements apply to companies listed on the stock exchange, which among others, requires listed companies to make continuous disclosures with respect to certain types of information.

2.3 Are there any public interest laws which apply to or influence corporate governance?

The legislative trend in Malaysia leans towards imposing responsibility for compliance on directors and officers of the company. Examples of public interest legislation with corporate governance elements include:

- the Employment Act 1955;
- the Occupational Safety and Health Act 1994;
- the Environmental Quality Act 1974;
- the Anti-Money Laundering and Anti-Terrorism Financing Act 2001; and
- the Personal Data Protection Act 2010.

The Whistleblower Protection Act 2010 prohibits the taking of any detrimental action against persons making disclosures of improper conduct in the public and private sectors.

2.4 Have there been any recent developments in any of the above laws? What are the recent changes to the above laws or rules and the reasons for such changes?

The introduction of the MCCG reinforces Malaysia's aim of strengthening corporate governance. The current MASB framework was made in conjunction with the MASB's plan to converge with the International Financial Reporting Standards (IFRSs) in 2012.

The exposure draft of the Companies Bill 2013 has recently been made available for public consultation and comment (see paragraph 1.2 above).

3. SHAREHOLDERS AND THE SHAREHOLDERS' MEETING

3.1 How are shareholders' interests represented in the company? How are the shareholders assured exercise of their rights? What is the highest governing body within the company structure if it is not the shareholders' meeting?

Shareholders' rights and interests are regulated by a company's articles of association (articles) and the provisions of the Companies Act. Where a company has in its articles a provision that delegates the management of the company's business to the directors, then as a general rule, the shareholders may not usurp such powers.

However, the Companies Act provides that certain proposals or transactions of the company shall remain subject to shareholders' approval.

Under section 132C of the Companies Act, an ordinary resolution of the shareholders of the company in a general meeting is required for disposals by directors of a substantial portion of the company's undertaking or property, or the acquisition of an undertaking or property of a substantial value.

Section 132E of the Companies Act provides that an ordinary resolution is also required for any substantial property transaction of a non-cash asset of a requisite value with a director or a substantial shareholder. The interested director or substantial shareholder is required to abstain from voting on the resolution in relation to the transaction or arrangement in the general meeting. The Listing Requirements also impose similar restrictions for related party transactions.

The Companies Act provides that certain proposals or transactions require the prior approval of the shareholders in a general meeting by way of a special resolution (ie of at least 75 per cent of the voting members). These include proposals:

- to alter the memorandum and articles of association;
- to convert a public company to a private company or vice versa;
- to reduce the share capital of a company;
- to pay interest out of capital in certain cases;
- to appoint an inspector to investigate a company's affairs; and
- to effect the winding-up of a company.

3.2 How is the shareholders' meeting conducted? Who may chair the meeting? May attendance (not voting) at the meeting be restricted only to the shareholders? Are the shareholders allowed to be accompanied by legal or other counsel?

General meetings of shareholders must be convened and conducted in accordance with the articles of the company. The articles may provide for appointment of the chairman of such general meeting.

The Companies Act provides that a general meeting called the 'annual general meeting' must be held once in every calendar year, and not more than 15 months after the holding of the last preceding annual general meeting. Certain matters must be conducted during such annual general meeting, eg the tabling of the company's profit-and-loss account and balance sheet, and the appointment of auditors.

All other general meetings of shareholders convened are known as 'extraordinary general meetings'. Extraordinary general meetings may be convened by the board, as it sees fit, or on the requisition of members in accordance with the Companies Act. In addition, the High Court also has the power to order such a meeting of a company.

Shareholders' meetings are typically private to the shareholders and the company. There are no specific provisions in the Companies Act which regulate who may attend a shareholders' meeting. Advisers may attend at the invitation of the company.

3.3 How are minority shareholders' rights protected?

Supermajority approval

For examples of proposals and transactions that require approval by way of shareholders' special resolution, see paragraph 3.1 above.

Remedy for oppression

Section 181 of the Companies Act provides judicial relief if: (i) the company's affairs are conducted or the directors' powers are exercised in a manner oppressive to one or more of the members or holders of debentures or in disregard of the interests of the member(s), shareholder(s) or holder(s) of debentures; or (ii) some act of the company has been done or is threatened or some resolution has been passed or is proposed which unfairly discriminates against or is otherwise prejudicial to one or more members or holders of debentures. When oppression is made out, the court may grant such relief as it thinks fit, including an order to: direct or prohibit any act or cancel or vary any transaction or resolution; regulate the conduct of the affairs of the company in the future; provide for the purchase of the shares or debentures of the company by other members or holder of debentures of the company or by the company itself; in the case of purchase of shares by the company, provide for a reduction accordingly of the company's capital; or provide that the company be wound up.

Contractual agreement

Shareholders may contract by way of a shareholders' agreement as to the rights and benefits of minorities.

3.4 Is shareholder activism encouraged or discouraged? If not encouraged, how is it regulated?

Minority Shareholder Watchdog Group

The Minority Shareholder Watchdog Group (MSWG) was established in 2000 as part of a broader capital market framework to protect the interests of minority shareholders.

3.5 How are professional shareholders (those minority shareholders who seek some extra benefit from companies by unduly and habitually influencing management by using their shareholding) treated by the law? Are they excluded from attending the shareholders' meeting? Are they criminally or otherwise publicly sanctioned?

The Companies Act does not distinguish between 'professional' shareholders and other shareholders, nor does it prescribe for different treatment of professional shareholders.

3.6 Are shareholders' benefits given to some of the shareholders by the company without resolution by the shareholders' meeting prohibited or regulated by the law or other rules?

Provided that the company's memorandum and articles permits the same, a company's share capital may be divided into different classes with different rights, whether in regards to dividend, voting, return of capital or otherwise.

With regards to public companies, the Malaysian Code on Takeovers and Mergers 2010 (Takeovers Code) requires any person involved in a takeover offer, merger or compulsory acquisition to provide fair and equal treatment to all shareholders, in particular, the minority shareholders.

4. DIRECTORS AND BOARD OF DIRECTORS

4.1 What are the functions and responsibilities of the directors and the board of directors? Do you have a one- or two-tier board system? What are the outside directors called?

Functions of the board

Section 131B of the Companies Act states that the business and affairs of a company must be managed by or under the direction of the board, subject to any modification, exception or limitation provided in the Companies Act or the company's articles.

Malaysia practices a single-tier board system; the board is permitted to delegate certain functions to a committee of the board.

Directors' duties

Directors have duties imposed on them under the Companies Act, common law, the company's articles and, where applicable, by contract.

Section 132(1) of the Companies Act provides that a director of a company shall at all times exercise his power for a proper purpose and in good faith in the best interest of the company.

Further, section 132(1A) states that a director should exercise reasonable care, skill and diligence with the knowledge, skill and experience which may reasonably be expected of a director having the same responsibilities and any additional knowledge, skill and experience which the director in fact has.

The Companies Act also codifies the following directors' duties:

- a director who makes a business judgment is deemed to meet the requirements under section 132(1A) and the equivalent duties under the common law and in equity if he makes such business judgment in good faith for a proper purpose; does not have a material personal interest in the subject matter of the business judgment; is informed about the subject matter of the business judgment to the extent the director reasonably believes to be appropriate under the circumstances; and reasonably believes that the business judgment is in the best interest of the company; and
- the duty of the director to be responsible for the actions of a delegate (see paragraph 4.3 below).

Disclosure of interests in contracts, property, offices, etc.

Section 131(1) of the Companies Act requires a director to declare his interest in a contract or proposed contract with the company to the board. Section 131A(1) of the Companies Act prohibits such director from participating in any discussion while the contract or proposed contract is being considered at the board meeting and from voting on the contract or proposed contract.

Types of directors

- *Executive director*: a salaried, full-time working director who is delegated with managerial or executive powers by the board to carry out the day-to-day management of the company's business.
- *Non-executive director*: a director who does not hold any salaried appointment with the company.
- *Independent director*: a director who is independent of management and is free from any business or other relationship which could interfere with his exercise of independent judgement or his ability to act in the best interests of an applicant or a listed company.
- *Non-independent director*: a director other than an independent director.

Under the Listing Requirements, every listed corporation must ensure that each of its directors, chief executive or chief financial officer has the character, experience, integrity, competence and time to effectively discharge his role as a director, chief executive or chief financial officer of the listed corporation.

4.2 What are the rules that may give rise to civil and criminal liability of the director(s)? How are those liabilities sought?

Criminal liability

Breach of the statutory duties set out in section 132 is an offence under the Companies Act, punishable by imprisonment for five years or a fine of RM 30,000. For other examples, see also paragraphs 2.1 and 2.3 above and paragraph 6.1 below.

Civil action by the company

The Companies Act provides that a director who is in breach of section 132 is liable to the company for any profit made by him or for any damage suffered by the company as a result of the breach. Other civil remedies available to the company include suing the director for return of specific property (in the case of misapplication of property) and applying to the court for a declaration that the exercise of power in breach of the director's duties to the company to be invalid.

Shareholders' derivative actions

See paragraph 11 below.

4.3 Does the board of directors have a committee system, eg, nomination committee, compensation committee, audit committee? If not required, is it common practice for companies? How does it function?

Subject to the provisions of the Companies Act, its articles, and any resolution of the board or shareholders, the board may delegate any of its powers. However, there is a presumption that the directors are responsible for the exercise of such delegated powers. The articles of a company would typically have an enabling provision for the directors to delegate any of their powers to committees.

It is not mandatory for a company to have a committee system. However, it is common practice, especially for larger companies, to set up the following committees.

Nominating committee

The MCCG recommends that the board should establish a nominating committee comprising exclusively of non-executive directors, a majority of whom should be independent. The nominating committee shall have the responsibility of overseeing the selection and assessment of directors, reviewing the board's succession plans and facilitating board induction and training programme.

Remuneration committee

The MCCG recommends that the board should establish a remuneration committee which consist exclusively, or comprises a majority of, non-executive directors to establish formal and transparent remuneration policies and procedures.

Audit committee

The MCCG summarises the following as responsibilities of an audit committee:

- to ensure that the financial statements comply with applicable financial reporting standards;
- to create policies and procedures to assess the suitability and independence of external auditors; and
- to review and monitor the suitability and independence of external auditors.

4.4 Is it a legal requirement to have an independent director or a third-party director? If so, how are they appointed? Is it required for listed companies?

The Listing Requirements provide that a listed company must ensure that at least two directors or one-third of its board (whichever is higher) are independent directors. If the number of directors of the listed company is not three or a multiple of three, then the number nearest one-third must be used.

A listed company must establish a nominating committee with the responsibility of identifying suitable candidates; this nominating committee must comprise exclusively of non-executive directors, a majority of whom must be independent.

4.5 How is the compensation for directors or officers determined? Can it be contested by the shareholders or the regulatory authorities?

What are the common rules or practices for the compensation of officers?

See paragraph 9.1 below.

4.6 How will the board handle a corporate crisis like an internal criminal case, violence, social media exposure or dawn raid by the authorities?

The MCCG states that it is the responsibility of the board to identify principal risks and ensure the implementation of appropriate internal controls and mitigation measures and to establish a sound framework to manage risk. The board should task management to prepare plans to handle such contingencies.

5. BOARD OF AUDITORS, AUDIT COMMITTEE, ACCOUNTING AUDITORS

5.1 How is the internal accounting and legal audit structured and conducted? Is an outside accounting audit required and, if so, how is it structured? Are there requirements to change the auditor each five years?

External audit

Every company must have auditors for the main purpose of auditing its accounts and reporting to the members of the company. The initial appointment of an auditor is made by the board at any time before the company's first annual general meeting. Subsequently, the company shall appoint the auditor at each annual general meeting of the company. However, the board is empowered to fill any casual vacancy in the office of the auditor unless such vacancy is created due to the removal of an auditor. There is no requirement for change of auditor for every five years. However, if the client of the auditor is a listed entity, then under the Malaysian Institute of Accountants By-Laws, the lead engagement partner of the audit firm should be rotated every five years.

Internal audit

There is no mandatory requirement for a private limited company to set up an independent internal audit function.

The Companies Act provides that the directors of a public company or a subsidiary of a public company shall have in place a system of internal controls that will provide reasonable assurance that:

- assets of the company are safeguarded against loss from unauthorised use or disposition; and
- all transactions are properly authorised and that they are recorded as necessary to enable the preparation of true and fair profit-and-loss accounts and balance sheets and to give a proper account of the assets.

The MCCG and the Listing Requirements provide that the board of a listed company should establish an internal audit function which reports directly to the audit committee. The head of the internal audit shall be responsible for providing assurances to the board that the internal controls are operating effectively. Internal auditors should also conduct regular reviews and appraisals of the effectiveness of the governance, risk management and internal controls processes within the company.

5.2 Do you have supervisory auditors? What is the function of the supervisory auditors' board?

See paragraph 5.1 above.

6. MARKET DISCLOSURE/TRANSPARENCY TO THE SHAREHOLDERS AND THE PUBLIC

6.1 What are the disclosure requirements for companies in your jurisdiction under company law, capital markets law or any other rules?

While not specifically provided for in the Companies Act, it is a duty of directors to furnish information to shareholders to enable the latter to make informed judgements.

Disclosure of information to shareholders in the usual course of business under the Companies Act

The directors of a company must lay before the company at its annual general meeting a profit-and-loss account for the period since the preceding account (or in the case of the first account, since the incorporation of the company) made up to a date not more than six months before the date of the meeting. A copy of every profit-and-loss account and balance sheet (including every document required by law to be attached thereto) which is to be laid before a company in general meeting accompanied by a copy of the auditor's report, must be sent to all persons entitled to receive notice of general meetings of the company.

If any director of a company fails to comply with the aforementioned requirements or to take all reasonable steps to secure compliance by the company with the same or has by his own wilful act been the cause of any default by the company thereunder, he shall be guilty of an offence under the Companies Act punishable by imprisonment for five years or a fine of RM 30,000, provided that a sentence of imprisonment shall not be passed unless in the opinion of the court dealing with the case, the offence was committed wilfully.

Disclosure of information to shareholders in specific circumstances under the Companies Act

The Companies Act imposes a duty on the company to furnish information to shareholders to assist them in making decisions under specific circumstances, for example:

- directors have a direct duty to explain to shareholders the effects of a proposed scheme of compromise or arrangement; default of this duty renders the company and every officer of the company who is in default guilty of an offence punishable by imprisonment for three years or a fine of RM 10,000;

- in the case of a proposal to remove a director of a public company from office before the natural expiration of his term of office, the company must furnish shareholders with the representations, if any, made by the affected director; and
- in the case of a proposal to remove its auditor, the company is required to circulate the representations, if any, made by the affected auditor.

Instances of public disclosure requirements include:

- *Requirement to issue and register prospectus.* A person is generally prohibited to issue, offer for subscription or purchase, to make an invitation to subscribe or purchase, securities, unless a prospectus in relation to the securities that is in compliance with the CMSA has been registered by the SC. Contravention of this prohibition is an offence, punishable on conviction, by a fine not exceeding RM 10,000,000 or imprisonment for a term not exceeding ten years or both.
- *Forms lodged with the Registrar of Companies.* A company is required to lodge with the Registrar of Companies certain statutory forms reporting the occurrence of certain actions and transactions undertaken by the company (eg the increase of authorised share capital, allotment of new shares, creation and discharge of certain charges, changes to the appointments of directors and secretaries, etc.). Any member of the public may review such documents on payment of a prescribed fee. Every company having a share capital must make a return made up to the date of the annual general meeting of the company in the year or a date not later than the 14th day after the date of the annual general meeting, in the prescribed form, and this return must be lodged with the Registrar of Companies within one month after its annual general meeting.
  Information that must be featured in such return include: a summary relating to the issued share capital of the company; particulars of the total amount of the indebtedness of the company in respect of all charges which are required to be registered with the Registrar of Companies; particulars of directors, managers and secretary(s) of the company that are required by the Companies Act to be contained in the relevant registers; and a copy of the company's last audited balance sheet and profit-and-loss accounts. If a company fails to comply with this requirement, the company and every officer is guilty of an offence under the Companies Act, the default penalty for which is RM 2,000.

Continuous disclosure requirements

In addition to the general requirements set out in the Companies Act above, Chapter 9 of the Listing Requirements sets out the continuing disclosure requirements that must be complied with, among others, by a listed company, its directors and advisors. A listed issuer must disclose to the public, all material information necessary for informed investing, and take reasonable steps to ensure that all who invest in its securities enjoy equal access to such information in accordance with the Listing Requirements.

Except for circumstances provided in the Listing Requirements, a listed issuer must make *immediate public disclosure* of any material information. Information is considered material if it is reasonably expected to have a material effect on the price, value or market activity of any of the listed issuer's securities or the decision of a holder of securities or the listed issuer or an investor in determining his choice of action.

In addition to the obligation to make immediate public disclosures of such material information, a listed issuer must also make periodic disclosures of its interim financial report that is prepared on a quarterly basis, its annual reports that include annual audited financial statements together with the auditors' and directors' reports on the listed issuer. Generally, the information that must be disclosed in an annual report includes:

- the particulars and qualifications of each director and the chief executive officer;
- a chairman's statement which represents the collective view of the board setting out a balanced summary of: the industry trend and development;
- a discussion and analysis of the group's performance during the year and the material factors underlying its results and financial position; and the prospects of the company;
- a narrative statement of the company's corporate governance practices with reference to the MCCG;
- a responsibility statement in respect of the financial year;
- the remuneration of directors for the financial year; and
- the particulars of all sanctions and/or penalties imposed on the company and its subsidiaries, directors or management by the relevant regulatory bodies.

In the event of any breach of any Listing Requirement, Bursa Malaysia may take or impose such actions or penalties as it considers appropriate. Bursa Malaysia will notify the SC of any decision to take or impose any action or penalty referred to in paragraph 16.19 of the Listing Requirements except where the decision is made in consultation with the SC. The types of actions and penalties Bursa Malaysia may take or impose for a breach of the Listing Requirements include:

- in relation to the listed company: issuance of a caution letter or a private or public reprimand; imposition of a fine not exceeding RM 1 million; suspension or trading of the listed securities; and any other action which Bursa Malaysia may deem appropriate, subject to consultation with the SC; and
- in relation to directors or officers of a listed company: issuance of a caution letter or a private or public reprimand; imposition of a fine not exceeding RM 1 million; imposition of a moratorium on or prohibition of dealings in the listed issuer's and/or other listed securities by the relevant director, officer or other person; and any other action which Bursa Malaysia may deem appropriate, subject to consultation with the SC.

6.2 What is the liability or responsibility of the board in relation to the company's disclosure requirements?

See paragraph 6.1 above.

7. M&A AND CORPORATE GOVERNANCE

7.1 Upon an M&A offer, how are the transparency and fairness rules of the company provided under the company and stock market laws and rules?

See paragraph 3.1 above for the Companies Act provision on related party transactions.

Mergers and acquisitions of public companies are regulated by the CMSA and the Takeovers Code issued pursuant to the CMSA which encapsulates principles and rules governing the conduct of all persons or parties involved in a takeover offer, merger or compulsory acquisition of shares.

The Takeovers Code applies to the following offers:

- *Mandatory offer*: a mandatory offer made when an acquirer (including parties acting in concert) has obtained control in a public company or when an acquirer acquires more than 2 per cent of the voting shares or voting rights in that company in any six-month period and such acquirer's holding is more than 33 per cent but not more than 50 per cent of the voting shares or voting rights of the public company during that six-month period.
- *Voluntary offer*: any offer that is not a mandatory offer.

Offer price

In all offers, where the offeror has purchased or agreed to purchase any voting shares or voting rights of the offeree during the offer period at a higher price than that in the offer document, the offeror must increase the price of the offer to not less than the highest price of the voting shares or voting rights that he has purchased or agreed to purchase.

In the case of mandatory offers, the offeror must offer an amount which is not less than the highest price paid or agreed to be paid by the offeror or any person acting in concert with the offeror for any voting shares or voting rights to which the offer relates, within six months prior to the beginning of the offer period.

Announcements and disclosures under the Takeovers Code

A person who is involved in an offer, merger or compulsory acquisition must observe good standards of commercial behaviour so that minority shareholders are given fair and equal opportunity to consider the merits and demerits of the offer, merger or compulsory acquisition. Such person must also provide fair and equal treatment to all shareholders, in particular, the minority shareholders.

The Takeovers Code requires an offeror who makes a takeover offer or proposes a possible takeover offer to immediately announce such takeover offer or possible takeover offer to the public by way of a press notice to at least three main newspapers. After the announcement, the offeror must give a written notice regarding the takeover offer to the board of the offeree, the SC and Bursa Malaysia (if the securities of the offeree or offeror are listed in Malaysia). In turn, the board of the offeree shall make an announcement upon receipt of the written notice from the offeror.

Listing Requirements

The Listing Requirements provides that a listed company must make an immediate announcement to Bursa Malaysia in relation to any information on an offer or possible offer which is required to be announced to Bursa Malaysia under the Takeovers Code. Upon completion of an offer, a listed company must furnish information in relation to its shareholding structure to ensure its compliance with the shareholding spread requirement.

There are also disclosure requirements under the Listing Requirements relating to the acquisition and disposal of assets by a listed company or its subsidiary.

8. PROXY FIGHTING

8.1 Is proxy fighting customarily conducted for control of the company management or what other items? How is it regulated under the company law or market regulations?

Section 149 of the Companies Act provides that a shareholder shall be entitled to appoint another person or persons as his proxy to attend and vote on his behalf at a members' meeting.

Proxy fighting is not specifically regulated in Malaysia. While there are generally no limitations as to who a shareholder may appoint as proxy, there may be indirect restrictions on the appointment of such persons, for example if they are related parties to a transaction.

9. OFFICERS' REMUNERATION RULES

9.1 How is remuneration of officers determined? By whom? Is there a role for the shareholders' meeting? Is there any mechanism for an independent body to review and evaluate them?

Directors

In the absence of a provision in the articles or a shareholders' resolution, a director of a company is not entitled to be paid for his services (*Tengku Dato' Ibrahim Petra bin Tengku Indra Petra & Ors v Perdana Petroleum Bhd (formerly known as Petra Perdana Bhd)* [2013] 8 MLJ 280). However, the articles of a company typically provide for the payment of remuneration of directors to be determined by the company in general meeting.

The Listing Requirements provides that fees payable to a director of a listed company should be a fixed sum and may not include a commission on, or percentage of, turnover. Fees payable to directors should not be increased except pursuant to a resolution passed at a general meeting, where notice of the proposed increase has been given in the notice convening the meeting.

For the MCCG recommendation to establish a remuneration committee, see paragraph 4.3 above. No director is permitted to participate in deciding their own remuneration.

The issue of the amount of directors' remuneration is an internal matter best left to be decided by the members themselves (*Guyler Magruder v Creative Software (M) Sdn Bhd & Ors* [1994] 3 CLJ 450). Unless there is evidence of oppression, it is not the function of the court to question whether payments or remuneration sanctioned by the company are excessive or improper (*Low Tien Sang & Sons Holding Sdn Bhd & Ors v How Kem Chin & Ors* [2000] 2 MLJ 334).

Secretaries

The remuneration of the secretary of a company is usually determined by the directors. The remuneration of a full-time salaried secretary of a company employed under a contract of service is normally provided in his letter of appointment just as any other employee of the company.

9.2 Is the mechanism of officers' remuneration publicly debated?

Not commonly; however, the MCCG recommends for board remuneration policies and procedures to be disclosed in the company's annual report. The Listing Requirements further require the remuneration of directors of the listed company to be disclosed in the listed company's annual report.

10. DIRECTORS' LIABILITIES, LIABILITY INSURANCE, INDEMNIFICATION

10.1 What are the directors' responsibilities and liabilities under the law? Can those liabilities be covered by insurance? Can it be indemnified by the company or other related parties?

See paragraphs 4.1 and 4.2 above for directors' responsibilities and liabilities under the law.

Section 140(1) of Companies Act generally prohibits a company from indemnifying any officer (which includes directors) or auditor against any liability which by law would otherwise attach to him in respect of any negligence, default, breach of duty or breach of trust. Any provision in the articles or in any contract with the company or otherwise, which has the effect of exempting or indemnifying the director for the above-mentioned liability is void. A company may, pursuant to its articles or otherwise, indemnify any officer or auditor against any liability incurred in defending any proceedings in which judgment is given in his favour or in which he is acquitted.

The civil liabilities of a director may be covered by directors' and officers' liability insurance.

11. SHAREHOLDERS' DERIVATIVE SUITS

11.1 Is a shareholder's derivative suit provided for by law in your jurisdiction? How is it enforced by the shareholders?

Statutory derivative action under the Companies Act

Section 181A of the Companies Act enables a complainant, with the leave of the court, to bring, intervene in or defend an action on behalf and in the name of the company. A complainant may be:

- a member of a company, or a person who is entitled to be registered as member of a company;
- a former member of a company if the application relates to circumstances in which the member ceased to be a member;
- any director of a company; or
- the Registrar of Companies, in the case of a declared company under Part IX of the Companies Act.

The procedure for obtaining leave of the court is prescribed in the Companies Act. In deciding whether or not leave shall be granted, the court shall take into account whether:

- the complainant is acting in good faith; and
- it appears *prima facie* to be in the best interest of the company that the application for leave be granted.

Shareholders' derivative actions under common law

Notwithstanding section 181A of Companies Act, the right to bring a shareholders' derivative action under common law is not abrogated. Under common law, a shareholder may bring action against a director who is in breach of his fiduciary duty in the following instances (*Tan Guan Eng v Ng Kweng Hee* [1992] 1 MLJ 487):

- the act in question is *ultra vires;*
- it is fraud on the minority;
- the act in question was a proposal or transaction which required the shareholders to resolve by special resolution, but failed to obtain such resolution;
- where the personal and individual rights of the shareholders have been invaded; or
- when the justice of the case requires it.

11.2 Have there been any recent relevant court cases on the subject?

Reported decisions in Malaysia which deal with the statutory derivative action provisions in the Companies Act are as follows:

***Celcom (M) Bhd v Mohd Shuaib Ishak* [2011] 3 MLJ 636**

It was held that the respondent (who sought to bring a derivative action under section 181 of the Companies Act) had failed to show that there was a direct causal nexus between the complaint and how he ceased to be a member. The Court of Appeal also stated that the statutory provision that enables complainants to bring a statutory derivative action should be restrictively applied, and stressed that it was crucial for the shareholder applying for leave to make a claim in a shareholder's derivative action under the Companies Act to show that he was acting in good faith. The onus of proof was on him on a balance of probabilities; he must show an honest belief on his part and the application must not have been brought for a collateral purpose. The Court reiterated that courts should not interfere and substitute their own judgment in what was a proper and prudent business and commercial decision of the directors.

***Lembaga Tabung Angkatan Tentera v Prime Utilities Bhd* [2013] 7 MLJ 831**
The plaintiff, a minority shareholder in the defendant company, had written several letters to the defendant demanding to know what action it had taken to recover the balance of a substantial sum of money it had given to a foreign asset-management company (Boston) for investment purposes. The plaintiff filed a leave application to commence proceedings against Boston on the defendant's behalf to account for the losses the defendant had suffered in the investment with Boston. The defendant had given RM 112 million but only RM 4 million was returned. The balance was owed for more than five years. Boston was wound up in another jurisdiction and the defendant failed to file any proof of its debt in the winding-up. The High Court granted leave to commence a derivative action and held that the plaintiff's complaints were not without basis or substance and the plaintiff as minority shareholder has the right to take a derivative action to protect the interests of the company.

12. SOCIAL INTEREST IN CORPORATE BEHAVIOUR

12.1 How is a company in your country expected to deal with the following issues? Corporate social responsibility; gender, racial and social diversification; environmental issues; ecology and corruption?

Companies are expected and encouraged to comply with all applicable laws and regulations.

Portugal

Maria da Conceição Cabaços **PLMJ, Law Firm**

1. GENERAL PRINCIPLES

1.1 What are the general principles of corporate governance in your jurisdiction? What are the main objectives of corporate governance principles in your jurisdiction? State also whether your legal system is based on common law or civil law.

Like the majority of countries in continental Europe that are members of the EU, Portugal's corporate environment is different to that of the UK, which in the 1990s was the first European country to welcome the corporate governance movement that had come from these, where it had begun around 20 years earlier.

In the first place, in contrast to the UK and, even more so, to the USA (both Anglo-Saxon systems), in Portugal (continental system) there is a smaller number of companies listed on the stock market – the main targets for the issue of corporate governance – and a lesser dispersal of share capital among the respective shareholders.

Furthermore, the percentage of shares held by institutional investors is also lower. These factors, taken together, lead to greater control of the management of companies by the dominant shareholders – either by means of the direct control of the decisions taken at the general meeting or by means of control of the management itself which, under the dominant organisational model in Portugal (one-tier system), those shareholders elect and in which they very often have a seat themselves.

It should also be noted that in this area Portugal did not suffer, at least directly, from the pressure of corporate scandals, unlike what happened in the USA (cases such as WorldCom, Nortel or Enron)and even in the UK (cases such as Maxwell and Brent Walker),which brought to the forefront of corporate governance concerns, the need for public scrutiny of the internal control mechanisms of companies or which led to the creation of measures that were binding in character or punitive in nature, such as the US Sarbanes-Oxley Act (SOX).

One can, therefore, say that the genesis of the framework of rules on corporate governance in Portugal may be found in the separation between ownership and management, and its aim, above all else, in making the interests of the stakeholders, the directors and the shareholders (owners) compatible – and among them, protecting and strengthening the rights of the minority shareholders.

The evolution seen over the last two decades in terms of information technology, allied to the liberalisation of the capital market and the growing internationalisation of companies, as well as the progressive increase in the influence of institutional investors, together, brought the objective of restoring confidence in the markets to centre stage among corporate governance concerns. This was to be achieved by means of measures aimed at increasing the transparency and independence of management, accountability (rendering of accounts, responsibility and key performance indicators (KPIs)) and encouraging the informed participation of the shareholders in the life of the company.

As a result, despite that fact that the most visible face of the handling of corporate governance in Portugal is based on the Portuguese Securities Market Commission's (*Comissão of the Mercado de Valores Mobiliários*) recommendations on corporate governance – in respect of which listed companies are required annually to disclose their degree of compliance under the mechanism of explain or comply – the Portuguese legal framework on this issue includes other principles that are mandatory in character and included in various pieces of legislation and regulation. These include:

- the obligation for the majority of the members of the supervisory and auditing bodies of the company to be independent;
- the obligation to disclose the remuneration of the company board members;
- rules on the liability of board members towards the company; and
- special rules for the election of directors by minority shareholders.

The Portuguese Commercial Companies Code also provides for the management and supervisory boards of the company to be bound by a set of duties, namely, (i) the *duty of care* and diligence of a manager conscientious in the exercise of his or her duties, and (ii) *duties of loyalty*, in the *interest of the company*, bearing in mind the *long-term interests of the members* and taking into account the interests of the other persons relevant to the sustainability of the company, including its workers, clients and creditors (*stakeholders*).

Another aspect of the framework of directors' duties is the Portuguese legal system's enshrinement of the 'business judgment rule', under which a director's liability is excluded if the director can prove that he or she acted on an informed basis, free of any personal interest and in accordance with criteria of sound business judgement.

1.2 Have there been any recent developments in the law, codes and rules of corporate governance?

See paragraphs 2.1 and 2.2.

1.3 Outline recent court cases and incidents involving corporate governance issues. Were there any significant corporate scandals or large unlawful corporate cases?

The cases of *Banco Português de Negócios* (BPN) and *Banco Privado Português* (BPP), two Portuguese private banks, illustrate perfectly how the incorrect application of and compliance with the main rules of corporate governance, in particular, the correct risk assessment and management of institutions, may have a serious impact on the solvency of a (financial) institution. The activity of supervising the actions of the two banks in question, namely the failures detected in that supervision, were also subject to lively discussion in Portugal and its main consequence was the strengthening of measures in this area.

1.4 Which law enforcement agency is in charge of enforcing corporate governance? May a criminal sanction be levied upon infringement of the corporate governance rules?

In Portugal, the mission of the Portuguese Securities Market Commission, also known by its initials 'CMVM', set up in April 1991, is to supervise and regulate the securities markets and derivative financial instruments (traditionally known as 'stock markets') and the activity of all those who operate in them.

In the context of its general supervision, the CMVM has to ensure compliance with the mandatory rules of corporate governance that apply to listed companies, and the application of fines for infringements of those rules.

In turn, the Commercial Companies Code and the Securities Code establish a set of obligations the breach of which may amount to an administrative or even criminal offence. This is the case for (i) the unlawful refusal to provide information to the shareholders by the board of the company, (ii) provision of false information on the life of the company, (iii) putting false or incomplete information in the notice of the general meeting, (iv) the market manipulation and the abuse of information by members of the management or supervisory boards of the company, by the shareholders or by the stakeholders, and (v) the failure to obey the lawful instructions and orders of the CMVM issued in the context of its supervisory role.

Furthermore, Law 28/2009 of 19 June, which revises the framework of sanctions for the financial sector in criminal and administrative offences, establishes the rules for the approval and disclosure of the remuneration policy of the members of the management and supervisory boards of public interest entities (which include listed companies).

2. SOURCES OF LAW

2.1 Which laws, codes or statutes govern company structures and organisations? Are there statutes like the Companies Act or other forms of law? Is there much relevant case law?

Portugal is a member of the EU and, as such, follows the standards set out by EU directives and regulations.

Portugal has a civil law and statute-based legal system. Court decisions are not the source of law but have value in the interpretation of legislation.

Portuguese companies are principally governed by two major laws: (i) the Commercial Companies Code containing the core legal framework applicable to all types of companies; and (ii) the Securities Code, which includes a relevant set of provisions specifically addressing publicly traded companies (listed companies).

Notwithstanding these two basic pieces of legislation, Portuguese law contains other mandatory regulations on companies and governance, such as:

- CMVM Regulation 10/2005 which amends CMVM Regulations 7/2001 and 4/2004 in corporate governance and the duties of information and which regulate the means and time limits for disclosing mandatory information;
- CMVM Regulation 5/2008 on the duties of information; and
- CMVM Regulation 1/2010 on governance of listed companies.

In addition to the above, corporate governance in Portugal is also subject to soft law: the Code of Corporate Governance of Listed Companies issued by the CMVM and approved in 2010 (the Corporate Governance Code). This code, presented in the form of recommendations, reflects international standards and recommendations on corporate governance best practice and adopts modern trends in corporate governance, as established by different institutions such as the OECD and the European Commission.

The provisions of the Corporate Governance Code are not mandatory. It sets out recommendations under the principle of 'comply or explain'. As previously noted, companies are legally required to issue an annual report describing their corporate structure and corporate governance practices, and stating the level of compliance with the Corporate Governance Code's recommendations. In the event they do not comply with any of those recommendations, they must give an explanation for their failure to comply.

Each year, the CMVM issues a public report stating the degree of compliance with the recommendations on corporate governance by the companies listed on the Portuguese regulated market and, therefore, subject to the Corporate Governance Code. The evaluation of the degree of compliance with the recommendations is left to the markets. The last Annual Report on Corporate Governance of Listed Companies in Portugal by the CMVM was published in 2012. According to this report, the average adoption level of the CMVM recommendations on corporate governance increased significantly from 74 per cent in 2010 to 89 per cent in 2011.

There is also a strong self-regulatory component in corporate governance. All companies have articles of association establishing the rules of organisation and operation of the company. These cover the relationships between shareholders and contain corporate rules (for example, shareholders' meetings, and powers and duties of directors, etc.). In the event of any discrepancy, legal provisions prevail over the articles of association.

Shareholders' agreements are common in Portugal. These agreements regulate matters not necessarily related to the governance and ownership of the company, where the rigidity of corporate law and the limited scope of the articles of association make it necessary to regulate these matters through separate agreements.

Shareholders' agreements generally regulate issues such as: (i) securities transfer mechanisms and limitations; (ii) voting criteria; (iii) financing requirements and capital calls; (iv) business plans and strategies; (v) non-compete agreements; and (vi) control of management and shareholders' meetings.

Finally, listed companies classified as credit institutions are subject to the rules of the Legal Framework for Credit Institutions and Financial Companies.

2.2 Which laws, codes or statutes regulate capital markets in your jurisdiction?

Capital markets in Portugal are regulated by the Securities Code and by CMVM regulations and instructions.

Decree-Law 357-C/2007 of 31 October (with the amendments introduced by Decree-Law 52/2010 of 26 May) provides the legal framework applicable to regulated markets management companies of multilateral trading facilities, management companies, clearing-house management companies acting as the central counterparty, settlement system management companies and management companies of the Central Securities Depositary. This Decree-Law partially transposes into Portuguese law the Markets in Financial Instruments Directive 2004/39/EC of the European Parliament and of the Council of 21 April (MiFID).

Ministerial Order 556/2005 of 27 June approves the list of regulated markets, for the purposes of Directive 93/22/EEC of 10 May.

Ministerial Order 913-I/2003 of 30 August (with the amendments introduced by Ministerial Order 1018/2004 (2nd Series) of 17 September and Ministerial Order 712/2005 of 25 August) establishes the new system of securities market supervision fees.

2.3 Are there any public interest laws which apply to or influence corporate governance?

Not applicable.

2.4 Have there been any recent developments in any of the above laws? What are the recent changes to the above laws or rules and the reasons for such changes?

Regulation 1/2010 issued by the CMVM acknowledged the possibility for listed companies to opt for an alternative corporate governance code to the one issued by the CMVM, provided that such a code:(i) complies with the principles and embodies corporate governance practices that, overall, ensure protection of shareholders' interests and corporate governance transparency that are not inferior to those established by the Corporate Governance Code issued by the CMVM; (ii) at least covers the matters laid down in the code issued by the CMVM; and (iii) is issued by an institution that brings together recognised experts in corporate governance matters and operates independently of any particular interests.

The Portuguese Issuers Association began running the self-assessment of alternative corporate governance practices alongside the regular assessment performed by the CMVM. In addition, the Portuguese Institute of Corporate Governance (PICG) recently put forward the first code of corporate governance produced by the private sector.

More recently, in March 2013, the CMVM placed the proposed draft

Regulation on Corporate Governance (repeals CMVM Regulation 1/2010) and draft amendment to the Corporate Governance Code for public consultation. The proposed draft includes, among other modifications, the possibility of partial compliance with the recommendations. This is an important change since, at the present, partial compliance is not admissible.

3. SHAREHOLDERS AND THE SHAREHOLDERS' MEETING

3.1 How are shareholders' interests represented in the company? How are the shareholders assured exercise of their rights? What is the highest governing body within the company structure if it is not the shareholders' meeting?

As a result of the lesser dispersal of the share capital, in the majority of listed companies in Portugal, it is frequent for a small number, or even a sole shareholder, to hold real control over the company. In these situations of concentration of ownership, the management of the company and a definition of its business strategy will always be closely associated with and bound to the interests pursued by the majority shareholder(s). The defence and protection of the minority shareholders, therefore, assumes particular relevance.

In terms of rules, it is in the Commercial Companies Code that we can find the regulation of the main rights and obligations of the shareholders and the legal mechanisms designed to ensure that the interests normally associated with the capacity shareholder are pursued: appreciation in the value of the respective stake, aimed at maximising the profits associated with the investment of capital.

This is the case, among others: (i) with the guarantee of mandatory distribution of a percentage of the profits, except if there is a provision in the articles of association or a shareholder resolution passed by a qualified majority to the contrary; (ii) with the right to permanent information on the facts relevant to the evolution of the company and its business and to the preparatory information for general meetings; and (iii) with the right to claim compensation, for themselves and/or the company, for any losses caused by the action of the members of the board of directors.

The law reserves the right to decide on the issues that are most relevant to the life of the company to the shareholders, by making them subject to resolutions taken at the highest level of decision-making in the company: the general meeting.

Among other matters, it falls to the shareholders to: (i) pass resolutions on the accounts of the company and on the proposal for application of the results; (ii) carry out a general assessment of the action of the management and supervision the company; (iii) decide on any alterations to the articles of association of the company; (iv) decide on any plan for merger or splitting up of the company or transformation of the company into a different type of company; (v) as a rule, elect the members of the management and supervisory boards of the company and, if applicable, remove them from their positions; and (vi) set the remuneration of the members of the management and supervisory boards.

However, on matters of management, the shareholders may only take decisions at the request of the board of directors.

3.2 How is the shareholders' meeting conducted? Who may chair the meeting? May attendance (not voting) at the meeting be restricted only to the shareholders? Are the shareholders allowed to be accompanied by legal or other counsel?

General meetings are conducted by the 'table of the general meeting', made up, at least, of a president and a secretary, elected for period not longer than four years. The requirements of independence and the rules on incompatibility of offices that apply to the supervisory body of the company also apply to the members of the table of the general meeting of the listed companies.

The recommendations of the Corporate Governance Code on this matter provide that the remuneration of the president of the table of the general meeting must be disclosed in the Annual Report on Corporate Governance.

The law reserves to the shareholders with voting rights the right to *vote* at the general meeting. However, it also allows shareholders with no voting rights and bondholders to attend the general meetings and even to participate in the discussion of the items on the agenda, except when there is a provision to the contrary in the articles of association.

The joint representatives of holders of preferential shares (preferred stock) without a vote and bondholders may also attend the meetings, but they have no right to participate in the discussion.

Rather than simply allowing it, the law requires the presence at general meetings of the members of the board of directors and of the supervisory and auditing bodies of the company, and, in the case of a general meeting to approve the accounts, that obligation extends to the chartered accountant(s) who examined them.

The shareholders may be represented at the general meeting. However, the participation of a shareholder accompanied by a consultant (legal or other) depends on the authorisation of the president of the table of the general meeting, and that authorisation may be revoked by the shareholders by a resolution to this effect.

3.3 How are minority shareholders' rights protected?

Both the Commercial Companies Code and the Securities Code contain a range of provisions aimed at protecting the minority shareholder, and making it possible for them to play an active role in the life of the company.

A highlight among these provisions is the general principle enshrined in the Commercial Companies Code – also appearing as a recommendation in the CMVM's Corporate Governance Code – of 'one share, one vote'. The aim of this principle is to ensure proportionality between voting rights and shareholder participation, and encouraging the participation of all shareholders.

Other important examples are as follows:

- Shareholders with a minimum of 10 per cent and a maximum of 20 per

cent of the share capital may be granted the possibility of appointing up to one-third of the company board members or, if applicable, the supervisory board, by means of special election mechanisms regulated by law.
- Any shareholder with shares corresponding to at least 10 per cent of the share capital may, under the legally defined conditions, apply to the court to appoint one more member and one more alternate member to the supervisory board of the company.
- Shareholders with shares corresponding to at least 2 per cent of the share capital may ask for a general meeting to be called and may also ask for new items to be included on the agenda of a general meeting that has already been called.

3.4 Is shareholder activism encouraged or discouraged? If not encouraged, how is it regulated?

The active participation of shareholders in the life of the company is greatly encouraged in Portugal. First, mechanisms that make it possible to hold general meetings using electronic means and to vote by post have been created. Second, the enshrinement of the principle of 'one share, one vote' together with the principle of the right of shareholders who hold at least one vote to participate in meetings, is aimed at reinforcing the idea that all shareholders are equal and all votes count and are important to the decision-making process.

There is also a prohibition on establishing periods greater than five days for sending declarations proving the deposit and blocking of shares to the table of the general meeting and, in the event of suspension of the works of the general meeting, the company must not require the blocking of the shares during the period suspension, which are factors that could discourage shareholders from participating in general meetings.

3.5 How are professional shareholders (those minority shareholders who seek some extra benefit from companies by unduly and habitually influencing management by using their shareholding) treated by the law? Are they excluded from attending the shareholders' meeting? Are they criminally or otherwise publicly sanctioned?

In Portugal there are no special rules aimed directly at 'professional shareholders'. However, the heavy concentration of share capital in the hands of a small number of shareholders, which is common in Portuguese listed companies, means there is no need for regulation on this matter. .

3.6 Are shareholders' benefits given to some of the shareholders by the company without resolution by the shareholders' meeting prohibited or regulated by the law or other rules?

The amendment of a company's articles of association (by which special rights/benefits may be granted) as well as the distribution of dividends in any form is always dependent on a resolution being passed by the shareholders.

The Corporate Governance Code recommends that the business of a listed company with shareholders that are in a situation of control or a group relationship with it, or have a qualified shareholding, must be carried on under normal market conditions. Whenever such business has significant relevance, it must be submitted to the prior opinion of the supervisory body of the company.

4. DIRECTORS AND BOARD OF DIRECTORS

4.1 What are the functions and responsibilities of the directors and the board of directors? Do you have a one- or two-tier board system? What are the outside directors called?

In Portugal, listed companies, as publicly traded companies, may choose between three organisational models:

- board of directors, statutory auditors board and chartered accountant or firm of chartered accountants (one-tier board system);
- board of directors, including an audit committee, and chartered accountant or firm of chartered accountants (the model commonly known as *Anglo-Saxon*); and
- executive board of directors, supervisory board and chartered accountant or firm of chartered accountants (two-tier board system).

The model used most commonly in Portugal is the one-tier board system, although the Anglo-Saxon model is adopted by larger companies.

In the one-tier system, the general principle is that the board of directors must decide on any matter related to the management of the company.

The rules of corporate governance on this matter recommend that the board of directors delegates to one or more managing directors, or to an executive committee made up of executive directors, the day-to-day management of the company, and the powers delegated must be identified in the annual report on corporate governance.

The board of directors must not delegate its power in respect of the definition of the strategy and general policies of the company, or in respect of any decisions, which because of the amount, risk or any special characteristics are deemed to be strategic for the company.

Other powers may not legally be delegated. This is the case with (i) calling general meetings, (ii) co-opting directors and (iii) the provision of security and personal and real guarantees by the company, among several others.

The delegation of powers does not prevent the board of directors from passing resolutions on the same matters and the non-executive directors continue to be liable for any losses caused by the acts or omissions of the executive directors if it is proved that they were aware of the mismanagement and did not take any steps to avoid it.

There must be enough non-executive directors to ensure the effective supervision, control and evaluation of the actions of the executive directors, and among them there must be an adequate number of independent directors.

4.2 What are the rules that may give rise to civil and criminal liability

of the director(s)? How are those liabilities sought?

The civil and criminal liability of the directors arises, essentially from the breach of the fiduciary duties by which they are bound in carrying out their work and from the information obligations, or the conditions of confidentiality that bind them in relation to the privileged information available to them in their capacity as a member of the board.

The Securities Code expressly regulates and classifies as crimes subject to a prison sentence of up to five years: (i) abuse of information; (ii) market manipulation; and (iii) disobedience.

In turn, the Commercial Companies Code also regulates a set of acts or omissions on the part of the directors that may give rise to criminal liability, namely: (i) the unlawful refusal to provide information; (ii) the provision of false information; (iii) improperly calling a general meeting; (iv) preventing the supervision of the operations of the company; (v) irregularities in the issuing of securities; (vi) the unlawful distribution of assets of the company; and (vii) the unlawful acquisition of shares and others.

These actions will only be punishable as crimes if there is intent and mere negligence or blame is insufficient to establish criminal liability.

The failure to comply with certain obligations to the tax authorities or the social security may give rise to criminal liability on the part of the directors.

Any practices of directors that may give rise to the application of fines or penalties in administrative proceedings are also extensively regulated by law.

Besides criminal liability, the directors are subject to civil liability, in general terms, for any losses their actions may cause to the company, the shareholders and the creditors of the company.

4.3 Does the board of directors have a committee system, eg, nomination committee, compensation committee, audit committee? If not required, is it common practice for companies? How does it function?

The articles of association of the company may include provision for the creation of specialised committees within the board of directors that are responsible for certain areas of management and these may include matters that may not be delegated to a director or an executive committee.

The recommendations on this matter are for the board of directors or the supervisory board, in accordance with the model adopted, to create any committees deemed necessary to: (i) ensure a competent and independent evaluation of the performance of the executive directors and for the evaluation of their overall performance, as a management of body the company; (ii) reflect on the appropriateness of the company governance model adopted and propose as any measures that may be appropriate to improve its performance; and (iii) identify candidates with the right profile to perform of the duties of director. In the context of the supervisory board, there must be a committee for financial matters.

In the case of the Anglo-Saxon model, some of the directors of the board of directors sit on the audit committee, which acts as the supervisory body of the company.

4.4 Is it a legal requirement to have an independent director or a third-party director? If so, how are they appointed? Is it required for listed companies?

The rules of corporate governance on this matter indicate the board of directors should include an adequate number of independent directors, taking in the size of the company and its shareholder structure and, in any event, this number may not be lower than a quarter of the total number of directors. The appointment of the independent directors is done in the same way as the appointment of the other directors, normally by election at the general meeting.

The characterisation and evaluation of the independence of the directors must take into account the applicable legal and regulatory rules on the requirements of independence and the rules on incompatibilities applicable to the members of the other corporate bodies. No director should be considered independent if he or she could not take up a membership position in another corporate body because of the applicable rules on incompatibilities and independence.

4.5 How is the compensation for directors or officers determined? Can it be contested by the shareholders or the regulatory authorities? What are the common rules or practices for the compensation of officers?

The remuneration of the corporate bodies, and in particular of the directors, is extensively regulated by the law and is the matter that is the focus of the greatest number of recommendations in the area of corporate governance.

The basic principles that govern the determination of the remuneration of the directors are, first of all the need for directors' remuneration to be structured so as to allow the interests of the directors to be brought into line with the long-term interests of the company and, second, the fact that it should be based on the evaluation of performance and discourage the assumption of excessive risk in decision-making by the management.

The general rule is that setting the level of remuneration for the management and supervisory bodies of companies is in the power of the general meeting (which may be in the hands of a remuneration committee appointed by it). In the case of the two-tier model, the remuneration of the members of the executive board is in the power of the supervisory board or a remuneration committee created within this body.

If the remuneration of the directors partially consists of a percentage of the profits earned in the financial year, the maximum value of this percentage must be set in the articles of association of the company. The remuneration of the members of the supervisory board, audit board and audit committee is made up exclusively of a fixed value.

In relation to listed companies, there commendations appearing in the Corporate Governance Code point to the remuneration of the executive directors being made up of a fixed portion and a variable portion, with the latter depending on performance evaluation that takes into account the real growth of the company and the wealth actually generated for the shareholders.

The board of directors, or the remuneration committee if one exists, must submit a declaration on the remuneration policy of the members of the board of directors and the supervisory board annually for approval by the general meeting.

The declaration must contain information on: (i) the mechanisms that make it possible to bring the interests of the members of the board of directors into line with the interests of the company; (ii) the criteria for defining the variable component of the remuneration of the directors, if there is one; (iii) the existence of share allocation or share option plans for members of the board of directors and the supervisory board; (iv) the possibility of payment of the variable component of the remuneration being made, in whole or in part, after clearance of the accounts for the financial year; and (v) the mechanisms for limiting variable remuneration, in the event the results show any relevant deterioration in the performance of the company.

The annual report on corporate governance must disclose the declaration on the remuneration policy, the annual amount of remuneration earned by the members of the board of directors and supervisory board, both as a total amount and individually, the different components that make up the variable remuneration of the directors and any remuneration earned for work done for other companies of the group.

The information to be disclosed in respect of the remuneration of the executive directors is even more detailed and must include the criteria on which the attribution of the various variable components of the remuneration, indicating the maximum limits of both the fixed and variable components and identifying the parameters and basis of any system of annual bonuses or any other non-pecuniary benefits. It must also identify the mechanisms and criteria for evaluation of the performance of the directors.

4.6 How will the board handle a corporate crisis like an internal criminal case, violence, social media exposure or dawn raid by the authorities?

The management of an internal crisis situation in the company, regardless of its characteristics, will be carried out with recourse to the general legal means available for the situation in question. The management must act in compliance with the laws applicable to the case and always respecting the duties to which it is subject in the exercise of its duties and the legitimate interests of the company it represents.

5. BOARD OF AUDITORS, AUDIT COMMITTEE, ACCOUNTING AUDITORS

5.1 How is the internal accounting and legal audit structured and conducted? Is an outside accounting audit required and, if so, how is it structured? Are there requirements to change the auditor each five years?

5.2 Do you have supervisory auditors? What is the function of the supervisory auditors' board?

The method of internal supervision of the activities of the company depends on the organisational model adopted.

As a rule (applicable to non-listed companies under a set of thresholds related to value of assets, turnover and/or number of employees), companies organised in accordance with the one-tier model have either a statutory auditors board, a collegiate body with a minimum of three members (one of whom a chartered accountant), or a single statutory auditor (also a chartered accountant). As mentioned above, listed companies (as well as companies issuing securities which are publicly traded) should have a statutory auditors board plus a chartered accountant or firm of chartered accountants.

In the Anglo-Saxon model, there will be an audit committee that is part of the board of directors and a chartered accountant.

The two-tier model includes a supervisory board that comprises a committee for financial matters and a chartered accountant.

All of the supervisory bodies identified above are required to:

- supervise the activities of the management body;
- ensure compliance with the law and the articles of association of the company;
- whenever it considers appropriate to do so, ensure that the accounting records of the company are in order;
- check that accounting policies and the criteria for calculating values adopted by the company lead to a correct evaluation of the assets and results;
- supervise the effectiveness of the system of risk management and internal control;
- receive any communications of irregularities presented by shareholders, employees of the company or other stakeholders; and
- issue an opinion on the management report and accounts of the company.

The internal supervisory body must prepare a report in its activity annually to inform the shareholders of the supervision it has carried out. According to the recommendation of the Corporate Governance Code this annual report must published on the company's website together with the financial statements.

The annual financial information in the financial statements of listed companies must be certified by a chartered accountant registered with the CMVM and subject to a report prepared by an external auditor also registered with the CMVM.

The chartered accountant(s) and external auditors of listed companies are appointed by the shareholders' general meeting on the basis of a proposal from the company's supervisory body – statutory auditors' board, audit committee or supervisory board, depending on the governance model adopted.

The external auditors of listed companies are liable for any losses caused to companies audited by them or to third parties by deficiencies in the report or opinion prepared. This liability is unlimited and shared jointly and with the appointed chartered accountant(s).

Listed companies are required to disclose the annual amount paid to the external auditor.

6. MARKET DISCLOSURE/TRANSPARENCY TO THE SHAREHOLDERS AND THE PUBLIC

6.1 What are the disclosure requirements for companies in your jurisdiction under company law, capital markets law or any other rules?

The duties of information imposed on companies in general are regulated in the Commercial Companies Code and in the Commercial Registration Code. Listed companies are subject to the additional regulations on this matter contained in the Securities Code and CMVM Regulation 5/2008, as well as the recommendations of the Corporate Governance Code.

The basic principle is that all the information relating to securities and to the issuing companies must be complete, true, up to date, clear, objective and lawful.

The directors are under an obligation to prepare and submit the management report and the accounts for the financial year (report and accounts) for consideration and approval by the shareholders, in within three months of the end of the financial year (as a rule).

In relation to listed companies, within four months of the end of the financial year: (i) the report and accounts, and other accounting documentation; (ii) the report prepared by the external auditor; and (iii) the declarations of compliance prepared by the internal auditors, must be published in the CMVM's Information Publishing System (an Internet site) and on the website of the company itself.

The management body of listed companies is also obliged to disclose interim financial information – half-yearly or quarterly, in accordance with the size of the company.

Additionally, the directors of listed companies must also ensure compliance with a vast number of duties of information aimed at guaranteeing existence of permanent contact with the market and respecting the principle of equality between shareholders by ensuring they all have the same level of access to information. The duties of information, the obligation to disclose privileged information of the company and the obligation to disclose information relating to the transactions with the shares of the company are particularly important.

The Corporate Governance Code provides that listed companies must publish a vast range of information on their websites. Besides financial and legal, they must publish a six-monthly calendar of corporate events and information and as well as the means of access to the Investor Support Office, which every company must have.

Finally, listed companies must prepare and publish a detailed annual report on the structure and practices of corporate governance it has adopted (Corporate Governance Report). This report must expressly identify the recommendations of the Corporate Governance Code that the company has decided to adopt and, for any it has not adopted, it must provide an explanation.

6.2 What is the liability or responsibility of the board in relation to the company's disclosure requirements?

The failure to comply with the obligations to provide information, as well as the provision of incorrect, incomplete, abusive or unlawful information will give rise to liability on the part of those responsible and, in the event of intent, even criminal liability.

7. M&A AND CORPORATE GOVERNANCE

7.1 Upon an M&A offer, how are the transparency and fairness rules of the company provided under the company and stock market laws and rules?

Once a listed company becomes aware of a decision to launch a takeover bid for more than one-third of the securities in the category subject to the bid, and until the result of the bid is known or until the end of the takeover proceedings, the company target cannot take any decision capable of altering in any relevant way the company's asset/financial situation. This restriction covers, with some exceptions established by law, acts putting into effect decisions taken prior to becoming aware of the launch of the bid.

On the bidder's side, from the moment of publication of the preliminary announcement of the bid up to the point at which the result of the bid is known, the bidder and anyone with whom the bidder is in a group relationship or control situation established by law, (i) may not trade outside the regulated market securities in the categories of those that are the subject of the bid or which form part of the consideration, except if they are authorised to do so by the CMVM, after first hearing the opinion of the target company (ii) must inform the CMVM on a daily basis about any transactions carried out in relation to any of the securities issued by the target company.

In terms of recommendations, it is a requirement that any measures taken by the target company aimed at preventing the success of takeover bids must respect the interests of the company and its shareholders. The articles of association of the companies that provide for a limitation on the number of votes that may be exercised by a single shareholder must establish that this provision in the articles has to be subject to a vote at the general meeting every five years and that the said limitation on the right to vote does not apply to this resolution.

Finally, the Corporate Governance Code recommends the company should not adopt defensive measures that have the effect of causing serious erosion in the assets of the target company in the case that the transfer in control of the company is successful, thus restricting the free transferability of the shares.

All processes aimed at acquiring control over listed companies are supervised and mediated by the CMVM, which is responsible for permanently evaluating whether or not the actions carried out by the various parties involved comply with the law.

8. PROXY FIGHTING

8.1 Is proxy fighting customarily conducted for control of the company management or what other items? How is it regulated under the company law or market regulations?

In Portugal, given the above-mentioned situation that a heavy concentration of the capital of the companies is in the hands of a single shareholder or of a small block of shareholders, this matter has no particular relevance in the context of regulation of corporate governance and is not subject to any mandatory provision in the law or even a recommendation in the Corporate Governance Code.

9. OFFICERS' REMUNERATION RULES

9.1 How is remuneration of officers determined? By whom? Is there a role for the shareholders' meeting? Is there any mechanism for an independent body to review and evaluate them?

See paragraph 4.5 above. The general rule for the determination of the remuneration of the members of the corporate bodies is that this is decided by the general meeting, or in the case of two-tier models, by the supervisory board..

9.2 Is the mechanism of officers' remuneration publicly debated?

See paragraph 4.5 above.

10. DIRECTORS' LIABILITIES, LIABILITY INSURANCE, INDEMNIFICATION

10.1 What are the directors' responsibilities and liabilities under the law? Can those liabilities be covered by insurance? Can it be indemnified by the company or other related parties?

The responsibility of the directors has already been addressed in paragraph 4.2 above.

In Portugal, the responsibility of each director must be guaranteed by an amount established in the articles of association of the company which, for listed companies, may not be less than EUR 250,000. The guarantee may be substituted by an insurance policy, the costs of which, at least up to the minimum value imposed by law, may not be paid by the company.

Listed companies may not dispense with this guarantee, even by a resolution of the shareholders. This is not the case with non-listed companies, where an exemption of guarantee may be granted.

11. SHAREHOLDERS' DERIVATIVE SUITS

11.1 Is a shareholder's derivative suit provided for by law in your jurisdiction? How is it enforced by the shareholders?

The Commercial Companies Code establishes and regulates civil liability actions brought by shareholders against directors to obtain damages for the company for any losses it has suffered as a result of the conduct of the directors against whom the action is brought.

In Portugal, this legal procedure is given the name *acção social de responsabilidade* (corporate liability action). Shareholders in public companies that hold at least 2 per cent of the share capital have legal standing to use this mechanism, whereas for other companies they must hold at least 5 per cent. The company will be joined as a party to the proceedings.

11.2 Have there been any recent relevant court cases on the subject?

We are not aware of the existence of any relevant case of this type in Portugal.

12. SOCIAL INTEREST IN CORPORATE BEHAVIOUR

12.1 How is a company in your country expected to deal with the following issues? Corporate social responsibility; gender, racial and social diversification; environmental issues; ecology and corruption?

Portuguese listed companies, like those in the rest of Europe, have been increasingly adopting social responsibility best practices; in particular, the concept of sustainable development by implementing policies to protect natural resources associated with the operations and practices to monitor environmental impact.

The adoption of codes of ethics and conduct has also been taking on special importance in the process of implementing social responsibility policies in companies, both internally in the management of human resources and externally in their relationships with the communities of which they form part.

The social responsibility and sustainability reports published annually by listed companies reflect the growing and positive evolution that has been witnessed in this area.

Russia

Vassily Rudomino, Anton Dzhuplin, Victoria Sivachenko &
Timur Akhundov **ALRUD**

1. GENERAL PRINCIPLES

1.1 What are the general principles of corporate governance in your jurisdiction? What are the main objectives of corporate governance principles in your jurisdiction? State also whether your legal system is based on common law or civil law.

The Russian legal system is based on the civil law.

General principles of the civil law and corporate governance are set out in the first part of the Civil Code of the Russian Federation (CC RF) and include the following: equability of participants of civil law relations, inviolability of property, freedom of agreement, impermissibility of arbitrary interference into private affairs, unhindered exercise of civil rights, and ensuring restoration of violated rights and their protection in court.

According to the CC RF, participants of civil law relations shall act in good faith when they establish, exercise or protect their rights or fulfil their civil duties. Moreover, under the recently enacted provision of the CC RF, fairness of participants of civil law relations and reasonableness of their actions shall be presumed.

Under the CC RF, if there are no relevant laws or customs which might be applicable to the legal issue, the parties and the court should be guided by the general principles and meaning of the civil legislation as well as requirements of honesty, reasonableness and justice.

However, current Russian legislation does not provide for the notions of such principles. Definitions of some of them are given in court practice of the Higher Arbitrazh Court or the Higher Court of the Russian Federation.

Generally accepted principles of corporate governance are also reflected in the Corporate Governance Code (Decree of the Federal Commission on the Securities Market of 4 April 2002 No. 421/r). According to the Corporate Governance Code, the principles of corporate conduct are fundamental guidelines underlying the formation, operation and enhancement of a company's system of corporate governance.

Under the Corporate Governance Code, corporate governance should be based on respect for the rights and lawful interests of all participants. Trust between all those engaged in corporate governance is at the root of the effective operation of a company and the ability to attract investment. The principles of corporate governance described in this chapter are aimed at the creation of trust in relations arising in connection with corporate management.

The general principles of corporate governance, although not directly specified in the Russian corporate legislation, are somehow reflected in the Russian Federal Law No. 14-FZ of 8 February 1998 'On Limited Liability Companies' (Law on LLC) and Federal Law No. 208-FZ of 26 December 1995 'On Joint Stock Companies' (Law on JSC).

Thus, according to the Law on LLC and the Law on JSC, when exercising his/her rights and performing his/her obligations a member of the board of directors of the company should act in the best interests of the company and exercise his/her rights and perform his/her obligations in respect of the company reasonably and in good faith.

1.2 Have there been any recent developments in the law, codes and rules of corporate governance?

There have been no recent significant developments in the legal acts in relation to corporate governance in Russia. In 2009–2010, there were made some changes with regard to the introduction of shareholders' agreements, regulation of limited liability companies, procedure of legal entities reorganisation, and change of requirements to business entities in case of inconformity of share capital to net assets value.

Recently, some amendments were introduced into the Civil Code with regard to fundamental principles of civil legislation – the establishment of corporate relations.

Thus, under recent amendments to the CC RF, the parties to civil relations should act in good faith when establishing, exercising and protecting their civil rights and performing their civil obligations. There was introduced a general rule under which no one is entitled to enjoy benefits resulting from illegal or inequitable conduct.

Under the recently adopted changes, the Civil Code recognises corporate relations as a separate type of civil relations arising out of participation in corporate entities and corporate governance. Therefore, resolutions adopted by corporate bodies become a new ground for establishing civil rights and obligations. A list of the remedies available was supplemented with a new option, being the invalidation of the corporate bodies' resolutions.

For more details, see paragraph 2.4 below.

1.3 Outline recent court cases and incidents involving corporate governance issues. Were there any significant corporate scandals or large unlawful corporate cases?

Merkuriy case (9th Appellate Commercial Court Ruling dated 17.09.2012 No. 09AP-27570/2012, case No. A40-104085/12-57-987)

This case illustrates one of the standard corporate war tools. The incident involved the largest self-regulatory organisation (SRO) of court-appointed trustees, 'Merkuriy', when several members of the organisation – who were not satisfied with the quality of work of the previous management – decided to hold a re-election of the chairman and dismiss General Director Artur Trapitsin in 2012. On 10 July, Vyacheslav Druzhinin became the head of 'Merkuriy' (he was elected by 95 per cent of the members meeting).

Artur Trapitsin contested the shareholders' meeting in which Vyacheslav

Druzhinin was elected the general director. 290 of 484 members of the shareholders' meeting voted under powers of attorney, which were held by Natalia Vasilenko. At the same time, 130 powers of attorney were in copies and scans, and therefore it was impossible to verify the validity of the signatures in the documents.

To stop the functioning of the company with the illegal management, Artur Trapitsin backdated the termination of the lease agreement of the company's office premises situated at Tsvetnoy Bulvar and thus made normal functioning of 'Merkuriy' impossible. The court trustees were thus unable to enter their cabinets and access to documents on a number of bankruptcy cases was blocked.

Artur Trapitsin announced that 'Merkuriy' had moved to offices located at Tverskaya-Yamskaya Street. He filed a claim to the court, challenging the results of the meeting.

The scandal resolved very quickly as the court ordered the interim measures blocking any further shares and real-estate transactions. In October 2012, the Arbitrazh Court of Moscow declared that the results of such election were null and void due to the lack of quorum.

1.4 Which law enforcement agency is in charge of enforcing corporate governance? May a criminal sanction be levied upon infringement of the corporate governance rules?

Though legal entities may not be subject to criminal prosecution in Russia, they may be liable under the Code of Administrative Offences of the Russian Federation dated 30 December 2001. Most of corporate procedures offences including those on securities markets are in the competence of the Federal Service on the Financial Markets. Although the general rule is that sanctions may be levied by the appropriate state authority within its competence (eg tax service charges for tax issues, anti-trust service charges for competition issues, etc.).

2. SOURCES OF LAW

2.1 Which laws, codes or statutes govern company structures and organisations? Are there statutes like the Companies Act or other forms of law? Is there much relevant case law?

The main legislative acts which regulate company structures and organisations in Russia are as follows:

- The CC RF, being the fundamental legislative act regulating corporate relations in the Russian Federation which provides for the definition of a legal entity, gives their classification and sets the general rules of their activities.

  According to the CC RF, all legal entities are divided into two categories: commercial and non-commercial. Commercial legal entities are identified as legal entities whose main purpose is to gain profit and which distribute the profit among their participants; whereas non-commercial legal entities do not count profit-making as the main purpose of their activity and do not distribute the profit among their participants.

The CC RF also distinguishes branches and representative offices which are not legal entities, but are rather bodies representing the interests of a legal entity (including the interests of a foreign legal entity in Russia). Heads of representative offices and branches are appointed by the company that they represent and act under powers of attorney.

- The Law on JSC, which deals with the majority of corporate issues regarding both types of joint stock companies (JSCs) in Russia, ie open joint stock companies (OJSCs) and closed joint stock companies (CJSCs). A JSC issues common or preferred shares in order to raise capital for its activities. A CJSC is a type of JSC, the shares of which may be allocated only to its founders or other predetermined set of persons. A CJSC is not entitled to offer its shares publicly or to an unlimited set of individuals; whereas an OJSC is generally entitled to offer its shares both publicly and privately.
- The Law on LLC, which provides regulation in respect of the other type of Russian commercial legal entities, ie limited liability companies (LLCs). The main difference between an LLC and a JSC is that the charter capital of a JSC consists of shares which are securities issued by the JSC; whereas the charter capital of an LLC consists of participatory shares which are not securities and fall outside the scope of Russian securities law, and therefore are not subject to registration as securities with the Federal Service on the Securities Market. The absence of necessity to issue shares in an LLC makes this form of legal entity more customary and flexible with the least burdensome statutory obligations.
- Federal Law No. 161-FZ dated 14 November 2002 'On State and Municipal Unitary Enterprises' (the Law on SUE and MUE). Under the Law on SUE and MUE, a unitary enterprise is a commercial organisation which doesn't have right of ownership of property. Only state and municipal enterprises can be set up in the form of unitary enterprises. Property of unitary enterprises is owned by the Russian Federation, subjects of the Russian Federation or municipal bodies.
- Federal Law No. 335-FZ dated 28 November 2011 'On Investment Partnership', which regulates peculiarities of simple partnership agreements concluded in execution of joint investment activity (investment partnership agreement), including legal status and liability of the parties of the investment partnership.
- Federal Law No. 380-FZ of 3 December 2011 'On Business Partnerships' (the Law on Business Partnerships), which regulates the legal status of business partnerships, rights and obligations of its participants, procedure of foundation and liquidation.
- Federal Law No. 156-FZ of 29 November 2001 'On Investment Funds' according to which investment fund is defined as an asset complex owned jointly by legal entities or individuals, but it is not considered as a legal entity.
- Federal Law No. 7-FZ of 12 January 1996 'On Non-commercial Organisations' (the Law on NCO), which specifies legal status, procedure of formation, reorganisation and liquidation of non-commercial

organisations, formation and use of property of non-commercial organisations, rights and obligations of its founders and sets out forms of non-commercial organisations.

Non-commercial organisations can be set up for charitable, cultural, educational managerial and other social purposes. Non-commercial organisations can be set up in the form of social and religious organisations, funds, state corporations, state companies, non-commercial partnerships, private institutions (state, municipal and budgetary institutions), autonomous non-commercial organisations and associations. It should be noted that a state corporation is set up by the Russian Federation on the basis of the federal law and, thus, is regulated by such law.

- Federal Law No. 129-FZ of 8 August 2001 'On the State Registration of Legal Entities and Individual Entrepreneurs' (the Law on State Registration) regulates issues connected with state registration of legal entities during their foundation, reorganisation and liquidation, as well as upon making amendments to constituent documents and state registration of individuals as individual entrepreneurs.

Court precedent is not considered as a source of law in Russia. However, rulings of the Supreme Arbitrazh Court and the Supreme Court, which are the courts of final instance, may be taken into account by the court of lower instance when making judgment.

In addition to the regulatory framework mentioned above, Russian companies are also subject to other laws, including laws on the registration of legal entities, bankruptcy, licensing, accounting and auditing.

2.2 Which laws, codes or statutes regulate capital markets in your jurisdiction?

The core legislation in the field of capital markets is the Federal Law No. 39-FZ of 22 April 1996 'On the Securities Market' (the Securities Market Law), which regulates issues relating to issuance and circulation of securities as well as peculiarities of creation and business activity of the professional participants of the securities market. This act also sets out liability of professional participants in the securities market with regard to breach of capital market legislation.

Additionally, the Federal Law No. 224-FZ of 27 July 2010 'On countering the illegal use of inside information and market manipulation and on amending certain legislative acts of the Russian Federation' regulates relations connected with financial instruments, foreign currency or goods admitted to trading on organised markets in the territory of the Russian Federation.

Besides, the Standards of Issuance of Securities and Registration of Securities Prospectuses enacted by the Order of the Federal Financial Market Service No. 07-4/pz-n of 25 January 2007, which regulate issuance of securities, issuer options, Russian depositary receipts and obligations of legal entities, as well as securities registration procedure, shall be taken into consideration.

2.3 Are there any public interest laws which apply to or influence corporate governance?

Establishment by a foreign investor of an enterprise in Russia may fall under the merger control exercised by the Federal Antitrust Service of the Russian Federation (FAS). The main legislative act for the purposes of the merger control is the Federal Law No. 135-FZ of 26 July 2006 'On Protection of the Competition' (the Competition Law). The Competition Law provides for the general regulation of the filing procedure; more detailed regulation is provided in the FAS decrees. Transactions and other actions falling under merger control, involve (i) fixed productive assets and/or intangible assets located or registered in the territory of Russia; or (ii) shares/rights in respect of Russian companies and non-commercial organisations; or (iii) shares/rights in respect of foreign companies or organisations, which supplied goods to Russia of an amount exceeding RUB 1 billion during the calendar year preceding the date of execution of the transaction.

There are a number of restrictions on foreign investments established under Russian law. Certain restrictions are imposed by the Federal Law 'On the Procedure of Foreign Investment in Companies having Strategic Importance for the Preservation of National Defence and State Security' No. 57-FZ of 29 April 2008 (the Strategic Investment Law). A strategic clearance according to the Strategic Investment Law is required if the target company is active in one of 42 spheres of strategic importance for national security and defence (for example, nuclear and radioactive materials, devices and waste; aviation and space; natural resources sector, etc.) or has a licence for conducting such activity (Strategic company). Any transaction leading to the establishment by a foreign investor or its group of persons of the control over a Strategic company falls within the scope of regulation of the Strategic Investment Law and requires approval of the Governmental Commission for Control over Foreign Investment in the Russian Federation chaired by the Prime Minister of Russia. The state body responsible for monitoring the foreign investments sphere is the FAS. In general, transactions entered into in breach of the Strategic Investments Law are null and void.

If foreign enterprises desire to develop real-estate projects in cooperation with Russian local government, the possible options include corporate and contractual forms of cooperation (on the basis of concession agreements). Under the Federal Law No. 115-FZ dated 21 July 2005 'On Concession Agreements' (the Law on Concessions), one party (concessionaire) shall at its own expense construct and/or reconstruct assets specified by the agreement, such as immovable property, complex of immovable and movable property (object), where the ownership right belongs to the other party (conceder . Under the concession agreement, the concessionaire undertakes its activities using (exploiting) the object and the conceder provides the concessionaire rights of possession and usage to the object under the provisions of the concession agreement.

A concession agreement is concluded by way of conducting an open or closed tender. The general rule is to conduct an open tender; a closed tender is conducted if the concession agreement is to be concluded for an object of strategic significance for the country's defence or if information constitutes a state secret. The tender winner is determined by the tender commission. The criteria for selecting the winning bidder are set in the tender documentation on a case-by-case basis.

However, in practice, such forms of cooperation as concession agreements between the state and a foreign investor are not widely used because the legislative provisions do not fully secure the foreign investors' interests.

A production sharing agreement (PSA) is a contract between one or more investors and the government in which rights to prospection, exploration and extraction of mineral resources from a specific area over a specified period of time are determined. The government hires the investor(s) as a contractor for the extraction of mineral resources, but the government still retains ownership of the resources. The investors administer the business at their own expense and risk sharing with the government part of the production output in accordance with the agreement.

2.4 Have there been any recent developments in any of the above laws? What are the recent changes to the above laws or rules and the reasons for such changes?

A draft bill to amend the Civil Code is currently being prepared in the State Duma (lower chamber of the Russian parliament). According to this draft bill, JSCs will be divided into public and non-public companies. A public JSC is a JSC whose shares and securities convertible to shares are publicly placed and publicly circulated. Non-public JSCs are those that do not fall under the description of public JSCs. There are some changes in the status of CJSCs in comparison to non-public JSCs, which are expected to be introduced into the new version of the Law on JSC; however, the general division between two types of JSCs will remain.

On 26 April 2013 the draft bill 'On Public Private Partnership' was approved by the State Duma in the first reading. According to the draft bill, a private partner can be recognised as an individual entrepreneur, a Russian or a foreign legal entity, excluding state corporations, state and municipal enterprises and legal entities wholly owned by the Russian Federation. It should be mentioned that there is no federal act regulating public-private partnerships nowadays. If the draft bill is adopted, it will enable the setting up of public-private partnerships at the regional level. A public partner will have obligations to provide property as well as to provide the right to use intellectual property – an outcome necessary for the fulfilment of obligations under public-private partnership. The draft bill will enable the conclusion a three-party agreement in case of attraction of financing from any third party . Moreover, the draft bill stipulates guarantees of rights and legally protected interests of private partners and creditors.

3. SHAREHOLDERS AND THE SHAREHOLDERS' MEETING

3.1 How are shareholders' interests represented in the company? How are the shareholders assured exercise of their rights? What is the highest governing body within the company structure if it is not the shareholders' meeting?

As described in paragraph 2 above, Russian law provides for several different types of legal entities. Most popular among them are JSCs and LLCs, and the legal regulation of these two forms is different in some respects.

The Law on LLC and the Law on JSC provide for the formation of the following management bodies in LLCs and JSCs:

- general meeting of participants/shareholders;
- board of directors;
- individual executive body (general director); and
- collective executive body (executive board, directorate, etc.).

The general meeting of the shareholders is the supreme body of the company, making more significant decisions with regard to the company's activity. The board of directors deals with the general management of the company's activity. The sole executive body (the general director or the managing company having the general director *ex officio* acting as a chairperson of such managing company) manages the current activities of the company.

The general meeting of participants (shareholders) and the individual executive body (general director) are the management bodies established in all JSCs and LLCs pursuant to the mandatory requirements of law; while the board of directors and the executive board are formed under the decision of the general meeting of founders/participants of the company in case the charter of the company contains the provisions on their formation. The board of directors is not obligatory for LLCs and for JSCs which have less than 50 shareholders with voting shares.

Shareholders of JSCs and participants of LLCs have a basic set of rights, including the right to participate in the management of the company, with some exceptions established by law; the right to obtain information on the company's activity as well as to have access to a company's documents, including its accounting books and other documents in the manner prescribed by the company's charter; the right to receive dividends and the right to receive a part of any distribution of a company's assets remaining after payments to creditors during liquidation proceedings. This list is not exhaustive: some other rights may be provided to shareholders by law or by the company's charter.

3.2 How is the shareholders' meeting conducted? Who may chair the meeting? May attendance (not voting) at the meeting be restricted only to the shareholders? Are the shareholders allowed to be accompanied by legal or other counsel?

Under the Law on LLC, the ordinary general meetings of participants shall be held no less than once per year and the extraordinary general meetings of participants is held in cases specified by the company's charter, as well as in any other cases if the interests of the company and its participants require convocation of such meeting.

Under the Law on JSC, the ordinary general meetings of shareholders shall be conducted at least once a year not earlier than two months and not later than six months after yearly closure. The annual results of JSC's activities (approval of annual reports, annual accounting balance sheets, decision of distribution of profits, etc.) shall be approved at such meetings. If the company is owned by one shareholder, such decisions shall be adopted in the form of a written resolution (without convocation of meeting). In case the company is owned by two or more shareholders, an additional special procedure and terms of notification, calling and holding of shareholders' meeting shall apply.

Any shareholders' general meetings which shall be convoked for any corporate purposes (approval of major or related-party transactions, appointment of general director, adoption of new charter edition, and other actions which are within the competence of shareholders) not related to approval of annual results of a company's activities are extraordinary. Such meetings shall be convoked and held in accordance with terms and requirements provided by the law.

3.3 How are minority shareholders' rights protected?

See paragraph 3.4. below

3.4 Is shareholder activism encouraged or discouraged? If not encouraged, how is it regulated?

In accordance with Article 31 of the Law on JSC, anyone, even the minority shareholder, has the following rights: (i) to participate in the general meeting of shareholders with the right to vote on all matters within its competence; (ii) to receive dividends; and (iii) in case of a company's liquidation – to receive a part of any distribution of a company's assets.

According to the Law on JSC, the extraordinary meeting of the shareholders shall be held by the decision of the board of directors (supervisory board) of the company based on its own initiative, requests of the internal audit commission (internal inspector), an auditor of the company and also any shareholders who jointly own no less than 10 per cent of the voting shares of the company at the date of submitting the request. The extraordinary meeting called at the request of the shareholders (or a shareholder) who jointly own(s) no less than 10 per cent of the voting shares of the company must be held within 40 days from the time of submitting the request to hold the extraordinary meeting. Therefore, minority shareholders who own jointly no less than 10 per cent of shares are entitled to require the holding of an extraordinary shareholders' meeting.

Under the Federal Law on JSC, shareholders (or a shareholder) who jointly own(s) no less than 2 per cent of the voting shares of the company are entitled to include the issues on the agenda of the annual shareholders' meeting and recommend candidates for the board of directors (supervisory board), collective executive board, internal audit commission (internal inspector) and counting commission of the company, whose number may not exceed the number of the members in a relevant body, and also a candidate for the position of chief executive officer.

Besides, a company or shareholder(s) jointly owning no less than 1 per cent of placed common shares of the company are entitled to file a lawsuit in court against a member of the board of directors (supervisory board), sole executive body (director, general director), member of collective executive body (management board, directorate) and also the management organisation or manager with regard to compensation of losses caused to the company.

Since 1 July 2006, a rule has come into force according to which a company or shareholder(s) are entitled to file a lawsuit in court against a member of the board of directors (supervisory board), sole executive body (director, general director), member of collective executive body (management board, directorate) and also the management regarding the losses caused due to their wrongful actions (or failure to act) violating the procedure for acquisition of shares of an OJSC provided for by Chapter XI.1 of the Federal Law on JSC. Thus, a minority shareholder may recover losses from an executive body caused by the actions of this executive body.

The court and arbitrary practice certifies the possibility of such recovery as well. In addition to the above-considered right for appeal of decisions of shareholders' meetings and board of directors, a shareholder has certain rights for appealing against the company's deals.

For instance, according to the CC RF, the deal effected by the legal entity in contradiction to the targets of its activity, definitely restricted in its charter documents, or by the legal entity, which has no licence for the performance of the relevant activity, may be recognised by the court as invalid upon the lawsuit of this legal entity, of its founder (participant), or of the state body, supervising over the activity of the legal entity, if it has been proved that the other party to the deal has known, or should have known, of the deal being illegal. The demand for use of the consequences of a void deal may be submitted by any interested party. A company's shareholder may be treated as such an interested party.

Besides, under the Law on JSC, a major or an interested-party transaction performed with a failure to comply with the corporate approval requirements may be invalidated on the basis of the lawsuit filed by a company or a shareholder thereof.

3.5 How are professional shareholders (those minority shareholders who seek some extra benefit from companies by unduly and habitually influencing management by using their shareholding) treated by the law? Are they excluded from attending the shareholders' meeting? Are they criminally or otherwise publicly sanctioned?

The Law on LLC contains no restrictions in this regard.

According to the Law on JSC, the holders of preferred shares of the company shall not be entitled to vote at a general shareholders' meeting unless the Law on JSC provides for otherwise.

Meanwhile, holders of preferred shares are entitled to participate in a general meeting of shareholders and vote on issues relating to (i) the reorganisation or liquidation of the company; and (ii) the introduction of amendments or addenda to the company's charter where such amendments or addenda restrict the rights of holders of preferred shares, including determination or increase of the amount of dividends and/or liquidation value payable on the preferred shares of the previous turn priority as well as providing holders of preferred shares of a different type of advantages in the order of payment of dividends and (or) liquidation value of the shares (Article 32, paragraph 4 of the Law on JSC). Holders of preferred shares are also entitled to participate and vote on issues included in the competence of the general meeting of the company's shareholders starting from the general meeting of shareholders following the annual general meeting that failed to adopt a decision on full payment or adopted a decision on partial payment of dividends on preferred shares irrespective of the reasons thereof.

The right of holders of preferred shares to participate in and vote at the general meeting of shareholders shall cease as from the date of the first payment of dividends on the shares in full (Article 32, paragraph 5 of the Law on JSC).

3.6 Are shareholders' benefits given to some of the shareholders by the company without resolution by the shareholders' meeting prohibited or regulated by the law or other rules?

The Law on LLC and the Law on JSC contain the possibility to attribute additional rights or obligations to one or more of the shareholders. These additional rights or obligations have to be unanimously approved by the participants/shareholders. Such additional rights are not transferred to the third party along with the share.

4. DIRECTORS AND BOARD OF DIRECTORS

4.1 What are the functions and responsibilities of the directors and the board of directors? Do you have a one- or two-tier board system? What are the outside directors called?

For the responsibilities and liabilities of the directors, see paragraph 10 below.

There is a three-tier directors' management system in Russia, which includes the board of directors (which may sometimes be called as supervisory counsel), collective executive body (the executive board) and sole executive body (the general director).

According to the legislator's concept, the board of directors is the body responsible for the strategy of the company's development, while the executive bard is a tactical body subordinate to the board of directors whose mission is to realise the business plan elaborated by the board of directors. The sole executive body is an intermediate between the company's corporate bodies and third parties from one side and the company's personnel from the other side.

Board of directors

As mentioned above, formation of the board of directors is not mandatory for LLCs and JSCs with less than 50 shareholders. In case the board of directors is not formed, its competence is by force of law delegated to the general meeting of shareholders/participants.

The procedure of formation of the board of directors and termination of the powers of its members is determined in the charter of the company. Members of the board of directors are elected by the general meeting of shareholders/participants.

The term of authority of the board of directors shall be determined in the charter of the company; no statutory limitations are imposed on the aforesaid term. The number of the board of directors members may not be less than five in JSCs. If the number of shareholders is more than 1,000, the board of directors shall consist of at least seven members and if the number of shareholders exceeds 10,000, no less than nine members of the board of directors are required.

Members of the board of directors are individuals who may be the participants/shareholders of the company. Members of the company's collective executive body (executive board) may not constitute more than a quarter of the membership of the board of directors of the company.

The chairman of the board of directors is elected from the members thereof under the procedure stipulated in the charter of the company or internal regulations for the board of directors. The general director of the company may not be simultaneously the chairman of its board of directors.

The competence of the board of directors is determined by the company's charter in compliance with provisions of law.

Elections to the board of directors are conducted using cumulative voting. At such voting, each share gives its owner the number of votes equal to the number of voting share multiplied by the number of members of the board of directors determined by the company's charter. Candidates having received the largest number of votes are deemed elected.

Collective executive body (CEB) – the executive board

The second tier of corporate management is represented by the executive board.

It may be formed in addition to the sole executive body of the company (the general director) in case the charter of the company expressly provides for its formation. Members of the executive board are elected by the general meeting of participants or board of directors (if such question is referred to its competence).

The term of authority of the executive board is determined in the charter of the company.

Members of the executive board are natural persons. Shareholders may be members of the company.

The functions of the chairman of the company's executive board are performed by the general director, except in the case where the powers of the company's individual executive body have been transferred to its manager.

The law does not provide for a definite list of authorities of the executive board. To its competence may be referred all questions which are not referred to the competence of the general meeting of participants and the board of directors of the company.

Sole executive body (SEB) – the general director (GD)

A company's sole executive body is the general director – the face of the company. He acts on behalf of the company without a power of attorney, represents its interests and complete transactions. The GD is entitled to issue powers of attorney for the right of representation on behalf of the company, including powers of attorney with right for subdelegation.

The GD issues orders on the appointment of the company's employees to relevant offices, on their transfer and dismissal, applies measures of encouragement and imposes disciplinary penalties.

Additionally, if preparation, convening and holding of the general meeting of shareholders (GMS) of the company falls within the competencies of the board of directors, the SEB shall have the right to demand the holding of the extraordinary GMS of the company. In a company which does not have a board of directors, making a decision on the convocation of the GMS and approval of its agenda generally falls within the competence of the GD .

The GD executes all other powers which are not assigned by law or the company's charter to the competences of the GMS, of the board of directors or the CEB. Under the Law on LLC and Law on JSC, the GD may not be limited in his power to enter into transactions on behalf of the company except for the cases that are directly referred by law to competences of other management bodies.

4.2 What are the rules that may give rise to civil and criminal liability of the director(s)? How are those liabilities sought?

See paragraph 10 below.

4.3 Does the board of directors have a committee system, eg, nomination committee, compensation committee, audit committee? If not required, is it common practice for companies? How does it function?

Current legislation of the Russian Federation does not provide for any mandatory requirements for the board of directors to have a committee system. Requirements with regard to a committee system, as a rule, are stipulated in the local documents of the company.

A committee system most often exists in major or transnational companies with foreign investments like TNK-BP, TGK-1. For instance, in TNK-BP there are three board committees: the audit committee, the compensation committee, and the health, safety and environment (HSE) committee; a committee system in TGK-1 comprises the audit committee, business strategy and investment committee, and the HR and remuneration committee.

4.4 Is it a legal requirement to have an independent director or a third-party director? If so, how are they appointed? Is it required for listed companies?

In OJSCs, if the number of shareholders exceeds 1,000 the decision to approve an interested-party deal shall be adopted by the board of directors of the company by the majority vote of independent directors who are not interested in the transaction.

If all the members of the board of directors of the company are deemed interested persons and/or are not independent directors, the transaction may be approved by the general meeting of shareholders according to the procedure specified in the Law on JSC.

According to the Law on JSC, an independent director is considered a member of the board of directors who is not or who had not been during the year preceding the decision taken:

- a person performing the functions of sole executive body of the company, in particular, its executive, member of the collective executive body, a person holding an office in the management bodies of the management company;
- a person whose spouse, parents, children, sibling and half-brothers and -sisters, step-parents and step-children are persons who hold an office in the mentioned management bodies; and
- an affiliated person of the company, except for a member of the board of directors of the company.

Russian legislation contains no special provisions on the procedure of appointing independent directors.

4.5 How is the compensation for directors or officers determined? Can it be contested by the shareholders or the regulatory authorities? What are the common rules or practices for the compensation of officers?

See paragraph 9 below.

4.6 How will the board handle a corporate crisis like an internal criminal case, violence, social media exposure or dawn raid by the authorities?

The board of directors does not have any rights and obligations to third parties. Yet, they must follow the general principles of corporate governance described in paragraph 1.1 above. The general director will be held liable for the actions prescribed by law (for the detailed description of the liability of the general director, see paragraph 10.1 below).

5. BOARD OF AUDITORS, AUDIT COMMITTEE, ACCOUNTING AUDITORS

5.1 How is the internal accounting and legal audit structured and conducted? Is an outside accounting audit required and, if so, how is it structured? Are there requirements to change the auditor each five years?

LLCs and JSCs are required to prepare financial statements for each calendar quarter and annual financial reporting. Currently, financial statements must be submitted to the tax authorities on a quarterly basis (no later than the 30th day of the month following the quarter) and the annual financial statements are filed within 90 days after the end of the reporting year. If the company fails to submit financial statements the penalty is established at RUR 200 (approx. $6) for each non-submitted document. An additional penalty is specified for responsible employees (general director) amounting to RUR 100–300 (approx. $3–10).

The external audit by an independent auditor for LLCs or CJSCs is mandatorily required if the volume of revenues from production sales for the previous business year exceeds RUR 400,000,000 (approx. $13,333,000) or volume of assets according to the annual balance sheet for the previous business year is more than RUR 60,000,000 (approx. $2,000,000). OJSCs should appoint an independent auditor in all cases. The current legislation does not provide for penalties for failure to appoint the external auditor (when required by the law). However, a new draft law prepared by the Ministry of Finance amending the Code on Administrative Offences proposes to introduce such a corporate penalty, amounting up to RUR 700,000 ($23,330).

The appointment of an internal auditor is obligatory for CJSCs and OJSCs in all cases and for an LLC if the number of its participants is more than 15. Nevertheless, LLCs may always appoint an internal auditor for the review of their financial and economic activities. Internal audit may be conducted either by the internal audit commission or an internal inspector. The term of the internal auditor's office as well as the number of members of the internal audit commission is stipulated by the charter.

At the demand of any participant/shareholder of the company an audit may be carried out by the professional auditor chosen by him. If such an audit has been carried out, the auditor's services shall be paid at the expense of the company's participant/shareholder who initiated this audit. Such expenses may be compensated to him by decision of the general meeting at the expense of the company's funds.

5.2 Do you have supervisory auditors? What is the function of the supervisory auditors' board?

Not applicable.

6. MARKET DISCLOSURE/TRANSPARENCY TO THE SHAREHOLDERS AND THE PUBLIC

6.1 What are the disclosure requirements for companies in your jurisdiction under company law, capital markets law or any other rules?

Basically, a company has two disclosure responsibilities: (i) to disclose company information to its shareholders/participants (private disclosure); and (ii) duty of public disclosure to third parties.

Private disclosure

According to the Federal Law 'On Security Market' and Resolution of the FSFR regarding Approval of the 'Regulations on Maintaining an Inscribed Securities' Owners Register', a shareholder owing more than 1 per cent of shares is entitled to demand, and the company is obliged to disclose to the shareholder names of the shareholders, quantity, type and nominal value of the owned shares.

According to the Law on JSC, the shareholders/participants have the right to receive, and the company is obliged to provide, the following information:

- articles of association of the company, duly registered amendments and

addenda thereto, other documents related to the state registration of the company;
- internal regulations of the company, information on the company's assets including the annual reports and financial statements, reports of independent appraisers, issues prospecta and securities reports;
- minutes of general meetings of shareholders, of the board of directors of the company, internal audit commission or internal inspector of the company and the collective executive body of the company;
- lists of affiliated persons of the company, as well as lists of the persons entitled to attend a general meeting of shareholders and to receive dividends, other lists compiled by the company for the purpose of exercising by shareholders of their rights in compliance with the requirements of the Law on JSC;
- notices of making shareholders' agreements forwarded to the company, as well as lists of the persons that have made such agreements; and
- judicial acts available to it in respect of a dispute which is connected with the company's establishment, its management or participation therein, in particular to rulings on initiation by arbitration court proceedings on a case and taking over of the statement of claim or application, on changing the ground or subject of the previous claim made.

In addition to the aforementioned documents, according to court practice a shareholder has the right to require other information relevant to the business activities of the company.

Public disclosure

The general principles of disclosure of information on the Russian stock market are specified in the Securities Market Law and Law on JSC.

The Securities Market Law sets out the general principles of disclosure of information relating to changes in the company's shareholders and controlling entities and there are also certain laws which set out additional disclosure requirements to such forms of entities as credit organisations, companies of strategic importance and others. Information disclosure protocol is specified by a number of regulations issued by the Federal Service for Financial Markets of the Russian Federation (FSFM), the federal body which is responsible for regulation, control and supervision of the capital markets in Russia.

The entities registered in Russia in the form of OJSCs with an unlimited number of possible shareholders and CJSCs/LLCs with the number of shareholders/participants limited to 50 which have publicly placed their bonds or other securities (the 'issuers' and solely the 'issuer') are subject to obligatory disclosure of information under Russian law as specified in the following paragraph.

The rules describing the procedure for disclosure requirements are set out in Order No. 11-46/pz-n dated 4 October 2011 of the FSFM 'On endorsing the Regulations on disclosure of information by the issuers of issuance securities' (as amended) (the Order). The Regulations on disclosure of information by the Issuers of securities endorsed by the Order (the Regulations) set out detailed requirements relating to disclosure of information by the issuers.

The Securities Law and the Federal Law on JSC only cover specific securities which are called issuance securities. A security is an issuance security if it:

- secures all property or non-property rights according to Securities Law;
- is placed by issues; and
- an issue grants equal terms and scope of the subscriber's rights regardless of the time of acquiring of such security.

For the purposes of this paragraph, indications of securities shall be read as issuance securities.

An issuer bears stock market public disclosure obligations if (i) it places securities through public placement or (ii) if the number of subscribers under private securities placement exceeds 500. This rule applies equally to CJSCs and OJSCs.

Therefore, if the issuer meets condition (i) or (ii), it shall disclose its information in the following forms:

- Mandatory disclosure data: it comprises the issuer's annual reports, the financial data, the list of subsidiaries, the content of the issuer's charter, the information on acquisition of more than 20 per cent of shares of another company, as well as some other data. As a general rule, this information is disclosed on the date this information is due to be prepared (eg, the annual reports have to be disclosed within three months after the end of the financial year) (the 'mandatory disclosure data').
- Substantial facts disclosure: it comprises those facts which may impact the share price. Generally, they have to be disclosed on the same day as they occur (the 'substantial facts').
- Quarterly report: a quarterly report is drawn up in the form fixed by the FSFM and cumulates necessary information on the issuer and its activities.

The list of mandatory disclosure data and substantial facts is determined in details by the Regulations. The disclosure scope of each substantial fact, its form and other terms is set out individually for each type of substantial fact. These rules may be found in clauses 6.2.1 to 6.2.50 of the Regulations.

6.2 What is the liability or responsibility of the board in relation to the company's disclosure requirements?

In case the company refuses to provide its shareholder with the aforementioned information, a shareholder may file a written claim to the Regional Office of FSFR addressed to its chief and demand bringing the company/company's director to administrative responsibility.

Administrative responsibility shall be as follows: failure of an issuer (the company) to submit the information, and also breaking by the said persons of the procedure for and time of submission thereof, as well as submission of incomplete information and/or unreliable information, and/or misleading information, if these actions (omission to act) do not contain a criminally punishable deed shall entail the imposition of an administrative fine on officials of between 20,000 and 30,000 roubles, and on legal entities of between 500,000 and 700,000 roubles.

7. M&A AND CORPORATE GOVERNANCE

7.1 Upon an M&A offer, how are the transparency and fairness rules of the company provided under the company and stock market laws and rules?

In Russia, M&A transactions may be performed by means of reorganisation or share transfer and each of the mentioned legal procedures has its own transparency and fairness rules.

Reorganisation of a Russian commercial entity can be made in the form of spin-off of a company from another, split up of one company into two or more independent companies, merger of two or more companies into one new entity and adhesion of one company to another. Since from the start of reorganisation creditors may claim pre-term discharge of the company's obligations, before reorganisation takes effect the companies participating in reorganisation are required to disclose information thereof through publications in a State Registration Herald.

Some specific provisions of the Russian law are applicable to acquisition of shares in OJSCs, eg mandatory offer and squeeze-out rules:

- Mandatory offer: a person who has acquired more than 30 per cent of shares of an OJSC (taking into account the shares owned by this person and its affiliates) is obliged to send a mandatory offer to other shareholders of the company to acquire their shares.
- Squeeze-out: a shareholder who as a result of a transaction with shares holds more than 95 per cent of shares of an OJSC (taking into account the shares owned by this person and its affiliates) may compel the remaining minority shareholders to sell their shares to him at his request and conversely such shareholder may be compelled to buy shares owned by such minority shareholders upon their request.

8. PROXY FIGHTING

8.1 Is proxy fighting customarily conducted for control of the company management or what other items? How is it regulated under the company law or market regulations?

According to Russian legislation, any shareholder that has the right to vote at the general shareholders' meeting may delegate this power to any other person under the power of attorney. Sometimes this leads to violations and, of course, this can be abused to acquire illegal control over the company (see the case described in paragraph 1.3).

There is a strict rule that the members of the board of directors and/or collective executive body may not delegate the right to vote to any other person.

This rule, however, does not extend to the sole executive body. Moreover, the general director has by virtue of law right to act on behalf of the company and thus powers of attorney issued by a GD do not require notarial form. However, they must be issued under the seal of the company.

9. OFFICERS' REMUNERATION RULES

9.1 How is remuneration of officers determined? By whom? Is there

a role for the shareholders' meeting? Is there any mechanism for an independent body to review and evaluate them?

The company is not obliged to fix the remuneration for the members of the board of directors or the CEB; moreover, the company may not guarantee such remuneration to the members of the board of directors or CEB.

The remuneration of the board of directors and CEB members has to be approved by the general meeting of shareholders/participants.

Unlike the CEB and board of directors members the general director is *de jure* an employee of the company and, therefore, gets his salary under the Labour Code of the Russian Federation. His additional remuneration may be determined either in the employment agreement or by the decision of the company's body, which is competent to appoint the general director.

The only remuneration of the general director which is legally binding is the termination compensation. According to the Labour Code of Russia, the company and the general director may at any time during employment agree on termination of employment on mutual agreement. On the last day of employment the employee receives final pay (salary for the time the employee has actually worked, compensation for holiday accrued but unused, compensation for expenses (if relevant) and compensation under the termination agreement (if any)).

Often this option implies that some compensation is paid to the employee; however, there are no legal requirements to the amount. The company may negotiate payment of compensation similar to the statutory entitlements the employee would/could get in case of, for example, dismissal due to redundancy (ie up to five monthly salaries). But in practice, the amount may be different depending on the results of negotiations between the company and the employee.

9.2 Is the mechanism of officers' remuneration publicly debated?

Not applicable.

10. DIRECTORS' LIABILITIES, LIABILITY INSURANCE, INDEMNIFICATION

10.1 What are the directors' responsibilities and liabilities under the law? Can those liabilities be covered by insurance? Can it be indemnified by the company or other related parties?

Directors' responsibilities

The Law on JSC contains more detailed legal provisions on the board of directors and its members; therefore, this paragraph will deal with the issues relating to JSC board of directors members.

The Law on JSC provides for a very general description of the responsibilities of the member of the board of directors. Specifically, according to the Law:

- When exercising his/her rights and performing his/her obligations the member of the board of directors of the company should act in the best interests of the company and exercise his/her rights and perform his/her obligations in respect of the company reasonably and in good faith.

- The member of the board of directors is obliged to inform the company in writing about shares of the company owned by him/her, specifying their quantity and categories (or types) no later than 10 days from the date of purchase of the shares.

The Law allows setting out more detailed and specific list of responsibilities of the board of directors and its members as well as liability for breach of such responsibilities in the internal documents of the JSC. Therefore, in practice, JSCs often adopt regulations on the board of directors that contain the list of responsibilities of the members of the board of directors.

On April 2002, the Federal Securities Commission of the Russian Federation by its decree approved the Corporate Code of Conduct that was developed for the purposes of improving management of JSCs in Russia, protection of rights and legitimate interests of shareholders as well as disclosure of information to investors. Such Corporate Code of Conduct touched on the issue of responsibilities of the members of the board of directors and set out the following responsibilities:

- To perform responsibilities reasonably and in good faith as well as in the best interests of the company. To this end to require provision by the officers of the company of additional information if such information is required to adopt a decision.
- To ensure that there is no conflict of interest between personal interests of the member of the board of directors and interests of the company and, if a conflict exists, to disclose it to the board of directors. To this end to abstain from voting on questions on an agenda in which he/she has personal interest.
- Actively participate in meetings of the board of directors and, when necessary, to call meetings of the board of directors to timely resolve matters.
- Not to disclose or use in private purposes or in the interest of third parties confidential information related to the company or insider information.

Although from the legal perspective the Corporate Code of Conduct is not considered as the mandatory ruling but rather serves as a guidance to Russian JSCs, in our view, the above list of responsibilities reflects responsibilities that members of the board of directors *de facto* have.

A member of the board of directors may have additional administrative responsibilities if he/she is elected as the chairperson of the board of directors.

Liability

Civil liability

The Member of the board of directors shall be liable to the company for any damages caused to the company if:

- he/she acted not in good faith, in the best interests of the company and without the proper discretion; and/or
- damages were caused as a result of the guilty actions (or omission to act) of the member of the board of directors.

When determining the grounds and extent of liability of the member of the board of directors, the ordinary course of business and other relevant circumstances of the matter must be taken into account.

Please note that the existing application practice with respect to responsibility of board members is not yet developed and remains rather ambiguous with respect to particular clarifications on what criteria shall be used to determine which actions may be considered as actions in good faith and best interests of the company, and, on the contrary, actions not in the good faith and best interest of the company. Therefore, when considering the case each court may interpret this in its own way.

In the event that liability is incurred by several members of the board of directors, their liability to the company shall be joint.

The company will be able to bring a claim against the member of the board of directors on compensation for damages caused to the company only if the company already suffered the damages by the time such a claim is brought. The possibility of incurring damages to the company in the future should not be taken into account.

It should be noted that the claimant bears onus probandi as to the amount of damages.

Since the Law does not limit the damages incurred by the company due to culpable actions of the member of the board of directors, the plaintiff is entitled to claim not only direct losses but also the lost profit.

If the member of the board of directors voted against a decision which caused damages to the company or did not participate in voting on such an issue, the member shall not be liable for the damages inflicted as a result of making such a decision except for cases when the above actions (or omission to act) of the member caused damages to the company.

Administrative and criminal liability

The member of the board of directors may also bear administrative and criminal liability.

The administrative liability of the member of the board of directors is specified by the Russian Code of Administrative Violations and generally includes an administrative penalty (ie, fine) and/or disqualification (ie, deprivation of the right to be a member of the board of directors, to manage a legal entity, etc.). For instance, misuse of insider information entails an administrative penalty between 30,000 RUR (approx. $1,000) and 50,000 RUR (approx. $1,600) or disqualification for a term of 1–2 years.

Administrative liability may be applied as a result of audits of the company by Russian controlling authorities initiated by these authorities, officers of the company or shareholders.

The criminal liability of the member of the board of directors is specified by the Russian Criminal Code. For example, misuse of insider information for making transactions with financial instruments if it inflicted large-scale damage (ie, more than 2,500,000 RUR (approx. $83,000)) or is connected to deriving large-scale revenue or avoidance of large-scale losses entails a penalty of between 300,000 RUR (approx. $10,000) and 500,000 RUR (approx. EUR 16,600) or a prison sentence of 2–4 years.

Criminal liability can be applied to the member of the board of directors only if he/she was found guilty by the respective court in Russia. Criminal proceedings may be initiated by Russian controlling authorities, officers of the company, shareholders or third parties that suffered damages.

Insurance issues
Under Russian law, a company is not obliged to insure the liability of the member of the board of directors. Such insurance is made on a voluntary basis at the discretion of each particular company. Terms and conditions of the insurance are set out by insurance companies.

The liability insurance is, usually, maintained by major Russian companies and, especially, Russian companies whose shares are listed on foreign stock markets.

As a rule, the insurance policy covers the risk of damages that may be caused by a member of the board of directors to a company that he/she will be obliged to compensate under the law, as well as compensation of court expenses that may be incurred by a company if court proceedings are initiated by third parties in connection with a violation. We note that this is only an example of insurance policy coverage and we would recommend that the client double-checks whether the insurance is maintained by the company and, if yes, what risks are covered by the insurance policy.

Indemnification
Russian law does not recognise the concept of indemnity as it is understood in common law; therefore, indemnity provisions stipulated in agreement between the company and its members of the board will hardly be enforceable in Russia. Furthermore, neither the company nor its shareholders (who are formally entitled to claim damages from members of the board (as the case may be)) may waive their claims (either existing or future) against members of the board.

11. SHAREHOLDERS' DERIVATIVE SUITS

11.1 Is a shareholder's derivative suit provided for by law in your jurisdiction? How is it enforced by the shareholders?

A shareholder is entitled to initiate court proceedings in order to invalidate the decision adopted by a general meeting of shareholders in violation of the requirements of the law and internal documents of the company. This is possible if two requirements are met:

- the shareholder has not taken part in the general meeting of shareholders or voted against the adoption of such decision; and
- his rights/legal interests have been violated by the said decision.

The application for declaring invalid a decision of a general meeting of shareholders may be filed with a court within three months as of the date when a shareholder learnt or was supposed to learn about the decision adopted and about the circumstances serving as a ground for declaring it invalid.

Besides, a shareholder/shareholders holding jointly not less than 1 per cent of the company's shares may file a claim to the court against a member of the board of directors, the SEB, a member of the CEB or the management company for compensation of damages caused to the company by their wrongful acts.

11.2 Have there been any recent relevant court cases on the subject?

These are two recent court cases in relation to shareholders' derivative suits:

Ruling of the Presidium of the Supreme Arbitrazh Court of the Russian Federation as of 15 January 2013 No. 11808/12 (case No. A59-2867/2010). In this case the shareholder contested the decisions of the board of directors of the bank and of the extraordinary shareholders' meeting. The claim was refused, as the claimant failed to prove that the bank made any hardships to the shareholder in exercising her rights to redeem the extra shares.

Ruling of Federal Arbitrazh Court of the Volgo-Vyatsky region as of 13 December 2012 (case No. A79-5172/2012). This case illustrates an action attacking the decision of the extraordinary shareholders' meeting in relation to new charter amendments. Shareholders claimed that the controversial clause stipulating prohibition of placement of shares and securities of the company was included in the text of the company's charter in breach of law. The claim was satisfied as the claimants demonstrated to the Court that such charter amendments have resulted in infringement of their rights and interests.

12. SOCIAL INTEREST IN CORPORATE BEHAVIOUR

12.1 How is a company in your country expected to deal with the following issues? Corporate social responsibility; gender, racial and social diversification; environmental issues; ecology and corruption?

Corporate social responsibility, gender, racial and social diversification

Currently, there are no requirements in Russian corporate governance legislation regarding social responsibility; gender, racial and social diversification.

Despite this fact, under the Labour Code of the Russian Federation, employers cannot refuse to sign the employment agreement or dismiss an employee (including a general director) for reasons of sexuality, gender or race.

Environmental issues and ecology

Most significant ecological issues in Russia are regulated by the Federal Law No. 7-FZ 'On environment protection' dated 10 January 2002 providing several prescriptions for companies preventing those activities which may harm the environment. Managers and officers of such companies should be aware of issues concerning the environment. Companies are liable to pay fines for any negative environmental impact that they cause. Such impact is preliminarily measured by the competent authorities – should the company be granted the right to such negative impact, it has the duty to monitor and report all the details of this negative impact.

Current Russian legislation also provides some tax exemptions for environmentally friendly entrepreneurial activity.

Under a Civil Code rule, construction contractors are required to protect the environment. Apart from that, the Code on Administrative Offences includes a series of rules prohibiting different types of activities which are detrimental to the environment.

Corruption

The Russian Federation has membership in several international organisations, including the Council of Europe Group of States Against Corruption (GRECO), OECD Working Group on Bribery in International Business Transactions, and some other FATF, UN and OECD conventions.

Main Russian anti-corruption laws include:

- The Federal Law 'On countering the legalisation of illegal earnings (money laundering) and the financing of terrorism' No. 115-FZ dated 7 August 2001.
- The Federal Law 'On Counteraction to Corruption' dated 25 December 2008.
- Codes for administrative offences and the Criminal Code.

Russian criminal law sets forth liability for the crimes (i) committed in Russia or (ii) by Russian citizens outside Russia, including the bribery of foreign officials (as per new changes in 2011).

Please note that there may be no criminal sanctions against legal entities. Only physical persons can be brought to criminal liability.

The Code on Administrative Offences, Article 19.28 'Unlawful remuneration on behalf of a legal entity' prohibits unlawful transfer, offer or promise made on behalf of or for the benefit of a legal entity of money, securities or other property, or unlawful rendering to such person of services with a monetary value, in return for the performance by the public official, or individual performing management functions in a commercial or other organisation, of action or inaction in the interest of such legal entity.

As of 2011, Russian law penalises companies for bribes with an administrative fine up to 100 times the amount of the bribe but not less than RUR 100 million (EUR 2.5 million) with the confiscation of money or other property given as a bribe.

In January 2013, a new set of anti-corruption regulations entered into force. These are aimed at implementing additional anticipatory measures for the prevention of corruption in companies.

Thus, as of 1 January 2013, according to Article 13.3 of the amended anti-corruption law (Federal Law of 25 December 2008 No. 273-FZ 'On Combating Corruption'), a company should develop specific measures for corruption prevention. This new article contains an approximate list of measures for corruption counteraction, which are *inter alia*: (i) the designation of officers responsible for anti-corruption measures; and (ii) the adoption of a corporate compliance and ethics code; prevention of drawing up informal reporting, etc.

While no exhaustive list of measures has been introduced by the legislator, a set of measures and procedures which are necessary to counter corruption in each company has to be determined, depending on the company's needs, risk assessment, specific activities and organisational structure.

Singapore

Annabelle Yip **WongPartnership LLP**

1. GENERAL PRINCIPLES

1.1 What are the general principles of corporate governance in your jurisdiction? What are the main objectives of corporate governance principles in your jurisdiction? State also whether your legal system is based on common law or civil law.

The Singapore legal system is based on the English common law system and Singapore law has its roots in English law. The general principles of Singapore corporate governance, being the system or framework of laws, regulations, customs, practices, processes and structures by which corporations are directed and controlled and which govern the relationship, rights and liabilities of corporations with its various stakeholders, have been traditionally rooted in English legal principles, enhanced by international best practices, as globalisation has influenced the convergence of corporate governance standards.

Singapore's approach to corporate governance has been a pragmatic, balanced one. It is mindful on the one hand of the importance of keeping up with global standards in line with Singapore's reputation as a hub for international business, and on the other, that the costs of compliance are kept under control such that companies of varying sizes and resources are still incentivised to do business and maintain their presence in Singapore and to continue to invest here.

The Singapore corporate governance regime comprises a mix of mandatory rules, captured mainly in the Companies Act (Chapter 50) (CA), Securities and Futures Act (Chapter 289) (SFA), the listing rules (Listing Rules) of the Singapore Exchange Securities Trading Limited (SGX), and best practice recommendations in the form of the Code of Corporate Governance (Code), as well as common law.

To carry on business in Singapore, a corporation must either be incorporated in Singapore or registered as a foreign company under the CA.

Companies incorporated in Singapore are managed by or under the direction or supervision of a board of directors (board). Directors are fiduciaries and obliged to act in the best interests of the company. This is generally understood also to refer to the collective interests of the company's shareholders. The collective interests of the company's employees can also be taken into account. If the company is insolvent, the board is bound to consider the interests of the company's creditors.

In line with an increasing global perspective of sustainable businesses that the interests of the company do not merely encompass the interests of shareholders, employees and (in the case of insolvency) creditors, but must necessarily encompass also the interests of other stakeholders, the Code provides that the role of the board includes setting the company's values and standards (including ethical standards), ensuring that obligations to shareholders and other stakeholders are understood and met, and considering sustainability issues (eg environmental and social factors) as part of its strategic formulation.

There are statutory requirements imposed on directors under the CA to act honestly and use reasonable diligence in the discharge of the duties of their office. Directors have duties of due care, skill and diligence under common law. The CA, as well as common law, also addresses issues of conflict of interests, acting for an improper purpose, and improper use of information or powers.

We will not cover in this chapter the more stringent sets of corporate governance requirements and guidelines issued by the Monetary Authority of Singapore (MAS) applicable to financial institutions, nor business structures other than corporations, nor the general laws relevant to corporations as they conduct their business in Singapore, such as laws prohibiting acts of corruption and competition law.

In this chapter, when we refer to provisions of the CA, they will apply to Singapore-incorporated companies, and when we refer to the SFA, Listing Rules and Code, they generally apply to corporations (both Singapore- and foreign-incorporated) which are listed on the SGX.

1.2 Have there been any recent developments in the law, codes and rules of corporate governance?

The area of corporate governance has been particularly fertile ground in Singapore in recent times, with extensive reviews undertaken.

The Securities and Futures (Amendment) Act 2009 provided for extensive amendments to be made to the SFA and has come progressively into force. Changes included a streamlining and updating of the regime for disclosure of interests by chief executive officers (CEOs), directors and substantial shareholders, and specific obligations for disclosure of interests in relation to listed business trusts and real-estate investment trusts, as well as new attributed liability provisions for prohibited market conduct, where corporations are made liable for the actions of their employees and officers if the offence was committed for the corporation's benefit and with its consent or connivance or attributable to its negligence, and officers in turn are made liable for civil penalties where a contravention by the corporation was as a result of the officer's consent or connivance or attributable to his neglect. Interestingly, the attributed liability provisions provide for defences based on corporate culture and compliance policies and procedures – a first for Singapore corporate governance regulations.

The Corporate Governance Council, comprising representatives from regulators, listed corporations, professionals and other key stakeholders, was set up to undertake a review of the Code. In May 2012, the 2012 version of the Code was issued, being the third iteration of the Code (the first two were issued in 2001 and 2005). Almost all of its provisions will take effect in respect of annual reports relating to financial years commencing on 1 November 2012.

A steering committee was set up to undertake a review of the CA. It issued a report on its recommendations in 2011, which was put up for public consultation. In October 2012, the Ministry of Finance released its response to the report, accepting most of the recommendations and modifying a few. In May 2012, the draft Companies (Amendment) Bill (CA Bill) implementing the recommendations was issued, again for public consultation. It is expected that by the end of 2012, the finalised CA Bill will be issued and passed, and will progressively come into force thereafter. The CA Bill will amend the CA extensively. Changes will be made to all areas, from provisions relating to directors, shareholder rights and meetings, to shares and share-related provisions, accounts and audit, general company administration and registration of charges.

1.3 Outline recent court cases and incidents involving corporate governance issues. Were there any significant corporate scandals or large unlawful corporate cases?

Corporate governance cases, ranging from cases on breaches of directors' fiduciary duties and prosecution of directors for failing to fulfil their duties of care, skill and diligence, to shareholder disputes, are a regular feature of Singapore law reports. Two notable recent cases are *Madhavan Peter v Public Prosecutor and other appeals* [2012] 4 SLR 613 (Airocean case) and *Lew Chee Fai Kevin v Monetary Authority of Singapore* [2012] 2 SLR 913 (Kevin Lew case), particularly for listed corporations. The Airocean case involved an acquittal of certain independent directors of the Singapore listed corporation Airocean Group Limited (Airocean). They had originally been found liable for their part in Airocean's breach of its obligation to immediately disclose material information under the Listing Rules and also for misleading statements made by Airocean.

The acquittal was a welcome relief to independent directors of listed corporations who were taken aback by the term of imprisonment to which one of the independent directors was initially sentenced, the first time a custodial sentence had been imposed on an independent director in Singapore. It also gave needed clarity to the interpretation of the disclosure obligation, and in particular, how courts would approach the question of whether the information was material such that it needed to be disclosed. The Kevin Lew case, as well as the Airocean case, also clarified the insider-trading offence under the SFA. Directors and management of listed corporations who want to deal in the securities of the listed corporations can now be guided by the principles set out in the two cases in deciding whether they are in a position to trade in the listed corporation's shares.

1.4 Which law enforcement agency is in charge of enforcing corporate governance? May a criminal sanction be levied upon infringement of the corporate governance rules?

Generally speaking, the Accounting and Corporate Regulatory Authority of

Singapore (ACRA) is the authority which administers the CA, and the MAS is the authority that enforces the provisions of the SFA.

The SGX is the initial enforcer of the Listing Rules. The SGX is both a listed securities exchange and a regulator. As a regulator, the penalties that the SGX can impose on corporations for breaches of the Listing Rules range from public censures and reprimands to suspensions and delisting for more serious breaches. In addition, in certain circumstances (eg where the SGX perceives that an offence may have been committed), the SGX will refer the matter to the MAS or another appropriate authority for further investigation and follow-up.

The CA provides for criminal sanctions in addition to disqualification and civil liability for a range of breaches. The SFA provides for criminal sanctions as well as civil penalties and civil liability (to a third party affected by the breach). The report of the steering committee for review of the CA stated that a few respondents had proposed the introduction of a civil penalty regime for the CA, and that this issue was the subject of a review by ACRA.

2. SOURCES OF LAW

2.1 Which laws, codes or statutes govern company structures and organisations? Are there statutes like the Companies Act or other forms of law? Is there much relevant case law?

See paragraphs 1.1 and 1.3 above.

2.2 Which laws, codes or statutes regulate capital markets in your jurisdiction?

See paragraph 1.1 above.

2.3 Are there any public interest laws which apply to or influence corporate governance?

The Code plays a key role in defining the standards of corporate governance best practice in Singapore. It goes beyond legal obligations and encourages listed corporations to meet its best practice recommendations. The Listing Rules require listed corporations to describe its corporate governance practices with specific reference to the principles of the Code in its annual report, and to disclose any deviation from any Code guideline together with an appropriate explanation for the deviation in its annual report.

In 2011, the SGX also issued a Guide to Sustainability Reporting for Listed Companies. For now, there is no requirement for listed corporations in Singapore to produce a sustainability report. However, in a speech made in March 2013, SGX's CEO indicated that the SGX would move to a comply-or-explain basis for sustainability reporting, although no timeline was given. The SGX will introduce more tools to help listed companies report on sustainability, and explore the possibility of setting up a Singapore sustainability index.

In addition, specific provisions of the CA require the court, the Registrar of Companies or the Minister to give due consideration to the 'public interest'. One example is the right of the Registrar, if he is satisfied that it is in the public interest to do so, to require a company which is otherwise exempt from audit to lodge audited accounts.

2.4 Have there been any recent developments in any of the above laws? What are the recent changes to the above laws or rules and the reasons for such changes?

See paragraph 1.2 above.

3. SHAREHOLDERS AND THE SHAREHOLDERS' MEETING

3.1 How are shareholders' interests represented in the company? How are the shareholders assured exercise of their rights? What is the highest governing body within the company structure if it is not the shareholders' meeting?

Under Singapore law, there are essentially two governing bodies within the company structure – the board and the shareholders.

The CA provides that the business of a company shall be managed by or under the direction of the directors, and the directors may exercise all the powers of a company except any power that the CA or the company's memorandum and articles of association (M&AA) require the company to exercise in general meeting. It follows that shareholders have a limited right to interfere in the day-to-day management of the business.

Certain decisions are reserved to shareholders under the CA, notwithstanding anything in the M&AA. For instance, directors may only issue shares of the company if they receive prior authority from shareholders to do so. Directors also shall not carry into effect any proposals for disposing of the whole or substantially the whole of the company's undertaking or property unless those proposals have been approved by shareholders. Other fundamental decisions such as amendment of the M&AA, and winding up of the company, may be effected only with shareholders' approval.

Directors, as a general rule, have to act in the best interests of the company and its shareholders as a whole. The M&AA generally provides that shareholders have the right to appoint and remove directors by ordinary resolution (for public companies, the CA provides additional safeguards and protection for directors in relation to their removal).

As duties of directors are owed to the company, as a general rule, only the company can sue directors for breach of their duties. As an extension of this principle, the CA provides for derivative actions, allowing any shareholder of the company, with the leave of the court, to bring an action in the name and on behalf of the company or to intervene in any action to which the company is a party, for the purpose of prosecuting, defending or discontinuing the action on behalf of the company. Although the derivative action is presently limited to companies other than public companies listed in Singapore, one of the proposals under the CA Bill is to extend the statutory derivative action to all companies. It follows that a shareholder may with leave of the court take out an action in the name and on behalf of the company against errant directors for breach of their fiduciary duties.

3.2 How is the shareholders' meeting conducted? Who may chair the meeting? May attendance (not voting) at the meeting be restricted only to the shareholders? Are the shareholders allowed to be accompanied by legal or other counsel?

The M&AA typically provides who will chair shareholders' meetings. For example, in the model articles set out in the Fourth Schedule of the CA, known as 'Table A', it is provided that the chairman of the board shall preside as chairman at general meetings, unless there is no such chairman or he is not present or is unwilling to act, in which event the members shall elect one of their number to chair the meeting.

In the absence of provision in the M&AA, the CA provides that any member elected by the members present may be chairman.

Generally speaking, attendance at the meeting is restricted only to shareholders and certain officers of the company, but the chairman has the discretion, if he deems fit, to admit observers into the meeting. Such observers may include the legal counsel of shareholders. The chairman may even permit such non-shareholders to address the meeting, if he deems it appropriate.

The M&AA typically also provides for the quorum for the meeting. In the absence of such provision, the CA provides that two members personally present shall form a quorum.

Subject to the M&AA, for companies with a share capital, resolutions can be passed either by show of hands or on a poll; on a show of hands, each member personally present and entitled to vote shall have one vote, and on a poll, each member shall have one vote in respect of each share held by him.

The CA provides for statutory rights to demand a poll, by *inter alia* not less than five members having the right to vote, or by a member or members representing not less than 10 per cent of the total voting rights of all members having a right to vote at the meeting (under the CA Bill, this will be reduced to 5 per cent).

For corporations, the CA provides for attendance at shareholders' meetings by their duly appointed representatives. Members are also entitled to appoint a proxy or proxies to attend and vote (only on a poll, unless the M&AA otherwise provides) in his place at the meeting, and proxies have the same right as the member to speak at the meeting.

The CA presently provides that unless the M&AA otherwise provides, a member shall not be entitled to appoint more than two proxies to attend and vote at the same meeting. The CA Bill, in a contentious amendment, provides for 'relevant intermediaries' to be able to appoint more than two proxies, provided that each proxy is appointed to exercise the rights attached to a different share or shares held by him, and each proxy shall also have the right to vote on a show of hands. 'Relevant intermediaries' are essentially banks or their wholly owned subsidiaries providing nominee services, capital markets licence holders providing custodial services, and the Central Provident Fund Board (in respect of shares purchased under Part IV of the Central Provident Fund (Investment Schemes) Regulations).

The CA also provides for a means for shareholders of a private company to pass resolutions by written means instead of at a shareholders' meeting. The CA Bill will extend the application of the provisions to public unlisted companies as well.

3.3 How are minority shareholders' rights protected?

Under the CA, any shareholder may apply to the court for a remedy on the ground that the affairs of the company are being conducted or the powers of the directors are being exercised in a manner oppressive to one or more shareholders (including himself) or in disregard of their interests as shareholder of the company, or that some act of the company has been done or is threatened or some shareholders' resolution has been passed or is proposed which unfairly discriminates against or is otherwise prejudicial to one or more shareholders (including himself). The court has wide powers to make such orders as it thinks fit to bring to an end or remedy the matter complained of, including directing or prohibiting any act, cancelling or varying any transaction, regulating the conduct of the company's affairs in future, requiring the purchase of shares by other members or by the company, or ordering the winding up of the company.

In addition, if a minority shareholder is sufficiently aggrieved such that it considers it no longer tenable for the company to continue in existence, it may, subject to it meeting the requirements under the CA, apply to the court for a winding up of the company. The court may order the winding up if, *inter alia*, the directors have acted in the affairs of the company in their own interests rather than in the interests of the members as a whole, or in any other manner whatever which appears to be unfair or unjust to other members, or the court is of the opinion that it is just and equitable that the company be wound up.

3.4 Is shareholder activism encouraged or discouraged? If not encouraged, how is it regulated?

Disruptive shareholder activism or shareholder agitation has generally not been an issue in Singapore and the authorities are quite neutral on this issue. Indeed, together with the Code, the Corporate Governance Council also issued an Annexure to the Code entitled 'The Role of Shareholders in Engaging with Companies in which they Invest', which acknowledges, *inter alia*, that active and constructive shareholder relations are crucial in ensuring that corporate governance standards are achieved and maintained, and shareholder inputs on governance matters are useful to strengthen the overall environment for good governance policies and practices, and to convey shareholders' expectations to the board.

3.5 How are professional shareholders (those minority shareholders who seek some extra benefit from companies by unduly and habitually influencing management by using their shareholding) treated by the law? Are they excluded from attending the shareholders' meeting? Are they criminally or otherwise publicly sanctioned?

Singapore law generally treats all shareholders equally. As long as a person, corporation or entity is named as a shareholder on the register of members of the company (in the case of private and public unlisted companies), or as a depositor in the register maintained by the Central (Depository) Pte Ltd, which presently operates the Central Depository System for the holding and transfer of book-entry securities (in the case of public listed companies), the law treats that person, corporation or entity as a member of the company with all the attendant shareholder rights.

Under the CA, notwithstanding any provision in the M&AA, all shareholders have a right to attend shareholders' general meetings and to speak and vote on any resolution, save for limited exceptions, where the M&AA provides that a shareholder may not vote unless all calls or other sums payable by him have been paid, and also where the shareholder holds preference shares and the M&AA provides such preference shareholders do not have the right to vote (except in the limited circumstances where the preference dividend remains in arrear and unpaid, or the resolution varies the rights attached to the preference shares or relates to the company's winding-up).

3.6 Are shareholders' benefits given to some of the shareholders by the company without resolution by the shareholders' meeting prohibited or regulated by the law or other rules?

The CA provides that the rights of preference shareholders with respect to repayment of capital, participation in surplus assets and profits, cumulative or non-cumulative dividends, voting and priority of payment of capital and dividend in relation to other shares or other classes of preference shares, must be set out in the M&AA. Accordingly, it will not be possible to grant such rights attached to shares without provision in the M&AA.

Besides such rights, it is possible for the board to enter into agreements with particular shareholders or which prefer particular shareholders or grant them certain benefits. In doing so, a director has a fiduciary duty to act in the company's best interests and avoid putting himself in a position where his duty and his interest conflict (see paragraph 1.1 above). If directors in doing so act in a manner which oppresses or unfairly prejudices the minority shareholders, minority shareholders have the remedies set out in paragraph 3.3 above, or can claim against the directors on behalf of the company through a derivative action as described in paragraph 3.1 above. (Of course, if the shareholder in question is a director or connected with a director, there are additional restrictions which apply because of his position as director rather than as shareholder.)

The Listing Rules contain a policy on thorough public dissemination of information, and make it clear that under no circumstances, save for limited exceptions, should disclosure of material information be made on an individual or selective basis to any persons, including shareholders, unless the information has previously been fully disclosed and disseminated to the public.

The Listing Rules also contain a chapter governing interested-person transactions. These are transactions between the listed corporation, any of its subsidiaries which is not listed on an approved exchange, or any of its associated companies which the listed group and its interested persons control and similarly not listed, on the one hand, and on the other hand, any director or controlling shareholder (ie a shareholder holding a 15 per cent or more stake in the company or which in fact exercises control over the company) or their associate (as defined in the Listing Rules), among others.

Depending on the value of the interested-person transaction entered into, an announcement, or an announcement and shareholders' approval, of the transaction, may be required. For recurrent transactions of a revenue or trading nature or those necessary for the listed corporation's day-to-day operations, the listed corporation may seek a general mandate from shareholders.

In the case where shareholders' approval is sought of a particular interested-person transaction or general mandate, an opinion from an independent financial adviser will have to be provided on whether the transaction is, or the methods or procedures in the general mandate are, sufficient to ensure that the transactions will be, carried out on normal commercial terms and not prejudicial to the interests of the issuer and its minority shareholders. The interested person and its associates must not vote on the resolution.

4. DIRECTORS AND BOARD OF DIRECTORS

4.1 What are the functions and responsibilities of the directors and the board of directors? Do you have a one- or two-tier board system? What are the outside directors called?

Singapore has a one-tier board system.

While private companies are not required under the CA to have independent directors, the Listing Rules require the boards of listed corporations to have at least two non-executive directors who are independent and free of any material business or financial connection with the listed corporation, and foreign-incorporated listed corporations must have at least two independent directors resident in Singapore.

The Code also recommends that at least one-third of the board comprises independent directors (and in certain cases, at least half of the board; this guideline, however, will not come into force until some years later). The Code defines an 'independent director' as one who has no relationship with the company, its related corporations, its 10 per cent shareholders or its officers that could interfere, or be reasonably perceived to interfere, with the exercise of the director's independent business judgement with a view to the best interests of the company.

4.2 What are the rules that may give rise to civil and criminal liability of the director(s)? How are those liabilities sought?

See paragraph 1.4 above.

4.3 Does the board of directors have a committee system, eg, nomination committee, compensation committee, audit committee?

If not required, is it common practice for companies? How does it function?

For private companies, there is no requirement to have board committees by law. The M&AA usually provides for the flexibility for the board to delegate certain functions to board committees.

For public-listed companies, the CA mandates the formation of an audit committee. In addition, the Code recommends the formation of three committees: the audit committee, remuneration committee (see paragraph 9.1 below) and nominating committee. The audit committee's duties include reviewing the scope and results of the external audit, significant financial-reporting issues and the effectiveness of internal audit functions. The nominating committee's duties include making recommendations to the board on board succession plans, determining the independence of directors, development of a process for board evaluation, and review of training and professional development programmes for the board.

In addition, the Code states that the board may establish a separate board risk committee to assist in overseeing the company's risk-management framework and policies.

4.4 Is it a legal requirement to have an independent director or a third-party director? If so, how are they appointed? Is it required for listed companies?

See paragraph 4.1 above.

4.5 How is the compensation for directors or officers determined? Can it be contested by the shareholders or the regulatory authorities? What are the common rules or practices for the compensation of officers?

See paragraph 9.1 below.

4.6 How will the board handle a corporate crisis like an internal criminal case, violence, social media exposure or dawn raid by the authorities?

Generally speaking, it will be advisable, if the matter is one that the board considers the company may not be sufficiently equipped or have the requisite resources to manage, for the board to appoint relevant advisors or consultants to advise the company. The CA provides that directors may rely on expert advice given by employees, professional advisors or experts who have the requisite competence and are reliable. In the Airocean case, the court also made it clear that reliance on legal advice without asking for counsel's reasons for giving such advice is not a reckless act. The court stated that clients have no duty to question their lawyers' advice and it would not be reasonable to expect or require them to do so, unless the advice is manifestly absurd, irrational or wrong. In the case, the court held that the company acted properly and prudently in seeking legal advice on whether or not to disclose what it knew.

5. BOARD OF AUDITORS, AUDIT COMMITTEE, ACCOUNTING AUDITORS

5.1 How is the internal accounting and legal audit structured and conducted? Is an outside accounting audit required and, if so, how is it structured? Are there requirements to change the auditor each five years?

The CA provides that every company and its directors and managers must cause to be kept such accounting and other records as will sufficiently explain the transactions and financial position of the company and enable true and fair profit-and-loss accounts and balance sheets, and any documents required to be attached thereto to be prepared from time to time, and cause those records to be kept in such manner as to enable them to be conveniently and properly audited.

The board is required to lay before shareholders within a specified time frame, at the annual general meeting (AGM), a profit-and-loss account and balance sheet (consolidated, in the case of a holding company, together with a balance sheet of the holding company) (collectively, accounts) which complies with the requirements of the Singapore financial-reporting standards and gives a true and fair view of the profit and loss and the state of affairs of the company, for and at the end of the relevant financial period respectively.

They must be accompanied by a directors' statement stating whether the accounts have been drawn up so as to give a true and fair view of the results of the business and state of affairs of the company and, where applicable, of all the relevant companies, for and at the end of the relevant financial period respectively, and whether at the date of the statement there are reasonable grounds to believe that the company will be able to pay its debts as and when they fall due.

Save for certain limited exceptions, the directors of the company must take reasonable steps to ensure that the accounts are audited and shall cause to be attached to the accounts a copy of the auditor's report.

The auditor must be registered or deemed to be registered under the Accountants Act (Chapter 2) (AA) as a public accountant. Where an accounting firm or accounting corporation is appointed as auditor, the appointment shall take effect and operate as if the partners of the firm at the time of the appointment or the directors or employees of the corporation who are public accountants at that time or practising as public accountants in that corporation, have been appointed as the auditors of the company.

Under the Listing Rules, listed corporations' auditing firms must be registered with ACRA, or registered with and/or regulated by an independent audit oversight body acceptable to the SGX, which should *inter alia* be a member of the International Forum of Independent Audit Regulators, or any other auditing firm acceptable by the SGX. The audit partner must not be in charge of more than five consecutive audits for a full financial year, regardless of the date of listing, and may return after two years. The SGX has the right to object to the appointment of an auditor or require a listed corporation to replace its auditor if the SGX is of the opinion *inter alia* that it is in the interest of shareholders to do so.

5.2 Do you have supervisory auditors? What is the function of the supervisory auditors' board?

The concept of a supervisory auditor is not applicable in Singapore. The AA provides for a practice-monitoring programme for public accountants (designed to ascertain whether they have complied with the prescribed standards, methods, procedures and other requirements when providing public accountancy services), under which, in order to remain in practice, a public accountant must successfully pass the practice review carried out thereunder. In practice, there are both 'hot reviews' which are done concurrently during the course of an audit, where the independent reviewer serves as mentor assisting the public accountant to review the quality of the audit process with the aim of improving it, and the public accountant's sign-off on the audit engagement is subject to the review having been completed, and 'cold reviews' which are peer reviews mandatory for public accountants who do not pass the practice review, which can be conducted after the completion of the audit engagement.

In addition, under the Listing Rules, the SGX may require a listed corporation to appoint a special auditor to review or investigate the listed corporation's affairs and report its findings to the SGX or the listed corporation's audit committee or such other party as the SGX may direct. The listed corporation may be required by the SGX to announce the findings of the special auditor.

6. MARKET DISCLOSURE/TRANSPARENCY TO THE SHAREHOLDERS AND THE PUBLIC

6.1 What are the disclosure requirements for companies in your jurisdiction under company law, capital markets law or any other rules?

Private companies are required to lodge certain information with ACRA under the CA, such as the names of their auditors, directors, company secretaries and shareholders, their share capital in number and classes of shares and quantum, their financial year-end, charges registered over their assets, and in most instances, their audited accounts. All such information is available for public search and extraction from the ACRA database in consideration of payment of a nominal fee. In addition, certain registers required to be maintained by companies under the CA are also subject to public inspection for a nominal fee.

The underlying fundamental rule of disclosure in the Listing Rules is that subject to certain limited exceptions, an issuer must announce any information known to the issuer concerning it or any of its subsidiaries or associated companies which is necessary to avoid the establishment of a false market in the issuer's securities, or would be likely to materially affect the price or value of its securities. The exceptions to disclosure are where it would be a breach of law to disclose the information, or where each of the following conditions applies:

Condition 1: a reasonable person would not expect the information to be disclosed;

Condition 2: the information is confidential; and

Condition 3: one or more of the following applies:
- the information concerns an incomplete proposal or negotiation;
- the information comprises matters of supposition or is insufficiently definite to warrant disclosure;
- the information is generated for the internal management purposes of the entity; and
- the information is a trade secret.

The Corporate Disclosure Policy in the Listing Rules addresses the likelihood of particular events requiring immediate disclosure, and deals with particular examples of circumstances encountered by listed corporations.

The Listing Rules also lists numerous items of information requiring immediate disclosure. For example, immediate announcement is required of any appointment or cessation of service of directors or key management and acquisitions and disposals of shares in subsidiaries and associated companies.

6.2 What is the liability or responsibility of the board in relation to the company's disclosure requirements?

The Airocean case serves as a useful indication of the SFA provisions which will be used against directors who the MAS considers to be responsible for the company's failure to make requisite disclosure or the company making misleading disclosure.

The SFA contains prohibitions against making statements or disseminating information that is false or misleading in a material particular and likely to induce persons to deal in securities or have the effect of raising, lowering, maintaining or stabilising the market price of securities, if, when the disclosing person makes the statement or disseminates the information, he does not care whether the information is true or false, or he knows or ought reasonably to know that it is false or misleading in a material particular. A listed corporation also shall not intentionally, recklessly or negligently fail to notify the securities exchange of such information as is required to be disclosed to it under the listing rules or other requirement of the securities exchange.

The SFA provides that where an offence under the SFA committed by a body corporate is proved to have been committed with the consent or connivance of, or to be attributable to any neglect on the part of an officer of the body corporate (which includes any director, among others), the officer as well as the body corporate shall be guilty of the offence.

7. M&A AND CORPORATE GOVERNANCE

7.1 Upon an M&A offer, how are the transparency and fairness rules of the company provided under the company and stock market laws and rules?

In Singapore, the takeover of listed corporations and unlisted public companies with more than 50 shareholders and net tangible assets of S$5 million or more is subject to the general principles and rules set out in the Singapore Code on Take-overs and Mergers (Take-over Code). The Take-over Code applies whether the acquirors are natural persons, companies or unincorporated bodies, and whether local or foreign. Accordingly, during an offer period, apart from complying with the continuing disclosure obligations under the Listing Rules (see paragraph 6.1 above), the acquirer and the company must be mindful of the obligations set out under the Take-over Code.

Shareholders must be given all the facts necessary to make an informed judgement on the merits or demerits of an offer. No relevant information should be withheld from shareholders. Such facts must be accurately and fairly presented and the information must be given to the shareholders early enough to enable them to make a decision in good time. Any document, advertisement or announcement issued in connection with an offer must, as with a prospectus, satisfy the highest standard of accuracy and present information adequately and fairly.

Shareholders will receive at least two documents during an offer period. An offer document will be issued by the acquiror. This is then followed by a response document issued by the board. Both documents are expected to contain certain information prescribed under the Take-over Code.

Information about the companies involved in an offer must be made equally available to all shareholders as nearly as possible at the same time and in the same manner. The acquiror, company and their respective advisers must not give information to some shareholders that is not made available to all shareholders. This principle, however, does not apply to the provision of information in confidence by the company to a bona fide potential acquiror or vice versa. However, such potential acquiror should be mindful of the restrictions on insider-trading should it subsequently decide to make an offer for the company.

8. PROXY FIGHTING

8.1 Is proxy fighting customarily conducted for control of the company management or what other items? How is it regulated under the company law or market regulations?

This is not generally an issue in Singapore. One reason may be that Singapore company law does not provide for cumulative voting for the election of directors, and indeed, in the recent review by the steering committee of the CA, the proposal to introduce cumulative voting was rejected.

9. OFFICERS' REMUNERATION RULES

9.1 How is remuneration of officers determined? By whom? Is there a role for the shareholders' meeting? Is there any mechanism for an independent body to review and evaluate them?

The CA effectively requires the provision or improvement of emoluments for directors in respect of their office to be approved by shareholders. 'Emoluments' is widely defined to include fees and percentages, sums paid by way of expenses allowance in so far as those sums are charged to income tax in Singapore, contributions paid under any pension scheme and any benefits received otherwise than in cash in respect of his services.

In addition, as a general rule, subject to certain exceptions, payments to directors by way of compensation for loss of office as an officer of the company or its subsidiary or as consideration in connection with his retirement from such office, are generally not lawful unless the payment has been disclosed to members and approved by them in general meeting.

Save as set out above, under the CA, shareholders have no say in the remuneration of officers. In particular, shareholders do not have a say on remuneration of key executives in the company, including executive directors (to the extent it relates to their employment remuneration).

The Code recommends that the board should establish a remuneration committee (RC). The RC should comprise at least three directors, the majority of whom, including the chairman, should be independent. All members of the RC should be non-executive directors. The RC should review and recommend to the board a general framework of remuneration for the board and key management personnel (comprising the CEO and other persons having authority and responsibility for planning, directing and controlling the activities of the company), and the specific remuneration packages for each director and the key management personnel, covering all aspects of remuneration.

9.2 Is the mechanism of officers' remuneration publicly debated?

The Code recommends that companies should fully disclose the remuneration of each individual director and CEO on a named basis, rounded to the nearest thousand dollars, and should also name and disclose the remuneration of at least the top-five key management personnel (who are not directors or the CEO) in bands of S$250,000. In each case, there should be a breakdown (in percentage or dollar terms) of remuneration earned through base/fixed salary, variable or performance-related income/bonuses, benefits in kind, stock options granted, share-based incentives and awards, and other long-term incentives. There are also other disclosures relating to remuneration recommended by the Code. As explained in paragraph 2.3 above, the Code applies on a comply-or-explain basis. As these disclosures or omission of disclosures are made in annual reports, it is not uncommon at AGMs for issues relating to remuneration to be queried and debated by shareholders.

10. DIRECTORS' LIABILITIES, LIABILITY INSURANCE, INDEMNIFICATION

10.1 What are the directors' responsibilities and liabilities under the law? Can those liabilities be covered by insurance? Can it be indemnified by the company or other related parties?

See paragraphs 1.1 and 1.4 above. The CA provides, *inter alia*, that any provision, whether in the M&AA or in any contract with a company or otherwise, for exempting a director or indemnifying him against any liability which by law would otherwise attach to him in respect of any negligence, default, breach of duty or breach of trust of which he may be guilty in relation to the company, shall be void. However, a company may purchase and maintain directors' liability insurance for its directors, and indemnify directors against any liability incurred in defending any civil or criminal proceedings in which judgment is given in his favour or in which he is acquitted or relief is granted to him by the court. The CA Bill will widen the exception to include indemnity against liability incurred to third parties, subject to conditions.

11. SHAREHOLDERS' DERIVATIVE SUITS

11.1 Is a shareholder's derivative suit provided for by law in your jurisdiction? How is it enforced by the shareholders?

See paragraph 3.1 above.

11.2 Have there been any recent relevant court cases on the subject?

The most recent case was a judgment of the Court of Appeal, which addressed the interpretation of section 216A(3)(b) of the CA, which requires that action may only be brought if the court is satisfied that the complainant was 'acting in good faith'. The Court found that it is not the questionable motivations of the applicant per se which amount to bad faith; instead, bad faith may be established where these questionable motivations constitute a personal purpose which indicates that the company's interests will not be served. The Court also noted from case law examined that good faith is dependent less on the motives which trigger the application for leave to bring the statutory derivative action and more on the purpose of the proposed derivative action, which must have an obvious nexus with the company's benefit or interests.

The Court also concluded that the onus should be on the complainant to establish good faith, ie there was no presumption of good faith in favour of the applicant, and endorsed the Australian position that the applicant lacks good faith where his collateral purpose amounts to an abuse of process.

Finally, the Court also interpreted section 216A(3)(c) of the CA, which requires that action may only be brought if the court is satisfied that 'it appears to be *prima facie* in the interests of the company that the action be brought, prosecuted, defended or discontinued'. The Court noted that to satisfy this requirement, the applicant must convince the Court that the company's claim would be legitimate and arguable.

12. SOCIAL INTEREST IN CORPORATE BEHAVIOUR

12.1 How is a company in your country expected to deal with the following issues? Corporate social responsibility; gender, racial and social diversification; environmental issues; ecology and corruption?

See paragraphs 1.1 and 2.3 above. Generally speaking, increasing numbers of Singapore corporations strive to be responsible corporate citizens, but the approach to corporate social responsibility has been patchy. Corruption is less of an issue in Singapore than in most places, Singapore being ranked fifth globally in the Corruption Perceptions Index 2012 of Transparency International. The Code states that the board and its committees should comprise directors who as a group provide an appropriate balance and diversity of skills, experience, gender and knowledge of the company, and they should also provide core competencies such as accounting or finance, business or management experience, industry knowledge, strategic planning experience and customer-based experience or knowledge. It is hoped that while the number of female directors on the boards of listed corporations in Singapore is low, that number will increase as corporations take cognisance of the recommendations for greater diversity in the Code.

Spain

Carlos Paredes Galego & Carlos Franco Duque
Uría Menéndez

1. GENERAL PRINCIPLES

1.1 What are the general principles of corporate governance in your jurisdiction? What are the main objectives of corporate governance principles in your jurisdiction? State also whether your legal system is based on common law or civil law.

The main principle of corporate governance in Spain is 'corporate interest'. Spanish corporate governance regulations use a narrow contractual interpretation of 'corporate interest', which values the common interests of shareholders. Therefore, directors should perform their duties with unity of purpose and independent judgement, according all shareholders equal treatment, and their performance should be guided at all times by the company's best interests.

This should not be understood to mean that shareholders' interests must be pursued at any price. Directors must ensure that the company satisfies its legal obligations in its dealing with stakeholders, fulfils its obligations and contracts in good faith, respects the customs and good practices of the sectors and territories in which it operates, and upholds any additional principles of social responsibility it has voluntarily committed to follow.

Spain has a civil law system based on statutes. Court decisions are not a source of law, but are of interpretative value.

1.2 Have there been any recent developments in the law, codes and rules of corporate governance?

Yes, among others, the following:

Securities market regulations

Law 2/2011 of 4 March, on Sustainable Economy (the SE Law) implemented important amendments to Law 24/1988 of 28 July on the Securities Market (SML). The SE Law was designed, among other aims, to foster transparency of remuneration policies of listed companies and financial institutions. It applies international principles of corporate governance in order to support solvency and to ensure that directors carry out appropriate risk management. The SE Law follows the European Commission's Recommendation 2009/3159/EC on remuneration policies in the financial services sector and the commitments undertaken at the G20 meeting held in London on 2 April 2009.

In particular, the SE Law establishes that the board of listed companies must prepare and submit, as a separate item on the agenda, an annual report on the remuneration of directors for an advisory vote at the general shareholders' meeting (GSM). This provision, which made the pre-existing recommendation on the 'say-on-pay' practice compulsory, was applied for the first time in the 2012 GSM season.

The SE Law also establishes that savings banks (*cajas de ahorros*) must prepare and submit, as a separate item on the agenda in the same way as listed companies, an annual report on the remuneration of directors and members of the supervisory committee for an advisory vote of the general assembly.

On 20 March 2013, the Ministry of Economy and Competitiveness approved Order ECC/461/2013, which updates the content required in annual reports on corporate governance (ARCG) and sets out the content required in the reports on remuneration. The development and approval of standard forms for those reports was delegated to the National Securities Market Commission (CNMV), who recently approved them through two ancillary rules (*Circular* 4/2013 and *Circular* 5/2013 of 12 June). The content of these circulars details the form, matters, structure and instructions for completing both the ARCG and the annual report on remuneration. These updated standard forms will apply for the 2014 GSM season.

National Reforms Programme

On 26 April 2013, the Spanish government approved the submission of the 2013 National Reforms Programme to the European Commission and an update of the 2013–2016 Stability Programme for Spain. These documents reflect Spain's future strategy on economic policy. With regard to corporate governance, the programme's aim is to reform and expand the current framework of corporate governance best practices in Spain in order to improve efficiency and accountability and, at the same time, set the bar for the highest standards of compliance.

To that end, the Spanish government created a special commission of experts in May 2013 to analyse international corporate governance best practices and propose measures to update and improve Spain's current framework. One of the aims of the reforms will be to bolster the role of the GSM in monitoring compensation policies for managing bodies and senior executives. In addition, the government announced that the recommendations contained in the Corporate Governance Code (see paragraph 2.1 below) will be improved and expanded, placing special emphasis on the supervision and the quality of information provided by companies regarding their compliance with the recommendations, in order to avoid mere box-ticking compliance. It also announced that it will analyse the possibility of preparing a 'code of best practice' for unlisted Spanish companies.

Financial sector

On 12 April 2013, the Spanish government approved Royal Decree 256/2013 (RD 256/2013), which incorporates the European Banking Authority's guidelines of 22 November 2012 on the assessment of the suitability of members of the management body and key function holders. RD 256/2013 empowers the Bank of Spain to assess the suitability of those individuals and introduces substantial changes to the current regime of requirements for commercial and professional reputation and experience. It also includes rules on good governance, particularly in relation to conflicts of interest.

RD 256/2013 has broadened the requirements of suitability for directors and general managers (*director general*) as well as officers with equivalent functions. Furthermore, these requirements have been extended to apply, for the first time, to those responsible for internal control functions and other key positions at the institution and at its parent company, as may be determined by the Bank of Spain. Institutions subject to RD 256/2013 must now have adequate resources and internal procedures to carry out the selection and ongoing assessment of people in affected positions.

Lastly, in respect of financial institutions that benefit from state aid, Royal Decree-Law 2/2011 of 18 February on reinforcing the financial sector sets out specific rules on the composition and functioning of the management body, while Royal Decree-Law 2/2012 (RDL 2/2012) of 3 February on the recapitalisation of the financial sector contains certain restrictions on executive remuneration (see paragraph 4.5 below).

Company law

The primary source of corporate legislation is Royal Legislative Decree 1/2010 of 2 July, which approves the consolidated text of the Capital Companies Law (LSC).

Amending the LSC, Law 25/2011 of 1 August (Law 25/2011), Royal Decree-Law 9/2012 of 16 March, and Law 1/2012 of 22 June (Law 1/2012) aimed to modernise specific aspects of the Spanish legal framework on companies contained in the LSC, simplify some of the formalistic provisions (especially the publication of announcements in the media) and reduce the costs and administrative burdens on companies. In order to achieve this, Law 25/2011 and Law 1/2012 allow for the approval of company websites (which are mandatory for listed companies), and set forth the requirements for their creation, reinforcing them as a means of communication with shareholders. Specifically, Law 1/2012 has allowed companies to address specific communications to their shareholders and debtors through their corporate webpages and has also permitted the notification of those communications to the shareholders electronically if shareholders have consented. As an example of those measures to develop the usefulness of corporate websites, a GSM can currently be called through an announcement via the company's website provided that the company's website had been created complying with the requirements set out in the LSC and recorded in the Commercial Registry, instead of by publishing an announcement in a newspaper and/or in the Official Gazette of the Commercial Registry (*Boletín Oficial del Registro Mercantil*, BORME). However, to make things more complicated, announcements by listed companies must be also published on the CNMV website and in the BORME. In the case of joint stock companies (*sociedades anónimas*) (SAs), Law 25/2011 has also removed the requirement for publicising (through a website or newspaper) agreements on a change of name, change of registered address or any other change to the company's object, which was a prerequisite for registration with the Companies Registry. Unfortunately, as indicated, those new provisions relating to the publication of notices by companies on their websites, while intending to simplify the regime and alleviate costs, have actually created a rather complex, highly bureaucratic procedure that makes a simple process such as calling a GSM a rather risky business in light of the formalistic approach of Spanish law.

Law 25/2011 also transposed Directive 2007/36/EC on the exercise of certain rights of shareholders in listed companies into Spanish law, removing obstacles that may hinder shareholders' access to information and deter them from voting. The law develops the regulation of proxy voting at the GSM, with a particular emphasis in case of conflict of interest of the proxy holder. The law stipulates, in this regard, that proxy holders affected by any of the situations that Law 25/2011 stipulates as a conflict of interest can vote if: (i) he/she has previously informed the represented shareholder about the existence of the conflict; and (ii) the proxy holder has received precise instructions on how he/she will vote.

In respect of announcing the calling of a GSM of a listed company, Law 25/2011 establishes that, in exceptional cases, an extraordinary GSM could be convened with 15 days' notice provided that: (i) all shareholders are offered an effective means of voting electronically; and (ii) it is expressly approved by an ordinary GSM, with a majority of at least two-thirds of the share capital with voting rights. The validity of this agreement cannot go beyond the date of the next ordinary GSM. The law requires that GSM documentation on corporate websites contain specific information that is available continuously from when the GSM is called until it takes place, including forms to apply for proxy voting and distance voting, unless the company sends these directly to each shareholder. In the event they cannot be available due to technical reasons, the website must contain information on how to obtain hard copies of these forms, and the company should send these to all shareholders who request them. The information framework for shareholders of listed companies has also been expanded, widening the right to request information in respect of any publicly available documents that the company has made available to the CNMV since the previous GSM, including the auditor's report. Directors are not obliged to respond if the information is clearly and directly available on the website in an FAQ format.

Finally, for non-listed companies (and only as from the five years following the registration of the incorporation of the company in the commercial registry), Law 25/2011 introduces a right for minority shareholders to request that the company acquire their stake in the event that, *inter alia*, the company does not distribute at least one-third of the previous year's distributable profits following the request of the shareholder. In view of the potentially negative financial effects of this 'withdrawal right', the rule has been suspended until 31 December 2014.

Further amending the LSC, Royal Decree-Law 9/2012 of 16 March and Law 1/2012 incorporate the rules contained in Directive 2009/109/EC of 16 September 2009 into Spanish law as regards reporting requirements in mergers and demergers. *Inter alia*, those regulations have established additional exceptions to the requirement of appointing financial experts for the valuation of in-kind contributions to SAs in certain mergers and capital increases. Law 1/2012 also introduced several amendments to the regulations for listed companies contained in the LSC and the SML, seeking to establish protective legislation against opportunistic tender-offers. Most importantly in relation to corporate governance, this law reinstates the possibility that the by-laws of SAs may limit the maximum number of voting rights a shareholder may have in the GSM (typically 10 per cent per shareholder), which was one of the most common anti-takeover instruments used by Spanish listed companies before 2010, when it was prohibited. Nevertheless, the limitation on voting rights will not apply where, following a takeover bid, an offeror has acquired 70 per cent or more of the target's share capital with voting rights (unless the offeror, its group companies or any other party acting in concert with them is not subject to similar breakthrough measures).

1.3 Outline recent court cases and incidents involving corporate governance issues. Were there any significant corporate scandals or large unlawful corporate cases?

One of the most representative recent court cases involving corporate governance issues was between two of Spain's largest listed companies. Actividades de Construcción y Servicios, S.A. (ACS), as an indirect shareholder of Iberdrola, S.A. (Iberdrola), had been requesting a seat on Iberdrola's board of directors pursuant to its right to appoint a director in accordance with the proportional representation system that allows minorities to get representation in the board. Iberdrola rejected each request, arguing that granting ACS a seat on the board would create a permanent conflict of interest given that the two companies were competitors in various sectors. At Iberdrola's 2010 GSM, ACS appointed a director who was immediately removed during the same meeting. ACS filed a claim challenging the dismissal. The court rejected the claim, holding that the dismissal was justified based on the need to preserve the company's interests against the damages resulting from the access to relevant information granted to a director appointed by a competing company. ACS appealed the ruling to the Supreme Court. A decision is pending.

Several corporate scandals have been made public within the context of the severe economic crisis Spain has been experiencing since 2008. The financial crisis has also revealed a number of shortcomings and limitations in the existing supervisory system. While various measures both at the European and domestic level have been taken, corporate governance reform remains an ongoing process. Examples of failed corporate governance include the recent scandal affecting a major Spanish fishing and food processing firm regarding alleged accounting failings and alleged corporate management irregularities in certain Spanish saving banks.

1.4 Which law enforcement agency is in charge of enforcing corporate governance? May a criminal sanction be levied upon infringement of the corporate governance rules?

In Spain, no single agency or organisation is entrusted with ensuring compliance with all of the mandatory rules regarding corporate governance, a concept which, understood in the broadest sense, includes any rules related to the management and control of companies. The enforcement of a specific corporate governance rule will depend on the nature and content of that rule. Within the scope of corporate governance rules, there are mandatory rules deriving from general corporate legislation, which are binding on all companies (both listed and unlisted), and mandatory rules which are only applicable to listed companies or to companies which have issued listed securities. Among the latter group, there exist: (i) organisational and disciplinary rules for the securities markets, which, if not fulfilled, may lead to an administrative sanction usually imposed by the CNMV, without prejudice to civil and commercial court proceedings also arising from non-compliance; and (ii) rules which, if not satisfied, may lead to civil or commercial proceedings before the relevant courts. There are also corporate governance recommendations for listed companies and entities issuing listed securities, although breach of these recommendations does not result in any sanction (see paragraph 2.1 below).

Spanish banking regulations also include mandatory regulations on an array of corporate governance issues (eg, suitability requirements for owners, directors and senior officers, executive pay, disclosure and reporting requirements). The Bank of Spain oversees the Spanish banking system, supervises and monitors banks' compliance with the law and imposes sanctions for non-compliance. As previously indicated, such sanctioning is without prejudice to civil and commercial court proceedings that may arise from non-compliance.

Aside from the CNMV and the Bank of Spain, companies that are engaged in other regulatory sectors are also subject to the supervision of the corresponding regulatory body.

As for criminal offences, although there is no explicit offence under Spanish criminal law for failure to comply with corporate governance rules, specific conduct closely related to the governance of Spanish companies may constitute a criminal offence (eg, those denominated 'corporate offences', such as accounting fraud, unlawful appropriation or transfer of company assets, depriving shareholders of their rights, obstruction of inspections carried out by authorities in regulated markets).

2. SOURCES OF LAW

2.1 Which laws, codes or statutes govern company structures and organisations? Are there statutes like the Companies Act or other forms of law? Is there much relevant case law?

Historically, the most common vehicle used in Spain for doing business was the SA, but the limited liability company (*sociedad de responsabilidad limitada*) (SL) has become more popular as a result of economical incorporation and management and greater flexibility. SLs are currently by far the most common type of business organisation. SAs are also used for larger investments and, since only SAs can be listed and issue debt, when a subsequent stock market listing or a debt issuance is contemplated. Both the SA and SL are limited liability companies (shareholders' liability is generally limited to their investment in the company's equity).

Under Spanish law there are other distinct corporate structures and organisations for doing business and the specific regulations that apply to each vary.

Limited liability companies (SAs and SLs) are primarily governed by the LSC, which includes the general corporate framework for listed companies previously contained in the SML. Apart from the LSC, specific ancillary regulations govern different corporate issues (eg, accounting audit, corporate reorganisations, transparency and disclosure, tender-offers).

Financial institutions are also subject to specific financial regulations that contain several rules on corporate governance. For reasons of brevity, this chapter will not address those rules, with the exception of specific issues of particular relevance for credit institutions, and will focus on general corporate governance rules applying to SLs and SAs (particularly listed companies).

Apart from these regulations, corporate governance in Spain is subject to a soft law rule: the Unified Code of Good Corporate Governance of Listed Companies approved in May 2006 by the CNMV (the CUBG or the Corporate Governance Code). The CUBG generally mirrors the international standards and recommendations on good governance practices set out by different entities and institutions such as the OECD, the Basel Committee on Banking Supervision and the European Commission. It sets out recommendations under the principle of 'comply or explain'. Companies are free to decide whether or not to follow the CUBG's recommendations, but they must give a reasoned explanation in their ARCG for any deviations from those recommendations. All listed companies (together with savings banks and entities issuing listed securities) are obligated to prepare an ARCG, in the recently renewed formats prescribed by the CNMV (see paragraph 1.2 above), including fairly extensive information regarding the company, such as that relating to: (i) ownership structure; (ii) organisation and functioning of the GSM; (iii) the board of directors (including, among other information, its composition, rules, committees, remuneration, relationship with 'significant shareholders', and procedures for the selection of directors); (iv) related-party transactions, including intra-group transactions; (v) risk management policies; (vi) main aspects of the risk monitoring and internal management system in relation to the process of issuing financial information; and (vii) an account of compliance with the CUBG recommendations and, as the case may be, reasons for non-compliance.

Although voluntary, the CUBG recommendations are provided within a framework of categories and concepts considered mandatory for all listed companies, irrespective of the size, market capitalisation or nature of their business. In this regard, the CNMV evaluates the degree of companies' compliance with the recommendations and it has powers to request additional explanations from any issuer regarding its corporate governance practice and information on its practice included in the ARCG, including the publication of amendments and the imposition of fines or other sanctions in the case of breaches of applicable law.

Given the time elapsed and the changes in the corporate environment since the CUBG's approval, an overall revision of CUBG is being carried out at the time of writing this chapter (see paragraph 1.2 above).

Case law

While the role of case law is inherently different in civil law than in common law, it nevertheless plays an important role in interpreting the law. It is fair to say that, depending on the particular issue of company law, there could very well be a substantial amount of relevant case law.

2.2 Which laws, codes or statutes regulate capital markets in your jurisdiction?

The SML is the primary source of Spanish securities market regulations. It governs the Spanish systems for trading in financial instruments and establishes the principles for their organisation and functioning and the rules regarding the financial instruments that are traded in those systems and the issuers of such instruments. It also contains rules on providing investment services and establishes a system of supervision, inspection, and discipline. The SML establishes the rules of conduct that apply generally to all participants in the Spanish securities markets, including primary rules on disclosure and transparency, market abuse, insider trading and takeover bids.

The SML has been developed and completed through a substantial number of secondary regulations approved by the Spanish government, in the form of Royal Decrees (*Reales Decretos*), and by the Ministry of Economy and Competitiveness, in the form of Ministerial Orders (*Órdenes Ministeriales*). Furthermore, ancillary rules issued by the CNMV (*Circulares*) implement and further develop Royal Decrees and Orders.

2.3 Are there any public interest laws which apply to or influence corporate governance?

In addition to the general company law rules which regulate standard corporate governance issues (see paragraph 1.2 above), there are also administrative law regulations which fall under the public interest umbrella, such as: (i) securities market regulations (eg, transparency and disclosure duties, market abuse); (ii) financial regulation regarding suitability of members of the management body and their salaries (see paragraph 1.2 above); and (iii) regulations on gender diversity in boards through the promotion of gender equality, which also impact corporate governance (see paragraph 12 below).

2.4 Have there been any recent developments in any of the above laws? What are the recent changes to the above laws or rules and the reasons for such changes?

See paragraph 1.4 above.

3. SHAREHOLDERS AND THE SHAREHOLDERS' MEETING

3.1 How are shareholders' interests represented in the company? How are the shareholders assured exercise of their rights? What is the highest governing body within the company structure if it is not the shareholders' meeting?

Although the GSM is a company's highest decision-making body, its non-permanent nature (being convened only with formal advance notification by the directors, except in the case of universal meetings in which all shareholders are present, or at the request of 5 per cent of the shareholders) and the fixed, formal nature of the decisions it can make (eg, appointment of directors, changes to the by-laws, appointment of auditors) means that the board of directors takes charge of the day-to-day management of the company.

To carry out this daily management, the board of directors must act in the interests of the company, which is understood to mean the common interest of shareholders. However, in a rather concentrated market such as Spain, it is not unusual for the board's decisions to give rise to conflicts between the interests of the majority and the minority shareholders due to the fact that some of the directors are often related to the controlling or significant shareholders (the so-called insider-outsider conflicts). In this case, the board must take a decision with the conflicted directors abstaining from debating and voting on the conflicting issue. For example, it is standard practice in a merger between a parent company and one of its subsidiaries that the ultimate approval of the transaction at the subsidiary's management body level is made by a committee of independent directors.

Shareholders' rights are protected at two different levels. First, the LSC contains several provisions protecting the interests of shareholders in general and minority shareholders in particular, including:

- Depending on the number of directors, shareholders of SAs can pool their shares in order to appoint a number of directors to the board in proportion to the share capital they hold in accordance with the proportional representation system.
- Shareholders holding at least 5 per cent of the share capital may: (i) request that the directors call a GSM with an agenda specified in the request and, if the directors fail to do so within two months, submit a judicial request that the meeting be called; (ii) in SAs, request the publication of a supplementary notice of a GSM that includes at least one additional agenda item; (iii) challenge certain board resolutions; (iv) seek enforcement action against directors (see *infra*); and (v) seek the removal and replacement of auditors by the courts, if justified reasons exist.
- Any shareholder may request that the directors provide information

on items in the agenda for the meeting (or any information made public through the CNMV since the last GSM or relating to the audit reports), which request the directors may only reject if they believe that the publicity of the information may be harmful to the company. The directors, however, may not refuse to give that information if the request has been made by shareholders representing at least 25 per cent of the company's share capital.

- The right to seek enforcement action against members of the management body through:
  (a) Company action: the company can file an action for liability against directors subject to the existence of a previous resolution approved at the GSM by an ordinary majority. The GSM may settle or waive the exercise of this action provided that there is no challenge by shareholders representing 5 per cent or more of the share capital. The general purpose of this action is to seek compensation for the company for any damages caused by fraudulent or negligent acts or omissions of directors contrary to law or the by-laws or for a breach of their corporate or fiduciary duties. Shareholders holding at least 5 per cent of the share capital also have standing to bring this action if it is not brought by the company, as do creditors if the company is insolvent. In all cases, any compensation awarded must be paid to the company.
  (b) Individual action: any third party (including shareholders) may file a claim for damages against the directors if their interests are compromised due to the directors' actions. The purpose of this action is to seek compensation for damages directly suffered by third parties not being damages caused indirectly through the company.
- Any shareholder may challenge any GSM resolution that is contrary to law or to the by-laws or that favours specific shareholders or any other third party to the company's detriment, provided that the shareholder voted against the resolution or was not present at the GSM.

Second, one of the CNMV's most important duties regarding listed companies is protecting the interests of minority shareholders. This protection is carried out through: (i) the assessment of complaints filed with the CNMV's Shareholder Information Office (*Oficina de Atención al Inversor*); (ii) the supervision and inspection of the technical and legal requirements on listed companies, and sanctioning of the same, where appropriate; and (iii) scrutinising the quality standards and accuracy of information publicly disclosed by listed companies.

3.2 How is the shareholders' meeting conducted? Who may chair the meeting? May attendance (not voting) at the meeting be restricted only to the shareholders? Are the shareholders allowed to be accompanied by legal or other counsel?

The GSM is conducted by the chairman (who chairs the meeting and has broad powers to moderate shareholders' speeches) and the secretary, who assists the president. Both of them, together with the other directors in attendance, normally constitute the presiding committee at the GSM. Unless otherwise specified in the by-laws or in the GSM's regulations, which all listed companies must approve, the chairman and the secretary of the GSM will be those of the board of directors and, in their absence, persons designated by the shareholders upon commencement of the meeting.

Generally, shareholders or their proxies attend the GSM. However, the chairman can allow anyone else to attend (eg, shareholders' counsel), although the GSM is authorised to revoke this permission. The directors must also attend the GSM. A public notary may also attend to draft the minutes of the meeting if directors or shareholders holding a minimum stake in the company (1 per cent for SAs and 5 per cent for SLs) so decide.

To conclude the meeting, the chairman will order a vote on the agenda items and announce the results of the votes. The shareholders exercise their right by voting for or against the resolutions, by abstaining or by voting in blank, as the case may be. In particular, listed companies must allow shareholders to participate through distance voting (eg, by post, electronically), and the by-laws may set out a procedure to allow shareholders an off-site exercise of their right to attend and vote at the GSM (eg, by broadcasting the meeting in real time). There are several examples of listed companies in Spain which currently allow their shareholders to fully participate in the GSM off-site (attending and voting remotely).

3.3 How are minority shareholders' rights protected?

See paragraph 3.1 above.

3.4 Is shareholder activism encouraged or discouraged? If not encouraged, how is it regulated?

As set out in paragraph 3.1, the shareholding structure of Spanish listed companies is somewhat concentrated. According to the most recent publicly available data for the fiscal year 2011 (see *www.cnmv.es*), while the free float in listed companies amounted to 37.5 per cent, 28.3 per cent of the share capital was held by significant shareholders represented in the board of directors and 32.5 per cent by non-director significant shareholders. The sum of 'significant shareholdings', including share packages in the hands of the board, exceeded 50 per cent of the share capital in 110 companies (73.8 per cent of the total), 19 of which were listed on the Ibex 35 Index, which includes the largest companies. In any case, the concentration level is higher in average in smaller companies.

This shareholding structure partly explains why the shareholder activism movement that has swept through the American and European markets over the past decade has been more muted in Spain. To date, the Spanish market has not seen significant shareholder action, except in very specific cases linked to disputes over the control of target companies, normally in the context of tender-offers or minority shareholders disagreeing with management.

Notwithstanding the above, it is worth noting that shareholder communication is gaining increasing importance, especially among the largest Spanish companies, which are also those in which the shareholding concentration level is more reduced and foreign shareholders are predominant. These companies have normally been among the first to comply with the 'say-on-pay' recommendation and regularly conduct both one-on-one and selective meetings with shareholders.

One additional matter to consider is the fact that GSMs do not function sufficiently, since there are high levels of shareholder apathy in respect of their rights to attend and vote. In spite of recent legislation to encourage shareholder participation (eg, by creating shareholders' forums) (see paragraph 1.1 above), as far as we are aware these attempts have been unsuccessful, as not only has the percentage of shareholders participating in GSMs not improved, but there has also been an increase in paperwork and costs for companies themselves.

Another attempt to activate shareholders' participation in the GSM is contained in the regulations on Spanish investment funds, which impose an obligation on management companies to exercise all political rights inherit to the shares in Spanish companies held by the funds they manage, provided that the shares represent at least 1 per cent of the share capital and have been held for one year or more. Lastly, the CUBG recommends that financial intermediaries actively exercise the political rights attached to the shares of the listed companies they hold and inform investors on the voting criteria.

3.5 How are professional shareholders (those minority shareholders who seek some extra benefit from companies by unduly and habitually influencing management by using their shareholding) treated by the law? Are they excluded from attending the shareholders' meeting? Are they criminally or otherwise publicly sanctioned?

This phenomenon has not become an issue in Spain yet and, as such, there is no specific legal treatment of it apart from being charged by the competent courts cost of proceedings initiated without cause or sound basis against companies.

3.6 Are shareholders' benefits given to some of the shareholders by the company without resolution by the shareholders' meeting prohibited or regulated by the law or other rules?

In general, shareholders in Spanish companies must be treated equally, in compliance with the principle of equal treatment of shareholders under equivalent circumstances. However, this general principle is compatible with the existence of different classes of shares with different rights attached to them (eg, ordinary shares and privileged shares which confer supplementary rights, such as a preference dividend). In principle, only corporate transactions (such as a reduction of capital) are subject to controls to avoid violating this principle. Therefore, any other type of transaction that takes place between the company and any of its shareholders (such as entering into a supply contract) does not need the approval of the GSM, since the board of directors or even managers of the company are capable of entering into such a transaction. However, a company can include different provisions in its by-laws to change the way that non-corporate transactions are governed. For example, there are some companies whose by-laws state that any type of transaction with a shareholder must be approved by the GSM. In listed companies it is standard practice that the approval of related party transactions is entrusted to the board (based on a prior report of a committee normally formed by a majority of independent directors), which should in turn apply the rules on conflicts of interest that prevent conflicted directors from participating and voting the specific transaction. There are also listed companies that require shareholders' approval for specific related-party transactions. Related parties include, among others, significant shareholders (ie, shareholders who own at least 3 per cent of the company's share capital) and directors.

Lastly, regarding listed companies, related-party transactions are specifically subject to public disclosure obligations under the SML, Order EHA/3050/2004 of 15 September and prescribed by the CUBG: listed companies must: (i) submit a report to the CNMV every six months disclosing transactions carried out with related parties, including 'significant shareholders'; and (ii) include information on related-party transactions in the ARCG.

4. DIRECTORS AND BOARD OF DIRECTORS

4.1 What are the functions and responsibilities of the directors and the board of directors? Do you have a one- or two-tier board system? What are the outside directors called?

Directors are entrusted with, and responsible for, the management and representation (before courts and outside courts *vis-à-vis* third parties) of the company in relation to all matters falling within the scope of ordinary business. To do so, they must have the widest authority and powers to adopt resolutions regarding all matters not assigned by the by-laws or the LSC to the GSM. As a general rule, the board entrusts the day-to-day management of the company to the executive bodies and focuses its activity on the general duty of supervision and decision on matters of particular importance. Directors have two basic duties: to act diligently and to be loyal to the interests of the company. The law sets out several obligations which are an expression of these two duties. For example, in order to fulfil their obligation of loyalty, directors must maintain the secrecy of all the confidential information which comes into their possession or avoid acting when a conflict of interest arises.

Spanish law provides for a standard one-tier board structure. Listed companies must have a board of directors. Only European Limited Companies (*Societas Europaea*) in Spain may opt for a two-tier board, in which directors assume the management of the company and the supervisory body controls their performance.

Outside directors, as opposed to internal or 'executive' directors (essentially, those which are also senior officers or employees in the company or its group companies), are denominated 'external directors' (*consejeros externos*). These external directors may be either: (i) proprietary directors (those holding, or representing or appointed by those holding, a significant or controlling stake in the company or which have otherwise been appointed due to their status as shareholders regardless whatever their holding is; or (ii) independent directors (see paragraph 4.4 below).

Finally, individuals who directly or indirectly are competitors of the company are barred from being directors (except with the express authorisation of the GSM).

4.2 What are the rules that may give rise to civil and criminal liability of the director(s)? How are those liabilities sought?

The general rule under the LSC is that directors shall be liable *vis-à-vis* the company, its creditors and the company's shareholders for any damage caused by them as a consequence of acts or omissions contrary to law or the by-laws or acts carried out in breach of the fiduciary duties inherent to the position of director. Liability would be imposed jointly and severally on all directors although, in certain circumstances, directors who did not participate in the approval or execution of (or who opposed to) the harmful resolution could be exonerated from liability. Regarding how to enforce these liabilities, see paragraph 3.1 above.

In addition to this general regime of civil liability, there are also other potential sources of civil liability for directors arising from breaches of corporate law (eg, if they failed to take the actions required under Spanish law to recapitalise or to wind up the company when its net worth had been reduced to less than one half of its share capital) or insolvency law (in case of fraudulent bankruptcy (*concurso culpable*) in certain circumstances). Directors can also face liability for the company's breaches of certain non-corporate related laws (eg, tax, labour, social security and environmental laws). Finally, directors may be criminally liable under the Spanish Criminal Code (eg, in case of 'corporate offences' (see paragraph 1.4 above)).

4.3 Does the board of directors have a committee system, eg, nomination committee, compensation committee, audit committee? If not required, is it common practice for companies? How does it function?

Spanish listed companies tend to have, in addition to a managing director holding delegated powers from the board, an executive committee with similar powers, that in practice operates as a reduced board.

Boards of directors of listed companies must have an audit committee (see paragraph 5.1 below).

The CUBG further recommends that a nomination or remuneration committee, or a single committee which performs both tasks (as is the common practice in Spanish listed companies), be created within the board. It is recommended that this committee be formed mostly of independent directors and chaired by one of these directors. The nomination and remuneration committees have advisory powers in matters such as the selection of candidates for the board, the right to make proposals (or inform of the proposals made by the board) relating to the appointment of directors and the right to propose (or inform of the proposal by the board) remuneration policies. Credit institutions that benefit from state aids must have either a nomination committee or a remuneration committee, or both.

4.4 Is it a legal requirement to have an independent director or a third-party director? If so, how are they appointed? Is it required for listed companies?

The CUBG recommends that companies strike a balance between external and internal directors. External directors should account for a wide majority of the board, while the number of executive directors should be limited to the minimum number necessary, taking into account the complexity of the corporate group and ownership interests. Under the CUBG, while proprietary directors should represent the 'significant shareholders' in a proportion that matches the capital that they represent, independent directors should represent at least one-third of all board members. The CUBG also states that the audit, nomination and remuneration committees should be exclusively composed of external directors and chaired by an independent director, and that a majority of nomination and remuneration committees must be independent directors.

Independent directors are essentially defined as those who, appointed for their personal or professional qualities, are in a position to perform their duties without being influenced by any connection with the company, its shareholders, or management. Order ECC/461/2013 lists a number of circumstances incompatible with acting as an independent director, such as having been an employee or an executive director during the preceding three or five years, respectively; receiving some significant payment or other form of compensation from the company or its group; or being in office uninterruptedly for more than 12 years.

Members of the board of directors must be appointed by the GSM. Although seldom used, the GSM may also designate 'substitute directors' to cover any vacancies that might arise on the board until new directors are appointed. Law also provides for subsidiary procedures for the appointment of directors, which alter the standard GSM appointment rule, denominated co-optation: the board of directors may designate a shareholder as a director in order to cover a vacancy until the following GSM is held.

Members of the board of directors can be removed by a resolution passed at the GSM, which can remove any director from their post without specifying a reason and without previously including a resolution for their removal in the agenda for the meeting.

4.5 How is the compensation for directors or officers determined? Can it be contested by the shareholders or the regulatory authorities? What are the common rules or practices for the compensation of officers?

Directors' remuneration for their supervisory duties: general framework

The position of director may, but need not necessarily be, remunerated. When the position is remunerated, the by-laws must expressly indicate that it is remunerated and the manner in which it is calculated. In general, companies are free to opt for the particular type or types of remuneration systems that they desire (eg, fixed annual remuneration, profit share, pension plans).

In the case of fixed remuneration schemes, the amount, or at a minimum a cap, of the aggregate remuneration to be paid to all directors must be decided by the GSM. Subject to these limitations, a company's by-laws may vest in the board of directors the authority to determine the amount of remuneration payable to each individual director, keeping in mind that all directors need not be remunerated on identical terms.

Where the remuneration system consists of a profit share, the by-laws must provide for the extent of the profit share or a maximum percentage thereof which, in the case of SLs, shall in no case exceed 10 per cent of the company's distributable profits. In the case of SAs, in order for remuneration of this nature to be payable to the directors, the shareholders' right to a dividend of 4 per cent (or any higher percentage established in the company's by-laws) of the company's paid-in share capital must have been previously recognised.

Finally, if remuneration involves delivery of the company's shares, that circumstance must be expressly indicated in the company's by-laws and will be subject to shareholder approval.

Executive directors' remuneration: the contractual nature doctrine (*doctrina del vínculo*)

One problem of particular practical relevance related to the need for directors' remuneration to be established in the by-laws, is when directors receive remuneration for carrying out their executive functions under an employment contract or a commercial law relationship separately from the remuneration they receive for exercising non-executive supervisory functions.

It is standard practice in Spanish companies for executive directors to sign employment contracts or rendering-of-service contracts which set out their salary and other remuneration for the 'executive functions', which can be concurrent with, and independent from, their purely corporate role of director. In many cases, the execution of executive directors' employment contracts and the remuneration provided for those tasks are authorised by the board without any other approval from the GSM other than the 'say-on-pay' role relating to the remuneration policy.

While far from being a settled issue, various Supreme Court judgments and certain scholars have supported the position that: (i) the executive functions of directors are not substantially different from their non-executive functions, forming part of the overall role of the director; and (ii) the same benefits cannot be simultaneously awarded under different legal guises (one derived from being a director of a company and the other derived from an employment or rendering-of-services contract with that company) and that, consequently, the relationship between the directors and the company should encompass both roles and their accompanying benefits. Specifically, this means that the corporate role of a director and the role of a senior executive under an employment contract are incompatible, and the first should take precedence over the second.

In accordance with this principle, known as the 'contractual nature doctrine', which we do not describe further in this chapter, and with academic commentary and case law, it has been suggested that employment contracts between a company and its executive directors could be invalid or void and that the remuneration awarded under these contracts could be lacking the necessary authority from the company's statutes if such remuneration is not established under the by-laws or through a resolution at the GSM. In our view, this doctrine is based on a fundamental misconception, as it equates the duties of directors in their position as executives (management duties) with those of non-executive directors (supervisory and advisory duties). It also ignores the fact that the duties of an executive director are fundamentally different from those of a non-executive director. Executive directors carry out daily activities as members of the board, whereas non-executive directors only attend the periodic board meetings (also attended by executive directors), in which they perform a merely supervisory role.

What the doctrine does not take into account is that the reason why executive directors receive specific remuneration is that the board has the authority to commission some of its members to carry out executive duties and also to determine, within this context, the remuneration due to them. This is the rule applied in surrounding jurisdictions, the approach of Spanish corporate governance codes, and the continued practice of Spanish companies.

Nevertheless, the prevailing case law is trending towards a scenario in which the remuneration of executive directors must be specifically approved by the shareholders and included, at least, as a maximum limit in the by-laws.

One reason for this may be current public opinion, which is hostile in the wake of certain cases of abuse and exacerbated by the economic crisis. However, in our view this is not the best means of preventing abuse; nor, apart from the 'say-on-pay' vote on the remuneration policy, does the GSM seem the most appropriate place for designing remuneration schemes to allow companies to attract, retain, and motivate the most qualified executives.

CUBG recommendations on directors' remuneration and disclosure

The CUBG contains various recommendations on directors' remuneration. By way of illustration, it recommends that external directors are not subject to variable remuneration systems which could compromise their objectivity or otherwise effectively result in a conflict of interest. That said, it acknowledges that a director that receives any variable remuneration need not necessarily forfeit the status of an independent director.

As to disclosure, the annual report on remuneration to be submitted for an advisory vote at the GSM must include complete, clear, and comprehensible information regarding the remuneration policy approved by the board for the current year and, if appropriate, the policy planned for future years, an overall summary on how the remuneration policy was applied during the fiscal year, and details on individual remuneration accrued by directors. The annual report on remuneration must be drafted in conformity with the standard format approved by the CNMV. Such report shall also specify the outcome of the advisory vote on the previous year's annual report on remuneration by the GSM and be published as a 'significant event' (*'hecho relevante'*).

Remuneration's regulatory control in financial institutions

Subject to certain exceptions, the remuneration paid to directors cannot generally be contested by regulatory authorities. As an exception, the Bank of Spain has authority over financial institutions regarding issues of directors and senior key executives' remuneration, which follow the Guidelines on Remuneration Policies and Practices approved by the Committee of European Banking Supervisors in December 2010. Specifically, under the SE Law, financial institutions and companies that render investment services must increase transparency of their remuneration policies and the consistency of such policies with the promotion of sound and effective risk management. To that end, the SE Law reinforced the Bank of Spain's role in the implementation and supervision of remuneration policies and the corporate governance rules of financial entities. In particular, the Bank of Spain is vested with powers to require financial institutions to limit variable components of their remuneration systems in order to preserve a solid capital basis. Both the requirements affecting the design and approval of remuneration policies and the corresponding supervisory powers of the Bank of Spain are comprehensively regulated by Royal Decree 771/2011 of 3 June, which amended specific regulations on capital requirements for financial institutions. Furthermore, RDL 2/2012 sets out specific restrictions for financial institutions that benefit from state aid, which affect both the *quantum* of the remuneration and its variable components and pension benefits associated with them, with the latter two items being reduced to zero in certain cases.

4.6 How will the board handle a corporate crisis like an internal criminal case, violence, social media exposure or dawn raid by the authorities?

It will normally set up a dedicated internal team (including an internal communication department) and hire expert lawyers, communication consultants and, as the case may be, investment banking advisors.

5. BOARD OF AUDITORS, AUDIT COMMITTEE, ACCOUNTING AUDITORS

5.1 How is the internal accounting and legal audit structured and

conducted? Is an outside accounting audit required and, if so, how is it structured? Are there requirements to change the auditor each five years?

Retaining external accounting auditors is compulsory for certain companies (eg, listed companies and companies issuing listed securities, financial intermediaries, insurance companies, companies exceeding certain thresholds in terms of turnover, total assets or number of employees).

Boards of directors of listed companies must have an audit committee. At least one of its members must have accounting or auditing knowledge. The role of the audit committee is primarily advisory in nature and refers to the supervision of auditing practices, the relationship with the external and internal auditors, paying special attention to the independence of external auditors, the oversight of risk management policies and the review of the financial information that the company has to make public.

Legislation sets out a system for the 'appointment and rotation' of external auditors, to ensure their independence. For instance, in companies with total turnover exceeding EUR 50 million, the lead auditor (but not the auditing firm itself) must rotate after seven years from the initial contract and may not audit the same company for a subsequent period of two years.

Lastly, listed companies and other financial institutions must have adequate internal procedures to oversee compliance with the securities market rules of conduct. In this regard, the CUBG recommends that supervision of compliance with the internal codes of conduct and corporate governance rules be entrusted to the audit committee, the remuneration committee or, if they exist as a separate body, the corporate governance or compliance committee.

5.2 Do you have supervisory auditors? What is the function of the supervisory auditors' board?

In Spain, an administrative body (*Instituto de Contabilidad y Auditoría de Cuentas* (ICAC)) monitors the manner in which auditors accomplish their duty of independence.

6. MARKET DISCLOSURE/TRANSPARENCY TO THE SHAREHOLDERS AND THE PUBLIC

6.1 What are the disclosure requirements for companies in your jurisdiction under company law, capital markets law or any other rules?

Standard corporate regulations require companies to provide general information to the commercial registry (memorandum and by-laws, directors, share capital, annual accounts, together with the management report and, if applicable, the audit report, etc.). In addition, directors must provide additional information to shareholders upon calling GSMs to decide certain specific matters (eg, amendments to the by-laws, mergers, spin-offs) as set out in detail in the corporate regulations.

Entities issuing listed securities are also subject to specific transparency and disclosure obligations, most of which arise from the Spanish regulations transposing Directives 2004/109/EC and 2007/14/EC. These obligations include, among others:

- Preparation and publication of specific periodical information (essentially, annual financial reports, biannual interim financials, intermediate management reports).
- Information regarding the company's transactions involving its own shares.
- Changes to the rights attached to the securities and information about debt issuances.
- Price-sensitive information (*'hechos relevantes'*).
- The ARCG and the directors' remuneration report.

In addition, shareholders of listed companies acquiring or transferring shares with voting rights must notify the company and the CNMV of their stake in the company when, as a result of the transaction, it reaches or falls below certain thresholds (3 per cent, 5 per cent, 10 per cent, 15 per cent, 20 per cent, 25 per cent, 30 per cent, 35 per cent, 40 per cent, 45 per cent, 50 per cent, 60 per cent, 70 per cent, 75 per cent, 80 per cent and 90 per cent).

Directors, senior officers and their family/arm's length ties must notify all transactions in the company's securities regardless of the percentage of share capital they represent.

Listed companies must have a corporate website to comply with the shareholders' right to information. The securities market regulations specify the minimum content to be included on the website.

Lastly, financial entities subject to special regulations (eg, credit entities, saving banks, investment services entities) are also subject to specific reporting and disclosure requirements on several matters (eg, financial statements, risks control).

6.2 What is the liability or responsibility of the board in relation to the company's disclosure requirements?

The company and its directors are responsible for disclosure.

The board must adopt a proactive approach on this matter, ensuring that the information regarding the company's activities and results provided to the market is accurate and faithful. The CUBG contains several recommendations emphasising the responsibility of the board to be accurate, especially regarding any issues that could affect share prices.

According to the SML, the company and its directors will be responsible for damage caused to shareholders due to incorrect or misleading information. Directors are also responsible for keeping the content of the company's website current to reflect documents filed with public registries.

7. M&A AND CORPORATE GOVERNANCE

7.1 Upon an M&A offer, how are the transparency and fairness rules of the company provided under the company and stock market laws and rules?

In the case of a voluntary bid, the decision to make a takeover bid must be announced as soon as it is adopted. Whoever falls within any of the cases that trigger the obligation to make a takeover bid must make public and disseminate the decision to the market immediately.

In all cases, the communication to the market must be made in the same manner as in the case of a 'significant event' (*'hecho relevante'*), and therefore: (i) the communication must be sent to the CNMV at the same time that it is disseminated by any other means and as soon as the event becomes known or the decision is adopted; and (ii) the content of the communication must be true, clear and complete, such that it is not misleading or deceptive. In addition, when the entity is an issuer of securities, it must disseminate the information through its website.

The takeover regulations establish the general principle of 'equal amount of information for competing offerors', to place all offerors on the same footing. The offeree company has a duty to guarantee that all competing offerors receive the same amount of information and potential good-faith offerors are under the same obligation. However, this principle does not imply an obligation on the offeree company to disclose any specific information. This principle would only apply after the offeree gives information to one potential offeror. In such case, it must then provide the same information to every competing offeror. The availability of information is conditional upon: (i) the information being specifically requested; (ii) such information having been previously provided to other existing or potential offerors; (iii) the recipient of the information duly ensuring its confidentiality, and such information being used for the sole purpose of making a takeover bid; and (iv) the information being necessary to make the bid.

In addition, Spanish regulations impose a requirement of passivity both on the offeree's board of directors and any executive body of the board (or anybody receiving powers therefrom), as well as the companies belonging to the offeree's group and persons acting in concert with any of the above. The purpose of this passivity rule is to eschew any possible interference with the bid by the offeree company, so before taking any action that may prevent the success of the bid, the management bodies of the offeree company must obtain the prior approval of the shareholders at a GSM. The only exception is that the offeree's board of directors does not need shareholder approval in order to seek other offers that compete with the original takeover bid, because, in so doing, the board not only causes no damage to the shareholders of the offeree company but rather complies with the fiduciary duties owed to the shareholders to maximise the value of the company.

8. PROXY FIGHTING

8.1 Is proxy fighting customarily conducted for control of the company management or what other items? How is it regulated under the company law or market regulations?

Proxy fighting is not common in Spain and has been seen only exceptionally in specific cases linked to disputes over the control of target companies, normally in the context of takeover bids or minority shareholders disagreeing with the management.

Corporate law contains specific rules on the delegation of votes, including the duty of the representative to duly inform the shareholder of conflicts of interest and specific rules if the representative is a director.

9. OFFICERS' REMUNERATION RULES

9.1 How is remuneration of officers determined? By whom? Is there a role for the shareholders' meeting? Is there any mechanism for an independent body to review and evaluate them?

The remuneration of senior executives will generally be as provided for in the corresponding employment contract and under applicable employment law. In the case of senior executives who are also directors, see paragraph 4.5 above.

For listed companies, the CUBG recommends that, as is the case with directors, the remuneration policies for senior executives be proposed to the board of directors by the remuneration committee. With respect to the remuneration of the senior executives of financial institutions, see paragraph 4.5 above.

9.2 Is the mechanism of officers' remuneration publicly debated?

Yes, in the context of the GSM's advisory vote on officers' remuneration policy.

10. DIRECTORS' LIABILITIES, LIABILITY INSURANCE, INDEMNIFICATION

10.1 What are the directors' responsibilities and liabilities under the law? Can those liabilities be covered by insurance? Can it be indemnified by the company or other related parties?

Directors' duties and liabilities are described in paragraph 4.1 above. Under Spanish law it is possible to purchase insurance policies to cover directors' liabilities to insure them against damages claims which may arise from actions taken in the scope of their regular duties. The core purpose of these policies is to provide financial protection for directors against the consequences of actual or alleged 'wrongful acts' when acting within the scope of their managerial duties. They do not cover fraud, criminal conduct or wilful misconduct. In addition, following the general criterion established by the Spanish insurance regulator, these policies do not cover fines or sanctions.

Although coverage may differ by insurer and is subject to negotiation, these policies usually do not cover claims brought by the company

Indemnification by the company or a related party

As a general matter, it is uncommon in Spain for a company to agree to directly indemnify its directors for damages incurred by them in their capacity as such. Indeed, there is a quite broad – albeit not unanimous – consensus among scholars that agreements of this nature could be deemed to be null and void on the ground that the liability regime of directors is mandatory and cannot be attenuated or excluded by the company and its directors. It is surprising that the scholars following the general consensus do not take issue with the 'external insurer' (through a policy insuring the liability of directors in which the premium is paid by the company) but nevertheless reject 'self-insurance' (ie, an indemnity between the company and the director).

On the other hand, according to this line of argument, the fact that an indemnification undertaking were to be given by a parent company (usually with respect to the proprietary director that it has appointed in the subsidiary) or by another related person would not resolve the risks of invalidity that these undertakings stir up and could even raise additional issues that exceed the scope of this chapter (eg, potential incompatibility with the duty of loyalty and corporate interest or the risk of the parent company being deemed a *de facto* director).

11. SHAREHOLDERS' DERIVATIVE SUITS

11.1 Is a shareholder's derivative suit provided for by law in your jurisdiction? How is it enforced by the shareholders?

Shareholders' derivative suits, understood as lawsuits brought by any shareholder on behalf of the company against third parties (who may or may not be the company's directors) allegedly causing harm to the company when the company has failed to take any measures against the wrongdoers, are not available under Spanish corporate law. Perhaps the only close equivalent would be the right of the company's shareholders to seek enforcement actions for damages against the management body through a 'subsidiary action' (see paragraph 3.1(a)).

11.2 Have there been any recent relevant court cases on the subject?

No. However, various related cases have shown that the best route for obtaining these judgments is in the criminal courts, where litigation costs are lower than in civil courts.

12. SOCIAL INTEREST IN CORPORATE BEHAVIOUR

12.1 How is a company in your country expected to deal with the following issues? Corporate social responsibility; gender, racial and social diversification; environmental issues; ecology and corruption?

During the 2000s, an increasing number of listed companies adopted internal policies on social responsibility and issued annual reports on their implementation. These reports, which were in all cases voluntary and – until recently – were not subject to any specific legal provisions, have become common practice in listed companies and show an upward trend in undertaking commitments with stakeholders. Beginning in 2011, corporate responsibility has been dealt with in the SE Law. Pursuant to the SE Law, listed companies may (but are under no obligation to) issue an annual report on corporate responsibility based on certain international standards, such as transparency of management, good corporate governance and commitment to responsible environmental practices. Any such report must state whether or not it has been verified by third parties. Reports issued by companies employing more than 1,000 individuals must be submitted to the National

Council for Corporate Responsibility for monitoring purposes. Under the SE Law, any company may request acknowledgement as being a socially responsible company.

Two principle measures have been taken in Spain with regard to gender diversity: the Spanish parliament approved Basic Law of 22 March 2007 on Effective Equality between Women and Men (the LOIHM) and the CNMV approved the CUBG, including a recommendation on this matter. The LOIHM calls for a balanced presence of women and men (no less than 40 per cent of either sex) on the boards of directors (not applicable to small- and medium-sized enterprises). The law does not contain express formal sanctions for failure to maintain this balance, although public authorities may, under certain circumstances, adopt positive discrimination in the bidding conditions for certain contracts.

The CUBG recommends that companies with few or no women on their boards explain the reasons for this situation and the measures taken to correct it, and make a specific effort to find potential candidates whenever they need to cover a vacancy. Moreover, the new standard format for the ARCG includes the obligation to explain the steps, if any, taken by the companies to promote a more equitable balance of women and men in the board of directors.

Finally, it is common for major listed companies to have additional internal policies forming part of their corporate governance systems, including anti-fraud and crime prevention policies.

Sweden

Peder Hammarskiöld & Sandra Hein
Hammarskiöld & Co.

1. GENERAL PRINCIPLES

1.1 What are the general principles of corporate governance in your jurisdiction? What are the main objectives of corporate governance principles in your jurisdiction? State also whether your legal system is based on common law or civil law.

The Swedish legal system is closer to the civil law system than to the common law system, but it has some particular features which makes it best described as pertaining to the 'Nordic' legal family. Written statutes are the principal source of law but for their interpretation preparatory works and case law play an important role.

The Swedish Code of Corporate Governance (the Corporate Governance Code) was first introduced on 1 July 2005, inspired by other European corporate governance codes such as the British Combined Code. The Swedish Corporate Governance Code is administered by the Corporate Governance Board and was last revised as of 1 February 2010. The Corporate Governance Code identifies as the main objectives of corporate governance, to ensure that companies are run in a way that is the most efficient from a shareholder perspective. The code emphasises that the investors' ability to rely upon this effectiveness is fundamental to their willingness to invest in the companies.

Historically, Swedish companies have to a large extent been controlled by a few large owners. Nowadays, institutional owners are the predominant owners, but many companies are still controlled by a small number of large owners. There is a tradition of active ownership, where owners for example often nominate representatives to the board of directors. It is common for listed companies to have shares of two classes, class A and B, where the class-A shares typically carry more votes than the class-B shares, but the difference may not exceed 10 to 1. In this way, the original owners of a company can ensure external funding and still maintain control over the company.

The board of directors and the managing director have a general duty of loyalty towards the company and are obliged to act in the best interest of the company. This includes a duty of secrecy where publicity could be detrimental to the company. Another fundamental principle of Swedish company law is the principle that all holders of a certain class of shares must be treated equally.

Swedish limited liability companies are either 'private' or 'public'. The fundamental difference is that only public companies are allowed to raise capital by means of public funding.

1.2 Have there been any recent developments in the law, codes and rules of corporate governance?

In order to facilitate for small companies, in 2010 the required minimum share capital for private companies was lowered from SEK 100,000 to SEK 50,000 and very small companies were exempt from the obligation to have an auditor.

As a result of Directive 2007/36/EC of the European Parliament and of the Council on the exercise of certain rights of shareholders in listed companies, some rules (regarding ie information to be made available to the shareholders in advance of a shareholders' meeting) have been amended.

The last version of the Corporate Governance Code entered into force on 1 February 2010. The changes included most importantly new rules on remuneration and director independence, as well as changes to the rules concerning audit committees.

1.3 Outline recent court cases and incidents involving corporate governance issues. Were there any significant corporate scandals or large unlawful corporate cases?

Recent court cases involving corporate governance issues include, for example, clarifications by the Swedish Supreme Court on board members' duties in case of capital deficit in the company – see, for example, the Supreme Court's ruling in NJA 2012 s 858.

There have been some large corporate scandals during the last years. A major scandal arose in 2012, when accusations were made that TeliaSonera, the dominant and half state-owned telecom company and mobile network operator in Sweden and Finland, had been involved in bribery and money laundering in connection with its establishment in Uzbekistan in 2007. A criminal investigation is currently ongoing.

In 2010, the Financial Supervisory Authority (*'Finansinspektionen'*) decided to revoke the licence for the niche bank HQ Bank AB and apply for mandatory liquidation of the bank. The sanctions were based on findings that, among other things, HQ Bank demonstrated serious deficiencies in its trading operations and a lack of effective risk management. As one of the consequences, the former parent company, HQ AB, has sued the former board members, managing director and auditors for damages.

Another recent corporate governance-related scandal in Sweden is the state-owned energy group Vattenfall's acquisition of the Dutch company Nuon Energy in 2009. In this deal, which is among the largest acquisitions ever by a state-owned company, Vattenfall has been heavily criticised for having paid a highly excessive purchase price for the shares.

1.4 Which law enforcement agency is in charge of enforcing corporate governance? May a criminal sanction be levied upon infringement of the corporate governance rules?

There is no central authority entrusted with enforcing corporate governance rules.

Compliance with certain stock market rules, for example related to insider trading, flagging and mandatory bids is monitored by the Swedish Financial Supervisory Authority.

The Swedish Companies Registration Office (*'Bolagsverket'*) is responsible for keeping a national public register of fundamental corporate data and it is also entrusted with certain disciplinary powers. The registration office can, for example, levy fines on or place a company in liquidation if the company fails to file annual reports or appoint and register directors of the board, auditors (if required) or certain other required officers.

Listed companies are also subject to stock market rules, ie Nasdaq OMX Stockholm's Rule Book for Issuers of 1 February 2012 and NGM Equity's Rules for companies whose shares are admitted to trading on NGM Equity of 1 July 2012. Compliance with these rules is monitored by the disciplinary committee of the respective market, which may impose sanctions in the forms of a warning, a fine or delisting. The fines that may be imposed are 1–15 annual fees.

In addition to the supervisory bodies described above, the Swedish Securities Council (*'Aktiemarknadsnämnden'*) evaluates actions on the stock market and issues written statements in order to contribute to the development of good practices on the stock market. The Council can issue statements on its own initiative or after a petition. It is also possible to seek a statement from the Securities Council in respect of a contemplated action.

Only in a limited number of cases can infringements of corporate governance rules result in criminal liability. These offences include most notably attempts to market or sell shares in private companies to the public, failure by the board of directors in private companies to correctly manage the company's share ledger, failure by the chairman of the board of directors to convene board meetings when required as well as the provision of certain loans or security from the company to shareholders or to someone else for the purpose of his acquisition of securities in the company.

2. SOURCES OF LAW

2.1 Which laws, codes or statutes govern company structures and organisations? Are there statutes like the Companies Act or other forms of law? Is there much relevant case law?

The organisation of Swedish limited liability companies is mainly governed by the Swedish Companies Act (SFS 2005:551) (the Companies Act). Supplementary rules apply to some particular types of companies, for example banks and insurance companies. There is a considerable amount of case law to take into account and new precedents are established from time to time.

The Companies Act is generally applicable to both private and public companies, but in several aspects the requirements on public companies are stricter than on private companies.

Fundamental rules about the company's organisation and operations are pursuant to the Companies Act to be set out in the articles of association which all companies must have in order to be duly incorporated.

In addition to the 'hard' law enacted in legislation, soft law has been developed in the form of the Corporate Governance Code. The code is based on a 'comply-or-explain' approach which allows for deviations as long as they are motivated in the company's annual corporate governance report. The code is applicable to all companies whose shares are traded on regulated markets in Sweden, ie NASDAQ OMX Stockholm and NGM Equity.

2.2 Which laws, codes or statutes regulate capital markets in your jurisdiction?

The capital market is regulated by several statutory laws. Among the most important legislative acts are the Securities Market Act (*'Lagen (2007:528) om värdepappersmarknaden'*), the Financial Instruments Trading Act (*'Lagen (1991:980) om handel med finansiella instrument'*), the Financial Instruments Accounts Act (*'Lagen (1998:1479) om kontoföring av finansiella instrument'*), the Market abuse penalties act (*'Lagen (2005:377) med straff för marknadsmissbruk vid handel med finansiella instrument'*) and the Act on Public Takeover Offers on the Stock Market (*'Lagen (2006:451) om offentliga uppköpserbjudanden'*). In addition, rules to prevent money laundering and terrorist financing may apply.

Companies listed on a Swedish regulated market must also comply with the listing rules of that market place, ie either Nasdaq OMX Stockholm's Rule Book for Issuers of 1 February 2012 or NGM Equity's Rules for companies whose shares are admitted to trading on NGM Equity of 1 July 2012. Listed companies must further also comply with the Corporate Governance Code, since the code according to the listing rules is considered to reflect good practices on the stock market.

2.3 Are there any public interest laws which apply to or influence corporate governance?

New and tougher legislation in the field of anti-corruption, for example, has increased the demands on effective internal controls and governance.

2.4 Have there been any recent developments in any of the above laws? What are the recent changes to the above laws or rules and the reasons for such changes?

See paragraph 12 below regarding the new anti-bribery legislation.

3. SHAREHOLDERS AND THE SHAREHOLDERS' MEETING

3.1 How are shareholders' interests represented in the company? How are the shareholders assured exercise of their rights? What is the highest governing body within the company structure if it is not the shareholders' meeting?

The shareholders exercise their rights of influence in the company via the shareholders' meeting. Certain important decisions require a resolution by the shareholders' meeting in order to be valid, for example appointment of board members and auditors, changes to the articles of association, increase or reduction of the share capital, issue of securities, payment of dividends and liquidation.

3.2 How is the shareholders' meeting conducted? Who may chair the meeting? May attendance (not voting) at the meeting be restricted only to the shareholders? Are the shareholders allowed to be accompanied by legal or other counsel?

The shareholders' meeting is to follow the agenda that is to be provided in advance, together with notice to attend the meeting. It is not permissible for the meeting to resolve on other matters than those set out in the agenda. The shareholders' meeting is to be held in the city in which the company maintains its registered office, unless all shareholders agree to hold the meeting somewhere else.

In companies with only one or few owners, shareholders' meetings are often conducted by means of circulating minutes from the meeting for signature by the owners. It is possible to allow shareholders to participate in the proceedings by telephone or videoconference.

Instead of attending a shareholders' meeting personally, a shareholder may be represented by a proxy holder who must be able to present a written proxy form signed and dated by the shareholder. A shareholder or proxy attending the meeting may also bring up to two advisors. Companies often ask shareholders who want to be represented by proxy at the meeting to submit a copy of their proxy forms in advance.

The shareholders' meeting is as a starting point restricted to shareholders, but other persons fulfilling a role at the meeting may also be present, including for example the chairman, the board of directors, auditors, meeting secretary etc. For listed companies, the Corporate Governance Code requires the managing director, the chairman of the board and as many board members as is required for the board to be quorate to be present at shareholders' meeting. At the annual shareholders' meeting, the code also requires the presence of at least one member of the nomination committee, one of the auditors and as far as possible all board members.

Further, the shareholders' meeting may also decide that a person who is not a shareholder may be present at the meeting or parts of the meeting, or otherwise follow the proceedings at the meeting. This right may also be laid down in the articles of association. For example, the public is often invited to attend annual shareholders' meeting in state-owned companies.

The chairman of the meeting is normally appointed by the shareholders' meeting. For listed companies, the Corporate Governance Code provides that the nomination committee is to prepare a proposal for chairman to the shareholders' meeting. The chairman may be any person who the meeting finds appropriate, but is typically the chairman of the board or a lawyer.

3.3 How are minority shareholders' rights protected?

The Companies Act includes several provisions intended to safeguard the rights of minority shareholders.

All shareholders have the right to attend shareholders' meetings (see paragraph 3.5 below). Majority and quorum requirements for resolutions by the shareholders' meeting are typically higher for decisions which may have more far-reaching consequences for the shareholders, such as, for example, a merger or a decision to issue new securities by deviation from the existing shareholders' pre-emptive rights.

Holders of one-tenth or more of all shares can require the general meeting to resolve to distribute a dividend that amounts to half the sum of the net profit of the year that is available for distribution to the shareholders. However, dividends forced by a minority according to the above may not exceed 5 per cent of the company's equity.

Holders of one-tenth of all shares or one-third of all shares represented at a meeting of shareholders can require the appointment of either (i) an extra auditor in the company who shall participate in the audit of the company together with the other auditors, or (ii) one or several examiners who shall conduct a special examination of the management and accounts of the company during a specified, past period of time or of particular actions or circumstances within the company.

Further, pursuant to the general principle of equal treatment of shareholders, the company may not favour or disfavour any shareholder in relation to any other holder of shares of the same class. Also, the shareholders' meeting, the board of directors as well as other representatives of the company are subject to a general prohibition from performing legal acts or taking any other measure which is likely to provide an undue advantage to the disadvantage of the company or any other shareholder.

Any shareholder can bring action against the company for the annulment of a resolution of the general meeting which has not been properly adopted or is otherwise contrary to the Companies Act or the company's articles of association.

See also paragraph 11 regarding shareholders' derivative suits.

3.4 Is shareholder activism encouraged or discouraged? If not encouraged, how is it regulated?

Active shareholders are generally considered to be a good thing from a Swedish corporate governance perspective.

3.5 How are professional shareholders (those minority shareholders who seek some extra benefit from companies by unduly and habitually influencing management by using their shareholding) treated by the law? Are they excluded from attending the shareholders' meeting? Are they criminally or otherwise publicly sanctioned?

All shareholders have the right to attend shareholders' meetings and state their views in relation to the issues dealt with at the meeting. If a shareholder so requests, the board of directors is also obliged to provide information in respect of any circumstances which may affect the assessment of a matter on the agenda and any circumstances which may affect the assessment of the company's or group's financial position, subject to the limitation that this may take place without significant harm to the company.

It is not possible to prohibit any shareholder from participating in a shareholders' meeting in advance of the meeting. At the meeting, the chairman is to make sure that the meeting is run efficiently and in good order. Shareholders wishing to make a statement can be asked to keep the statement brief and to the point and if necessary a time limit can be set.

3.6 Are shareholders' benefits given to some of the shareholders by the company without resolution by the shareholders' meeting prohibited or regulated by the law or other rules?

The company may not favour certain shareholders before other shareholders unless the disfavoured shareholders give their consent.

4. DIRECTORS AND BOARD OF DIRECTORS

4.1 What are the functions and responsibilities of the directors and the board of directors? Do you have a one- or two-tier board system? What are the outside directors called?

All companies must have a board of directors, which is the body in charge of the company's business and its organisation. Sweden has a one-tier board system. The board of directors is responsible to ensure that the company's organisation in respect of accounting, management of funds and the company's financial position in general includes satisfactory controls. The Corporate Governance Code adds some clarifications about the tasks of the board by expressing, for example, that the board is to establish the overall operational goals and strategy of the company and that the board is to ensure that there is a satisfactory process for monitoring the company's compliance with laws and other regulations relevant to the company's operations.

If the company has a managing director, the managing director will assume the primary responsibility for the company's day-to-day business, the company's compliance with laws, its bookkeeping and typically also to some extent, the organisation of the company.

The board has to issue written instructions governing: (i) reporting to the board of information as is required for the board's assessment of the company's financial position, management of funds and accounting; (ii) rules of procedures for the board's work; and (iii) the allocation of work between the board of directors on the one hand and the managing director and other organs established by the board of directors on the other, for example committees.

Public companies must always have a managing director but in private companies this is optional. The managing director may be a board member but does not have to be. In a public company the managing director may not be the chairman of the board. It is the board of directors that appoints, instructs and supervises the managing director. The board of directors also decides on the signatory powers within the company, within certain boundaries.

In addition, as expressed in the Corporate Governance Code '*directors are to devote the necessary time and care, and to ensure that they have the competence required, to effectively protect and promote the interests of the company and its owners'* (see the introductory section to section 5.1 of the code).

4.2 What are the rules that may give rise to civil and criminal liability of the director(s)? How are those liabilities sought?

The most important provisions regarding civil liability of directors are laid down in Chapter 29 of the Companies Act. These rules are, however, only applicable where the directors have caused damage 'in the performance of his or her duties as directors'. Where the liability provisions in Chapter 29 do not apply, the general Swedish Tort Liability Act (*'skadeståndslagen (1972:07)'*) or other legislation which may contain liability provisions for specific areas of business may apply. The Tort Liability Act is more restrictive than the Companies Act and does not provide any remedy for pure economic loss where the damaging act is not a criminal act.

The Companies Act distinguishes between on the one hand damage that has been caused to 'the company' and on the other hand damage that has been caused to 'a shareholder or other person'. In relation to the company, directors of the board and the managing director can be held liable for any negligent or wilful acts or omissions in the performance of their duties as directors. In relation to shareholders or other persons, directors can only be held liable pursuant to the Companies Act where the damage is a result of the director's violation of the Companies Act, the applicable annual reports legislation, the company's articles of association, or rules governing prospectuses.

Actions for damages against board members or the managing director must be brought in general courts.

In addition to the general rules governing directors' liability for damages described above, directors who in a situation of suspected capital deficit in the company fail to comply with certain procedures set out in Chapter 25 of the Swedish Companies Act, may be held liable for debts incurred by the company during the period of their failure. Also, directors may be personally held liable for unpaid taxes if the company in a situation of threatening insolvency fails to apply for bankruptcy or reorganisation before the taxes fall due.

Where crimes are committed within the company's operations, the starting point is typically that liability lies with the executive management and the board of directors. Such officers and directors may not only be held liable for acts that they have actually committed, but also for failure to take action against wrongdoings that he or she was, or should have been aware of.

In addition to criminal law in general, the Companies Act provides criminal liability for violation of certain of its rules (see paragraph 1.4 above).

4.3 Does the board of directors have a committee system, eg, nomination committee, compensation committee, audit committee?

If not required, is it common practice for companies? How does it function?

The Companies Act allows for the board to establish the committees the board sees fit, and if so, in the board's rules of procedure clarify the allocation of work between the board and the committee. Listed companies are by law required to have an audit committee. Companies applying the Corporate Governance Code are required by the code to have a nomination committee and a remuneration committee.

The members of the audit committee may not be employed by the company. At least one committee member must be independent and be experienced in accounting or auditing. Pursuant to the Corporate Governance Code, the audit committee is to consist of at least three board members and that the majority of the members are to be independent in relation to the company and its management. At least one of the members who are independent in relation to the company and its management must also be independent of the larger shareholders.

Pursuant to the Corporate Governance Code, the shareholders' meeting is to appoint members of the nomination committee, or to prescribe procedures for how such committee members are to be appointed. The main tasks for the nomination committee are to prepare the shareholders' meeting's resolutions regarding appointment of board members and auditors as well as regarding compensation to board members and auditors. The nomination committee is to consist of at least three members of which one person is to be the chair. The majority of the committee's members is to be independent in relation to the company and its management. The managing director or other members of the management may not be appointed to the nomination committee. At least one of the committee's members is to be independent in relation to the largest shareholder in terms of voting power, or group of shareholders acting in concert in the governance of the company.

The main tasks of the remuneration committee required by the Corporate Governance Code, are to: (i) prepare the board's decisions on issues concerning principles for remuneration, remunerations and other terms of employment for the executive management; (ii) monitor and evaluate programmes for variable remuneration, both ongoing and those that have ended during the year, for the executive management; and (iii) monitor and evaluate the application of the guidelines for remuneration that the annual shareholders' meeting is legally obliged to establish, as well as the current remuneration structures and levels in the company.

The remuneration committee is established by the board and the chairman of the board may also chair the committee. The other members of the committee, appointed to the board by the shareholders' meeting, are to be independent of the company and its executive management. In addition, one employee representative may attend and participate in remuneration committee meetings (see paragraph 4.4 below). Alternatively, the tasks of the remuneration committee may instead be performed by the entire board of directors, provided that no board members that are part of the executive management participate in the committee's work.

4.4 Is it a legal requirement to have an independent director or a third-party director? If so, how are they appointed? Is it required for listed companies?

The Corporate Governance Code provides that, in listed companies, the majority of the directors elected by the shareholders' meeting are to be independent of the company and its executive management. No more than one member of the board may be a member of the executive management of the company or a subsidiary. At least two of the members of the board who are independent of the company and its executive management are also to be independent in relation to the company's major shareholders.

Also, in addition to the directors appointed to the board by the shareholders' meeting, in all private or public companies which on average have more than 25 employees during a financial year, the trade unions are entitled to appoint two representatives. (The act on board representation for employees in joint stock companies (*'Lagen 1987:1245 om styrelserepresentation för de privatanställda'*).

4.5 How is the compensation for directors or officers determined? Can it be contested by the shareholders or the regulatory authorities? What are the common rules or practices for the compensation of officers?

It is the shareholders' meeting that resolves on any compensation to the board of directors, normally at the annual general shareholders' meeting. The decision is to specify the compensation to each of the directors.

In listed companies it is common that the managing director as well as top management participate in stock-option programmes and similar incentive programmes. With respect to board members, the Corporate Governance Code provides that non-executive members of the board are not to participate in programmes designed for the executive management or other employees. Remuneration of non-executive board members is further not to include share options. The Corporate Governance Code contains various other rules on incentive schemes.

It is the board of directors that decides on the remuneration and other terms of employment for the managing director, but the decision is to comply with guidelines issued by the shareholders' meeting, in accordance with a proposal by the board. The shareholders must at each annual general meeting adopt guidelines for salaries and any other remuneration to the managing director and other top management, including stock-option programmes.

It should be noted that, in listed companies, a resolution by the shareholders' meeting to issue securities to board directors or to the managing director by deviation from the existing shareholders' preferential rights is subject to particularly strict quorum rules, ie the resolution must be supported by a 90 per cent majority of the votes cast as well as of the shares represented at the meeting.

In companies applying the Corporate Governance Code, the board's decision on remuneration to the managing director and other executive managers should be prepared by the remuneration committee. Further, the code requires that all share and share price-related incentive programmes for the executive management (including the managing director) be approved by the shareholders' meeting.

All decisions on remuneration which are taken by the shareholders' meeting can be challenged by any shareholders bringing action for annulment in court. Decisions on remuneration which are made by the board of directors or by the managing director cannot be challenged as to their validity, but should the decision cause damage to the company or the shareholders, shareholders have certain possibilities to bring action for compensation of damages against directors.

There is no authority that can contest resolutions on remuneration or other compensation to board members or other officials. However, with respect to listed companies, the disciplinary committees of the regulated market where the company's securities are traded may impose sanction for violations of laws, regulations and the applicable listing rules, including, for example, good practices on the stock market.

4.6 How will the board handle a corporate crisis like an internal criminal case, violence, social media exposure or dawn raid by the authorities?

How the board will handle a corporate crisis depends, of course, on the type of company and crisis it faces. General measures that may be considered include, for example, establishing a task force to be in charge of the company's handling of the issue, defining a strategy for communication internally and externally, ensuring document retention, conducting an investigation, seeking advice from external attorneys, as well as having contacts with the police or other relevant authorities.

5. BOARD OF AUDITORS, AUDIT COMMITTEE, ACCOUNTING AUDITORS

5.1 How is the internal accounting and legal audit structured and conducted? Is an outside accounting audit required and, if so, how is it structured? Are there requirements to change the auditor each five years?

As further described in paragraph 4.1 above, the responsibility to organise and monitor the company's accounting, fund management, financial position and reporting vest in the board of directors and the managing director.

All companies must have an external auditor unless the company or group (as applicable) is so small that it: (i) has no more than three employees; (ii) the company's reported balance sheet total for each of the two most recent financial years has not exceeded SEK 1.5 million; and (iii) the company's reported net turnover for each of the two most recent financial years has not exceeded SEK 3 million.

The auditor shall examine the company's annual report and accounts, as well as the management by the board of directors and the managing director. The audit shall be as detailed and extensive as required by generally accepted auditing standards. After the end of each financial year, the auditor is to submit an auditor's report to the annual shareholders' meeting. If the company is a parent company, the audit and the report will also encompass corresponding measures with respect to the group. In conjunction with the audit, the auditor shall provide the board of directors and the managing director with any criticisms and observations required by generally accepted accounting standards.

Listed companies must change auditors after seven years. An auditor who has served for a period of seven years may not be appointed auditor again until two years have passed since he or she resigned as auditor. During the two-year period, the former auditor may not participate in any audits of the company in question. The obligation to change auditors only applies to auditors in person and not to audit firms. This means that a listed company can maintain the same audit firm for more than seven years, as long as the person conducting the audits is replaced after seven years.

5.2 Do you have supervisory auditors? What is the function of the supervisory auditors' board?

There are no supervisory auditors under Swedish law, but see paragraph 3.3 above regarding the minority's right to have general and special examiners appointed.

6. MARKET DISCLOSURE/TRANSPARENCY TO THE SHAREHOLDERS AND THE PUBLIC

6.1 What are the disclosure requirements for companies in your jurisdiction under company law, capital markets law or any other rules?

Listed companies have a general duty to disclose information about decisions and facts that are price sensitive as soon as possible. In addition, the listing rules applicable to the regulated markets contain several specific requirements on information to be disclosed, including among many other things financial reports, audit reports, unexpected and significant deviation in financial result or position, notice to attend shareholders' meetings, resolutions by the shareholders' meeting, issue of securities, changes in board of directors, management and auditors, share-based incentive programmes, closely related-party transactions, business acquisitions and divestitures, substantive changes to the company, its ownership structure or its business activities, decisions regarding listing, and information required by another trading venue.

6.2 What is the liability or responsibility of the board in relation to the company's disclosure requirements?

A company that fails to comply with disclosure requirements can be subject to sanctions by the disciplinary committee on the market where its securities are traded. The sanction could be a warning, fines or ultimately delisting. Fines are incurred on the company and not on its directors or officers, but if fines are imposed on the company as a result of negligence by its directors of officers, this could give rise to liability in damages for the directors or officers.

7. M&A AND CORPORATE GOVERNANCE

7.1 Upon an M&A offer, how are the transparency and fairness rules of the company provided under the company and stock market laws and rules?

Public takeovers in Sweden are governed by the Swedish Act on Public Takeovers on the Stock Market (*'Lagen (2006:451) om offentliga uppköpserbjudanden på aktiemarknaden'*) (the Takeover Act), which is based on Directive 2004/25/EC on takeover bids. In addition, the takeover rules of the respective stock markets apply. These rules codify, for example, the general principles expressed in the directive, such as fair and equal treatment of shareholders, duty to provide clear and correct information, etc.

A public offer may only be made if the bidder has undertaken to comply with the takeover rules of the stock exchange where the shares in question are listed. Failure to make such an undertaking may result in substantial fines.

As soon as a decision has been made to launch a public offer, it must be disclosed together with the main terms and other information. When a public offer is made, or plans for a public offer are disclosed, the Financial Supervisory Authority must at the same time be informed. Within four weeks from the date when an offer is announced, the offeror must prepare an offering document and apply for its approval by the Financial Supervisory Authority. Once the offering document has been approved it must be made public. Both the company making the offer and the target company also have duties of information towards their employees.

The board of directors or the managing director of the company may not take defensive measures, intended to impair the conditions for the launching or implementation of the bid, without a resolution adopted by the general meeting of shareholders. This applies as well when the aforementioned persons have received information originating from the offeror that a public bid is imminent.

In order to ensure that the shareholders have an exit opportunity in case of a takeover, the Takeover Act provides for mandatory bids. Anyone who, alone or together with a related party, becomes the owner of the equivalent of 30 per cent or more of the votes in a listed company must immediately announce the size of its shareholding and within four weeks from that date launch a public offer to acquire the rest of the shares.

Transparency is also enhanced by the flagging rules in the Financial Instruments Trading Act (*'Lagen (1991:980) om handel med finansiella instrument'*), obliging shareholders to disclose changes in their shareholdings which mean that the holding (in shares or votes) reaches, exceeds or falls below any of the threshold values 5, 10, 15, 20, 25, 30, 50, 66 (two-thirds) or

90 per cent.

Compliance with the takeover rules is primarily monitored by the Financial Supervisory Authority, which has right to request information and impose sanctions.

8. PROXY FIGHTING

8.1 Is proxy fighting customarily conducted for control of the company management or what other items? How is it regulated under the company law or market regulations?

Proxy fighting is not very common in Sweden. As set out in paragraph 3.2 above, a shareholder may be represented by proxy at a shareholders' meeting and the same proxy may represent one or more shareholders.

Listed companies are obliged by law to provide forms for powers of attorney via their website during a period of three weeks before the shareholders' meeting. These powers of attorney are to be standard forms, intended to give only a general authorisation to represent a shareholder, without any voting instructions, and they may not refer to any particular person as proxy.

There are limited possibilities for the company to arrange for the collection of proxies on the company's expense. First, the articles of association must allow for collection of proxies on the company's expense. If they do, the board may decide to provide the shareholders with a proxy form in connection with notice to attend the shareholders' meeting. The form is to be used to empower a person named in the form to represent the shareholder at the shareholders' meeting and vote according with the instructions in the form. The form must present the proposed resolutions together with two alternative answers headed 'yes' or 'no', which are to be presented in equal fashion.

Similarly, voting by regular mail in advance of the shareholders' meeting is allowed if the articles of association permit it. The shareholders will then use a form provided by the company in which the proposals to the meeting are listed together with the two alternative answers 'yes' or 'no', presented in an equal fashion.

9. OFFICERS' REMUNERATION RULES

9.1 How is remuneration of officers determined? By whom? Is there a role for the shareholders' meeting? Is there any mechanism for an independent body to review and evaluate them?

See paragraph 4.5 above.

9.2 Is the mechanism of officers' remuneration publicly debated?

Remuneration to directors of the board and other officers are among the corporate governance issues which are most frequently addressed by media and debated. These 'fat cats' discussions often focus on remunerations being too generous, with too low demands on performance.

10. DIRECTORS' LIABILITIES, LIABILITY INSURANCE,

INDEMNIFICATION

10.1 What are the directors' responsibilities and liabilities under the law? Can those liabilities be covered by insurance? Can it be indemnified by the company or other related parties?

As regards directors' responsibilities and liabilities, see paragraphs 4.1 and 4.2 above.

A company may provide insurance to cover liability for its board of directors and managing director, and this is often done, in particular in larger companies.

One reason why directors' and officers' insurance is common, is that a company cannot undertake to indemnify and hold harmless the members of the board of directors or the managing director for claims for damages to the company. If the company has a claim for liability in damages against a director of the board or managing director, any settlement must be approved by the shareholders' meeting, whereby holders of a tenth of the shares have blocking powers. It is in principle possible for a company, typically a parent company, to undertake to indemnify directors in another group company. However, rules on minority protection or capital protection should be considered with respect to the indemnifying company. Further, it is to some extent also possible for a company to agree to indemnify directors for liability claims from a third party, to the extent the claim refers to a violation of rules for protection of third-party rights only.

11. SHAREHOLDERS' DERIVATIVE SUITS

11.1 Is a shareholder's derivative suit provided for by law in your jurisdiction? How is it enforced by the shareholders?

Shareholders representing at least one-tenth of the shares in the company may in their own name bring an action for damages to the company against board members, founders, the managing director, auditors, general or special examiners or other shareholders. This right can only be exercised where shareholders representing at least one-tenth of the shares in the company have at the shareholders' meeting supported a resolution to bring such action in damages or, with respect to board members or the managing director, have voted against a resolution regarding discharge from liability.

11.2 Have there been any recent relevant court cases on the subject?

Shareholders' derivative suits are rather unusual in Sweden and there are no relevant recent Supreme Court cases.

12. SOCIAL INTEREST IN CORPORATE BEHAVIOUR

12.1 How is a company in your country expected to deal with the following issues? Corporate social responsibility; gender, racial and social diversification; environmental issues; ecology and corruption?

Although not a formal requirement, most large companies have a sustainability policy and publish sustainability reports on an annual basis, describing the company's work with corporate social responsibility issues such as environmental, social and ethical issues. Also, the Corporate

Governance Code provides an obligation for the board of directors to define necessary guidelines to govern the company's ethical conduct.

With respect to board composition, the Corporate Governance Code provides that the board members elected by the shareholders' meeting are collectively to exhibit diversity and that the company is to strive for equal gender distribution on the board, but there is no sanction to be imposed if this goal is not met. A discussion about whether or not to impose gender quotas has been ongoing for some years, but the issue is controversial.

Anti-corruption issues have attracted a growing interest and awareness during the last years. New legislation entered into force on 1 July 2012. This included, for example, the introduction of two new crimes: 'negligent financing of bribery' and 'influence peddling'.

There are no formal requirements on measures that companies must take to prevent corruption but in order to minimise such risks it is, generally speaking, advisable to at least: implement clear policies, provide training of staff, have routines for controls and follow-up, implement a whistleblower or speak-up policy and perform due diligence of business partners. Depending on the size and operations of the company, internal audits should be considered as a valuable tool to help detect wrongdoings.

Taiwan

Chun-yih Cheng
Formosa Transnational Attorneys at Law

1. GENERAL PRINCIPLES

1.1 What are the general principles of corporate governance in your jurisdiction? What are the main objectives of corporate governance principles in your jurisdiction? State also whether your legal system is based on common law or civil law.

Taiwan is a civil law country. The emphasis of the legal system is placed on statutes rather than case law. Corporate governance in Taiwan has no clear definition and can be defined in several ways. From the legal point of view, corporate governance may be deemed as a vehicle of decision-making and power allocation among shareholders, directors, managers and other interested parties; from the financial point of view, the purpose of corporate governance is to maximise the shareholders' value and stakeholders' rewards.

Under the Corporate Governance Best Practice Principles for TWSE/GTSM Listed Companies (Principles), in order to assist companies listed on the Taiwan Stock Exchange Corporation (TWSE) and the GreTai Securities Market (GTSM, collectively referred to as 'listed companies') to establish a sound corporate governance system, and to promote the integrity of the securities market, the TWSE and GTSM have jointly adopted these Principles to be followed by listed companies. Listed companies are advised to promulgate their own corporate governance principles in accordance with these Principles.

According to the Principles, when setting up the corporate governance system, in addition to complying with relevant laws, regulations, articles of incorporation, contracts signed with the TWSE or GTSM and other relevant regulations, a listed company shall follow the following principles:

- Establish an effective corporate governance framework.
- Protect the rights and interests of shareholders.
- Strengthen the powers of the board of directors.
- Fulfil the function of supervisors.
- Respect the rights and interests of stakeholders.
- Enhance information transparency.

Given the above, corporate governance refers to a guidance and management mechanisms to implement the liability of the operators of the company for the purpose to strengthen the corporate performance and to protect the shareholders' interests by taking into account other stakeholders' interests. Therefore, we can say that the main objective of corporate governance is to improve the company's operation and to get maximum benefit therefrom for stakeholders.

1.2 Have there been any recent developments in the law, codes and rules of corporate governance?

The legal basis of corporate governance in Taiwan primarily arises from the application of the Company Act, the Securities and Exchange Act (SEA), and their related rules and regulations. In 2012, relevant laws and regulations have been amended for the purpose to achieve the goal of corporate governance development. The purposes of such amendments are as follows:

- to require company to add the exercising of voting right via e-voting platform;
- to allow split voting by shareholders holding shares for others to divide their share votes;
- to implement the requirement for companies to establish a remuneration committee;
- to strengthen the disclosure of information relating to public tender offerings, and to ensure reasonable pricing;
- to strengthen the role of the board of directors; and
- to enhance the transparency of corporate information.

In order to strengthen corporate governance, the Financial Supervisory Commission (FSC) expressed its intentions to propose relevant law, regulations, self-regulatory and market mechanisms to enhance the competitiveness of enterprises and the protection of shareholders' interests in May 2013. The main directions of said proposal include establishment of a corporate governance evaluation mechanism, requiring listed companies to have independent directors and audit committee, extension of compulsory company-wide adoption of electronic voting, and strengthen dialogue with stakeholders.

1.3 Outline recent court cases and incidents involving corporate governance issues. Were there any significant corporate scandals or large unlawful corporate cases?

According to the Annual Report 2012 of the Securities and Futures Investors Protection Center (*http://220.130.32.146/webdata/證券投資人+交易人保護中心_年報_低.pdf*), as of the end of 2012, there were 81 cases pending before courts. The Center has filed class-action litigations on behalf of investors, by the end of 2012, there are 22 cases which have been won with final judgments, including the cases of Tong Lung Metal Industry (false financial statement, misleading prospectus), Infodisk Technology (insider trading in 2000), Taiwan Fertilizer (stock price manipulation) and Procomp (misleading prospectus). By the end of 2012, the Center has helped investors collect compensations totalling NT$2.059 billion. In order to strengthen the corporate governance mechanism, according to the law, the Center has the right to file lawsuits on behalf of companies and request the court to discharge directors/supervisors as wrongdoers. In case of any listed company's directors/supervisors whose behaviours are harmful to the company's interest or violate the law or articles of incorporation, the

Center would file a lawsuit against the wrongdoing directors/supervisors for compensation or request discharge of their positions from the company. As of the end of 2012, the Center has filed 18 derivative suits on behalf of companies and another eight requesting the court to discharge wrongdoing company directors/supervisors from their positions.

1.4 Which law enforcement agency is in charge of enforcing corporate governance? May a criminal sanction be levied upon infringement of the corporate governance rules?

For non-listed companies in Taiwan, the authority in charge of enforcing corporate governance is the Ministry of Economic Affairs. As for listed companies, they should be governed by the Securities and Futures Bureau of the FSC, which is the authority responsible for the legislative environment of corporate governance by companies with stocks listed on the TWSE and GTSM. The TWSE or GTSM have also carried out the establishment of standards, supervision and execution in a self-disciplinary regulatory manner.

2. SOURCES OF LAW

2.1 Which laws, codes or statutes govern company structures and organisations? Are there statutes like the Companies Act or other forms of law? Is there much relevant case law?

The Company Act is the main law governing company structures and organisations in Taiwan. The Company Act provides four categories of companies: unlimited company, hybrid-unlimited company, limited company, and company limited by shares, and the most popular form of which is company limited by shares. According to the Company Act, a company limited by shares is a company organised by two or more or one government or corporate shareholder, with the total capital of the company being divided into shares and each shareholder being liable for the company in an amount equal to the total value of shares subscribed. In addition, a company limited by shares must have at least three directors and at least one supervisor. The basic regulatory model is a check-and-balance structure that consists of board of directors, supervisor(s) and shareholders' meeting. In addition to the Company Act, the Mergers and Acquisitions Act, the SEA, the Fair Trade Act and other secondary legislations promulgated by relevant authorities are also relevant to corporate matters in Taiwan.

Being a civil law jurisdiction, the reliance on case law is less than common law jurisdictions. Only those Supreme Court judgments that have been selected by the Supreme Court as precedents have the force of law.

2.2 Which laws, codes or statutes regulate capital markets in your jurisdiction?

In Taiwan, the administration and supervision of the offering, issuance, and trading of securities issued by a public company are governed by the SEA. In addition to the SEA, the securities authorities have, by the power vested under the SEA, issued regulations/rules regarding the administration of public companies, which are also important directives for corporate governance. Those regulations/rules include, but are not limited to, Regulations Governing Procedure for Board of Directors Meetings of Public Companies, Regulations Governing Appointment of Independent Directors and Compliance Matters for Public Companies, and Regulations Governing the Exercise of Powers by Audit Committees of Public Companies. Take the Regulations Governing Procedure for Board of Directors Meetings of Public Companies (BOD Regulations), for example, it is provided for in the BOD Regulations that a public company shall adopt rules of procedure for meetings of its board of directors; the main agenda items, operational procedures, required content of meeting minutes, public announcements, and other compliance requirements for board meetings shall be handled in accordance with these BOD Regulations.

2.3 Are there any public interest laws which apply to or influence corporate governance?

Under the Corporate Governance Best Practice Principles for TWSE/GTSM Listed Companies, in developing its normal business and maximising the shareholders' interest, a listed company shall pay attention to consumers' interest, environmental protection of community and public interest issues, and shall have high regard for the social responsibility of the company.

Moreover, in order to assist listed companies to fulfil their corporate social responsibility initiatives and to promote economic, social and environmental balance and sustainable development, the TWSE and GTSM hereby jointly adopt the Corporate Social Responsibility Best-Practice Principles for TWSE/GTSM Listed Companies (Corporate Social Responsibility Principles) to be followed by listed companies. Listed companies are advised to promulgate their own corporate social responsibility principles in accordance with the Corporate Social Responsibility Principles to manage their environmental and social risks and impact.

According to the Corporate Social Responsibility Principles, in fulfilling corporate social responsibility initiatives, listed companies shall, in its corporate management and operations, give due consideration to the social mores and the rights and interests of the interested parties and, while pursuing sustainable operations and profits, also give due consideration to the environment, society and corporate governance. To implement corporate social responsibility initiatives, listed companies are advised to follow the principles below:

- Exercise corporate governance.
- Foster a sustainable environment.
- Preserve public welfare.

2.4 Have there been any recent developments in any of the above laws? What are the recent changes to the above laws or rules and the reasons for such changes?

As the shareholders often leverage their limited liability to hollow out the assets of their company so that creditors who are injured cannot pursue the liabilities of the shareholders, on 14 January 2013, the Legislative Yuan adopted the amendment to Article 154 of the Company Act. In the future, if any of a company's shareholders misuses the juristic person status of the company to the extent that the company assumes certain debts which are obviously and materially difficult for the company to repay, such shareholders shall still be liable for repayment.

3. SHAREHOLDERS AND THE SHAREHOLDERS' MEETING

3.1 How are shareholders' interests represented in the company? How are the shareholders assured exercise of their rights? What is the highest governing body within the company structure if it is not the shareholders' meeting?

Shareholders, as the owners of the company, are the highest governing body within the company structure in Taiwan. According to the Company Act, shareholders may, for example, exercise the following rights to play an important role in corporate governance to:

- elect and discharge directors and supervisor(s);
- submit the shareholder proposal to the shareholders' meeting to increase their participation in company affairs;
- determine the remuneration of directors and supervisor(s);
- modify or alter the company's articles of incorporation; and
- approve material transaction of the company.

In order to encourage shareholders to actively participate in the shareholders' meeting to exercise their shareholders' rights, the Corporate Governance Best Practice Principles for TWSE/GTSM Listed Companies requires listed companies shall encourage its shareholders to actively participate in its corporate governance and hold shareholders' meetings on the premises of legal, effective and safe proceedings. Moreover, listed companies shall seek all ways and methods, including fully exploring technologies for information disclosure, so as to enhance the attendance rate of shareholders at the shareholders' meeting.

For the purpose of allowing shareholders to learn about the meeting procedures and contents ahead of a shareholders' meeting and to attend such meeting and exercise their rights actively, the FSC amended the Regulations Governing Content and Compliance Requirements for Shareholders' Meeting Agenda Handbooks of Public Companies in December 2009. The amended regulations require that 21 days before a company is to convene a regular shareholders' meeting, it shall prepare an electronic file of the shareholders' meeting agenda handbook and the supplemental materials, and upload it to the Market Observation Post System (MOPS).

Further, according to the SEA, an annual report must be published in no less than three months after the end of each fiscal year. That makes the shareholders' meeting generally held after that period of time to have advanced knowledge of the annual report. In order to solve the problem of conflicting schedule of shareholders' meetings for different listed companies, FSC has coordinated with government-invested companies to hold their annual shareholders' meeting on different dates and has limited the number of shareholders' meeting on the same date.

3.2 How is the shareholders' meeting conducted? Who may chair the meeting? May attendance (not voting) at the meeting be restricted only to the shareholders? Are the shareholders allowed to be accompanied by legal or other counsel?

Unless otherwise provided by law or regulation, the shareholders' meetings shall be convened by the board of directors. For a listed company, it shall prepare electronic versions of the shareholders' meeting notice and proxy forms, and the originals and explanatory materials relating to all proposals, and upload them to the MOPS before 30 days of the date of a regular shareholders' meeting (or before 15 days of the date of a special shareholders' meeting). Also, the company shall prepare electronic versions of the shareholders' meeting agenda and supplemental meeting materials and upload them to the MOPS. In addition, the company shall also have prepared the shareholders' meeting agenda and supplemental meeting materials and made them available for review by shareholders at any time. With the consent of the addressee, the meeting notice may be given in electronic form. If a shareholders' meeting is convened by the board of directors, the meeting agenda shall be set by the board of directors, and the meeting shall proceed in the order set by the agenda, which may not be changed without a resolution of the shareholders' meeting.

If a shareholders' meeting is convened by the board of directors, the meeting shall be chaired by the chairman of the board. When the chairman of the board is on leave or for any reason unable to exercise the powers of the chairman, the vice chairman shall act in place of the chairman. Absent the vice chairman, a director appointed by the chairman or, without such appointment, a director elected among the directors shall preside over the shareholders' meeting.

For each shareholders' meeting, a shareholder may appoint a proxy to attend the meeting by providing the proxy form issued by the company and stating the scope of the proxy's authorisation. A shareholder may issue only one proxy form and appoint only one proxy for any given shareholders' meeting, and shall deliver the proxy form to the company.

Under Taiwanese laws, the company may appoint its attorneys, certified public accountants (CPA), or related persons retained by it to attend a shareholders' meeting in a non-voting capacity. There is no law/regulation regulating whether a shareholder can be accompanied by legal or other counsel to attend a shareholders' meeting. But in practice, it is generally not allowed. According to the Company Act, the statements and records of accounts prepared by the board of directors and the report made by the supervisors shall be made available at the head office for inspection at any time by the shareholders, 10 days prior to the regular shareholders' meeting. The shareholders may bring their attorneys or CPAs for such an inspection.

3.3 How are minority shareholders' rights protected?

Regarding the rights of the minority shareholders under Taiwanese laws, other than the rights commonly owned by each shareholder, such as receiving dividends, attending shareholders' meeting and pre-emptive right to subscribe for new shares in proportion to the shareholding, the minority shareholders are entitled to exercise the following rights:

- propose to the company a proposal for discussion at a regular shareholders' meeting;
- request the board of directors to call a special shareholders' meeting;
- convene a shareholders' meeting after obtaining an approval from the competent authority;
- propose to the company in writing a roster of director candidates;
- initiate a lawsuit in the court for a judgment on the discharge of the director;
- request in writing the supervisor(s) of the company to initiate, for the company, a lawsuit against a director of the company;
- apply to the court for appointment of inspector to inspect the business operations, financial accounts and the property of the company;
- initiate a lawsuit in the court for annulment of the resolution that is in violation of any applicable laws, regulations and/or the articles of incorporation;
- request the board of directors to discontinue the unlawful act;
- apply to the court for rendering a ruling for the dissolution of the company;
- exercise the rights of the a company's affiliated company to claim against the company for the payment of the indemnity to the affiliated company; and
- waive his voting right and request the company to buy back, shares of the split and consolidated or merged company he holds at the prevailing market price.

3.4 Is shareholder activism encouraged or discouraged? If not encouraged, how is it regulated?

The Corporate Governance Best Practice Principles for TWSE/GTSM Listed Companies (Principles) requests that a listed company shall establish a corporate governance system which ensures shareholders' rights of being fully informed of, participating in and making decisions over important matters of the company. Moreover, a listed company shall encourage its shareholders to actively participate in its corporate governance and hold shareholders' meetings on the premises of legal, effective and safe proceedings. A listed company shall seek all ways and means, including fully exploring technologies for information disclosure, so as to enhance the attendance rate of shareholders at the shareholders' meeting and ensure the exercise of shareholders' rights by shareholders at the shareholders' meeting in accordance with laws. Given the above, we would say that shareholder activism is encouraged.

3.5 How are professional shareholders (those minority shareholders

who seek some extra benefit from companies by unduly and habitually influencing management by using their shareholding) treated by the law? Are they excluded from attending the shareholders' meeting? Are they criminally or otherwise publicly sanctioned?

Under Taiwanese laws, a company shall treat all shareholders fairly. But a company may set up internal rules to maintain the order of the shareholders' meeting. According to the template issued by the competent authority in this regard, except with the consent of the chairman of the shareholders' meeting, a shareholder may not speak more than twice on the same proposal, and a single speech may not exceed five minutes. If the shareholder's speech violates the rules or exceeds the scope of the agenda item, the chairman may terminate the speech. Moreover, when an attending shareholder is speaking, other shareholders may not speak or interrupt; the chairman shall stop any violation. The chairman may direct the security personnel to help maintain order at the meeting place. At the place of a shareholders' meeting, if a shareholder attempts to speak through any device other than the equipment set up by the company, the chairman may prevent the shareholder from so doing. When a shareholder violates the rules of procedure and defies the chairman's correction, obstructing the proceedings and refusing to heed calls to stop, the chairman may direct the security personnel to expel the shareholder from the meeting.

If the professional shareholders' activities are considered constituting the crimes under Taiwanese criminal law (usually, offences of coercion, offences of intimidation for endanger security, and offences of intimidation), such shareholders may be criminally punished with imprisonment.

3.6 Are shareholders' benefits given to some of the shareholders by the company without resolution by the shareholders' meeting prohibited or regulated by the law or other rules?

Based on shareholder equality, it is not allowed to give benefit only to some of the shareholders.

4. DIRECTORS AND BOARD OF DIRECTORS

4.1 What are the functions and responsibilities of the directors and the board of directors? Do you have a one- or two-tier board system? What are the outside directors called?

The director individually acts as the responsible person of a company and is a member of the board of directors of a company. The board of directors generally functions as the central management body of the company and is responsible for policy/decision-making, execution and supervision of the businesses and matters of the company. According to Taiwan's Company Act, unless otherwise provided for under the laws or the articles of incorporation of the company that it should be executed in accordance with the resolutions of the shareholders' meeting, the business operation of a company shall be executed in accordance with the resolution of its board of directors. Except for companies listed on the TWSE or GTSM, which are required by the SEA and FSC to establish an audit committee, most Taiwanese companies operate with a special two-tier system (board of directors and supervisors). In Taiwan, external directors are called 'independent directors'.

4.2 What are the rules that may give rise to civil and criminal liability of the director(s)? How are those liabilities sought?

Regulations that may give rise to civil and or criminal liability of a director include, among others, the various provisions under the Civil Code, the Company Act, the Business Entity Accounting Act, the SEA, and the Criminal Code. Depending on the specific industry in which the company operates, a director is also subject to the regulations that may impose civil and criminal liabilities, such as the Banking Act and the Insurance Law. In most cases, criminal procedures utilised to pursue a director's potential criminal offence are initiated through the indictment of a prosecutor. With respect to civil liability, any party, including a third party or the company itself, that suffered damages or losses due to the act or omission of a director of a company may initiate litigation against the director in court. Derivative suits against directors are also available in Taiwan. See paragraph 11 below for details.

4.3 Does the board of directors have a committee system, eg, nomination committee, compensation committee, audit committee? If not required, is it common practice for companies? How does it function?

Under the SEA, a company listed on the TWSE or GTSM must establish a remuneration committee. The members of a remuneration committee must be appointed by the board of directors and there should be at least three members. The remuneration committee is designed to prescribe and periodically examine the performance review and remuneration policy, system, standards, and structure for directors, supervisors and managerial officers; periodically evaluate and prescribe the remuneration of the directors, supervisors, and managerial officers; and submit their recommendation for deliberation by the board of directors. When performing the above-identified duties, the remuneration committee must follow the principles below:

- Make reference to the typical pay levels adopted by peer companies, and take into consideration the reasonableness of the correlation between remuneration and individual performance, the company's business performance, and future risk exposure in the performance assessment and remuneration.
- Do not produce incentives for the directors or managerial officers to engage in activities in the pursuit of remuneration exceeding the risks that the company can tolerate.
- Take into consideration the characteristics of the industry and the nature of the company's business when determining the ratio of bonus payout based on the short-term performance of its directors and senior management, and the time for payment of the variable part of such

remuneration.

Should the board of directors resolve to decline the adoption or to modify the recommendation of the remuneration committee, such resolution must have the consent of a majority of the directors in attendance at a meeting attended by two-thirds or more of the entire board, in which the resolution shall have given the aforementioned principles comprehensive consideration, and shall have specifically explained whether the remuneration passed by the board exceeds in any way the recommendation of the remuneration committee. If the remuneration passed by the board of directors exceeds the recommendation of the remuneration committee, the circumstances and cause for the difference must be specified in the board meeting minutes, and must be publicly announced and reported on the MOPS within two days from the date of passage by the board of directors.

4.4 Is it a legal requirement to have an independent director or a third-party director? If so, how are they appointed? Is it required for listed companies?

The SEA provides that a public company may appoint independent directors in accordance with its articles of incorporation. That is, a listed company may, in view of the company's scale, shareholder structure, and or operational needs, stipulate in its articles of incorporation the appointment of independent directors, which shall be no less than two and comprise no less than one-fifth of the number of board of directors. Further, under the authorisation of the SEA, the FSC orders that listed financial holding companies, banks, bills finance companies, insurance companies, securities investment trust enterprises, integrated securities firms, listed (either on the TWSE or the GTSM) futures commission merchants, and listed (either on the TWSE or the GTSM) companies in non-financial industries with paid-in capital exceeding NT$10 billion must stipulate in their articles of incorporation the appointment of independent directors, which must be no less than two and which must comprise no less than one-fifth of the number of directors on the board of directors.

The FSC has promulgated the Regulations Governing the Appointment of Independent Directors and Compliance Matters for Public Companies to regulate the professional qualifications, restrictions on shareholdings and concurrent positions held, assessment of independence, method of nomination, and other matters for compliance with respect to independent directors. In general, independent directors must possess professional knowledge and there are restrictions on their shareholdings and the positions they may concurrently hold. They must maintain independence within the scope of their directorial duties, and may not have any direct or indirect interest in the company.

The election of independent directors at a public company must adopt a candidate nomination system, and such system must be expressly stated in the articles of incorporation of the company, and the shareholders must elect independent directors from among those listed in the slate of independent director candidates. In addition to the board of directors, shareholder(s) with shareholdings of 1 per cent or more of the total number of issued shares may also submit a candidate list in writing to the company, and such candidates will be evaluated by the board of directors with respect to the qualifications of the candidates. The election of the independent directors of a public company must proceed along with the election of general directors in accordance with the Company Act, but under separately calculated numbers.

4.5 How is the compensation for directors or officers determined? Can it be contested by the shareholders or the regulatory authorities? What are the common rules or practices for the compensation of officers?

According to the Company Act, unless otherwise provided for in the articles of incorporation of the company, the compensation/remuneration of directors must be approved by the shareholders' meeting. It is common in practice to set forth in the articles of incorporation of a company that the board of directors is authorised to determine the compensation for the directors, taking into account their extent and the value of their services provided for the management of the company and the standards of the domestic and overseas industry. The compensation of officers is usually decided by the board of directors. Unless it is in violation of the articles of incorporation of the company or the resolution of the shareholders' meeting, a compensation for director or managerial officer cannot be legally challenged.

4.6 How will the board handle a corporate crisis like an internal criminal case, violence, social media exposure or dawn raid by the authorities?

A public company is required by law that, in the event of the occurrence of any matters that may affect the price of the company's shares and the shareholders' interests, the company must disclose such information within two days upon the occurrence by uploading the matters to the MOPS to comply with its announcement and reporting obligations. The TWSE or the GTSM may also ask the company involved to make announcement or clarification by holding press conferences.

5. BOARD OF AUDITORS, AUDIT COMMITTEE, ACCOUNTING AUDITORS

5.1 How is the internal accounting and legal audit structured and conducted? Is an outside accounting audit required and, if so, how is it structured? Are there requirements to change the auditor each five years?

The financial report of a public company shall be jointly audited and attested to by two or more CPAs of a joint CPA firm or incorporated CPA firm pursuant to Article 15 of the Certified Public Accountant Act. The first time that a joint CPA firm or incorporated CPA firm applies to conduct the auditing and attesting business for the financial report of a public company, it shall file the application and its attachments with the FSC for approval.

A listed company shall select a professional, responsible and independent CPA to be its external auditor, who shall perform regular reviews of the financial conditions and internal control measures of the company. With regard to the irregularity or deficiency discovered and disclosed by the auditor during the review, and the concrete measures for improvement or prevention suggested by the auditor, the company shall faithfully implement improvement actions. Moreover, a listed company shall evaluate the independence of the CPA regularly and no less frequently than once annually. In the event that the company engages the same CPA without replacement for seven years consecutively, or if the CPA is subject to disciplinary actions or other circumstances prejudicial to the independence of the CPA, the company shall review the necessity of replacing the CPA.

5.2 Do you have supervisory auditors? What is the function of the supervisory auditors' board?

There will be two types of corporate governance legal framework for public companies in Taiwan: a supervisor system consisting of shareholders' meeting, board of directors, supervisor(s), and an audit committee system consisting of shareholders' meeting, board of directors, and audit committee (within the board). According to the SEA, a listed company shall establish either an audit committee or a supervisor. The competent authority may, however, in view of the company's scale, type of operations, or other essential considerations, order it to establish an audit committee in lieu of a supervisor.

Under the Company Act, supervisors of a company shall be elected by the shareholders' meeting, and at least one supervisor shall have a domicile within the territory of Taiwan. The number of supervisors should be not less than two in public companies. As to TWSE listed companies, it should have at least three supervisors who lack significant family and business relationships with directors.

A supervisor shall be familiar with the relevant laws and regulations, understand the rights, obligations, and duties of directors of the company and the functions, duties, and operation of each department, and attend meetings of the board of directors to supervise the operations and to state his/her opinions when appropriate so as to control or discover any abnormal situation early on. Also, a supervisor shall supervise the implementation of the operations of the company, and the performance of duties by directors and managers, and care for the enforcement of the internal control system so as to reduce the financial and operational risks of the company. Where a director, for himself/herself or on behalf of others, enters into a sale/purchase or loan transaction, or conducts any legal act with the company, a supervisor shall act as the representative of the company. In the event that the company has set up an audit committee, an independent director member of the audit committee shall act as the representative of the company in the above situation. With regard to review of documents, a supervisor shall have the rights to investigate the operational and financial conditions of the company from time to time, and the relevant departments in the company shall provide the books or documents that will be needed for the supervisor's review. When reviewing the finance or operations of the company, a supervisor may retain attorneys or CPAs on behalf of the company to perform the review; however, the company shall inform the relevant persons of their confidentiality obligations.

As to an audit committee, it is provided for in the SEA that the audit committee shall be composed of the entire number of independent directors. It shall not be fewer than three persons in number, one of whom shall be convener, and at least one of whom shall have accounting or financial expertise. The independent directors shall be elected by the shareholders' meeting. A majority of the members of audit committee shall constitute a quorum to transact business. According to the SEA, the following matters shall be subject to the consent of half or more of all audit committee members and be submitted to the board of directors for a resolution:

(a) adoption or amendment of an internal control system;
(b) assessment of the effectiveness of the internal control system;
(c) adoption or amendment of the handling procedures for financial or operational actions of material significance, such as acquisition or disposal of assets, derivatives trading, extension of monetary loans to others, or endorsements or guarantees for others;
(d) a matter bearing on the personal interest of a director;
(e) a material asset or derivatives transaction;
(f) a material monetary loan, endorsement, or provision of guarantee;
(g) the offering, issuance, or private placement of any equity-type securities;
(h) the hiring or dismissal of a CPA, or the compensation given thereto;
(i) the appointment or discharge of a financial, accounting, or internal auditing officer;
(j) annual and semi-annual financial reports; or
(k) any other material matter so required by the company or the competent authority.

Any matter (other than (j) above) that has not been approved with the consent of half or more of all audit committee members may be undertaken upon the consent of two-thirds or more of all directors. The FSC has announced the Regulations Governing the Exercise of Powers by Audit Committees of Public Companies to implement the audit committee requirement under the SEA.

6. MARKET DISCLOSURE/TRANSPARENCY TO THE SHAREHOLDERS AND THE PUBLIC

6.1 What are the disclosure requirements for companies in your jurisdiction under company law, capital markets law or any other rules?

In Taiwan, the disclosure requirements that a public company, including a company listed on the TWSE/GTSM, are subject to include disclosure in the primary market and disclosure in the secondary market, and the latter may consist of regular and special disclosures. The prospectus is the most material document in the disclosure process of listing. Currently, the main contents of the prospectus must include, among others, operating conditions, operating and capital budgeting plans, financial conditions, important resolutions, articles of incorporation, and the Corporate Governance Self-assessment Report. With respect to the disclosure requirements in the secondary market, the regular disclosure items include monthly operations' condition, periodical financial reporting, financial forecast (not mandatory), annual report and meeting minutes, and insider-trading information. The special disclosure items include timely disclosure of material information, the declaration and publication of acquisitions and disposal of assets, and others such as solicitation for proxies and capital increase by case.

6.2 What is the liability or responsibility of the board in relation to the company's disclosure requirements?

Failing to comply with the disclosure requirements may subject the responsible persons of such failure to comply to an administrative fine, civil compensation and/or criminal liability.

7. M&A AND CORPORATE GOVERNANCE

7.1 Upon an M&A offer, how are the transparency and fairness rules of the company provided under the company and stock market laws and rules?

In Taiwan, a public company is not required to disclose an M&A deal by uploading the matters to the MOPS until a material memorandum, strategic alliance, cooperation, or any other material contract has been executed. Under the Business Mergers and Acquisitions Act, a public company must, before the convention of a board of directors' meeting to approve any resolution on merger/acquisition matters, seek opinions from an independent expert on the justification for the share exchange ratio or distribution of cash or other assets to shareholders, and report the opinions to the board of directors and at the shareholders' meeting. However, when a resolution by a shareholders' meeting is not required for such types of merger/acquisition, the above opinions need not be reported at the shareholders' meeting. If a shareholder has expressed an objection to the merger/acquisition deal in accordance with the manners provided by the relevant laws, the shareholder may request the company to buy back his/her shares at a then fair price.

8. PROXY FIGHTING

8.1 Is proxy fighting customarily conducted for control of the company management or what other items? How is it regulated under the company law or market regulations?

In Taiwan, solicitations of proxy are commonly used to seek control of the board of directors in a company. According to the Company Act, a shareholder may appoint a proxy to attend the shareholders' meeting on his/her/its behalf by executing a power of attorney printed by the company stating therein the scope of power authorised to the proxy. To regulate the use of proxies specifically for public companies, the FSC has promulgated the Regulations Governing the Use of Proxies for Attendance at Shareholders' Meetings of Public Companies, which set forth the formalities of proxies, qualifications for proxies solicitors, and particulars that must be included in writing and advertisements of proxies solicitation, restrictions on the use of proxies (eg, a proxy cannot be obtained in exchange for money or other interest, other than for souvenirs at a shareholders' meeting).

9. OFFICERS' REMUNERATION RULES

9.1 How is remuneration of officers determined? By whom? Is there a role for the shareholders' meeting? Is there any mechanism for an independent body to review and evaluate them?

The board of directors has the authority and discretion to determine and approve the remuneration of managerial officers of a company. In general, the shareholders' meeting plays no role in the determination of the remuneration of managerial officers. Under the SEA, a company listed on the TWSE or the GTSM must establish a remuneration committee responsible for prescribing and periodically examining the performance review and remuneration policy, system, standards, and structure for directors, supervisors and managerial officers; periodically evaluating and prescribing the remuneration of the directors, supervisors, and managerial officers, and submitting their recommendations for deliberation by the board of directors. See paragraph 1.3 for more details as to how the remuneration committee functions.

9.2 Is the mechanism of officers' remuneration publicly debated?

The mechanism of the managerial officers' remuneration is less publicly debated, in comparison with the same for directors and supervisors.

10. DIRECTORS' LIABILITIES, LIABILITY INSURANCE, INDEMNIFICATION

10.1 What are the directors' responsibilities and liabilities under the law? Can those liabilities be covered by insurance? Can it be indemnified by the company or other related parties?

According to Taiwan's Company Act, the mandate relationship under the Civil Code will apply to the relationship between the company and its directors, unless otherwise provided by the Company Act. The Company Act stipulates the special duties of the directors. Under Company Act, the principal duties of a director include:

- The duty of loyalty and the duty of care.
- The duty of non-competition.
- The duty to report to the supervisor when the company is likely to incur substantial damages.
- The duty to act in accordance with the laws, the articles of incorporation, and the resolutions adopted at the shareholders' meetings.
- The duty to declare to the relevant authority the amount of the

company's shares held by a director at the time he is elected and during the term of his office.
- The duty to notify the company of the creation or cancellation of a pledge of the company's shares held by a director.
- The duty to sign or affix his seal to the securities issued by the company.

According to Article 23 of the Company Act, a director shall have loyalty to the company and shall execute the due care of a good administrator in conducting the business of the company; if he/she has acted contrary to this provision, he/she shall be liable for damage sustained by the company. Further, if a director has, in the course of conducting business operations, violated any law or regulation and thus caused damage to a third party, he/she shall be liable, jointly and severally, with the company, for the damage sustained by such a third party.

A director's liabilities under the applicable laws and the company's articles of incorporation cannot be limited or waived. According to the Corporate Social Responsibility Best Practice Principles, a company listed on the TWSE or the GTSM may procure liability insurance to cover director's liability in accordance with its articles of incorporation or resolution of shareholders' meeting.

11. SHAREHOLDERS' DERIVATIVE SUITS

11.1 Is a shareholder's derivative suit provided for by law in your jurisdiction? How is it enforced by the shareholders?

Taiwan's Company Act provides that if a director/supervisor has committed any act that results in material damages to the company or which is in serious violation of applicable laws and/or regulations in the course of performing his/her duties, but the director/supervisor has not been discharged by a resolution of the shareholders' meeting, the shareholder(s) holding 3 per cent in aggregate or more of the total number of outstanding shares of the company may, within 30 days after that shareholders' meeting, institute a lawsuit in the court for a judgment in respect of such matter. Also, a shareholder(s) who has/have been continuously holding 3 per cent or more in aggregate of the total number of the outstanding shares of the company for more than one year may request in writing that the supervisor of the company (or the board of directors, in the case of a supervisor) institute, for the company, an action against a director (or supervisor) of the company; in case the supervisor (or the board of directors) fails to institute an action within 30 days after having received the above request, the above requesting shareholders may institute the action for the company; and under such circumstance, the court may, on the petition of the defendant, order the suing shareholders to furnish an appropriate security. In case the suing shareholders become the losing party in that lawsuit and thus cause damage to the company, the suing shareholders shall be liable for indemnifying the company for such damage. Given to the above provision, shareholders' derivative suits have been rare in the past.

However, since 2009, after the amendment of the Securities Investor and Futures Trader Protection Act, when the Securities and Futures Investors

Protection Center (SFIPC) discovers conduct by a director (or supervisor) of a company listed on either the TWSE/GTSM in the course of performing his or her duties that is materially injurious to the company or is in violation of laws, regulations, and/or provisions of the company's articles of incorporation, the SFIPC may, without the applications of the above-mentioned provisions of the Company Act imposed on the shareholder, request the supervisors (or the board of directors) of the company to institute an action against the director (or supervisor) on behalf of the company. If the supervisors (or the board of directors) fail to institute an action within 30 days after receiving the request made by the SFIPC, the SFIPC may institute the action on behalf of the company. The SFIPC may also institute a lawsuit in court for an order dismissing the given director/supervisor.

11.2 Have there been any recent relevant court cases on the subject?

Shareholders' derivative suits were rare in the past. However, more cases have evolved after the amendment of the Securities Investor and Futures Trader Protection Act in 2009, which authorises the Securities and Futures Investors Protection Center to initiate lawsuits for shareholders.

12. SOCIAL INTEREST IN CORPORATE BEHAVIOUR

12.1 How is a company in your country expected to deal with the following issues? Corporate social responsibility; gender, racial and social diversification; environmental issues; ecology and corruption?

In order to assist listed companies to better understand and fulfil their corporate social responsibility and to promote economic, social, and environmental balance and sustainable development, the TWSE and the GTSM have jointly promulgated the Corporate Social Responsibility Best Practices Principles for TWSE/GTSM Listed Companies for reference when they establish their own corporate social responsibility principles. Listed companies are required to disclose how they perform social responsibility in their annual report and prospectus, which must cover the structure and results of their carrying out their social responsibility programme with respect to the environment, community service, social welfare, consumer rights, human rights, safety and sanitation, and other social responsibilities.

Thailand

Kedsara Luengruengtip **Dej-Udom & Associates**

1. GENERAL PRINCIPLES

1.1 What are the general principles of corporate governance in your jurisdiction? What are the main objectives of corporate governance principles in your jurisdiction? State also whether your legal system is based on common law or civil law.

Thailand's legal system is based on civil law, and the general principles of corporate governance (CG) in Thailand regulate the relationship between the board of directors of a company, its management team, and its shareholders in guiding the company and monitoring its operation.

A company with good CG principles will establish a transparent working environment to enhance the company's competitiveness, to preserve capital, and to increase its shareholders' long-term value from their investment. This also means that the company has efficient, transparent and audited management systems that create trust and confidence among its shareholders, investors, and all related parties. At the core of CG is the role of the board of directors in managing business operations by monitoring, directing and controlling the management in order to serve the interest of the shareholders. The directors are acting as the link between the shareholders and management, and thus have an essential role in establishing good CG. Good CG also dictates the company's rules, regulations and mechanisms which ensure the protection of the rights of the shareholders.

1.2 Have there been any recent developments in the law, codes and rules of corporate governance?

Recently, a World Bank report analysed Thailand's CG framework. This report on the observance of standards and codes confirms that Thailand is a regional leader in CG with a relatively comprehensive framework and has achieved high levels of compliance in a number of key areas.

Corporate governance reform has been a priority since the 1997 Asian financial crisis. The Thai government designated 2002 as a year of good CG. On 5 February 2002, the cabinet appointed the National Corporate Governance Committee (NCGC) to set out policies, measures and schemes to upgrade the level of CG in Thai business. The NCGC consists of the Prime Minister or assigned Deputy Prime Minister as the chairman with committee members that consist of representatives from the Ministry of Commerce, the Ministry of Finance, the Bank of Thailand, the Securities Exchange Commission, the Stock Exchange of Thailand, and the industrial sector.

In 2002, the Stock Exchange of Thailand (SET) set out the Principles of

Good Corporate Governance (Principles) as a guideline for listed companies to implement. In 2006, the Principles were revised to be comprehensive and comparable to the Principles of Corporate Governance of the Organisation for Economic Cooperation and Development (OECD) and recommendations in the World Bank's Reports on the Observance of Standards and Codes (CG-ROSC).

Listed companies are required to disclose the implementation of the said Principles in their annual report, including their reason(s) for non-implementation.

In July 2002, the SET had set up the Corporate Governance Center to provide consulting services to and exchange ideas about CG practices with directors and executives of listed companies.

Per the incorporation of the private sector, the Thai Institute of Directors was established in 1999 and has provided director training and knowledge to board members to enable them to perform their duties and responsibilities efficiently, and meet good CG standards.

1.3 Outline recent court cases and incidents involving corporate governance issues. Were there any significant corporate scandals or large unlawful corporate cases?

In practice, most cases were settled at the Office of the Securities and Exchange Commission by the payment of fines for varying offences. These offences include non-compliance with business conduct of business operators, failure to submit financial statements of the listed companies, failure of securities holding of directors and executives, dissemination of false or misleading information, market manipulation, and insider trading and takeover.

1.4 Which law enforcement agency is in charge of enforcing corporate governance? May a criminal sanction be levied upon infringement of the corporate governance rules?

The Department of Business Development (DBD) in the Ministry of Commerce has authority over all companies and is in charge as a record keeper. The Securities and Exchange Commission (SEC) is responsible for oversight of securities companies and has authority over public limited companies whose shares are listed on the SET (listed companies) and other issuers, dealers, brokers and fund managers. The Bank of Thailand (BOT) has authority over commercial banks and other lenders. The BOT can issue regulations and guidelines, conduct examinations and inspections and also has the power to take enforcement actions. The SEC's powers include administrative actions such as dispensing warning letters, fines, and implementing suspension and removal of licences.

However, the SEC may not initiate civil actions in court and may not exact damages on behalf of the shareholders. The SEC has no prosecutorial powers, but it may refer criminal cases to the inquiry official of the Economic Crime Investigation Division of the Royal Thai Police or the special investigator of the Department of Special Investigation in the

Ministry of Justice.

Additionally, the SEC can take enforcement actions related to takeovers, market manipulation, insider trading, and corporate fraud. In February 2012, the courts sentenced 26 defendants in two cases for fraud in listed companies. It also actively enforces securities rules not directly related to CG.

2. SOURCES OF LAW

2.1 Which laws, codes or statutes govern company structures and organisations? Are there statutes like the Companies Act or other forms of law? Is there much relevant case law?

Company laws in Thailand include the Thai Civil and Commercial Code, usually referred to as the CCC, for private companies, and the Public Limited Companies Act B.E. 2535 (1992) as amended up to No. 3 B.E. 2551 (the PLC) for public limited companies. In addition, public limited companies whose shares are listed on the SET and companies that are issuing securities to the public shall comply with the Securities and Exchange Act B.E. 2535 as amended up to No. 4 B.E. 2551 (2008) (the SEA) and notifications of the SET and the Capital Market Supervisory Board of the SEC. In addition, laws governing specific business apply to certain types of business such as (i) the Banking Act for banking and finance businesses, and (ii) the Life Insurance and the Assurance Business Act for life and property insurance businesses, etc.

2.2 Which laws, codes or statutes regulate capital markets in your jurisdiction?

The Public Limited Company Act B.E. 2535 (1992) and its amendments, the Securities and Exchange Act B.E. 2535 (1992) and its amendments, the notifications of the Stock Exchange of Thailand and the Capital Market Supervisory Board of the Securities and Exchange Commission.

2.3 Are there any public interest laws which apply to or influence corporate governance?

Generally, the CCC states that an act is void if its object is expressly prohibited by law or is impossible or is contrary to public order or good morals. The said provision covers the public interest transaction which applies to every person.

In addition, there are specific laws governing specific business, such as the Banking Act, Insurance Act, Factory Act, Customs Act, Revenue Code, Food and Drug Act, Environment Act, Industry Act, etc. The provisions of these laws specify that an operator must also manage its business in a manner that complies with these specific laws. Practically, the operator must consider and set the rule outlining the responsibilities or proper practices as a code of conduct. The operator and/or its representatives shall be liable for civil and/or criminal penalty if they fail to comply with specific laws.

2.4 Have there been any recent developments in any of the above

laws? What are the recent changes to the above laws or rules and the reasons for such changes?

The amendment to the Securities and Exchange Act B.E. 2535 (1992) No. 4 B.E. 2551 (2008) reinforces the commitment to CG development of all parties in the capital market and the efficiency of the SEC's supervision. The said amendment modifies the governance of publicly traded companies, the duties and responsibilities of the directors and executives, and the shareholders' meeting.

3. SHAREHOLDERS AND THE SHAREHOLDERS' MEETING

3.1 How are shareholders' interests represented in the company? How are the shareholders assured exercise of their rights? What is the highest governing body within the company structure if it is not the shareholders' meeting?

The meeting of shareholders is the highest governing body in the company management hierarchy. Under the CCC and PLC Act, the shareholders have the basic right to control the company by attending and voting at the shareholders' meeting for matters that are proposed by the board of directors.

According to law, there are specific matters that require an approval of the shareholders' meeting. In ordinary cases these require a majority vote of the shareholders who attend the meeting and cast their votes. In case of a deadlock, an equality of votes, the chairman of the meeting shall cast an additional vote as the deciding vote. Certain cases require a vote of not less than three-fourths of the total number of votes of shareholders who attend the meeting and have the right to vote. This includes the increase or decrease of capital and amendment of the memorandum of association or the articles of association.

In addition, the PLC Act prescribes certain essential matters that require the votes of not less than three-fourths of the total number of votes of shareholders who attend the meeting and have the right to vote:

- the sale or transfer of the whole or important parts of the business of the company to other persons;
- the purchase or acceptance of transfer of the business of other companies or private companies by the company;
- the making, amending or terminating of contracts with respect to the granting of hire of the whole or important parts of the business of the company;
- the entrustment of the management of the business of the company to any other person; and
- the amalgamation of the business with other persons with the purpose of profit-and-loss sharing.

There may be additional requirements according to each company's articles of association.

The Capital Market Supervisory Board's regulations specify additional rules that require a listed company to seek an approval of the shareholders' meeting for significant transactions such as the acquisition or disposal of material assets, or a connected transaction between the company and connected persons.

With regard to the right for requesting an extraordinary meeting of shareholders, under the CCC, the shareholders holding not less than one-fifth of the shares of a company may request in writing to the board to call for a shareholders' meeting. For a public limited company, the shareholders holding shares amounting to not less than one-fifth of the total number of shares sold or shareholders amounting to not less than 25 persons holding shares amounting to not less than one-tenth of the total number of shares sold may, by subscribing their names, request the board of directors to call an extraordinary meeting at any time, but the reasons for calling such meeting shall be clearly stated in such request. In this regard, the board of directors shall proceed to call a meeting of shareholders to be held within one month from the date the request is received from the shareholders.

Under the SEA, shareholders who hold shares and have the right to vote amounting to not less than 5 per cent of the total number of the voting rights of the company may submit a written proposal in order to request the board of directors to include such proposal as an agenda of the shareholders' meeting.

3.2 How is the shareholders' meeting conducted? Who may chair the meeting? May attendance (not voting) at the meeting be restricted only to the shareholders? Are the shareholders allowed to be accompanied by legal or other counsel?

The board of directors shall call a meeting of shareholders which is an annual ordinary meeting of shareholders within four months of the last day of the accounting year of a company. Any meetings of shareholders other than this shall be called extraordinary meetings. The chairman of the board shall preside over the meetings of shareholders. If there is no chairman or there is a vice-chairman, but such vice-chairman is unable to perform his or her duty, the shareholders present shall elect one among themselves to preside over the meeting

For a quorum of the shareholders' meeting, at least one-fourth of the capital of the company is required for a limited company according to the CCC. For a public limited company, the quorum would be at least 25 persons or not less than one-half of the total number of shareholders, and in either case, such shareholders shall hold shares amounting to not less than one-third of the total number of shares sold according to the PLC Act.

Under Thai laws, only shareholders have the right to join the meeting and exercise their vote. Nevertheless, they can assign their rights to other persons by following the rules regarding for proxy in the CCC, PLC Act and SEC accordingly. A person without a proxy or approval from the company cannot participate in the meeting.

Nonetheless, there can be 'proxy solicitation' where the proxy solicitor requests to attend the meeting and vote on the behalf of the shareholders. It is recognised in practice; however, the proxy solicitor must comply with the specific SEC rules such as the clear scope of the influences to be used in the decision-making in writing, the realm of the decision, and reliable identification of the proxy solicitor.

3.3 How are minority shareholders' rights protected?

Shareholders' protection rights are listed in the CCC, PLC Act and SEA. For example, minority shareholders may:

- request in writing to the board to call for a shareholders meeting;
- request the competent officer to appoint an inspector to examine the business of company;
- receive the notice of shareholders' meeting in advance not less than seven days for general matters; 14 days for some issues such as increase or decrease of capital and amendment of the articles of association and memorandum of association;
- file a motion with the court to cancel any resolution passed at irregular general meeting; and
- bring a derivative suit to the court to claim compensation on behalf of the company against directors.

3.4 Is shareholder activism encouraged or discouraged? If not encouraged, how is it regulated?

Shareholder activism is encouraged and regulated and prescribed by the CCC, SEA and SEC, including but not limited to the:

- right to propose agendas for the shareholders' meetings;
- right to bring an action against the directors and executives for illegal or unethical acts by the company to court;
- veto rights on employee stock plans (no veto right from shareholders higher than 5–10 per cent), and discounted securities offering securities (no veto right from shareholders higher than 10 per cent).

3.5 How are professional shareholders (those minority shareholders who seek some extra benefit from companies by unduly and habitually influencing management by using their shareholding) treated by the law? Are they excluded from attending the shareholders' meeting? Are they criminally or otherwise publicly sanctioned?

There are no specific regulations regarding professional shareholders in Thailand. Nonetheless, should any shareholder act in a way that could cause a disruption to, negatively influence, or act in bad faith to the company, an authorised director can exercise his or her rights on the behalf of the company to proceed with a civil or criminal lawsuit against such shareholder.

3.6 Are shareholders' benefits given to some of the shareholders by the company without resolution by the shareholders' meeting prohibited or regulated by the law or other rules?

The CCC does not stipulate any legal requirement for giving benefits to shareholders. On the other hand, the SET issued regulations regarding connected transactions between a listed company and its major shareholders (holding at more than 10 per cent of the issued shares with voting rights including shares held by related persons) whereby such must be disclosed to or approved by the board of directors or the shareholders' meeting.

The SEC deems that a connected transaction may lead to a conflict of interest between a listed company and a connected person. The company must ensure transparency when making a decision to enter into a connected transaction and to ensure that a listed company has means to eliminate the conflict of interest with honesty and integrity in a sound, ethical and independent framework together with complete disclosure. The procedure requirements depend on the types of transactions and transaction value, ie, disclosure to the SET. These are transactions that exceed more than either 1 million Baht but less than 20 million, or 0.03 per cent but less than 3 per cent of net tangible assets, whichever is higher. For shareholders' approval, the requirement is for transactions exceeding 20 million Baht or 3 per cent of net tangible assets, whichever is higher.

4. DIRECTORS AND BOARD OF DIRECTORS

4.1 What are the functions and responsibilities of the directors and the board of directors? Do you have a one- or two-tier board system? What are the outside directors called?

Thai companies have a one-tier board system. For every category of Thai company, the board of directors has the power and duty to manage the business of the company in accordance with the company's business objectives, articles of association, and shareholder resolutions, and to perform their duties with loyalty and care to preserve the interests of the company. The scope of powers and duties of the board of directors will depend on the articles of association and the shareholders' resolutions of those companies.

A public limited company must have a board of directors that consists of at least five directors to conduct the business of the company with not less than half of whom must reside within the kingdom. There must be no restrictions to prevent a shareholder from becoming a director. The board of directors shall hold a meeting at least once every three months in the locality in which the head office of the company is located or in a nearby area, unless it is stipulated in the articles of association that the meeting can be held elsewhere.

The SEA Amended No. 4. B.E. 2551 (2008) provides a clearer scope of the duties and liabilities of directors and executives. Any matter approved by the director or executive that, at the time of considering such matter, his/her decision has met the following requirements shall be deemed that the said director or executive has performed his/her duty with responsibility and due care (this is an equivalent to the 'business judgment rule') – honestly, made with reliable information, and sincerely believed to be sufficient and without conflict of interest.

According to the SEC rules, the directors, management, executives, and auditors of listed companies shall prepare a report for the SEC on their securities holdings, their spouses' and any minor children's holdings.

4.2 What are the rules that may give rise to civil and criminal liability of the director(s)? How are those liabilities sought?

Under civil law, directors are legally responsible to the company and shareholders.

Under the legal responsibility to the company, if the company or shareholders believe that the directors caused damages to the company, the company or shareholders may file a derivative suit against a director.

For liabilities under criminal law, when the company violates the law (eg by failure to file relevant documents as required by law, insider trading, etc.), the law imposes the penalty and the director responsible for its operations shall be subject to the penalty as well. There are illegal acts by individuals, eg fraud, scams, or insider dealings, and in such cases, any director committing an offence can be prosecuted. The punishment for such offences appears in the PLC Act and the SEA. Directors of listed companies are liable for more severe penalties under the SEA than those of non-listed public companies, for instance, a fine penalty and 5–10 years' imprisonment in case of fraud or swindle, since the public's invested in such a company.

4.3 Does the board of directors have a committee system, eg, nomination committee, compensation committee, audit committee? If not required, is it common practice for companies? How does it function?

For a limited company and a public limited company whose shares are not listed on the stock market, there is no requirement to set up a sub-committee. Only listed companies require an audit committee which must consist of at least three independent directors according to the SEC notification.

An audit committee has duties as delegated by the board of directors and include basic responsibilities, such as: reviewing the company's financial reporting process to ensure that it is accurate and adequate; reviewing the company's internal control system and internal audit system; reviewing the company's compliance with the law on securities and exchange, the Exchange's regulations, and the laws relating to the company's business; and preparing and disclosing the company's annual report. In its performance of such duties, the audit committee must be directly responsible to the company's board of directors, while the company's board of directors shall remain responsible to third parties for the operations of the company.

In its performance of duties, if it is found or suspected that there is a transaction or any of the listed acts which may materially affect the company's financial condition and operating results, the audit committee shall report it to the board of directors for rectification within the period of time that the audit committee deems fit.

If the company's board of directors or management fails to make rectification within the period of time, any audit committee member may report the transaction or act to the Office of the SEC.

In addition, the Principles 2012 recommend that a remuneration committee and a nomination committee should be set up. However, this is not a mandatory requirement.

4.4 Is it a legal requirement to have an independent director or a third-party director? If so, how are they appointed? Is it required for listed companies?

For a limited company and a public company, the laws do not stipulate the requirement of a third-party director. Nonetheless, for a listed company, at least one-third of the total board members of the company must comprise independent directors but no fewer than three independent directors.
The SEC's regulation states the specific qualifications for the independent director itself in order to maintain its independence that include not holding more than 1 per cent of the company's shares and not having an occupation with inappropriate relations with the company's business, ie, an auditor or a lawyer.

4.5 How is the compensation for directors or officers determined? Can it be contested by the shareholders or the regulatory authorities? What are the common rules or practices for the compensation of officers?

According to the PLC Act, a public limited company shall not pay money or give any property to a director unless it is a payment of remuneration under the articles of association of the company. In the case where the articles of association of the company do not stipulate such payment, the payment of remuneration shall be in accordance with the resolution of the meeting of shareholders based on a vote of not less than two-thirds of the total number of votes of the shareholders attending the meeting.

According to the Principles, board remuneration should be comparable to the industry level in which the company operates, and reflect the experience, obligations, scope of work, accountability and responsibilities and contributions of each director. For the remuneration of top executives that does not require obtaining an approval from the shareholders' meeting, the said principle provides that the remuneration should be in accordance with the board of directors' policy and within the limits approved by the shareholders. For the best interest of the company, all executive salaries, bonuses and other long-term compensation should correspond to the performance of each given executive.

4.6 How will the board handle a corporate crisis like an internal criminal case, violence, social media exposure or dawn raid by the authorities?

There are no regulations or other guidelines in this regard. This may vary according to each company's policies regarding to 'damage control' without derogating from the disclosure requirements for the public.

5. BOARD OF AUDITORS, AUDIT COMMITTEE, ACCOUNTING AUDITORS

5.1 How is the internal accounting and legal audit structured and

conducted? Is an outside accounting audit required and, if so, how is it structured? Are there requirements to change the auditor each five years?

A limited company is required to hire an external licensed auditor, and the auditor shall be elected every year at an ordinary meeting of shareholders. The auditor shall not be a director, staff, employee or person holding any position or having any duty in the company. With regard to listed companies, they must have an auditor approved by the SEC as their auditor. The SEC rules require audit partners with a particular client to rotate after five years. Note that the audit committee of a listed company's board should choose the auditor and propose the same to the board of directors for consideration and further propose his/her appointment to the shareholders' meeting for consideration and approval.

5.2 Do you have supervisory auditors? What is the function of the supervisory auditors' board?

Not applicable.

6. MARKET DISCLOSURE/TRANSPARENCY TO THE SHAREHOLDERS AND THE PUBLIC

6.1 What are the disclosure requirements for companies in your jurisdiction under company law, capital markets law or any other rules?

As required by law, all companies must prepare audited financial statements. There are different requirements for each company category. A public limited company is required to prepare a board of directors' report which contains the following details subject to the particulars as prescribed in the Ministerial Regulations:

- the name, location of the head office, category of business, number and type of all the shares sold of the company including the number and type of shares of affiliated companies held by the company or private company in which the company holds 10 per cent or more of the number of shares sold of such other company or private company (if any);
- the interest of directors in any contract made with the company and numbers of shares held in the company; and
- remuneration, shares, debentures, or other benefits which directors receive from the company, together with the names of directors.

A listed company has the duty to disclose any information which may affect the market price of the listed company, investors' decisions or shareholders' interests. There are certain compulsory disclosures that are required by law or the SET's regulations:

- Periodic disclosure: financial statements, ie, (i) quarterly financial statements, (ii) yearly financial statements, (iii) annual registration information, and (iv) annual reports.
- Non-periodic disclosures: at the occurrence of an important event, eg, acquisition of sale of significant assets, connected transactions,

mergers and or consolidation, change in shareholder structure, increase or decrease of capital, declarations of payment or non-payment of dividends, a change in any key management, a change in the company's objectives, etc.

In addition, a listed company shall employ reasonable procedures to ensure that all who invest in its securities enjoy equal access to such information. To comply with this fundamental principle, the SET issued the Disclosure Guidelines for Listed Companies' Management in 2005, which covers the following matters:

- immediate public disclosure of material information;
- thorough public dissemination;
- clarification or confirmation of rumours and reports;
- response to unusual market activity;
- unwarranted promotional disclosure; and
- insider trading.

6.2 What is the liability or responsibility of the board in relation to the company's disclosure requirements?

In any company, non-compliance with the disclosure rules, such as the non-filing of audited financial statements, brings a fine penalty against the company and also the authorised directors. The fines will be imposed on the company and the authorised directors.

For a listed company under the SEA Act, the directors and the executives must provide information or any other reports in relation to the business prepared by the company for the purpose of disclosure to shareholders or the public as specified in the notifications of the Capital Market Supervisory Board and the SET.

7. M&A AND CORPORATE GOVERNANCE

7.1 Upon an M&A offer, how are the transparency and fairness rules of the company provided under the company and stock market laws and rules?

In terms of a merger and acquisition of assets or shares, certain disclosures and voting rules and requirements will apply. For example, according to the PLC Act, a public limited company must obtain a vote of not less than three-fourths of the total number of votes from shareholders who attend the meeting and have the right to vote in the following cases:

- the sale or transfer of the whole or important parts of the business of the company to other persons;
- the purchase or acceptance of transfer of the business of other companies; and
- the making, amending or terminating of contracts with respect to the granting of a hire of the whole or important parts of the business of the company, the entrustment of the management of the business of the company to any other person or the amalgamation of the business with other persons with the purpose of profit-and-loss sharing.

In addition, the Capital Market Supervisory Board's regulations specify additional rules that require a listed company to seek an approval of the shareholders' meeting for acquisition or disposal of assets that value transaction calculated an amount exceeding 50 per cent.

The amalgamation of a limited company must obtain an approval from the shareholders' meeting as a special resolution. The votes shall not be less than three-fourths of the total number of votes of the shareholders attending the meeting. Note that before such shareholders' meeting, a board of directors' meeting must be convened to call such shareholders' meeting. Later on, the company shall notify its creditors in writing and also publish in a newspaper the resolution of the amalgamation and specify in the notification that any objection thereto shall be submitted within 60 days of the convened meeting.

The amalgamation of a public limited company under the PLC Act requires a resolution of the shareholders' meeting by a vote of not less than three-fourths of the total number of votes of the shareholders attending the meeting and having the right to vote, and in the case of an amalgamation with a private company, a special resolution of the shareholders' meeting as prescribed in the CCC is required. Moreover, once the board of directors of the listed company resolves to allow the company to amalgamate with the other, the listed company is also required to disclose information in accordance with the relevant regulations of the SET.

In the case where a shareholder raises an objection to the amalgamation, the company shall arrange for the purchase of shares belonging to such shareholder. If such shareholder does not agree to sell his or her shares within 14 days from the date of receipt of the purchase offer, the company shall proceed with the amalgamation, and it shall be deemed that such shareholder is a shareholder of the company formed by the amalgamation.

For a public limited company, it shall notify its creditors in writing of the resolution of the amalgamation within 14 days from the date on which the meeting of shareholders passes such resolution and shall specify in the notification that any objection thereto shall be submitted within two months from the date on which the creditors received the notice of such resolution. The company shall also have the notice of such resolution published in a newspaper within the above-mentioned 14-day period. If an objection is raised, the company cannot be amalgamated unless it has paid its debts or given security for the debts.

8. PROXY FIGHTING

8.1 Is proxy fighting customarily conducted for control of the company management or what other items? How is it regulated under the company law or market regulations?

Vote lobbying for the shareholders' meeting is prohibited under Thai law. Nevertheless, the SEA provides that solicitation, leading, or doing any act in a general manner to the shareholders of the company with a view to enticing the shareholders to give proxy to the person doing such act or any other persons to attend and vote at the shareholders' meeting on their behalf, shall comply with the rules, conditions and procedures as specified in the notification of the Capital Market Supervisory Board.

So far, there are no court rulings or SEC opinions as to the issue of proxy fighting as customary in other jurisdictions, eg, the USA, etc.

9. OFFICERS' REMUNERATION RULES

9.1 How is remuneration of officers determined? By whom? Is there a role for the shareholders' meeting? Is there any mechanism for an independent body to review and evaluate them?

See paragraph 4.5.

9.2 Is the mechanism of officers' remuneration publicly debated?

No. It is based solely on the company's associations, the meeting of shareholders and the special remuneration committee (not in every company) that determines the remuneration of the officers.

10. DIRECTORS' LIABILITIES, LIABILITY INSURANCE, INDEMNIFICATION

10.1 What are the directors' responsibilities and liabilities under the law? Can those liabilities be covered by insurance? Can it be indemnified by the company or other related parties?

Under the CCC, PLC Act and SEC, there are similar principles regarding acts of the directors. The main responsibilities are conducting the business of the company to comply with the laws, the objects and the articles of association of the company, and the resolutions of the meeting of shareholders, in good faith and with care to preserve the interests of the company, and the directors cannot compete against the normal business of the company. Thus, the details vary depending on the company category and are detailed in the PLC Act and SEA.

Directors' and officers' insurance provides coverage for claims brought against the directors and officers of a company for actual or alleged breach of duty, neglect, misstatements, error and omissions. Typically, coverage includes advancement of defence costs granted prior to final disposition of a claim for individuals when the company cannot provide such costs, and reimbursement for indemnification of directors and officers for any judgments, settlements and defence costs associated with the cover claims when the company has indemnified the insured for loss.

11. SHAREHOLDERS' DERIVATIVE SUITS

11.1 Is a shareholder's derivative suit provided for by law in your jurisdiction? How is it enforced by the shareholders?

Generally, under Thai law, shareholders' derivative suits are available only for a civil claim for damages against the director(s) of a company, not a third party, who cause damage to the company. The derivative suit can be made by the shareholder only once it is found that the company itself fails to do so.

However, there are some different criteria for instigation of a suit against a director under the applicable laws, such as the CCC, PLC and SEA.

For instance, any shareholder of a limited company is authorised by the CCC to file a court suit against the director, regardless of the minimum required number of shares held by such shareholder.

For a public limited company, shareholder(s) holding shares amounting to not less than 5 per cent of the total number of company shares sold could instigate a civil claim against the director of a public limited company according to the PLC. The shareholders may apply for a court order for the removal of such directors.

In addition, the SEA, which is mainly applicable to a listed company, requires that such claim can be made by any one or more shareholders holding shares amounting to not less than 5 per cent of the total number of voting rights of the company. The shareholder who instigates such a court case for the company may receive an actual and reasonable expense claim as the court thinks fit.

11.2 Have there been any recent relevant court cases on the subject?

The most recent case is *Dika* 2481/2552. The case held the position that the derivative suit against the director should be filed only when the company refuses to file for damages against such director. Moreover, the derivative suits must be filed against the director, not a third party. Additionally, the claim must be for compensation only.

12. SOCIAL INTEREST IN CORPORATE BEHAVIOUR

12.1 How is a company in your country expected to deal with the following issues? Corporate social responsibility; gender, racial and social diversification; environmental issues; ecology and corruption?

The SET's focus on corporate social responsibility (CSR) started as early as 2006 when a CSR Working Group was established. The SET also has a CSR Club, established in 2009, that helps promote CSR among listed companies by sharing information, knowledge and best practice.

The guidance document is largely based on ISO 26000, but draws on a number of international CSR instruments including the UN Global Compact and GRI. It also integrates social responsibility with other relevant principles and guidelines for Thai companies. The details herein include organisational governance, human rights, labour practices, the environment, fair operating practices, consumer issues, community development with additional specific emphasis on anti-corruption and communication and reporting. A breakdown of the samples of the regulations related to is as follows:

- Environment: Environment Development and Preservation Act B.E. 2535, Industrial and Factory Act B.E. 2535 and Ordinances from the Ministry of Industry, Energy Act B.E. 2535 and Orders from Office of the National Environment Board, Ordinances and Orders from the Ministry of Science and Technology.
- Social: Abatement of Taxation in Charitable Payment in Supports and Development of Disables' Life Act B.E. 2550, Revenue Act and its orders and/or Ordinances.
- Consumer: Consumer Act B.E. 2522.

- Safety: ISO 18000, Management of Safety in Life and Health for Working Environment Act B.E. 2549.
- Labour: Labor Act B.E. 2551, Improvement and Development of Working Skilled B.E. 2545, International Labour Standard based on the ILO (International Labour Organisation).
- Gender, Racial and Social Diversification: Labor Act B.E. 2551.
- Corruption: Anti Money Laundering Act, Act of Counter Corruption Civil Service Act, Act of Governing Liability for Wrongful Acts of Competent Officers, Act of Criminal Procedure for persons holding political positions Act.

Turkey

Kayra Üçer & Zeynep Ahu Sazci
Hergüner Bilgen Özeke Attorney Partnership

1. GENERAL PRINCIPLES

1.1 What are the general principles of corporate governance in your jurisdiction? What are the main objectives of corporate governance principles in your jurisdiction? State also whether your legal system is based on common law or civil law.

A historical weakness of corporate governance in Turkey (a civil law jurisdiction) is that dominant shareholders tend to control a significant portion of Turkish companies. This has meant that many of the formal rights of shareholders have been ineffective in practice, and has necessitated a legislative framework that stipulates extensive shareholder protection mechanisms. The investor-friendly governance culture recently introduced by the Turkish Commercial Code (the New TCC) in July 2012 rests on equal treatment, transparency, and effective shareholder participation principles. The New TCC was published in the *Official Gazette* dated 14 February 2011 and numbered 27846, replacing the former Turkish Commercial Code which had been in force since 1956.

1.2 Have there been any recent developments in the law, codes and rules of corporate governance?

The corporate governance concept was first introduced to a Turkish audience in 2003 based on the OECD's corporate governance rules by the Capital Markets Board of Turkey (the CMB Principles). Until very recently, the CMB Principles were considered to be a set of rules applicable only to companies listed on Borsa Istanbul (formerly known as the Istanbul Stock Exchange) (the ISE) on a comply-or-explain basis.

The CMB's corporate governance communiqué (the Corporate Governance Communiqué) came into force in December 2011 (the communiqué numbered IV-56 published in the *Official Gazette* dated 30 December 2011 and numbered 28158). The Corporate Governance Communiqué lists 20 corporate governance principles and mandates that listed companies abide by them, making an exception for a small group remaining below certain thresholds in terms of overall market value and the market value of their floating shares. The mandatory principles mainly focus on effective shareholder participation in general assembly meetings, maintaining efficient disclosure mechanisms and transparency, appointment of independent directors and formation of committees.

The Corporate Governance Communiqué divides listed companies into three groups: (i) companies with a market value exceeding TL 3 billion and an average value of floating shares exceeding TL 750 million (the first group); (ii) companies with a market value exceeding TL 1 billion and an average value of floating shares exceeding TL 250 million (the second group); and (iii) the remaining listed companies (the third group). The third group does not cover the companies traded on the Emerging Companies Market or the Watchlist Market. Listed companies in the first group are required to comply with the mandatory corporate governance principles listed under the Corporate Governance Communiqué in their entirety. The CMB has refrained from imposing 'one-size-fits-all' solutions to the extent possible. Since any problems of poor governance of the first group are likely to have a larger impact, not only on individual companies but also on the market in general, the companies in this group are subject to higher standards of investor protection. The second and the third groups, on the other hand, are exempt from compliance with certain principles. Despite their relatively limited audience, this communiqué was perceived as a positive deviation from the comply-or-explain system, giving listed companies a stronger incentive for adherence. In addition, in order to enhance enforcement mechanisms for listed companies, the CMB is authorised to issue administrative fines, seek judicial orders to invalidate non-compliant transactions in case companies fail to comply with mandatory principles, amend non-compliant companies' articles of association (AoA) or seek injunctive relief as necessary.

In addition to the adoption of the above-mentioned CMB communiqué, the Turkish Commercial Code, which entered into force in 1954, was replaced with the New TCC. Likewise, the Capital Markets Law dated 1981, applicable to listed companies only, was replaced with the New Capital Markets Law (the New CML) in December 2012 (published in the *Official Gazette* dated 30 December 2012 and numbered 28513). Both the New TCC and the New CML now openly recognise the main principles of equality, transparency, accountability and responsibility, providing these concepts with robust legal recognition. The inclusion of these principles in the New TCC extends their application to non-listed companies as well.

1.3 Outline recent court cases and incidents involving corporate governance issues. Were there any significant corporate scandals or large unlawful corporate cases?

Turkey has not been a scene for significant corporate scandals or large unlawful corporate cases. Therefore, the structural corporate governance reforms in Turkey were not derived from major corporate scandals or large unlawful corporate cases, as in many countries. The main deficiency of the Turkish corporate environment has rather been that the substantial control of block-holding families over the governance of corporate entities curbs minority shareholder protection, sustainability and transparency.

As an emerging market, the main motive is to attract local and foreign investors in return for lower capital costs. Responsive to these distinctive features of the Turkish corporate system and the governance issues triggering the global financial crisis, the legislature and the regulatory institutions have chosen to provide reassurance to investors by promoting corporate governance obligations, such as shareholder participation, disclosure and independence and supporting these rules with the CMB's broad authorities for intervention in case of non-compliance.

1.4 Which law enforcement agency is in charge of enforcing corporate governance? May a criminal sanction be levied upon infringement of the corporate governance rules?

The CMB is the regulatory body for listed companies and has certain regulatory and supervisory powers based on which it can issue administrative fines and other sanctions on listed companies that fail to comply with the relevant legislation.

In addition, certain actions have been specified as a crime under the New CML, such as manipulation and insider trading which would require criminal sanctions.

2. SOURCES OF LAW

2.1 Which laws, codes or statutes govern company structures and organisations? Are there statutes like the Companies Act or other forms of law? Is there much relevant case law?

In the current Turkish corporate law system, the corporate governance framework comprises: (i) the New TCC, governing all sorts of companies; and (ii) the New CML and secondary legislation (ie, regulations, communiqués and CMB decisions) issued by the CMB, which are applicable only to listed companies. Under the New CML, in addition to the listed companies, companies with more than 500 shareholders will also be considered publicly held and must file a listing application within two years. Since both laws have very recently gone through transformation, case law has not yet emerged.

2.2 Which laws, codes or statutes regulate capital markets in your jurisdiction?

The main piece of legislation specifically applicable to capital markets and listed companies is the New CML and the communiqués issued by the CMB in relation to certain particular matters (eg, issuance of bonds, investment funds, public offerings etc.). It is also noteworthy that the CMB issued two new communiqués regarding public offerings and issuance of debt instruments in June 2013. In addition, the New TCC is also applicable to all companies regardless of whether they are listed or not.

2.3 Are there any public interest laws which apply to or influence corporate governance?

There are no public interest laws which apply to or influence corporate governance.

2.4 Have there been any recent developments in any of the above laws? What are the recent changes to the above laws or rules and the

reasons for such changes?
See paragraphs 1.2 and 2.2 above.

3. SHAREHOLDERS AND THE SHAREHOLDERS' MEETING

3.1 How are shareholders' interests represented in the company? How are the shareholders assured exercise of their rights? What is the highest governing body within the company structure if it is not the shareholders' meeting?

Shareholders are represented at the general assembly meeting of shareholders. Ordinary meetings are to be held annually, whereas extraordinary meetings may be held whenever the need arises.

Certain matters are reserved for shareholders, including amendments to the company's AoA, director appointments and resolutions as to their terms of office, compensation and removal, distribution of dividends, and the sale of a significant portion of the company's assets; voting on these matters is the shareholders' exclusive and inalienable right. Companies may determine other reserved matters under their AoA.

In order to secure participation and oversight by shareholders in listed companies, material transactions and related-party transactions are rendered subject to shareholder approval if they are not approved by the majority of the independent directors sitting on the board of directors (BoD). In addition, the New CML couples this rule with exit rights granted to shareholders objecting to these material transactions; in other words, dissenting shareholders can sell their shares in the company and exit.

For transparency and equality purposes, shareholders are equipped with an extensive right of access to information. This right is highly protected and cannot be eliminated by an amendment to the company's AoA or a shareholders' or BoD resolution. Shareholders are entitled to review financial statements, as well as the annual and audit reports of the company, at least two weeks in advance of the annual general assembly meeting. Financial statements must be available for shareholder examination for the entire year at the company headquarters and at its branches. Listed companies have to meet additional disclosure requirements prior to general assembly meetings. They must announce, on their website, the shareholding structure of the company as of the meeting date, any changes in the management or business structure of the company or its subsidiaries, the removal of directors and grounds for such removal, together with information on nominees, and information as to any amendments to the AoA.

3.2 How is the shareholders' meeting conducted? Who may chair the meeting? May attendance (not voting) at the meeting be restricted only to the shareholders? Are the shareholders allowed to be accompanied by legal or other counsel?

Companies must convene the general assembly of shareholders annually within the three months following the end of each fiscal year. If necessary, more meetings can be held on a voluntary basis. The main agenda of items to be discussed at general assembly meetings are, among others, the release and appointment of directors, financial tables, annual reports, and the amounts of dividends to be distributed. For informed voting purposes, it is essential that the meeting and the agenda be announced to the shareholders three weeks in advance for listed companies, and two weeks for non-listed companies. The announcement requirement can be eliminated in the absence of opposition from any of the shareholders, which appears to be more practicable for non-public companies with a smaller number of shareholders.

Chairman of the meeting can be anyone elected by the general assembly unless otherwise stated in the AoA of the company. Shareholders or their representatives registered on the attendance sheet prepared by the BoD, BoD members, auditor, if any, ministry representative, if appointed, and the persons to be elected or appointed for the meeting chairmanship can enter the meeting place. If the other directors, employees of the company or guests, counsels, audiovisual technicians, press members shall be present at the meeting place, such situation shall be indicated in an internal directive separately.

It is also worth mentioning that Turkey has been one of the very few countries to adopt the 'e-general assembly system'. As of July 2012, shareholders have the option to attend general assembly meetings virtually. Listed companies are now obligated to have e-general assembly meetings. Virtual meetings will have the exact legal consequences of a physical meeting. The new system is expected to encourage and facilitate participation by foreign investors and domestic investors alike. Shareholders can vote in the general assembly meeting by giving a power of representation to another shareholder or a third person.

3.3 How are minority shareholders' rights protected?

Under Turkish law, a shareholder or a group of shareholders owning shares of at least 10 per cent (in publicly held companies: 5 per cent) of the share capital of a privately held company may enjoy the minority shareholders' rights granted under the New TCC. There are no provisions under Turkish law restricting the inclusion of these rights in the AoA or shareholders' agreements. However, failure to do so would not hinder the applicability or enforceability of these rights.

It must be noted that the threshold for the minority shareholding may be decreased by the AoA of the company (ie, the 10 per cent threshold may be decreased to a 7 per cent threshold). In addition, additional positive minority rights may be provided to minority shareholders in the AoA.

The minority rights regulated under the New TCC (which are also applicable to publicly held companies) are as follows:

- Postponement of the financial statement discussions: minority shareholders are entitled to request postponement of the financial statement discussions for one month. The main purpose of this provision is to give the minority shareholders a chance to review the financial statement in greater detail. If a satisfactory explanation cannot be given as to the issues objected to by the minority shareholders regarding the financial statement, the minority shareholders may request the delay of the financial statement discussions for a second and final time.

- Appointment of an independent auditor: each shareholder has the right to request the appointment of an independent auditor whenever it necessitates exercising its shareholders' rights in the general assembly meeting, although it is not included in the agenda, and provided that the information or evaluation right has already been exercised.
- Request for a general assembly meeting and addition of an item to the meeting agenda: minority shareholders may, via notary public, request that an extraordinary general assembly meeting be convened, or that an item to the agenda of the general assembly meeting be added, if a date has already been established for the meeting.
- Rights with respect to settlement and release: responsibilities of the BoD, auditors, and incorporators with respect to the incorporation and capital increase of a company cannot be settled or released unless four years have passed since the incorporation. Subsequent to such four-year period, a settlement or release may only be validated upon the approval of the general assembly. However, a settlement or release cannot be granted if the minority shareholders vote against such settlement or release.
- Right to request the dissolution of the company: for just cause, minority shareholders may request the dissolution of the company by filing a lawsuit before the commercial court that has jurisdiction. Instead of dissolution, the court may decide upon termination of the plaintiff minority shareholders' shareholding in the company in return for the market value of their shares as any other appropriate and acceptable solution.
- Right to request issuance of share certificates: upon request by the minority shareholders, the company is obliged to issue registered share certificates and to distribute such to each shareholder holding registered shares. The provision's intention is to prevent share transfer restrictions by not giving share certificates, proof of shareholding and pressure, especially being exerted by the management of a closed company, or a family of companies, by not issuing/distributing share certificates.
- Right to request the replacement of the auditor: the competent commercial court may replace the auditor of the company upon the request of the minority shareholders or the BoD, if there are just causes regarding the auditor itself, especially if there is doubt as to the auditor's neutrality, by hearing both the auditor and those concerned.
- Right of representation in the BoD: minority shareholders and a certain group of shareholders may be granted the right of being represented in the BoD by the AoA. Accordingly, certain BoD members may be elected from among certain groups of shareholders or minority shareholders, or they may be granted the right to nominate BoD members to be elected. The nominee of, or a shareholder among, minority shareholders, or a certain group of shareholders, must be elected as a member of the BoD,

unless just cause exists not to do so. The representation right thereof cannot exceed half of the BoD members in publicly held companies.

3.4 Is shareholder activism encouraged or discouraged? If not encouraged, how is it regulated?

Even though there are certain individual efforts by activist shareholders or entities such as the Stock Exchange Investors Association (BORYAD), shareholder activism remains a relatively small force for investor protection. Instead, regulatory bodies, such as the CMB, exercise supervisory powers in order to maintain such protection.

3.5 How are professional shareholders (those minority shareholders who seek some extra benefit from companies by unduly and habitually influencing management by using their shareholding) treated by the law? Are they excluded from attending the shareholders' meeting? Are they criminally or otherwise publicly sanctioned?

Professional shareholders do not constitute a major or common problem in Turkey.

3.6 Are shareholders' benefits given to some of the shareholders by the company without resolution by the shareholders' meeting prohibited or regulated by the law or other rules?

Under Turkish Law, shareholders' benefits such as dividends may only be distributed following a resolution adopted by the general assembly of shareholders.

4. DIRECTORS AND BOARD OF DIRECTORS

4.1 What are the functions and responsibilities of the directors and the board of directors? Do you have a one- or two-tier board system? What are the outside directors called?

The BoD is a one-tier governance and representation body. The composition of the BoD slightly differs for listed and non-listed companies. In terms of quantity, a non-listed company BoD is allowed to function with a single director, whereas there is a requirement of at least five directors for listed companies.

The New TCC clarifies the distinction between the BoD's representation and governance functions, which are both delegable. The BoD is equipped with extensive governance powers, except for certain matters that must be exclusively and indispensably resolved by the shareholders. The governance power can be partially or wholly delegated to one or more directors or third persons through an internal company by-law to be prepared by the BoD, provided that the company's AoA permits such delegation.

Attending BoD meetings and voting are inalienable duties of directors and may not be exercised through proxy. Directors are expected to personally attend the meetings and participate in the adoption of decisions. Moreover, certain duties and authorities are defined to be exclusive to the BoD. These duties and authorities are, among others: (i) high-level governance of the company; (ii) determining the company's management organisation; (iii) establishing the necessary regime for financial planning (eg, accounting, financial auditing and financial planning); (iv) appointing and removing the management and other authorised signatories; (v) overseeing the management's compliance with the legislation and the BoD's directions; and (vi) keeping company books, preparing annual activity and corporate governance reports, and implementing general assembly resolutions. The BoD's exclusive duties and authorities may not be delegated, restricted or eliminated by a provision in the company's AoA or a general assembly resolution and must be resolved by the BoD itself.

Directors owe a duty of loyalty and a duty of care to their company. The duty of loyalty under the New TCC requires directors to protect the interests of the company in compliance with the principles of good faith. The standard for the duty of care introduced by the New TCC echoes the well-known 'business judgment rule'. The legislature, however, has left the scope of the Turkish business judgment rule unclear, and deferred the interpretation surrounding the new standard to the Turkish courts.

Outside directors are called 'independent directors'. Independent directors are mandatory for listed companies and must comply with the independence criteria named under the Corporate Governance Communiqué.

4.2 What are the rules that may give rise to civil and criminal liability of the director(s)? How are those liabilities sought?

As a general principle under Turkish law, members of the BoD will generally be liable for actions taken during their term to the extent that their fault is proven. They would be held responsible on a pro rata basis with respect to the proportion of fault found to be attributable to them. In addition, they will not be liable for the actions taken by previous BoD members.

The New TCC enables delegation of governance duties, provided that the AoA of the company allows such delegation and the BoD has adopted bylaws (*iç yönerge*) structuring the delegation of governance duties. The by-laws of a company will, in particular, determine the duties, positions and reporting chain. Therefore, the BoD may delegate governance duties to certain BoD members or to third parties.

The power to represent and bind a company is vested in any two of the BoD members, unless the BoD is comprised of one member, or a specific scheme is specified in the AoA on how the company will be represented or bound to override the statutory default. The BoD may delegate its powers to represent and bind the company to individual BoD members or third parties. However, at least one BoD member must always retain the power of representation.

In the event that the powers are delegated, those who delegated their powers may not be held liable, unless they are proven to have failed exercising due care in electing the competent persons to delegate their powers to. It should be highlighted that if a power is delegated, and this power may not be so delegated according to applicable law or the AoA, such delegation is unlawful, and the BoD member(s) will still be held liable despite the delegation.

The shareholders of the company – *inter alia* – have the right to file a lawsuit against the BoD members. If fault may not be attributed to him/her, a BoD member shall not be held liable. BoD members shall not be held liable, especially in instances where powers are duly delegated. If the BoD members are released by a general assembly resolution once, the release may not be cancelled by another general assembly resolution. However, the shareholders who object to such resolution have the right to file a lawsuit against the BoD members within six months starting from the resolution date. Lawsuits related to the liability of BoD members may be filed within two years starting from the time of the act or action triggering the alleged liability being discovered. In any event, a lawsuit may be filed within five years starting from the occurrence of such act or action attracting scrutiny. The lawsuit must be filed with the court where the headquarters of the company are located.

The New TCC regulates both civil and criminal liabilities of the BoD members. In principle, crimes set forth under the New TCC are prosecuted without the need for complaint.

4.3 Does the board of directors have a committee system, eg, nomination committee, compensation committee, audit committee? If not required, is it common practice for companies? How does it function?

Listed companies are required to form: (i) an audit committee; (ii) a corporate governance committee; (iii) a nomination committee; (iv) an early risk detection committee; and (v) a remuneration committee within the BoD. The audit committee must be composed entirely of independent directors. All committees must be chaired by an independent director and must comprise a majority of independent directors. In order to secure independent functioning, the general manager of the company is prohibited from participating in these committees. The duties, working principles and members of the committees must be determined by the BoD and disclosed to public. Early risk detection committees, audit committees and compensation committees are not mandatory for banks.

Early risk detection committees have also become increasingly important in the last few years, perhaps as a lesson learned from the global financial crisis, and are now mandatory for all companies under the New TCC, excluding banks. Early risk detection committees report to the BoD once every two months and alert directors to any potential risks and threats that the company may face, in order to allow directors to take the necessary precautions. In practice, companies not only form special early risk detection committees, but also closely cooperate with insurance companies. Insurance companies provide companies risk consultancy services as well as legal due diligence in order to detect any potential risks.

4.4 Is it a legal requirement to have an independent director or a

third-party director? If so, how are they appointed? Is it required for listed companies?

Independent directors are required for listed companies. Independent directors are expected to protect the interests of all shareholders and the company itself. The mandatory ratio for listed company BoD is one independent director to every three non-independent directors. A BoD, in any case, must have at least two independent directors. The Corporate Governance Communiqué provides an exception for banks where the number of independent directors is limited to three, regardless of the size of the BoD. Non-listed companies may also choose to appoint independent directors on a voluntary basis.

The independence criteria are provided by the Corporate Governance Communiqué. While certain items on the list (eg, possessing strong moral standards, the ability to preserve impartiality) appear to be incapable of objective articulation, the most notable requirements are as follows:

- no relationship in terms of employment, shareholding or material commercial transactions with the company, its related parties or entities related, in terms of management or capital, to the shareholders of the company with 10 per cent or more of the company's shares within the last five years;
- no shareholding, employment or management relationship with the significant suppliers of the company; and
- no shareholding in excess of 1 per cent of the common shares in the company.

The foregoing independence criteria do not apply to banks.

As a general rule, all directors are appointed and removed by shareholders at the general assembly meeting, save for exceptional circumstances where the BoD itself overtakes such duty and temporarily appoints directors to vacant seats. However, appointment of independent members is subject to certain additional rules. For instance, a director who has served for more than six years within the last 10 years may not be appointed as an independent director. Banks are held exempt from this limitation.

As an example of the stricter corporate governance obligations imposed on the first group named under the Corporate Governance Communiqué, excluding banks, the BoD must follow a different procedure for the determination and appointment of independent directors. The BoD will put together a list of nominees in line with the recommendation of the company's nomination committee and submit it to the CMB for approval at least 60 days prior to the upcoming general assembly meeting. The CMB runs a background check for the names on the list. Nominees approved by the CMB within the 30-day review period can be appointed as independent directors. Persons appointed as independent directors must sign a declaration acknowledging the independence criteria specified under the Corporate Governance Communiqué and representing their compliance with such criteria.

Despite a very small number of exceptions, there is a trend towards compliance by a majority of the listed companies in Turkey. The CMB's extensive authorities must have played a role in maintaining this adherence. In case of non-compliance with the independent director requirement, the CMB can apply to court to have independent directors appointed from among a list of names it has identified or will identify itself.

4.5 How is the compensation for directors or officers determined? Can it be contested by the shareholders or the regulatory authorities? What are the common rules or practices for the compensation of officers?

The compensation for BoD members is determined by the general assembly of shareholders if not determined under the AoA of the company.

Under the Corporate Governance Communiqué, the remuneration packages for a listed company's independent directors cannot include stock options or performance-based compensation. As a reflection of the 'say-on-pay' concept, compensation policies of listed companies must be disclosed to shareholders in the general assembly meeting in order to give the latter an opportunity to present their opinion. Such policies must also be disclosed on the company's website.

4.6 How will the board handle a corporate crisis like an internal criminal case, violence, social media exposure or dawn raid by the authorities?

The best measure that a BoD can adopt in such cases is accurately informing the investors, through various public disclosures, assuring them that the situation is under control. Since transparency is one of the most vital principles under the new TCC and the relevant communiqués, keeping the public informed would prevent negative financial consequences to the extent possible.

5. BOARD OF AUDITORS, AUDIT COMMITTEE, ACCOUNTING AUDITORS

5.1 How is the internal accounting and legal audit structured and conducted? Is an outside accounting audit required and, if so, how is it structured? Are there requirements to change the auditor each five years?

The companies subject to independent audit have been announced by a Council of Ministers decree on 23 January 2013 (published in the *Official Gazette* dated 23 January 2013 and numbered 28537). As a general rule, companies satisfying two of the following criteria will be subject to the website and independent audit requirements: having: (i) an asset value of TL 50 million (approximately EUR 20 million) or more; (ii) net sales revenue of TL 200 million (approximately EUR 80 million) or more; or (iii) 500 or more employees. In addition, listed companies, banks and rating agencies are other notable entities named under the decree.

The New TCC sets forth certain conflict of interest restrictions as to the eligibility of appointed independent auditors. Accordingly, among others, if the independent auditor: (i) is a shareholder in the company to be audited; (ii) is a manager or employee of the company within the last three years prior to his/her appointment; or (iii) is a BoD member, manager or a shareholder holding more than 20 per cent of shares of any companies that are affiliated with the company to be audited. Moreover, in the event that an independent audit company is hired for the audit of the company and if this audit company assigned the same auditor to the relevant company for seven years, the audit company shall not assign the same auditor to the same company for at least two years.

Under the TCC, non-listed companies will be audited by an independent auditor in compliance with the Turkish Accounting Standards (TAS), which is in line with International Financial Reporting Standards (IFRS). Under the relevant articles of the TCC, independent auditors will be appointed by the general assembly of shareholders GA.

Under the CMB regulations, publicly held companies must be audited in line with the standards detailed under the CMB Communiqué on the Independent Audit Standards in the Capital Markets (the Audit Communiqué), which are in line with the International Auditing Standards. Even though advising on the differences between the accounting and auditing principles applicable to publicly held and private Turkish companies is outside the area of our expertise, in general it is possible to say that the professional standards used by independent auditors in Turkey can be considered compatible with international standards.

Under the TCC, auditing activities will be performed by independent audit firms, independent accounting financial advisors or sworn financial accountants in accordance with the TAS. The scope of the audit will include audit of financial statements and/or consolidated financial statements and annual report. Auditors will have to be appointed by the GA with respect to each fiscal year.

In April 2013, an amendment was made to the New TCC, which sets forth that any and all companies are subject to audit. The law indicates that details of which type of audit that companies will be subject to will be stipulated by a regulation, which is not yet promulgated.

5.2 Do you have supervisory auditors? What is the function of the supervisory auditors' board?

Not applicable.

6. MARKET DISCLOSURE/TRANSPARENCY TO THE SHAREHOLDERS AND THE PUBLIC

6.1 What are the disclosure requirements for companies in your jurisdiction under company law, capital markets law or any other rules?

Access to information is one of the key privileges promoted by the legislation for the protection of investors. The Corporate Governance Communiqué recommends listed companies to have in place a disclosure policy regulating the content, manner, means and frequency of disclosures and press conferences to be made by the company.

The CMB published a very detailed communiqué and comprehensive guidelines in 2009 regarding the disclosure obligations of listed companies (the Disclosure Communiqué) (published in the *Official Gazette* dated 6 February 2009 and numbered 27133). As a general principle, the Disclosure Communiqué stipulates that 'inside information' that relates to transactions or events that may influence the value of a company's securities or the investment decisions of a company's shareholders must be immediately disclosed. Rather than identifying an exhaustive list of events requiring disclosure, the Disclosure Communiqué leaves specific disclosure decisions to the companies' individual discretion on a case-by-case basis. Certain changes in share ownership or management control must be publicly disclosed within three business days by persons concluding such transactions (eg, any direct or indirect acquisition of 5 per cent, 10 per cent, 15 per cent, 20 per cent, 25 per cent, 33.33 per cent, 50 per cent, 66.66 per cent or 75 per cent or more of the share capital or voting rights). The New TCC introduces a similar disclosure requirement for share acquisitions in non-listed companies.

To encourage disclosure on the part of non-listed companies, the New TCC has expanded the scope of the website requirement. The New TCC requires certain companies to set up a publicly accessible website by July 2013, and mandates that the website contain a large number of disclosures, such as the annual financial statements, announcements, and minutes for shareholders' meetings. Companies that will be subject to this requirement are companies that will also be subject to independent audit.

The primary means for disclosure are company websites and the 'Public Disclosure Platform' (KAP, available at *www.kap.gov.tr*), which is a web-based platform that allows listed companies to electronically post disclosures in a timely, complete and accurate manner. KAP serves as an up-to-date archive that is highly accessible by all stakeholders of a listed company. Active and efficient use of the company website is also encouraged. In addition to other mandatory disclosures, listed companies must disclose, on their website, the company's trade registry information, current shareholding structure, information on privileged shares, an up-to-date consolidated copy of the AoA, financial statements, annual activity reports, general assembly meeting agendas, disclosure, remuneration and dividend distribution policies, and information on related-party transactions pertaining to the last five years. Any information displayed on the companies' websites must be constantly updated. The mandatory contents of the annual activity reports have also been determined in detail by a regulation (published in the *Official Gazette* dated 28 August 2012 and numbered 28395). As per this regulation, annual activity reports must consist of a general information section (including general corporate information on the company such as headquarters, shareholding and management structures, privileged shares) followed by information on financial benefits provided to the directors and the executive management, the company's research and development activities, the company's activities and any materials developments regarding the activities (eg, investments, internal audit and control systems, pending lawsuits and sanctions imposed, evaluation of performance and targets), the financial status of the company, evaluation of potential risks (eg, risk-management policies and activities of the early risk detection committee) and any other matters that may affect shareholders' rights. In order to give companies stronger incentives for compliance with corporate governance principles, the Corporate Governance Communiqué also requires listed companies to disclose, in their annual reports, the extent of their compliance with CMB Principles.

6.2 What is the liability or responsibility of the board in relation to the company's disclosure requirements?

As the representation body of a company, the BoD must comply with the disclosure requirements. The New TCC stipulates that failure to comply with the disclosure requirements in relation to certain share transfers in relation to group companies may cause the relevant voting rights to freeze. Also, in the event that it is a listed company that fails to comply with the above-mentioned disclosure requirements, the CMB has the authority to issue administrative fines. These cases may be considered as a breach of the duty of care by the BoD.

7. M&A AND CORPORATE GOVERNANCE

7.1 Upon an M&A offer, how are the transparency and fairness rules of the company provided under the company and stock market laws and rules?

The Disclosure Communiqué does not specifically spell out at what stage negotiations must be disclosed by listed companies, and leaves specific disclosure decisions to the companies' individual discretion on a case-by-case basis. As a general principle set forth under the Disclosure Communiqué, any events that may influence the value of the shares or the investment decisions of the investors must be disclosed to public.

The guidelines attached to the Disclosure Communiqué lists certain exemplary cases, which potentially need to be disclosed. The fact of being engaged in acquisition discussions needs to be disclosed if there is only one potential buyer and one target company, the intention to reach an agreement is evident, and if there is a meeting of the parties' minds concrete enough to influence the value of the shares and the investment decisions of the investors.

8. PROXY FIGHTING

8.1 Is proxy fighting customarily conducted for control of the company management or what other items? How is it regulated under the company law or market regulations?

Proxy fighting is not a common issue in the Turkish corporate system.

9. OFFICERS' REMUNERATION RULES

9.1 How is remuneration of officers determined? By whom? Is there a role for the shareholders' meeting? Is there any mechanism for an

independent body to review and evaluate them?
See paragraph 4.5 above.

9.2 Is the mechanism of officers' remuneration publicly debated?
Not applicable.

10. DIRECTORS' LIABILITIES, LIABILITY INSURANCE, INDEMNIFICATION

10.1 What are the directors' responsibilities and liabilities under the law? Can those liabilities be covered by insurance? Can it be indemnified by the company or other related parties?

Insurance for director liability has become common practice for listed companies, particularly following the revival of the Turkish capital markets in the last five years. Companies are allowed to maintain insurance for damages that may arise as a result of the directors' fault. The New TCC requires directors' and officers' insurance coverage exceeding a quarter of the company's share capital to be disclosed to public.

Directors may also be held liable for the company's tax or other public debts to the extent that they cannot be collected from the company.

11. SHAREHOLDERS' DERIVATIVE SUITS

11.1 Is a shareholder's derivative suit provided for by law in your jurisdiction? How is it enforced by the shareholders?

Under Turkish law, the shareholders of the company have the right to file a lawsuit against the BoD members.

11.2 Have there been any recent relevant court cases on the subject?

There are no recent major court cases.

12. SOCIAL INTEREST IN CORPORATE BEHAVIOUR

12.1 How is a company in your country expected to deal with the following issues? Corporate social responsibility; gender, racial and social diversification; environmental issues; ecology and corruption?

Social responsibility obligations to society at large remain as a recommendation linked to the comply-or-explain principle for listed companies. The Corporate Governance Communiqué defines stakeholders as a company's employees, creditors, customers, suppliers, non-governmental organisation and the like. Listed companies are recommended to develop governance models in order to support participation by these stakeholders and employees in particular. They must protect the rights of stakeholder groups and provide them accessible compensation mechanisms in cases of breach. The importance of maintaining customer satisfaction and product and service quality is specifically emphasised under the Corporate Governance Communiqué.

Listed companies are encouraged to adopt established universal standards in terms of human rights and combat against bribery and adopt moral standards regarding the environment, consumer rights and public health.

They must disclose in their annual report any social responsibility activities that have an environmental or social aspect to it. Most companies consider these social responsibility activities as a means of marketing and increasing goodwill. Sponsorship activities and social responsibility projects in cooperation with non-governmental organisations are the most significant efforts and they tend to generally be focused on education, such as providing assistance for female students in financial hardship.

UK

Charles Martin & Mark Slade **Macfarlanes LLP**

1. GENERAL PRINCIPLES

1.1 What are the general principles of corporate governance in your jurisdiction? What are the main objectives of corporate governance principles in your jurisdiction? State also whether your legal system is based on common law or civil law.

Corporate governance principles in England and Wales arose out of the common law and, in particular, the fiduciary obligations of directors, many of which have now been enshrined in statute, including the overriding duty to promote the success of the company for the benefit of its members as a whole.

Although the UK Corporate Governance Code (the Code) only applies to listed companies, its underlying principles are of wider application. The first version of the Code was produced by the Cadbury Committee in 1992 and describes corporate governance as:

'the system by which companies are directed and controlled. Boards of directors are responsible for the governance of their companies. The shareholders' role in governance is to appoint the directors and the auditors and to satisfy themselves that an appropriate governance structure is in place. The responsibilities of the board include setting the company's strategic aims, providing the leadership to put them into effect, supervising the management of the business and reporting to shareholders on their stewardship. The board's actions are subject to laws, regulations and the shareholders in general meeting.'

One of the hallmarks of corporate governance in England and Wales is the 'comply or explain' approach pursuant to which companies either comply with relevant corporate governance provisions or provide an explanation as to why they have not complied (for example, the Code recognises that some of its provisions may be disproportionate for smaller listed companies, in particular those new to listing).

1.2 Have there been any recent developments in the law, codes and rules of corporate governance?

The financial crisis covering broadly the period from 2007 to 2009 led to widespread criticism of the governance of UK banks. Specific criticisms included:

- remuneration which encouraged excessive risk taking;
- an impotent regulator; and
- weakness of non-executive directors.

In response, the Government commissioned a review by Sir David Walker into corporate governance of UK banks (the Walker Review), the final recommendations of which were published in November 2009. At the same time, the Financial Reporting Council (FRC) announced a review of the Combined Code (at the time, the overarching corporate governance code for UK companies). The Financial Services Authority (FSA) also appointed a new chairman and chief executive who were charged with reforming regulatory oversight.

The Walker Review made 39 recommendations, which included:

- strengthening the role of non-executive directors through training and dedicated support, as well as providing greater time commitments than has been the case in the past;
- the creation of a Stewardship Code by the FRC to cover principles of best practice in stewardship by institutional investors and fund managers;
- extending the terms of reference of the remuneration committee to oversight of remuneration policy and outcomes in respect of all 'high-end' employees, as well as disclosure of remuneration of high-end employees (in bands); and
- the deferral of incentive payments to align rewards with sustainable performance for executive board members and 'high-end' employees.

The FRC and the FSA were the principal bodies tasked with implementing the recommendations of the Walker Review.

On 28 May 2010, the FRC published the final version of the Code, which replaced the Combined Code. Key changes introduced in the Code include:

- an upgrading from a supporting principle to a main principle of the principle that the non-executive directors should constructively challenge and help develop proposals on strategy;
- evaluation of the board of FTSE 350 companies should be externally facilitated at least every three years and all directors of FTSE 350 companies should be subject to annual election by shareholders;
- the effectiveness of the company's risk management and internal control systems should be reviewed annually; and
- performance-related elements of executive directors' remuneration should be stretching and designed to promote the long-term success of the company.

The Code has been subsequently updated. A summary of the Code is set out at paragraph 2.1 below.

In July 2010, the FRC published the Stewardship Code. On 1 January 2010, the FSA's remuneration code came into force. Both Codes have been subsequently updated and a summary of their provisions is respectively set out at paragraphs 3.4 and 9 below. Another fundamental change to remuneration in listed companies is that votes on remuneration reports will become binding after October 2013 (see paragraph 9 below for further details).

The regulatory functions of the FSA were split with effect from 2013 pursuant to the so-called 'twin peaks' model, under which banks, building societies and major investment firms have two groups of supervisors, one focusing on prudential (the Prudential Regulatory Authority (the PRA)) and one focusing on conduct (the Financial Conduct Authority (FCA)). All other regulated firms are supervised by the FCA.

The Bribery Act 2010 came into force in April 2011. Its implementation responded to criticism by, among others, the OECD Group on Bribery, which stated in 2008 that it was,

'...disappointed and seriously concerned with the unsatisfactory implementation of the [OECD Anti-Bribery] Convention by the UK. The continued failure... to address deficiencies in its laws on bribery of foreign public officials and on corporate liability for foreign bribery has hindered investigations...'

Further details of the Bribery Act are set out at paragraph 4.2 below.

One further report which may lead to further reform in corporate governance is the Kay Review of UK Equity Markets and Long-Term Decision Making, which reported in July 2012. It concluded that equity capital markets have evolved in a way that encourages short-termism, resulting in companies making bad long-term decisions which ultimately result in poorer returns for investors. Its key recommendations were:

- Remuneration: directors' remuneration should be restructured so that bonuses are paid in shares which must be held significantly beyond the director's employment in the company. Asset management firms should also restructure pay to be based on long-term performance incentives.
- Culture: regulatory authorities at EU and domestic level should apply fiduciary standards to all relationships in the investment chain and the Law Commission should be asked to review the legal concept of fiduciary duty in the investment context. Company directors, asset managers and asset holders should adopt Good Practice Statements to promote stewardship and long-term decision-making. The Stewardship Code should be developed to incorporate a more expansive concept of stewardship.
- Increased engagement: an investors' forum should be established to facilitate engagement in companies by investors. Companies should consult long-term investors over major board appointments.
- Supply of information: mandatory quarterly reporting obligations should be removed and high-quality, succinct narrative reporting should be encouraged.

Although beyond the scope of this chapter, the Alternative Investment Fund Managers Directive is also having significant corporate governance consequences for managers of alternative assets.

1.3 Outline recent court cases and incidents involving corporate governance issues. Were there any significant corporate scandals or large unlawful corporate cases?

The main feature of corporate governance in England and Wales in recent times has been the rise of shareholder activism, with a group of activist hedge funds having emerged in Europe with goals including:

- changes of corporate strategy;
- improvement of business performance;
- addressing management issues; and
- influencing corporate events.

The rise of these activist shareholders led to the so-called 'shareholder spring' of 2012, where corporate governance issues and, in particular, executive pay received significant media attention. Investors, frustrated that poor performance by listed companies coincided with increasing remuneration packages, voted against executive pay packages at a significant number of annual general meetings held by FTSE 100 companies in spring 2012 (albeit that these votes were non-binding). High-profile companies affected included Aviva (whose chief executive left after investors failed to approve the company's remuneration report), Trinity Mirror, William Hill, Cairn Energy and WPP (where more than 60 per cent of investors voted against the remuneration report).

There have been a number of significant corporate scandals in recent years, mainly affecting the banking industry.

UBS trader Kweku Adeboli was sentenced to seven years in prison for fraud in 2012 involving authorised trading leading to losses for UBS of approximately £1.4 billion. UBS was fined £29.7 million by the FSA (the forerunner to the FCA) for defective systems and controls which led to the loss. Similarly, J.P. Morgan lost $2 billion in a single week as a result of an ineffectively hedged position taken by a single trader in London.

Several banks were embroiled in the LIBOR rigging scandal, which led to the resignation of Bob Diamond, the chief executive of Barclays, and a number of very significant fines, as well as a criminal investigation. A number of banks were also involved in a scandal involving the mis-selling of complex derivative instruments.

A number of international companies, including Google, Starbucks and Amazon, faced heavy criticism for adopting strategies which (although not illegal) sought to minimise the amount of tax which they paid in the UK.

1.4 Which law enforcement agency is in charge of enforcing corporate governance? May a criminal sanction be levied upon infringement of the corporate governance rules?

A wide variety of bodies enforce corporate governance in England and Wales, reflecting the multiplicity of corporate governance sources (see sources of law in paragraphs 2.1 and 2.2 below). Breaching certain corporate governance rules gives rise to criminal sanctions (as detailed in paragraph 4.2 below).

2. SOURCES OF LAW

2.1 Which laws, codes or statutes govern company structures and organisations? Are there statutes like the Companies Act or other forms of law? Is there much relevant case law?

The primary piece of legislation which governs company structures in England and Wales is the Companies Act 2006 (the Companies Act).

Other key sources of corporate governance law, regulation and code include:

- Promulgations of the FRC
  - *the Code*

As noted above, the Code is a key source of corporate governance regulation for premium listed companies. Under the Listing Rules made by the FCA (the Listing Rules), a listed company is required to include in its annual report:

- a statement setting out how the company has applied the Main Principles set out in the Code in a manner that would enable shareholders to evaluate how the principles have been applied; and
- a statement as to whether the company has:
  - complied throughout the accounting period with all relevant provisions set out in Code; or
  - not complied throughout the accounting period with all relevant provisions set out in the Code and if so, setting out:
    - those provisions, if any it has not complied with;
    - in the case of any provisions whose requirements are of a continuing nature, the period within which, if any, it did not comply with some or all of those provisions; and
    - the company's reasons for non-compliance.

The Code is divided into five sections and consists of main principles, supporting principles (which provide more detail on the main principles) and code provisions (which provide concrete action points for companies), with further details in schedules and appendices.

The main principles of the Code are as follows:

- Section A: Leadership
  - Every company should be headed by an effective board which is collectively responsible for the long-term success of the company.
  - There should be a clear division of responsibilities at the head of the company between the running of the board and the executive responsibility for the running of the company's business. No one individual should have unfettered powers of decision.
  - The chairman is responsible for leadership of the board and ensuring its effectiveness on all aspects of its role.
  - As part of their role as members of a unitary board, non-executive directors should constructively challenge and help develop proposals on strategy.
- Section B: Effectiveness
  - The board and its committees should have an appropriate balance of skills, experience, independence and knowledge of the company to enable them to discharge their respective duties and responsibilities effectively.
  - There should be a formal, rigorous and transparent procedure for the appointment of new directors to the board.
  - All directors should be able to allocate sufficient time to the company to discharge their responsibilities effectively.
  - All directors should receive induction on joining the board and should regularly update and refresh their skills and knowledge.
  - The board should be supplied in a timely manner with information in a form and of a quality appropriate to enable it to discharge its

duties.
    - The board should undertake a formal and rigorous annual evaluation of its own performance and that of its committees and individual directors.
    - All directors should be submitted for re-election at regular intervals, subject to continued satisfactory performance.
- Section C: Accountability
    - The board should present a fair, balanced and understandable assessment of the company's position and prospects.
    - The board is responsible for determining the nature and extent of the significant risks it is willing to take in achieving its strategic objectives. The board should maintain sound risk management and internal control systems.
    - The board should establish formal and transparent arrangements for considering how they should apply the corporate reporting, risk management and internal control principles, and for maintaining an appropriate relationship with the company's auditors.
- Section D: Remuneration
    - Levels of remuneration should be sufficient to attract, retain and motivate directors of the quality required to run the company successfully, but a company should avoid paying more than is necessary for this purpose. A significant proportion of executive directors' remuneration should be structured so as to link rewards to corporate and individual performance.
    - There should be a formal and transparent procedure for developing policy on executive remuneration and for fixing the remuneration packages of individual directors. No director should be involved in deciding his or her own remuneration.
- Section E: Relations with Shareholders
    - There should be a dialogue with shareholders based on the mutual understanding of objectives. The board as a whole has responsibility for ensuring that a satisfactory dialogue with shareholders takes place.
    - The board should use the AGM to communicate with investors and to encourage their participation.

- *the Stewardship Code* (see paragraph 3.4 below)
- *FRC guidance*
  The guidance below largely gives effect to the Code:
    - guidance on board effectiveness (March 2011), formerly the Higgs Guidance;
    - guidance on audit committees (September 2012);
    - going concern and liquidity risk – guidance for directors of UK companies (2009); and
    - internal control revised guidance for directors on the Combined Code (2005), formally the Turnbull Guidance.
- the Bribery Act 2010 (see paragraph 4.2 below);

- prudential regulation made by the PRA and conduct-based regulation made by the FCA in each case for regulated firms (most of which is beyond the scope of this chapter);
- the FCA's Remuneration Code (see paragraph 9 below);
- institutional guidance from organisations such as the Association of British Insurers (ABI), Pension & Investment Research Consultants (PIRC), the National Association of Pensions Funds (NAPF) and the Institute of Chartered Secretaries and Administrators (ICSA);
- corporate governance guides for particular types of companies, such as the Corporate Governance Guide for Investment Companies produced by the Association of Investment Companies and the Corporate Governance Guidelines for Small and Mid-Size Quoted Companies produced by the Quoted Companies Alliance;
- a very significant body of case law; and
- the sources listed in paragraph 2.2 below.

2.2 Which laws, codes or statutes regulate capital markets in your jurisdiction?

In addition to the sources listed in paragraph 2.1 above, the following laws, rules and regulations are the key sources of capital markets law, code and regulation in England and Wales:

- the Financial Services and Markets Act 2000 (FSMA), which is the principal piece of securities legislation in England and Wales;
- the Listing Rules;
- the Model Code, which is a share-dealing code with which premium listed companies must apply;
- the Prospectus Rules;
- the City Code on Takeovers and Mergers (the Takeover Code) promulgated by the Panel on Takeovers and Mergers (the Panel), which regulates takeovers;
- the Disclosure and Transparency Rules (the DTRs);
- the Admission and Disclosure Rules of London Stock Exchange Plc;
- rules of other markets, eg the AIM Rules for Companies of London Stock Exchange Plc; and
- the Criminal Justice Act 1993, which among other things, makes insider dealing a criminal offence.

2.3 Are there any public interest laws which apply to or influence corporate governance?

Not applicable.

2.4 Have there been any recent developments in any of the above laws? What are the recent changes to the above laws or rules and the reasons for such changes?

See paragraph 1.2 above.

3. SHAREHOLDERS AND THE SHAREHOLDERS' MEETING

3.1 How are shareholders' interests represented in the company? How are the shareholders assured exercise of their rights? What is the highest governing body within the company structure if it is not the shareholders' meeting?

The key sources of shareholders' rights are:

- shareholders agreements;
- articles of association; and
- the Companies Act, as amended by the Companies (Shareholders' Rights) Regulations 2009.

Shareholders agreements

A shareholders agreement is a contract between shareholders and a company containing key provisions on, for example, their personal rights and obligations.

Articles of association

Articles of association (articles) are a publicly filed contract between a company and its shareholders governing aspects of the running of the company and the powers and rights of shareholders and directors. The articles supplement and, where expressly permitted by the Companies Act, may also vary the provisions of the Companies Act.

The Companies Act ensures protection of the rights contained in a company's articles by providing that the articles may only be amended by a special resolution (ie a resolution passed by not less than 75 per cent of shareholders' voting). Certain articles may also be 'entrenched', whereby the articles may specify that a particular procedure (for example the requirement for unanimous shareholder approval) must be followed to amend a particular article.

While the Companies Act provides template articles (the Model Articles) which may be adopted by a company, a company is free to amend the Model Articles or to use an entirely new set of articles.

The Companies Act and Companies (Shareholders' Rights) Regulations 2009

The shareholders' meeting is the highest form of governing body within a company, and as such the Companies Act reserves certain matters for shareholder decision only.

If shareholders consider that the acts of directors are in breach of their duties, they may bring a derivative claim as detailed at paragraph 11 below. The Companies Act also provides a number of methods for shareholders to ensure that points they wish to discuss may be brought before other shareholders and the directors. For example:

- shareholders holding at least 5 per cent of such of the paid up share capital as carries the voting rights in a company can demand a general meeting of the shareholders;
- shareholders holding at least 5 per cent of the voting rights in a company can require a company to circulate a statement detailing a

proposed resolution at a general meeting;
- shareholders in traded companies have the right to have their questions answered at general meetings;
- the articles of a traded company can no longer provide for the chairman to have a casting vote in the event of a deadlock at shareholder meetings; and
- shareholders in a quoted company may require the directors to obtain an independent report on any poll taken.

Failure by officers of the company to observe these rights is an offence.

3.2 How is the shareholders' meeting conducted? Who may chair the meeting? May attendance (not voting) at the meeting be restricted only to the shareholders? Are the shareholders allowed to be accompanied by legal or other counsel?

Calling shareholder meetings

A shareholders' meeting may be called either by the directors or by a request from shareholders holding at least 5 per cent of the paid-up share capital to the directors. If the directors fail to call the general meeting following a request from the shareholders, the Companies Act allows shareholders to call the meeting themselves.

At least 14 days' notice of the meeting must be provided to the shareholders, and in the case of the annual general meeting of a public company at least 21 days' notice must be provided. The Companies Act contains detailed guidance on the form the notice must take and to whom it must be delivered.

Voting

The Code provides that the company should propose a separate resolution for each separate issue to be considered. Voting on these resolutions will be by an ordinary resolution (a simple majority) unless the Companies Act or model articles provide that a higher threshold must be passed, such as a special resolution.

Shareholders also have the right to demand the circulation of a written resolution as opposed to voting at the meeting or, if voting at the meeting, may demand a poll vote as opposed to voting on a show of hands. PIRC considers a poll vote to be the most appropriate way for listed companies to undertake business at general meetings.

Chairing

The Companies Act allows the company's articles to dictate who may chair the meeting. The Model Articles state that the chairman shall be appointed by the directors. If he is not present or has not been elected then the directors present, or if none are present, the shareholders, must appoint a director or shareholder to chair the meeting as the first item of business.

Subject to any provision in the articles, the Companies Act provides that a shareholder may be elected as the chairman of a general meeting by the passing of an ordinary resolution.

Attendance

Under the Companies Act, shareholders, their proxies, the representatives of any corporate shareholders and the company's auditors are allowed to attend general meetings.

In most other respects, attendance may be dictated by the articles. The Model Articles, for example, allow directors to attend and speak at general meetings (whether or not they are shareholders) and the Code recommends that all directors and the chairmen of the audit, remuneration and nomination committees should attend an annual general meeting.

The Model Articles also provide the chairman of the meeting with the power to permit other persons to attend and speak at the meeting, which could, if requested, include legal counsel.

3.3 How are minority shareholders' rights protected?

Minority shareholders' rights are frequently protected by way of contract, usually in a shareholders' agreement and/or articles of association. In addition to these contractual protections, certain protections are afforded by law and regulation, the key ones being set out below.

Unfair prejudice

The Companies Act provides that a member of a company may apply to court by petition on the ground:

- that the company's affairs are being or have been conducted in a manner that is unfairly prejudicial to the interests of members generally or of some part of its members (including at least the member bringing the action); or
- that an actual or proposed act or omission of the company (including an act or omission of on its behalf) is or would be so prejudicial.

If the petition is well founded, the court may make such order as it thinks fit for giving relief in respect of the matters complained of. Without prejudice to the court's general discretion, the Companies Act provides that the court's order may:

- regulate the conduct of the company's affairs in the future;
- require the company:
  - to refrain from doing or continuing an act complained of; or
  - to do an act that the petitioner has complained that it has omitted to do;
- authorise civil proceedings to be brought in the name and on behalf of the company by such person or persons and on such terms as the court may direct;
- require the company not to make any, or any specified, alterations in its articles without the leave of the court; and
- provide for the purchase of the shares of any members of the company by other members or by the company itself and, in the case of a purchase by the company itself, the reduction of the company's capital

accordingly.

Pre-emption rights

The Companies Act provides that a company must not allot equity securities to a person on any terms unless:

- it has made an offer to each person who holds ordinary shares in the company to allot to him on the same or more favourable terms a proportion of those securities that is as nearly as practicable equal to the proportion in nominal value held by him of the ordinary share capital of the company; and
- the period during which any such offer may be accepted has expired or the company has received notice of the acceptance or refusal of every offer so made.

Statutory pre-emption rights may be disapplied by special resolution, either in relation to a specific allotment or generally.

Class rights

The Companies Act protects holders of different classes of shares by providing that rights attached to a class of a company's shares may only be varied in accordance with provisions in the company's articles or where the company's articles contain no such provisions, if the holders of the shares of that class consent to the variation. The consent required is consent in writing from at least three-quarters in nominal value of the issued shares of that class.

Listing principles

The listing principles set out in the Listing Rules provide that a listed company must ensure that it treats all holders of the same class of its listed equity shares that are in the same position equally in respect of rights attaching to such listed equity shares.

Takeover Code

The Takeover Code provides as a general principle that all holders of the same class of securities of an offeree company must be afforded equivalent treatment by an offeror. There are a number of specific rules which further this general principle.

3.4 Is shareholder activism encouraged or discouraged? If not encouraged, how is it regulated?

Shareholder activism is strongly encouraged. The Stewardship Code encourages an active dialogue between companies and their shareholders. The Stewardship Code explains the purpose of stewardship as follows:

'For investors, stewardship is more than just voting. Activities may include monitoring and engaging with companies on matters such as strategy, performance, risk, capital structure, and corporate governance, including culture and remuneration. Engagement is purposeful dialogue with companies on these matters as well as on issues that are the immediate subject of votes at general meetings.'

The Stewardship Code's overriding objective is to protect and enhance the value that accrues to the ultimate beneficiary. In furtherance of that objective it sets out seven principles, which provide that institutional investors should:

- publicly disclose their policy on how they will discharge their stewardship responsibilities;
- have a robust policy on managing conflicts of interest in relation to stewardship which should be publicly disclosed;
- monitor their investee companies;
- establish clear guidelines on when and how they will escalate their stewardship activities;
- be willing to act collectively with other investors where appropriate;
- have a clear policy on voting and disclosure of voting activity; and
- periodically report on their stewardship and voting activities.

There is also significant institutional guidance in this area, most notably ICSA guidance on enhancing stewardship dialogue.

3.5 How are professional shareholders (those minority shareholders who seek some extra benefit from companies by unduly and habitually influencing management by using their shareholding) treated by the law? Are they excluded from attending the shareholders' meeting? Are they criminally or otherwise publicly sanctioned?

As shareholder activism is strongly encouraged to maintain board accountability, there are no significant laws which prevent shareholders from exercising their rights, even where this may be categorised as 'nuisance' activism. Directors who prevent shareholders from exercising their rights to, for example, call a meeting or place an item on a meeting's agenda, will be guilty of an offence under the Companies Act.

Campaigners have therefore been able to use minority shareholdings in public companies to promote their own agendas. For example, in 2008 a chef used a minority shareholding in a major supermarket chain to propose a resolution at the company's AGM relating to an improvement in the living standards of poultry. The resolution was duly circulated and voted on at the company's AGM, and although not passed, received widespread press coverage.

While companies cannot prevent shareholders exercising their rights in this manner, they may be able to mitigate related wasted expenditure. If requests sufficient to require the company to include a matter in the business to be dealt with at a general meeting are not received before the end of the financial year, the company can require that the relevant shareholder pays the costs incurred with complying with the request (which may include costs for printing and circulating the item). In the above 2008 example, the shareholder was required to pay for the company's costs (of circa £90,000) in complying with the request.

The company may also introduce a code of conduct for shareholders' meetings, specifying that disruptive behaviour may result in expulsion from the meeting at the discretion of the chairman.

3.6 Are shareholders' benefits given to some of the shareholders by the company without resolution by the shareholders' meeting prohibited or regulated by the law or other rules?

In addition to the overriding duty of directors to promote the success of the company for the benefit of its members as a whole, there are a number of protections contained in regulation and statute which seek to protect shareholders as a whole from deals which might be done with certain shareholders or directors and their connected persons.

Related party transaction

The Listing Rules provide protections for shareholders in relation (broadly) to transactions which are between a listed company and a related party. A related party is:

- a person who is (or was within the 12 months before the date of the transaction or arrangement) a substantial shareholder (being a person (broadly) who is entitled to exercise or control at least 10 per cent or more of the votes at a general meeting of the company);
- a person who is (or was within 12 months before the date of the transaction or arrangement) a director of the company, its subsidiary undertaking or parent undertaking or a fellow subsidiary undertaking of its parent undertaking;
- a person exercising significant influence over the company; or
- any associate of any of the persons referred to above.

The protections depend on the size of the transaction. Larger related party transactions require, among other things, shareholder approval. Smaller related party transactions require, among other things, the company's listing sponsor to provide the FCA with written confirmation that the terms of the proposed transaction or arrangement with the related party are fair and reasonable so far as the shareholders of the listed company are concerned.

Protection of minorities

See paragraph 3.3 above.

Companies Act protections

The Companies Act principally provides protection for shareholders in relation to transactions with directors. Shareholder approval is required for, *inter alia*, certain substantial property transactions with directors and their connected persons and loans to directors and their connected persons.

Issues and repurchases of shares also (generally) require shareholder approval and a company must have sufficient distributable reserves to make a distribution to shareholders.

4. DIRECTORS AND BOARD OF DIRECTORS

4.1 What are the functions and responsibilities of the directors and the board of directors? Do you have a one- or two-tier board system? What are the outside directors called?

Companies in England and Wales have a single-tier board structure. There is no equivalent of a management board and a supervisory board, although many companies (particularly listed companies) have an operating board below the main board of the company. There is no requirement for a board to have non-executive or independent directors (although see paragraph 4.4 below). All directors are collectively responsible for the success of the company and have the same legal duties, although non-executive directors are likely to have less detailed knowledge about the business than the executive directors and this may be relevant in assessing the knowledge, skill and experience expected of them.

The Companies Act sets out seven general duties of directors. The general duties of a director are:

- to act within the company's constitution and to only exercise powers for the purpose for which they are conferred;
- to act in the way that director considers, in good faith, would be most likely to promote the success of the company for the benefit of its members as a whole;
- to exercise independent judgement;
- to exercise reasonable care, skill and diligence;
- to avoid conflicts of interest;
- not to accept benefits from a third party conferred by reason of being a director or doing or not doing anything as a director; and
- to declare an interest in a proposed transaction or arrangement with the company.

Outside of these duties and a number of specific duties imposed by statute and regulations which will affect directors in different areas of the business (examples include purchase of the company's own shares, distribution of profits and assets, preparation of annual accounts and in insolvency situations (see the section on wrongful trading at paragraph 4.2 below)) directors are free to run the company as they see fit. Companies frequently divide responsibilities between directors; for example, finance, commercial and human resources functions might all be headed by a different director in a larger company (see also the discussion on committees at paragraph 4.3 below), albeit that all directors remain responsible for decisions taken by the company.

4.2 What are the rules that may give rise to civil and criminal liability of the director(s)? How are those liabilities sought?

Criminal Liability

Key pieces of legislation pursuant to which directors may face criminal liability include:

- The Fraud Act 2006

  The Fraud Act 2006 comprises three basic offences:

  - fraud by false representation;
  - fraud by failure to disclose information (which there is a legal duty to disclose); and
  - fraud by abuse of position.

- The Bribery Act 2010

There are four main offences under the Bribery Act:

  - a general offence relating to bribing another, ie promising, offering or giving a financial or other advantage to another person to induce or reward a person regarding improper performance of a certain function or activity; and offering, promising or giving financial or other advantage to another person, where it is known or believed that the acceptance of the advantage would constitute improper performance;
  - a general offence relating to being bribed; requesting, agreeing to receive or accepting a bribe;
  - an offence of bribing a foreign public official to obtain/retain business; and
  - a strict liability offence for commercial organisations where they fail to prevent bribery by those acting on their behalf.

A director who consents or connives at the commission of the first three offences will also commit the relevant offence.

The Ministry of Justice has published guidance about procedures which relevant commercial organisations can put in place to prevent persons associated with them from bribing.

- Gross negligence manslaughter

If a company's negligent act or acts cause a person's death and a director was the 'directing mind' within the organisation then that director can be liable at common law for the offence of gross negligence manslaughter.

Criminal acts are likely to be prosecuted by the Director of Public Prosecutions or the Serious Fraud Office.

Civil liability

- Breach of duty

A director may incur liability to a company if that director has breached any of the duties owed to the company described at paragraph 4.1 above. In addition to actions initiated by the company, shareholders can initiate actions against directors for breaches of duty, as described at paragraph 11 below.

- Wrongful trading

The Insolvency Act 1986 imposes upon directors some of the strictest standards, which they face in carrying out their duties. In particular, directors risk incurring personal liability to contribute to the assets of the company available to creditors where it is found in the course of winding up a company that the directors have wrongfully traded. A director (subject to certain defences) will have wrongfully traded where:

  - the company of which he was a director has gone into insolvent liquidation; and
  - at some time before the commencement of the liquidation of the company the director knew or ought to have concluded, that there was no reasonable prospect that the company would avoid going into insolvent liquidation.

Applications for a declaration of wrongful trading are made to the court by liquidators. There is also the associated criminal offence of fraudulent trading.

- Disqualification

A person may be disqualified from being a director of any company (for up to 15 years in some cases) for certain breaches of duty or other wrongdoing, including persistent failure to file returns, accounts or other documents with the Registrar of Companies, fraud, behaviour amounting to wrongful or fraudulent trading or conduct which the court considers demonstrates that the director is unfit to hold such office, such as conviction for an indictable offence.

4.3 Does the board of directors have a committee system, eg, nomination committee, compensation committee, audit committee? If not required, is it common practice for companies? How does it function?

Companies usually have provisions in their articles of association permitting the use of board committees and many companies have committees in place, albeit that it may not be necessary or appropriate for a small private company to operate through committees.

For listed companies, the Code recommends the appointment of:

- a nomination committee which should lead the process for board appointments and make recommendations to the board;
- a remuneration committee which should have responsibility for setting remuneration for all executive directors and the chairman, as well as recommending and monitoring the level and structure of remuneration for senior management; and
- an audit committee which should consider how to apply financial reporting and internal control procedures and establish and make arrangements for maintaining an appropriate relationship with the issuer's auditors.

4.4 Is it a legal requirement to have an independent director or a third-party director? If so, how are they appointed? Is it required for listed companies?

There is no legal requirement for a company to have independent directors. However, the Code provides that, for listed companies, except for smaller companies (being companies below the FTSE 350), at least half the board, excluding the chairman, should comprise non-executive directors determined by the board to be independent. A smaller company should have at least two independent non-executive directors.

The nomination committee of a listed company will lead the process for board appointments and make recommendations to the board. The Code considers that the following factors may be relevant to any determination of independence.

If the director:

- has been an employee of the company or group within the last five

years;
- has, or has had within the last three years a material business relationship with the company either directly, or as a partner, shareholder, director or senior employee of a body that has such a relationship with the company;
- has received or receives additional remuneration from the company apart from a director's fee, participates in the company's share option or a performance-related pay scheme, or is a member of the company's pension scheme;
- holds close family ties with any of the company's advisers, directors or senior employees;
- holds cross-directorships or has significant links with other directors through involvement in other companies or bodies;
- represents a significant shareholder; or
- has served on the board for more than nine years from the date of their first election.

4.5 How is the compensation for directors or officers determined? Can it be contested by the shareholders or the regulatory authorities? What are the common rules or practices for the compensation of officers?

See paragraph 9.1 below.

4.6 How will the board handle a corporate crisis like an internal criminal case, violence, social media exposure or dawn raid by the authorities?

The same duties and responsibilities outlined in paragraph 4.1 above continue to apply in a corporate crisis. To discharge those duties and responsibilities, however, the board may need to meet more regularly (including outside usual business hours) and information flow and access to relevant advisers will necessarily be more critical. Boards usually have policies in place for dealing with corporate crises, including information cascades.

5. BOARD OF AUDITORS, AUDIT COMMITTEE, ACCOUNTING AUDITORS

5.1 How is the internal accounting and legal audit structured and conducted? Is an outside accounting audit required and, if so, how is it structured? Are there requirements to change the auditor each five years?

Internal accounting and auditing

Companies have a duty under the Companies Act to maintain adequate accounting records. The directors are responsible for ensuring that proper accounts are prepared and audited by the company's auditors each year.

The accounts must contain the following:

- a profit-and-loss account for the past financial year;

- a balance sheet as at the end of the financial year approved by the board and signed by a director on its behalf;
- a statement that so far as each of the directors is aware there is no information needed by the company's auditors in connection with preparing their report of which the company's auditors are unaware; and that each director has taken all the steps that he ought to have taken as a director in order to make himself aware of any such information and to establish that the company's auditors are aware of that information;
- a business review, in the directors' report: (i) containing a balanced and comprehensive analysis of the development and performance of the company's business (and of its subsidiaries) during the financial year and of their position at the end of it; and (ii) using, to the extent necessary for an understanding of the development, performance or position of the company's business, analysis using financial and other key performance indicators including information relating to environmental matters and employee matters;
- a statement of the amount (if any) which the directors recommend should be paid as dividend; and
- a report by the auditors stating whether in their opinion the balance sheet and profit-and-loss account have been properly prepared and give a true and fair view of the financial state of affairs of the company. In the case of a company which is required to report under, or has adopted, International Financial Reporting Standards, the accounts must be 'fairly presented'.

The Companies Act expressly states that the purpose of the business review is to help the members assess how the directors have performed their duty to promote the success of the company for the benefit of the members as a whole.

The directors of a quoted company (ie one whose equity share capital is officially listed in the UK or another EEA state or is admitted to dealing on either the New York Stock Exchange or Nasdaq) must also:

- prepare a remuneration report setting out certain information regarding directors' remuneration; and
- include in the business review, to the extent necessary for an understanding of the development, performance or position of the company's business: (i) the main trends and factors likely to affect the future development, performance and position of the company's business; (ii) information about environmental matters, the company's employees and social and community issues; and (iii) information about persons with whom the company has contractual or other arrangements which are essential to the business of the company.

The directors' report (which contains the business review) and the remuneration report must be approved by the board and signed by a director or the secretary. The profit-and-loss account and the balance sheet must also be approved by the board of directors, one of whom must sign the balance sheet. The accounts are then sent to the auditors for them to report on. It is this final version which is put before the members in general meeting.

In the case of a public company, copies of the accounts must be sent to the shareholders in advance of the meeting (usually the company's AGM) at which the accounts are to be presented to the shareholders. A copy of the accounts, having been approved by the board, must also be filed with the Registrar of Companies. All of this must be done within six months following the end of the relevant financial year. Companies also have the option of sending a summary financial statement to those shareholders which want the summary instead of a copy of the full accounts.

A private company must send copies of its accounts to the shareholders and file its accounts with Registrar of Companies. It must send out its accounts no later than nine months following the end of the relevant financial year or, if earlier, the date on which it files its accounts with Registrar of Companies.

Both the company and the directors (except those who took all reasonable steps to secure compliance) are liable to a fine for failure to comply with these requirements.

Companies subject to the DTRs have increased financial reporting requirements (see paragraph 6.1 below).

Companies should have sufficient systems and controls in place to enable accurate financial reporting to take place.

For listed companies, the auditing of the company's accounts will be overseen by the company's audit committee. The Code states that the committee should consist of at least three independent non-executive directors, at least one of whom should have recent and relevant financial experience. The FRC Guidance on Audit Committees states that the level of financial experience of the other members of the committee will vary according to the nature of the company.

In relation to the internal audit, the committee's roles include:

- reviewing the effectiveness of the internal audit;
- recruiting the company's head of internal audit;
- reviewing the company's internal control and risk-management systems; and
- monitoring the integrity of the financial statements of the company and any formal announcements relating to the company's financial performance.

The audit committee is also responsible for overseeing the company's external audit. This role includes primary responsibility for the appointment of the external auditor and, where requested by the board, advising on whether the annual accounts provide a fair, balanced and understandable view of the company for the shareholders.

External auditing

With the exception of certain small, subsidiary or dormant companies, companies are required by the Companies Act to have their accounts audited. The shareholders of a company which would fall into the small, subsidiary or dormant company exceptions may nevertheless require that company to produce audited accounts.

When auditing the accounts, the auditor must make an independent report to the shareholders that the accounts give a true and fair view of the company's affairs, and that the accounts have been prepared in accordance with the law and financial report framework. The audit itself must be carried out in accordance with the Auditing Practices Board's (APB) International Standards on Auditing (UK and Ireland).

Although auditors must be re-appointed annually, currently there is no requirement to change auditors periodically. The APB's Ethical Standard 3, however, provides for rotation of individual partners, including that the audit engagement partner should be rotated at least every five years. The Code provides that FTSE 350 companies should put the external audit contract out to tender at least every 10 years. Following an investigation into competition in the audit market by the UK Competition Commission, the Competition Commission proposed (in July 2013) that FTSE 350 companies should put the external audit contract out to tender at least every five years. It further proposed that the FRC's Audit Quality Review team should review every audit engagement in the FTSE 350 on average every five years.

5.2 Do you have supervisory auditors? What is the function of the supervisory auditors' board?

Supervision of auditors at a company level is provided by the audit committee, as detailed above at paragraph 5.1.

Independent oversight of the auditing profession at a national level is provided by the FRC through recognised supervisory bodies (RSBs). These are the major accountancy professional bodies: the Institute of Chartered Accountants in England and Wales, the Institute of Chartered Accountants in Scotland, the Institute of Chartered Accountants in Ireland and the Association of Chartered Certified Accountants. Audit firms must be registered with an RSB and will be subject to its supervision.

6. MARKET DISCLOSURE/TRANSPARENCY TO THE SHAREHOLDERS AND THE PUBLIC

6.1 What are the disclosure requirements for companies in your jurisdiction under company law, capital markets law or any other rules?

Companies Act

There are a considerable number of matters affecting a company in respect of which details must be sent to the Registrar of Companies within a specified period following the relevant event (which are then publicly accessible). Among the most important of these documents and events are:

- the annual return, which is designed to ensure that information at Companies House is kept reasonably up to date and that changes to the company's directors, shareholders and share capital are noted;
- changes in the articles;
- purchases by the company of its own shares;
- special resolutions of the shareholders, including those in writing;

- ordinary resolutions, including those in writing, to give authority to allot shares;
- creation of registrable charges (eg mortgages) over the company's property; and
- the allotment of shares.

See paragraph 5.1 above in relation to the requirement to produce and file accounts.

Capital markets law

- Periodic financial reporting

DTR 4 sets out requirements for periodic financial reporting by issuers.

- *Annual financial reporting*

An issuer must make public an annual financial report at the latest four months after the end of each financial year, which includes:

- audited financial statements;
- a management report containing a fair review of the issuer's business and the principal risks and uncertainties facing the issuer; and
- responsibility statements.

Detailed contents requirements are also set out in the Companies Act, the Listing Rules and institutional codes and guidance.

- *Half-yearly financial reporting*

An issuer must also make public a half-yearly report covering the first six months of the financial year not later than two months after the end of the period to which it relates. The report must include:

- condensed financial statements;
- an interim management statement giving an indication of important events that have occurred during the first six months of the financial year, and their impact on the condensed set of financial statements, and a description of the principal risks and uncertainties for the remaining six months of the financial year; and
- responsibility statements from persons responsible within the issuer.

- *Interim management statements*

An issuer is required to make public a statement by its management during the first six-month period of the financial year and another statement by its management during the second six-month period. The relevant statement must be made in a period between 10 weeks after the beginning, and six weeks before the end of the relevant six-month period. The interim management statement must provide:

- an explanation of material events and transactions that have taken place during the relevant period and their impact on the financial position of the issuer and its controlled undertakings; and
- a general description of the financial position and performance of the issuer and its controlled undertakings during the relevant period.

- Disclosure of inside information by issuers

Under DTR 2, issuers must immediately announce information to the market if, broadly, it is precise, it affects the issuer and/or its securities and its announcement would be likely to have a significant effect on the price of the issuer's shares (including that it is information of that kind which a reasonable investor would be likely to use as part of the basis of its investment decisions (Inside Information)).

The announcement of Inside Information may be delayed by an issuer so as not to prejudice its legitimate interest (eg when it is negotiating a contract) provided that:

- such omission would not be likely to mislead the public;
- any person receiving the information owes the issuer a duty of confidentiality; and
- the issuer is able to ensure the confidentiality of that information.

- Notification of substantial shareholdings

Under DTR 5, a person must notify the issuer and the FCA (using the prescribed form TR-1) of the percentage of voting rights that person holds through direct or indirect holding of certain financial instruments if the percentage of those voting rights reaches, exceeds or falls below certain thresholds. The relevant thresholds are 3 per cent and each 1 per cent threshold thereafter up to 100 per cent. For non-UK issuers, the relevant thresholds are 5 per cent, 10 per cent, 15 per cent, 20 per cent, 25 per cent, 30 per cent, 50 per cent and 75 per cent.

The notification must be made as soon as possible but broadly within four trading days in the case of a non-UK issuer and two trading days in the case of a UK issuer of the event which changed that person's voting rights. The issuer is then obliged to make public all of the information contained in the notification by the end of the trading day following receipt of the notification if it is a UK issuer and not later than the end of the third day following receipt of the notification if it is a non-UK issuer.

Under DTR 3, all 'persons discharging managerial responsibility' (being directors and all senior managers with regular access to inside information) and their connected persons must notify all transactions conducted on their own account in the shares of the issuer or derivatives or any other financial instruments relating to those shares within four business days of the day on which the transaction occurred. The issuer must then release the information via a regulatory information service by no later than the end of the business day following the receipt of the information by the issuer.

A public company also has the power under the Companies Act to compel shareholders and those it reasonably suspects are shareholders to provide details of who ultimately owns those shares.

- Market abuse/insider dealing

Legislation imposing sanctions for market abuse (civil liability) and insider dealing (criminal liability) is set out respectively in FSMA and the Criminal Justice Act 1993.

6.2 What is the liability or responsibility of the board in relation to the company's disclosure requirements?

Failure to comply with disclosure requirement may result in a range of sanctions for a company and its board members, including fines, public and private censure and, in extreme cases, delisting.

7. M&A AND CORPORATE GOVERNANCE

7.1 Upon an M&A offer, how are the transparency and fairness rules of the company provided under the company and stock market laws and rules?

When a public company (or a certain type of private company) is involved in a takeover, the general principles of conduct and specific rules of the Takeover Code apply.

The Takeover Code is mainly concerned with regulating the conduct of the parties to takeovers to ensure that there is a 'level playing field'.

The general principles

The rules set out in the Takeover Code all stem from six general principles, which include the following:

- all holders of the same class of securities of an offeree company must be afforded equivalent treatment by an offeror; and
- the board of the offeree company must act in the interests of the company as a whole.

Other restrictions

Among other things, the Takeover Code imposes the obligation that before any announcement of a takeover is made, anyone who is privy to confidential information (especially price-sensitive information) about an offer must treat that information as secret. The information should only be disclosed on a need-to-know basis and recipients must be told of the information's secrecy.

The Takeover Code also imposes restrictions on dealings by persons with unpublished price-sensitive information and on frustrating action which might be taken in defending against a hostile takeover.

The rules in the Takeover Code cover such matters as the making of the first approach; the shares during the offer period; the timing and revision of the offer; and the contents of offer documents.

Sanctions

The Panel can:

- give directions to secure compliance with the Takeover Code;
- make rulings requiring the payment of compensation to holders or former holders of securities (including making such payments subject to interest); and
- seek enforcement by the courts.

In addition, failing to comply with certain rules constitutes a criminal offence. Proceedings for the offence may only be brought in England and Wales by or with the consent of the Secretary of State or the Director of Public Prosecutions.

8. PROXY FIGHTING

8.1 Is proxy fighting customarily conducted for control of the company management or what other items? How is it regulated under the company law or market regulations?

Proxy fighting is less common in UK board rooms than their US counterparts although, as with other some other European countries, it is becoming increasingly common in the UK.

Proxy fighting is used in particular where:

- target shareholder approval is required for the acquisition of a target by a bidder; or
- majority investors or shareholder groups wish to implement a change in the boardroom.

There is no specific legislation regulating proxy fights but a number of bodies have made recommendations in this area. The Hedge Fund Working Group has, for example, recommended that hedge fund managers should have a proxy voting policy. Certain tools are available to activist shareholders in proxy fights, in particular, the powers under the Companies Act to:

- require the circulation of a statement;
- require circulation of a resolution for a public company's AGM;
- include matters in business dealt with at a public company's AGM;
- require an independent report on a poll taken at a general meeting of a public company; and
- require website publication of audit concern.

9. OFFICERS' REMUNERATION RULES

9.1 How is remuneration of officers determined? By whom? Is there a role for the shareholders' meeting? Is there any mechanism for an independent body to review and evaluate them?

Officers' remuneration is generally determined by the board of directors (and its remuneration committee if the company has one) but with certain restrictions imposed by statute and regulation for listed and certain regulated companies.

While previously votes on remuneration reports were advisory only, with effect from 1 October 2013 (by way of amendment to the Companies Act) UK incorporated companies whose shares are admitted to trading on the London Stock Exchange, an EEA exchange, NASDAQ or the New York Stock Exchange will be subject to binding shareholder votes on remuneration.

The new rules provide that remuneration reports for these companies need to be split into two sections: an implementation report (which is, broadly, a backward-looking review of directors' remuneration in the financial year) (the Implementation Report) and a policy report (which sets out the company's policy on remuneration) (the Policy Report).

The Implementation Report will continue to be the subject of an advisory vote at each AGM. The Policy Report must be put to a shareholder vote at least every three years. If a company makes any remuneration payment to a director which is not consistent with the last Policy Report approved by shareholders:

- that payment is void;
- the director holds any money transferred on trust for the company; and
- any director who authorised the payment is personally liable to the company.

The first Policy Report must be put to shareholders at the company's AGM held in the first financial year after 1 October 2013 and take effect no later than the start of the next financial year. If the Policy Report is not approved at that meeting, the company will have to put a revised Policy Report to shareholders as, unless it has an approved Policy Report, the company will not be able to pay directors from the date the legislation becomes effective.

The Remuneration Code (the RC) which forms part of the FCA and PRA handbooks is a code which applies in some form to all banks and building societies and most investment firms. The RC divides firms into three tiers (based mainly on the available capital resources of the firm) and allows them to apply the principles of the code differently depending on which tier they fall into (with Tier three firms being able to apply many of the requirements of the RC proportionately).

The RC affects the remuneration of 'Code Staff' which is, very broadly, senior management, risk takers and staff engaged with control functions. Staff members whose current remuneration takes them into the same bracket as senior management or risk takers, whose professional activities have a material impact on the firm's risk profile also need to be assessed to see if they qualify as Code Staff. Key elements of the Code include:

- deferral of between 40 per cent and 60 per cent of Code Staff's remuneration for a minimum of three to five years;
- 50 per cent of all variable remuneration for Code Staff to be provided in the form of shares or the equivalent;
- variable remuneration for Code Staff to be linked to performance and significantly reduced in the case of subdued or negative performance of the firm, including clawback mechanisms; and
- public disclosure of remuneration policy.

The text of a new European Directive (CRD IV) has been approved by the European Parliament and is likely to impose further restrictions in relation to remuneration, including:

- potentially widening the scope of the definition Code Staff;
- further limiting a firm's ability to award guaranteed variable remuneration;
- a maximum ratio (1:1) of fixed to variable components of remuneration (rising to 2:1) with shareholder approval; and
- additional disclosure in relation to those earning more than EUR 1 million per annum.

Institutional Guidance for listed companies is also significant in this area, in particular the ABI Principles of Remuneration.

9.2 Is the mechanism of officers' remuneration publicly debated?

See paragraph 9.1 above.

10. DIRECTORS' LIABILITIES, LIABILITY INSURANCE, INDEMNIFICATION

10.1 What are the directors' responsibilities and liabilities under the law? Can those liabilities be covered by insurance? Can it be indemnified by the company or other related parties?

See paragraphs 4.1 and 4.2 above in relation to directors' responsibilities and liabilities under the law.

Provisions which seek to exempt any director from any liability arising from his negligence, default, breach of duty or breach of trust in relation to a company are void. Any indemnities for directors of a company or any associated companies against such liabilities are also void. This is the case whether the provision is contained in the articles, in a separate contract with the company or otherwise.

There are, however, three exceptions to these restrictions:

- Insurance

Companies can purchase insurance to cover the restricted liabilities. Directors' and officers' liability insurance policies will, of course, always be subject to certain exclusions and limitations.

- 'Qualifying third-party indemnity provisions'

Provisions are permitted which do not provide an indemnity against any liability incurred by the director:

  - to the company or an associated company;
  - to pay a fine imposed in any criminal proceedings or a penalty imposed by a regulatory authority;
  - in defending criminal proceedings in which he is convicted or in defending any civil proceedings brought by the company or any associated company in which judgment is given against him; or
  - in connection with certain applications for relief by the court in which the court refuses to grant relief.

- 'Qualifying pension scheme indemnity provisions'

Provisions are permitted which indemnify a director of a company that is a trustee of an occupational pension scheme against liability incurred in connection with the company's activity as a trustee of the scheme. Any such provision must not indemnify the director against any liability incurred by the director:

  - to pay a fine imposed in any criminal proceedings or a penalty imposed by a regulatory authority; or
  - in defending criminal proceedings in which he is convicted.

Directors' and officers' liability insurance and the details of any qualifying third-party or pension scheme indemnity provisions have to be disclosed in the company's annual report and accounts. In addition, shareholders may inspect the terms of any such indemnities, in the same way as they are entitled to see copies of directors' service agreements.

11. SHAREHOLDERS' DERIVATIVE SUITS

11.1 Is a shareholder's derivative suit provided for by law in your jurisdiction? How is it enforced by the shareholders?

A director's duties are owed to the company and not to any other person, so generally only the company can take action to enforce them. However, in certain circumstances, shareholders may be able to bring a derivative claim under the Companies Act 2006 on the company's behalf for any breach.

The derivative claim procedure applies to any claim arising from negligence, default, breach of duty or breach of trust by a director of the company. The cause of action must be the company's and may be against the director or another person (if against another person, that person will have had to be involved in the breach, for example by inducing or knowingly assisting the director to act as he did). The claimant need not have been a shareholder at the time the claim arose but must be a shareholder in order to bring the claim.

There is a two-stage procedure which applies to derivative claims. First, the claimant must show a *prima facie* case and then the court must give or refuse permission to continue the claim.

In considering whether to give permission, the court must have regard to various factors including:

- whether the member is acting in good faith;
- the importance that a person acting in accordance with the duty to promote the success of the company would attach to continuing the action;
- the possibility and the likelihood of ratification; and
- whether the member could in fact continue the claim in his own right.

The person bringing the derivative claim could end up bearing the costs if the claim is dismissed and the court determines that it was unmerited. If a derivative claim is successful, any damages awarded will go to the company, not to the shareholder bringing the claim.

11.2 Have there been any recent relevant court cases on the subject?

Recent case law on shareholder derivative actions has largely been limited to procedural matters but the cases have emphasised that courts will only permit shareholders' derivative claims in limited circumstances.

In *Joseph Cyril Edward Bamford v John Henry Harvey & Avro Heritage Ltd* [2012] EWHC 2858 (Ch), the court refused to grant permission for a director, who was a 50 per cent shareholder in a company, to continue a derivative claim against another company director, also a 50 per cent shareholder in the company on the basis that a claim could be brought under the shareholders' agreement between the two parties. Similarly, in *Seven Holdings Ltd, Re* [2011] EWHC 1893 (Ch), the court refused to grant permission for a shareholder director to bring certain derivative claims against another director on the basis that an ordinary director would not seek to prosecute some of the claims made, and that a liquidator could deal with some of the disputes more efficiently.

Recent claims have, however, been allowed to continue where the court felt that a derivatives claim was a suitable method for pursuing the claim. For example, in *Phillips v Fryer* [2013] B.C.C. 176, the court granted permission for a shareholder to continue derivative claims on the basis that a director seeking to promote the success of the company would have pursued the claims, and that the directors defending the claims did not demonstrate any convincing defences.

12. SOCIAL INTEREST IN CORPORATE BEHAVIOUR

12.1 How is a company in your country expected to deal with the following issues? Corporate social responsibility; gender, racial and social diversification; environmental issues; ecology and corruption?

There is no one piece of legislation governing corporate and social responsibility (CSR) in England and Wales but the concept is referred to in the main company law statutes and codes in England.

Directors' duties and governance

In complying with the Companies Act duty to promote the success of the company for the benefit of its members as a whole, a director must have regard to the following matters (among other matters):

- the interests of the company's employees;
- the need to foster the company's business relationships with suppliers, customers and others;
- the impact of the company's operations on the community and the environment; and
- the desirability of the company maintaining a reputation for high standards of business conduct.

Narrative reporting and disclosure of CSR matters

Companies are required to include in the directors' report which accompanies their annual financial statements information to help shareholders assess how well the directors have complied with the duties referred to above. Quoted companies are also required to include an 'enhanced business review' within the directors' report, containing information about environmental matters, the company's employees, social and community issues and a statement regarding the company's policies on these matters and the effectiveness of those policies. Draft legislation (the Companies Act 2006 (Strategic Report and Directors' Report) Regulations 2013) proposes to replace the enhanced business review with a strategic report, in which the reporting requirements for a quoted company would include additional items such as consideration of human rights issues.

Investor groups also publish non-binding guidelines for companies on the CSR management and reporting. For example, the ABI has published Guidelines on Responsible Investment Disclosure, which states, among other things, the environmental, social and governance disclosures that the ABI would expect to be included in listed companies' annual reports.

Gender and racial and social diversification

Companies in England and Wales operate under a suite of legislation intended to promote equality and prevent discrimination, including the Equality Act 2010, the Employment Equality (Age) Regulations 2006 and the

Disability Discrimination Act 1995.

Gender equality is the area which has received most attention in recent years, principally through the Equality Act 2010.

The majority of the current statutory regime regarding gender equality is contained in the Equality Act 2010. One section of that Act provides the power to require employers with 250 or more employees to publish details of the wages of their male and female employees for the purpose of exposing any gender differences in pay.

The statutes are supplemented by non-binding recommendations. The Davies Report was commissioned by the Government in 2011 to report on 'Women on boards', and made 10 non-binding recommendations for furthering gender equality in corporations. These included:

- the chairman of a company should disclose information to shareholders on how that company addresses diversity in its annual reports;
- companies should establish gender policies and report on the progress of achieving the objectives in those policies; and
- FTSE 100 boards should aim for a minimum of 25 per cent female representation by 2015.

Draft European legislation goes further, proposing binding quotas for female representation.

Environmental and ecological issues

Companies in England and Wales are affected by a considerable volume of environmental legislation. A number of recent developments have arisen out the Climate Change Act 2008, which introduced a number of new targets and requirements. For example, the Greenhouse Gas Emissions (Directors' Reports) Regulations 2013 will, with effect from October 2013, require quoted companies to include details of the company's greenhouse gas emissions in directors' reports.

UK investor groups are also active in producing guidelines in this area. For example, PIRC stated in its 16th edition of the UK Shareholder Voting Guidelines 2012 that it expects listed companies to publish a comprehensive environmental policy.

Corruption

A summary of the Bribery Act 2010 is set out at paragraph 4.2 above. Other pieces of legislation designed to address corruption include the Proceeds of Crime Act 2002 and the Money Laundering Regulations 2007 which, between them, introduced due diligence, reporting and record-keeping requirements for UK corporate entities in order to detect and prevent those entities being used for money laundering purposes.

USA

Adam O. Emmerich, Sabastian V. Niles & Andrew D. Kenny
Wachtell, Lipton, Rosen & Katz

1. GENERAL PRINCIPLES

1.1 What are the general principles of corporate governance in your jurisdiction? What are the main objectives of corporate governance principles in your jurisdiction? State also whether your legal system is based on common law or civil law.

The US legal system consists of a combination of state and federal common law, statutory law and rules and regulations of various government agencies, including in the area of securities law and rules applicable to publicly listed companies promulgated by the US Securities and Exchange Commission (the SEC) and self-regulatory organisations, such as the stock exchanges, which are supervised by the SEC. In addition to these sources and judge-made law (principally of the Delaware Court of Chancery, as most US corporations are incorporated in the state of Delaware), the US corporate governance regime derives from a variety of non-legal sources, including best practice recommendations and guidelines and proposals advanced by shareholders, proxy advisory firms and various interest groups. Moreover, the ability of corporations and their shareholders to privately order the vast majority of their governance arrangements and the structure of the US market – in which most public companies now have widely dispersed and diversified shareholder bases, controlling shareholders are rare and institutional investor intermediaries of varying types hold more than 70 per cent of publicly traded securities (as compared with less than 10 per cent in the 1950s) – strongly influence corporate governance.

In the USA, a unitary board of directors, elected by shareholders and subject to fiduciary duties, is charged with overseeing the corporation's business and affairs. Directors are fiduciaries of the corporation and its shareholders and are expected to focus on promoting and developing the long-term and sustainable success of the company. See paragraph 4.1 for a discussion of fiduciary duties, including the duties of care, loyalty, good faith and candour. Unlike some jurisdictions where shareholders directly determine key business matters, such as dividend policy and material acquisitions, the US model is director-centric, giving boards broad authority to exercise their business judgement on most matters. Courts will typically not second-guess business decisions of the board where the 'business judgment rule' applies, which involves a rebuttable presumption that directors are discharging their duties in good faith, on an informed basis and in a manner the directors reasonably believe to be in the best interests of the corporation and its shareholders. '[H]elp[ing] the corporation build long-term, sustainable growth in value for shareholders and, by extension, other stakeholders' has been described by the NYSE Commission on Corporate Governance as the 'fundamental objective' of the board.

Principles of transparency are implemented through a disclosure-based securities law regime designed to provide timely information to shareholders about the corporation and material developments.

1.2 Have there been any recent developments in the law, codes and rules of corporate governance?

Within a relatively stable framework of state law and federal regulation, incremental developments in corporate governance-related laws and practices have occurred in recent years, with more fundamental shifts having occurred in prior periods, such as those wrought by the Sarbanes-Oxley Act of 2002 (Sarbanes-Oxley) or the focus of boards shifting from business strategy towards a more compliance-oriented posture aimed at oversight and monitoring. Principal areas of governance pressure and change include risk management, executive compensation (see paragraphs 4.5, 9.1 and 9.2), board structure, director elections, takeover defences and the extent to which matters of corporate strategy and even ordinary business decisions should be determined by shareholders instead of the board (see paragraphs 3.4 and 8.1).

- Most US public companies now have annually elected boards. In 2002, 61 per cent of S&P 500 companies had classified boards in which a third of the board is elected each year; that percentage is now down to only 17 per cent. 84 per cent of S&P 500 companies now elect directors by a majority of votes cast (instead of a plurality voting standard) with incumbent directors who are not re-elected by majority vote having to tender their resignations. These changes have increased the power of shareholders and proxy advisory firms. For example, the most influential proxy advisory firm, Institutional Shareholder Services (ISS), will recommend a 'withhold' or 'against' vote against directors if the board is insufficiently responsive to shareholder proposals that receive the support of a majority of the shares cast in a previous year.
- 57 per cent of S&P 500 companies are led by a combined chairman and CEO, down from 75 per cent in 2002. 92 per cent of S&P 500 company boards have a lead or presiding director (which position may be filled by the independent chairman).
- Nearly 60 per cent of major corporations today have boards whose only non-independent member is the CEO (as contrasted to 31 per cent in 2002), even though the rules of the stock exchanges require public company boards to have only a majority of independent directors and there has been renewed interest in whether the presence on the board of a meaningful minority of directors with prior history or familiarity with the company and its industry may actually enhance board effectiveness. The voting guidelines of many institutional investors and governance advisory organisations often specify that a 'substantial' majority or a specific percentage of the board must be independent as defined by

criteria stricter than the stock exchange definitions.

- The Dodd-Frank Wall Street Reform and Consumer Protection Act of 2010 (Dodd-Frank) eliminated broker discretionary voting for the election of directors and executive compensation. In 2012, the NYSE eliminated broker discretionary voting on many governance items. As a result, brokers can no longer vote on such matters on behalf of clients who fail to provide voting instructions. These changes are considered to have made it harder for companies to achieve majority votes on company-sponsored proposals, including director elections.
- In 2011, the SEC permitted shareholders to include, in the company's proxy statement through the Rule 14a-8 shareholder proposal process, proposed bylaw amendments that would permit shareholders to nominate director candidates through the company's own proxy statement. Prior Dodd-Frank-related rule-making in which the SEC required companies to provide such 'proxy access' for shareholder-nominated directors was struck down by the courts.

1.3 Outline recent court cases and incidents involving corporate governance issues. Were there any significant corporate scandals or large unlawful corporate cases?

Risk oversight is highly scrutinised. For example, proxy advisory firms like ISS have added material failures of risk oversight to the list of factors considered in recommending 'against' or 'withhold' votes in director elections – but note that this addition is not intended to 'penalize boards for taking prudent business risks or for exhibiting reasonable risk appetite'. Illustrative examples of what ISS considers a failure of risk oversight include bribery, large or serial fines or sanctions from regulatory bodies, significant adverse legal judgments or settlements, and significant hedging or pledging of company stock. Recent high-profile incidents involving perceived failures of effective oversight include the 'London whale' trading losses at JPMorgan Chase – which resulted in 'withhold the vote' campaigns against certain independent directors involved in the board's oversight function and an ultimately unsuccessful shareholder proposal to separate the board chairman and CEO positions – and Hewlett-Packard's nearly $9 billion write-down of its Autonomy acquisition amid accusations of inadequate due diligence, which resulted in the chairman of the board relinquishing his chairmanship and two other directors stepping down after receiving bare majorities of votes in uncontested elections following the write-down. Recent court cases have underscored expectations that directors will be active and engaged, particularly where potential 'red flags' revealing corporate malfeasance may be present, and that resigning from a board may not necessarily immunise directors from liability.

1.4 Which law enforcement agency is in charge of enforcing corporate governance? May a criminal sanction be levied upon infringement of the corporate governance rules?

Corporate governance, generally speaking, is traditionally not a matter of criminal or civil enforcement by law enforcement agencies. Fiduciary duties imposed by state statutory and common law are primarily enforced via private lawsuits brought by shareholders.

The SEC and the US Department of Justice (DOJ) enforce federal securities laws, including Sarbanes-Oxley, which provides for civil, criminal and administrative penalties. Many of the securities laws may also be enforced by private lawsuits.

Companies that violate substantive civil or criminal law may be subjected to remedies (or agree to settlements) that touch on corporate governance matters, such as enhancing ethics and compliance programmes or appointing an external, independent compliance monitor. Under the Federal Sentencing Guidelines and the DOJ's Principles of Federal Prosecution, sentencing may take into account the effectiveness of a company's compliance programme and active director oversight.

2. SOURCES OF LAW

2.1 Which laws, codes or statutes govern company structures and organisations? Are there statutes like the Companies Act or other forms of law? Is there much relevant case law?

There is no overarching federal corporate code in the USA, and company structure and organisation are primarily a matter of state statutory law. Each of the 50 states has its own corporate code, with Delaware's General Corporation Law being by far the most prominent, since the majority of US public companies are incorporated in Delaware. A variety of company structures are permissible under state law, including corporate, limited liability company, partnership and sole proprietorship forms, and companies can be quickly formed with minimal procedural hurdles to act in furtherance of any lawful purpose. Most state laws take an enabling approach, in which corporations and their shareholders have the ability to engage in private ordering of their governance and organisational arrangements through their charters and bylaws. The Delaware courts, particularly the Delaware Court of Chancery, a specialised business court, have developed an immense body of case law interpreting the Delaware General Corporation Law (and equivalent laws applicable to non-corporate entities), including with respect to various corporate governance topics. These cases, while not legally binding outside Delaware, have wide influence.

For listed companies, stock exchange listing rules and regulations, such as the NYSE Listing Manual and the NASDAQ Marketplace Rules, may also implicate company structures and organisations and are adopted with the approval of the SEC. Listing rules address several important aspects of corporate governance, including director independence, the nature and composition of various board committees, meetings of non-management and independent directors in executive session, shareholder voting rights, regulation of dual-class stock structures, and the content and public disclosure of corporate governance guidelines and codes of business conduct.

2.2 Which laws, codes or statutes regulate capital markets in your

jurisdiction?

US capital markets are primarily governed by: (i) the federal securities laws, particularly the Securities Act of 1933, the Securities Exchange Act of 1934, and the rules and regulations of the SEC promulgated under those Acts, which include, among others, proxy rules, tender offer rules and ownership reporting rules for directors, officers and significant shareholders; (ii) stock exchange listing rules, predominantly those of the NYSE and the NASDAQ; and (iii) the rules and regulations of the Financial Industry Regulatory Authority (FINRA), a market-wide self-regulatory organisation that regulates securities firms doing business in the USA, including member brokerage firms and exchange markets. The stock exchanges and FINRA play a significant role in promoting fair and transparent capital markets and are subject to oversight by the SEC. Both Sarbanes-Oxley and Dodd-Frank included provisions relating to capital markets, many of which operated to amend and expand provisions of the 1933 and 1934 Acts. Certain state securities laws, including 'blue sky' laws, also regulate the offering and sale of securities.

2.3 Are there any public interest laws which apply to or influence corporate governance?

Generally, no. For example, with respect to board composition, there are no requirements for labour or government representation (or other mandated representation for particular constituencies) on the board of directors, nor are there gender or racial diversity requirements. However, with respect to diversity, public companies are required to disclose whether, and if so how, diversity is considered in identifying director nominees and how diversity policies are implemented and assessed.

2.4 Have there been any recent developments in any of the above laws? What are the recent changes to the above laws or rules and the reasons for such changes?

- In 2013, Delaware adopted legislation enabling the formation of for-profit 'public benefit' corporations that seek to promote one or more specific public benefits identified in the corporation's certificate of incorporation. Directors of public benefit corporations would have fiduciary duties to conduct the corporation's affairs for the benefit not only of shareholders, but also in the broader public interest.
- In April 2012, Congress enacted the Jumpstart Our Business Startups (JOBS) Act to ease reporting requirements for 'emerging growth companies' and facilitate private capital formation. Related rule-making is underway.
- New SEC and stock exchange listing rules have been adopted concerning conflicts of interest involving compensation consultants, enhanced criteria for compensation committee independence, expanded compensation committee authority and responsibility over advisors and mandated independence assessments for compensation committee advisors.

- Various rule-makings related to Dodd-Frank are still pending, including with respect to new 'pay equity' and 'pay for performance' disclosures, compensation clawback policies and hedging of stock.
- Rule-making is also pending before the SEC for (i) the elimination of regulatory loopholes that enable activist hedge funds to rapidly accumulate significant and even controlling stakes in public companies without timely notice to the market and (ii) modernisation of the reporting periods in which institutional investors must report their shareholdings in public companies.

3. SHAREHOLDERS AND THE SHAREHOLDERS' MEETING

3.1 How are shareholders' interests represented in the company? How are the shareholders assured exercise of their rights? What is the highest governing body within the company structure if it is not the shareholders' meeting?

As discussed in paragraph 4.1, a unitary board of directors, all of whose members must be elected by the shareholders and each of whom is charged with acting in the best interests of the company and its shareholders, is the highest governing body of the public corporation. Shareholders' interests are represented through the shares they hold in the company. Most public companies in the USA have a single class of voting common stock entitled to one vote per share, although dual-class stock structures are permitted (such as those seen at several major technology and media companies). In the proto-typical case, shareholder interests are protected by virtue of the equal treatment generally afforded to shareholders by law, fiduciary duties owed to the company and its shareholders, and by one-vote-per-share operating in the context of widely dispersed share ownership. Courts will carefully scrutinise any improper curtailment of shareholder rights and apply heightened scrutiny to board actions that negatively impact a shareholder's right to vote. See paragraph 3.3 for a discussion of shareholder rights.

3.2 How is the shareholders' meeting conducted? Who may chair the meeting? May attendance (not voting) at the meeting be restricted only to the shareholders? Are the shareholders allowed to be accompanied by legal or other counsel?

Shareholders' meetings are typically held annually, as provided by state law and the organisational documents of the company. Annual and special meetings may be convened by the board and, to the extent provided for in the company's charter or bylaws, shareholders satisfying certain ownership requirements (which vary across companies) may have the right to call special meetings of the shareholders. The board sets the agenda of the meeting, and many companies have adopted advance notice bylaws that require shareholders to provide advance notice and satisfy other procedural requirements in order to propose business at a meeting.

Shareholders' meetings are usually held in person, although companies are increasingly experimenting with 'virtual' shareholders' meetings conducted entirely online. Each meeting has a 'record date' fixed by the board, and only persons holding shares as of such date are entitled to vote. Advance notice of the meeting must be given to shareholders by specified deadlines, and such notice must set forth the matters to be considered at the meeting. When items are subject to a shareholder vote, the company must provide shareholders with comprehensive proxy statements containing the recommendation of the board, information about the proposals to be considered, disclosure of interests of directors and officers that may differ from the general interests of shareholders and other mandatory items.

Meetings are conducted in accordance with the company's charter and bylaws, and the chairman of the board (who is often the CEO of the company) usually chairs the meeting. Depending on the topic at issue, the specific vote requirement for shareholder action may be a majority of the outstanding shares, a majority of the shares present and entitled to vote, a majority of voted shares, or a plurality of voted shares. In certain cases involving related party transactions, the standard is voluntarily tightened to count only votes of unaffiliated or disinterested shareholders. Actions taken at a meeting will not be effective in the absence of a sufficient quorum of shares being represented at the meeting. The specific quorum requirement is generally specified in the company's bylaws.

Companies may, but are not required to, restrict attendance at shareholders' meetings to shareholders entitled to vote. Although uncommon in practice (except in the context of proxy fights), shareholders generally may be accompanied by legal or other counsel.

3.3 How are minority shareholders' rights protected?

As an initial matter, most large public companies in the USA have a widely dispersed shareholder base and hence no majority or controlling shareholder exists with the power, even in theory, to 'exploit' minority shareholders. In addition, most public companies have a single class of voting common stock with each share entitled to one vote. Under Delaware law, generally speaking, all shareholders must be treated equally (such as with respect to dividends). In the rare case of a public company with a controlling shareholder, transactions between the company and the controlling shareholder are subject to heightened legal scrutiny and in practice are generally subject to the review and approval of independent directors who are unaffiliated with the controlling shareholder.

Shareholders also have various rights. For example, shareholders are generally entitled to communicate with other shareholders and attend, participate and vote in person or by proxy at meetings; action taken at a meeting will not be effective if too few shares are represented and quorum requirements are not met. In addition, shareholders generally have the right to elect directors; nominate their own director candidates in compliance with company bylaws; remove directors (albeit in certain cases, such as with a classified board, only at certain intervals or for cause); adopt certain forms of corporate bylaws and approve (but not initiate) charter amendments; receive dividends on a pro rata basis to the extent declared by the board; approve charter amendments and fundamental transactions (such as mergers, sales of all or substantially all of a company's assets, dissolutions or changes in the form of entity); require that shareholders' meetings be held annually; for certain transactions (such as cash-out mergers), exercise appraisal rights and receive the fair value of their shares if they do not vote in favour of the transaction; call special shareholders' meetings to the extent provided under the company's organisational documents; inspect the books and records of the company and obtain its shareholder list for proper purposes; and submit proposals for shareholder vote (including through use of the company's own proxy statement without charge if certain requirements are met). Shareholders of listed companies have additional voting rights established by stock exchange rules, including with respect to certain issuances of common stock. Where there is no controlling shareholder, as is usually the case, the outcome of voting decisions depends on the aggregate of widely held votes.

Finally, shareholders can sue directors for violating fiduciary duties or federal securities laws and petition courts to review results of shareholder votes, including the validity of the election, appointment, removal or resignation of directors and the rights of such persons to continue to hold office. Shareholders can also engage the board directly, either by working constructively with the board to propose and effect strategic or governance changes or conducting an adversarial proxy contest to replace part or all of the board.

3.4 Is shareholder activism encouraged or discouraged? If not encouraged, how is it regulated?

Corporate governance laws and practices have evolved over time to enhance the power of activist shareholders and, consequently, the existing legal and regulatory regime greatly facilitates shareholder activism. Indeed, the last two decades have witnessed a slow but steady shift in the balance of power from boards of directors and corporate management to institutional shareholders and other institutional activists. Changes in SEC rules and stock exchange listing requirements, supplemented by federal and state legislation, have provided activists with a variety of tools for organising public and private campaigns to advance their governance and economic agendas. Hedge funds and other activist shareholders frequently press boards and management, who are often under pressure to achieve quarterly financial targets, to take actions that will boost immediate stock prices – such as stock buybacks, special dividends, spin-offs and other corporate reorganisations – even at the expense of long-term performance. Discussions between companies and activists concerning potential changes often involve the implicit (and sometimes explicit) threat of an election contest, proxy fight and aggressive public campaign to remove the current board and management if the activist's demands are not met. In addition, under current law, activists can accumulate substantial stakes in companies without prior notice, and use derivative/synthetic arrangements to acquire voting positions that are not commensurate with their economic stake in the company. In order to counteract the undesirable effects of shareholder activism, the disproportionate power of activist hedge funds and the outsized influence of one-size-fits-all recommendations by proxy advisory firms, long-term investors – and the companies in which they invest – are encouraged to constructively resolve governance and other issues through direct, pragmatic and case-by-case engagement on the merits.

See paragraphs 1.2, 3.5 and 8.1 for related discussions of activism.

3.5 How are professional shareholders (those minority shareholders who seek some extra benefit from companies by unduly and habitually influencing management by using their shareholding) treated by the law? Are they excluded from attending the shareholders' meeting? Are they criminally or otherwise publicly sanctioned?

US corporate law generally treats all shareholders of the same class equally. Shareholders may generally pressure management and exercise their rights freely and self-interestedly, even to the extent of imposing significant costs on the company or proposing actions that may not be in the best interests of the company and its shareholders collectively. Unlike the board of directors, non-controlling shareholders owe no fiduciary or other duties to their fellow shareholders or to the company.

The phenomenon of 'professional shareholders' – in the sense of shareholders that threaten to disrupt annual meetings in hopes of being paid off, as sometimes occurs in certain other countries – largely does not exist in the USA, although certain practices, such as 'strike suit' litigation against a company by plaintiffs firms in order to extract a settlement or receive legal fees, do exist. In the 1980s, some corporate raiders practised 'greenmail' in which they would purchase large blocks of shares in public companies and then threaten a takeover unless the corporation bought back those same shares at a higher price than the raider had paid for them. While lucrative for a short period, such practices are rare today, although companies do from time to time buy back shares in a lump from an individual shareholder, such as a former activist.

See paragraph 3.2 for a discussion of the shareholders' meeting and paragraph 3.4 for a discussion of shareholder activism.

3.6 Are shareholders' benefits given to some of the shareholders by the company without resolution by the shareholders' meeting prohibited or regulated by the law or other rules?

Selective benefits given to a subset of shareholders are generally prohibited or regulated by law, which by and large requires that all shareholders of the same class be equally treated. Holders of preferred shares may have preferences or priorities of superior rank to those of common shareholders. While 'related party' transactions are generally rare due to the dispersed nature of ownership at most large public companies, a company may enter into transactions or arrangements with its directors, officers and significant shareholders on terms not available to all shareholders, subject to the board's exercise of its fiduciary duties and compliance with applicable stock exchange requirements (such as public disclosure, review by disinterested directors and shareholder approval in the case of certain stock issuances to directors or officers).

4. DIRECTORS AND BOARD OF DIRECTORS

4.1 What are the functions and responsibilities of the directors and the board of directors? Do you have a one- or two-tier board system? What are the outside directors called?

US companies are managed under the direction of a single-tiered, unitary board of directors, elected by the shareholders and subject to fiduciary duties, and with full control over the company's business and affairs. The board's basic responsibility is to exercise its business judgement and act in a manner reasonably believed to be in the best interests of the company and its shareholders (see paragraphs 1.1 and 4.2).

Directors owe the corporation and its shareholders fiduciary duties such as the duty of care and the duty of loyalty. The duty of care encompasses the obligation to act on an informed basis after due consideration and appropriate deliberation. The duty of loyalty encompasses the obligation to act in the best interests of the corporation and the shareholders, as opposed to the directors' personal interests. Corollary duties – such as duties of good faith and duties of candour and disclosure to shareholders when submitting matters for shareholder action – also often apply. The board is generally entitled to take into account long-term as well as short-term interests and set the appropriate time frame for achievement of corporate objectives. The interests of non-shareholder constituencies may also be considered for their impact on creating corporate and shareholder value, and many states formally permit boards to consider the interests of non-shareholder constituencies such as employees, business partners and local communities.

Effective boards typically perform dual roles: (i) advisor to and business partner of management; and (ii) monitor and overseer of management. Boards typically delegate day-to-day management to the CEO and other senior management, all of whom serve at the pleasure of the board. Outside directors are typically referred to as 'non-management' directors and as 'independent' directors where they qualify as such under applicable rules (see paragraph 4.4). Core board responsibilities include:

- establishing the appropriate 'tone at the top';
- choosing and monitoring the performance of the CEO and establishing succession plans;
- monitoring corporate performance and providing advice to management as a strategic partner;
- evaluating and approving the company's annual operating plan, long-term strategy and major corporate actions;
- determining risk appetite, setting standards for managing risk and monitoring risk management;
- planning for and dealing with crises;
- determining executive compensation;
- interviewing and nominating director candidates and monitoring the board's performance and effectiveness;

- taking centre stage in any proposed transaction that creates a potential conflict between the best interests of shareholders and those of management;
- setting high standards for corporate social responsibility;
- monitoring compliance;
- supporting long-term relationships with shareholders; and
- overseeing relations with government, community and other constituents.

4.2 What are the rules that may give rise to civil and criminal liability of the director(s)? How are those liabilities sought?

- *Breach of fiduciary duties.* Directors owe fiduciary duties, including duties of care and loyalty, to the corporation and its shareholders (or, in certain cases involving insolvent or near-insolvent companies, to its creditors) in their capacity as directors by virtue of state corporation statutes and common law. Directors may rely on management and advisors when making decisions so long as they have no reason to believe such reliance is not reasonable. Personal liability for failure of oversight for business risks is subject to an extremely high burden of proof and is typically limited to sustained, systemic and conscious failures of the board. These statutory and common-law duties are generally enforced by private actions alleging breach brought by shareholders against directors directly or derivatively on behalf of the corporation.
- *Illegal dividends.* Subject to state law and knowledge requirements, directors may be jointly and severally liable for the payment of unlawful dividends or unlawful stock repurchases or redemptions by the corporation for the full amount unlawfully paid.
- *Breach of securities laws.* Violations of US federal securities laws can result in civil and criminal liabilities and administrative penalties. The SEC and the DOJ have various enforcement powers, and violations of securities laws can also be enforced by private civil suits brought by shareholders. State securities laws are enforced by state securities regulators. In addition to the anti-fraud prohibitions discussed in paragraph 6.2 concerning intentional or reckless misrepresentations or material omissions made in securities offering documents or certain other SEC filings, securities laws also prohibit 'insider trading', which is the violation of the Rule 10b-5 prohibition on trading in company securities while in the possession of material non-public information. Directors may also be held criminally liable for fraudulently influencing, coercing or misleading an accounting firm during an audit with the intention of rendering the audit report misleading, or for knowingly destroying, altering or concealing records with the intent to obstruct, influence or impede any official proceeding (punishable by imprisonment of up to 20 years).
- *Fraud, theft and corrupt payments.* A director can be criminally liable under US federal law for fraud and theft, such as the misappropriation of corporate funds through the use of mail or electronic communications

as part of an intentional scheme to defraud another of money or property. The Foreign Corrupt Practices Act (FCPA) makes it a crime for the company or any of its directors, officers or employees to bribe any foreign official, political party or candidate for political office to curry business favours. The FCPA also prohibits any person from directly or indirectly falsifying the company's books, and directors and officers cannot make materially false, misleading or incomplete statements to an accountant in connection with a required audit or any filing with the SEC.

- *Other laws.* US federal bankruptcy laws and other insolvency provisions, such as laws prohibiting fraudulent conveyances, may also give rise to director liability, as may the Fair Labor Standards Act, which guarantees employees federal minimum wages and overtime compensation, depending on the level of control exercised by the director. Other state and federal laws may also give rise to liability under certain circumstances.

4.3 Does the board of directors have a committee system, eg, nomination committee, compensation committee, audit committee? If not required, is it common practice for companies? How does it function?

No particular committee system is mandated by state law, but the board of directors is generally authorised to delegate powers to committees (and determine their membership), although certain powers cannot be delegated (such as declaring dividends, amending the organisational documents or recommending or adopting fundamental transactions). At public companies, board committees typically perform a significant portion of the board's work and provide reports and recommendations to the full board. Certain committees, such as audit, nominating and governance, and compensation committees, are required for publicly traded companies and must consist of independent directors and fulfil certain minimum duties. Each of the nominating, compensation and audit committees must have a written charter that specifies its purpose and responsibilities.

Other permanent or ad hoc committees may be created as needed, such as to handle succession planning, risk management, health and safety or public policy matters. Special committees can also be created to deal with a crisis or handle conflict transactions. Dodd-Frank requires certain financial institutions to have a separate, fully independent risk committee and that an 'appropriate committee' review derivatives activities involving entry into covered 'swap transactions' involving certain 'commercial end-user' exemptions.

4.4 Is it a legal requirement to have an independent director or a third-party director? If so, how are they appointed? Is it required for listed companies?

No particular board composition is mandated by state law, but stock exchange listing rules applicable to publicly traded companies typically require that a majority of the board consist of independent directors, as defined by stock exchange rules, and that certain responsibilities be handled by independent board committees (see paragraph 4.3). Independent directors, like non-independent directors, are elected by the shareholders, and the board determines which director candidates to submit to the shareholders, typically on the recommendation of the nominating and governance committee, and which directors to appoint to the various committees. In order for a director to qualify as 'independent', the board of directors generally must affirmatively determine that he or she has no material relationship with the company and that other 'bright-line' independence standards are met. Some companies voluntarily impose a higher minimum number of independent directors or stricter independence criteria than those required by stock exchange listing rules.

4.5 How is the compensation for directors or officers determined? Can it be contested by the shareholders or the regulatory authorities? What are the common rules or practices for the compensation of officers?

The board of directors has the legal authority to determine compensation for directors and officers. At public companies, stock exchange rules mandate that committees of the board play a central role in compensation decisions. On account of these requirements, an independent compensation committee of the board usually determines and approves the CEO's compensation. Non-CEO executive officer compensation is also usually determined by the independent compensation committee, although stock exchange rules permit the full board to make such determinations after receiving the compensation committee's recommendation. Heightened independence rules apply to the members of compensation committees and committee advisors. Using an independent compensation committee also facilitates tax deductibility of certain compensation.

Compensation philosophies and programmes are often developed with the input of third-party compensation consultants. The appropriate mix of fixed compensation (eg, annual base salary) and variable compensation (ie, short- and long-term performance incentives), as well as the form of compensation (eg, stock options, restricted shares, restricted stock units or cash-based payments) vary among companies, as determined by the compensation committee in its business judgement based on the particular needs of the business. Equity-based components are common, and shareholder approval is required of most equity compensation plans under stock exchange rules, including those involving grants of equity-based awards to directors and officers. In addition, Dodd-Frank's requirement of non-binding shareholder advisory votes on executive compensation, popularised as 'say-on-pay', provides shareholders with means for expressing dissatisfaction with compensation practices, which may also be expressed directly to the company outside of the annual meeting context. While these votes are non-binding, companies that receive low approval ratings face intense pressure to modify executive compensation programmes. Courts typically respect compensation decisions so long as the directors act on an informed basis, in good faith and not in their personal self-interest. Except in the case of certain financial institutions (where special 'safety and soundness' provisions apply), regulators generally cannot contest compensation decisions.

4.6 How will the board handle a corporate crisis like an internal criminal case, violence, social media exposure or dawn raid by the authorities?

The board of directors, along with senior management as appropriate, is expected to provide careful guidance and leadership in steering the company through a crisis if and when one arises. The specific circumstances will dictate the appropriate handling of the situation, including as to whether to conduct an internal investigation and the form and content of any responsive or remedial action. Advance planning and preparedness is recommended.

5. BOARD OF AUDITORS, AUDIT COMMITTEE, ACCOUNTING AUDITORS

5.1 How is the internal accounting and legal audit structured and conducted? Is an outside accounting audit required and, if so, how is it structured? Are there requirements to change the auditor each five years?

A public company's accounting and audit function involves an independent committee of the board (referred to as the audit committee), external independent auditors, internal auditors and senior management. Public companies must have adequate internal controls over financial reporting, and publicly filed annual and quarterly reports must contain related certifications from the CEO and CFO. All public companies must have their financial statements audited annually by a registered independent accounting firm in compliance with US generally accepted accounting principles and generally accepted auditing standards (US GAAP and US GAAS). The company's external auditor – in the case of large public companies, usually one of the major registered public accounting firms – must publicly file its signed annual report attesting to the quality of the audit and the company's internal control over financial reporting. The federal securities laws require prompt disclosure with respect to changes in the external auditor and any revision to or inability to rely on prior audited financial statements. There is no entity-level auditor rotation requirement, but the partner in charge of the audit must be rotated at least once every five years.

Federal law and stock exchange rules require that an independent audit committee of the board (comprised of 'financially literate' members, none of whom may accept consulting or advisory fees from the issuer, with 'comply or explain' disclosure required if no members qualify as a 'financial expert') be responsible for the appointment, compensation, retention and oversight of the independent auditor and for oversight of certain internal audit function-related matters. While not required, shareholders are typically asked to ratify such auditor's appointment.

5.2 Do you have supervisory auditors? What is the function of the supervisory auditors' board?

Generally, not applicable. The annual financial statements of public companies must be audited by a registered independent accounting firm as discussed above. The Public Company Accounting Oversight Board, a federal-level agency created by Sarbanes-Oxley, generally oversees accounting firms and public company audits.

6. MARKET DISCLOSURE/TRANSPARENCY TO THE SHAREHOLDERS AND THE PUBLIC

6.1 What are the disclosure requirements for companies in your jurisdiction under company law, capital markets law or any other rules?

The federal securities laws require public companies to file annual, quarterly and periodic 'current' reports triggered by the occurrence of specified events. The contents of such reports are prescribed by law, and false and misleading statements are generally prohibited. Annual reports contain audited financial statements and comprehensive information about the business, performance and relevant risk factors; quarterly reports contain unaudited interim financial statements and other business information; and current reports disclose the occurrence of certain material events, such as entry into material agreements, completion of significant acquisitions or dispositions of assets, and changes in officers or directors and amendments to the corporation's charter or bylaws. Regulation FD generally prohibits selective disclosure of material information.

When items are brought before the shareholders for their approval, such as for election of directors or consideration of significant transactions such as mergers or the sale of all or substantially all corporate assets, proxy statements containing the recommendation of the board, information about the proposals to be considered, disclosure of interests of directors and officers that may differ from the general interests of shareholders and other mandatory items must be filed. Proxy statements for the annual meetings at which directors are elected contain extensive information about the board and senior management, director and executive compensation, auditor information, and other matters. Anti-fraud rules generally prohibit public disclosures from containing material misstatements or omissions of material facts. While the SEC does not opine on the merits of a securities offering or corporate actions, SEC clearance is required for certain disclosure documents before they become effective.

6.2 What is the liability or responsibility of the board in relation to the company's disclosure requirements?

As part of its oversight role, the board has ultimate responsibility for overseeing management's implementation of adequate disclosure controls and procedures. Under the federal securities laws, directors can be held liable for their material misstatements or omissions of material facts in public filings. In some cases, liability is limited to circumstances where the director acted with *scienter* (actual knowledge or reckless disregard), and various defences, including demonstrating appropriate due diligence, may be available. Violations of the corollary fiduciary duties of candour and disclosure may also result in liability.

7. M&A AND CORPORATE GOVERNANCE

7.1 Upon an M&A offer, how are the transparency and fairness rules of the company provided under the company and stock market laws and rules?

In the case of a tender offer, various disclosure requirements operate to ensure that shareholders are sufficiently informed to assess the offer. Federal securities laws require that the offer be held open for a minimum of 20 business days, and while the bidder is not required to bid for any specific maximum or minimum percentage of shares, all shareholders must be given the opportunity to participate in the offer, receive the same consideration and withdraw their shares from the offer for a specified period of time.

M&A transactions are required to be announced to the market at the time the parties have entered into a definitive agreement, and where shareholder approval is required for the transaction to be consummated, a proxy statement setting forth all material information is required to be made available to all shareholders entitled to vote on the transaction. Prior to reaching such definitive agreement, the bidder and target generally have no disclosure obligations, including with respect to preliminary discussions, and to the extent takeover rumours emerge or inquiries are made, 'no comment' is the typical response.

8. PROXY FIGHTING

8.1 Is proxy fighting customarily conducted for control of the company management or what other items? How is it regulated under the company law or market regulations?

See paragraph 3.4 for a discussion of shareholder activism generally. Proxy fights have become a common feature of the US landscape, and the frequency of election contests has recently increased, particularly among large public companies. Activist shareholders and hostile bidders may nominate their own director candidates and conduct campaigns for full or partial board control or threaten to do so to pressure the company to enact desired changes. 'Withhold' campaigns – in which shareholders are encouraged to withhold votes from or vote against incumbent directors running unopposed – also occur and can have a significant impact at companies with majority voting standards or policies. Precatory resolutions encouraging the company to enact governance or business changes may also be submitted at the shareholders' meeting; if such non-binding resolutions receive majority support by shareholders and the board determines not to adopt the changes, the board may be subject to criticism and adverse vote recommendations from proxy advisory firms at the next year's annual meeting.

Proxy fights are regulated by: (i) federal securities laws, primarily with respect to communications with shareholders, including prohibitions on making false and misleading statements and required filings such as proxy statements; (ii) corporate organisational documents, such as with respect to advance notice bylaw requirements for director nominations or other proposed business and as to the number of election cycles required to replace the full board; and (iii) state law fiduciary duties, with respect to the actions of the board.

9. OFFICERS' REMUNERATION RULES

9.1 How is remuneration of officers determined? By whom? Is there a role for the shareholders' meeting? Is there any mechanism for an independent body to review and evaluate them?

See paragraph 4.5.

9.2 Is the mechanism of officers' remuneration publicly debated?

Executive compensation – particularly the degree of alignment between executive pay and performance and the magnitude and components of pay packages – has been one of the most hotly debated issues over the past several years. Mandatory, but non-binding, 'say-on-pay' votes are conducted annually at most publicly traded companies, and in addition to negative publicity, failed votes can result in proxy advisory firms recommending that shareholders withhold their votes from members of the compensation committee and, in egregious cases, from the entire board. Director compensation has also become an increasingly debated topic.

10. DIRECTORS' LIABILITIES, LIABILITY INSURANCE, INDEMNIFICATION

10.1 What are the directors' responsibilities and liabilities under the law? Can those liabilities be covered by insurance? Can it be indemnified by the company or other related parties?

See paragraphs 4.1 and 4.2 for a discussion of board functions, responsibilities and liabilities. Most states generally allow the corporate charter to limit directors' personal liability to the corporation or its shareholders, except in the case of liability arising out of breaches of the duty of loyalty, intentional misconduct, illegal dividends or transactions from which the director derives an improper personal benefit.

Most state laws also expressly permit corporations to purchase insurance on behalf of current or former directors (as well as officers), including for non-indemnifiable matters, and nearly all companies purchase such insurance and negotiate appropriate coverage limits.

Indemnification, including expense reimbursement, is also expressly permitted and, in certain cases, is mandatory (such as where a director is wholly successful on the merits in defending against a suit involving his or her conduct as a director). Indemnification is generally not available to the extent the director acted in bad faith or against the interests of the corporation, and certain federal laws prohibit indemnification for specified violations. The SEC has taken the position that indemnification of officers, directors or control persons for Securities Act liability arising out of knowing violations of the law is unenforceable as against public policy. In the case of a derivative suit, indemnification may be limited to defence costs and not extend to monetary damages or amounts paid in settlement.

11. SHAREHOLDERS' DERIVATIVE SUITS

11.1 Is a shareholder's derivative suit provided for by law in your jurisdiction? How is it enforced by the shareholders?

Shareholders may, and often do, bring derivative suits on behalf of the corporation against the corporation's directors and officers pursuant to state corporation law. Such derivative suits are often used to allege breaches of fiduciary duties. Certain procedural requirements must be met in order to proceed with such suits, including, subject to certain exceptions, compliance with 'demand' procedures whereby the corporation is given the opportunity to initiate the suit itself.

11.2 Have there been any recent relevant court cases on the subject?

US corporations and their directors and officers have increasingly faced duplicative shareholder derivative suits filed in multiple forums. A recent innovation responding to this problem is board adoption of exclusive forum selection bylaws, which require shareholders bringing derivative claims or other claims involving breaches of fiduciary duties (or otherwise addressing violations of state law or the internal affairs of the corporation) to file such lawsuits in a single forum, such as the issuer's state of incorporation. In June 2013, following uncertainty as to the validity of such bylaws, the Court of Chancery for the State of Delaware – where most US public companies are incorporated – declared the adoption of such bylaws to be a legitimate subject for board action, with shareholders retaining the right to challenge enforcement of such bylaws on a case-by-case, fact-specific basis.

12. SOCIAL INTEREST IN CORPORATE BEHAVIOUR

12.1 How is a company in your country expected to deal with the following issues? Corporate social responsibility; gender, racial and social diversification; environmental issues; ecology and corruption?

Corporate social responsibility, including treatment of environmental, social and ethical issues, is an appropriate matter of business judgement for the board, and the modern public company is expected to set, and meet, high standards of social responsibility. Related risks are expected to be addressed through robust risk oversight and management processes. Companies often voluntarily disclose performance and policies in this area. Specific disclosure requirements may apply in some of these areas, such as climate change, board diversity policies and environmental topics. Substantive law may also apply, such as for anti-bribery, anti-corruption and anti-discrimination rules or environmental mandates. Shareholder proposals often involve sustainability, environmental and social issues, including greenhouse gas emissions and renewable-energy concerns; international labour standards and human rights; and diversity, equality and non-discrimination issues, particularly with respect to sexual orientation.

Vietnam

Vo Ha Duyen & Nguyen Anh Hao **VILAF**

The below describes the basic principles for corporate governance under Vietnamese laws. There are several different types of companies in Vietnam, of which the two major types are limited liability company (LLC) and joint stock company (JSC). JSCs are divided into several sub-types, including a non-public JSC, a public JSC which is not listed, and a public, listed JSC. As a JSC is the most popular form of company in Vietnam, this article focuses on JSCs, including non-public and public JSCs. We will also briefly discuss LLCs.

A JSC of which the majority or minority of shares are held by the state is also considered to be a JSC under the Enterprise Law and is subject to the same corporate governance requirements for a JSC under the Enterprise Law.

An enterprise that is a one-member LLC wholly owned by the state is regulated separately under Vietnamese laws and is not a subject of this article.

1. GENERAL PRINCIPLES

1.1 What are the general principles of corporate governance in your jurisdiction? What are the main objectives of corporate governance principles in your jurisdiction? State also whether your legal system is based on common law or civil law.

In general, although there are no specific regulations covering all general principles of corporate governance, several of them may be found in:

- the Enterprise Law of 2005 (the Enterprise Law), which governs, among others, the corporate governance of a non-public company; and
- the Securities Law of 2006 as amended in 2010 (the Securities Law), which governs, among others, the corporate governance of a public company.

For a non-public company, the Enterprise Law requires the members of the members' council, being the capital owners or their authorised representatives, (the MC), the president, the director/general director (the general director) and internal inspector (if any) of a LLC, the directors on the board of management (the BOM), the general director and other managers of a JSC:

- to exercise assigned rights and duties in an honest, careful, and optimal manner to ensure the maximum legitimate interests of the company and its shareholders/owners (Articles 56.1.a, 72.1.a and 119.1.b of the Enterprise Law);
- to be loyal to the company's benefits and shareholders/owners; not to use business information, know-how and opportunities; not to abuse their position, power, and use the company's assets for benefit or of any other organisations or individuals (Articles 56.1.b, 72.1.b and 119.1.c of

the Enterprise Law); and

- to inform promptly, sufficiently, and exactly the company or other companies that they or their related persons own or have capital contributions or controlling shares (Articles 56.1.c, 72.1.d and 119.1.d of the Enterprise Law).

For public companies, the corporate governance of public companies must comply with the Securities Law, the Enterprise Law, and other relevant laws (Article 28.1 of the Securities Law). However, directors on the BOM must, in addition to those required under the Enterprise Law (Article 13 of Circular 121):

- fulfil their duties truthfully, carefully, and in the best interest of the shareholders and the company;
- attend all BOM meetings and give opinion about the issues discussed;
- report the company of the wages that they receive from the subsidiaries, affiliated companies, and other organisations in which they are the representatives of the contributed capital of such company/organisation; and
- report their or their related person's transactions with respect to the shares issued by the company to the State Securities Commission (SSC) and disclose the information about such transactions as prescribed by law.

The above-listed obligations appear to be designed, among others: (i) to ensure an effective managerial structure and ensure transparency; (ii) to protect the rights of owners and the company; and (iii) to encourage fair and impartial treatment among shareholders/owners.

Vietnam's legal system is based on the civil law system.

1.2 Have there been any recent developments in the law, codes and rules of corporate governance?

Recently, the Vietnamese Government adopted Decree No. 102/2010/ND-CP dated 1 October 2010 guiding of the implementation of the Enterprise Law (Decree 102).

One of the most significant provisions under Decree 102 is the right of a member of the MC on its behalf or on behalf of a LLC to sue the chairman of the MC or the general director of the LLC and the right of a shareholder/group of shareholders representing at least 1 per cent of the total ordinary shares of a JSC for at least six consecutive months to request the inspection board of the JSC (the inspection board) to sue a director or the general director in one of the following cases (Articles 19.1 and 25.1 of Decree 102):

- the chairman of MC, a director or the general director: (i) fails to properly exercise his/her vested rights and perform his/her assigned duties; (ii) fails to implement or fails to properly and promptly implement decisions of the BOM; (iii) exercises his/her vested rights and performs his/her assigned duties in contravention of laws, the company's charter or a resolution of the general meeting of shareholders (the GMS);
- the chairman of MC, members of the BOM or the general director

has used business information, know-how, and opportunities of the company for their own interest or for other organisations and individuals' interest;
- the chairman of MC, a director or the general director has abused his/her position, post, and the company's assets for their own interest or for other organisations and individuals' interest; or
- other breaches specified by law and the company charter.

Additionally, on 26 July 2012, the Ministry of Finance issued Circular 121 No. 121/2012/TT-BTC dated 26 July 2012 on the governance of public companies. Similar to Decree 102, Circular 121 specifically gives shareholders the right to protect their interests in the JSC such as the right to request the relevant authority to cancel a decision of the GMS or of the BOM which is against the law or which violates the legitimate fundamental rights and interests of the shareholders (Article 3.2 of Circular 121). In addition, Circular 121 also provides more specific provisions on the rights and responsibilities of the inspection board. For example, if the inspection board detects violations of the directors, general director, and other management staff, the inspection board must report to the BOM in writing within 48 hours and request the violator(s) to provide measures to remedy such violation. The inspection board must report directly to the SSC if the violation continues without being remedied in seven days (Article 21.4 of Circular 121).

1.3 Outline recent court cases and incidents involving corporate governance issues. Were there any significant corporate scandals or large unlawful corporate cases?

Vietnam does not have an official case precedents system. Therefore, information regarding cases involving corporate governance issues is not publicly available. Based on limited publicly available information, the following are some related cases for reference:

- The FPT Corporation case highlighted several problems of corporate governance in listed companies. This case illustrated 'poor' investor protection due to: (i) 'weak' law enforcement; (ii) the lack of regulations on the rights of shareholders to sue directors of the BOM in the past; (iii) the ineffective role of the JSC's shareholders in the corporate governance process; and (iv) 'weak' information disclosure and transparency in listed companies in Vietnam.
- The Bien Hoa Confectionary Corporation (BIBICA) case raised questions about: (i) the accounting and auditing standards of listed companies; (ii) the breaches of the BOM and the general director of BIBICA in relation to their duties of care and diligence as required by law and BIBICA's charter; and (iii) the ineffective role of securities regulator in dealing with such incidents.
- The Vietnam Petroleum Transport JSC (VIPCO) case raised questions about investor protection, especially the discrimination between state shareholder and other shareholders (including minority shareholders). This case is a significant example of 'poor' corporate governance in

equitised state-owned enterprises.

Unfortunately, the final judgments of the court regarding the above cases have not been made public.

1.4 Which law enforcement agency is in charge of enforcing corporate governance? May a criminal sanction be levied upon infringement of the corporate governance rules?

There is no specific authority in charge of enforcing corporate governance in Vietnam. In general, the law enforcement agencies in charge of enforcing corporate governance in Vietnam may contain, among others, the following:

- the relevant court;
- the People's Procuracy;
- the SSC with respect to public companies and other companies operating in the securities sector;
- the relevant licensing authority (eg provincial Departments of Planning and Investment and provincial industrial zone management authority, etc.); and
- the Ministry of Public Security.

Under the Vietnamese Penal Code as amended from time to time (the Penal Code), the followings appear to be most relevant to infringements of the corporate governance rules:

- abusing position and/or power to deliberately act against the state's regulations on economic management causing serious consequences (Article 165 of the Penal Code);
- abusing positions and/or powers to establish illegal funds (Article 166 of the Penal Code);
- making false reports on data and/or documents which are clearly untruthful causing serious consequences to the elaboration and implementation of socio-economic plans of the state (Article 167 of the Penal Code);
- illegally using charter capital supplementation reserve funds of credit institutions to distribute dividends causing serious consequences (Article 178 of the Penal Code);
- intentionally disclosing false information or concealing truths in securities activities causing serious consequences (Article 181a of the Penal Code);
- using insider information for securities trading (Article 181b of the Penal Code); and/or
- manipulating securities prices causing serious consequences (Article 181c of the Penal Code).

2. SOURCES OF LAW

2.1 Which laws, codes or statutes govern company structures and organisations? Are there statutes like the Companies Act or other forms of law? Is there much relevant case law?

In general, the legal framework for corporate governance may include the Enterprise Law, the Securities Law, and their implementing regulations.

2.2 Which laws, codes or statutes regulate capital markets in your jurisdiction?

The Securities Law and its implementing regulations issued by the Ministry of Finance of Vietnam (and its relevant departments) regulate the capital market in Vietnam.

2.3 Are there any public interest laws which apply to or influence corporate governance?

No, but the Vietnam Civil Code (which generally governs contractual and non-contractual relationships) as amended from time to time (the Civil Code), contains certain basic principles which may apply to corporate governance. For instance, the Civil Code governs the relationship between the legal representative of a company who can be either the general director or chairman/president (as determined by the company's charter), the 'person' he/she represents (ie the company) and the extent of such representative's liability to the person he represents and third parties relying on his representation.

2.4 Have there been any recent developments in any of the above laws? What are the recent changes to the above laws or rules and the reasons for such changes?

See paragraph 1.2 above.

3. SHAREHOLDERS AND THE SHAREHOLDERS' MEETING

3.1 How are shareholders' interests represented in the company? How are the shareholders assured exercise of their rights? What is the highest governing body within the company structure if it is not the shareholders' meeting?

A GMS applies only to a JSC. An LLC does not have a GMS. In the LLC with two capital owners or more, the capital owners make decision through the MC of the LLC or in the LLC with one capital owner, through the president or the MC of the LLC.

In a JSC, shareholders can exercise their rights by way of participating in and voting at every GMS directly or through their authorised representative(s). More specifically, the Enterprise Law gives a shareholder in a JSC the following rights (Article 79.1 of the Enterprise Law):

- to participate and speak in all GMS and exercise the right to vote directly or through an authorised representative(s) in which each ordinary share carries a vote;
- to receive dividend at the level set by the GMS;
- to be given priority in buying newly issued shares pro rata to the amount of ordinary shares held by each shareholder in the JSC;
- to freely transfer their shares to other shareholders and those who are other than shareholders except for the founding shareholders within the first three years for the incorporation of the JSC;
- to review, search, and extract information in the list of shareholders holding voting rights and request correction of inaccurate information;

- to review, search, and extract or copy the JSC's charter, the minutes book of GMS and resolutions of the GMS;
- to receive part of the remaining property in proportion to the shares contributed to the JSC where the JSC is dissolved or goes bankrupt;
- to exercise other rights provided for by the Enterprise Law or by the JSC's charter.

In general, the BOM and the general director of the JSC will have the right to decide on all matters that do not fall under the authority of the GMS (Article 108.1 of the Enterprise Law).

3.2 How is the shareholders' meeting conducted? Who may chair the meeting? May attendance (not voting) at the meeting be restricted only to the shareholders? Are the shareholders allowed to be accompanied by legal or other counsel?

The GMS must hold a meeting at least once a year. The location of a meeting of the GMS must be within the territory of Vietnam. The GMS may have extraordinary meetings in addition to its annual meetings (Article 97.1 of the Enterprise Law).

An extraordinary GMS may be convened by the BOM at any time in certain circumstances provided by law such as at the request of a shareholder or group of shareholders holding more than 10 per cent of the outstanding ordinary shares for a period of six consecutive months or longer (Article 97.3 of the Enterprise Law).

The GMS must hold an annual meeting within four months from the end of the fiscal year, extendable up to six months subject to an approval of the relevant licensing authority (Article 97.2 of the Enterprise Law).

The required quorum for the first meeting of the GMS is 65 per cent of the outstanding voting shares. If the first meeting fails, the second meeting may be convened within 30 days of the first meeting and the required quorum will be 51 per cent of the outstanding voting shares. If the second meeting fails, the third meeting may be convened within 20 days from the second meeting and no quorum will be required (Article 102 of the Enterprise Law).

The chairman of the BOM will chair the GMS. Alternatively, the person who signs the decision to convene a meeting of the GMS will guide the shareholders to elect the chair of the meeting and the person who receives the highest number of votes will chair the meeting (Article 103.2 of the Enterprise Law).

A shareholder being an individual or an authorised representative of an institutional shareholder may participate in the GMS in person or authorise another person in writing to do so (Article 101 of the Enterprise Law). The person authorised to attend a meeting of the GMS must submit the authorisation document before attending the session (Article 101.2 of the Enterprise Law). Currently, the law is silent whether legal counsel of shareholders may accompany the shareholder to attend the meeting. Thus, this issue will be subject to the JSC's decision.

3.3 How are minority shareholders' rights protected?

In general, Vietnamese laws protect minority shareholders' rights with the following:

- Derivative suit:
  A shareholder or a group of shareholders holding at least 1 per cent of the outstanding ordinary shares for six consecutive months may request the inspection board to initiate a lawsuit against a director or the general director in one of the following cases (Article 25 of Decree 102):
  - the director or the general director fails to properly exercise his/ her vested rights and perform his/ her assigned duties; fails to implement or to properly and promptly implement decisions of the BOM; exercises his/her vested rights and performs his/her assigned duties in contravention of law, the JSC's charter or a resolution of the GMS;
  - the director of the BOM or the general director has used business information, know-how, and opportunities of the JSC for their own interest or for other organisations and individuals' interest;
  - the director of the BOM or the general director has abused his/her position, post and the JSC's assets for their own interest or for other organisations' and individuals' interest; or
  - other cases specified by the law and the JSC's charter.

  Within 15 days after receiving the above-mentioned request, the inspection board must reply to the shareholder(s) in writing to acknowledge the receipt of the request and carry out procedures for instituting a lawsuit (Article 25.2 of Decree 102). In case the inspection board fails to do so or the JSC does not have an inspection board, such shareholder or group of shareholders may file a lawsuit against such director or the general director (Article 25.3 of Decree 102).
- Related-party transaction (under Article 120 of the Enterprise Law, a related party transaction is a transaction between the company and: (i) shareholders, authorised representatives of shareholders that own more than 35 per cent of total ordinary shares of the company and their related persons; (ii) members of the BOM, the general director; and (iii) companies in which members of the BOM, the inspection board, the general director, and other managers of a JSC are shareholders or where their related person holds more than 35 per cent of the capital):
  A related-party transaction needs to be approved in accordance with the procedures required by laws and the shareholder having a related interest in the transaction is not allowed to vote. If the transaction is not approved in accordance with the procedures required by law, it may be declared void.
- Right to accumulative votes:
  Essentially, accumulative voting means that shareholders have the right to form a group in order to nominate a candidate/s and to cast cumulative votes for their candidates for positions on the BOM or the inspection board. The number of candidates of each group that has the right to nominate generally depends on the number of candidates to be decided by the GMS and the aggregate shareholding ratio of each group

(Articles 29.2 and 3 of Decree 102).

- General obligations of large shareholders:
  The Securities Law prohibits large shareholders from taking advantage of their shareholding to cause damage to the rights and interests of the JSC and other shareholders (Article 14 of Circular 121).
- General rights of a shareholder or group of shareholders who hold, within at least six consecutive months, more than 10 per cent of ordinary shares or a smaller percentage as provided for in the JSC's charter:
  Such shareholder or group has the following rights (Article 79.2 of Enterprise Law):
  - to nominate candidates to the BOM and the inspection board (if any);
  - to review and extract the minutes book and other resolutions of the BOM, mid-year and annual financial statements made according to the forms of the Vietnamese accounting system and other reports of the inspection board;
  - to request the convening of the GMS in the cases specified in the Enterprise Law;
  - to request the inspection board to check each specific problem related to the management and operation of the JSC when it is necessary; and
  - other rights as provided for by the Enterprise Law and the JSC's charter.
- Certain obligations of the management positions as discussed in paragraph 1.1. above.

3.4 Is shareholder activism encouraged or discouraged? If not encouraged, how is it regulated?

Vietnamese law does not have the concept of shareholder activism. With respect to the rights of shareholders, see paragraph 3.1. above. .

3.5 How are professional shareholders (those minority shareholders who seek some extra benefit from companies by unduly and habitually influencing management by using their shareholding) treated by the law? Are they excluded from attending the shareholders' meeting? Are they criminally or otherwise publicly sanctioned?

The Securities Law defines '*professional securities investors*' to include a commercial bank, financial institution, finance leasing company, insurance business organisation, investment fund manager and securities company (Article 6.11 of the Securities Law).

In general, if it is a holder of ordinary shares, a professional securities investor will have rights and obligations similar to those of other ordinary shareholders, including the right to attend the GMS. Note that the holders of preferential dividend shares or of preferential redemption shares are not allowed to, among others, attend and vote at the GMS (Articles 82 and 83 of the Enterprise Law).

See paragraph 1.4. above regarding the possible criminal responsibilities for the infringements of the corporate governance rules.

3.6 Are shareholders' benefits given to some of the shareholders by the company without resolution by the shareholders' meeting prohibited or regulated by the law or other rules?

Each share of the same class gives the holder equal rights, obligations, and interests (Article 78.5 of the Enterprise Law and Article 3.1(b) of Circular 121). Therefore, any special benefits given to some of the shareholders of the JSC as compared with other same-class shareholders are not legally recognised.

4. DIRECTORS AND BOARD OF DIRECTORS

4.1 What are the functions and responsibilities of the directors and the board of directors? Do you have a one- or two-tier board system? What are the outside directors called?

See paragraph 1.1. above regarding, among others, the rights and obligations of the directors on the BOM.

Functions and obligations of the BOM

The Enterprise Law regulates only a one-tier BOM. In practice, a large public company by its own policy may organise an executive board below the BOM.

The BOM has the right to decide on all matters that do not fall into the authority of the GMS and with exceptions to those which have been authorised to the general director and/or chairman of the BOM. More specifically, the BOM has the following rights and duties (Article 108 of the Enterprise Law and Article 14 of Circular 121):

- to decide on the development strategy, medium-term development plans, and annual business plans of the JSC;
- to propose the types of shares and the total number of shares of each type allowed to be offered;
- to decide on the sale offer of new shares within the number of shares of each type allowed to be offered; determine the additional mobilisation of capital in other forms;
- to set the price of shares offered and bonds issued by the JSC;
- to decide on the redemption of shares as provided for the Enterprise Law;
- to make decisions on investment plans and projects falling under its competence and within the limit provided for by the Enterprise Law or the JSC's charter;
- to make decisions on market development, marketing, and technology solutions; to approve contracts of sale, purchase, borrowing, lending or any other contracts worth 50 per cent or more of the total value of assets recorded in the JSC's latest financial statement, or a smaller percentage provided for in the JSC's charter, except for related-party contracts and transactions defined in the Enterprise Law;

- to appoint, remove from office, dismiss, sign or terminate contracts with the general director and other key managers of the JSC as provided for in the JSC's charter; to decide on salary and other benefits applied to such persons; to appoint its authorised representatives to exercise the ownership right over shares or capital contributions in other companies, and to decide on allowances and other benefits to be applied to such persons;
- to supervise and direct the general director and other managers in managing day-to-day business activities of the JSC;
- to decide on the organisational structure, management rules within the JSC; to make decisions on the setting up of subsidiary companies, branches, representative offices, and on the contribution of capital to or buying of shares from other companies;
- to approve the agenda, materials used in sessions of the GMS, convene sessions of the GMS or collect written opinions for the adoption of decisions of the GMS;
- to submit annual financial statements to the GMS;
- to propose the amount of dividend to be paid, timing, and procedures for payment of dividend or the settlement of losses incurred during the course of business operations;
- to propose reorganisation, dissolution or bankruptcy of the JSC; and
- to have other rights and duties as provided for by the Enterprise Law and the JSC's charter.

The BOM may opt to have its decisions adopted by voting at its meetings, by collecting written opinions or other ways as provided for in the JSC's charter.

If the JSC has more than 11 individual shareholders or one institutional shareholder holding more than 50 per cent of the total shares of the JSC, the JSC must have the inspection board. Otherwise, the JSC may, at the decision of the GMS, have the inspection board. In general, the inspection board has the right and obligation to inspect the operations of the BOM and the general director and report to the GMS.

In a public company, at least one-third of the directors of the BOM must be 'non-executive directors,' which are defined as directors who are not the general director, deputy general director, chief accountant or other management position appointed by the BOM. In a large-scale public company or a listed company, at least one-third of the directors of the BOM must be 'independent directors'. The definition of 'independent directors' is discussed in paragraph 4.4 below.

4.2 What are the rules that may give rise to civil and criminal liability of the director(s)? How are those liabilities sought?

See paragraphs 1.2 and 1.4 above.

4.3 Does the board of directors have a committee system, eg, nomination committee, compensation committee, audit committee? If not required, is it common practice for companies? How does it

function?

In general, the Securities Law and Enterprise Law give the JSC substantial flexibility in establishing their governance structure.

Notwithstanding, in the corporate structure of a large-scale public company or of a listed company, the BOM is required to set up a committee system to assist the BOM in its operations, including the Development Policy Committee, Human Resources Committee, Remuneration Committee, and other Board Committees as decided by the GMS from time-to-time. In case that the BOM does not set up the above-mentioned committees, it needs to appoint each director to be in charge of each area such as remuneration or human resources (Article 32 of Circular 121).

4.4 Is it a legal requirement to have an independent director or a third-party director? If so, how are they appointed? Is it required for listed companies?

A non-public JSC is not required to have an independent director. It will mainly be subject to a decision of the GMS.

In a public company, at least one-third of the directors of the BOM must be 'non-executive directors,' which are defined as directors who are not the general director, deputy general director, chief accountant or other management position appointed by the BOM.

In a large-scale public JSC or a listed JSC at least one-third of directors of the BOM are required to be independent directors (Article 30 of Circular 121). The independent director of the BOM is a director satisfying the following conditions (Article 2.3 of Circular 121):

- being a non-executive director of the BOM and not related to the general director, deputy general director, chief accountant, and other managers appointed by the BOM;
- not being a director, the general director or deputy general director of any subsidiary, affiliate or another company controlled by the JSC;
- not being a large shareholder or the representative of a large shareholder or a related person of a large shareholder of the JSC;
- not working for any organisations that provided the JSC with legal consulting or audit services within the previous two years; and
- not being a partner or a related person of a partner with the JSC in a transaction the value of which accounts for at least 30 per cent of the total revenue or the total value of goods and services purchased by the JSC within the previous two years.

4.5 How is the compensation for directors or officers determined? Can it be contested by the shareholders or the regulatory authorities? What are the common rules or practices for the compensation of officers?

In general, the JSC has the right to decide the salary of its employees as long as the salary is not lower than the minimum salary levels set out by law.

Unless otherwise provided for in the JSC's charter, the remuneration, salaries, and other benefits of the directors on the BOM and the general director will be paid based on the business operation results and the following (Article 117 of the Enterprise Law):

- Directors are entitled to remuneration and bonuses. The remuneration is calculated based on the number of working days needed to complete their tasks multiplied by the daily remuneration. The BOM estimates the remuneration for each director on the principle of consensus. The total remuneration of the BOM will be determined by the GMS in its annual meetings.
- Directors can be reimbursed of all expenses such as meals and accommodation, travel expenses, and other reasonable expenses that they have paid to fulfil their assigned tasks.
- The general director will be entitled to salary and bonuses.

For the members of the inspection board, unless otherwise provided for in the JSC's charter, remuneration and other benefits for members of the inspection board will be paid according to the following provisions:

- Members of the inspection board will receive remuneration based on the work done and other benefits as decided by the GMS. The GMS will decide on the total remuneration and the annual operation budget for the inspection board based on the estimated number of working days, volume, and nature of work and the average daily remuneration of members.
- Members of the inspection board will be paid for meals, accommodation, travel expenses, and fees for hiring independent consultancy services at a reasonable level. The total remuneration and expenses will not exceed the total annual budget for operations of the inspection board approved by the GMS, unless otherwise decided by the GMS.
- Remuneration and operations expenses of the inspection board will be accounted as business expenses of the company according to the provisions of law on enterprise income tax and other relevant laws, and will be presented in a separate section of the company's annual financial statement.

The Enterprise Law gives the BOM the right to decide the salaries of the general director and other managers of the JSC. The general director has the right to decide on the salaries of all other employees which do not fall into the authority of the BOM (Articles 108.2.h and 116.3.e of the Enterprise Law).

Remuneration of the directors of the BOM, the members of the inspection board and salaries of the general director or other managers of the JSC will be accounted as business expenses of the JSC and must be presented in a separate section of the JSC's annual financial statements and reported to the GMS at its annual meetings (Articles 117.3 and 125.3 of the Enterprise Law).

4.6 How will the board handle a corporate crisis like an internal criminal case, violence, social media exposure or dawn raid by the authorities?

There is no specific regulatory model under the Enterprise Law to handle a corporate crisis. The practice may vary subject to the nature of the crisis and the internal policies of each company.

5. BOARD OF AUDITORS, AUDIT COMMITTEE, ACCOUNTING AUDITORS

5.1 How is the internal accounting and legal audit structured and conducted? Is an outside accounting audit required and, if so, how is it structured? Are there requirements to change the auditor each five years?

A company incorporated in Vietnam is required to maintain its internal accounting system in compliance with the Vietnam Accounting System (Article 37 of the Law on Independent Audit dated 29 March 2011). Accounting books of a foreign-invested company or of a public company must be audited by an independent audit firm licensed to operate in Vietnam (Article 37.1 of the Law on Independent Audit). A local company does not need to have its accounting books audited unless it is a public company, a finance company, an insurance company or a credit institution. Vietnamese laws do not require a company to change its audit every five years, but the audit firm is restricted from arranging the same auditing officer to audit a company for five consecutive years if such company is a public company, a finance company, an insurance company or a credit institution (Article 58.1 of the Law on Independent Auditing).

5.2 Do you have supervisory auditors? What is the function of the supervisory auditors' board?

The Enterprise Law requires an inspection board to be established in a JSC with more than 11 individual shareholders or with one institutional shareholder owning more than 51 per cent of the outstanding shares of the JSC (Article 95 of the Enterprise Law). An inspection board includes three to five members.

The members of the inspection board are selected and appointed by the GMS.

The members of the inspection board elect one of them to be the head of the inspection board. The rights and duties of the head of the inspection board are stipulated in the charter of the JSC. More than half of the members of the inspection board must permanently reside in Vietnam.

At least one member of the inspection board must be an independent accountant or auditor and not a staff member of the accounting/financial department of the JSC or of an auditing company that audits the JSC's financial statements (Article 123 of the Enterprise Law). In addition, in order to ensure the independence of the inspection board, members of the inspection board may not hold managerial positions in the JSC. A member of the inspection board need not be a shareholder or the employee of the JSC (Article 122.2 of the Enterprise Law).

The Enterprise Law gives the inspection board the following rights and duties (Article 123 of the Enterprise Law):

- to inspect the management and direction by the BOM and the general

director of the JSC; to be responsible to the GMS for the performance of its assigned tasks;
- to verify the reasonableness, legality, truthfulness and prudency of business management and direction, accounting and statistical work, and making of financial statements;
- to verify business reports, annual and biannual financial statements of the company, and evaluation reports on the management of the BOM;
- to submit to the regular meetings of the GM the appraisal reports on annual financial statements and business reports of the JSC and the evaluation reports on the management of the BOM;
- to check accounting books and other materials of the JSC and the management and direction of the JSC's activities at any time if necessary or under a decision of the GMS or at the request of individual shareholders or group of shareholders in accordance with the Enterprise Law;
- in case there is a request from individual shareholders or a group of shareholders provided for by the Enterprise Law, to investigate within seven working days from the date of receipt thereof and send an explanation report on investigated issues to the BOM, the requesting shareholder or group of shareholders within seven working days from the date of completion of the investigation. The investigation by the inspection board must neither obstruct the normal operations of the BOM nor disrupt the management of business operations of the JSC;
- to propose to the BOM or the GMS measures to adjust and improve organisational and business management structures of the JSC;
- to promptly send a written notice to the BOM to request the cessation of such violations and the remedy of consequences when members of the BOM and/or the general director are discovered to have violated the obligations of managers provided for in the Enterprise Law;
- to exercise other rights and perform other duties in accordance with the Enterprise Law, the JSC's charter and decisions of the GMS; and
- to use independent consultants to perform assigned duties.

The inspection board may consult with the BOM before it submits reports, conclusions, and recommendations to the GMS (Article 123 of the Enterprise Law).

6. MARKET DISCLOSURE/TRANSPARENCY TO THE SHAREHOLDERS AND THE PUBLIC

6.1 What are the disclosure requirements for companies in your jurisdiction under company law, capital markets law or any other rules?

The remuneration of the directors and general director must be displayed in a separate section of the annual financial report and reported to the GMS (Article 117.3 of the Enterprise Law).

A public company is subject to more stringent internal disclosure and public disclosure requirements under the Securities Law and its implementing regulations regarding acts and transactions involving the directors, general director, large shareholders and/or management positions.

In addition, the public company needs to meet the following requirements when disclosing information (Article 3 Circular 52/2012/TT-BTC):

- the information disclosure must be sufficient, accurate, and punctual as prescribed by law;
- the information disclosure must be made by the legal representative of the company or the person authorised to disclose information. The legal representative of the company will be responsible for the accuracy, the punctuality, and the adequacy of the information disclosed by the person authorised to disclose;
- the company will register one person authorised to disclose information with the SSC and the relevant stock exchange and if the company changes the authorised person, it will need to notify the SSC and the stock exchange in writing at least five days before the replacement;
- for information affecting the share price, the legal representative of the company or the person authorised to disclose information must verify or correct such information within 24 hours from receipt of such information or requests of the relevant authority;
- the information disclosure must be made concurrently with the report to the SSC and the stock exchange on the disclosed information contents;
- the language of information disclosure generally must be Vietnamese.

6.2 What is the liability or responsibility of the board in relation to the company's disclosure requirements?

A director on the BOM, a member of the inspection board or the general director of a public company ('manager') is obliged to report to the BOM and conduct a public disclosure in relation any of the following transactions:

- transactions between the public company and any other company of which the above manager is a founding capital owner, a director on the BOM or general director during the preceding three years;
- transactions between the public company and any other company of which a related person of the manager is a director on the BOM, general director or large shareholder;
- transactions [with the public company] which may render a benefit to the manager (Article 28 of Circular 121).

A manager is also obliged to report to the BOM any transaction between a subsidiary of the public company or another company that the public company controls and the manager or a related person of the manager. Within 24 hours after such a transaction is approved by the BOM or the GMS pursuant to its charter, the transaction must be publicly disclosed on the public company's website and reported to the SSC. Such transactions must also be reported in the public company's annual reports (Article 23 of Circular 121).

In general, failure to comply with certain disclosure requirements may be subject to an administrative penalty of up to VND 90 million (Article 33.4 of

Decree 85/2010/ND-CP).

In an extreme case, a disclosure violation as part of a larger violating act might establish a crime under the Penal Code (Article 181a, 181b, 181c of the Penal Code). See paragraph 1.4. above.

In addition, if the related-party transaction is not disclosed and approved by the GMS or the BOM as required, such transaction may be considered as void and the relevant person must compensate the JSC for all damages and all benefits generated from such a transaction must be returned to the JSC (Article 120 of the Enterprise Law).

7. M&A AND CORPORATE GOVERNANCE

7.1 Upon an M&A offer, how are the transparency and fairness rules of the company provided under the company and stock market laws and rules?

Secondary shares

Generally, in an LLC, existing capital owners are entitled to the pre-emptive rights proportional to their existing capital holding with respect to the capital interests offered for sale by a capital owner.

In a JSC, generally secondary shares are freely transferred. In a public JSC, an investor may be required to conduct a tender offer in certain cases (such as when it intends to acquire at least 25 per cent of the outstanding ordinary shares of the public company) unless its transaction is specifically approved by the GMS (Article 32.1 of the Law on Securities).

There are public disclosure requirements with respect to '*insider shareholder's transactions*' and '*large shareholder's transactions*' with respect to public companies (Article 28.1 of Circular 52/2012/TT-BTC).

An individual or organisation or a group of related persons holding at least 5 per cent of the shares in a public company is considered as a *large shareholder* and subject to certain reporting requirements when certain changes to its shareholding occur under the securities laws (Article 29 of the Law on Securities).

A large shareholder (including a group of related persons holding an aggregate of 5 per cent) is required to report each of the following changes to the public company, the SSC and the relevant stock exchange within seven days after such change (Article 29.3 of the Law on Securities):

- there is a change in the number of shares owned by such large shareholder in excess of 1 per cent of the outstanding shares in the public company; or
- it is no longer a large shareholder.

An insider shareholder is a shareholder that is also a director on the BOM, general director, deputy general director, chief accountant or finance manager of the public company (Article 2.3 of Circular 52/2012/TT-BTC). An insider shareholder is required to notify the listed company, the SSC and the relevant stock exchange at least three working days prior to her trade of any shares of such listed company (Article 28.1 of Circular 52/2012/TT-BTC). Generally, the trade may not begin until at least 24 hours after the publication of the information on the stock exchange. The trade must be completed within 30 days after the date of notification to the SSC and the stock exchange. The result of the trade must be reported to the same agencies within three days after completion (Article 28 of Circular 52).

Primary shares

Generally, existing shareholders even in a JSC have the pre-emptive rights proportional to their existing shareholding in the issue of new shares by the company.

A private placement of shares to third parties or other than in the exercise of such pre-emptive rights must be approved by the GMS (Article 4.1(a) of Decree 58/2012/ND-CP).

8. PROXY FIGHTING

8.1 Is proxy fighting customarily conducted for control of the company management or what other items? How is it regulated under the company law or market regulations?

Proxy fighting does occur especially in corporate hostile takeover. There is no specific regulation addressing proxy fighting.

9. OFFICERS' REMUNERATION RULES

9.1 How is remuneration of officers determined? By whom? Is there a role for the shareholders' meeting? Is there any mechanism for an independent body to review and evaluate them?

See paragraph 4.5 above. Under Vietnamese law, there is no independent body to review and evaluate remuneration of officers as long as the salary of an officer is not lower than the minimum regulatory salary.

9.2 Is the mechanism of officers' remuneration publicly debated?

No, to the best of our knowledge.

10. DIRECTORS' LIABILITIES, LIABILITY INSURANCE, INDEMNIFICATION

10.1 What are the directors' responsibilities and liabilities under the law? Can those liabilities be covered by insurance? Can it be indemnified by the company or other related parties?

See paragraph 6.1 above regarding the functions and responsibilities of the directors of the BOM. The law is silent on directors' liability insurance though some insurance firms do offer this coverage in Vietnam. The law is also silent about indemnity agreements.

11. SHAREHOLDERS' DERIVATIVE SUITS

11.1 Is a shareholder's derivative suit provided for by law in your jurisdiction? How is it enforced by the shareholders?

See paragraph 3.3 above. Since 2010, Decree 102 has provided an explicit legal framework for the capital owners in an LLC to file a lawsuit in their names or on behalf of the LLC, or the shareholders in a JSC to file a lawsuit against the managers of such LLC or JSC for their breach of duties.

11.2 Have there been any recent relevant court cases on the subject?

Vietnam does not have an official case precedents system.

In the case of Hanoi Concrete Construction Joint Stock Company (VIBEX JSC), a group of shareholders holding 10.92 per cent shares initiated a lawsuit against the chairman of the BOM in the Ha Noi People's Court claiming that:

- while such a group had nominated a person who was a shareholder and met the conditions provided in the JSC's charter to be a director of the BOM for the term from 2011 to 2015, the nomination was rejected with unacceptable reasons; and
- the annual GMS of VIBEX JSC for electing five directors of the BOM and the inspection board for the term from 2011 to 2015 was conducted illegally.

Unfortunately, the final judgment of the court for the above-mentioned case was not made available to the public.

12. SOCIAL INTEREST IN CORPORATE BEHAVIOUR

12.1 How is a company in your country expected to deal with the following issues? Corporate social responsibility; gender, racial and social diversification; environmental issues; ecology and corruption?

- Corporate social responsibility:
  This is generally encouraged by policy but the tax laws do not seem to encourage charity contributions (Article 6.2.21 to 6.2.24 of Circular 123/2012/TT-BTC). Under current tax law, such contributions are not considered deductible expenses, except certain cases as provided by laws.
- Gender, racial and social diversification:
  Under the Vietnamese Labour Code, gender, racial, and social discriminations are strictly prohibited. However, the law does not specifically require gender, racial or social diversification (Article 8 of the Vietnamese Labor Code).
- Environmental issues:
  The Vietnamese Environment Protection Law requires companies to meet certain environmental standards and/or to obtain certain approvals when the companies operate in certain specific business sectors.
- Corruption:
  In general, giving or receiving bribes is considered a crime and is strictly prohibited by the Penal Code.

Contact details

GENERAL EDITOR
Akira Kawamura
Anderson Mori & Tomotsune
Akasaka K-Tower, 2-7
Motoakasaka 1-chome, Minato-ku
Tokyo 107-0051
Japan
T: +81 3 6888 1028
F: +81 3 6888 3028
E: akira.kawamura@amt-law.com
W: www.amt-law.com/en

AUSTRALIA
Hiroyuki Kano & Andrew Hay
Clayton Utz
L28 Riparian Plaza, 71 Eagle Street
Brisbane, Queensland 4000
Australia
F: +61 7 3292 7262
F: +61 7 3221 9669
E: hkano@claytonutz.com
W: www.claytonutz.com

BRAZIL
Marta Viegas
Tozzini Freire
Rua Borges Lagoa, 1328
Vila Clementino
São Paulo 04038-904
Brazil
T: +55 11 5086 5233
F: +55 11 5086 5555
E: mviegas@tozzinifreire.com.br
W: www.tozzinifreire.com.br

CANADA
Jay M. Hoffman & James Klotz
Miller Thomson LLP
40 King Street West, Suite 5800
Scotia Plaza, PO Box 1011
Toronto ON M5H 3S1
Canada
T: +416 595 8508/597 4373
F: +416 595 8695
E: jhoffman@millerthomson.com
E: jklotz@millerthomson.com
W: www.millerthomson.com

CHINA
Xu Ping & Wei Kao
King & Wood Mallesons
20F, East Tower
World Financial Centre
1 Dongsanhuan Zhonglu
Chaoyang District
Beijing 100020
People's Republic of China
T:+86 10 5878 5012/5296
F:+86 10 5878 5577
E: xuping@cn.kwm.com
E: wei.kao@cn.kwm.com
W: www.kwm.com

FRANCE
Jacques Buhart & Nicolas Lafont
McDermott Will & Emery AARPI
23 rue de l'Université
Paris 75007
France
T: +33 1 81 69 15 00
F: +33 1 81 69 15 15
E: jbuhart@mwe.com
E: nlafont@mwe.com
W: www.mwe.com

GERMANY
Prof. Dr Jörg Rodewald
Luther Rechtsanwaltsgesellschaft mbH
Friedrichstraße 140
Berlin 10117
Germany
T: +49 30 52133 21189
F: +49 30 52133 110
E: joerg.rodewald@luther-lawfirm.com
W: www.luther-lawfirm.com

Dr Jörgen Tielmann, LL.M.
Luther Rechtsanwaltsgesellschaft mbH
Gänsemarkt 45
20354 Hamburg
Germany
T: +49 40 18067 16829
F: +49 40 18067 110
E: joergen.tielmann@luther-lawfirm.com
W: www.luther-lawfirm.com

HONG KONG

George A. Ribeiro, Dominic W. L. Hui & Ricky W. K. Sun
Ribeiro Hui
1303-5, 13th Floor, Wilson House
19–27 Wyndham Street, Central
Hong Kong
T: +852 2537 0686
F: +862 2537 7636
E: g.ribeiro@ribeirohui.com
E: d.hui@ribeirohui.com
E: r.sun@ribeirohui.com
W: www.ribeirohui.com

HUNGARY

Richard Lock & Pál Rahóty
Lakatos, Köves and Partners
Madách Imre út 14
Budapest 1075
Hungary
T: +36 1 429 1300
F: +36 1 429 1390
E: info@lakatoskoves.hu
W: www.lakatoskoves.hu

INDIA

Rajiv K. Luthra, Sundeep Dudeja & Vaibhav Kakkar
Luthra and Luthra Law Offices
103 Ashoka Estate, Barakhamba Rd
New Delhi, Delhi 110001
India
T: +91 11 4121 5100
F: +91 11 2372 3909
E: delhi@luthra.com
W: www.luthra.com

INDONESIA

Tony Budidjaja & Juni Dani
Budidjaja & Associates
The Landmark Center Tower II, Fl. 8
Jalan Jenderal Sudirman No. 1
Jakarta 12910
Indonesia
T: +62 21 520 1600
F: +62 21 520 1700
E: lawyers@budidjaja.com
W: www.budidjaja.com

ISRAEL

Rachel Levitan & Yael Navon
Levitan Sharon & Co., Advocates and Notaries
57 Yigal Alon Street
Tel Aviv 67891
Israel
T: +972 3 688 6768
F: +972 3 688 6769
E: rachellevitan@levitansharon.co.il
E: yaelf@levitansharon.co.il
W: www.levitansharon.co.il

ITALY

Claudio Visco & Ernesto Pucci
Macchi di Cellere Gangemi
via Cuboni 12
Rome 00197
Italy
T: +39 06 362 141
F: +39 06 322 2159
E: c.visco@macchi-gangemi.com
W: www.macchi-gangemi.com

JAPAN

Hiroki Kodate
Anderson Mori & Tomotsune
Akasaka K-Tower, 2-7
Motoakasaka 1-chome, Minato-ku
Tokyo 107-0051
Japan
T: +81 3 6888 1064
F: +81 3 6888 3064
E: hiroki.kodate@amt-law.com
W: www.amt-law.com/en

KOREA

Gene-Oh (Gene) Kim & Heon-Yup Lee
Kim & Chang
39 Sajik-ro 8-gil
(Seyang Bldg., Naeja-dong)
Jongno-gu
Seoul 110-720
Korea
T: +82 2 3703 1261/1585
F: +82 2 737 9091~3
E: gokim@kimchang.com
E: hylee3@kimchang.com
W: www.kimchang.com

MALAYSIA

Kar Han Lim
Zaid Ibrahim & Co
Level 19 Menara Milenium, Jalan
Damanlela, Pusat Bandar Damansara
Kuala Lumpur
Wilayah Persekutuan 50490
Malaysia
T: +603 2087 9999
F: +603 2094 4888
E: kar.han.lim@zicolaw.com
W: www.zicolaw.com

PORTUGAL

Maria da Conceição Cabaços
PLMJ, Law Firm
Lisbon (Head Office)
Av. da Liberdade, 224, Edifício
Eurolex, 1250-148 Lisboa, Portugal
T: +351 213 197 300
F: +351 213 197 400
E: plmjlaw@plmj.pt
W: www.plmj.com

Oporto Office
Rua S. João de Brito, 605-E, 1º–1.2,
4100-455 Porto, Portugal
T: +351 226 074 700

Faro Office
R. Pinheiro Chagas, 16 - 2º Drtº
8000-406 Faro, Portugal
T: +351 289 887 630

RUSSIA

Vassily Rudomino, Anton Dzhuplin,
Victoria Sivachenko &
Timur Akhundov
ALRUD Law Firm
17 Skakovaya Street
Building 2, 6th Floor
Moscow 125040
Russia
T: +7 495 234 96 92
F: +7 495 956 37 18
E: info@alrud.com
W: www.alrud.com

SINGAPORE

Annabelle Yip
WongPartnership LLP
12 Marina Boulevard Level 28
Marina Bay Financial Centre Tower 3
Singapore 018982
T: +65 6416 8249
F: +65 6532 5711
E: annabelle.yip@wongpartnership.com
W: wongpartnership.com

SPAIN

Carlos Paredes Galego &
Carlos Franco Duque
Uría Menéndez
Príncipe de Vergara 187
Plaza de Rodrigo Uría
Madrid 28002
Spain
T: +34 915 860 400
F: +34 915 860 403/4
E: carlos.paredes@uria.com
E: carlos.franco@uria.com
W: www.uria.com

SWEDEN

Peder Hammarskiöld & Sandra Hein
Advokatfirman Hammarskiöld & Co.
Skeppsbron 42, PO Box 2278
Stockholm SE-103 17
Sweden
T: +46 8 578 450 00

F: +46 8 578 450 99
E: peder.hammarskiold@hammarskiold.se
E: sandra.hein@hammarskiold.se
W: www.hammarskiold.se

TAIWAN

Chun-yih Cheng
Formosa Transnational Attorneys at Law
13F Lotus Building
136 Jen Ai Road, Section 3
Taipei City 106
Republic of China (Taiwan)
T: +886 2 2755 7366
F: +886 2 2708 6035
E: chun-yih.cheng@taiwanlaw.com
W: www.taiwanlaw.com

THAILAND

Kedsara Luengruengtip
Dej-Udom & Associates
Attorneys-at-Law
Charn Issara Tower I, 9th Floor
942/142-3 Rama IV Road
Suriyawong Sub-District
Bang-rak District
Bangkok 10500
Thailand
T: +66 2 233 0055/0068
F: +66 2 236 6681/+66 2 233 0227
E: dej-udom@dejudom.com
W: www.dejudomlaw.com

TURKEY

Kayra Üçer & Zeynep Ahu Sazci
Hergüner Bilgen Özeke Attorney Partnership
Süleyman Seba Cad. Sıraevler 55
Akaretler Beşiktaş
Istanbul 34357
Turkey
T: +90 212 310 18 00
F: +90 212 310 18 99
E: kucer@herguner.av.tr
E: zasazci@herguner.av.tr
W: www.herguner.av.tr

UK

Charles Martin & Mark Slade
Macfarlanes LLP
20 Cursitor Street
London EC4A 1LT
England
T: +44 20 7831 9222
F: +44 20 7831 9607
E: charles.martin@macfarlanes.com
E: mark.slade@macfarlanes.com
W: www.macfarlanes.com

USA

Adam O. Emmerich, Sabastian V. Niles & Andrew D. Kenny
Wachtell, Lipton, Rosen & Katz
51 West 52nd Street
New York
NY 10019
USA
T: +212 403 1000
F: +212 403 2000
E: AOEmmerich@wlrk.com
E: SVNiles@wlrk.com
E: ADKenny@wlrk.com
W: www.wlrk.com

VIETNAM

Vo Ha Duyen & Nguyen Anh Hao
Vietnam International Law Firm (VILAF)
Ho Chi Minh City Head Office
Suite 404–406, Kumho Asiana Plaza Saigon, 39 Le Duan, District 1
Ho Chi Minh City, Vietnam
T: +84 8 3827 7300
F: +84 8 3827 7303

Hanoi Branch Office
Suite 603, HCO Building (Melia)
44B Ly Thuong Kiet Street
Hanoi, Vietnam
T: +84 4 3934 8530
F: +84 4 3934 8531
E: duyen@vilaf.com.vn
E: hao@vilaf.com.vn
W: www.vilaf.com